Folds of Past, Present and Future

Folds of Past, Present and Future

—

Reconfiguring Contemporary Histories of Education

Edited by Sarah Van Ruyskensvelde, Geert Thyssen,
Frederik Herman, Angelo Van Gorp and
Pieter Verstraete

ISBN 978-3-11-125575-0
e-ISBN (PDF) 978-3-11-062345-1
e-ISBN (EPUB) 978-3-11-062372-7

Library of Congress Control Number: 2021939830

Bibliographic Information published by the Deutsche Nationalbibliothek
The Deutsche Nationalbibliothek lists this publication in the Deutsche Nationalbibliografie;
detailed bibliographic data are available on the Internet at http://dnb.dnb.de.

© 2023 Walter de Gruyter GmbH, Berlin/Boston
This volume is text- and page-identical with the hardback published in 2021.
Cover Image: Portrait of Marc Depaepe, 2010. Photo by Ginette Dumortier. Bellegem,
Belgium. Used with the permission of Ginette Dumortier.
Printing and binding: CPI books GmbH, Leck

www.degruyter.com

Liber Amicorum for Emeritus Professor Marc Depaepe

Table of Contents

Acknowledgements —— XI

Note on the editors —— XIII

List of Contributors —— XV

Geert Thyssen, Pieter Verstraete, Frederik Herman, Angelo Van Gorp and Sarah Van Ruyskensvelde
Introduction —— 1

1 Leaving Marks of Inquiry: Ravels of Theory, Methodology, and History of Educational Historiography

Antonio Fco. Canales (Universidad Complutense de Madrid, Spain)
The Cultural History of Education: Between the Siren Song of Philosophy and the Discrete Charm of the Philosophy of the Social Sciences —— 39

Lynn Fendler (Michigan State University, USA)
Critical Powers of Historical Framing: Continuity and Representation —— 59

Joyce Goodman (University of Winchester, UK)
Concentric Circles and Magnetic Currents: Moral Disarmament at the League of Nations International Institute of Educational Cinematography, 1931–34 —— 81

Thomas S. Popkewitz (University of Wisconsin–Madison, USA)
The Study of Education. On Rethinking History with the Help of Marc Depaepe —— 103

2 The Politics of Diversity: Gender, Culture, and Post-colonial Education

Ian Grosvenor (University of Birmingham, UK)
Engaging with "the Act of Looking Back, [and] of Seeing with Fresh Eyes": the Colonial Experience and Pedagogies of Display —— 129

Mathieu Zana Etambala (RMCA/UGent/KU Leuven, Belgium)
A Virtual Visit to the Renovated Royal Museum for Central Africa. Two Major Challenges: Decolonization and Africanization —— 147

Rebecca Rogers (Université de Paris, France)
French Variations on the Educational Civilizing Mission (19th – 20th century). *Cherchez les missionaires, cherchez les femmes!* —— 175

Eckhardt Fuchs (Technische Universität Braunschweig, Germany)
Textbooks in their Contexts: Textbook Studies Revisited —— 195

3 Flood Lands of Pedagogy: Meanderings between Empiricism, Theory, and Practice

Eva Matthes (Augsburg University, Germany)
"Geisteswissenschaftliche Pädagogik," Teacher Training and Educational Science – Different Concepts and Attributions of Significance. Germany, 1900 – 2000 —— 217

András Németh and Éva Szabolcs (ELTE Eötvös Loránd University, Hungary)
Educational Science as an Academic Discipline in Hungary (1867 – 1953): Turns and Developmental Phases —— 249

Iveta Kestere, Zanda Rubene and Iveta Ozola (University of Latvia, Latvia)
Educational Sciences Between "Real" Moscow and the "Imaginary" West: The Case of Latvia (1989 – 1999) —— 267

Marcelo Caruso, Daniel Przygoda and Friedrich Schollmayer (Humboldt-Universität zu Berlin, Germany)
"Pedagogic" – A Preliminary Thesis on a Lexical Innovation during the European Enlightenment —— 289

4 Walking the Line: The Attraction of Psychology and Medicine in Educational Theory and Practice

Jürgen Oelkers (University of Zürich, Switzerland)
From Herbart to Dewey: On the Historical Irresistibility of Learning Psychology —— 313

Kaat Wils (KU Leuven, Belgium)
The Promises of Suggestion. Hypnosis, Education, and the Dangers of Modernity in Belgium around 1900 —— 337

Nelleke Bakker (University of Groningen, the Netherlands)
MBD and De-educationalization: a Countertendency in the pre-ADHD Era —— 359

5 Turns Taking Turns: Concepts, Approaches, and Methodologies in the Making

Jeroen J.H. Dekker (Rijksuniversiteit Groningen, the Netherlands)
Dangerous, Seductive, and Innovative. Visual Sources for the History of Education —— 383

María del Mar del Pozo Andrés (University of Alcalá, Spain) and Sjaak Braster (Erasmus University of Rotterdam, The Netherlands)
Teachers Acting as Photographers: The Progressive Image of the Cervantes School of Madrid (1918–1936) —— 405

Nele Reyniers (KU Leuven, Belgium)
Sound as an Archival Source in the History of Education for Children with Mental Disabilities. —— 433

Inés Dussel (DIE-CINVESTAV, México)
What Might a Material Turn to Educational Histories Add to the History of Education? Proof-eating the Pudding —— 449

Antonio Viñao (University of Murcia, Spain)
School culture(s): Historiography of a Polysemic Concept —— 469

Index —— 489

Acknowledgements

This book, dedicated to Emeritus Professor Marc Depaepe, could not have been realized without the help of many. Some of the book chapters included in this volume were first presented at a symposium organized in November 2018 on the occasion of Marc Depaepe being awarded emeritus status. Hence, special thanks go to Prof. Dr. Ian Grosvenor, Prof. Dr. Rebecca Rogers, and Assoc. Prof. Dr. Antonio Canales for their thought-provoking keynote speeches reworked as chapters for this book. Also, we would like to thank Josefine-Charlotte Soen and Annick Decabooter for their logistical support in celebrating Em. Prof. Dr. (Dr.) Depaepe. We thank the Subfaculty of Psychology and Education Sciences at Kulak, the KULAK rectorate, as well as the KU Leuven Faculty of Psychology and Education Sciences for their financial support of this event. Furthermore, the publication of this book would not have been realized without the continuous support of the colleagues and friends of Marc Depaepe who responded with much enthusiasm to our invitation to contribute to this volume. We are also very grateful for the funding we received from the *Stichting Paedagogica Historica* for the publication of this book volume. Last, but certainly not least, our special thanks go to Maria Leon who supported us in the much-dreaded final editing and correction process.

Note on the editors

Frederik Herman has been a lecturer at the School of Education of the University of Applied Sciences and Arts Northwestern Switzerland since March 2018 and the Schwyz University of Teacher Education since June 2019. He is specializing in the social and cultural history of education. He completed his doctorate on twentieth-century school culture at the University of Leuven, Belgium, in 2010. Frederik joined the FAMOSO project at the University of Luxembourg as a postdoctoral researcher in March 2013 and was a member of the Institute of Education and Society and later of the Luxembourg Centre for Contemporary and Digital History until February 2018. His publications have dealt with topics such as school culture and materialities of schooling; psychophysiology, professional orientation, and vocational training; cultural learning, heritage making, and identity construction; and visual histories of schooling. He recently guest- and co-edited the special issues *Bodies and Minds in Education* (History of Education, 2019; with Michèle Hofmann) and *Cultivating Children and Youth: Transnational Explorations of the Urban and the Natural* (History of Education, 2020; with Ian Grosvenor and Siân L. Roberts) as well as a volume of essays, *Fabricating Modern Societies: Education, Bodies, and Minds in the Age of Steel* (Leiden: Brill, 2019, with Karin Priem).

Geert Thyssen is Associate Professor in Educational Sciences at the Western Norway University of Applied Sciences (HVL), Bergen, Norway. Over the past 20 years, his research has ventured mainly into the (new) social and cultural history of education but frequently crossed disciplinary boundaries. His work so far has focused on educational reform, health education, body-sensory education, and "meaning and sense making" in education, with particular attention to in/equality, inclusion and exclusion, and diversity relating to particular childhoods and social categories produced. He is a member of the Executive Committee of the History of Education Society UK, co-convenor of Network 17 (Histories of Education) of the European Educational Research Association (EERA), as well as scientific board member for a number of history of education and education journals. He has successfully attracted external funding as PI/CI for a number of research projects. His most recent work centers on "timespacematters" of education, on education and "senses of belonging" relating to food and street music, and, in line with previous research on school "dropout", also on issues concerning Ph.D. completion. Among his latest (co-)publications is a special issue of *The Senses and Society* ("Learning to Make Sense – Interdisciplinary Perspectives on Sensory Education and Embodied Enculturation", with Ian Grosvenor).

Angelo Van Gorp is Professor of History of Education at the University of Koblenz-Landau, Campus Landau, Germany. By focusing on past responses to social questions in both educational theory/research and practices, he attempts to enrich current and future debates on related topics. In his research he offers historical perspectives on appropriation processes of progressive education, on urbanity and social inequality as well as on educational media, particularly social or documentary photography, and film. In his most recent research he explores the potential of a socially engaged educational history in relation to a participatory approach.

Sarah Van Ruyskensvelde is Assistant Professor in the History of Education at KU Leuven. Over the past years, she has published on a broad range of topics within the history of education, including the history of education in times of conflict and war, the history of the education sciences in Belgium, and the history of residential youth care. Also, some of her most recent publications reflect on innovative approaches and methods of historical source investigation. Apart from publishing single- and multiple-authored academic publications on a wide array of topics in the field of the History of Education, she is also a board member of the Belgian-Dutch Association for the History of Education (BENGOO) and is co-convenor of and reviewer for Network 17: Histories of Education within the European Education Research Association. In the past, she has acted as an editorial assistant board member of *Paedagogica Historica*, as well as member of the editorial board of the *Tijdschrift voor Onderwijsrecht en Onderwijsbeleid*. Her current and forthcoming work centers on the scientization of primary and secondary education in Belgium, and the development of an "ontological" approach to historical source materials. For instance, her research project *Attention, please! Conceptualizations of attention and the psychologization of primary education, 1842–1980* has recently been awarded funding of the Flemish Fund for Fundamental Research (FWO), and will be initiated in the fall of 2021.

Pieter Verstraete is Professor of History of Education at the Research Unit for Education, Culture and Society (KU Leuven, Belgium). His main research interests are the history of disability and special education, educational histories of contagious diseases (for example leprosy in Belgian-Congo), and the role played by sounds and silences in the history of education. He is president of the Belgian-Dutch Society for the History of Education and curator of the annual Leuven DisABILITY Filmfestival. He currently examines the role played by silence in the history of education: *Silence in the classroom – A modern history of schooling* (Leuven University Press – to be published October 2021).

List of Contributors

Antonio Fco. Canales (Barcelona, 1966) is Associate Professor in History of Education at the Universidad Complutense de Madrid (Spain). He is a specialist in the history of Spain during the twentieth century, with especial attention to education, gender, and science. He is the author of books such as *Las otras derechas* (Madrid: Marcial Pons, 2006) and co-editor of *La larga noche de la educación española* (Madrid: Biblioteca Nueva, 2015), *Science Policies and Twentieth-Century Dictatorships* (London: Routledge, 2016), and *Women's Education in Southern Europe. Historical Perspectives (19th–20th Centuries), Vol 1–4* (Roma, Aracne, 2017, 2018, 2019 and 2021). He has published articles in journals such as *Paedagogica Historica*, *History of Education*, *Gender and Education*, *Revista de Educación*, *Bordón*, *Educación XX1*, *Ayer*, *Historia Social*, and *Historia Contemporánea*. He is the leader of the National Research Project *The boundary between science and politics and science in the boundary: Spanish science, 1907–1975* (FFI2015–64529-P). He is member of the Executives Committees of ISCHE and the Spanish Society of History of Education (SEDHE), and editor-in-chief of its journal *Historia y Memoria de la Educación*.

Lynn Fendler is Professor Emerita, Michigan State University, USA. For 20 years in the Department of Teacher Education, she taught courses in educational foundations, curriculum theory, philosophy, and historiography. Since 2000, Professor Fendler has been a member of the Research Community Philosophy and History of the Discipline of Education: Evaluation and Evolution of the Criteria for Educational Research. In 2010–11 she served as Visiting Professor in Languages, Culture, Media, and Identities at the University of Luxembourg. Her research interests include ethics of knowledge, historiography, genealogy, educational research, and the philosophy of food. Professor Fendler is the author of *Michel Foucault* in the Bloomsbury (formerly Continuum) Library of Educational Thought, which introduces Foucault's philosophical, genealogical, and literary critique to teachers.

Joyce Goodman is Professor of History of Education at The University of Winchester UK and *chercheure associée* at CERLIS.eu. Her research explores how women's work in and for education during the interwar period intersected with internationalism and empire, particularly through entanglements of women's international and regional organizations, schooling, and higher education. She is currently working on a book entitled *Rosa Branson Art, Life and Education* (Winchester University Press, forthcoming). Her previous books include *Girls'*

Secondary Education in the Western World (Palgrave, 2014 pbk), with James Albisetti and Rebecca Rogers; *Women and Education: Major Themes in Education* (Routledge, 2011, 4 volumes), with Jane Martin; and *Social Change in the History of Education: The British Experience in International Context* (Routledge, 2008), with Gary McCulloch and William Richardson. Joyce is an honorary member of the ISCHE and of Network 17 of EERA. For her publications, see www.joyce-goodman.org.uk. She tweets as @joycehisted.

Thomas Popkewitz is a Professor in the Department of Curriculum and Instruction, The University of Wisconsin–Madison, USA. His studies focus on the systems of reason that govern curriculum reforms, the sciences of education, teacher education, and policy. His research crosses the fields of curriculum studies, the political sociology of education, cultural history, and transnational studies to understand the politics of educational knowledge and the paradoxes of exclusion and abjection in efforts to include. His most recent publications are: *The Impracticality of Practical Research: A History of Sciences of Change That Conserve* (University of Michigan Press, 2020); Thomas S. Popkewitz, Daniel Pettersson, and Kai-Jung Hsiao, eds., *The International Emergence of Educational Sciences in the Post-World War Two Years: Quantification, Visualization, and Making Kinds of People* (Routledge, 2021); and a special issue on Curriculum History in the Spanish journal *Historia De La Educación* (with Miguel Pereyra). With Swedish colleagues, he is studying international student assessments to understand the changing relations of science, policy, and society.

Ian Grosvenor is Emeritus Professor of Urban Educational History at the University of Birmingham. He is currently Director of the Arts and Humanities Research Council funded *Voices of War and Peace: First World War Engagement Centre*. Current research focuses on the relationship between the academy and communities and the co-production and co-design of research; pandemics and histories of education; and populism, anti-fascism, and education. He was Managing Editor of the international journal *Paedagogica Historica* from 2008–2020.

Mathieu Zana Etambala (Kinshasa, DRC /1955) holds a Doctorate in Modern History. He was affiliated to KU Leuven until July 2020. Since August 2020, he has been working as an expert for a working group of the Federal Parliament responsible for an investigation into Belgium's colonial past. From February 2021 he has taught an introductory course on the history of Africa at the University of Ghent (UGent).

Rebecca Rogers is professor in the history of education at Université de Paris (France) and a member of the research laboratory Cerlis (Centre de recherches sur les liens sociaux). She has published widely in both English and French on the history of French girls' education and on historiography in the history of education or gender history. Her publications include *A Frenchwoman's Imperial Story: Madame Luce in Nineteenth-century Algeria* (Stanford University Press, 2013) and an edited volume with Françoise Laot: *Les sciences de l'éducation. Emergence d'un champ de recherches dans l'après-guerre* (Presses universitaires de Rennes, 2015). President of the International Standing Conference for the History of Education between 2015 and 2018, she is active on the board of *Histoire de l'éducation*, *Paedagogica Historica*, as well as editor of *Clio. Femmes, Genre, Histoire*.

Eckhardt Fuchs is Director of the Georg Eckert Institute for International Textbook Research and Professor for History of Education/Comparative Education at the Technical University Braunschweig. He has worked in a variety of academic institutions and served as a visiting professor in Sydney, Umeå, Tokyo, and Seoul. His research interests include the global history of modern education, international education policies, and textbook development. He has published ten books and more than 100 articles and chapters on these issues including *The Palgrave Handbook of Textbook Studies* (2018), *Textbooks and War. Historical and Multinational Perspectives* (2018), *Connecting Histories of Education: Transactions, Transculturalism and Transnationalism* (2014), and *Transnationalizing the History of Education* (2012). He served as president of ISCHE from 2012 to 2015.

Eva Matthes has been full professor for educational science at the University of Augsburg since October 2000. She is specialized in the history of pedagogical ideas, institutions, professions, and media. She completed her doctorate on W. Klafki's contribution to the development of educational science in 1991 and her habilitation on the dealing of *Geisteswissenschaftliche Pädagogik* with National Socialism after 1945 in 1997, both at the University of Erlangen-Nürnberg. In 1998–1999 she led the Theodor Litt Research Center at the University of Leipzig. Eva was President of the *Sektion Historische Bildungsforschung* in the *Deutsche Gesellschaft für Erziehungswissenschaft (DGfE)* from September 2011–September 2015. She has been President of *IGSBi* (*International Society for the Research on Textbooks and Edcuational Media*) since 2001. Her publications deal with topics such as educational classics; educational and didactical theories; the development of educational science and pedagogical professions; and educational media. She recently co-edited *Europa und Bildungsmedien/Europe *and Educational Media* (2019, with Annemarie Augschöll and Sylvia Schütze); *Migration und Bildungsmedien/Migration and Educational Media* (2020, with Sylvia Schütze) as well as the special issue *Holocaust Education in der Migrationsgesellschaft* (*Bildung und Erziehung*, with Elisabeth Meilhammer).

András Németh is a professor at the Eötvös Loránd University Faculty of Education and Psychology Institute of Education, and the head of the Research Group for Historical, Theoretical, and Comparative Education. His main field of interest is theoretical, historical, and comparative pedagogy, reform pedagogy and life reform, history of profession, pedagogical historical anthropology, and the development of educational science in Hungary and Central European countries.

Éva Szabolcs is a professor at the Eötvös Loránd University Faculty of Education and Psychology Institute of Education, and a member of the Research Group for Historical, Theoretical, and Comparative Education. Her main field of interest is educational science during the socialist period in Hungary, childhood studies, and the research methodology of educational science.

Iveta Kestere is Professor for History of Education at the Faculty of Education, Psychology, and Art (University of Latvia). She is also acting as scientific expert in Education at the Council of Sciences of the Republic of Latvia. Her current research projects are focusing on the creation and training of the "New Soviet Man" (in collaboration with the University of Vilnius, Lithuania), visual propaganda in education under European totalitarian regimes (in collaboration with the University of Vic, Spain), and childhood representations within Latvian museums (Scientific Council of Latvia). Her other research work concerns the history of educational sciences and the history of teacher training. She is the author and co-editor of several books, such as the collected volume (co-edited with Ene-Silvia Sarv and Irena Stonkuviene) *Pedagogy and Educational Sciences in the Post-Soviet Baltic States, 1990–2004: Changes and Challenges* (Riga: University of Latvia Press, 2020). Kestere was an invited researcher and guest lecturer at the KU Leuven (Belgium), at the Georg Eckert Institute for International Textbook Research (Germany), and at Vilnius University (Lithuania). She was member of Executive Board of International Standing Conference for the History of Education (ISCHE) from 2011 to 2014. She is currently Link Convenor for Network 17, Histories of Education (European Conference on Educational Research, ECER)/European Education Research Association (EERA).

Zanda Rubene is Professor for Philosophy of Education at the University of Latvia, Vice Dean of the Faculty of Pedagogy, Psychology, and Art, and Head of the

Doctoral Study program "Education Sciences." She also operates as scientific expert in Education at the Council of Sciences of the Republic of Latvia. She completed her doctorate on critical thinking as a pedagogical phenomenon at the University of Latvia, in 2004. Her main research interests are philosophy of education, critical thinking, and childhood studies (including Soviet childhood and digital childhood), on which she widely published. She authored the book *Sapere Aude! Critical Thinking in University Studies in Latvia* (2004) and co-authored the book *Introduction to Media Pedagogy* (2008). She also co-edited the special issue *Education and Power: Historical Perspectives* (Paedagogica Historica, 2015; with Iveta Kestere and Irena Stonkuviene; editor in Chief: Jeroen Dekker).

Iveta Ozola is a teacher of German, and Board Member and lecturer at the Institute of Lifelong Learning and Culture *"Vitae"* in Riga (Latvia). She completed her doctorate on geneses of educational sciences from the 1920s to 1960s in Latvia at the University of Latvia in 2014. In her professional career she has been a researcher at the Scientific Institute of Pedagogy at the University of Latvia. For several years, she has had presentations and publications at the *Theodor-Litt-Symposium* in Leipzig (Germany). Her academic interests include development of educational sciences and pedagogy in Latvia and Germany.

Marcelo Caruso has studied at the Universidad de Buenos Aires (BA, 1993), at the University in Munich (PhD, 2001), and at the Humboldt-Universität zu Berlin (Habilitation, 2008). Professor for History of Education at Humboldt-Universität zu Berlin since 2011. Managing Director of the *Zeitschrift für Pädagogik* (since 2015) and *Paedagogica Historica* (since 2021). Recent books: *Geschichte der Bildung und der Erziehung. Medienentwicklung und Medienwandel* (Paderborn, 2019); (ed. together with Daniel Maul) *Decolonization(s) and Education: New Men and New Polities* (Frankfurt/M., 2020); and *El espíritu y la mecánica. El orden de la enseñanza como construcción cultural (Prusia, Dinamarca/Schleswig-Holstein, España, 1800–1870)* (Frankfurt, 2021).

Daniel Przygoda is a research assistant at the Department of History of Education at the Humboldt-Universität zu Berlin and a former assistant in the field of teacher education for theory and history of schooling. His PhD studies focus on the emergence, implementation, variance, and transformation of the adjective "pädagogisch" (pedagogical) during the so-called "bridge time" (denotes the period between 1750 and 1850).

Friedrich Schollmeyer has been assistant at the Department of History of Education at the Humboldt-Universität zu Berlin. An associate to the *Kolleg Globale*

Bildung at the University of Jena/Germany, he researched as an assistant at the Institute for Bildung and Culture. His research is the philosophy of Bildung both in the eighteenth and twentieth century, having completed his doctorate on the Jewish Swiss cultural anthropologist Michael Landmann (1913–1984) this year.

Prof. em. Dr. Dr. h.c. Jürgen Oelkers is retired Professor of "Allgemeine Pädagogik" at the University of Zürich. His research focusses on international progressive education, American pragmatism, and history of educational knowledge.

Kaat Wils is full professor of modern European cultural history at KU Leuven. She has worked on the history of intellectual and scientific culture, the history of the social and biomedical sciences, history of education, gender history, and the teaching and learning of history. She is currently working on a cultural history of the therapeutic use of magnetism and hypnosis in Belgium in the long nineteenth century.

Nelleke Bakker has recently retired as associate professor of history of education at the University of Groningen, the Netherlands. She has published books and articles on the history of childhood, education, parenting, schooling, gender and education, child sciences, and education studies. In recent years her research has focused on child health arrangements, special education, and the influences of child psychiatry, child psychology, and special education studies on child-rearing and education.

Jeroen J.H. Dekker is Honorary Professor of History and Theory of Education at the Rijksuniversiteit Groningen. He was visiting professor at the European University Institute (Florence), Columbia University (New York), and the University of Sassari, and visiting Fellow at the Max Planck Institute for Human Development (Berlin). A former President and Honorary Life Member of ISCHE, he is Editor of *Paedagogica Historica*. His publications, among them *A Cultural History of Education in the Renaissance* (2020, editor), *Educational Ambitions in History* (2010), *The Will to Change the Child* (2001), and *Het verlangen naar opvoeden* (2006), deal with long-term history of education, childhood, parenting, and children at risk from early modern Europe to the present.

Sjaak Braster is Associate Professor of Sociology at the Erasmus School of Social and Behavioural Sciences, Erasmus University of Rotterdam, The Netherlands. He was Professor of History of Education at Utrecht University from 2003 till 2010. He also was Chairman of the Division Educational Policy of the Dutch Association for Educational Research (VOR). His main research lines are sociology of education and educational policy, and the analysis of new sources and new methodologies in the history of education. Recent book publications are: *The black box of schooling: A cultural history of the classroom.* (Brussels: Peter Lang, 2011; with Ian Grosvenor and María del Mar del Pozo Andrés) and *A history of popular education: Educating the people of the world* (New York: Routledge, 2013; with Frank Simon and Ian Grosvenor). Recent articles are: "From savages to capitalists: Progressive images of education in the UK and the USA (1920–1939)", *History of Education* 49, no. 4 (2020): 571–595 (with Maria del Mar del Pozo Andrés); "The progressive child: Images of new education in the New Era, 1920–1939", *History of Education and Children's Literature* 48, no. 4 (2018): 443–451.

María del Mar del Pozo Andrés is Full Professor of Theory and History of Education at the University of Alcalá (Madrid, Spain). In 2000–2006 she was Secretary of the Spanish Society of Educational Sciences and Deputy Director of the journal *Bordón.Revista de Pedagogía*. In 2005–2013 she was Secretary of the Spanish Society for the History of Education. From 2006–2012 she was member of the Executive Committee of the International Standing Conference for the History of Education (ISCHE). Since 2014 she has been co-editor-in-Chief of *Paedagogica Historica*. Her main lines of research and publications are: the role of education in the building of national identities, urban education, teachers training, transnational dimensions of pedagogical movements (with particular attention to Progressive Education), iconography and education, women and education, ethnography of the school, and history of curriculum. She recently coedited the special issues "Images of the European Child" (*History of Education & Children's Literature*, 2018), "Fotografía, propaganda y educación" (*Historia y Memoria de la Educación*, 2018), and edited the catalogue *Madrid, educational city (1898–1938). Memory of the Public School. Essays for an exhibition* (Madrid: Ayuntamiento de Madrid, 2019). A recent article is "The visual turn in the history of education: Origins, methodologies and examples", in *Handbook of historical studies in education*, edited by Tanya Fitzgerald, 893–908 (New York: Springer, 2020, with S. Braster).

Nele Reyniers is a PhD student at the Centre for History of Education of the KU Leuven, Belgium. She graduated as Master of Arts in History at the University of Ghent in 2016. In 2018 she started her PhD project "The sound of abnormality. The first educational initiatives for children with mental disabilities in Belgium from a Sound Studies perspective, 1857–1940"

Inés Dussel is currently Professor and Researcher at the Department of Educational Research, CINVESTAV, Mexico. She acted as the Director of the Education Area, Latin American School for the Social Sciences (Argentina), from 2001 to 2008. She has published extensively on issues related to the historical production of schooling and pedagogy, particularly on its material and visual cultures. She is currently doing research on the intersections between schools and digital visual culture.

Antonio Viñao is honorary professor of Theory and History of Education at the University of Murcia (Spain). Member of the Executive Committee of the ISCHE (1994–2000), president of the Spanish Society of History of Education (2001–2005), and director of the Centre for Studies of Educational Memory (2009–2013) of the University of Murcia, as well as of the journal *Historia y Memoria de la Educación* (2014–2019), his main areas of research are history of literacy (reading and writing as cultural practices) and schooling, history of school culture and heritage (textbooks and school subjects, school spaces and times, school cultures and educational reforms, school memory), and secondary education.

Geert Thyssen, Pieter Verstraete, Frederik Herman, Angelo Van Gorp and Sarah Van Ruyskensvelde
Introduction

Today and tomorrow, and yesterday, too (...)
I'm a man of contradictions, I'm a man of many moods
I'll play Beethoven's sonatas, and Chopin's preludes
I contain multitudes[1]

For we are made of lines. ... Or rather, of bundles of lines (...).[2]

Since each of us was several, there was already quite a crowd.[3]

This book gathers lines. More specifically, it gathers lines of materials, people, and places, and memories, affects and imaginaries. As a peer reviewed scientific publication threading together contemporary, scholarly incisions on the subject of education, it draws in a range of disciplinary fields: from the history and philosophy of education, to visual, material, sensory and culture studies, to science studies, to colonial and race studies, to gender and queer studies, to name but a few. As a *Liber Amicorum* cordially dedicated to Emeritus Professor Dr. Marc Depaepe, in turn it joins key lines of research that have run through his 40-plus year long career so far: the historiography of education; the (post-)colonial history of education; the scientization of education, or the latter's formation as a discipline (sometimes referred to as "pedagogy", "educational sciences", "education studies" etc.) – with reference to educationalization and related notions of medicalization and psychologization; and the "new" cultural history of education. These lines of research, trailing on materially not least via Depaepe's countless high quality (co-)publications critically yet amicably engaged with here, constitute different sections of the book which, like the contributions bound therein, however, in *Deleuzeguattarian* fashion may be read through one another as plateaus. The contributions themselves gather materials, in written as well as visual-material forms, which embody and in turn body forth knowledge and practice that will no doubt tangle with other movement, beyond any specific disciplines.

The book, however, also gathers people and places, and that which one might imagine to be of a less material kind. Yet, "gathering" here – even of

---

1 Bob Dylan, *I Contain Multitudes* (2020), Columbia Records.
2 Gilles Deleuze and Félix Guattari, *A Thousand Plateaus: Capitalism and Schizophrenia*, trans. B. Massumi (London: Continuum, [1987] 2004), 215 and 223.
3 Deleuze and Guattari, *Thousand Plateaus*, 3.

such things – is understood with Tim Ingold (in this matter inspired by Heidegger) as the actual gathering of "drawn threads" that are "drawn into other knots with other threads."[4] It is the doing that for Ingold helps become all "living beings," human or non-human, whom he conceives (informed by Deleuze and Guattari) as "bundles of lines"; they are "gathering"-s that develop along paths, thereby always leaving "trails."[5] Each place thus emerges as a "knot of stories,"[6] a path along which people and things "lay trails."[7] This book is alive in gathering precisely such knots, as it joins paths along which its contributors and Depaepe have laid trails: conferences and similar places of amical and scientific exchange and circulation, museums or exhibitions, university sites but also less formal places, along which alike minds may have met and ideas trailed on. People, as similar knots or "knotting"-s,[8] in Ingoldian terms likewise make up the "texture" that helps breathe life into the book. Indeed, all knots or gatherings "whose constituent strands, as they become tied up with other strands, in other knots"[9] form a "meshwork": the "ever-ramifying web" of tangled "lines of growth" and movement that Deleuze and Guattari have figured as a *haecceity* comprised of rhizomatic "lines of flight", "lines of drift", or "lines of becoming".[10]

"Entangled" with this book – that is: inseparable from it,[11] even if they may not have directly contributed to it – are a number of persons whose paths have touched Depaepe's and helped shape his research lines. One such person is Emeritus Professor Dr. Frank Simon, whom Depaepe himself has often called his *compagnon de route*, but whom in terms of lines of flight, which can only

---

4 Tim Ingold, *Lines: A Brief History* (London and New York: Routledge, 2007), 169.
5 Ingold, *Lines*, 75–81; Tim Ingold, "Bindings against Boundaries: Entanglements of Life in an Open World," *Environment and Planning A* 40 (2008): 1796–1810; Tim Ingold, "Bringing Things to Life: Creative Entanglements in a World of Materials," 2010, 4 (http://eprints.ncrm.ac.uk/1306/1/0510_creative_entanglements.pdf, accessed April 21, 2015); Tim Ingold, *Being Alive: Essays on Movement, Knowledge and Description* (Oxon/New York: Routledge, 2011), 3–4, 10, 12–13. See also Deleuze and Guattari, *Thousand Plateaus*, 223–225.
6 Tim Ingold, "Against Space: Place, Movement, Knowledge," in *Boundless Worlds: An Anthropological Approach to Movement*, ed. Peter W. Kirby (Oxford: Berghahn, 2009), 41; Ingold, *Being Alive*, 149.
7 Ingold, "Against Space," 33.
8 Tim Ingold, *The Life of Lines* (London and New York: Routledge, 2015), 18.
9 Ingold, *Being Alive*, 70.
10 Deleuze and Guattari, *Thousand Plateaus*, 62, 215, 223–226, 290; see also Ingold, *Lines*, 80; Ingold, *Being Alive*, 86.
11 Karen Barad, *Meeting the Universe Halfway: Quantum Physics and the Entanglement of Matter and Meaning* (Durham: Duke University Press, 2007), 3. Ingold figures "entanglement" rather as a dense "interlacing". See Ingold, *Being Alive*, 71.

be seized in the in-between,[12] is best seen as a crowd formed together with Depaepe. Other people worth mentioning are Depaepe's late mentor Maurits de Vroede, who helped to carve out certain paths along which Depaepe's career was to unfold (for instance, that of the historiography and scientization of education); his wife Ginette, who not only helped make his career and impressive academic track record and an enriching family life possible, but whose former profession as kindergarten teacher no doubt contributed to Depaepe's excursions into the history of early childhood education. Family has "mattered" in other ways still that are co-constitutive of at least one of the plateaus of this book. Indeed, Depaepe's great aunt, Sister Maria Adonia Depaepe, can also be seen knotted into the texture of his research into (post-)colonial education in the former Belgian Congo.[13]

That said, with Deleuze and Guattari and Ingold, it is worth diverting attention away from matter already formed. For them, the "essential relation, in a world of life is (…) [that] between *materials* and *forces*,"[14] as one of lively becoming. For Deleuze and Guattari, indeed all is "matter-flow", ever moving, reconfiguring and enfolding: that which "can only be *followed*."[15] This applies also to the book section introductions that follow, which consecutively focus on marks left by educational historiography; politics of diversity pervading the history of post-colonial education; meanderings towards the multi-current discipline of pedagogy; the thin line at times walked between pedagogy and psychology and pedagogy and medicine in this discipline forming movement, and the ever-alternating turns characterizing the new cultural history of education. Without further ado, therefore, we advise the reader to adopt a rule of thumb Ingold has devised from this: *"follow the materials"*,[16] wherever readings thereof may lead.

---

12 Deleuze and Guattari, *Thousand Plateaus*, 323.
13 Marc Depaepe [in cooperation with René Lefebvre, Mathieu Zana Aziza Etambala], *"Tot Glorie van God en tot Zaligheid der Zielen". Brieven van Moeder Marie Adonia Depaepe over haar leven en werk als Zuster van Liefde in Belgisch Kongo (1909–1961)* (Antwerp: Standaard Uitgeverij, 1992).
14 Ingold, *Being Alive*, 210; Deleuze and Guattari, *Thousand Plateaus*, 377.
15 Deleuze and Guattari, *Thousand Plateaus*, 451; cited also in Ingold, *Being Alive*, 213.
16 Ingold, *Being Alive*, 213.

Section 1: Leaving Marks of Inquiry: Ravels of Theory, Methodology, and History of Educational Historiography

Geert Thyssen

Enmeshed through, and across, the contributions featuring in the first section of this book are considerations regarding that which Depaepe has referred to as the "theory, methodology and history of educational historiography."[17] Each of the four contributions included indeed touch upon aspects of theory and methodology which are key to historiography of education while inscribing themselves – either more or less explicitly – within a history of historiographic tradition (as well as a history of education). They do so in rather different ways, and it is worth noting from the start that two of the four contributors do not identify as historians of education. As such, the authors and contributions are drawn into and mark a body of scholarly enterprise which, in line with Depaepe's repeated stress on the importance of interdisciplinarity and disciplinarity in this area of scientific endeavor,[18] shows "not (...) a single, flat developmental line" but "multiple developmental lines (with their specific pace and own dynamics)"[19] that tangle in ways that matter.

Here, we employ Karen Barad's onto-ethico-epistemological work to analyze some of the ways that "lines of flight"[20] concerning historiography of education embraided through the contributions in this section might indeed make a difference, or rather differences that "matter" as both "significance" and "substance" and that are thus worth "attuning" one's "analytical apparatus" to.[21] Tracing the descent of the term historiography helps illuminate why posthumanist "grand theory" *à la* Barad does have something to offer here, however "fashionable" its current status. Historiography indeed gathers two ancient Greek words that each refer to practices or doing-s: *historia* (ἱστορία), denoting the act of inquiring or seeking knowledge, but also knowledge affected by such inquiry, and thus in a way the effecting itself of particular knowledge, and *graphein* (γραφειν), point-

---

17 Marc Depaepe, "Why Even Today Educational Historiography is not an Unnecessary Luxury: Focusing on four Themes from Forty-Four Years of Research," *Espacio, Tiempo y Educación* 7 (2020): 227, accessed February 26, 2021, doi: http://dx.doi.org/10.14516/ete.335.
18 See, for instance, Marc Depaepe, "The Ten Commandments of Good Practices in History of Education Research," *Zeitschrift für Pädagogische Historiographie* 16 (2010): 33.
19 Depaepe, "Why Even Today," 241.
20 Deleuze and Guattari, *Thousand Plateaus*, 62, 224–226.
21 Cf. Barad, *Meeting the Universe Halfway*, 3, 36, 72–73.

ing to the act of writing, but also of drawing.²² Engagement with historiography of education, then, is about "writing(s) or drawing(s)-together of knowledge (seeking) pertaining to education", that is: about the making of knowledge-producing "imprints" concerning education. In other words, historiography of education is about "inscriptions"²³ coming about through the very act of inquiry into matters of education.

In Barad's terms, historiography of education is about "agential cuts" being "enacted", or boundaries being stabilized, which cause particular "phenomena" to be configured in particular ways. A phenomenon is thereby seen as a "congealing of agency": a cause-and-effect of action implicating the very apparatus(es) producing the phenomenon as inseparable from it, that is: of "intra-action",²⁴ not interaction (which implies separate elements):

> An agential cut effects a local separability of different 'component parts' of the phenomenon, one of which ('the cause') expresses itself in effecting and marking the other ('the effect'). … Whether it is thought of as a 'measurement,' or as part of the universe making itself intelligible to another part in its ongoing differentiating intelligibility and materialization, is a matter of preference. Either way, what is important about causal intra-actions is the fact that marks are left on bodies.²⁵

To suggest historiography of education is about marks of inquiry being left on bodies, is to point to material-discursive effects, a bodying forth of meaningful differences in which it is implicated. With Barad, it is also to point to responsibility called upon for inscriptions made. Obviously, here, marks of inquiry may be assumed to have a bearing on some kind(s) of past(s) and on education (however conceived), but historiography of education as an endeavor of "inscribing meaningful difference making" has much broader relevance. Although no longer conceived "as a form of social action",²⁶ as was the case within the tradition of

---

22 On the etymology of history, see https://time.com/4824551/history-word-origins/, accessed January 20, 2021.
23 In Barad's post-humanist theory, neither "human" or "non-human" apparatuses are thought to act as "inscription devices"; imprints/inscriptions or marks left are seen as "intra-acting" agencies entangled through the production, by an "apparatus", of a "phenomenon" inseparable from it, as both a "being configured" and "configuring". Karen Barad, "Posthumanist Performativity: Toward an Understanding of How Matter Comes to Matter," *Signs* 28 (2003): 816.
24 Barad, *Meeting the Universe Halfway*, 33, 56, 139–140, 151, 170. See also Joyce Goodman, "Circulating Objects and (Vernacular) Cosmopolitan Subjectivities," *Bildungsgeschichte: International Journal for the Historiography of Education* 17 (2017): 116–118.
25 Barad, "Posthumanist Performativity," 824.
26 Cristiano Casalini and Laura Madella, "Tracking Three Traditions in the Historiography of Education Toward Comparative Methods," *Revista Española de Educación Comparada* 34 (2019): 32.

(radical) revisionism, historiography of education, Lynn Fendler (2017) has noted, remains "inescapably political because perceptions are shaped by specific lenses that make some things visible and other things invisible."[27] Indeed, to quote Depaepe, it "possesses its own [material-]discursive power" as it produces "discourse[s] about discourses,"[28] and particular "ways of seeing"[29] (and other ways of engaging with and being in the world).[30] The very contributions in this section each adopt different approaches, thus exemplifying what Fendler (2017) has termed "specific ways (…)[that] research shapes what it is possible to see as 'history' and as 'education'."[31] Insofar then as the contributions in this section and the book overall can be seen (as we believe they can) as an "effort to balance the values of truth, justice, and beauty,"[32] to quote David Labaree, they surely have wider purchase beyond the boundaries of the history of education and cognate disciplines.

We will now briefly zoom into the various contributions in this section, starting with that by Antonio Canales, who approaches the historiography of education from the vantage point of a particular strand of philosophy of social sciences, namely: that of analytical Marxism and more specifically Jon Elster's program of micro-foundations, rather than that of any grand philosophy *à la* Foucault espousing postmodernism. Particularly as a critique of linguistic proposals, historiography here is configured as a "craft" (cf. Marc Bloch) bound by clear rules described as "materialist, empiricist and realist." These terms in no way refer to "new materialisms". In fact, Canales' approach firmly inscribes itself in the classic tradition of social constructivism, based on representational theory, with knowledge being built on "objects of study" thought to represent

---

[27] Lynn Fendler, "Apertures of Documentation: Reading Images in Educational History," *Paedagogica Historica* 53 (2017): 751.
[28] Depaepe, "Ten Commandments," 32.
[29] Depaepe, "Ten Commandments," 33; cited also in Fendler, "Apertures of Documentation." After António Nóvoa, "Ways of Saying, Ways of Seeing. Public Images of Teachers (19th–20th Centuries)," *Paedagogica Historica* 36 (2000): 21–52.
[30] See, for instance, Ian Grosvenor, "Back to the Future or Towards a Sensory History of Schooling," *History of Education* 41 (2012): 675–687; Pieter Verstraete and Josephine Hoegaerts, "Educational Soundscapes: Tuning in to Sounds and Silences in the History of Education," *Paedagogica Historica* 53 (2017): 491–497; Geert Thyssen and Ian Grosvenor, "Introduction: Learning to Make Sense – Interdisciplinary Perspectives on Sensory Education and Embodied Enculturation," *The Senses and Society* 14 (2019): 119–130.
[31] Fendler, "Apertures of Documentation," 751.
[32] David Labaree, "A Sermon on Educational Research," *Bildungsgeschichte: International Journal for the Historiography of Education* 2 (2012): 74; cited in António Nóvoa, "Letter to a Young Educational Historian," *Historia y Memoria de la Educación* 1 (2015): 48.

"things of the world", if contingent on "cultural categories". The stress is on method and indeed mathematics and modelling, so as to arrive at theory and explanations offering the "most plausible account",[33] rather than the other way around, which is framed as reverting to idealism and functionalism. For Canales this is about proper use of "historical sources" seen as "empirical evidence of a past reality that exists outside of us." Adhering to the agreed specific procedures of the craft ensures objectivity – here viewed as "correspondence" established via "interpretive mediation" involving "intentional-causal explanations" as "chains of connections between antecedent and consequent." "Difference that matters" emerges between Canales' "materialist, post-linguistic" account and a Baradian "new materialist, post-humanist" one, which likewise configures objectivity in causal terms, but as "accountability" to precise agential intra-actions "effecting" "local determinacy" not through some mediation from the outside but "within phenomena" thus produced.[34] The approach Canales proposes locates discursivity at the intentional level of actions considered and related context only, not at the level of effects or that of interpretation. This helps to produce straightforward, causal explanations for the countless historical examples of unintended consequences highlighted in much of Depaepe's work. Yet on a Baradian account anything is "material-discursive", including that which for Canales regards representation or interpretation and which is reconfigured as "diffraction": just another kind of agential intra-action or cut co-constitutive of a historical phenomenon, re-diffractions ("re-turnings") of which may help reveal exclusions embodied therein.[35]

Exclusions are also key to Lynn Fendler's contribution on historiography, "critical and effective" forms of which, she suggests, have shown a commitment to "specificity of time and place". Such a commitment is required to produce what Fendler has previously termed "lever histories" able to open up possibilities for "understand[ing] ourselves in the world."[36] This entails troubling of dominant, exclusionary "truth making", she argues here. In particular, Fendler addresses exclusions that come with invocations of "continuity" and

---

33 Depaepe, "Ten Commandments," 33; Marc Depaepe, "History of Education Anno 1992: 'A Tale Told by an Idiot, Full of Sound and Fury, Signifying Nothing'? Presidential Address ISCHE XIV," *History of Education* 22 (1993): 1–10.
34 Barad, "Posthumanist Performativity," 821; Barad, *Meeting the Universe Halfway*, 93, 135.
35 Karen Barad, "Diffracting Diffraction: Cutting Together-Apart," *Parallax* 20 (2014): 168; Geert Thyssen and Frederik Herman, "Re-Turning Matters of Body_Mind: Articulations of Ill-/Health and Energy/Fatigue Gathered through Vocational and Health Education," *History of Education* 48 (2019): 502.
36 Fendler, "Apertures of Documentation," 759.

"representation" – two tropes which, she contends, "dehistoricize history" when they present themselves as universally applicable. Fendler's approach to these tropes "baked into history" is a Foucauldian one, like Tom Popkewitz's, employing "historical examples as pedagogical apparatuses for confronting the limits of thought." Here Fendler uses three examples in which continuity tends to be assumed – from tutoring to common schools; from rats to humans; and from statistical probability to scientific certainty – as well as four examples of levels at which representation usually operates unquestioned – that of archives; that of structuralist analyses; that of generalizations from past to present or future; and that of linear, expository writings. She shows how in each of the three examples of truth-making continuity things or questions that matter for education are excluded from mattering, and biases, injustices, and inequities reinscribed. Similarly, Fendler reveals truth shaped by assumptions of representation to be exclusionary in that they obscure gaps and perpetuate silences, impose a conceptual logic to a tapestry of perspectives inevitably marginalizing some of these, prioritize inference damaging specificity and diversity of experience, and write out the messiness of life. Fendler then offers up a number of critical alternatives available. Substitutes to continuity proposed, for instance, include: genealogy, key to which are chance and specific mobilizations of power allowing for a richer texture of experiences and historical possibilities; and Afrofuturism which also strips historiography of its deterministic features and enables de-centering from hegemonic accounts of history. Fendler likewise points to several alternatives to representation, among which are: strong objectivity as presentation of richer historical texture including context neglected from positions of privilege – as well as surface reading unhindered by structuralist interpreting and montage of gaps critically employing material absent from the archive; critical fabulation as a means to exhaust limits posed by archives in representing for instance the enslaved and using narration to perform what cannot be represented of their lives; indigenous epistemologies that addresses "violence of historical representation"; and poetry- and other arts-based approaches to research like exhibition projects entangling history with heritage, or fiction as a source and medium. Other alternatives to continuity and representation could have been added here still, like counterfactualism[37] working with what if-s to point at complex aspects to as yet excluded forms of what Barad terms "differential becoming"[38] of past, present, and future. Approaches like these based on "non-representational

---

[37] Jeremy Black, *Other Pasts, Different presents, Alternative Futures* (Indianapolis: Indiana University Press, 2015).
[38] Barad, *Meeting the Universe Halfway*, 170.

theories"³⁹ confront scholars with the entanglement of temporalities and spatialities studied and inscribed, and resulting inclusions or exclusions.

Such entanglement of temporalities and spatialities is explicitly explored by Joyce Goodman in her contribution, which can be read as a non-linear, non-expository text seemingly dealing with two distinct approaches to film, education, internationalism, and Empire in the context of 1930s "moral disarmament", yet really working through the issue of how temporal and spatial aspects can be inscribed in histories of education.⁴⁰ Goodman works with three articles issued in the International Review of Educational Cinematography by Evelyn Wrench and Germaine Dulac.⁴¹ She first teases out spatial and temporal dimensions underpinning Wrench's writing, focusing on a concentric circles diagram he uses, which she suggests is grounded in classical physics' second law of thermodynamics on energy quality, enabling a "unidirectional" notion of temporality that Henri Bergson has referred to as one of "differences of degree". Goodman figures the "arrow of time", thus infusing Wrench's work as linked to its spatial conception of internationalism, moving from the "self" to the national to the international. This imaginary of "enrichment" or "enlargement" for her reveals a notion of "abstract"/"absolute" space and time, configured in terms of the "discrete, discontinuous and homogeneous." Goodman argues this affirms a self-centered modern Western "style of reason" and related "identity politics" giving way to "evolutionary taxonomies" of the backward/advanced or racially inferior/superior, etc. Goodman contrasts this space/time model with that of "temporal indeterminacy" undergirding Dulac's account, which she contends is more closely aligned with quantum physics and what Bergson has called "differences in

---

39 See also Lynn Fendler, "The Ethics of Materiality: Some Insights from Non-Representational Theory," in *Educational Research: Material Culture and Its Representation*, ed. Marc Depaepe and Paul Smeyers (Dordrecht: Springer, 2014), 115–132; Lynn Fendler and Paul Smeyers, "Focusing on Presentation Instead of Representation: Perspectives on Representational and Non-Representational Language-Games for Educational History and Theory," *Paedagogica Historica* 51 (2015): 691–701; Goodman, "Circulating Objects," 118, 124.
40 See also Goodman, "Circulating Objects," 122; Joyce Goodman, "Suzanne Karpelès (1890–1969): Thinking with the Width and Thickness of Time," *Bildungsgeschichte: International Journal for the Historiography of Education* 8 (2018): 231–244; Joyce Goodman and Sue Anderson-Faithful, "Turning and Twisting Histories of Women's Education: Matters of Strategy," *Women's History Review* 29 (2019): 377–395; Joyce Goodman, "Afterword: Histories of Women's Higher Education, Time, and Temporalities," *Paedagogica Historica* 56 (2020): 847–856.
41 Wrench was founder of the Overseas League, the English-Speaking Union, and the All Peoples' Association; Dulac in turn was artistic and newsreels director at Gaumont-Franco-Films-Aubert, founder of France-Actualités, film producer, teacher, lecturer, film theorist and activist, feminist and pacifist.

kind". Dulac's framing of the educative work of newsreels towards internationalism as one of allowing spectators to sense not only the "infinitely great" but also an inconspicuous world of the "infinitely small" placed "on the same plane" disrupts Wrench's concentric circles model. As Goodman shows, in Dulac's approach to newsreels, in particular the "little incidents" to which they can expose the "self", the latter is "thrown out of (...)[its] own environment and out of (...)[its] own circle." She suggests that Dulac's focus on "life-matter" of such everyday "slow-burn" events resonates with Bergson's concept of *élan vital* and of "duration": "the lived movement of temporality" – the latter being conceived as "heterogeneous, (...) continuous and interpenetrating." It is within duration, Goodman notes, Bergson imagines "differences in kind" to be experienced, which are about the "unique" and the "incomparable" of lived events. She then argues that the "turbulence" of "little incidents" from newsreels envisaged by Dulac effect what Michel Serres terms a "space of passage" or "transience", where "friction" associated with "exposure" opens up new possibilities. Finally, Goodman draws on Alfred North Whitehead to figure both Wrench's and Dulac's temporal- spatial models not as absolute epistemological opposites but as each tainted by "abstraction" whereby the "fullness to existence" is not wholly grasped; both entail artificial separation of what Whitehead sees as "events", mental or otherwise, which he situates "on the same plane." From this notion of "event", it makes sense for her, instead, to consider Wrench's and Dulac's spatial-temporal thinking concerning film, education, and internationalism as "counterpoints" entangled within the same fabric. Goodman's theorizing here is clearly informed by Barad's, in which similarly there are no things that happen in time or space and can be seized as such, but rather intra-actions as "differential spacetimematterings of the world."[42]

Tom Popkewitz's chapter likewise can be seen to entangle the historical and historiographical in that he deploys "history of the present" to explore "modern school" as a "double inscription of science" – "as a mode of interpreting, organizing pedagogy and as a quality of the mind in rationalizing children's thinking" –, which he argues is evident most clearly from pragmatism and the writings of John Dewey. Popkewitz figures all of these as "agents", be they of specific kinds, thereby dissolving, with reference to Barad, the boundaries between epistemology and ontology and shifting attention to material effects. He first defines history of the present as to do with bringing to bear the "entanglement of different historical lines" that are "activated to give intelligibility to the matters of the present," here: present-day "knowledge or systems of reason" of

---

42 Barad, *Meeting the Universe Halfway*, 182.

science governing schooling. As Foucauldian genealogy, it is about "historicizing", here as "excavating" of conditions that make features of the curriculum, teaching, and learning intelligible and actionable such that "particular kinds of people, subjectivities and differences are fabricated" and the very "materiality of schooling" is affected. Popkewitz then historicizes the reason of schooling Dewey and his writings embodied through the notions of "indigenous foreigner", "conceptual personae" (Deleuze and Guattari), and "traveling libraries" (Depaepe). He argues each of these theoretical-methodological frames undercut a "semiotic realism" that works to "romanticize" the archive as a "site to find the given words, and how their rendering change over time and space." The figure of indigenous foreigner thus points to imaginaries of belonging enacted around Dewey's work upon its "travelling into" historical spaces, such that "hopes, desires and fears about future" are projected into it as "native" to these precise spaces. In turn, the figure of conceptual personae for Popkewitz helps grasp the "assembling" of this work "through the interstices of different moving historical lines" enabling such "phantasma of collective belonging and subjectivity." Yet, Depaepe's image of traveling libraries for him best embodies the iterative efforts expended in producing it upon its arrival, not as stable text but as "grids of practices" attuned to particular cultural sites where it is "articulated as part of a tapestry of 'thought' occurring at the interstices of the collective readings." For Popkewitz, archival documents are thus best "viewed as events helping to problematize what is seen."[43] He further elaborates on this using two exemplars, the "idea of social improvement" and "the modern school as a historical project in the making of people", connected as agents in grids of practices like Dewey's texts in ways that "indigenous foreigner" and "travelling libraries" help capture. Popkewitz argues that with the effecting of school, through the idea of improvement, as inscription of particular pedagogical proposals, "a memory of the past that orders time as a regular and irreversible quality of human life (...)[and] connects with notions of development in the sciences" as "desires of the present' gets embodied within the inscription. Relatedly, he contends, the inscription of school as a historical project in the making of people imbued with "anticipatory change embodied in the notion of improvement" entails "double gestures". That is, as "partial folds" in school's becoming, "comparativeness is activated" and specific groups of children "abjected from the spaces of belonging," often paradoxically, Popkewitz suggests, in "efforts to include."

---

[43] Alessandra Arce Hai, Frank Simon, and Marc Depaepe, "From Practice to Theory, Ovide Decroly for Brazilian Classrooms: A Tale of Appropriation," *History of Education* 45 (2016): 795.

Section 2: The Politics of Diversity: Gender, Culture, and Post-colonial Education

Pieter Verstraete

In an often-cited article published in *History of Education* in 2003, the British scholar Richard Aldrich identified three important duties for the historian of education.[44] Given the scientific nature of their work, the historian of education had an important duty to the truth. He or she could not invent historical data and had to come up with a historical narrative that approached as closely as possible the historical truth – although Aldrich obviously recognized the fact that a faithful reconstruction of the past is sheer impossible. Besides aiming at a truthful reconstruction of the past, the historian of education also had an important duty to the present, that is, to his or her fellow human beings. Too many people look at the world as if it consists only of black and white. When they are confronted with good news, they are seized with pure ecstasy. Bad news, on the contrary, leads to intellectual paralysis and doomsday thinking. The historian of education therefore needed to produce historical narratives that invite people to think twice and resist the tendency to oversimplify human life. The third duty Aldrich identified had to do with all those voices that were and still are neglected, oppressed, and not heard. Way too many life stories of human beings are buried in the catacombs of archives. Even more have been denied access to the depositories of historical source material or the narratives assembled in historiographical overviews. This un/conscious historical bias has been the outcome of divergent discriminatory processes deeply rooted in cultural values and norms, political ideals, and economical ambitions. Unveiling the underlying mechanism of human suppression and neglect, according to Aldrich, symbolized an important step towards the creation of inclusionary environments.

The different chapters included in the section (post)colonial histories of education demonstrate that Aldrich's plea has not fallen on deaf ears. Historians of education in particular and historians in general have come up with narratives, stories, theories, public events, and scholarly conferences systematically deconstructing historical practices of "othering." In this way the discipline of history of education has tried to keep pace with societal change, notably instances of traditionally marginalized people deciding to stand up and speak up against historical injustices, such as genocide, suppression, slavery, and economic exploita-

---

44 Richard Aldrich, "The three duties of the historian of education." *History of Education* 32 (2003): 133–143.

tion – to name but a few. Probably the most well-known of these today is the Black Lives Matter movement which gained prominence after the inhumane treatment and death-provoking suffocation of the African-American George Floyd by mainly white policemen. The reactions triggered by that horrifying event led to mass demonstrations all over the world as well as increased sensibility to (post)colonial injustices. To give just one example, we could mention the Belgian events that took place in the wake of the American Black Lives Matter movement and stimulated several people to initiate discussions and demonstrations concerning the public visibility of colonial authority. One of the pressing issues had to do with the public statues of the Belgian King Leopold II, who founded what later was to become the Belgian Congo. These tangible monuments, according to the demonstrators, continued to justify the historical injustices that the Congolese people underwent during the colonial area. But the unquestioned visibility of colonial history not only affected those who had by then passed away. It still poses innumerable problems, challenges, and obstacles to the emancipatory ambitions of the African community living in Belgium today.

The four (post)colonial historical essays which we have collected in this section not only aim to answer Aldrich's plea but also want to innovate the research being undertaken in the field of history of education. They do so in a twofold way. The first two chapters, written by Ian Grosvenor and Zana Etambala, are constructed around the fruitful intersection of history and heritage research. Although several authors have given critical accounts of how history and heritage relate to one another,[45] the intersection of the two nevertheless constitutes an interesting educational space which is continuously re-invented by actors coming from divergent fields. This in particular becomes clear when one thinks about the museum as an informal educational space where visitors are exposed to historical objects, narratives, and events. If the constructed nature of the museum can be applied to all museums – whether dedicated to architecture, the natural sciences, toys, or comic books – it probably becomes most clear in museums focusing on colonial history. The chapter of Zana Etambala offers an intimate account of the recent renovation of the Royal Museum of Central Africa. The critical reading of Etambala contrasts sharply with the at times heraldic messages about the renovation's decolonizing approach. Both the chapter of Etambala and the chapter of Grosvenor implicitly advocate a critical reappraisal by historians of education of those informal learning environments pervaded by colonial attitudes, imperial prejudices, and Eurocentric epistemologies.

---

45 See for instance David Lowenthal. *The heritage crusade and the spoils of history* (Cambridge: Cambridge University Press, 1998).

Whereas the chapters of Etambala and Grosvenor in particular direct our attention towards educational spaces related to cultural heritage (both tangible and intangible), the essays of Rebecca Rogers and Eckhardt Fuchs zoom in on the importance of adopting an intersectional lens when dealing with (post)colonial histories. Intersectionality refers to the idea that human experiences are not determined by single differences like race, class, gender, sexual preference or disability.[46] The outlook of someone's life is always shaped by them being simultaneously a woman, having dark skin, belonging to the upper class, being lesbian, and blind – to give but one concrete example. Historians of education interested in the history of colonial enterprises cannot understand the impact of imperial regimes when solely focusing on race. In order to understand and come to terms with the complex mechanisms that eradicated the memory of innumerable colonized individuals, historians of education need to include several differences at the same time. And this is precisely what Rebecca Rogers does in her essay on French historiography that points at the telling absence of women in (post)colonial histories. Eckhardt Fuchs in his turn focuses on textbook research. He gives a broad overview of the different trajectories that are currently available for scholars interested in deconstructing the colonial powers present in the school manuals we use for the instruction of children in primary schools.

Section 3: Flood Lands of Pedagogy: Meanderings between Empiricism, Theory, and Practice

Frederik Herman

This section deals with the formation of pedagogy (*Pädagogik, pedagogiek, pédagogie*) as a discipline or, in other words, the development of the "science of education" – the more systematic socio-scientific examination of educational processes – from the late nineteenth century onwards. Two short definitions of pedagogy – taken from two manuals for (General) Pedagogy from the beginning of the twentieth century – seamlessly integrate the discipline's cornerstones: scientific inquiry ("empirical pedagogy"), theorization ("theoretical pedagogy"), and practical guidelines ("practical pedagogy" and "methodolatry"):

---

[46] Kimberlé W. Crenshaw, "Demarginalizing the Intersection of Race and Sex: A Black Feminist Critique of Antidiscrimination Doctrine, Feminist Theory and Antiracist Politics," *University of Chicago Legal Forum* (1989): 139–167.

Pedagogy, or the science of education, is the set of principles, methods and procedures that a wise teacher applies while raising/educating children. Usually, manuals for pedagogy offer an overabundance of directions and advice from which to choose. Depending on the nature of the school in which he/she teaches, his/her personal aptitudes and his/her experience, the teacher applies the principles which guide him/her, the methods he/she follows and the procedures he/she employs.[47]

Pedagogy is not the same as education. It is the theory. It is a science which results from the experience of centuries, from the study of the child and from the examination of methods which suit each kind of knowledge. It gives the rules to follow in order to educate the child and train him/her in virtue.[48]

Of course, these descriptions, made for future teachers, sketch a harmonious, unproblematic, and symbiotic interplay between these three dimensions and, therewith, a kind of homogeneity and orderly image of the discipline – how else would one present the discipline to future practitioners? The strained relation or even the gap between lower and higher pedagogy – as Marc Depaepe and others named the practical knowledge generated by teachers and the empirical based and theoretically loftier pedagogy developed at universities, respectively[49] – is for instance elegantly disregarded. So, the authors of these pieces were probably concealing purposefully (and unaware of changes yet to come) that the discipline was in permanent transition, struggled with its multifaceted

---

47 Edmond Gabriel, *Manuel de pédagogie – à l'usage des écoles catholiques* (Tours: Imprimerie Mame, 1909), 1. Translated by the section editor.
48 Louis Riboulet, *Manuel de pédagogie générale – à l'usage des écoles normales, des candidats au Brevet supérieur et de tous les éducateurs* (Lyon: Imprimerie Emmanuel Vitte, 1930), 7. Translated by the section editor.
49 Elsewhere, Marc Depaepe refers to this tension as the paradox between "praxis-oriented theory" and "theory-based praxis". Marc Depaepe, "Praktijkgerichte theorie versus theoriegerichte praktijk: Een 'historische' paradox in de pedagogiek?," in *Paradoxen van pedagogisering: Handboek pedagogische historiografie*, ed. Marc Depaepe, Frank Simon, and Angelo Van Gorp (Leuven: Acco, 2005), 442–466. See also Marc Depaepe, Frank Simon, and Angelo Van Gorp, "The 'Good Practices of Jozef Emiel Verheyen – schoolman and Professor of Education at the Ghent University: A case of using educationally correct discourse at the right place and the right time," in *Educational Research: Why 'What Works' Doesn't Work*, ed. Paul Smeyers and Marc Depaepe (Dordrecht: Springer, 2006), 17–36; Marc Depaepe et al., *Order in Progress: Everyday Educational Practice in Primary Schools, Belgium, 1880–1970* (Leuven: Leuven University Press, 2000); Marc Depaepe, "The Practical and Professional Relevance of Educational Research and Pedagogical Knowledge from the Perspective of History: Reflections on the Belgian Case in its International Background," *European Educational Research Journal* 1 (2002): 360–379.

nature, and did not really manage to formulate its own "pedagogical foundations" (*pädagogische Grundgedanken*).[50]

The development of the "science of education" is thus characterized by an ongoing search for the discipline's profile (e.g., its role within society, its position within the existing scientific field, its epistemological orientation, and its institutional affiliation) and a permanent drifting in between the abovementioned empiricism, theory, and practice – which has in turn resulted in a dazzling plurality.[51] With the so-called empirical or realistic turn (scientization of education) and the associated, more structural institutional and academic embedment (e.g., the establishment of Faculties of Educational Sciences), the discipline positioned itself as a quasi-autonomous field of research that strongly depended on, and turned towards, developing auxiliary sciences, such as developmental psychology, educational psychology, educational sociology, and didactics. The eagerness to borrow from "foreign' disciplines – for instance, due to the young discipline's lack of proper theoretical frameworks –, made it quasi-immediately a repository of various empirical, theoretical, and practical approaches. Moreover, next to its interdisciplinary hybridity, which has contributed to the discipline's plurality, also evolutions within the discipline itself (e.g., paradigm shifts and specializations) and developments of (and within) field(s) of application have further pluralized "pedagogy".

An epistemological plurality was established through various competing schools of thought that developed in the course of the twentieth century – schools adopting different stances on such questions as: how can one understand education or pedagogy as science(s)? What are the goals of educational/pedagogical sciences? What empirical methods are appropriate?[52] Among significant shifts were turns towards the hermeneutics and phenomenology oriented *Geisteswissenschaftliche Pädagogik* (ca. 1900 – e.g., Nohl, Litt, Spranger, and Flitner), the positivist and empirical/experimental educational sciences (ca. 1960 – e.g. Roth, Brezinka), and critical pedagogy (ca. 1970 – Mollenhauer, Heydorn), respectively.[53] These subsequent paradigm shifts resulted, on the one hand, in what Gert Biesta has called a "diachronical plurality" and, on the other hand, in a "synchronic plurality" – as older and newer epistemological

---

50 Dietrich Benner, *Allgemeine Pädagogik: Eine systematisch-problemgeschichtliche Einführung in die Grundstruktur pädagogischen Denkens und Handelns* (Weinheim, Basel: Beltz Juventa, 2015), 5.
51 Siebren Miedema, "De Pluraliteit van de pedagogiek," in *Pedagogik in Meervoud*, ed. Siebren Miedema (Houten/Diegem: Bohn Stafleu Van Loghum, 1997), 13.
52 Margrit Stein, *Allgemeine Pädagogik* (München: Ernst Reinhardt Verlag, 2017), 16.
53 Stein, *Allgemeine Pädagogik*, 17.

approaches co-existed and interacted with one another.⁵⁴ Likewise, the '*Innendifferenzierung*'⁵⁵ or gradual specialization, and thus crystallization, of subdisciplines (e.g., systematic, comparative, historical, social, and vocational pedagogy), specific subject areas, and fields of application (e.g., intercultural, peace, environmental and media pedagogy/education) have further diversified the field.⁵⁶ Furthermore, the "practice field" – the "playground" of educationists/pedagogues – over time developed and further diversified and expanded, not least due to the ongoing educationalization (*Pädagogisierung*) of modernizing society – transforming issues previously foreign to education/pedagogy into educational/pedagogical questions.⁵⁷ This urged the discipline of education, which saw itself as a "practical" science (*Handlungswissenschaft*), to further inflect. Finally, while adopting a comparative stance – for instance, towards different institutions, regions or countries –, one is confronted with many variations within applied and developed scientific methods, theories, ways of thinking and talking about education, as well as within a multifarious praxis.

Consequently, exploring and writing the history of the "science of education" implies dealing with this plurality and thus presupposes a willingness to travel along the meanderings of this "multi-current" discipline – as Depaepe himself called it – and an eagerness to collect driftwood left behind on its flood lands. The following four contributions focusing on the development of the science(s) of education between 1850 and 2000 in different countries (Latvia, Hungary, Germany) explicitly shed light on specific dimensions of the discipline's multifaceted nature, be it in terms of (3.1) the various stances taken with-

---

54 Gert Biesta, "Pluraliteit, pragmatisme en pedagogiek," *Comenius* 10 (1990): 7–30.
55 See e.g. Niklas Luhmann, "Zur Innendifferenzierung des Gesellschaftssystems: Schichtung und funktionale Differenzierung," *Soziale Welt* 68 (2017): 5–23.
56 Stein, *Allgemeine Pädagogik*, 13.
57 For more information, see Marc Depaepe, "Educationalisation: A key concept in understanding the basic processes in the history of western education," *History of Education Review* 27 (1998): 16–28; Marc Depaepe, "Dealing with the paradoxes of educationalization: Beyond the limits of "New" Cultural History of Education," *Revista Educação & Cidadania* 7 (2008): 11–31; Marc Depaepe and Paul Smeyers, "Educationalisation as an ongoing modernization process," *Educational Theory* 58 (2008): 379–389; Marc Depaepe et al., "About pedagogization: From the perspective of the History of Education," in *Educational research: The educationalisation of social problems*, ed. Paul Smeyers and Marc Depaepe (Dordrecht: Springer, 2008). See also Daniel Tröhler, "Die Pädagogisierung des Selbst und die Pädagogisierung der Welt," in *Selbstgesteuertes Lernen: Interdisziplinäre Kritik eines suggestiven Konzepts – Mit Nachbemerkungen zum Corona-Lockdown*, ed. Damian Miller and Jürgen Oelkers (Weinheim, Basel: Beltz Juventa, 2021), 52–74; Andrea De Vincenti et al., *Pädagogisierung des 'guten Lebens'. Bildungshistorische Perspektiven auf Ambitionen und Dynamiken im 20. Jahrhundert* (Bern: Bibliothek am Guisanplatz, 2020).

in the *Geisteswissenschaftliche Pädagogik*, (3.2) the diachronic plurality of the discipline, (3.3) the exposure to plurality after a period of dictatorship and, finally, (3.4) the conceptual diversity and ambiguity of the adjective "pedagogic/-al ".

How should primary and secondary school teachers be educated and where should their education take place (e. g., at a university or at teacher education colleges)? These questions are at the core of the contribution *"Geisteswissenschaftliche Pädagogik", teacher training and educational science – different concepts and attributions of significance. Germany, 1900–2000*. Eva Matthes explores the writings of Eduard Spranger, Theodor Litt, Herman Nohl, Wilhelm Flitner, Erich Weniger, and Albert Reble – the "dynasty" of representatives of the *Geisteswissenschaftliche Pädagogik* – in which they took positions with regard to (re)orientation and institutionalization of teacher training in Germany during the twentieth century. Matthes reveals that, despite the fact that these influential German educational thinkers belonged to the same "school of thought", different stances were taken with regard to future teachers' roles, the position of "educational sciences" within teacher education programs, terrain covered by the discipline (including, for instance, subject matter relating to psychology, sociology, anthropology, and didactics), the theoretical, academic or practical nature of teacher education, the educationalization or translation of "unpractical" and "unworldly" sciences, etc.

In their contribution, *Educational science as an academic discipline in Hungary (1867–1953): Turns and developmental phases*, András Németh and Éva Szabolcs investigate how pedagogy developed into a more or less independent discipline, became institutionalized, and was permanently reframed (in terms of goals, methods, etc.). The authors distinguish four major developmental phases, characterized by specific shifts: (1) the incorporation of pedagogy within the existing university system; (2) the turn towards science-based approaches; (3) pedagogy's orientation towards the *Geisteswissenschaften*; and (4) its political instrumentalization under the Soviet regime. While writing this (national) history of the discipline – focusing on and contextualizing the major protagonists, their institutions, and instruments –, the authors are crystal clear that this can only be understood as a history of traveling educational ideas, reception, and adaptation/appropriation, as an ongoing struggle for institutional stability and a permanent search for a proper profile (between modernization and self-preservation, and between existing and developing sciences and disciplines).

The next chapter, *Educational sciences between "real" Moscow and the "imaginary" West: The case of Latvia (1989–1999)*, picks up where the previous one ended, namely: the period after the Soviet dictatorship. Iveta Kestere, Zanda Rubene, and Iveta Ozola reflect – in some cases as "experts by experience" – on the re-orientation, re-institutionalization, and internationalization (*in casu* Westernization) of the educational sciences in Latvia after the fall of the Iron Curtain. This transitional phase, the so-called "hour zero," was strongly characterized by the eagerness to get rid of the old yoke, on the one hand, and to belong to the West, on the other hand. The regained freedom, that came with political and intellectual liberation, inaugurated a new era for the discipline and academic staff involved. However, the speedy emancipation process aspired and restoration of the discipline's reputation envisaged – with a view to playing a significant role in the academic world, both on the national and international level – was decelerated by a variety of factors. In the chapter, the authors elaborate on such barriers to change (for instance, on the level of finances and organization, the academic curriculum and theoretical approaches, and the available human resources and skills) and the applied coping strategies (e.g., a turn towards Germany with its strong tradition of *Geisteswissenschaftliche Pädagogik*). Probably more important here is the fact that the insider's perspective allows us to gain a better insight into the broad range of feelings – from excitement to a sense of being overwhelmed, to gratefulness, to insecurity, to fear (e.g., concerning self-image and esteem among academic staff, new independencies, ambiguity with regard to academic "development support") – that have accompanied changes and influenced associated decision-making processes. As such, the authors' contribution is a call for historians of education dealing with the history of the science(s) of pedagogy to consider also the associated history of emotions and mentalities.

Not the development of the discipline, but rather the conceptual history of derived adjectives – such as pedagogic and pedagogical – in different language contexts (German, French, and English) are at the core of this section's last chapter, entitled *Pedagogic – A preliminary thesis on a lexical innovation during the European Enlightenment*. In their contribution, Marcelo Caruso, Daniel Przygoda, and Friedrich Schollmayer explore the historical emergence of these adjectives as well as the varying uses and meanings. With their conceptual history approach – surely an underexplored domain within the history of education – and their specific focus on the adjectives (rather than the nouns), they take up the call to explore and gain deeper insight into the educational jargon –,[58] be it its emergence, expansion, circulation, perception, connotation, differentiation, and appropriation over time. Their exploration clearly demonstrates how the adjective "pedagogic" in different linguistic environments and by different groups of users was assigned different meanings, from rather negative (e.g., pedagogic as pedantic) to more positive ones, and was used in different ways (e.g., as descriptor or qualifier). Thus, with their contribution the authors not only hint at a

---

[58] See, for instance, Depaepe, "Ten Commandments," 32.

plurivalent and ambiguous conceptual field hiding behind these adjectives, but they also make historians of education aware of the importance of critically assessing educational concepts previously used, as well as those currently used to write about the past.

Section 4: Walking the Line: The Attraction of Psychology and Medicine in Educational Theory and Practice

Angelo Van Gorp

> I keep the ends out for the tie that binds,
> Because you're mine, I walk the line[59]

Whereas in the previous section the discipline formation of pedagogy and educational science has been discussed mainly from the perspective of educationalization, and more specifically from its institutional and rhetorical dimension, the fourth section shows that more knots can be found on the plateau of disciplinarization. This section focuses on the notions of psychologization and medicalization, two central processes of modernity that contributed to the process of individualization in western culture.[60] Both notions refer to the exponential growth and impact of psychology and medicine respectively throughout the nineteenth and twentieth centuries in almost every walk of life, including educational theory and practice. Based on his research on the development of the empirical-an-

---

[59] Johnny Cash, *I Walk the Line* (1956), Sun Records.
[60] Eduardo Crespo and Amparo Serrano, "The Psychologisation of Work, the Deregulation of Work and the Government of Will," *Annual Review of Critical Psychology* 8 (2010): 44. On psychologization, see for instance, from a Foucauldian point of view: Nikolas Rose, *The Psychological Complex: Psychology, Politics, and Society in England, 1869–1939* (London: Routledge/Kegan Paul, 1985); Nikolas Rose, *Inventing our Selves: Psychology, Power and Personhood* (Cambridge: Cambridge University Press, 1996); Nikolas Rose, *Governing the Soul: The Shaping of the Private Self* (London: Free Association Books, 1999), second edition. See also: Mathew Thomson, *Psychological Subjects: Identity, Culture, and Health in Twentieth-Century Britain* (Oxford/New York: Oxford University Press, 2006); Ole Jacob Madsen and Svend Brinkmann, "The Disappearance of Psychologisation?," *Annual Review of Critical Psychology* 8 (2010): 179–199; Jan De Vos, *Psychologisation in Times of Globalisation* (London: Routledge, 2012); Jan De Vos, *Psychologization and the Subject of Late Modernity* (New York: Palgrave Macmillan, 2013). On medicalization, see for instance: Robert A. Nye, "The Evolution of the Concept of Medicalization in the Late Twentieth Century," *Journal of History of the Behavioral Sciences* 39 (2003): 115–129; Peter Conrad, *The Medicalization of Society: On the Transformation of Human Conditions into Treatable Disorders* (Baltimore: Johns Hopkins University Press, 2007).

alytical paradigm in the history of educational science, Marc Depaepe laid a trail that paid attention to a discipline developed increasingly "in the direction of positivism and experimental science."[61] From the late nineteenth century onwards, this direction was further shaped by approaches such as child study, pedology, and educational psychology.[62] As Depaepe argued, "(m)any forms of research existed side by side, conflicting with each other and mixed up, both in terms of methodology and content."[63] The aforementioned empirical-analytical disciplines were highly diverse and in the ongoing germination and differentiation process of educational science it remained difficult to distinguish between disciplinary fields of psychology and pedagogy.[64]

In his analysis of this development, Depaepe, together with Paul Smeyers, draws attention to the growing interest in psychology within the field of pedagogy, which he relates to "the illusion of certainty" that is "very attractive, almost irresistible" for educational researchers.[65] This is picked up further by Jürgen Oelkers, who in his contribution to this volume discusses what he calls "the historical irresistibility" of learning psychology in educational theory. With his contribution, Oelkers elaborates on an older contribution to a German volume that discussed the "psychologization" of pedagogy.[66] In this essay, Oelkers emphasized that the dependence of pedagogy on psychology is "a structural fact that

---

[61] Marc Depaepe, "Struggling with the Historical Attractiveness of Psychology for Educational Research: Illustrated by the Case of Nazi-Germany," in *Between Educationalization and Appropriation: Selected Writings on the History of Modern Educational Systems*, ed. Marc Depaepe (Leuven: Leuven University Press, 2012), 408. Originally published in Paul Smeyers and Marc Depaepe, ed. *Educational Research: The Attraction of Psychology* (Dordrecht: Springer, 2012), 11–31.
[62] Marc Depaepe, *Zum Wohl des Kindes? Pädologie, pädagogische Psychologie und experimentelle Pädagogik in Europa und den USA, 1890–1940* (Weinheim/Leuven: Deutscher Studien Verlag/Leuven University Press, 1993).
[63] Depaepe, "Struggling," 413.
[64] Niklas Luhmann, *Essays on Self-Reference* (New York: Columbia University Press, 1990). See also: Rudolf Stichweh, "Die Autopoiesis der Wissenschaft," in *Theorie als Passion. Niklas Luhmann zum 60. Geburtstag*, ed. Dirk Baecker et al. (Frankfurt am Main: Suhrkamp, 1987), 447–481; Angelo Van Gorp, Marc Depaepe, and Frank Simon, "Backing the Actor as Agent in Discipline Formation: An Example of the 'Secondary Disciplinarization' of the Educational Sciences, based on the Networks of Ovide Decroly (1901–1931)," *Paedagogica Historica* 40 (2004): 591–616.
[65] Paul Smeyers and Marc Depaepe, "Making Sense of the Attraction of Psychology: On the Strengths and Weaknesses for Education and Educational Research," in *Educational Research: The Attraction of Psychology*, ed. Paul Smeyers and Marc Depaepe (Dordrecht: Springer, 2012), 4.
[66] Jürgen Oelkers, "Einige historische Erfahrungen im Verhältnis von Psychologie und Pädagogik," in *Die Psychologisierung der Pädagogik. Übel, Notwendigkeit, Fehldiagnose*, ed. Roland Reichenbach and Fritz Oser (Weinheim/München: Juventa, 2002), 12–28.

has played a part in the continuity of the history of pedagogy." It is the "normal relationship – a constant which has unfolded throughout history."[67] In his actual contribution, Oelkers introduces the notion of learning as cognitive "problem solving." In that respect, he wonders how cognitive learning psychology became so irresistible that today it is hardly challenged anymore. In order to answer this question, he deploys what he terms an "interdisciplinary history," starting with Herbart's pedagogy and philosophy, in the framework of which Herbart had developed his conceptualization of psychology. By the end of the nineteenth century, however, Herbart's "new" psychology seemed to have remained an "old" psychology from where there was no route to a psychology of learning, at least not a direct one. In order to illustrate this point, Oelkers first introduces the "new" psychology before discussing in detail Thorndike's position towards Herbart and Dewey, respectively, and explaining the success of "problem solving."

In discussions on Thorndike and Dewey, it is often stated that "Thorndike won (and) Dewey lost."[68] It is important, however, to distinguish between *Rezeptions-* und *Wirkungsgeschichte*, as Depaepe and colleagues explained in their examination of Dewey's influence on Belgian education.[69] In this regard, Depaepe's research on the Belgian educational reformer Ovide Decroly (1871–1932), which he conducted together with Frank Simon and Angelo Van Gorp, reveals that both Dewey and Thorndike, among other psychologists, inspired Decroly in the design of his method as well as in the development of psychological tests, educational games, and films as didactic tools. The Decroly case also shows that scientific expertise within the empirical-analytical paradigm was not only, and in this case not even primarily, based on pedagogy and psychology.[70] Indeed, although he is often regarded as a "psycho-pédagogue,"[71] it was

---

[67] As discussed in Depaepe, "Struggling," 415. With his continuity hypothesis applied to the history of "Reformpädagogik," Oelkers has been an important source of inspiration in regard to Depaepe's critical stance towards the history of new education. See in particular: Jürgen Oelkers, *Reformpädagogik: Eine kritische Dogmengeschichte* (Weinheim, Basel: Juventa, 2005) fourth edition; Jürgen Oelkers, "Reformpädagogik vor der Reformpädagogik," *Paedagogica Historica* 42 (2006): 15–48.
[68] Ellen C. Lagemann, *An elusive science: The troubling history of education research* (Chicago/London: The University of Chicago Press, 2000), xi. As quoted in Depaepe, "Struggling," 409.
[69] Tom De Coster et al., "Dewey in Belgium: A Libation for Modernity?," in *Inventing the Modern Self and John Dewey: Modernities and the Traveling of Pragmatism in Education*, ed. Thomas S. Popkewitz (New York: Palgrave Macmillan, 2005), 85–109.
[70] This long-running research project finds a provisional culmination point in a biography and supplemental material, the publication of which is planned for the end of 2021: Marc Depaepe,

particularly the medical standpoint that made Decroly a specialist, also in his capacity of educational reformer.[72] Also other key figures in the fields of pedagogy and psychology were medical doctors, Maria Montessori and Edouard Claparède perhaps being the most illustrious examples. It underlines that, in addition to the intertwining processes of educationalization and psychologization, the related notion of medicalization played a decisive role as well. This becomes clear in the two contributions by Kaat Wils and Nelleke Bakker, respectively.

In her contribution, Kaat Wils discusses the promises of suggestion for both medicine and education. She describes how educationalists in Belgium around 1900 became intrigued by the role of suggestion in education. Interest in the topic remained lively until at least the First World War, as the International Conference of Pedology in Brussels (1911) demonstrates. Alongside a medical approach, in which hypnosis and suggestion functioned as therapeutic tools to cure behavioral problems in children, a much broader interpretation of suggestion as a specific way to communicate with students had gained interest as well. The belief in the benefits of integrating insights from medicine into education also fostered educationalists' wider interest in suggestion as a teaching method. Suggestion was presented as an extension of the intensive individual therapy that doctors provided. The belief in the beneficial effects of suggestion shared by those educators and doctors was, however, paralleled by a common anxiety about the negative role of suggestion in contemporary society. In her contribution, Wils focuses on the birth of the paradox that would also reverberate in the field of education: hypnosis and suggestion were perceived as both a disease and cure, both a danger and solution for a society whose members were considered to suffer from new, modern illnesses. Relegating hypnosis to the strictly medical domain appeared to be an elegant way out of this paradox.[73]

Frank Simon, and Angelo Van Gorp, *Ovide Decroly (1871–1932): Une approche atypique?* (in preparation).
71 See, for example: Yann Diener, *On agite un enfant: L'État, les psychothérapeutes et les psychotropes* (Paris: La Fabrique Éditions, 2011).
72 Depaepe, "Struggling," 412.
73 In addition to her research on history education, Kaat Wils focusses on history of science, for instance on positivism and on the history of sociology and medicine. Marc Depaepe participated in a conference she co-organized on the notion of medicalization: Marc Depaepe, "De markt van het kind: Over de medicalisering van opvoeding en onderwijs," in *De zieke natie: Over de medicalisering van de samenleving, 1860–1914*, ed. Liesbet Nys et al. (Groningen: Historische Uitgeverij, 2002), 260–278. With regard to medical history, see also: Frank Huisman, Joris Vandendriessche, and Kaat Wils, "Blurring Boundaries: Towards a Medical History of the Twentieth Century," *Low Countries Historical Review* 132 (2017): 3–15.

As Frederik Herman already emphasized in his introduction to the third section, in the course of the twentieth century numerous research areas as well as methodological paradigms supplemented the already heterogeneous empirical-analytical paradigm, leading to the educational sciences "manifesting themselves increasingly 'in the plural' from the end of the 1960s."[74] In this development, as Nelleke Bakker explains in her contribution, neuroscience became ever more attractive to both psychologists and educationalists.[75] In response to the notion of educationalization, she explores the possibility of a process of "de-educationalization," by examining the way school-based children's problems, such as inattention and overactivity, were perceived and treated from the 1960s to the 1980s, that is: the pre-Attention Deficit Hyperactivity Disorder (ADHD) era. She focusses on the Netherlands, where the most prominent forerunner of ADHD, Minimal Brain Damage/Dysfunction (MBD), was diagnosed frequently. She concludes that MBD has played a significant role in preparing the path towards a bio-medicalization, hence de-educationalization, of the problems discussed.[76]

---

74 Depaepe, "Struggling," 408.
75 See also: Smeyers and Depaepe, "Making Sense"; Jeroen J.H. Dekker, "Children at Risk in History: A Story of Expansion," *Paedagogica Historica* 45 (2009): 17–36; and from a Foucauldian perspective: Nikolas Rose, *The Politics of Life itself: Biomedicine, Power, and Subjectivity in the Twenty-First Century* (Princeton: Princeton University Press, 2007); Nikolas Rose and Joelle M. Abi-Rached, *Neuro: The New Brain Sciences and the Management of the Mind* (Princeton: Princeton University Press, 2013).
76 In her research, Nelleke Bakker focusses on the medicalization of education, for instance on the development of special education, the role of school doctors, and the relation between psychology and education. See, for instance: Nelleke Bakker, "Monitoring Child Health: School Doctors at Work in a Dutch Rural Area (1930–1970)," *History of Education* 45 (2016): 813–830; Nelleke Bakker, "A culture of Knowledge Production: Testing and Observation of Dutch Children with Learning and Behavioural Problems (1949–1985)," *Paedagogica Historica* 53 (2017): 7–23; Nelleke Bakker, "Child Guidance, Dynamic Psychology and the Psychopathologisation of Child-Rearing Culture (c.1920–1940): A Transnational Perspective," *History of Education* 49 (2020): 617–635.

Section 5: Turns Taking Turns: Concepts, Approaches, and Methodologies in the Making

Sarah Van Ruyskensvelde

That the History of Education, a field of study that has paid attention to historical patterns of continuity and change,[77] is itself continuously evolving is perhaps best illustrated by the methodological-conceptual shifts that have occurred within the field. Influenced by developments in related fields of study, such as history, philosophy or sociology, historians of education have searched for new ways to approach the educational past and reconsidered their relationship towards that past. This fifth book section discusses some of the prominent methodological approaches, theoretical concepts, and debates that have emerged within new social and cultural histories of education, through the lens of different topical foci, ranging from disability history to the history of progressive education, to the history of school uniforms. With this discussion of the debates, shifts, and tensions that have surrounded the methods, approaches, and theoretical lenses of history of education research, it is aimed at a revalorization of the dialogues within the history of education that might lead to new pathways for future research. After all, the past is never "really over", nor is the search for ways to write history. And although Marc Depaepe himself has, at times, been critical about the many turns that steered "the gaze" of historians of education in particular directions,[78] his research has fueled methodological and theoretical renewal within the discipline. A particular case in point is the twentieth ISCHE conference session in Kortrijk that was organized by Marc Depaepe and colleagues. While historians of education had begun to explore visual source materials such as paintings as "gateways" to the past, the 1998 conference in Kortrijk was in fact the first to address the potential of the visual for history of education research in particular. Since then, and under the influence of the pictural and visual turns,[79] visual materials have gained their permanent place in the historian of education's "source box." Yet, the latter's methodological habitus towards visual sources, as Jeroen Dekker calls it in his contribution to this volume, has also

---

[77] Marc Depaepe has contributed a great deal to the study of continuity and change in the history of education. See, for instance: Marc Depaepe et.al., *Order in progress*.
[78] See, for instance, Marc Depaepe, *Between Educationalization and Appropriation: Selected Writings on the History of Modern Educational Systems* (Leuven: Leuven University Press, 2012).
[79] See, for instance, Ulrike Mietzner, Kevin Myers, and Nick Peim, eds., *Visual History. Images of Education* (Bern: Peter Lang, 2005); Ian Grosvenor, Martin Lawn, and Kate Rousmanière, *Silences and Images. The Social History of the Classroom* (New York: Peter Lang, 1999).

changed throughout the years. Whereas, for some time, visual sources were approached as mirrors of a past reality, there is an increasing consensus upon the fact that – following Elizabeth Edwards – visual materials are agents in a much larger ecology, in which past, present, and future intersect.[80]

The latter idea is represented in the two contributions to this volume which, albeit through different topical lenses, deal with the potential of visual sources for history of education research. Both Jeroen Dekker's chapter "Dangerous, seductive, and innovative. Visual sources for the history of education", and Maria del Mar del Pozo Andrés and Sjaak Braster's chapter "Teachers acting as Photographers: The Progressive image of the Cervantes School of Madrid (1918–1936)" develop a shared importance of "triangulating" visual materials with other sources to put together the pieces of the puzzle. More specifically, the seventeenth-century emblem books Jeroen Dekker investigates on their strength, educational meaning, and relationship with educational reality are a combination of text and image. They include "a caption with information on the meaning, an image showing part of the emblem's story, [and] finally a text onto which the emblem has been based (...)." In a similar vein, in their chapter on the progressive Cervantes School in Madrid, del Mar del Pozo Andrès and Braster introduce the notion of visibility to advocate a holistic approach to educational research that combines visual sources with textual ones. In doing so, both contributions develop a complementary understanding of the potential of visual sources for history of education research. Following Frank Ankersmit, Dekker advances a convincing argument regarding the potential of visual sources to bring historians of education "in closer contact with the realities studied, not by mirroring those realities but by referring to aspects of them." In del Mar del Pozo Andrés and Brasters' contribution, visual sources are in essence acknowledged for their potential to inform a "montage of gaps"[81] around the aspects of historical reality that the written documentary archive does not reveal. They argue that the photographic materials they used for their study, as other visual sources, give visibility to the "occult" discourses of the school that are not made explicit in textual materials, because of their supposedly trivial or self-evident nature. As a result, the image speaks perhaps louder than the words of textual sources, as they are a condensed representation of aspects of historical reality.

---

80 Elizabeth Edwards, *The camera as historian: amateur photographers and historical imagination, 1885–1918* (Durham: Duke University Press, 2012).
81 Cf. Catherine Burke and Ian Grosvenor, "An exploration of the Writing and Reading of a Life: The 'Body Parts' of the Victorian School Architect E.R. Robson," in *Rethinking the History of Education. Transnational Perspectives on Its Questions, Methods, and Knowledge*, ed. Thomas S. Popkewitz, 205 (New York: Palgrave Macmillan, 2013).

Surely, the emergence and continued importance of "the visual" in history of education research should be considered within broader paradigmatic developments. With the advent of the new cultural history of education in the 1990s came also a growing concern within history of education research for "the ordinary and the mundane". Rather than studying macro-level systems, theories or policies, historians of education turned their attention to opening the black box of schooling,[82] shedding light not only on aspects of daily school life, but also addressing the experiences of teachers or pupils. Inevitably, this shift required a methodological shift too, as the written archive often represents an "institutional gaze."[83] In recent years, visual sources, and methodologies to investigate aspects of the lives of "common people" have been complemented with other (sensory) approaches.[84] This is exemplified by Nele Reyniers's study that explores sound as an archival source. Starting from the case study of Catholic asylums for children with mental disabilities in nineteenth-century Belgium, Reyniers investigates how mental disability was socially and culturally constructed along acoustic lines. "Sound as an archival source in the history of education for children with mental disabilities" uses personal files to document how "education experts", such as medical doctors, observed and interpreted the sounds produced by, and silences of, institutionalized mentally disabled children. In doing so, she convincingly demonstrates how sounds and silences became firmly entrenched in normative notions of "otherness". Drawing on Bakker, she concludes that "sounds and also silences produced by children were psychopathologized in the late nineteenth and twentieth century (...)." But perhaps even more important than Reyniers' contribution to the historical scholarship on educational initiatives for disabled children is the attention her chapter directs towards the potential of the acoustic for the history of education. While established in other disciplinary fields, historians of education have only recently begun to explore a sound studies approach. Informed by amongst others Vehkahlathi, Rice, and Van Drenth, Reyniers explores the importance of the acoustic to look beyond the "institutional gaze" to which the historian of education is so often condemned. By documenting how children's vocality, speech, and language were part of their labelling, Reyniers convincingly draws attention to the logics behind knowledge production within institutional contexts.

---

82 Sjaak Braster, Ian Grosvenor, and María del Mar del Pozo Andrés, *The black box of schooling: A cultural history of the classroom* (Brussels: Peter Lang, 2011).
83 See, for instance, the work of Ann Laura Stoler, *Along the Archival Grain: Epistemic Anxieties and Colonial Common Sense* (Princeton, NJ: Princeton University Press, 2009).
84 See, for instance, Grosvenor, "Back to the Future,"; Verstraete and Hoegaerts, "Educational soundscapes"; Thyssen and Grosvenor, "Learning to make sense".

The inclusion of senses other than vision in the history of education relates to ongoing calls for the adoption of inter- and multi-sensory approaches[85] within the history of education. To some extent, this also resonates with Inés Dussel's chapter on the question of "What might a material turn to educational history add to the history of education?" While the importance of the material turn has been widely recognized in history of education research, Dussel tells the story of her own research into the history of school uniforms to reveal the changing perspectives on, and approaches to, the materialities of schooling.[86] More specifically, she explains how she moved from investigating school uniforms, along Foucauldian lines, as materials to govern and regulate bodies, to developing sensitivity to their material qualities (such as texture and design) to investigate the "meshwork in which objects were inscribed". In doing so, she addresses two important implications of the shift in theoretical conceptualizations and methodological approaches to the material in history of education research. First, engaging with the conceptual frameworks of Latour and Ingold, among others, Dussel underlines how objects have moved from being considered as reflections of human action to being conceived as full-blown participants in a meshwork. As such, she stresses the importance of acknowledging material objects (in education) in their capacity to act. Second, she highlights how materials have gone from being understood as "static objects" to being explored as "things

---

[85] See, for instance, David Howes, "Cultural Synaesthesia: Neuropsychological versus Anthropological Approaches to the Study of Intersensoriality," *Intellectica* 55 (2011): 139–157.

[86] Marc Depaepe and colleagues have published a great deal on the history of materialities of schooling, in general, and on the history of the school desk and school architecture, in particular. See, for instance, Frederik Herman, Angelo Van Gorp, Frank Simon, and Marc Depaepe, "The school desk: from concept to object," *History of Education* 40 (2011): 97–117; Marc Depaepe, Frank Simon, and Pieter Verstraete, "Valorising the Cultural Heritage of the School Desk Through Historical Research," in *Educational Research: Material Culture and Its Representation. Educational Research*, ed. Paul Smeyers and Marc Depaepe, 13–30 (Cham: Springer, 2014); Marc Depaepe, Frank Simon, Frederik Herman, and Angelo Van Gorp, "Brodsky's hygienische Klappschulbank: Zu leicht für die schulische Mentalität?," *Zeitschrift für Pädagogik* 52 (2012): 50–65. On school architecture, see, for instance, Frederik Herman, Angelo Van Gorp, Frank Simon, Bruno Vanobbergen, and Marc Depaepe, "Modern architecture meets new education. Renaat Braem's design and the Brussels Decrolyschool (1946)," *Belgisch Tijdschrift voor Nieuwste Geschiedenis/Journal of Belgian History* XLI (2011): 135–166; Frederik Herman, Angelo Van Gorp, and Marc Depaepe, "Auf den Spuren von Diskurs, Traum und Wirklichkeit der Architektonischen Formgebung in Decroly's Ermitage," *Zeitschrift für Pädagogik* 57 (2011): 928–951; Frederik Herman, Angelo Van Gorp, Frank Simon, and Marc Depaepe, "The organic growth of the Decroly School in Brussels: from villa to school, from living room to classroom," in *The Black Box of Schooling. A Cultural History of the Classroom*, ed. Sjaak Braster, Ian Grosvenor, and Maria del Mar del Pozo Andrés, 241–259 (Brussels: Peter Lang, 2011).

always in the making" that continue to change in the course of their lives and as a result of their interactions with other objects and actors.

In doing so, Dussel's contribution reaffirms that education should not only be understood in terms of human interactions, but that objects are entirely constitutive of educational practices and discourses too. With the latter, we touch upon the notion of school culture that is the central point of attention in the final book chapter to this section. In "School Culture(s): Historiography of a Polysemic Concept", Antonio Viñao discusses the origins and development of the use and (multiple) meanings of the notion of school culture in close relation to major "paradigmatic" tendencies within the historiography of education. The importance of his contribution can barely be overestimated: the notion of school culture is firmly anchored within the new cultural history of education and has theoretically underpinned much of the research into the black box of schooling.[87] While initially introduced and conceptualized by Dominique Julia as the complex interplay between norms and practices that regulate schools, school culture has turned out to be a complex concept, partly due to the ambiguity surrounding the definition of culture itself. Viñao's book chapter discusses how history of education research has evolved from understanding school culture as a singular, coherent, and homogenous concept to a plural concept that acknowledges the layered nature of the multiple sub-culture(s) within the institution of the school.

Although different and heterogeneous in topical focus, what all these chapters demonstrate is that the history of education is a polysemic thing in itself that is – to paraphrase Dussel – constantly in the making. But turns taking turns themselves is what fuels methodological and theoretical renewal within the discipline.

Bibliography

Aldrich, Richard. "The three duties of the historian of education." *History of education* 32 (2003): 133–143.
Bakker, Nelleke. "Monitoring Child Health: School Doctors at Work in a Dutch Rural Area (1930–1970)." *History of Education* 45 (2016): 813–830.
Bakker, Nelleke. "A Culture of Knowledge Production: Testing and Observation of Dutch Children with Learning and Behavioural Problems (1949–1985)." *Paedagogica Historica* 53 (2017): 7–23.

---

[87] Cf. Braster, Grosvenor and del Mar del Pozo Andrès, *The Black Box of Schooling*.

Bakker, Nelleke. "Child Guidance, Dynamic Psychology and the Psychopathologisation of Child-Rearing Culture (c.1920–1940): A Transnational Perspective." *History of Education* 49 (2020): 617–635.

Barad, Karen. "Posthumanist Performativity: Toward an Understanding of How Matter Comes to Matter." *Signs* 28 (2003): 801–831.

Barad, Karen. *Meeting the Universe Halfway: Quantum Physics and the Entanglement of Matter and Meaning.* Durham: Duke University Press, 2007.

Barad, Karen. "Diffracting Diffraction: Cutting Together-Apart." *Parallax* 20 (2014): 168–187.

Black, Jeremy. *Other Pasts, Different Presents, Alternative Futures.* Indianapolis: Indiana University Press, 2015.

Benner, Dietrich. *Allgemeine Pädagogik: Eine systematisch-problemgeschichtliche Einführung in die Grundstruktur pädagogischen Denkens und Handelns.* Weinheim/Basel: Beltz Juventa, 2015.

Biesta, Gert. "Pluraliteit, pragmatisme en pedagogiek." *Comenius* 10 (1990): 7–30.

Braster, Sjaak, Ian Grosvenor, and María del Mar del Pozo Andrés. *The Black Box of Schooling: a Cultural History of the Classroom.* Brussels: Peter Lang, 2011.

Burke, Catherine, and Ian Grosvenor. "An exploration of the Writing and Reading of a Life: The 'Body Parts' of the Victorian School Architect E.R. Robson." In *Rethinking the History of Education. Transnational Perspectives on its Questions, Methods, and Knowledge*, edited by Thomas S. Popkewitz, 201–220. New York: Palgrave Macmillan, 2013.

Casalini, Cristiano, and Laura Madella. "Tracking Three Traditions in the Historiography of Education Toward Comparative Methods." *Revista Española de Educación Comparada* 34 (2019): 19–40.

Cash, Johnny. *I Walk the Line.* Sun Records, 1956.

Conrad, Peter. *The Medicalization of Society: On the Transformation of Human Conditions into Treatable Disorders.* Baltimore: Johns Hopkins University Press, 2007.

Coster, Tom De, Marc Depaepe, Frank Simon, and Angelo Van Gorp. "Dewey in Belgium: A Libation for Modernity?" In *Inventing the Modern Self and John Dewey: Modernities and the Traveling of Pragmatism in Education*, edited by Thomas S. Popkewitz, 85–109. New York: Palgrave Macmillan, 2005.

Crenshaw, Kimberlé W. "Demarginalizing the Intersection of Race and Sex: A Black Feminist Critique of Antidiscrimination Doctrine, Feminist Theory and Antiracist Politics." *University of Chicago Legal Forum* 1989 (1989): 139–167.

Crespo, Eduardo, and Amparo Serrano. "The Psychologisation of Work, the Deregulation of Work and the Government of Will." *Annual Review of Critical Psychology* 8 (2010): 43–61.

Dekker, Jeroen J.H. "Children at Risk in History: A Story of Expansion." *Paedagogica Historica* 45 (2009): 17–36.

Deleuze, Gilles, and Félix Guattari. *On the Line.* Translated by J. Johnston. New York: Semiotext(e), 1983.

Deleuze, Gilles, and Félix Guattari. *A Thousand Plateaus: Capitalism and Schizophrenia.* Translated by B. Massumi. London: Continuum, [1987] 2004.

Depaepe, Marc [in cooperation with René Lefebvre, and Mathieu Zana Aziza Etambala]. *"Tot Glorie van God en tot Zaligheid der Zielen." Brieven van Moeder Marie Adonia Depaepe over haar leven en werk als Zuster van Liefde in Belgisch Kongo (1909–1961).* Antwerpen: Standaard Uitgeverij, 1992.

Depaepe, Marc. *Zum Wohl des Kindes? Pädologie, pädagogische Psychologie und experimentelle Pädagogik in Europa und den USA, 1890–1940*. Weinheim/Leuven: Deutscher Studien Verlag/Leuven University Press, 1993.

Depaepe, Marc. "Educationalisation: A key concept in understanding the basic processes in the history of western education." *History of Education Review* 27 (1998): 16–28.

Depaepe, Marc, et al. *Order in Progress: Everyday Educational Practice in Primary Schools, Belgium, 1880–1970*. Leuven: Leuven University Press, 2000.

Depaepe, Marc. "De markt van het kind: Over de medicalisering van opvoeding en onderwijs." In *De zieke natie: Over de medicalisering van de samenleving, 1860–1914*, edited by Liesbet Nys, Henk de Smaele, Jo Tollebeek, and Kaat Wils, 260–278. Groningen: Historische Uitgeverij, 2002.

Depaepe, Marc. "The Practical and Professional Relevance of Educational Research and Pedagogical Knowledge from the Perspective of History: reflections on the Belgian case in its international background." *European Educational Research Journal* 1 (2002): 360–379.

Depaepe, Marc. "Praktijkgerichte theorie versus theoriegerichte praktijk: Een 'historische' paradox in de pedagogiek?" In *Paradoxen van pedagogisering: Handboek pedagogische historiografie*, edited by Marc Depaepe, Frank Simon, and Angelo Van Gorp, 442–466. Leuven: Acco, 2005.

Depaepe, Marc. "Dealing with the Paradoxes of Educationalization: Beyond the Limits of "New" Cultural History of Education." *Revista Educação & Cidadania* 7 (2008): 11–31.

Depaepe, Marc. "Struggling with the Historical Attractiveness of Psychology for Educational Research: Illustrated by the Case of Nazi-Germany." In *Between Educationalization and Appropriation: Selected Writings on the History of Modern Educational Systems*, edited by Marc Depaepe, 405–431. Leuven: Leuven University Press, 2012.

Depaepe, Marc. *Between Educationalization and Appropriation: Selected Writings on the History of Modern Educational Systems*. Leuven: Leuven University Press, 2012.

Depaepe, Marc, Frank Simon, and Angelo Van Gorp, "The 'Good Practices of Jozef Emiel Verheyen – schoolman and Professor of Education at the Ghent University: A Case of Using Educationally Correct Discourse at the Right Place and the Right Time." In *Educational Research: Why 'What Works' Doesn't Work*, edited by Paul Smeyers and Marc Depaepe, 17–36. Dordrecht: Springer, 2006.

Depaepe, Marc, Frank Simon, and Angelo Van Gorp. *Ovide Decroly (1871–1932): Une approche atypique?*. In preparation.

Depaepe, Marc, Frederik Herman, Melanie Surmont, Angelo Van Gorp, and Frank Simon. "About Pedagogization: From the Perspective of the History of Education." In *Educational Research: The Educationalisation of Social Problems*, edited by Paul Smeyers and Marc Depaepe, 13–30. Dordrecht: Springer, 2008.

Depaepe, Marc, and Paul Smeyers. "Educationalisation as an Ongoing Modernization Process." *Educational Theory* 58 (2008): 379–389.

Depaepe, Marc. "The Ten Commandments of Good Practices in History of Education Research." *Zeitschrift für pädagogische Historiographie* 16 (2010): 31–34.

Depaepe, Marc, Frank Simon, Frederik Herman, and Angelo Van Gorp. "Brodsky's hygienische Klappschulbank: Zu leicht für die schulische Mentalität?" *Zeitschrift für Pädagogik* 52 (2012): 50–65.

Depaepe, Marc, Frank Simon, and Pieter Verstraete, "Valorising the Cultural Heritage of the School Desk Through Historical Research." In *Educational Research: Material Culture and Its Representation. Educational Research*, edited by Paul Smeyers and Marc Depaepe, 13–30. Cham: Springer, 2014.

Depaepe, Marc. "Why Even Today Educational Historiography is not an Unnecessary Luxury. Focusing on four Themes from Forty-Four Years of Research." *Espacio, Tiempo y Educación* 7, no. 1 (2020): 227–246. Accessed February 26, 2021. Doi: http://dx.doi.org/10.14516/ete.335.

De Vincenti, Andrea, Norbert Grube, Michèle Hofmann, and Lukas Boser, eds. *Pädagogisierung des 'guten Lebens'. Bildungshistorische Perspektiven auf Ambitionen und Dynamiken im 20. Jahrhundert.* Bern: Bibliothek am Guisanplatz, 2020.

De Vos, Jan. *Psychologisation in Times of Globalisation.* London: Routledge, 2012.

De Vos, Jan. *Psychologization and the Subject of Late Modernity.* New York: Palgrave Macmillan, 2013.

Diener, Yann. *On agite un enfant: L'État, les psychothérapeutes et les psychotropes.* Paris: La Fabrique Éditions, 2011.

Dylan, Bob. *I Contain Multitudes.* Columbia Records, 2020.

Edwards, Elizabeth. *The Camera as Historian: Amateur Photographers and Historical Imagination, 1885–1918.* Durham: Duke University Press, 2012.

Fendler, Lynn. "The Ethics of Materiality: Some Insights from Non-Representational Theory." In *Educational Research: Material Culture and Its Representation*, edited by Marc Depaepe and Paul Smeyers, 115–132. Dordrecht: Springer, 2014.

Fendler, Lynn. "Apertures of Documentation: Reading Images in Educational History." *Paedagogica Historica* 53 (2017): 751–762.

Fendler, Lynn, and Paul Smeyers. "Focusing on Presentation Instead of Representation: Perspectives on Representational and Non-Representational Language-Games for Educational History and Theory." *Paedagogica Historica* 51 (2015): 691–701.

Gabriel, Edmond. *Manuel de pédagogie – à l'usage des écoles catholiques.* Tours: Imprimerie Mame, 1909.

Goodman, Joyce. "Circulating Objects and (Vernacular) Cosmopolitan Subjectivities." *Bildungsgeschichte: International Journal for the Historiography of Education* 17 (2017): 115–126.

Goodman, Joyce. "Suzanne Karpelès (1890–1969): Thinking with the Width and Thickness of Time." *Bildungsgeschichte: International Journal for the Historiography of Education* 8 (2018): 231–244.

Goodman, Joyce. "Afterword: Histories of Women's Higher Education, Time, and Temporalities." *Paedagogica Historica* 56 (2020): 847–856.

Goodman, Joyce, and Sue Anderson-Faithful. "Turning and Twisting Histories of Women's Education: Matters of Strategy." *Women's History Review* 29 (2019): 377–395.

Grosvenor, Ian. "Back to the Future or Towards a Sensory History of Schooling." *History of Education* 41 (2012): 675–687.

Grosvenor, Ian, Martin Lawn, and Kate Rousmanière. *Silences and Images. The Social History of the Classroom.* New York: Peter Lang, 1999.

Hai, Alessandra Arce, Frank Simon, and Marc Depaepe. "From Practice to Theory, Ovide Decroly for Brazilian Classrooms: A Tale of Appropriation." *History of Education* 45 (2016): 794–812.

Herman, Frederik, Angelo Van Gorp, Frank Simon, and Marc Depaepe. "The school desk: from concept to object." *History of Education* 40 (2011): 97–117.
Herman, Frederik, Angelo Van Gorp, Frank Simon, Bruno Vanobbergen, and Marc Depaepe. "Modern architecture meets new education. Renaat Braem's design and the Brussels Decrolyschool (1946)." *Belgisch Tijdschrift voor Nieuwste Geschiedenis/Journal of Belgian History* XLI (2011): 135–166.
Herman, Frederik, Angelo Van Gorp, and Marc Depaepe. "Auf den Spuren von Diskurs, Traum und Wirklichkeit der Architektonischen Formgebung in Decroly's Ermitage." *Zeitschrift für Pädagogik* 57 (2011): 928–951.
Herman, Frederik, Angelo Van Gorp, Frank Simon, and Marc Depaepe, "The organic growth of the Decroly School in Brussels: from villa to school, from living room to classroom." In *The Black Box of Schooling. A Cultural History of the Classroom*, edited by Sjaak Braster, Ian Grosvenor, and Maria del Mar del Pozo Andrés, 241–259. Brussels: Peter Lang, 2011.
Howes, David. "Cultural Synaesthesia: Neuropsychological versus Anthropological Approaches to the Study of Intersensoriality." *Intellectica* 55 (2011): 139–157.
Huisman, Frank, Joris Vandendriessche, and Kaat Wils. "Blurring Boundaries: Towards a Medical History of the Twentieth Century." *Low Countries Historical Review* 132 (2017): 3–15.
Ingold, Tim. *Lines: A Brief History*. London/New York: Routledge, 2007.
Ingold, Tim. "Against Space: Place, Movement, Knowledge." In *Boundless Worlds: An Anthropological Approach to Movement*, edited by Peter W. Kirby. Oxford: Berghahn, 2009.
Ingold, Tim. "Bindings against Boundaries: Entanglements of Life in an Open World." *Environment and Planning A* 40 (2008): 1796–1810.
Ingold, Tim. "Bringing Things to Life: Creative Entanglements in a World of Materials." 2010. Accessed April 21, 2015. http://eprints.ncrm.ac.uk/1306/1/0510_creative_entanglements.pdf.
Ingold, Tim. *Being Alive: Essays on Movement, Knowledge and Description*. Oxon/New York: Routledge, 2011.
Labaree David. "A Sermon on Educational Research." *International Journal for the Historiography of Education* 2 (2012): 78–87.
Lagemann, Ellen C. *An Elusive Science: The Troubling History of Education Research*. Chicago/London: The University of Chicago Press, 2000.
Lowenthal, David. *The heritage crusade and the spoils of history*. Cambridge: Cambridge University Press, 1998.
Luhmann, Niklas. *Essays on Self-Reference*. New York: Columbia University Press, 1990.
Luhmann, Niklas. "Zur Innendifferenzierung des Gesellschaftssystems: Schichtung und funktionale Differenzierung." *Soziale Welt* 68 (2017): 5–23.
Madsen, Ole Jacob, and Svend Brinkmann. "The Disappearance of Psychologisation?" *Annual Review of Critical Psychology* 8 (2010): 179–199.
Miedema, Siebren. "De pluraliteit van de pedagogiek." In *Pedagogik in Meervoud*, edited by Siebren Miedema, 13–21. Houten/Diegem: Bohn Stafleu Van Loghum, 1997.
Mietzner, Ulrike, Kevin Myers, and Nick Peim, eds. *Visual History. Images of Education*. Bern: Peter Lang, 2005.

Nóvoa, António. "Ways of Saying, Ways of Seeing. Public Images of Teachers (19th–20th Centuries)." *Paedagogica Historica* 36 (2000): 21–52.
Nóvoa, António. "Letter to a Young Educational Historian." *Historia y Memoria de la Educación* 1 (2015): 23–58.
Nye, Robert A. "The Evolution of the Concept of Medicalization in the Late Twentieth Century." *Journal of History of the Behavioral Sciences* 39 (2003): 115–129.
Oelkers, Jürgen. "Einige historische Erfahrungen im Verhältnis von Psychologie und Pädagogik." In *Die Psychologisierung der Pädagogik. Übel, Notwendigkeit, Fehldiagnose*, edited by Roland Reichenbach and Fritz Oser, 12–28. Weinheim/München: Juventa, 2002.
Oelkers, Jürgen. *Reformpädagogik: Eine kritische Dogmengeschichte*. Weinheim: Juventa, 2005, fourth edition.
Oelkers, Jürgen. "Reformpädagogik vor der Reformpädagogik." *Paedagogica Historica* 42 (2006): 15–48.
Riboulet, Louis. *Manuel de pédagogie générale – à l'usage des écoles normales, des candidats au Brevet supérieur et de tous les éducateurs*. Lyon: Imprimerie Emmanuel Vitte, 1930.
Rose, Nikolas. *The psychological complex: Psychology, politics, and society in England, 1869–1939*. London: Routledge/Kegan Paul, 1985.
Rose, Nikolas. *Inventing Our Selves: Psychology, Power and Personhood*. Cambridge: Cambridge University Press, 1996.
Rose, Nikolas. *Governing the Soul: The Shaping of the Private Self*. London: Free Association Books, 1999, second edition.
Rose, Nikolas. *The Politics of Life Itself: Biomedicine, Power, and Subjectivity in the Twenty-First century*. Princeton: Princeton University Press, 2007.
Rose, Nikolas, and Joelle M. Abi-Rached. *Neuro: The New Brain Sciences and the Management of the Mind*. Princeton: Princeton University Press, 2013.
Smeyers, Paul, and Marc Depaepe, eds. *Educational Research: The Attraction of Psychology*. Dordrecht: Springer, 2012.
Smeyers, Paul, and Marc Depaepe. "Making Sense of the Attraction of Psychology: On the Strengths and Weaknesses for Education and Educational Research." In *Educational Research: The Attraction of Psychology*, edited by Paul Smeyers and Marc Depaepe, 1–10. Dordrecht: Springer, 2012.
Stein, Margrit. *Allgemeine Pädagogik*. München: Ernst Reinhardt Verlag, 2017.
Stichweh, Rudolf. "Die Autopoiesis der Wissenschaft." In *Theorie als Passion. Niklas Luhmann zum 60. Geburtstag*, edited by Dirk Baecker, Jürgen Markowitz, Rudolf Stichweh, Hartmann Tyrell, and Helmut Willke, 447–481. Frankfurt am Main: Suhrkamp, 1987.
Stoler, Ann Laura. *Along the Archival Grain: Epistemic Anxieties and Colonial Common Sense*. Princeton, NJ: Princeton University Press, 2009.
Thomson, Mathew. *Psychological Subjects: Identity, Culture, and Health in Twentieth-Century Britain*. Oxford/New York: Oxford University Press, 2006.
Thyssen, Geert, and Frederik Herman. "Re-Turning Matters of Body_Mind: Articulations of Ill-/Health and Energy/Fatigue Gathered through Vocational and Health Education." *History of Education* 48 (2019): 496–515.

Thyssen, Geert, and Ian Grosvenor. "Introduction: Learning to Make Sense – Interdisciplinary Perspectives on Sensory Education and Embodied Enculturation." *The Senses and Society* 14 (2019): 119–130.

Tröhler, Daniel. "Die Pädagogisierung des Selbst und die Pädagogisierung der Welt." in *Selbstgesteuertes Lernen: Interdisziplinäre Kritik eines suggestiven Konzepts – Mit Nachbemerkungen zum Corona-Lockdown*, edited by Damian Miller and Jürgen Oelkers, 52–74. Weinheim Basel: Beltz Juventa, 2021.

Van Gorp, Angelo, Marc Depaepe, and Frank Simon. "Backing the Actor as Agent in Discipline Formation: An Example of the 'Secondary Disciplinarization' of the Educational Sciences, Based on the Networks of Ovide Decroly (1901–1931)." *Paedagogica Historica* 40 (2004): 591–616.

Verstraete, Pieter, and Josephine Hoegaerts. "Educational Soundscapes: Tuning in to Sounds and Silences in the History of Education." *Paedagogica Historica* 53 (2017): 491–497.

1 Leaving Marks of Inquiry: Ravels of Theory, Methodology, and History of Educational Historiography

Section editor: Geert Thyssen

Antonio Fco. Canales (Universidad Complutense de Madrid, Spain)

The Cultural History of Education: Between the Siren Song of Philosophy and the Discrete Charm of the Philosophy of the Social Sciences

Abstract: This chapter presents some reflections on the history of education. The starting point is that the renewal and development of research in the field should resist the seduction of Philosophy with a capital P and instead take into account the much more modest contributions offered by the philosophy of the social sciences. To defend this approach, the program of micro-foundations, developed by Jon Elster and others, is presented as a way to address some of the concerns of cultural historians of education, and to integrate most of the new approaches to the history of education in a theoretical and methodological framework that appears to be more solid than those of the postmodern proposals. The final proposal is to reformulate the main theoretical approaches as mid-range theories able to be empirically researched.

Keywords: philosophy of social sciences; theory of history; micro-foundations thesis; mid-range theories

During the last decade of the twentieth century, history was characterized by a far-reaching debate that called into question many of the discipline's widely accepted truths. Some authors went as far as to suggest a paradigm shift,[1] although establishing just what new hegemony was taking the place of the former reign of social history is no easy task. Faced with the demise of the comfortable certain-

---

Note: This work has been conducted in the framework of the National Research Project The boundary between science and politics and science in the boundary: Spanish science, 1907– 1975, MINECO/FEDER FFI2015–64529-P.

1 "This theoretical shift is giving rise to a new change of historical paradigm." Patrick Joyce, foreword to *Postsocial History: An introduction*, by Miguel Angel Cabrera (Oxford: Lexington Books, 2004), xiii. See also Carlos Barros, "The Return of History," in *History Under Debate: International Reflection on the Discipline*, ed. Carlos Barros and Lawrence J. McCrank (New York: The Haworth Press, 2004), 4; Carlos Barros, "History Under Debate Manifesto," in *History Under Debate*, 53.

ties with which they had been trained, some authors succumbed to the siren song of Philosophy with a capital P, venturing in search of answers into realms that traditionally had only been visited by historians on rare occasions. Others, such as Marc Depaepe, chose instead to explore a humbler, less showy path of renewal,[2] as part of a group of "more pragmatically-oriented researchers, who, while going along with the so-called contemporary 'turns' in cultural history in general (...), attempted to incorporate them critically and heuristically into a more sophisticated interpretation, rather than following them slavishly."[3] Such renewal was much more in keeping with the historian's practice, or what one could call *le métier d'historien*, to borrow from Marc Bloch's famous posthumous essay.[4] *Métier* here refers to a notion the historian must be careful not to lose sight of when navigating the turbulent waters of historiographic debate. Researching history is a craft, and like all crafts, it has rules. The aim of this chapter is to explore the possibilities for the renewal of this craft through recourse to the theoretical aid of the philosophy of science, and more specifically, the philosophy of social sciences.

The Postmodernist Challenge

During the 1980s, dissatisfaction with the existing paradigm of social history gave rise to multiple proposals that emerged from reflections taking place within the discipline. Some warned that the plurality of historiographic proposals would lead to a crumbling of history, in the words of François Dosse.[5] The risk was that the structural understanding of the past that had been built by social history would be weakened and fragmented into a multitude of kaleidoscopic visions. However, the debate took a sudden change of course, making a qualitative leap with the emergence of a group of proposals linked to Foucault and the lin-

---

[2] E.g., Marc Depaepe, "Educationalisation: A Key Concept in Understanding the Basic Processes in the History of Western Education," in *Between Educationalization and Appropriation*, ed. Marc Depaepe (Leuven: Leuven University Press, 2012), 128–129.
[3] Marc Depaepe and Frank Simon, "At the Intersection of Anecdotal Stories and Great Narratives: Reflections on the Cooperation Between Educational Historians and Educational Philosophers," in *Past, Present, and Future Possibilities for Philosophy and History of Education*, ed. Stefan Ramaekers and Naomi Hodgson (Dordrecht: Springer, 2018), 17.
[4] Marc Bloch, *Apologie pour l'histoire ou Métier d'historien* (Paris: Armand Collin, 1949).
[5] François Dosse, *L'Histoire en miettes: Des Annales à la "nouvelle histoire"* (Paris: La Découverte, 1987).

guistic turn; in simple terms, we can refer to this change as the postmodernist challenge.

Before scrutinizing the effect that these approaches have had on history, it is important that we clarify this initial point: unlike other proposals that had previously been debated, postmodernism is not an approach that arises out of history; nor does it specifically relate to history. Postmodernism is a philosophical questioning of modernity, a questioning of the foundations upon which Western thought has been based since at least the Enlightenment. What is at stake is not a particular conception of history as a discipline, but rather our inherited conception of the world. The certainties upon which our societies are built waver in the face of a discursive conception of such key notions as Reason, Justice, Progress or Democracy. In fact, given the magnitude of the challenge, I for one feel that it is as a citizen, rather than as a historian, that one should feel more concerned or alarmed by this discourse. In the face of the social, moral, and existential unease we are drawn into by the crisis in the narrative of modernity, a lack of faith in history as privileged knowledge of the past becomes a rather innocuous matter.

To return to history – which is our craft and the way we earn our living –, the postmodernist challenge, despite its tangential nature in relation to history or, if you will, its transversal relationship to thought in general, seems to have become the central point around which the historiographic debate revolves. Alongside it having become an academic trend, two factors have helped put postmodernist approaches center stage. The first is the insistence and forcefulness with which its advocates warned of a terminal crisis in social history. The second is the way in which they were able to convince historians that beyond their field a fully-fledged intellectual revolution was taking place, and that historians risked being left behind. With regard to this, G. Eley and K. Nield denounced the apocalyptic and apodictic tone used by the proponents of this approach.[6] In truth, the postmodernist approaches are in themselves an example of the centrality of the language that they champion; it is their forceful rhetoric that seems to have established so firmly the notion that social history is dead. The discourse, then, has created its own reality.

In any case, what is certain is that the proposals associated with postmodernism succeeded in demolishing the solid structural bases on which social history was founded. Now, in the wake of this, it is not a question of tearfully evoking a past Arcadia, but of rebuilding the discipline following this radical

---

[6] Geoff Eley and Keith Nield, "Starting over: The Present, the Post-Modern and the Moment of Social History," *Social History* 20 (1995): 355.

questioning. This is where the true challenge lies, since so many of the seemingly attractive, seductive proposals for reconstruction actually threaten to destroy the discipline itself. The debate is far-reaching and the positions are varied, but in my opinion any present-day historian who positions themself within what is generally understood to be the new cultural history has an obligation to take a stand on at least two key issues: the role of subjects and the nature of history as a discipline.

With regard to the role of subjects, following the linguistic turn, discourses are said to be independent of individuals; they are said to be given, determined by the prevailing conceptual framework's potential for evolution. This approach is in principle acceptable (who is going to argue against the constrictions of historical actions?). Nonetheless, at its core lie two very dangerous possible future lines of development. The first concerns a return to the purest metaphysical idealism. Where do these conceptual frameworks come from? Are they in some way a human product, despite being alien to individuals, or do they float in some galactic space, colliding from time to time with the earth and changing our discursive possibilities for interpreting the world? The second risk is linked to the return to a new structural determinism, which this time is not socio-economic, but linguistic. In the words of Foucault, quoted by Popkewitz in a seminal book on historiography of education:

> One has to dispense with the constituent subject, to get rid of the subject itself, that's to say, to arrive at an analysis which can account for the constitution of the subject within a historical framework. And this is what I would call genealogy, that is, a form of history which can account for the constitution of knowledge, discourses, domains of objects etc., without having to make reference to a transcendental subject which is either in relation to the field of events or runs in its empty sameness throughout the course of history.[7]

What is left here of the human experience in history for which Edward P. Thompson fought so courageously and for so long from the trenches of social history?[8] According to Popkewitz, Franklin, and Pereyra, we find ourselves facing a de-

---

[7] Michel Foucault, "Truth and Power," in *Power/Knowledge: Selected Interviews and Other Writings, 1972–1977*, ed. Colin Gordon (New York: Pantheon Books, 1972), 117. Cited by Thomas S. Popkewitz, "The Production of Reason and Power: Curriculum History and Intellectual Traditions," in *Cultural History and Education: Critical Essays on Knowledge and Schooling*, ed. Thomas S. Popkewitz, Barry M. Franklin, and Miguel A. Pereyra (New York: RoutledgeFalmer, 2001), 165.
[8] Edward P. Thompson, *The Poverty of Theory and Other Essays* (London: Merlin Press, 1978).

centered subject.⁹ In fact, the question we have to ask ourselves here is whether the subject is even present. One might think that this de-centered subject seems even more dead than Althusser's subject, which Thompson fought against. At this point, one needs to retrace one's steps and search for a more promising route.

The second crucial issue that any historian must confront concerns the effects of this genealogy on the discipline itself. Of course it is important, as Depaepe noted, to be aware of the historicity of historiography.[10] But this is quite different from asserting that history as a discipline is nothing more than a mere discursive construction. Understanding history as a text of texts can lead to intriguing discussions on narrativity and other more philosophical issues, i.e. Philosophy with a capital P, but it signals the end of history as a discipline as it has been understood for the last two centuries. Thus, we alight at another landing point, one which, notwithstanding what Kavafis may have thought, leads us to reassess the purpose of the journey.

For, if we continue along this track, we have no alternative but to become philosophers. But that is not what we are. As Depaepe has pointed out on several occasions, we have not been taught to look at the world from a philosophical perspective, but rather, from a historical one.[11] That is what we know how to do and why we are historians. As historians we have no choice but to stand and defend the craft that provides us with a living.

The Rules of the Craft

As historians, like Ulysses, we must resist the seductive Siren (and Triton) songs by tying ourselves tightly to the mast of our craft. The key is to keep in mind that being a historian is a craft and as such is concerned with a set of skills and rules, not the features of the end product. Within any discipline there is bound to be disagreement about the end products; this is perfectly normal, especially in the social sciences. The widely accepted notion of Kuhn's paradigm shift has been applied very little to the social sciences, especially history, despite the ef-

---

9 Thomas S. Popkewitz, Miguel A. Pereyra, and Barry M. Franklin, "History, the Problem of Knowledge, and the New Cultural History of Schooling: An Introduction," in *Cultural History and Education*, 20.
10 Depaepe, "Educationalisation: A Key Concept," 122.
11 Marc Depaepe, "Philosophy and History of Education: Time to Bridge the Gap?," *Educational Philosophy and Theory* 39 (2007): 28–43.

forts of numerous authors.[12] As Larry Laudan has stated, "It is difficult, for instance, to find any lengthy period in the history of any science in the last 300 years when the Kuhnian picture of 'normal science' prevails."[13] This leads him to propose the concept of the research tradition, a concept that is far less popular than the Kuhn paradigm but far more in keeping with the practice of the social science disciplines, where research traditions co-exist, compete, and even debate with one another. Disagreement about theories, then, is not a flaw in the social disciplines, but a constituent part of them. Nevertheless, to use Evandro Agazzi's formulation, disagreement over the interpretation of the world cannot be extended to the manner in which the discipline builds its objects of study from the things of the world.[14] This process of construction is a feature of the rules of objectification that define the discipline itself.

At this point, it is worth revisiting a thinker who was cast aside in the social history paradigm and seems totally rejected today: Leopold von Ranke. Depaepe, with customary equanimity and discretion, says that little theory can be developed from von Ranke's ideal.[15] This is certainly true. However, Ranke's value lies not in his having produced historical theory – he was no Marx –, but rather in something that precedes this and is much more important, although is often passed over[16]: the establishment of the rules of the historian's craft, which had never before been discussed within the discipline. These rules basically determine the use of historical sources as empirical evidence of a past reality that exists outside of us. Underlying these rules are materialist, empiricist, and realist assumptions, all of them essential to the discipline, but above all there is the conviction that history as a discipline is a way of accessing past reality that is

---

12 Traian Stoianovich, *French historical method: The Annales paradigm* (Ithaca: Cornell University Press, 1976); Georg G. Iggers, *New Directions in European Historiography* (Middletown: Wesleyan University Press, 1984). Both have been commented on by Gonzalo Pasamar, "El concepto de *paradigma* y su importancia en historia de la historiografía," in *La situación de la historia: Ensayos de historiografía*, ed. Miguel A. Cabrera and Marie McMahon (La Laguna: Universidad de La Laguna, 2002), 152. See also Carlos Barros, "The Return of History," 3–41.

13 Larry Laudan, "A Problem-Solving Approach to Scientific Progress," in *Scientific Revolutions*, ed. Ian Hacking (Oxford: Oxford University Press, 1981), 153.

14 For this author's perspective, see Evandro Agazzi, "Il significato dell'oggettività nel discorso scientifico," *L'oggettività della conoscenza scientifica*, ed. Fabio Minazzi (Franco Angeli: Milano, 1996), 19–35; Evandro Agazzi, "Problemi di epistemologia contemporanea," *Quaderni della Società Filosofica Italiana* 1–2 (1979): 31–61.

15 Depaepe, "Philosophy and History of Education," 36.

16 Depaepe himself dismisses this question as secondary in relation to the historicism of von Ranke. Marc Depaepe, "Dealing with Paradoxes of Educationalization: Beyond the Limits of 'New' Cultural History of Education?," in *Between Educationalization and Appropriation*, 140.

superior to all others. Patrick Joyce states that "What is at issue is not the existence of the real, but – given that the real can only ever be apprehended through our cultural categories – which version of the real should predominate."[17] This perspective, which could lead to a lengthy theoretical debate on relativism, is in practice hardly controversial; matters can be resolved using viable, practical criteria to establish correspondence between different versions and the empirical evidence that is available.

Clearly, there is no one today who still defends objectivity – which is, after all, what is at issue here – as the apprehension of the final essence of things, much less that of things from the past. A number of authors, including Longino, Kitcher, and Hacking among others, have attempted to theorize updated, acceptable forms of objectivity with concepts such as "degrees of objectivity" or "intersubjectivity."[18] In new approaches such as these, agreement between practitioners of the discipline as to the rules of objectivization takes precedence over all else. Empirical evidence, however, has much to tell us. The margin of interpretative possibilities of an occurrence is not infinite and is based upon the empirical evidence available, regardless of the different political or ideological theories and perspectives from which the event may be viewed. Subsequently, the discussion initiated by Patrick Joyce regarding which version of reality ought to prevail does not refer to philosophical speculation but rather to the specific, agreed procedures, in our case, those accepted by the colleagues who practice our craft. As P. Zagorín affirmed, objectivity as a guiding principle of our profession "was not a chimera, but an intrinsic aspect of historical reason which could not be abandoned as an aim or standard without also abandoning history itself as one of the foremost of the human and social sciences."[19] Of course, there are many other ways of approaching the past... but they are not history. In the words of Depaepe, "it is difficult to place the writing of history (of education) – even the post-modernistic history – outside the perspective of an entitlement to truth."[20] In terms of the postlinguistic turn, history is undoubtedly a text, but it is not just any text.

---

17 Patrick Joyce, "The End of Social History?," *Social History* 20 (1995): 78.
18 Helen Longino, *Science as Social Knowledge* (Princeton: Princeton University Press, 1990); Philip Kitcher, *The Advancement of Science: Science without Legend, Objectivity without Illusions* (Oxford, Oxford University Press, 1993); Ian Hacking, *Representing and Intervening: Introductory Topics in the Philosophy of Natural Science* (Cambridge University Press, Cambridge, 1983).
19 Pérez Zagorin, "History, the Referent, and Narrative: Reflections on Postmodernism Now," *History and Theory* 38 (1999): 2.
20 Marc Depaepe, "After the Ten Commandments... the Sermon? Comments on David Labaree's Research Recommendations," in *Between Educationalization and Appropriation*, 474.

It does not seem unreasonable to defend the requirement that the theoretical efforts of historians should develop around these rules that define our craft. Of course, to do so we must turn to philosophy, but not to the great speculative metaphysical subject of Philosophy with a capital P, but instead to the humble philosophy that entails a meta-reflection on science, which in this case is none other than the philosophy of the social sciences. In essence, my proposal is to explore the possibilities offered by one general theoretical framework that relates to social sciences, namely, that proposed by analytical Marxism and its thesis of micro-foundations.

The Thesis of Micro-foundations

The thesis of micro-foundations is a materialist and empiricist proposal that is radically opposed to functionalist holism. In contrast to the vague general and metaphysical frameworks of structuralism, it stresses the importance of paying attention to the microphysics of social events. Authors such as Jon Elster, John Roemer, Erik O. Wright, and Philippe van Parijs propose focusing analysis on the most basic components of social reality and opening up their black box to see how their internal processes work.[21] This is something that fits perfectly with our views regarding research in education, where the call to open up the black box has been a classic demand since the 1960s, from sociologist Stephen Ball's micropolitics of the school up to, in our field, the famous 1995 article by Depaepe and Simon, or a recent collection of studies on the new cultural history of education.[22]

---

21 For the exposition of the basic principles of this trend I have followed Amparo Gómez Rodríguez, "El programa analítico y el debate de los microfundamentos," in *Filosofía y metodología de las ciencias sociales*, ed. Amparo Gómez Rodríguez (Madrid: Alianza, 2003), 78–93. See also Amparo Gómez Rodríguez, "The Micro-Foundations of Social Explanation," *Epistemologia: Rivista italiana di filosofia della scienza* 32 (2009): 95–112. For the source literature, see Jon Elster, *Nuts and Bolts for the Social Sciences* (Cambridge: Cambridge University Press, 1989); John Roemer, *A General Theory of Exploitation and Class* (Cambridge Mass.: Harvard University Press, 1982); Erik O. Wright, *Classes* (London: Verso, 1985); Philippe van Parijs, *Marxism Recycled* (Cambridge; Cambridge University Press, 1992).

22 Stephen Ball, *The Micro-Politics of the School: Towards a Theory of School Organization* (London: Methuen, 1987); Marc Depaepe and Frank Simon, "Is There Any Place for the History of 'Education' in the 'History of Education'?," *Paedagogica Historica* 31 (1995): 10; Sjaak Braster, Ian Grosvenor and María del Mar del Pozo Andrés, eds., *The Black Box of Schooling: A Cultural History of the Classroom* (Brussels: Peter Lang, 2011).

The thesis of micro-foundations argues that social theory should be reconstructed using the contemporary tools of methodology, mathematics, and model construction. This revision leads to a substantial research program on the methodological foundations of social sciences through the critical analysis of theories, concepts, and explanations. The assumptions on which this analysis is based are that:
A) Social concepts must be specified and refined, establishing their empirical and theoretical basis;
B) Theories must be based on empirical research, following accepted standards of scientific practice; they cannot be based on mere speculation;
C) Social explanations must form chains of connections between antecedent and consequent.

The key to the whole program lies in this last point and in the critique of the functional explanation. It is accepted that the functional explanation is sustainable in some scientific fields, because there is an underlying causal theory which takes the feedback mechanism into account. In biology, as in cybernetics or the thermostat on a heater, the functional explanation is ultimately a form of shorthand for referring to a series of causal mechanisms. In the social sciences, however, these causal chains are unknown, but are simply metaphysically stated. A refinement of social explanations is then called for, requiring a return to causal and intentional explanations. The appropriate paradigm for the social sciences is, therefore, a combined causal-intentional explanation: an intentional explanation of actions and a causal explanation of their consequences.[23]

Narratives, Meanings, and Hermeneutics

With the reassessment of subjects and their intentions, this approach places the role of discourses, cultural categories, and theoretical frameworks front and center. This puts the program in a position where it can make a significant contribution to addressing many of our dissatisfactions with social history, while at the same time embedding these responses within a solid theoretical framework. To start with, the proposal of micro-foundations is realistic and materialistic, being at one remove from the underlying idealism of the new postmodernist proposals. Historical actors do not construct their reality in the postmodernist way,

---

[23] Jon Elster, "Marxism, Functionalism, and Game Theory: The Case for Methodological Individualism," *Theory and Society* 11 (1982): 463.

since the real world exists outside them; what they do is interpret it in order to act. Of course, they do not do this *ex-novo*, but from certain established conceptual frameworks that are inherent to their times.

The central role afforded to interpretive mediation now allows us to take into account a perspective that has traditionally been regarded as lying at the opposite end of the spectrum to that of a concept of history that strives for generality or a basis in science: Dilthey and his hermeneutics. As Depaepe stated: "We have to search for a language in which we can gradually 'understand' cultural actions that are alien to us, and the best approach to such rapprochement is probably provided by hermeneutics – old-fashioned though it may be – (...)."[24] Depaepe is absolutely right and there is no reason he should feel a need to apologize for his sympathies, as hermeneutics play an important part in historical explanations. Any intentional explanation requires a hermeneutic moment, since it is not possible to properly explain intentional actions unless their meaning is understood first. It is necessary, as advocates of hermeneutics rightly claim, to understand the reasons that have motivated the action, but in the case of history, it is just as important to understand the context in which that action arises, as it is in relation to that particular context that the action acquires sense and meaning. However, taking into consideration the comprehension of sense and meaning does not imply any objection to the aims of generality and objectivity of historical knowledge. Any such risk in this direction is thwarted by the classical synthesis posited by Max Weber, who stated that understanding constitutes the first step of social explanation.[25] Firstly we understand, then we explain.

Furthermore, the thesis of micro-foundations questions the extreme idealism implicit in the idea popularized by followers of the linguistic turn, namely, that the same historical situation can be evaluated differently depending on the current discourses. Regarding this point, we must remember António Nóvoa's argument – following Martin Jay – that the border between the text and the world must be dissolved.[26] From a materialistic perspective, such a border does not exist; anything else is pure idealism. It is not that there is a situation on one hand and discourses through which to interpret it on the other; rather, discourses form part of the situation itself, as "components of the world" in Depaepe's

---

[24] Depaepe, "Philosophy and History of Education," 38.
[25] Fritz Ringer, *Max Weber's Methodology: The Unification of the Cultural and Social Sciences* (Cambridge, Mass.: Harvard University Press, 1997), 92–100; Amparo Gómez Rodríguez, *Filosofía y metodología*, 46–50.
[26] António Nóvoa, "Texts, Images, and Memories: Writing 'New' Histories of Education," in *Cultural History and Education*, 46.

terms.[27] Therefore, situations in which different conceptual frameworks are present are simply not the same situation.

Thus, the thesis of micro-foundations allows us to integrate central issues raised by the linguistic turn, such as discursive mediation and hermeneutics, while dispensing with those aspects which pose a challenge to the discipline. Thanks to the linguistic turn, we now know that discourses, cultural categories, and conceptual frameworks are indissoluble aspects of historical reality and that they play a central role in the consideration of human actions. We are forced to accept, therefore, the discursive mediation of the action. This is what compels historians to objectify discourses, cultural categories, and theoretical frameworks for analysis, as we do with the other elements contained in a historical situation. However, to conclude the process at this point with the interpretation of reality within conceptual frameworks would again show naive idealism.

The Objective Logic of Actions Undertaken

The importance of discourses and understanding is limited to this phase in which action is being considered. Once an action has been taken, it ceases to be within the control of those who took it and triggers a series of causal consequences that take over implacably, regardless of the intentions and discursive frameworks of those who took the action. The unintended consequences of actions occupy a central position in the thesis of micro-foundations, building upon a question raised by Georg Henrik von Wright several years earlier.[28] This serves to demonstrate how little this perspective has in common with either the proactive, idealistic, traditional individualism or with the new discursivity. The consequences of actions escape those who carry them out, be they individuals or groups, due to the fact that these consequences never occur in isolation or independently; they take place within a strategic and non-parametric context, one that is not constructed discursively but which instead imposes its own uncompromising logic. These logical chains can lead to unintended, unforeseeable

---

27 "Good historic research presupposes that the researcher approaches the representational structures of the group (...) as components of the world." Marc Depaepe, "How Should the History of Education be Written? Some Reflections about the Nature of the Discipline from the Perspective of the Reception of our Work," *Studies in Philosophy and Education* 23 (2004): 337.
28 Amparo Gómez Rodríguez, "Acciones, razones y valores en la filosofía de Georg Henrik von Wright," introduction to *Sobre la libertad humana*, edited by Georg H. von Wright (Barcelona: Paidós, 2002), 17; Georg Henrik von Wright, *Norm and Action* (London: Routledge and Kegan Paul, 1963).

results which often contradict the initial intention of those who initiated the process.

The history of education is full of examples of these unintended, unforeseeable results that ended up becoming established, often against the wishes and intentions of those who set the process in motion. Brian Simon illustrated this paradox using the example of the educational policies of czarist Russia, which in its attempt to provide technical education that would serve the country's economic development produced instead a nihilist intellectual class that played an important part in destabilizing czarism rather than consolidating it.[29] A similar case occurred in Spain in the 1960s, when Franco's drive to popularize university education, which was meant to consolidate a sense of national consensus, led instead to the creation of one of the principal movements of political opposition to the regime.[30] Nor was it Franco's intention, after the Spanish Civil War, to promote the position of women in secondary education; and yet this was the unintended consequence of suppressing coeducation in secondary schools and encouraging private religious day schools for girls, since this model satisfied the ambitions of social selection and sexual segregation of the middle classes to a much greater degree than the public coeducational schools promoted and defended by the Second Republic.[31] Examples of this sort abound.

In fact, a great many historical processes can be interpreted in this sense, as causal concatenations of unintended consequences. At this point it is necessary to recall Elster's reference to the Scottish Enlightenment thinker Adam Ferguson's affirmation that "History is the result of human action, not of human design."[32] It is the task of the historian to establish the logic that explains these processes – which are neither intentional nor discursive – in a reliable way, through empirical research and the use of theories on human interaction such as the Game Theory, the Collective Action Theory or the Rational Choice Theory.

---

[29] Brian Simon, "Can Education Change Society?," in *The RoutledgeFalmer Reader in History of Education*, ed. Gary McCulloch (London: RoutledgeFalmer, 2005), 139–150.

[30] Elena Hernández Sandoica, Marc Baldó, and Miguel Angel Ruiz Carnicer, *Estudiantes contra Franco (1939–1975): Oposición política y movilización juvenil* (Madrid: La Esfera de los Libros, 2007).

[31] Antonio F. Canales, "Little Intellectuals: Girls' Academic Secondary Education under Francoism: Projects, Realities and Paradoxes," *Gender and Education* 244 (2012): 375–391.

[32] Jon Elster, *Nuts and Bolts for the Social Sciences* (Cambridge: Cambridge University Press, 1989), 91.

A Research Program for the History of Education Using Mid-range Theories

This appeal to empirical research emphasizes the idea that the program of microfoundations is not just another historiographic fad, but rather a research program. An initial step in the program would be the reconstruction of classical explanatory frameworks in the history of education in terms of acceptable intentional and causal interaction, removing their functional components.

In an exhaustive study published during the heyday of social history in the late 1970s, Fritz Ringer, trapped in the functional net, attempted to resolve the dysfunctional anomaly between the needs of an industrial society on the one hand, and on the other, the persistence across Europe of a secondary education that clung to the teaching of classical humanities.[33] From the perspective of a functional paradigm, the only way out of this situation was to remove this dysfunctionality by finding a way of conferring a new function on this fascination for the classics. Thus, he resorted to the theory of Latin as a barrier to explain the dominant position of the classics in secondary education as a need of the reproduction of the bourgeois class.[34]

While the results of this research continue to be extremely valuable for the field, they still need to be stripped of their functionalist components and reformulated in intentional and causal terms. It is not the segregating effect of Latin that is in question, but rather the lack of awareness of this effect among the bourgeoisie, which is a vital requirement for the functional explanation. In functionalist terms, within a social structure the reproduction of social classes is a need that determines the actions of its individuals, regardless of their individual consciousness. Against this structural determination, the explanation of the segregating effects of Latin should be reformulated from the perspective of the micro-foundations thesis either as an intentional result of bourgeois strategies or as an unintentional consequence of actions aimed at some other objective. In the first case, if the bourgeois agents were aware of this reproductive effect

---

33 Fritz K. Ringer, *Education and Society in Modern Europe* (Bloomington: Indiana University Press, 1979), 18–22.
34 See the 1925 classic: Edmond Goblot, *La barrière et le niveau* (Brionne, Éditions Gérard Monfort, 1984), 8. See also Pierre Bourdieu and Jean-Claude Passeron, *La reproduction* (Paris, Éditions de Minuit, 1970), 204; Abram de Swaan, *In Care of the State: Health Care, Education and Welfare in Europe and the USA in the Modern Era* (Cambridge: Polity: 1988), 85–87; Antonio Viñao, *Política y Educación en los orígenes de la España contemporánea* (Madrid: Siglo XXI, 1982), 449–54.

and sought to achieve it, we would no longer be dealing with a functional explanation but rather with an intentional one, which would pose no explicative problem at all. It would simply be a matter of locating the empirical evidence that supports the two extremes: that the segregating intent truly existed and, more importantly, that it drove the actions of the bourgeois agents in educational matters. In the second case, a non-intentional explanation would be based on the premise that the continuation of Latin was not due to any attempt to segregate but to other reasons such as tradition, emulation of the aristocracy or simply a belief in Latin's educational value. This lack of intentionality, however, in no way changes the segregating effects, which become an unforeseen and unintended consequence, albeit one that is ultimately welcome. The two logics were not mutually exclusive in the bourgeois circles of nineteenth century Europe. In both cases, the crucial point is that with this reformulation the final word on the explanation of the phenomenon does not come from theories about the structure of bourgeois society and its need to reproduce itself; the final word comes from pure, old-fashioned historical research. And there is certainly no shortage of historical archives full of additional empirical evidence to pursue this line of research.

The focus, then, should not be on grand theories, but rather on medium-level explanatory frameworks. The program of micro-foundations argues that in the current state of the social sciences, and therefore of history, it is preferable to be satisfied with modest low-level generalizations which are well-founded than to propose great general laws that are empty, theoretically ill-defined, and have barely been tested with empirical research. This is not a new idea; Merton anticipated it in sociology two decades earlier.[35] We do not need grand theories about society, and much less a great Theory of Society to replace the one that collapsed with the Berlin Wall. What we need are mid-range theories about the range of phenomena that we study, obtained from theoretical hypotheses that are subjected to empirical corroboration.

This is precisely the territory in which the great masters of the history of education, such as Depaepe, position themselves, and they do so out of a sense of pure devotion to their craft. A book published in Spain in 2008, which pulverized the existing history of education and went on to establish a new paradigm, illustrates this position well.[36] In their contributions, both Depaepe and the other

---

35 Robert K. Merton, *Social Theory and Social Structure* (New York: The Free Press, 1968), 39–45.
36 Antonio Viñao, "La escuela y la escolaridad como objetos históricos: Facetas y problemas de la Historia de la Educación," in *Pensar críticamente la educación escolar: Perspectivas y controversias historiográficas*, ed. Juan Mainer (Zaragoza: Prensas Universitarias de Zaragoza, 2008), 83–118; Marc Depaepe, "Perspectiva histórica de la continuidad y el cambio en la historia de

great master, Antonio Viñao, offered a fairly extensive and detailed analysis of the linguistic turn and Foucauldian genealogy, demonstrating, as you might expect, their mastery of the theoretical literature of the field. However, ultimately, they redirect what at first seemed to be a radical epistemological challenge towards a much humbler reconsideration of the main lines of research in our field. By their own means, they reached the destination theoretically marked by the program of micro-foundations, that is, mid-range theories, since that is what the grammar of schooling, the grammar of educationalization or the languages of education in fact are.

The grammar of schooling could well be considered one of these mid-range theories. This is the expression that Larry Cuban and David Tyack used to defend the ongoing existence of practices firmly embedded in schools, practices which undermine any attempts at educational reform. Beneath the interminable pedagogical theorizing and lively political-pedagogical debates, school practices remain virtually unchanged, and what goes on in the classroom today is very much akin to what went on nearly a century ago.[37]

This grammar of schooling finds, in Depaepe's opinion, an unavoidable complement in the grammar of educationalization, which focuses on practices that lead to an infantilization of children and young people and to the ethical and controlling elements of their social behavior.[38] This perspective opens the door to a historicization of Pedagogy in a broader and much more critical sense than we find in the traditional, more limited study of pedagogical ideas. An examination of the ways in which Pedagogy has legitimized (or questioned) forms of social domination at different times makes for a potentially stimulating line of research, especially if we are to comprehend the peculiar fusion of the principles of rationality and redemption that characterize the field.

This religious backdrop that we find in pedagogical discourse is taken up by Daniel Tröhler in his languages of education, another approach that we could consider to be a mid-range theory. Tröhler sees the languages of education as in-

---

la escuela: ¿Una paradoja de la "nueva" historia cultural de la educación?," in *Pensar críticamente*, 173–204.

37 David Tyack and Larry Cuban, *Tinkering toward Utopia: A Century of Public School Reform* (Cambridge, Mass.: Harvard University Press, 1995).
38 Depaepe, "Dealing with Paradoxes," 158; Marc Depaepe and Paul Smeyers, "Educationalization as an Ongoing Modernization Process," *Educational Theory* 48 (2008): 379–389; Marc Depaepe, "The Practical and Professional Relevance of Educational Research and Pedagogical Knowledge from the Perspective of History: Reflections on the Belgian Case in its International Background," *European Educational Research Journal* 1 (2002): 361–362; Depaepe, "Educationalisation: A Key Concept," 126.

terpretative frameworks that serve to construct in a normative way the social reality that we perceive.[39] According to this author, the languages of Republicanism, Protestantism, and Lutheranism can be said to constitute the main practical paths in the historical development of education. This perspective coincides to a certain extent with the linguistic turn in that a central role is given to language as well as to associated operations that are concerned with the construction of meanings and symbolic mediation. However, it rejects Foucauldian metaphysics completely, situating itself unequivocally in the terrain of social-cultural history practice.[40] Even more importantly, languages, in addition to being historical, are empirical; we are dealing with linguistic nuances that are actually used and therefore can be contrasted through research using empirical evidence.

All of these mid-range theories offer a wide gamut of theoretical hypotheses of unquestionable historiographic potential. Rather than demanding adherence to them – or a requirement to position oneself in relation to them –, they are simply calling for research to be undertaken. With the appropriate formulation, each one of them could constitute a stimulating research program and provide lines of work in our field over the coming years.

We could even go as far as reformulating certain ideas of Foucault's disciples and interpret them as mid-range theories, in spite of their epistemological radicalness. In fact, if we dispense with all of its challenging rhetoric (this is, after all, a question of language), the part of the Foucauldian approximation that we are left with consists of a sensible and perfectly assumable perspective that highlights the disciplinary and regulatory component of educational systems together with the legitimizing role of knowledge, including history.[41] This represents an extraordinarily rich and suggestive perspective, one that calls into question the framework of progress and emancipation in which the process has traditionally been framed, as well as the neutrality of the discourse associated with it – including that of scientists and scholars. Once again, with this reformulation we see the possibility of a rich range of theoretical hypotheses to be investigated historically, that is, empirically, as opposed to being subjected to philosophical speculation or meta-theorization.

---

[39] Daniel Tröhler, *Languages of Education: Protestant Legacies, National Identities, and Global Aspirations* (New York and London: Routledge, 2011).

[40] "Languages are not metaphysical entities. Nothing can constitute the langue that has never belonged to parole. On the other hand, parole is only possible as a social product due to the background provided by a certain langue?" Tröhler, *Languages of Education*, 5.

[41] See Depaepe's exposition of the ideas of Foucault and their application to the history of education: Depaepe, "Philosophy and History of Education," 35–37.

In his Ten Commandments, Depaepe proposes "Developing Theoretical and Conceptual Frameworks from within the History of Education" and calls for

> the production of more fine-grained explanatory models on the history of education from within: specific interpretive schemas that are not at all intended to serve as manuals for contemporary interventions but to enter more structure (and thereby more insight) into the chaos of the educational past.[42]

Producing these more fine-grained explanatory models is precisely the aim of mid-range theories. The future of research in the history of education lies in understanding these theoretical hypotheses for precisely what they are: hypothetical propositions on the behavior or expression of the varied phenomena that are to be investigated. To conduct this research, rather than philosophizing about the meaning of knowledge and society, these hypothetical propositions must be made operational so that they may be empirically investigated and contrasted with available evidence. Obviously, from this perspective, the empiricism of the British tradition is not a defect, as claimed by Kevin Myers[43], but on the contrary is a great virtue.

In summary, in this text we have attempted to defend the proposal of microfoundations as a path of renewal for historiography, one that offers a response to the dissatisfaction underlying recent historiographic developments. It even reconciles us with discarded traditions from the past such as hermeneutics, but without gazing into the self-destructive abysses of idealism, anti-realism or historicist subjectivism. Furthermore, and this may be its main merit, it provides these answers using a theoretical and methodological framework that meets the social sciences' standards of rigor while at the same time serving to enhance our craft. In this sense there is probably no better conclusion to this text than Depaepe's idea that the history of education has the methodological duty to increasingly be history.[44] We are quite certain that this involves compromising on the rules of the craft... and some visits to dusty archives and *hémérothèques*.

---

42 Marc Depaepe, "The Ten Commandments of Good Practices in History of Education Research," in *Between Educationalization and Appropriation*, 468.
43 Kevin Myers, "Immigrants and Ethnic Minorities in the History of Education," *Paedagogica Historica* 45 (2009): 804, cited by Gary McCulloch, *The Struggle for the History of Education* (New York: Routledge, 2011), 78.
44 Depaepe, "Philosophy and History of Education," 40.

Bibliography

Agazzi, Evandro. "Problemi di epistemologia contemporánea." *Quaderni della Società Filosofica Italiana* 1–2 (1979): 31–61.
Agazzi, Evandro. "Il significato dell'oggettività nel discorso scientifico." In *L'oggettività della conoscenza scientifica*, edited by Fabio Minazzi, 19–35. Franco Angeli: Milano, 1996.
Ball, Stephen. *The Micro-Politics of the School: Towards a Theory of School Organization*. London: Methuen, 1987.
Barros, Carlos. "The Return of History." In *History Under Debate. International Reflection on the Discipline*, edited by Carlos Barros and Lawrence J. McCrank, 3–41. New York: The Haworth Press, 2004.
Barros, Carlos. "History Under Debate Manifesto." In *History Under Debate. International Reflection on the Discipline*, edited by Carlos Barros and Lawrence J. McCrank, 43–55. New York: The Haworth Press, 2004.
Bloch, Marc. *Apologie pour l'histoire ou Métier d'historien*. Paris: Armand Collin, 1949.
Braster, Sjaak, Ian Grosvenor, and María del Mar del Pozo Andrés, eds. *The Black Box of Schooling: A Cultural History of the Classroom*. Brussels: Peter Lang, 2011.
Cabrera, Miguel Angel. *Postsocial History: An Introduction*. Oxford: Lexington Books, 2004.
Canales, Antonio F. "Little Intellectuals. Girls' Academic Secondary Education under Francoism: Projects, Realities and Paradoxes." *Gender and Education* 24 (2012): 375–391.
Depaepe, Marc. "The Practical and Professional Relevance of Educational Research and Pedagogical Knowledge from the Perspective of History: Reflections on the Belgian Case in its International Background." *European Educational Research Journal* 1 (2002): 360–379.
Depaepe, Marc. "How Should the History of Education be Written? Some Reflections about the Nature of the Discipline from the Perspective of the Reception of our Work." *Studies in Philosophy and Education* 23 (2004): 333–345.
Depaepe, Marc. "Philosophy and History of Education: Time to Bridge the Gap?" *Educational Philosophy and Theory* 39 (2007): 28–43.
Depaepe, Marc. "Perspectiva histórica de la continuidad y el cambio en la historia de la escuela: ¿una paradoja de la "nueva" historia cultural de la educación?" In *Pensar críticamente la educación escolar: Perspectivas y controversias historiográficas*, edited by Juan Mainer, 173–204. Zaragoza: Prensas Universitarias de Zaragoza, 2008.
Depaepe, Marc. "Educationalisation: A Key Concept in Understanding the Basic Processes in the History of Western Education." In *Between Educationalization and Appropriation*, edited by Marc Depaepe, 121–138. Leuven: Leuven University Press, 2012.
Depaepe, Marc. "Dealing with Paradoxes of Educationalization: Beyond the Limits of 'New' Cultural History of Education?" In *Between Educationalization and Appropriation*, edited by Marc Depaepe, 139–166. Leuven: Leuven University Press, 2012.
Depaepe, Marc. "The Ten Commandments of Good Practices in History of Education Research." In *Between Educationalization and Appropriation*, edited by Marc Depaepe, 463–469. Leuven: Leuven University Press, 2012.
Depaepe, Marc. "After the Ten Commandments... the Sermon? Comments on David Labaree's Research Recommendations." In *Between Educationalization and Appropriation*, edited by Marc Depaepe, 471–476. Leuven: Leuven University Press, 2012.

Depaepe, Marc, and Frank Simon. "Is There Any Place for the History of 'Education' in the 'History of Education'?" *Paedagogica Historica* 31 (1995): 9–16.

Depaepe, Marc, and Frank Simon. "At the Intersection of Anecdotal Stories and Great Narratives: Reflections on the Cooperation Between Educational Historians and Educational Philosophers." In *Past, Present, and Future Possibilities for Philosophy and History of Education,* edited by Stefan Ramaekers and Naomi Hodgson, 15–31. Dordrecht: Springer, 2018.

Depaepe, Marc, and Paul Smeyers. "Educationalization as an Ongoing Modernization Process." *Educational Theory* 48 (2008): 379–389.

Dosse, François. *L'Histoire en miettes. Des Annales à la "nouvelle histoire."* Paris: La Découverte, 1987.

Eley, Geoff, and Keith Nield. "Starting over: The Present, the Post-Modern and the Moment of Social History." *Social History* 20 (1995): 355–364.

Elster, Jon. "Marxism, Functionalism, and Game Theory. The Case for Methodological Individualism." *Theory and Society* 11 (1982): 453–482.

Elster, Jon. *Nuts and Bolts for the Social Sciences.* Cambridge: Cambridge University Press, 1989.

Foucault, Michel. "Truth and Power." In *Power/Knowledge: Selected Interviews and Other Writings, 1972–1977*, edited by Colin Gordon, 109–133. New York: Pantheon Books, 1972.

Goblot, Edmond. *La barrière et le niveau.* Brionne, Éditions Gérard Monfort, 1984.

Gómez Rodríguez, Amparo. "Acciones, razones y valores en la filosofía de Georg Henrik von Wright." Introduction to *Sobre la libertad humana*, edited by Georg H. von Wright, 9–50. Barcelona: Paidós, 2002.

Gómez Rodríguez, Amparo. *Filosofía y metodología de las ciencias sociales.* Madrid: Alianza, 2003.

Gómez Rodríguez, Amparo. "The Micro-Foundations of Social Explanation." *Epistemologia: Rivista italiana di filosofia della scienza* 32 (2009): 95–112.

Hacking, Ian. *Representing and Intervening: Introductory Topics in the Philosophy of Natural Science.* Cambridge University Press, Cambridge, 1983.

Hernández Sandoica, Elena, Marc Baldó, and Miguel Angel Ruiz Carnicer. *Estudiantes contra Franco (1939–1975): Oposición política y movilización juvenil.* Madrid: La Esfera de los Libros, 2007.

Iggers, Georg G. *New directions in European Historiography.* Middletown: Wesleyan University Press, 1984.

Kitcher, Philip. *The Advancement of Science: Science without Legend, Objectivity without Illusions.* Oxford, Oxford University Press, 1993.

Laudan, Larry. "A Problem-Solving Approach to Scientific Progress." In *Scientific Revolutions*, edited by Ian Hacking, 144–155. Oxford: Oxford University Press, 1981.

Longino, Helen. *Science as Social Knowledge.* Princeton: Princeton University Press, 1990.

McCulloch, Gary. *The Struggle for the History of Education.* New York: Routledge, 2011.

Merton, Robert K. *Social Theory and Social Structure.* New York: The Free Press, 1968.

Myers, Kevin. "Immigrants and Ethnic Minorities in the History of Education." *Paedagogica Historica* 45 (2009): 801–816.

Nóvoa, António. "Texts, Images, and Memories: Writing 'New' Histories of Education." In *Cultural History and Education: Critical Essays on Knowledge and Schooling,* edited by

Thomas S. Popkewitz, Barry M. Franklin, and Miguel A. Pereyra, 45–66. New York: RoutledgeFalmer, 2001.
Parijs, Philippe van. *Marxism Recycled*. Cambridge, Cambridge University Press, 1992.
Pasamar, Gonzalo. "El concepto de *paradigma* y su importancia en historia de la historiografía." In *La situación de la Historia: Ensayos de historiografía*, edited by Miguel A. Cabrera and Marie McMahon, 133–156. La Laguna: Universidad de La Laguna, 2002.
Popkewitz, Thomas S., Miguel A. Pereyra, and Barry M. Franklin. "History, the Problem of Knowledge, and the New Cultural History of Schooling: An Introduction." In *Cultural History and Education: Critical Essays on Knowledge and Schooling*, edited by Thomas S. Popkewitz, Barry M. Franklin, and Miguel A. Pereyra, 3–42. New York: RoutledgeFalmer, 2001.
Popkewitz, Thomas S. "The Production of Reason and Power: Curriculum History and Intellectual Traditions." In *Cultural History and Education: Critical Essays on Knowledge and Schooling*, edited by Thomas S. Popkewitz, Barry M. Franklin, and Miguel A. Pereyra, 151–183. New York: RoutledgeFalmer, 2001.
Ringer, Fritz K. *Education and Society in Modern Europe*. Bloomington: Indiana University Press, 1979.
Ringer, Fritz. *Max Weber's Methodology: The Unification of the Cultural and Social Sciences*. Cambridge, Mass.: Harvard University Press, 1997.
Roemer, John. *A General Theory of Exploitation and Class*. Cambridge Mass.: Harvard University Press, 1982.
Simon, Brian. "Can Education Change Society?." In *The RoutledgeFalmer Reader in History of Education*, edited by Gary McCulloch, 139–150. London: RoutledgeFalmer, 2005.
Stoianovich, Traian. *French Historical Method: The Annales paradigm*. Ithaca: Cornell University Press, 1976.
Swaan, Abram de. *In Care of the State: Health Care, Education and Welfare in Europe and the USA in the Modern Era*. Cambridge: Polity: 1988.
Thompson, Edward P. *The Poverty of Theory and Other Essays*. London: Merlin Press, 1978.
Tröhler, Daniel. *Languages of Education: Protestant Legacies, National Identities, and Global Aspirations*. New York and London: Routledge, 2011.
Tyack, David, and Larry Cuban. *Tinkering toward Utopia: A Century of Public School Reform*. Cambridge, Mass.: Harvard University Press, 1995.
Viñao, Antonio. *Política y Educación en los orígenes de la España contemporánea*. Madrid: Siglo XXI, 1982.
Viñao, Antonio. "La escuela y la escolaridad como objetos históricos: Facetas y problemas de la Historia de la Educación." In *Pensar críticamente la educación escolar: Perspectivas y controversias historiográficas*, edited by Juan Mainer, 83–118. Zaragoza: Prensas Universitarias de Zaragoza, 2008.
Wright, Erik O. *Classes*. London: Verso, 1985.
Wright, Georg H. von. *Norm and Action*. London: Routledge and Kegan Paul, 1963.
Zagorin, Perez. "History, the Referent, and Narrative: Reflections on Postmodernism Now." *History and Theory* 38 (1999): 1–24.

Lynn Fendler (Michigan State University, USA)
Critical Powers of Historical Framing: Continuity and Representation

Abstract: This chapter problematizes issues of continuity and representation in educational history by drawing critical attention to the ways continuity and representation can dehistoricize history and exclude non-mainstream perspectives from history. Examples from educational history include assumed continuities from tutoring to common schools, rats to humans, and statistical probability to scientific certainty. Problematic representational issues include the curation of archival sources, structuralist analyses, generalizations from past to present or future, and formal constraints of historical writing that are usually linear and expository. The chapter ends by offering several examples of alternatives to historical continuity and representation, including genealogy, nonrepresentational theories, Afrofuturism, critical fabulation, and arts-infused historiography.

Keywords: historiography; genealogy; continuity; representation; statistical probability; new materialism; Afrofuturism

Philosophy enjoys a kind of intellectual superiority in scholarly worlds, and historians have at times expressed frustration with an academic hierarchy that celebrates philosophy over history. As Depaepe wrote: "the philosopher's focus on what is more general is not only a potential source of irritation to historical researchers but can also sometimes result in feelings of inferiority with respect to fundamental, philosophical, systematic and/or theoretical approaches to education as a discipline, as there still exists – or appears to exist – a kind of 'natural' hierarchy between a theoretical (often normative) and a descriptive (often idiosyncratic) 'view'."[1]

Following from Depaepe's characterization of history as a discipline committed to specificity in time and place, I argue in this chapter that a commitment to historical specificity provides us with critical leverage that can serve to crumble dominating assumptions about truth, and incorporate a greater range of diverse perspectives for scholarship in which historical thinking plays a role. Depaepe has referred to this critical approach to scholarship as "demythologizing histo-

---

[1] Marc Depaepe, "Philosophy and History of Education: Time to Bridge the Gap?," *Educational Philosophy and Theory* 39 (2007): 28–43.

https://doi.org/10.1515/9783110623451-006

ry."² Analytic philosophy has at times been ahistorical whenever it favored eternal, fundamental, and systematic truths, which Kant called analytic. Analytic truths, over time, have enacted gate-keeping functions, such as the reproduction of existing power hierarchies through the establishment of eternal – unchanging and unchangeable – canonical knowledge and evaluation criteria. It is precisely because of this epistemological preference for unchanging – i.e., ahistorical – truths that philosophy has been granted its lofty intellectual status. At the same time, analytical traditions of truth-making have also functioned to perpetuate the inequitable dominance of a set of particular, narrow, and privileged perspectives and simultaneously to exclude a wide diversity of epistemological possibilities for historical study.

In contrast to this particular approach to analytic philosophy, historiography has for the most part sustained a commitment to specificity in time and place, or what Kant called synthetic truths. As Depaepe wrote: "An Archimedean fulcrum from which one would be able to read and move the world does not seem to be available in history. Human knowledge (...) is always relative because of its sociohistorical determination."³

This chapter sets aside scholarly thinking that appeals to the eternal and universal, and highlights instead critical affordances of scholarly inquiry committed to specificity in time and place. Nietzsche's *Wirkungsgeschichte* and Foucault's *l'histoire effective* are both approaches that highlight critical potentials for historical research that rejects eternal truths in favor of historical specificity. To develop the idea of critical and effective educational history,⁴ I focus in this chapter on two vexing theoretical issues of historiography: continuity and representation. Claims of continuity and representation have posed dangers for historical work insofar as continuity and representation can invoke eternal and universal (i.e., ahistorical and metaphysical) mechanisms that function (usually unintentionally) to undermine commitments to specificity of time and place. In addition, these dehistoricized tropes of continuity and representation have also functioned to exclude a great many diverse perspectives from history as a discipline and a scholarly practice. My aim in this chapter is to call attention to these two tropes – continuity and representation – which, if not problematized, tend to dehistoricize historiography, which in turn restricts the scope of per-

---

2 Depaepe, "Philosophy and History of Education," 31.
3 Marc Depaepe, "History of Education Anno 1992: 'A Tale Told by an Idiot, Full of Sound and Fury, Signifying Nothing'?," *History of Education* 22 (1992): 7.
4 Mitchell Dean, *Critical and Effective Histories: Foucault's Methods and Historical Sociology* (New York: Routledge 1994).

spectives that are available for historiography, and deprives historiography of particular kinds of critical leverage.

Continuity

One of Foucault's most salient contributions to the discipline of history is his 1971 essay "Nietzsche, Genealogy History," in which he argued that origins are products of metaphysics. According to Foucault's genealogical stance, history proceeds not continuously or according to any pattern, but by accident and events that are generated by power relations. To make this point, Foucault (following Nietzsche) problematized the search for origins. According to Foucault, for us to make a claim about origins, we must establish a metaphysical break (discontinuity), justified on the basis of (ahistorical and essential) inventions such as progress, telos, cycles, or dialectic. Claims of origin may serve ideological purposes, such as inventing truths to support a particular position, or establishing historical identities. In that way, a break or rupture can serve as a marker for the origin of something new and allegedly true.[5] The establishment of historical breaks is usually called periodization. For example, many versions of European history posit that the period of the Enlightenment constituted a break from an earlier Medieval period, and that Modernity ought to be seen as continuous with Enlightenment. In his *Archeology of Knowledge*, however, Foucault problematized both the discontinuity between Medieval and Enlightenment, and the continuity between Enlightenment and Modernity, by calling attention to the ways a particular kind of rationality was privileged in this periodization. Historical periodization, including both continuities and discontinuities, includes claims about origins and endings; in this way, periodization contributes to the invention of truths. In Foucault's words, "Truth is undoubtedly the sort of error that cannot be refuted because it was hardened into an unalterable form in the long baking process of history."[6]

In the following section, I describe three examples of continuity that have been widely accepted and baked into history, particularly in discourses of educational foundations. I chose these examples in order to draw critical attention to some damaging truth-making effects of imposing metaphysical continuities in

---

[5] Alison Moore, "Historicising Historical Theory's History of Cultural Historiography," *Cosmos and History: The Journal of Natural and Social Philosophy* 12 (2016): 257–291.
[6] Michel Foucault, "Nietzsche, Genealogy, History," in *Michel Foucault: Aesthetics, Method and Epistemology*, ed. James D. Faubion, vol. 2 of *Essential Works of Foucault, 1954–1984*, ed. James D. Faubion (New York: The New Press, 1978/1998), 144.

historical narratives. Readers will recognize my approach as being akin to Foucault's critical and effective history that uses historical examples as pedagogical apparatuses for confronting the limits of thought.

From Tutoring to Common Schools

The first example of a truth-making continuity is the common narrative thread that connects Socratic or Rousseauian tutoring with the establishment of common schools. We can see this continuity enacted in textbooks of educational foundations, and in reference works that begin with Plato, move on to include the works of Jean-Jacques Rousseau (sometimes after a short pit stop at John Locke), and continue seamlessly to describe the schooling recommendations of Johann Heinrich Pestalozzi and Horace Mann.[7] It is difficult to figure out why educational textbooks would consistently present this continuous narrative because 1830s Massachusetts common schools clearly have nothing in common with Plato's agora or Emile's fictional state of nature in eighteenth century Europe. So why do textbooks of educational foundations narrate a historical continuity from Plato to Rousseau to Mann?[8]

We cannot know with any certainty why educational discourses would perpetuate an assumption of continuity between tutoring and common schooling. But, as an exercise in critical thinking, we can imagine some possibilities. First, we can imagine that a continuous narrative of schooling might be useful for making schools appear to be necessary for the advancement of civilization. Schooling might be perceived as indispensable for the establishment of respectable society if only schooling could be seen as a natural outgrowth of *paideia* and *didakton*, practices from "the cradle of Western civilization" in classical Greece. Along the same lines, a continuous narrative from tutoring to common schooling might be seen as a crucial component of democracy because both *Emile* and *The Social Contract* were written by the same famous person, Rousseau. Another possibility is that a continuous narrative could be useful for obscuring the fact that tutoring in Classical Greece and in Enlightenment Geneva was accessible only to privileged elite male citizens of those respective societies

---

[7] See, e.g., Steven M. Cahn, *Classic and Contemporary Readings in the Philosophy of Education* (New York, NY: McGraw-Hill, 1996).

[8] For another critique of historical continuity, see e.g., Marc Depaepe, "The Practical and Professional Relevance of Educational Research and Pedagogical Knowledge from the Perspective of History: Reflections on the Belgian Case in its International Background," *European Educational Research Journal* 1 (2002): 360–379.

(especially since Sophie's education was not the same as Emile's). A continuous historiographical narrative has the chance to convey the impression that schooling is an indispensable component for the development of civilization and common good. Finally, another possibility is that a long-standing history contributes to the status and gravitas of education as a scholarly profession. By locating the origins of schooling in the fifth century BCE, education can be perceived as a grandiose enterprise, and a longstanding integral component of Western culture.

But what if we rejected the narrative that traces a continuous history of education from Greece to the present? Education might be perceived differently if the continuity between tutoring and common schooling were replaced with a different, non-continuous story. In *Discipline and Punish*, for example, rather than a reiterating a historical continuity tracing schools back to Classical Greece, Foucault instead established a genealogical resemblance between prisons and schools. In this genealogical approach, education as an object of study is not construed as a continuation of Plato's agora or Emile's state of nature, but rather as a contemporaneous development of modern institutions of governance for surveillance and punishment. Foucault's non-continuous approach has made it possible for us to perceive different phenomena in the history of education, such as the disciplinary surveillance mechanisms of the Lancaster method and the normalization of bodies enacted by the shape of school desks. In this way, the genealogical (rather than continuous) approach to historical scholarship opens the door for inclusion of minoritized and silenced perspectives into the history of education.

From Rats to Humans

Another continuity widely perpetuated in discourses of educational history is the continuity of learning between rats and humans. Prior to the twentieth century, the term learn made sense only as a transitive verb: learn a language, learn good manners, learn calculus. However, Edward Thorndike's early twentieth century work in psychology was based on his experimental work with lab rats. As part of the invention of educational psychology, Edward Thorndike's work reconceptualized learning from a transitive process (e.g., learn a language) into an abstract faculty of transfer. In his classic book *Human Learning*, Thorndike's Lecture 11 is titled "The Evolution of Learning in General." To illustrate the phenomenon of learning, Thorndike cited studies that document learning by earthworms, snails, cockroaches, crabs, and crayfish. Defining learning as a capacity shared across the animal kingdom, Thorndike theorized learning as a psychological phenomenon that is separate from reasoning, evolutionary adaptation, literacy, emotional response, deliberation, insight, or invention:

> Here we have the most widespread sort of learning in the world. There need be no reasoning, no process of inference or comparison; there need be no thinking about things, no putting two and two together; there need be no ideas–the animal may not think of the box or of the food or of the act he is to perform.[9]

Previous conceptions of mental capacities distinguished "low level" habit formation from "high level" abstraction, inference, and generalization. Thorndike's theory is a critique of the distinction between these low and high levels. For Thorndike, there are not two qualitatively different kinds of intellect; rather, learning in general forms the basis for all intellectual capacities. For Thorndike, differences in intelligence are not qualitative but quantitative; the more associations there are, the greater the intelligence. For Thorndike, there is no Bloom's taxonomy of capacities, no qualitative difference between habit formation and innovation. Rather, there is a continuity between rat learning and human learning:

> [A] simple quantitative variation in the number of neurone connections, causes *the appearance* of what we call ideas, insights, reasoning, and the like, is its harmony with the facts about the differences amongst individual human beings in the degree of development of these *so-called* higher powers.[10]

To investigate whether habit formation and reasoning were qualitatively the same or different, Thorndike (and his associate John Tilton) conducted a research experiment. They administered to the same children two tests: one test of habit formation (language information and mathematical information) and another test of reasoning (language reasoning and mathematical reasoning). Thorndike and Tilton found that the results across both tests had "very close" correspondence:

> Quantity of associative learning and ability to deal with abstract qualities and relations (...) are intimately related in mental dynamics and presumably depend upon a common cause (...). [The] human capacity to learn developed from the general mammalian and primate capacity by a quantitative extension.[11]

---

9 Edward L. Thorndike, *Human Learning* (New York: The Century Company, 1931), 14.
10 Thorndike, *Human Learning*, 171 (emphases added).
11 Thorndike, *Human Learning*, 177.

A closer look at Thorndike's theory helps to clarify the parameters of learning as it was formulated in the early days of educational psychology and allows us to raise questions about the establishment of a continuity between rat learning and human learning.

Based on Thorndike's research, educational psychologists generally conducted research on the assumption that there were not two separate types of intellectual development (habit formation and reasoning), but only one type, namely learning. These days, we can understand the impulse to conceptualize learning this way if we put Thorndike's research in the historical context of the U.S. Progressive Era when science and efficiency were celebrated as promising new approaches for improving society. Furthermore, Thorndike's psychology reflects Enlightenment beliefs in human capacities: if we understand learning as the fundamental building block of animal adaptation, then we do not have to appeal to any transcendent deity or mechanism. If learning is seen as the basis for all improvement, human agents are then put in a position to manage and control that process.

Depaepe has called this historical process educationalization, i.e., the belief that schools can solve social problems. Educationalization is commensurate with a modern worldview in which humans are seen as the agents of progress and development. If learning – and not endowment – is the basis for advancing humanity, then science gives us mechanisms of management that help humans administer social institutions such as schools, just as we are able to manage the behavior of rats in a laboratory by a system of rewards and punishments. Thorndike's theory of learning was compelling in the context of the Progressive Era because it promised human agency and scientific management for the cause of social betterment.

The optimism and clarity of Thorndike's reified notion of learning has been woven into continuous narratives about the history of education. This continuity has made it relatively easy for people these days to perceive learning as a neutral and desirable focus for schooling. The continuity of learning (as established on the basis of Thorndike's research) has been appealing because it conveys the optimistic impression that we can make a difference in the world if we use incentives and disincentives to manage people and social institutions like schools. When narratives enact continuity between rat learning and human education, it does not matter anymore what we learn; it only matters that we learn. In these continuous narratives, learning becomes a value unto itself; in the process, questions about values – the purposes of learning, and purposes of education other than learning – have been foreclosed.[12]

From Statistical Probability to Scientific Certainty

The third and final example of a truth-making continuity in the history of education is the use of the bell curve as a basis for designing, revising, and reporting results for standardized tests (e.g., SAT, ACT, GRE, PISA). Educational histories have trusted that the bell curve is a scientific model of the distribution of things – and particularly intellectual capacities – in the world. However, the history of statistics tells us that is not true.

German mathematician Carl Friedrich Gauss formalized the bell curve in the early nineteenth century as a depiction of binomial probability distribution. The bell curve was imported into "moral statistics" in the mid nineteenth century with the work of Belgian statistician, Adolphe Quetelet. In mathematics, the bell curve is a perfectly appropriate depiction of binomial probability density: the more times you flip a coin, the higher the probability that you will get an equal number of heads and tails. The history of the bell curve shows unequivocally that the importation of the bell curve from mathematics into social sciences was based not on science or empirical evidence, but on theology. Quetelet was a devoutly religious person, and he believed that a God-created universe would have to be symmetrical. Quetelet promoted *"statistique morale,"* in which the job of the statistician was to reveal the divine symmetry of the universe by designing and tweaking statistical measurements until they could be displayed on a bell curve.

The bell curve was invented as a mathematical display of binomial random variables, not as a depiction of empirical things in the universe. The bell curve is usually portrayed in the history of education as an indicator of progress in which social sciences were made more rigorous by becoming more mathematical. In a continuous historical narrative, the bell curve became a scientific fact, an invented truth, and a realistic model of phenomena in the human world. The continuity from math to social science has perpetuated a damaging perspective on variations in human capacities, namely the invention of "intelligence," and the construction of racial hierarchies as if they were scientific. The historical continuity

---

[12] For further discussion on "learnification" as a hegemonic educational goal, see Gert Biesta, "What is Education For? On Good Education, Teacher Judgement, and Educational Professionalism," *European Journal of Education, Research, and Development* 50 (2015): 75–87.

of the bell curve has validated an unjust basis for sorting people and legitimizing existing race-based privileges and hierarchies.

The previous section provided three examples of how historical discourses have imported continuity as ahistorical metaphysical constructs that have, over time, created the appearance of eternal truths. Continuities can create the impression of laws of nature, as if they were not specific to time and place, and therefore appear to be universally true, in a Cartesian sense. Insofar as the elements of continuous narratives are not specific to time and place, they are ahistorical, and they serve to perpetuate existing hierarchies, injustices, privileges, and exclusions.

Alternatives to Continuity

One well-known historiographical approach that provides us with a critical alternative to continuity is Foucault's genealogy. "Nietzsche, Genealogy, History" begins by problematizing all attempts to establish origins; it continues by historicizing any imposition of metaphysics to shape historical narratives. In place of continuity Foucault argued that history is shaped by chance and power. Quoting Nietzsche's *Dawn,* Foucault wrote that history cannot be explained by anything other than "the iron hand of necessity shaking the dice-box of chance."[13] As an example of *Wirkungsgeschichte,* Foucault's invocation of chance strips inevitability from the historical narrative. If change in history occurs by historically specific mobilizations of power (not by cause and effect), then humans are not subject to determinism; rather, humans become constructed as having a greater range of options. In other words, we are freer. In this way, Foucault's genealogical alternative to continuous history provides us with critical possibilities for emancipation and inclusion of a wider array of diverse perspectives.

Another alternative to continuity in historiographical narratives is Afrofuturism. Because available histories of Black and African cultures have been shaped by violence and colonialism, one critical approach to inclusivity is to reframe the narrative away from assumptions of continuity, and to problematize linear relationships among past-present-future. Most histories of people from African cultures center enslavement as a determining event. These histories prioritize the historical period when African people were captured and enslaved by dominant, imperial, and colonizing powers. By centering enslavement, these histories efface historical periods when African cultures were thriving, and leading cultural

---

13 Foucault, "Nietzsche, Genealogy, History," 381.

developments in governance, arts, and medicine. Afrofuturism is an approach to historiography in which enslavement is not denied but is also not posited as the inevitable condition for people of African descent. When enslavement is no longer seen as inevitable, it becomes possible to narrate African history from more humanizing perspectives. It is telling to realize that much Afrofuturism is designated as "fantasy." However, Afrofuturism can be regarded as fantasy only insofar as previous – imperial and supremacist – versions of history have been accepted as true. As Thrasher wrote:

> Seeing black people as aliens, and imagining ourselves on other worlds, is radical, Womack noted, because black people have had their imaginations "hijacked": we have been duped into only believing one narrative about ourselves. And this creates a co-constitutive process in which we imagine a limited sense of possibility and create limited lives in this image.[14]

The next section explores a second vexing theoretical issue for historiography, namely: representation.

Representation

The so-called "crisis of representation" has been debated across several disciplinary fields since the end of the twentieth century. Cultural studies, political theory, history, and philosophy have all confronted challenges to semiotic systems of representation in research and epistemology. One chapter of Foucault's *Archeology of Knowledge* is dedicated to locating representation as a historically specific episteme: "the search for roots could appear (or reappear) only when the analysis of the attributive sentence or the notion of the noun as an analytic sign of representation had been developed."[15] Representation can occur at several different epistemological levels in scientific research, and representation most often has a reductionist effect. That is, in the process of conducting research, it is often the case that complexities are simplified, irregularities are smoothed over, serendipity is quietly forgotten, and contradictions are edited out of manuscripts.

---

14 Steven W. Thrasher, "Afrofuturism: Reimagining Science and the Future from a Black Perspective," *The Guardian*, December 7, 2015, accessed September 26, 2020, https://www.theguardian.com/culture/2015/dec/07/afrofuturism-black-identity-future-science-technology.
15 Michel Foucault, *The Archaeology of Knowledge and the Discourse on Language* (New York: Pantheon, 1972), 168.

In *Laboratory Life: The Construction of Scientific Facts*, Bruno Latour and Steve Woolgar studied the historical processes of scientific research.[16] Their ethnographic study was in essence a history of how scientific facts were invented. Latour and Woolgar described several sequential steps involved in the research process under investigation: from the initial inspiration, to the laboratory bench, to lab notes, to research team meetings, to conference presentations, to drafts of manuscripts, and finally to edited articles for publication. For each step, the record of the research process is represented in various written and spoken languages. In *Laboratory Life*, the process of going from one step to the next is called a "translation." That is, bench notes are translated into language for conversations in research team meetings; research team conversations are translated into language and formats for conference presentations; conference presentations are translated into drafts of articles; and manuscripts are translated into final form for publication in journals and books. As is the case for all translations, elements from a previous stage are represented in the subsequent stage by different vocabulary, analytical framings, and sequences of presentation suitable for the next stage. And as is the case for all translations, there is never a precise correspondence between words in different languages. Something is always lost in translation. Latour and Woolgar's historical study of the construction of scientific facts is parallel with the invention of historical facts. This section outlines four levels where representation has functioned theoretically to shape truths of historical research: archival sources, structuralist analyses, generalized implications, and written reports.

Archives are Always Already Curated

Representation can operate at the level of the archive because not everything from the past remains extant, and so historians are obligated to draw inferences from a "representative" sample of archival materials. Archival materials are not necessarily representative because "typically only about five percent of most organizational records will be preserved permanently in the organization's archives."[17] As outlined by the curators at the Region of Peel Archives in Ontario, Canada:

---

16 Bruno Latour and Steve Woolgar, *Laboratory Life: The Construction of Scientific Facts* (Princeton, NJ: Princeton University Press, 1979).
17 Archives @PAMA, https://peelarchivesblog.com/2018/04/04/what-do-archivists-keep-or-not/, accessed September 26, 2020.

> There's more to an archival record than its age.
> Archives don't keep everything.
> "Everything" doesn't exist to keep.[18]

Some things are not recorded, and therefore cannot be present in any archive (e.g., smells, tastes, emotions, mental states). Other things may be recorded, but may be missing from archives (e.g., shopping lists, "low-level" memos, and travel documents). Depending on historically specific sets of circumstances (e.g., capacity of storage sites, persuasions of archival curators, idiosyncratic indexing schemes), archival materials may be more or less accessible to researchers. Yet other things may have been recorded and archived, but then erased from archives by disasters (fire, flood, bombing), neglect, or by political-ideological actions of censorship, genocide, and contempt. All of these historically specific circumstances contribute to problems with assumptions about representation in archives.

Issues of representation in educational historiography have been addressed variously by different scholars. Burke and Grosvenor, for example, used the evocative term "montage of gaps" to call attention to historiographical possibilities that are made possible when historians depart from extant materials to address gaps as sources of historical inquiry.[19] Their approach takes into account the problems of representation that are inevitable because recorded material is limited, and offers historians a way to imagine greater possibilities beyond inference from extant material.

At another level, researchers make (implicit or explicit) decisions about which phenomena in the world shall "count" as being representative of the object of study. In the case of educational history, objects of study that are regularly included are textbooks, classrooms, lesson plans, teachers' records, student-produced work, photographs, school architecture and furniture, and educational policy documents. But what about modes of transportation to and from school, or the smells of disinfectant, or the Coca-Cola vending machines in the hallways, or the family's routines for choosing school clothes and backpacks? Many features of schooling are not readily understood as being worthy objects of study that represent education. The work of educational historian Catherine Burke

---

[18] Archives @PAMA, https://peelarchivesblog.com/2018/04/04/what-do-archivists-keep-or-not/, accessed September 26, 2020.
[19] Catherine Burke and Ian Grosvenor, "The 'Body Parts' of the Victorian School Architect E.R. Robson or an Exploration of the Writing and Reading of a Life," in *Rethinking the History of Education: Transnational Perspectives on its Questions, Methods, and Knowledge*, ed. Thomas S. Popkewitz (New York: Palgrave Publishers, 2013), 201–220.

has expanded the scope of things that have been included in educational histories to school lunches,[20] pockets,[21] and footwear.[22] Archives function as filters in educational research because some things are regularly represented in archives, and other things are not represented.

Structuralist Analyses

A second level at which representation operates in historiography occurs when structuralism governs the approach to analysis. Structuralism posits a two-tiered system of reality: *langue* and *parole*. Structuralist approaches to scientific research do not focus on the messy surface layer of *parole*, but rather on the regularized, tidied up layer of *langue*. In a structuralist epistemology, the proper object of study is not surface phenomena, but underlying concepts – the representations of the surface phenomena. Concepts are invented by scholars, and so when analysis is based on concepts, an expert perspective is privileged, and non-expert perspectives can be dismissed as invalid or uninformed. In this way, a structuralist approach to analysis can function to perpetuate systemic privileges of historiography by excluding the perspectives of those who have been under-represented in established institutions of scholarly production.

Depaepe et al. called attention to problematic theoretical issues posed by representation in historiography by asking questions about the purposes of history:

> What is history for?: Should we integrate [popular accounts] into a scientific account? Or should we seek conflict? Or should we learn to live with these 'paradoxes' of historic representation? (...) They force us to continue to think about how we present the past: as history 'for' the people, or as history 'with' and 'by the people.'[23]

---

20 Catherine Burke, "Contested Desires: The Edible Landscape of School," Paedagogica *Historica* 41 (2005): 571–587.
21 Catherine Burke, "Nature Tables and Pocket Museums: From the Leicestershire Classroom to the Mountain View Center for Environmental Education, Colorado," *Pedagogia Oggi* 17 (2019): 17–30.
22 Catherine Burke, "Feet, Footwear and 'Being Alive' in the Modern School," *Paedagogica Historica* 54 (2018): 32–47.
23 Marc Depaepe, Frank Simon, and Pieter Verstraete, "Valorising the Cultural Heritage of the School Desk Through Historical Research," in *Educational Research: Material Culture and Its Representation*, ed. Paul Smeyers and Marc Depaepe (Dordrecht: Springer, 2014), 27.

Structuralism has at times been considered scientific partly because conceptualizations help to tidy up the messiness of practice. Concepts are invented by experts in ways that are not always accessible by ordinary people. In this way, much modern research is a self-perpetuating and exclusionary approach to knowledge creation and gatekeeping. It is precisely because of the exclusionary epistemology of structuralist analyses that much academic discourse has been accused of being elitist and inaccessible.[24]

Generalized Implications for the Present

A third level at which representation operates in educational history occurs when implications from individual studies are generalized as if they applied to other events, times, and places. This is related to analytical thinking, as described previously. In some cases, a historical study may be interpreted to provide us with clues about what will happen in the future, as George Santayana[25] so famously warned. Many research projects are designed to draw inferences from samples to a larger population (i.e., reliability). Analogously, historical studies might allow a small sample of artifacts to stand in as evidence for an event or trend (even as many historians warn against such generalizations). Sample-based representation happens when findings from the study of a single school are generalized to apply to schools in other times or places. When inferences are drawn from samples, then the research is shaped by mechanisms of representation.

Most nineteenth century educational research was idiothetic, that is, specific case studies that were focused on unique individuals, and not meant to be generalized beyond the immediate object of inquiry. In the twentieth century, however, along with efficiency and large-scale organizational administration, trends in research design shifted from idiothetic to nomothetic, that is, from the study of unique individuals to the study of large groups. To increase efficiency in the research process, it was assumed that representative samples could be created from which inferences could be drawn to make claims about a broader array of cases. With the trend toward generalization, inference became the highest priority for analysis in social-scientific studies. Inference is now the primary consideration in all educational research, and idiothetic research is generally regarded

---

[24] For further discussion on elitism vs. populism in scholarly work, see Lynn Fendler, "An Information Reformation? Research Expertise in a Populist Context," *Journal of the Philosophy of Education* 53 (2020): 694–710.
[25] "Those who cannot remember the past are condemned to repeat it."

to be less valuable because it cannot be "scaled up." As Gigerenzer and Marewski wrote:

> The qualifier *inference* indicates that among all scientific tools – such as hypothesis formulation, systematic observation, descriptive statistics, minimizing measurement error, and independent replication – the inference from a sample to population grew to be considered the most crucial part of research.[26]

As inference has taken on more prominence in research, other scholarly values have decreased in importance, including observation, measurement, and contextualization. Much educational historiography is idiothetic, that is, focused on a specific time, place, and event. However, to the extent that historical research is conducted or interpreted for purposes of generalization to other times and places, inference tends to take precedence over other historiographical research tools such as observation and thick description. In that way, representation functions as a problematic tool of generalization that may obscure variation and diversity in human life.

Linear Expository Writing

> Historical truth is merely a function of what is possible to write.
> Marianne Larsen, 2011

It is commonplace for historical research to be reported in a chronological exposition arranged from oldest to newest. This approach to historical reporting is a relatively modern style. The conventional chronological format for historical writing does not aim to capture the research process itself, which would be a faithful account of how the research was conducted: first we went to the older newspapers, which in turn led us to the archives, which in turn led us to some court documents. Instead, the conventional chronological arrangement for historical is meant to represent the past *wie es eigentlich gewesen*.

But even when the format of the report departs from the most conventional chronological arrangement, representation is still operating insofar as conventional scholarly formats are meant to represent complicated and messy life worlds that surround and shape every research project.

---

26 Gerd Gigerenzer and Julian N. Marewski, "Surrogate Science: The Idol of a Universal Method for Scientific Inference," *Journal of Management* 41 (2015), 425.

Cultural historian Natalie Zemon Davis regularly used conditional verb tenses (i.e., "could be") in her historical writing in an effort to convey cautious uncertainty in the face of limited evidence:

> The use of the conditional is a safeguard for the historian. More and more it seems I have to use it... [W]hen I took off in pursuit of the ideas, feelings, conflicts, and dreams of particular persons, I sometimes encountered big gaps in the documentation, especially since I was often tracking people who had left no written traces.[27]

Finally, linear expository writing – which characterizes most scholarly authorship in a modern ethos – is itself representational insofar as it is meant to open a window on the world. The world is dynamic, sprawling, and multidimensional, but scholarly writing is usually linear, with starting and ending points that are fixed on the page. Writing formats put us in a position to make decisions about where the story begins and where it ends (harkening back to origins and periodization), and those decisions function as representations that construct truths, just as Latour and Woolgar's translations construct scientific facts.

As Sobe wrote:

> The challenge that we face as historians of education is to recognize the interaction between the historically constituted temporalities we study and the temporalities produced/imposed by the tools and methods we use to conduct these studies.[28]

Historians generally maintain commitments to specificity in time and place. With that being the case, it becomes important to recognize that our tools of writing and analysis are also specific to time and place. There are no independent variables in history.[29]

---

[27] Natalie Zemon Davis, *A Passion for History: Conversations with Denis Crouzet* (Kirksville, MO: Truman State University Press, 2010), 5–6.
[28] Noah Sobe, "Entanglement and Transnationalism in the History of American Education," in *Rethinking the History of Education: Transnational Perspectives on its Questions, Methods, and Knowledge*, ed. Thomas S. Popkewitz (New York: Palgrave Publishers, 2013), 100.
[29] Lynn Fendler, "There Are no Independent Variables in History," in *Rethinking the History of Education*, 264–291.

Alternatives to Representation

Most scholars have been educated to read in a mode that Best and Marcus called "symptomatic reading."[30] Symptomatic reading is based on representation and structuralism: the assumption that meanings are "hidden, repressed, deep, and in need of detection and disclosure by an interpreter." If expertise is premised on the belief that all reading should be symptomatic, then the possibilities for interpretation tend to be limited by existing structuralist constraints about signs and symbols. Structuralism establishes conventions with respect to which phenomena may be counted as proper objects of study and which phenomena should be counted as mere ephemeral epiphenomena. Those conventions are exclusive; they perpetuate existing privileges for some kinds of interpretations while disallowing others. Best and Marcus' work presents a critical intervention poised to confront the limitations on "the way we read now." They conclude that "producing accurate accounts of surfaces is not antithetical to critique."[31]

To address issues of representation and suggest alternatives, philosopher of science Sandra Harding has advanced a "strong objectivity proposal." Her thesis is that trends in modern research that have been called "objective" have been reductionist insofar as most research was conducted by and about men, and then the results were generalized to all people. Harding distinguished strong objectivity from weak objectivity:

> Strong objectivity (...) demands interrogation of just which cultural commitments can advance growth of the kinds of knowledge a particular community desires. Weak objectivity has been too narrowly focused to detect the values and interests that most powerfully shape research. Yet in another respect it has been too broadly focused to maximize objectivity. It demanded that all social values and interests originating outside research processes be eliminated from them.[32]

Harding noted that, by conventional agreement, research reports do not include values and other aspects of the personal lives of the researchers, even when we cannot be certain whether values and life events may have had an impact on the research process. Harding advocates "strong objectivity," an approach to writing

---

[30] Stephen Best and Sharon Marcus, "Surface Reading: An Introduction," *Representations* 108 (2009): 1.
[31] Best and Marcus, "Surface Reading," 18.
[32] Sandra Harding, *Objectivity and Diversity: Another Logic of Scientific Research* (Chicago: University of Chicago Press, 2015), 36.

that deliberately attends to elements of time and place that may have been neglected by researchers from privileged sites, and that have shaped the written historical narrative. The "strong objectivity hypothesis" is less reductionist than conventional approaches to research because it demands inclusion of elements of time and place that are sometimes personal and sometimes environmental. By including contextual elements of time and place, the research process relies less on representation and more on presentation of a broader array of contextual elements. Harding wrote about the natural sciences, but her theory of strong objectivity pertains equally to educational history, especially to the degree any historiographical project includes consideration of specific time and place, who and how, as influential elements of the historical record.

Similarly, Saidya Hartman also problematized representation in the historical record by calling attention to the role of power relations in shaping what counts as evidence in historiography:

> For theorists, conceptual problems proliferate: how to listen for the dominated in the archives of the dominant? How, for example, might one recover the experiences of enslaved people – barred from literacy on threat of torture, sale, or death – from the records of owners and traders without amplifying the violence that confined them there?[33]

Addressing the impossibility of representing that which has never been recorded, Hartman coined the term "critical fabulation" to describe efforts of historians to "paint as full a picture of the lives of the captives as possible":

> straining against the limits of the archive to write a cultural history of the captive, and, at the same time, enacting the impossibility of representing the lives of the captives precisely through the process of narration... The method guiding this writing practice is best described as critical fabulation.[34]

A third example of alternatives to representation is offered in studies of indigenous epistemologies. In her forward to Wilma Mankiller's book, Gloria Steinem, for example, addressed violence of historical representation by focusing on Native American history that has been largely ignored by the scholarly community. Steinem wrote: "Most of us never learned that they [Native Americans] had democratic forms of self-governance before Greece and without slavery, irrigation systems and astronomical calendars as advanced as those of Rome, and medi-

---

[33] Sam Huber, "Saidiya Hartman Unravels the Archive," *The Nation*, May 1, 2019, accessed September 26, 2020, https://www.thenation.com/article/saidiya-hartmans-astounding-history-of-the-forgotten-sexual-modernists-in-20th-century-black-life/.
[34] Saidya Hartman, "Venus in Two Acts," *Small Axe* 12 (2008): 11.

cine using herbs and psychotherapeutic skills when Europe was relying on 'humours' and leeches."[35]

A fourth example of nonrepresentational language is poetic inquiry, and other arts-based approaches to research. In poetry, writing is not only representational, but also material in rhythm, intonation, rhyme, and meter schemes. In recognition of the research potential of nonrepresentational language, Depaepe, Simon, and Verstraete remarked on the possibility of allowing exhibition projects to be counted as a Master's thesis: "this would be an ideal possibility for creating a bridge between the academic world and the public world. In terms of the history of education, this would enable us to scan alternative ways of finding out about the past: heritage, collective memory, tradition."[36]

Educational historian Natalie Z. Davis opened alternatives to representation by exploring the use of fiction as both historical sources and as media for historical reports:[37]

> A good historical film should pose questions to the viewer. But planning and visualizing a historical film are fascinating for the historian or the historically minded filmmaker. So many situations arise [in film] for which you would not need to seek evidence if you were writing a prose nonfiction text: conversations, movements, encounters. The imagination is constantly at work here...[38]

Similarly, cultural historian Trinh T. Minh-ha remarked on the indispensability of poetry and literature as historical sources in any attempt to write about Vietnam: "No book, no substantial study on the history, culture and civilization of Vietnam written by Vietnamese can do without the body of tales, which constitute the core of a popular literature widely spread among all classes of its society."[39]

Alternatives to representation in research have been formulated as "nonrepresentational theories" by geographers in the United Kingdom. Nonrepresentational theories can be characterized as one example of new materialisms. Nonrepresentational theories strip away epistemological classifications that separate *langue* from *parole*, and allow all things to share the same plane of immanence:

---

35 Gloria Steinem, introduction to *Every Day Is a Good Day: Reflections by Contemporary Indigenous Women*, by Wilma Mankiller (New York: Fulcrum Publishing, 2011), xvii.
36 Depaepe, Simon, and Verstraete, "Valorising the Cultural Heritage of the School Desk," 27.
37 Natalie Zemon Davis, *Fiction in the Archives: Pardon Tales and Their Tellers in Sixteenth-Century France* (Palo Alto: Stanford University Press, 1990).
38 Davis, *A Passion for History*, 23.
39 Trinh T. Minh-ha, *Elsewhere, within here: Immigration, Refugeeism and the Boundary Event* (New York: Routledge, 2010), 17.

beliefs, atmospheres, sensations ideas, toys, music, ghosts, dance therapies, footpaths, pained bodies, trance music, reindeer, plants, boredom, fat, anxieties, vampires, cars, enchantment, nanotechnologies, water voles, GM foods, landscapes, drugs, money, racialised bodies, political demonstrations.[40]

In this way, nonrepresentational theories provide us with mechanisms to jettison the last vestiges of structuralism from research epistemologies. New materialisms in general, and nonrepresentational theories in particular, provide alternatives for writing histories that problematize both continuity and representation. Structuralism posited a two-tiered universe that separated surface epiphenomena from a representational abstract reality. In contrast, new materialisms reject that separation and put everything on the same material plane. One critical dimension of new materialism is that it challenges previous conventions of representation, coherence, and continuity. Those challenges invite departures from tradition, especially traditions that sustain existing privileges and hierarchies as they are represented in scholarly knowledge production.

New materialisms have arisen partly in response to the trends of abstraction and inference (e.g., suspicious or structuralist readings) that have taken over compositions and interpretations in historiography and other disciplines. The emphasis on inference is a contemporary trend that has sustained representational readings. Representations require expertise in order to be interpreted. When that happens, experts are put at an advantage, and ordinary people have more difficulty gaining access to the complicated and esoteric tools that have become necessary for the production of research knowledge. New materialist approaches to research (also shaped by power relations) have not yet solidified into established practices, and so they still (for the time being, anyway) offer some critical leverage that have the potential to untether us from past restrictions, and to diversify research approaches.

Conclusion

Continuity and representation have functioned in educational histories in the role of *deus ex machina* to include some knowledge as truth and exclude other knowledge as mythology or folklore. In some times and places, continuity and representation appear out of nowhere into historical narratives to save the day, by fabricating coherence out of chaotic and random world events. In efforts

---

40 Ben Anderson and Paul Harrison, introduction to *Taking-Place: Non-Representational Theories and Geography*, by Ben Anderson and Paul Harrison, eds. (Farnham: Ashgate, 2010), 14.

to make history appear coherent or believable, discourses around educational history have at times imported from outside history some independent variables, some unwavering points of anchor, such as continuity and/or representation, that function to stabilize a historical narrative. Continuity and representation are themselves exempted from history, as fabrications of an imaginary God's eye view of the world. As if we could stand outside history! There is nothing in any historical record *per se* that says continuity and representation exist, in all times and in all places, and are necessary for historiography. Continuity and representation are dehistoricized concepts that convey the appearance of being universally true and helpful for promoting a particular worldview, however, continuity and representation belong more properly in a particular passing phase of historiography, limited to a few decades of our modern era.

If educational historians would like to avoid the use of independent—ahistorical—variables, and strive instead for the no-exemptions policy of writing history, then there are many more educational histories to be written. When we make efforts to historicize history, it does mean that certain kinds of historical research projects will fall by the wayside. At the same time, it also means that many new, exciting, and different historical projects, from many more diverse voices and perspectives, have become available for study.

Bibliography

Anderson, Ben, and Paul Harrison. Introduction to *Taking-Place: Non-Representational Theories and Geography*, edited by Ben Anderson and Paul Harrison, 1–14. Farnham: Ashgate, 2010.
Archives @PAMA. https://peelarchivesblog.com/2018/04/04/what-do-archivists-keep-or-not/. Accessed September 26, 2020.
Best, Stephen, and Sharon Marcus. "Surface Reading: An Introduction," *Representations* 108 (2009): 1–21.
Burke, Catherine. "Contested Desires: The Edible Landscape of School." *Paedagogica Historica* 41 (2005): 571–587.
Burke, Catherine. "Feet, Footwear and 'Being alive' in the Modern School." *Paedagogica Historica* 54 (2018): 32–47.
Burke, Catherine. "Nature Tables and Pocket Museums: From the Leicestershire Classroom to the Mountain View Center for Environmental Education, Colorado." *Pedagogia Oggi* 17 (2019): 17–30.
Burke, Catherine, and Ian Grosvenor. "The 'Body Parts' of the Victorian School Architect E.R. Robson or an Exploration of the Writing and Reading of a Life." In *Rethinking the History of Education: Transnational Perspectives on its Questions, Methods, and Knowledge*, edited by Thomas S. Popkewitz, 201–220. New York: Palgrave, 2013.
Davis, Natalie Zemon. *Fiction in the Archives: Pardon Tales and Their Tellers in Sixteenth-Century France*. Palo Alto: Stanford University Press, 1990.

Davis, Natalie Zemon. *A Passion for History: Conversations with Denis Crouzet*, Kirksville, MO: Truman State University Press, 2010.

Dean, Mitchell. *Critical and Effective Histories: Foucault's Methods and Historical Sociology* New York: Routledge, 1994.

Depaepe, Marc. "History of Education Anno 1992: 'A Tale Told by an Idiot, Full of Sound and Fury, Signifying Nothing'?" *History of Education* 22 (1992): 1–10.

Depaepe, Marc. "Philosophy and History of Education: Time to Bridge the Gap?." *Educational Philosophy and Theory* 39 (2007): 28–43.

Depaepe, Marc, Frank Simon, and Pieter Verstraete, "Valorising the Cultural Heritage of the School Desk Through Historical Research." In *Educational Research: Material Culture and Its Representation*, edited by Paul Smeyers and Marc Depaepe, 13–30. Dordrecht: Springer, 2014.

Fendler, Lynn. "There Are no Independent Variables in History." In *Rethinking the History of Education: Transnational Perspectives on its Questions, Methods, and Knowledge*, edited by Thomas S. Popkewitz, 264–291. New York: Palgrave, 2013.

Foucault, Michel. *The Archaeology of Knowledge and the Discourse on Language*. New York: Pantheon, 1972.

Foucault, Michel. "Nietzsche, Genealogy, History." In *Michel Foucault: Aesthetics, Method and Epistemology*, edited by James D. Faubion, vol. 2 of *Essential Works of Foucault, 1954–1984*, edited by James D. Faubion. New York: The New Press, 1978/1998.

Gigerenzer, Gerd, and Julian N. Marewski, "Surrogate Science: The Idol of a Universal Method for Scientific Inference." *Journal of Management* 41 (2015): 421–440.

Harding, Sandra. *Objectivity and Diversity: Another Logic of Scientific Research*. Chicago: University of Chicago Press, 2015.

Hartman, Saidya. "Venus in Two Acts." *Small Axe* 12 (2008): 1–14.

Huber, Sam. "Saidiya Hartman Unravels the Archive." *The Nation*, May 1, 2019. Accessed September 26, 2020. https://www.thenation.com/article/saidiya-hartmans-astounding-history-of-the-forgotten-sexual-modernists-in-20th-century-black-life/.

Latour, Bruno, and Steve Woolgar. *Laboratory Life: The Construction of Scientific Facts*. Princeton, NJ: Princeton University Press, 1979.

Moore, Alison. "Historicising Historical Theory's History of Cultural Historiography." *Cosmos and History: The Journal of Natural and Social Philosophy* 12 (2016): 257–291.

Sobe, Noah. "Entanglement and Transnationalism in the History of American Education." In *Rethinking the History of Education: Transnational Perspectives on its Questions, Methods, and Knowledge*, edited by Thomas S. Popkewitz, 93–107. New York: Palgrave, 2013.

Steinem, Gloria. Introduction to *Every Day Is a Good Day: Reflections by Contemporary Indigenous Women,* by Wilma Mankiller, xv–xxvi. New York: Fulcrum Publishing, 2011.

Thorndike, Edward L. *Human Learning*. New York: The Century Company, 1931.

Trinh, T. Ming-ha, *Elsewhere, within here: Immigration, Refugeeism and the Boundary Event*. New York: Routledge, 2010.

Thrasher, Steven W. "Afrofuturism: Reimagining Science and the Future from a Black Perspective." *The Guardian*, December 7, 2015. Accessed September 26, 2020. https://www.theguardian.com/culture/2015/dec/07/afrofuturism-black-identity-future-science-technology.

Joyce Goodman (University of Winchester, UK)
Concentric Circles and Magnetic Currents: Moral Disarmament at the League of Nations International Institute of Educational Cinematography, 1931–34

Abstract: This chapter explores spatial and temporal elements in configurations that entangle education, internationalism, and empire in three articles published in the International Review of Educational Cinematography (IREC). In the first article Evelyn Wrench (1934) deploys a concentric circles spatial model that places the self at the center and sees world-mindedness as the result of learning to negotiate ever-widening circles of relationships (family, region, nation, international/empire/world). Following Papastephanou (2016), the chapter argues that Wrench deploys a cultural-cognitive model of the enlargement and enrichment of a cosmopolitan self associated with linear temporal notions of progress and of abstract space that constitutes a style of reason thought to invoke a less parochial existence via a pedagogy in which individuals learn to negotiate distance between self and other in an imperialist frame aligned with notions of territorial expansion. Analysis of two IREC articles by Germaine Dulac (1931, 1934) draws on Grosz's (2004) analysis of Bergsonian temporalities to trace how Dulac's thinking disrupts the concentric circles model by gesturing towards quantum notions of timespacematter that dislodge the human from the center of analysis through little incidents, thereby creating what Serres (1991) calls a space of passage or transience where learning comes via friction in what Tsing (2011) terms zones of awkward engagement. The conclusion argues that rather than situating the articles by Wrench and Dulac across an epistemological break, their understandings of how to foster international understanding and friendship might be approached via Whitehead's (1920, 1925, 1927, 1935) theorization of abstraction and the Event, as spatial and temporal counterpoints that coexisted and knotted together in the fabric that constituted 1930s moral disarmament.

Keywords: moral disarmament; cinematography; quantum physics; temporalities, spatialities

Introduction

During the 1920s and early 1930s the view that no amount of international arbitration or economic cooperation would prevent the return of war unless people abandoned chauvinistic impulses and embraced cross-national understanding was articulated through what the League of Nations termed moral disarmament. Moral disarmament was concerned with countermanding pernicious feelings inimical to international understanding. In 1932 the Romanian George Oprescu told the League's International Committee of Intellectual Co-operation (ICIC):

> It cannot be denied that very often nations foster a feeling of hatred for other nations ... that misunderstood pride and patriotism are the greatest enemies of mutual understanding between peoples; that the love for one's mother-country stifles the love we owe to mankind to the community of nations. Efforts are being made to remedy this state of affairs by extirpating these pernicious feelings from the hearts of men.[1]

At both the ICIC (established 1922) and the League's Ad Hoc Committee of Moral Disarmament (established 1932)[2] film appeared as a concern for moral disarmament because of its potential to promote cultural misrepresentation and Americanization. But it was also portrayed as a means to foster the spirit of internationalism even after talking films disrupted earlier notions of silent film as a universal language.[3] The League's International Institute of Educational Cinematography (IIEC), founded in Rome in 1928 and funded by Mussolini's government, linked educationists, internationalists, humanitarians, and the cinema industry around an agenda that saw educational cinematography as a positive mechanism for fostering international friendship in the pursuit of peace. The

---

1 League of Nations Intellectual Co-operation Organisation, "The International Committee on Intellectual Co-operation and Moral Disarmament. Extract from the Minutes of the Fourteenth Plenary Session of the I.C.I.C. Geneva, July 21, 1932," *Information Bulletin of the League of Nations Intellectual Co-operation Organisation* 1 (1932): 132.
2 The Ad Hoc Committee on Moral Disarmament, established within the Conference for the Reduction and Limitation of Armaments (1932–34), progressed moral disarmament via nation states and the ICIC additionally through associations. See Elly Hermon, "Le désarmement moral, facteur dans les relations internationales pendant l'entre-deux-guerres," *Guerres mondiales et conflits contemporains* 39 (1989): 23–36. For teachers and moral disarmament, see Mona L. Siegel, *The Moral Disarmament of France: Education, Pacifism, and Patriotism, 1914–1940* (Cambridge: Cambridge University Press, 2004), 3.
3 Joyce Goodman, "'Shaping the Mentality of Races and Especially of Young People': The League of Nations and the Educational Cinematography Congress, 1934," in *League of Nations: Histories, Legacies and Impact*, ed. Joy Damousi and Patricia O'Brien (Melbourne: Melbourne University Press, 2018), 197–213.

IIEC worked to facilitate international agreements around the circulation of educational film, conducted empirical studies on children, young people, and film, held conferences on educational cinematography, and disseminated its work via the multilingual journal, *The International Review of Educational Cinematography (IREC)*.⁴

This chapter focuses on articles from two contributors to *IREC*, both of whom sought to foster the international spirit at the heart of moral disarmament. Writing in the context of the IIEC's 1934 conference, Evelyn Wrench, the founder of the Overseas League, the English-Speaking Union, and the All Peoples' Association, portrays cinema as a "wonderful instrument of unity" to "unite the coming generation in the bonds of friendship."⁵ In his article Wrench includes a concentric circles diagram to illustrate his argument that fostering international understanding and international friendship moves through nationalism to internationalism.⁶ The first part of the chapter discusses the spatial-temporal understandings that thread through Wrench's concentric circles diagram, which the chapter argues are grounded in the second law of thermodynamics and resonate with what Bergson terms differences of degree. The second section discusses two papers which film producer, teacher, lecturer, film theorist and activist, feminist, and pacifist Germaine Dulac⁷ delivered at conferences held at the IIEC in 1931 and 1934.⁸ When outlining how cinematography fosters international

---

4 Christel Taillibert, L'institut International Du Cinématographe Éducatif: Regards sur le rôle du cinema éducatif dans la politique internationale du fascism italien (Paris: L'Harmattan, 1999); Zoe Druick, "The International Educational Cinematograph Institute, Reactionary Modernism and the Formation of Film Studies," *Canadian Journal of Film Studies* 16 (2007): 80–97; Benjamin G. Martin, *The Nazi–Fascist New Order for European Culture* (Cambridge Mass: Harvard University Press, 2016); Andrew Higson, "Cultural Policy and Industrial Practice: Film Europe and the International Film Congresses of the 1920s," in *"Film Europe" and "Film America": Cinema, Commerce and Cultural Exchange, 1920–1939*, ed. Andrew Higson and Richard Maltby (Exeter: University of Exeter Press, 1999), 117–131. The IIEC operated until Italy's withdrawal from the League in 1937, see Hilla Wehberg, "Fate of an International Film Institute," *The Public Opinion Quarterly* 2 (1938): 483–485.
5 Evelyn Wrench, "Children of the World," *International Review of Educational Cinematography* 6 (1934): 272–273.
6 For languages of international understanding, moral disarmament and the "international mind" see Joyce Goodman, "Women and International Intellectual Co-operation," *Paedagogica Historica* 48 (2012): 357–368.
7 Tami Williams, *Germaine Dulac: A Cinema of Sensations* (Illinois: University of Illinois Press, 2014), 187.
8 Germaine Dulac, "The Meaning of Cinema," *International Review of Educational Cinematography* 12 (1931): 1089–1099 [delivered at the conference organized at the IIEC by the International Council of Women, see Joyce Goodman, "The Buddhist Institute at Phnom Penh, the Internation-

understanding and friendship, Dulac argues that the newsreel "puts the most opposed mentalities into communication [and] joins in a magnetic current the most divergent races of the world."⁹ She disrupts the geometry of the concentric circles approach by describing the film spectator thrown out of their own circle, which she considers to be a key moment in creating affection and understanding between peoples.¹⁰ The chapter argues that Dulac's account is underpinned by a temporal indeterminacy that resonates with the new physics of subatomic particles and with what Bergson terms differences in kind. The conclusion draws on the thinking of Alfred North Whitehead to suggest that rather than locating these two approaches across an epistemological break, they might be approached as co-existing counterpoints in the spatial-temporal knots of early 1930s moral disarmament.

Internationalism, Concentric Circles, and Differences of Degree: Rationalizing Time and Space

The concentric circles diagram of internationalism that Wrench deploys seeks to illustrate "the way our various loyalties should dovetail into one another," which Wrench argues is necessary to inculcate internationalism and to "extirpate ... pernicious feelings from the hearts of men."¹¹ Wrench's diagram moves through nationalism to internationalism.¹² The individual is to be a good citizen of their town before they can be a good patriot of their country, and they are to be a good citizen of their country before they can give loyal allegiance to Europe and the World. The same doctrine is true of the young, notes Wrench: "[t]hey should love their countries as well as the greater units of Europe and the World."¹³ For Wrench this is a question of inculcating "the right kind of loyalty."¹⁴ Reso-

---

al Council of Women and the Rome International Institute for Educational Cinematography: Intersections of Internationalism and Imperialism, 1931–34," *History of Education* 47 (2018): 415–431)]; Germaine Dulac, "The Educational and Social Value of the Newsreel," *International Review of Educational Cinematography* (1934): 545–560.
9 Dulac, "Educational and Social Value of the Newsreel," 546.
10 Dulac, "Meaning of Cinema," 1090, 1094.
11 Wrench, "Children of the World," 272.
12 Wrench, "Children of the World," 272.
13 Wrench, "Children of the World," 272.
14 Wrench, "Children of the World," 272.

nating with moral disarmament discourse at the League, he maintains that "[w]e shall never get lasting peace in the world until we disencumber our minds of wrong thinking."[15] Youth are to love their family but not hate other families; be proud of their school or university but not hate "other seats of learning"[16]; love their town or districts but not hate neighboring towns or districts; love their country but not hate neighboring countries; love their race but not hate other races; love their continent but not hate other continents. Wrench notes that this means "[n]o Europe *versus* America or *versus* Asia theories."[17] He is also concerned about "relations of the white and coloured races" and with whether "the rising tide of colour" will make a clash between East and West inevitable, which he considers will be key problems for the world during the next 100 years.[18]

Wrench condemns many commercial films for stirring up race-hatred but argues that so long as films are carefully prepared by experts in film-production and by child psychologists the cinema can play a decisive role in preventing "racial war."[19] He portrays silent and talking films as "wonderful instrument[s] for uniting the coming generation in the bonds of friendship"[20]; and he calls on delegates at the 1934 IIEC conference to draw up a syllabus in which world leaders would "give a talk in simple words to children of other nations on why we should be friends."[21] He suggests that Mussolini might provide the first talk in French, English, and German, followed by "talkies" from other world leaders. He also advocates the establishment of an exchange library of films with titles like "Why European Boys and Girls should be Friends," "We are all Europeans," "What other Countries can teach us," "Why War is stupid" and "Human Nature *does* change."[22] To foster a sense of civic duty in the young, the library is also to contain films on topics like the preservation of wild life, kindness to animals, and keeping street and public parks clean.

Wrench adopts a Eurocentric approach and imagines Europe integrating along the lines of the British commonwealth. Wrench was a staunch imperialist who transferred his enthusiasm from the idea of imperial unity to that of eventual world unity. In 1910 he founded the Overseas League for British citizens; in

---

15 Wrench, "Children of the World," 272.
16 Wrench, "Children of the World," 272.
17 Wrench, "Children of the World," 273.
18 Wrench, "Children of the World," 273.
19 Wrench, "Children of the World," 273.
20 Wrench, "Children of the World," 272.
21 Wrench, "Children of the World," 273.
22 Wrench, "Children of the World," 273.

1918 he established the English-Speaking Union to promote friendship and cooperation between the British empire and the United States via exchanges, travelling fellowships, lectures, and social events; and in 1929 he set up the All Peoples' Association, open to all nations, which aimed to promote international amity in general and Anglo-German understanding in particular.[23] In his own youth, Wrench notes, he had been "intensely interested in the welfare of the British empire" and would have loved to have seen films about men like French Canadian Sir Wildrid Laurier, South Africans Paul Kruger and Cecil Rhodes, New Zealander Richard Seddon, and Australian Alfred Deakin.[24] Wrench's model of increasing European integration parallels the cooperation he imagines to characterize the British commonwealth:

> We live in an age of integration. On the continent of Europe we have witnessed the growing international unity of Italy and Germany. During the past half century strong forces have been at work unifying the far-flung British commonwealth.[25]

In discussing international integration Wrench deploys an evolutionary unidirectional temporality of "next steps" that moves forward from the heritage of Europe's "splendid past." He comments: "we have got past [the] stage in our evolution" where "in the Middle Ages Perugia had hated and fought with Assisi and England in Scotland." The "next step" for Europeans is to "create a European ethos and set "an example to the rest of the world" by instilling into the minds of children in all "our countries" that in addition to their local loyalty, they are European.[26]

Wrench's concentric circle diagram places the self at the center of the circles. As Maria Papastephanou argues, in spatial terms, a concentric model with the self at the center constitutes an individualistic cultural-cognitive model of the enlargement and enrichment of the self and a style of reason thought to invoke a less parochial existence. She describes the concentric circles model as an approach immersed in Western ways of maintaining the coherence of a Western-rooted modern self via a successful negotiation of distance between self and

---

[23] The Overseas League, founded as the Overseas Club, changed its name in 1918 after amalgamating with the Patriotic League of Britons Overseas. The All People's Association was wound up in 1936 in the face of the rise of Nazism. Alex May, "Wrench, Sir (John) Evelyn Leslie (1882–1966), Promoter of the British Empire and Author," *Oxford Dictionary of National Biography*, accessed October 18, 2019, https://www.oxforddnb.com/view/10.1093/ref:odnb/9780198614128.001.0001/odnb-9780198614128-e-37031.
[24] Wrench, "Children of the World," 273.
[25] Wrench, "Children of the World," 273.
[26] Wrench, "Children of the World," 273.

other. She also sees the concentric circles model as a way of affirming identity politics because it raises "one's secure self-image to an exemplary status."[27] It is the self, Papastephanou comments, who is the center of attention and the primary beneficiary of this intercultural formation because it is the self who entertains feelings of patriotism and cosmopolitanism.[28]

The unidirectional temporality that underpins Wrench's diagram of international friendship and its move through nationalism to internationalism is informed by the temporal irreversibility that British astronomer Arthur Eddington called "the arrow of time."[29] This view of temporal irreversibility is grounded in nineteenth century scientific understandings of the laws of thermodynamics, which were elaborated in the realm of physics from the 1840s and impacted on a range of fields, including literature, biology, psychoanalysis, and history.[30] The two laws of thermodynamics are concerned with energy. In the first law of thermodynamics, which deals with the transformation of energy (its quantity), the total energy of the system remains constant and is never created or destroyed. The second law of thermodynamics (which refers to energy quality)[31] says nothing about the "flow of time" or about the moment called "now" and its movement into the future;[32] but as Richard Morris outlines, it enables future and past to be distinguished because what is termed entropy constitutes a process in which the amount of energy remains constant but useful energy diminishes due to its dissipation into heat and is rendered unavailable for work.[33] The second law of thermodynamics also illustrates that where no energy is expended

---

27 Maria Papastephanou, *Thinking Differently About Cosmopolitanism: Theory, Eccentricity, and the Globalized World* (Boulder: Paradigm Publishers, 2015), kindle locs. 427, 1627–1631, 1640–1641, 2417–2420; quotation at 1627–1631; see also Maria Papastephanou, "Concentric, Vernacular and Rhizomatic Cosmopolitanisms," in *Cosmopolitanism: Educational, Philosophical and Historical Perspectives*, ed. Marianna Papastephanou (Switzerland: Springer International Publishing, 2016), 215–228;

28 Papastephanou, *Thinking Differently About Cosmopolitanism*, 2417–2420. For cosmopolitanism and intellectual cooperation see Joyce Goodman, "Cosmopolitan Women Educators, 1920–1939: Inside/Outside Activism and Abjection," *Paedagogica Historica* 46 (2010): 69–83.

29 Richard Morris, *Time's Arrows: Scientific Attitudes toward Time* (New York: Simon and Schuster, 1985), 121.

30 Mary Ann Doane, *The Emergence of Cinematic Time: Modernity, Contingency, the Archive* (Cambridge MA: Harvard University Press, 2002), 114; Michel Serres, *Hermes, with an Introduction by Josué V. Harari and David F. Bell* (Baltimore: Johns Hopkins University Press, 1982), 71–83.

31 Entropy represents the amount of energy no longer capable of being transformed into work. See Michael Alhadeff-Jones, *Time and the Rhythms of Emancipatory Education: Rethinking the Temporal Complexity of Self and Society* (London: Routledge, 2016), 22.

32 Morris, *Time's Arrows*, 121.

33 Morris, *Time's Arrows*, 121, 122; Alhadeff-Jones, *Time and Emancipatory Education*, 22.

the spontaneous flow of heat always takes place in the same direction (from warm to cold).³⁴ As Michael Alhadeff-Jones comments, with the second law of thermodynamics future and past can be distinguished because the measure of entropy enables an observer to distinguish processes on a "before" and "after" basis, which introduced the idea that time has a directionality and shifted conceptions of time from a Newtonian temporal model based on symmetry and reversibility to theories based on irreversibility and unidirectionality.³⁵ While there is no cause-and-effect relation between theoretical physics and history, as Mary Ann Doane notes, as soon as the theory of energy is injected with a temporal directionality, the ideas of both historical progress and historical decline become possible. In addition, argues Doane, the temporal irreversibility of the second law of thermodynamics manifests itself in the diminishing possibility of differentiation because the logic of the law dictates that as entropy increases, there will be less and less difference, leading to a non-dynamic homogeneity.³⁶ These differences can be measured quantitatively and mapped in a forward moving notion of time that is irreversible and unidirectional.

Wrench's thermodynamic concentric circles diagram of international friendship is informed by the type of abstracted, divisible, and measurable organization of temporality that Henri Bergson terms differences of degree, and which he construes as "differences of magnitude, quantitative differences of more or less measurable differences."³⁷ As Elizabeth Grosz explains, if quantitative differences are measurable they indicate spatial differences (i.e. differences between things that can be marked or characterized through measurement).³⁸ Differences of degree are discrete, discontinuous, and homogenous.³⁹ They are the juxtaposition of points and repeatable units that tend to be addressed as if they are absolute (i.e. existing independently of humankind).⁴⁰ These repeatable units mea-

---

34 Morris, *Time's Arrows*, 111 uses the example of when a piece of hot iron is plunged into water the iron is cooled and some water evaporates and no blacksmith ever heated iron by putting it into a water bath; and where there is no expenditure of energy, heat will always flow from a warm object to a cool one, but the reverse process is never observed. However, the ability to do useful work is lost – after the hot and cold objects come into equilibrium this would be impossible.
35 Alhadeff-Jones, *Time and Emancipatory Education*, 22.
36 Doane, *Cinematic Time*, 115, 117.
37 Elizabeth Grosz, *The Nick of Time: Politics, Evolution, and the Untimely* (Durham: Duke University Press, 2004), 158.
38 Grosz, *The Nick of Time*, 159.
39 Grosz, *The Nick of Time*, 159.
40 Keith Robinson, ed., *Deleuze, Whitehead, Bergson: Rhizomatic Connections* (Basingstoke: Palgrave, 2008), 224; Sanja Perovic, "Year 1 and Year 61 of the French Revolution: The Revolutionary

sure time spatially as distance in a Cartesian view of (abstract) space also thought to be independent of persons.[41] "[W]hen we speak of time," writes Bergson, "more often than not we think of homogeneous milieus where the events or facts of consciousness line themselves up, juxtaposing themselves as if in space."[42] Location in abstract/absolute space/time provides the means to identify the individuality and uniqueness of persons, things, and processes.[43] As Dipresh Chakrabarty argues, concepts grounded on notions of abstract/absolute space/time work to demarcate difference and racialize populations by assigning so called primitive societies to slots in evolutionary taxonomies that reinterpreted time as distance in categories of savage, barbaric, and civilized.[44] The cultural-cognitive concentric circles model imagines the enrichment and enlargement of the self in similar ways.[45] While the second law of thermodynamics points to an increasing homogenization based on a diminishing possibility of differentiation, the spatialized, linear trajectory of the concentric circles model also supports the potential for "dividing practices"[46] around normative descriptions of the desired pupil based on their ability to move through nationalism to internationalism, which simultaneously constructs a problematic counterpart without those qualities.[47]

In deploying a concentric circles diagram to illustrate the growth of international friendship, Wrench builds on the simple, one dimensional common-sense version of time through which public and practical life proceeds. In the spatial-temporal frame underpinning his diagram two things are thought to be contemporary if they inhabit the same segment of time and space: objects are said to co-

---

Calendar and Auguste Comte," in *Breaking up Time: Negotiating the Borders between Present, Past and Future*, ed. Chris Lorenz and Berber Bevernage (Gottingen: Vandenhoek & Ruprecht, 2013), 87.
41 David Harvey, *Cosmopolitanism and the Geographies of Freedom* (New York, Chichester: Columbia University Press, 2009).
42 Henri Bergson, *Time and Free Will: An Essay on the Immediate Data of Consciousness*, trans. Frank L. Pogson (London: George Allen and Unwin, 1921), 90.
43 Harvey, *Cosmopolitanism*; Henri Lefebvre, *The Production of Space* (London: Wiley, 1992).
44 Dipesh Chakrabarty, *Provincializing Europe: Postcolonial Thought and Historical Difference* (Princeton, N.J.: Princeton University Press, 2000).
45 Papastephanou, "Concentric, Vernacular and Rhizomatic Cosmopolitanisms," 217; Papastephanou, *Thinking Differently*, kindle loc. 427.
46 Thomas S. Popkewitz, *Cosmopolitanism and the Age of School Reform: Science, Education, and Making Society by Making the Child* (London: Routledge, 2012), 4.
47 Julie McLeod, "Educating for 'World-Mindedness': Cosmopolitanism, Localism and Schooling the Adolescent Citizen in Interwar Australia," *Journal of Educational Administration and History* 44 (2012): 339–359.

exist, pre-exist or follow on from each other,⁴⁸ space is imagined as separate from place, and time becomes the abstract time on the calendar or the clock.⁴⁹ But this was not the only spatial-temporal approach to fostering international friendship carried in *IREC*. As the following section illustrates, Dulac's theorization of the contribution of newsreels to international understanding and friendship in her 1931 and 1934 *IREC* articles disrupts the geometry of the concentric circles model of internationalism through a spatial-temporal frame associated with "the world of the infinitely small" that aligns with what Bergson terms differences in kind.

Internationalism, Newsreels, and Differences in Kind: Movement, Turbulence, and the World of the Infinitely Small

Like Wrench, Dulac is critical of aspects of commercial film but views the newsreel as a "great social educator" with the potential for inculcating international friendship.⁵⁰ At a point when newsreels were gaining in importance, she turned from directing fiction films to write, direct, and produce narrative fiction features, shorts, and newsreels.⁵¹ She contributed to the development of non-fiction film through her work as artistic director and director of newsreels at Gaumont-Franco-Films-Aubert, one of France's largest and longest standing production houses, and through France-Actualités, which she established in November 1931 as a French company of talking newsreels and documentary films and where she was sole director. This was one of only five or six international newsreel journals, at a time which included the US newsreels Paramount and Fox Movietone and their French counterparts Pathé Natan and Éclaire Journal. From 1937 Dulac would also advise the ICIC about the use of newsreels to foster international understanding.⁵²

---

48 Michael Halewood, *A.N. Whitehead and Social Theory: Tracing a Culture of Thought* (London: Anthem Press, 2013), 34.
49 António Nóvoa and Tali Yariv-Mashal, "Comparative Research in Education: A Mode of Governance or a Historical Journey?" *Comparative Education* 39 (2003): 431.
50 Dulac, "Educational and Social Value of the Newsreel," 546.
51 Tami Williams, *Germaine Dulac: A Cinema of Sensations* (Illinois, University of Illinois Press, 2014), 166.
52 This paragraph draws heavily on Williams, *Germaine Dulac*, 158, 166, 176.

During the 1920s and 1930s Dulac was vice president of the Women's Committee for Moral Disarmament,[53] and her writing on newsreels aligns with League moral disarmament discourse. She portrays newsreels enabling individuals to become familiar with outstanding figures of the "national world" and of the "international chessboard" in ways that are not possible through books, newspapers, and manuals.[54] She argues that newsreels penetrate the heart of diplomatic debates, enabling the observer to see something of the "infinitely great" major problems of the day in the alliances and disputes of nations, and that newsreels facilitate the growth of fraternity by providing individuals with opportunities to learn about the manufacture of products in distant corners of the globe.[55] She also writes that ideas circulating via the newsreel enable sorrows to become common, less strange, and less abstract, and so help to create bonds and promote understanding. But in Dulac's argument it is not just that newsreels enable the observer to see something of the "infinitely great" major problems of the day. When it comes to international understanding and friendship it is also a question of "little incidents" and the "infinitely small" which she places on the same plane as the "infinitely great" and which she argues are important factors in breaking down barriers and uniting "classes, races, sentiments, joys and happiness":[56]

> (...) each people was encircled in its particular customs and thought itself the centre of the world. Now that the life of their peoples is made clear in its appealing movement still breathing warmly of its customs and habits, without transposition, we begin to understand that even if it is always foreign to us in its detail, in its great and effective lines it is the same as our own. Thus the Cinema leads us to understand the entire world and to the inevitable conclusion that above all questions of race and country, there is humanity and that in humanity there are things infinitely small and infinitely great.[57]

It is this concern with the "little incidents" of the everyday that Dulac argues differentiates her approach from that of US and French newsreel houses. She writes that the latter focus on sudden and important "blockbuster" grand events, whereas she focuses on the "subtle (...) slow-burn" type of event "that evolves as

---

53 Williams, *Germaine Dulac*, 28, 29, 188. The Women's Committee for Moral Disarmament was established in France in 1925.
54 Dulac, "Educational and Social Value of the Newsreel," 546.
55 Dulac, "Educational and Social Value of the Newsreel," 546–548.
56 Dulac, "Educational and Social Value of the Newsreel," 546, 548.
57 Dulac, "Meaning of Cinema," 1094.

the days go by."⁵⁸ In noting that the "true meaning" of "slow-burn" events becomes clearer only with time⁵⁹ Dulac situates her newsreel practice within an indeterminate temporality that resonates with the newly developing physics of subatomic particles that brought an experience of indeterminacy to characterize not only mathematical knowledge of the physical world, but also values, language, and social life.⁶⁰

Dulac's interest in the world of the "infinitely small" was fostered through scientific and educational film and particularly through the microcinematography of Jean Comandon, whose films she projected during a number of her conference talks from the 1920s and whose microcinematography techniques she interwove within her earlier avant-garde practice. As Paula Amad argues, Commandon traversed the visible and invisible by bringing into visibility "slices of life teeming with vitality."⁶¹ His techniques of microcinematography and time-lapse in his experimentation in scientific films of plant growth and cell division used the camera to illustrate what had previously been invisible dimensions of nature's daily life.⁶² In a similar vein Dulac writes that it is the focus on life-matter that renders the existence of the individual less isolated and encourages them to leave their own "petty circles."⁶³ As a consequence, "the least village [comes into] communication with the entire universe, the least individual with all men."⁶⁴ This stress on "life" resonates with Bergson's notion of élan vital – "the vital impetus of force that propels life forward from its beginnings and through all its varieties and forms"⁶⁵ – which Bergson construes together with what he terms duration (durée réelle) – the lived movement of temporality – and with a notion of intuition as the method of entering into duration's undivided flow. As Keith Robinson explains, duration is heterogeneous, qualitative, continuous, and interpenetrating, and the creative dynamism and indivisible move-

---

58 Germaine Dulac, "Cinema at the Service of History: The Role of Newsreels" (1936), trans. Siân Reynolds, in "Screening the Past 12 – Germaine Dulac and Newsreel – 3 Articles, Introduction – March 2001," accessed September 10, 2020, http://www.screeningthepast.com/issue-12-classics-re-runs/germaine-dulac-and-newsreel-3-articles/. Also cited in Paula Amad, *Counter-Archive: Film, the Everyday, and Albert Kahn's Archives de la Planète* (New York: Columbia University Press, 2010), 164.
59 Dulac, "Cinema at the Service of History," 164.
60 For developments in quantum physics around uncertainty see Suzanne Guerlac, *Thinking in Time: An Introduction to Henri Bergson* (Ithaca: Cornell University Press, 2006), 14–41.
61 Amad, *Counter-Archive*, 242.
62 Amad, *Counter-Archive*, 212.
63 Dulac, "Meaning of Cinema," 1107.
64 Dulac, "Meaning of Cinema," 1107.
65 Robinson, *Rhizomatic Connections*, 224.

ment of "the time of life (...) the mobility of time itself."⁶⁶ It is within duration, writes Bergson, that differences of kind are experienced. These are the qualitative temporal differences that are incomparable and unique and constitutive of the particularity of events. They are impossible to measure or to describe in numerical terms but are discernible in and for conscious mental life, comments Elizabeth Grosz.⁶⁷

Amad argues that advances in the manipulation of the speed and scale of the camera's vision expanded the parameters of film's synthesizing capacities as a universal visual language and enabled film to portray not only "global and cultural difference discovered in far and foreign lands" and "the life of their peoples" but also to uncover "that which was near and familiar yet undetectable to the naked eye (...) or simply beneath the habitual radar of the human gaze."⁶⁸ In her cinematic practice (which she terms extended cinema) Dulac builds on the notion of the camera as a powerful eye able to capture the invisible: "that which our eye cannot see [and which] exists materially but is outside our range of visual perception."⁶⁹ She describes the slow motion camera exploring "the domain of minute things in nature" and showing us visually "dramas and beauties which our too synthetic eye does not perceive."⁷⁰ For Dulac, the educative role of the cinema lies in its ability to render perceptible things "whose existence we have always known and never understood."⁷¹

Siegfried Kracauer refers to inter-war views of the "uplifting" effects of films that were thought to enable those whose sensibilities had been blunted by the predominance of technology and analytical thinking to resume "sensuous and immediate contact with life."⁷² In this vein Dulac notes that newsreels reveal the "truth of life" and enable individuals to "see it, live it and not only fancy it."⁷³ She writes that through the newsreel "humanity is uplifted above its individual characteristics and through a gradual comprehension of life begins to forget and forgo its hates⁷⁴ as wider knowledge of the world is portrayed that frees "the sense of the individual and tune[s] his spirit with the general universality of

---

66 Robinson, *Rhizomatic Connections*, 224.
67 Grosz, *Nick of Time*, 159.
68 Amad, *Counter-Archive*, 212.
69 Dulac, "Meaning of Cinema," 1093.
70 Dulac, "Meaning of Cinema," 1093.
71 Dulac, "Meaning of Cinema," 1092.
72 Siegfried Kracauer, *Theory of Film: The Redemption of Physical Reality, with an Introduction by Miriam B Hansen* (Princeton New Jersey: Princeton University Press, 1997), 170.
73 Dulac, "Educational and Social Value of the Newsreel," 546.
74 Dulac, "Educational and Social Value of the Newsreel," 546.

mankind."⁷⁵ Dulac's orientation to "the art of movement and the visual rhythms of life and the imagination,"⁷⁶ revealed by the powerful eye of the camera, underpins her argument that spontaneity is central to the newsreel film-making process.⁷⁷ She comments: "what is the newsreel? It's the event of the day, captured in its movement and life, and thus in its truth by the camera and the microphone."⁷⁸ For Dulac the camera lens and the microphone deliver the real and invent nothing, as Williams notes. Central to this conception of the newsreel and its capacity for objectivity and its ability to deliver "truth" is the unpredictability of the subject matter itself, which is not to be prepared like a studio scene, or to be overlaid with commentary, as Williams describes.⁷⁹

Dulac's recourse to unpredictability rests in turn, on her belief that it is the registering of movement that makes film an art in itself;⁸⁰ and that it is the powerful eye of the camera that registers "the spirit which comes out of movement."⁸¹ But this is not the type of movement associated with the spatial-temporal frames of Wrench's linear trajectory from A to B (through nationalism to internationalism). In Dulac's configuration of international understanding and friendship, as the powerful eye of the camera attacks "minute shades of difference",⁸² individuals encounter the turbulence without which, Tim Cresswell comments, there can be no movement.⁸³ Unlike the linear trajectory of Wrench's concentric circles diagram, in Dulac's approach the spectator is thrown out of their circle:

> It is impossible to deny that the Cinema vastly increases our knowledge. At every moment it throws us out of our own environment and out of our own circle, our own knowledge, into worlds of which we were ignorant. It moves about, grasps forms, their rhythm and spirit by attacking those minute shades of difference which conceal instinct. It is a powerful eye added to our own which is much too limited.⁸⁴

---

75 Dulac, "Educational and Social Value of the Newsreel," 546–547.
76 Germaine Dulac, "La cinégraphie intégrale," in Marcel Lapierre, ed., *Anthologie du cinéma* (Paris: La Novelle Edition, 1946), 157–168, cited in Kracauer, *Theory of Film*, 184.
77 Dulac, "Meaning of Cinema," 1091.
78 Cited in Williams, *Germaine Dulac*, 182.
79 Williams, *Germaine Dulac*, 183, 187.
80 Dulac, "Meaning of Cinema," 1090
81 Dulac, "Meaning of Cinema," 1092.
82 Dulac, "Meaning of Cinema," 1091.
83 Tim Cresswell, *On the Move: Mobility in the Modern Western World* (New York: Routledge, 2006), 265; see also the description of turbulence in Serres, *Hermes*, 75.
84 Dulac, "Meaning of Cinema," 1091.

As individuals are thrown out of their own environment and out of their own circle and their own "knowledge (...) into worlds of which (...) [they] were ignorant,"[85] they encounter friction as they brush up against lives, intelligences, joy, and misery that are hitherto unfamiliar:

> We range every moment into mysteries and marvels with which we are unacquainted and we brush up against lives, intelligences, joy and misery that we should not have suspected. The cinema shows them to us, uncovers them to our gaze, renders them sensible to us so that they may become familiar. This simply by the power of the lens, mathematically related to the speed at which the film travels.[86]

Turbulence from newsreels' "little incidents" and from "movement still breathing warmly" of custom and habits[87] creates what Michel Serres calls a space of passage. All learning, writes Serres, comes through passage in the third place, where space is sown with sites of exposure and time is deployed. Serres describes this space of passage as a state of phase change "between equilibrium and disequilibrium, between being and nothingness" and a space where sensitivity to possibility or capacity comes from the exposure to "the other" without which Serres argues there is no learning.[88] Paraphrasing Anna Tsing, it is in these "zones of awkward engagement" that new realities are made through friction and exposure and international connections can be made powerful but can also get in the way of the smooth operation of international power.[89]

Mobilities with different configurations of time and space emerge in Dulac's and Wrench's deployment of circles as they account for international understanding and friendship. Dulac's recourse to duration as a heterogenous indeterminate mode of temporality, passage, or transience aligns with Bergson's differences in kind and his view that mobilities of duration are accessible only by placing oneself within duration.[90] Wrench's model exemplifies a unidirectional and spatializing temporality associated with thermodynamics that resonates with Bergson's view that spatialization is inherent to the intellect and aligns

---

85 Dulac, "Meaning of Cinema," 1091.
86 Dulac, "Meaning of Cinema," 1091.
87 Dulac, "Meaning of Cinema," 1094.
88 Michel Serres, *The Troubadour of Knowledge*, trans. Sheila F. Glaser and William Paulson (Ann Arbor: University of Michigan Press, 1991), 8–9, 12.
89 Anna L. Tsing, *Friction: An Ethnography of Global Connection* (Princeton: Princeton University Press, 2011), 6.
90 Didier Debaise, "The Emergence of a Speculative Empiricism: Whitehead Reading Bergson," in *Deleuze, Whitehead, Bergson: Rhizomatic Connections*, ed. Keith Robinson (Basingstoke: Palgrave, 2008), 81.

with a temporality that he characterizes as differences of degree. Both Dulac and Wrench reserve a place for the national in fostering international understanding and friendship. Wrench's diagram moves explicitly through nationalism to internationalism. Despite Dulac's stress on the universality of film and her antipathy to nationalism, her attention to the everyday lives of peoples where "movement still breath[es] warmly" of custom and habits[91] resonates with her view that although "spiritual and social internationalism might appear," films from each country bear the marks of their origin and remain national in particular ways.[92]

In 1933 the poet Paul Valéry argued that the "world of the infinitely small" had challenged the "old idea of unification, of explication of the universe," determinism and causality,[93] which Gaston Bachelard would subsequently frame as an epistemological break.[94] Thinking with Alfred North Whitehead, however, suggests that situating Wrench and Dulac across an epistemological break would constitute what Whitehead terms a bifurcation of nature in which a scientific conception of the world and a subjective experience of the world would be divided.[95] Whitehead's theorization of the event suggests an alternative reading in which the divergent spatialities-temporalities of Wrench's and Dulac's approaches to fostering international understanding and friendship constitute spatial-temporal counterpoints knotted together in 1930s moral disarmament, to which the conclusion turns.

Conclusion: Spatialities-temporalities of Moral Disarmament as Event

As Didier Debaise outlines, Whitehead shares Bergson's view that the central feature of reality is becoming or process, and he also understands the "real" as a fundamental movement or creative force that expresses itself as a process of occasions. Like Bergson, too, Whitehead critiques the spatialization thought to occur as movement is translated spatially and temporally into points and succes-

---

[91] Dulac, "Meaning of Cinema," 1094.
[92] Dulac, "Meaning of Cinema," 1094
[93] Paul Valéry, Œvres Complètes. 2 Vols. (Paris: Gallimard, 1987), cited in Guerlac, Thinking in Time, 16.
[94] Gaston Bachelard, Formation of the Scientific Mind: A Contribution to a Psychoanalysis of Objective Knowledge (Manchester: Clinamen Press, 2002), cited in Guerlac, Thinking in Time, 17.
[95] Maria Tamboukou, "Challenging the Bifurcation of Nature: Women Workers' Education through Process Philosophy," History of Education 49 (2020): 313–326; Didier Debaise, Nature as Event: The Lure of the Possible (Durham: Duke University Press, 2017), 7.

sions, ignoring the fluency of the world and analyzing the world in terms of static categories. But as Debaise charts, Whitehead parts company with Bergson over the latter's view that spatialization is an inherent necessity of the intellect. For Whitehead the mind is the meeting place of what we know and how we know: "the nature apprehended in awareness" and the "nature which is the cause of awareness."[96]

Whitehead argues that all thought and thinking involves abstraction which arises from the process of selection whereby some elements are combined but not all elements of existence.[97] The error, argues Whitehead, lies in the way abstractions are mistaken for concrete realities[98] and treated as though they are concretely real and a "fact,"[99] a process that Whitehead terms the "fallacy of misplaced concreteness."[100] As Michael Halewood summarizes, Whitehead does not overlook the work that abstractions do in the world, but he insists that they do not explain as much as they think they do: "for every abstraction neglects the influx of the factors omitted into the factors retained."[101] As Halewood comments, Whitehead considers that there is a fullness to existence that is not captured by abstractions of knowledge. In Wrench's approach, the division of space and time into points and instants and the notion that time is an uninterrupted flow within which things occur[102] are made possible by the work of abstraction. Similarly, Dulac's recourse to the infinitely small and the infinitely great exemplifies the work of abstraction, despite the notions of movement and life that she deploys.

As Steven Shaviro argues, Whitehead treats entities that are on different scales, levels of reflexivity, and complexity in the same manner. He does not separate how we know from what we know and he sees no reason why mental events should be treated any differently than any other sort of events – they are all parts of the same stream of experience. Shaviro comments that for Whitehead, categories are not imposed by the mind. Rather, they are immanent to the

---

96 Alfred North Whitehead, *The Concept of Nature* (Cambridge: Cambridge University Press, 1920 [1964 edn.]), 31; see Debaise, *Nature as Event*, 12.
97 Michael Halewood, *A.N. Whitehead and Social Theory: Tracing a Culture of Thought* (London: Anthem Press, 2013), 147.
98 Alfred North Whitehead, *Science and the Modern World* (Cambridge University Press, 1925 [1967 edn.]), 56, cited in Halewood, *Whitehead and Social Theory*, 51; Debaise, *Nature as Event*, 24
99 Halewood, *A.N. Whitehead and Social Theory*, 157.
100 Whitehead, *The Concept of Nature*, 20–21.
101 Alfred North Whitehead, *Modes of Thought* (New York: Free Press, 1938 [1968 edn.]), 196.
102 Alfred North Whitehead, *Symbolism: Its Meaning and Effect* (New York: Fordham University Press, 1927), 35.

"data" – the events or actual occasions – out of which they arise by a process of abstraction.[103] Consistent with this line of thinking, Whitehead's theory of the event situates theoretical, abstract, and operative elements on the same plane.[104] Events do not "happen to" things: rather "events themselves *are* the only things."[105] Events are fundamental – a happening, an occurrence, an occasion, a phenomenon – and things or substances can be variously viewed as "effects," "products" or temporary "structures" of events.[106] There is no mere time which is filled up with events and happenings. There are simply events and happenings through which we experience and within which we find ourselves.[107] Paraphrasing Debaise, the passage of time is an event, as are the perspectives through which we experience it and the parts of it that we differentiate and spatialize in our perception.[108] As Maria Tamboukou explains, events happen and disappear and then conceptual abstractions are constructed to account for them.[109] Thinking with Whitehead's notion of event suggests that rather than located across an epistemological break, the space-times of Wrench's concentric circles diagram and Dulac's newsreels might be approached as spatial and temporal counterpoints that coexist and are knotted together in the fabric that constituted 1930s moral disarmament.

Bibliography

Alhadeff-Jones, Michael. *Time and the Rhythms of Emancipatory Education: Rethinking the Temporal Complexity of Self and Society.* London: Routledge, 2016.

Bachelard, Gaston. *Formation of the Scientific Mind: A Contribution to a Psychoanalysis of Objective Knowledge.* Manchester: Clinamen Press, 2002.

Bergson, Henri. *Time and Free Will: An Essay on the Immediate Data of Consciousness.* Translated by Frank L Pogson. London: George Allen and Unwin, 1921.

Chakrabarty, Dipesh. *Provincializing Europe: Postcolonial Thought and Historical Difference.* Princeton, N.J.: Princeton University Press, 2000.

Cresswell, Tim. *On the Move: Mobility in the Modern Western World.* New York: Routledge, 2006.

---

[103] Steven Shaviro, "Deleuze's Encounter with Whitehead," accessed October 12, 2019, http://www.shaviro.com/Othertexts/DeleuzeWhitehead.pdf.
[104] Debaise, *Nature as Event*, 33.
[105] Shaviro, "Deleuze's Encounter with Whitehead," 7. Italics in the original.
[106] Robinson, *Rhizomatic Connections*, 226.
[107] Halewood, *A.N. Whitehead and Social Theory*, 127.
[108] Debaise, *Nature as Event*, 30.
[109] Tamboukou, "Challenging the Bifurcation of Nature," 313–326.

Debaise, Didier. *Nature as Event: The Lure of the Possible*. Durham: Duke University Press, 2017.
Debaise, Didier. "The Emergence of a Speculative Empiricism: Whitehead Reading Bergson." In *Deleuze, Whitehead, Bergson: Rhizomatic Connections*, edited by Keith Robinson, 77–88. Basingstoke: Palgrave, 2008.
Doane, Mary Ann. *The Emergence of Cinematic Time: Modernity, Contingency, the Archive*. Cambridge MA: Harvard University Press, 2002.
Dulac, Germaine. "The Meaning of Cinema." *International Review of Educational Cinematography* 12 (1931): 1089–1099.
Dulac, Germaine. "The Educational and Social Value of the Newsreel." *International Review of Educational Cinematography* 15 (1934): 545–560.
Dulac, Germaine. "La cinégraphie intégrale." In *Anthologie du cinéma*, edited by Marcel Lapierre, 157–168. Paris: La Nouvelle Edition, 1946.
Dulac, Germaine. "Cinema at the Service of History: The Role of Newsreels" (1936). Translated by Siân Reynolds. In "Screening the Past 12 – Germaine Dulac and Newsreel – 3 Articles, Introduction – March 2001." Accessed September 10, 2020. http://www.screeningthepast.com/issue-12-classics-re-runs/germaine-dulac-and-newsreel-3-articles/.
Druick, Zoe. "The International Educational Cinematograph Institute, Reactionary Modernism and the Formation of Film Studies." *Canadian Journal of Film Studies* 16 (2007): 80–97.
Goodman, Joyce. "Cosmopolitan Women Educators, 1920–1939: Inside/Outside Activism and Abjection." *Paedagogica Historica* 46 (2010): 69–83.
Goodman, Joyce. "Women and International Intellectual Co-operation." *Paedagogica Historica* 48 (2012): 357–68.
Goodman, Joyce. "The Buddhist Institute at Phnom Penh, the International Council of Women and the Rome International Institute for Educational Cinematography: Intersections of Internationalism and Imperialism, 1931–34." *History of Education* 47 (2018): 415–431.
Goodman, Joyce. "'Shaping the Mentality of Races and Especially of Young People': The League of Nations and the Educational Cinematography Congress, 1934." In *League of Nations: Histories, Legacies and Impact*, edited by Joy Damousi and Patricia O'Brien, 197–213. Melbourne: Melbourne University Press, 2018.
Grosz, Elizabeth. *The Nick of Time: Politics, Evolution, and the Untimely*. Durham: Duke University Press, 2004.
Guerlac, Suzanne. *Thinking in Time: An Introduction to Henri Bergson*. Ithaca: Cornell University Press, 2006.
Halewood, Michael. *A.N. Whitehead and Social Theory: Tracing a Culture of Thought*. London: Anthem Press, 2013.
Harvey, David. *Cosmopolitanism and the Geographies of Freedom*. New York/Chichester: Columbia University Press, 2009.
Hermon, Elly. "Le désarmement moral, facteur dans les relations internationales pendant l'entre-deux-guerres." *Guerres mondiales et conflits contemporains* 156 (1989): 23–36.
Higson, Andrew. "Cultural Policy and Industrial Practice: Film Europe and the International Film Congresses of the 1920s." In *"Film Europe" and "Film America": Cinema, Commerce and Cultural Exchange, 1920–1939*, edited by Andrew Higson and Richard Maltby, 117–131. Exeter: University of Exeter Press, 1999.
Kracauer, Siegfried. *Theory of Film: The Redemption of Physical Reality, with an Introduction by Miriam B Hansen*. Princeton, New Jersey: Princeton University Press, 1997.

League of Nations Intellectual Co-operation Organisation. "The International Committee on Intellectual Co-operation and Moral Disarmament. Extract from the Minutes of the Fourteenth Plenary Session of the I.C.I.C. Geneva, July 21, 1932." *Information Bulletin of the League of Nations Intellectual Co-operation Organisation* 1 (1932): 132–138.

Lefebvre, Henri. *The Production of Space*. London: Wiley, 1992.

Martin, Benjamin G. *The Nazi-Fascist New Order for European Culture*. Cambridge, Mass.: Harvard University Press, 2016.

May, Alex. "Wrench, Sir (John) Evelyn Leslie (1882–1966), Promoter of the British Empire and Author." Oxford Dictionary of National Biography. Accessed October 18, 2019. https://www.oxforddnb.com/view/10.1093/ref:odnb/9780198614128.001.0001/odnb-9780198614128-e-37031.

McLeod, Julie. "Educating for 'World-Mindedness': Cosmopolitanism, Localism and Schooling the Adolescent Citizen in Interwar Australia." *Journal of Educational Administration and History* 44 (2012): 339–359.

Morris, Richard. *Time's Arrows: Scientific Attitudes toward Time*. New York: Simon and Schuster, 1985.

Nóvoa António, and Tali Yariv-Mashal. "Comparative Research in Education: A Mode of Governance or a Historical Journey?" *Comparative Education* 39 (2003): 423–438.

Papastephanou, Maria. *Thinking Differently About Cosmopolitanism: Theory, Eccentricity, and the Globalized World*. Boulder: Paradigm Publishers, 2015.

Papastephanou, Maria. "Concentric, Vernacular and Rhizomatic Cosmopolitanisms." In *Cosmopolitanism: Educational, Philosophical and Historical Perspectives*, edited by Marianna Papastephanou, 215–228. Switzerland: Springer International Publishing, 2016.

Perovic, Sanja. "Year 1 and Year 61 of the French Revolution: The Revolutionary Calendar and Auguste Comte." In *Breaking up Time: Negotiating the Borders between Present, Past and Future*, edited by Chris Lorenz and Berber Bevernage, 87–99. Gottingen: Vandenhoek & Ruprecht, 2013.

Popkewitz, Thomas S. *Cosmopolitanism and the Age of School Reform: Science, Education, and Making Society by Making the Child*. London: Routledge, 2012.

Robinson, Keith, ed. *Deleuze, Whitehead, Bergson: Rhizomatic Connections*. Basingstoke: Palgrave, 2008.

Serres, Michel. *Hermes, with an Introduction by Josué V. Harari and David F. Bell*. Baltimore: Johns Hopkins University Press, 1982.

Serres, Michel. *The Troubadour of Knowledge*. Translated by Sheila F. Glaser and William Paulson. Ann Arbor: University of Michigan Press, 1991.

Shaviro, Steven. "Deleuze's Encounter with Whitehead." Accessed October 12, 2019. http://www.shaviro.com/Othertexts/DeleuzeWhitehead.pdf.

Siegel, Mona L. *The Moral Disarmament of France: Education, Pacifism, and Patriotism, 1914–1940*. Cambridge: Cambridge University Press, 2004.

Tamboukou, Maria. "Challenging the Bifurcation of Nature: Women Workers' Education through Process Philosophy." *History of Education* 49 (2020): 313–326.

Taillibert, Christel. *L'institut International Du Cinématographe Éducatif. Regards sur le rôle du cinema éducatif dans la politique internationale du fascisme italien*. Paris: L'Harmattan, 1999.

Tsing, Anna L. *Friction: An Ethnography of Global Connection*. Princeton: Princeton University Press, 2011.
Valéry, Paul. *Œvres Complètes. 2 Vols.* Paris: Gallimard, 1987.
Wehberg, Hilla. "Fate of an International Film Institute." *The Public Opinion Quarterly* 2 (1938): 483–485.
Whitehead, Alfred North. *The Concept of Nature*. Cambridge: Cambridge University Press, 1920 [1964 edn.].
Whitehead, Alfred North. *Science and the Modern World*. Cambridge University Press, 1925 [1967 edn].
Whitehead, Alfred North. *Symbolism: Its Meaning and Effect*. New York: Fordham University Press, 1927.
Whitehead, Alfred North. *Modes of Thought*. New York: Free Press, 1938 [1968 edn].
Williams, Tami. *Germaine Dulac: A Cinema of Sensations*. Illinois: University of Illinois Press, 2014.
Wrench, Evelyn. "Children of the World." *International Review of Educational Cinematography* 6 (1934): 272–273.

Thomas S. Popkewitz (University of Wisconsin–Madison, USA)
The Study of Education. On Rethinking History with the Help of Marc Depaepe

Abstract: One of the distinguishing characteristics of the modern school is the double inscription of science: as a mode of interpreting and organizing pedagogy, and as a psychological quality of the mind to be interiorized in rationalizing children's thinking. The chapter explores these inscriptions as *a History of the Present*. The connections to the present, however, are not about how the past is reproduced or for applying the present to define the past. The chapter asks about the uneven historical lines activated in contemporary knowledge or systems of reason that order the curriculum, teaching, and research about the child. The "reason" of science is viewed as a historical "actor" in governing the relation between collective belonging and individuality. The historical interest is the entry point to my conversations with the work of Marc Depaepe. The historical strategy critically cuts into the historian's chimera of a semiotic realism that connects with positivism and empiricism to romanticize the archive. The chapter moves across multiple disciplinary literatures. It draws on an attitude of the Enlightenment's cosmopolitanism that folds into contemporary social/cultural theory and non-representational philosophy. The notions of indigenous foreigner and traveling libraries provide a frame for thinking historically about the dynamic complexities and differences appropriate for historical theory and methods.

Keywords: history of the present; the reason of schooling; critical histories; political sociology of knowledge; historical philosophy of science

Introduction

For a long time, I have studied the relation of school reform to the sciences of education. This interest was expressed earlier in writing about paradigms of research and more recently in thinking about the history of the social and psychological sciences. This focus on the past should be of no surprise to historians who think about modernity and/or the modern school. One of the distinguishing characteristics of the modern school is the inscription of science; as a mode of interpreting, organizing pedagogy, and as a quality of the mind in rationalizing children's thinking. The inscriptions of science as a mode of thinking are best expressed in John Dewey's concern with scientific methods and his anthropological psychology associated with "intelligent action."

These studies of schooling and science are framed as *History of the Present*. It is an intellectual strategy to think about science as a historical "actor" in the governing of the modern school. That governing is in principles generated about the relation between collective belonging and individuality in pedagogy and research. The connections to the present are not about how the past is reproduced or for applying the present to define the past. Rather, it is to ask about the uneven historical lines activated in contemporary knowledge or systems of reason about the curriculum, teaching, and children. These historical interests are my entry points to the work of Depaepe.[1] Depaepe's historical analyses have continually explored how schooling and its research are performed at the intersection of different historical lines that are never merely that of the school.

This essay continues my conversation with Depaepe about historicizing schooling and its research. The chapter explores a strategy of historicizing that has different contours from what typically (but not always) populates the history of education.[2] The discussion emerges through the intersection with scholarship in the history of science, cultural studies, non-representational philosophy, and

---

[1] Marc Depaepe, "Social and Personal Factors in the Inception of Experimental Research in Education (1890–1914)," *History of Education* 16 (1987): 275–298; Marc Depaepe, "Differences and Similarities in the Development of Educational Psychology in Germany and the United States before 1945," *Paedagogica Historica* 33 (1997): 69–97; Marc Depaepe, "The Practical and the Professional Relevance of Educational Research and Pedagogical Knowledge from the Perspective of History," In *Philosophy and History of the Discipline of Education: Evaluation and Evolution of the Criteria for Educational Research*, ed. Paul Smeyers and Marc Depaepe (Leuven: University of Leuven, 2001): 49–72; Marc Depaepe [et al.], *Order in Progress: Everyday Education Practice in Primary Schools: Belgium 1880–1970* (Leuven: Leuven University Press, 2000); Paul Smeyers and Marc Depaepe, eds., *Educational Research: The Educationalization of Social Problems* (Dordrecht: Springer, 2008). As I was writing this, I remembered a chapter in which I refected on this trajectory: Thomas S. Popkewitz "The Past as the Future of the Social and Educational Sciences," in *Education Systems in Historical, Cultural, and Sociological Perspectives*, ed. Daniel Tröhler and Raghild Barbu (Leiden: Brill/Sense, 2011), 163–180.

[2] See, e.g. Jorge Ramos do Ó, "The Disciplinary Terrains of Soul and Self-Government in the First Map of the Educational Sciences," in *Beyond Empiricism: On Criteria for Educational Research (Studia Paedagogica 34)*, ed. Paul Smeyers and Marc Depaepe (Leuven: Leuven University Press, 2003), 105–116; Thomas S. Popkewitz, ed., *Inventing the Modern Self and John Dewey: Modernities and the Traveling of Pragmatism in Education* (New York: Palgrave Macmillan Press, 2005); Thomas S. Popkewitz, ed., *The "Reason" of Schooling: Historicizing Curriculum Studies, Pedagogy, and Teacher Education* (New York: Routledge, 2015); Thomas S. Popkewitz, "What is 'Really' Taught as the Content of School Subjects? Teaching School Subjects as an Alchemy," *High School Journal* 101 (2018): 77–89; Thomas S. Popkewitz, *The Impracticality of Practical Research: A History of Sciences of Change that Conserve* (Ann Arbor: University of Michigan Press, 2020); Thomas S. Popkewitz, Barry Franklin, and Miguel Pereyra, ed., *Cultural History and Education: Critical Studies on Knowledge and Schooling* (New York: Routledge, 2001).

curriculum studies.³ Initially, I explore this as a History of the Present and then move to think about the history of schooling through notions of indigenous foreigner and traveling libraries. The two notions bring into view the relation of theory and method that works against the historian's chimera of a semiotic realism that romanticizes the archive,⁴ a point where my conversation with Depaepe's scholarship enters again. The final sections consider aspects of this historicizing through examining the notion of social improvement and schooling as the making of kinds of people. As the chapter moves across multiple disciplinary literatures, I provide limited but hopefully relevant references for readers to pursue where appropriate.

The History of the Present (with the Presence of Depaepe)

History of the Present is to make visible the entanglement of different historical lines that are activated to give intelligibility to the matters of the present.⁵ This interest focuses on the knowledge or the reason of schooling that orders and classifies the practices of schooling. The principles generated in teaching and the school curriculum are practices that order and classify modes of life about kinds of people and their differences – the citizen, the creative learner, and the problem solver whose qualities and characteristics are different from "the child left behind," the immigrant, and the reluctant learner.⁶

---

3 See, e.g., Popkewitz, *Impracticality of Practical Research*; Thomas S. Popkewitz, Daniel Pettersson, and Kai-Jung Hsiao, eds., *The International Emergence of Educational Sciences in the Post-World War Two Years: Quantification, Visualization, and Making Kinds of People* (New York: Routledge, 2021).
4 I explore the notion of the archive and the notion of romanticizing in Thomas S. Popkewitz, "How Theory Acts as the Retrieval Apparatus in Methods: Historical Thoughts on Romanticized Intellectual Practices," in *Handbook of Historical Studies in Education: Debates, Tensions and Directions*, ed. Tanya Fitzgerald (New York: Springer, 2020), 153–169.
5 This historicizing as entanglements is nicely articulated in comparative and historical studies by Noah Sobe, *Provincializing the Worldly Citizen: Yugoslav Student and Teacher Travel and Slavic Cosmopolitanism in the Interwar Era* (New York: Peter Lang, 2008); Noah Sobe, "Entanglements and Transnationalism in the History of American Education," in *Rethinking the History of Education: An Intercontinental Perspective on the Questions, Methods, and Knowledge of Schools*, ed. Thomas S. Popkewitz (New York: Palgrave Macmillan, 2013), 93–108.
6 For the fabricating of the kinds of people that examines a range of historical phenomena, see Karin Priem and Frederik Herman, eds., *Fabricating Modern Societies: Education, Bodies, and Minds in the Age of Steel* (Leiden: Brill, 2019).

The study of the reason of schooling is not only about "ideas" and discourses but also its material effects. What is thought, talked about, and done in schools is entangled with cultural and social principles that form as the political in modernity. That political is related to how power in modernity operates less through brute force (although it is still present) but more through how knowledge orders and classifies the (im)possibilities of experience. Governing gave attention to human reason and rationality that were hallmarks of the European and American Enlightenments. Its cosmopolitanism was brought into the spaces of action of family life, the pedagogical projects of the modern school and the formation of the human sciences.[7]

Schooling as a privileged place in modernity is well documented in neo-institutional studies.[8] My concern, however, is not with the institutionalization of schooling. It is with the double qualities of social contract expressed in the phrase "We, the people." That double quality of individual freedom of the contract was its attachments with the bonds of collective belonging, the latter often signified as "the common good," and of the nation. The principles of governing were also transported and (re)visioned as adaptive education in the colonial context.[9] In both western and colonial schools, the pedagogical projects and institu-

---

[7] Thomas S. Popkewitz, *Cosmopolitanism and the Age of School Reform: Science, Education, and Making Society by Making the Child* (New York: Routledge, 2008).

[8] John W. Meyer et al., *School Knowledge for the Masses and National Primary Curriculum Categories in the Twentieth Century* (Washington, DC: Falmer Press, 1992); David P. Baker, *The Schooled Society: The Educational Transformation of Global Culture* (Stanford: Stanford University Press, 2014). I will beg the question of modernity as a concept here except to briefly say my interest is related to the emergence of science as a political theology in the long nineteenth century and as a mode of consciousness in what Berger, Berger, and Kellner call "the homeless mind." I use the latter differently than Berger et al., however, to explore a particular way of reasoning about the world and self, discussed in Popkewitz, *Cosmopolitanism and the Age of School Reform*; Popkewitz, *Impracticality of Practical Research*.

[9] Marc Depaepe, "Why Even Today Educational Historiography is not an Unnecessary Luxury: Focusing on four Themes from Forty-Four Years of Research," *Espacio, Tiempo y Educación* 7 (2020): 227–246, accessed April 10, 2020, http://dx.doi.org/10.14516/ete.335; Christopher Kirchgasler, "Building Bridges and Colonial Residues: Transnational School Reforms and the Making of Human Kinds" (PhD diss., University of Wisconsin-Madison, 2017); Kathryn L. Kirchgasler, "Scientific Americans: Historicizing the Making of Differences in Early 20th-Century US Science Education," in *A Political Sociology of Educational Knowledge: Studies of Exclusions and Difference*, ed. Thomas S. Popkewitz, Jennifer Diaz, and Christopher Kirchgasler (New York: Routledge, 2017), 89–104; Ana Isabel Madeira, "Portuguese, French, and British Discourses on Colonial Education: Church-State Relations, School Expansion, and Missionary Competition in Africa, 1890–1930," *Paedagogica Historica* 41 (2005): 31–60.

tional structures of the schools connected the human sciences as social technologies to relate subjectivities and sociality.

The technologies of knowledge are the political that bring into view what Foucault speaks of as governmentality and Rancière calls the partition of the sensible and, I would add, of affect or sensibilities.[10] The distinctions, differentiations, and divisions embodied in the psychologies of learning and pedagogical knowledge partition the sensible (and not sensible) through, for example, talking about the child's "learning." Learning as a way of reasoning about the child brings into existence particular conceptions about "human nature" that the pedagogical practices activate. Concepts of development that permeate the psychologies of the child and learning, for example, entail practices about what is sensible (and not sensible). These sensibilities relate, for example, to fabrications of the nature of the child and society that become the object of development that organize the modern European and American school and its sciences. That nature and development of the child in the educational sciences were at the interstices of biology and cultural theses about the modes of life that one should live.[11]

It is obvious I think from the above that knowledge or "reasoning" about schooling requires a lot of backstage or historical work. That historical work requires something different from making the empirical object of historical studies as asking how children learn, childhood develops, and competence is gained; or tracing the national evolution of the institutional development and growth of the school as a testimonial of modernity. The empirical object of historical studies is genealogically to excavate how particular kinds of people, subjectivities, and differences are fabricated and have the material effects in schooling, concerns that relate back to the scholarship of Depaepe.[12] If I take the New Education and American Progressive Education studies, for example, they are studied as events

---

10 Michel Foucault, "Governmentality," in *The Foucault Effect: Studies in Governmentality: With Two Lectures by and an Interview with Michel Foucault*, ed. Graham Burchell, Colin Gordon, and Peter Miller (Chicago: University of Chicago Press, [1976] 1991), 87–104; Jacques Rancière, *The Politics of Aesthetics*, trans. Gabriel Rockhill (New York: Bloomsbury Academic, 2004). I link the two literatures to emphasize the relation of epistemology and ontology as historical questions about the knowledge (reason) as the effects of power and the political of modernity. I am less interested in Rancière's notion of hierarchies of experts that brings back a structural theory of power. My focus is with Rancière's partition of the sensible as the political and policing in that expertise gives attention to particular characteristic of knowledge in modernity. Homologous to Foucault's notions of productive power and police, the partition of the sensible "acts" materially to generate modes of existence and the production of differences.
11 Depaepe, "Social and Personal Factors"; Depaepe, "Differences and Similarities."
12 See, e.g., Depaepe, "Why Even Today Educational Historiography."

rather than as landmarks that testify to the place of education in modernity. Historicizing is to understand the conditions that give intelligibility to its teaching practices, inscriptions of the curriculum, and psychologies of learning.[13] The school is explored as the interstices of historical lines that embody cultural principles, notions of society and individual/collective belonging and individuality, political theories and salvation themes as well as institutional patterns.[14]

The historical concern with the reason of school brings together what contemporary analytical philosophical traditions have separated; the ontological from epistemological evoked as a semiotic realism. This realism places emphasis on archival methods as technologies organizing data. Yet if we take into account historical studies of "data" and visual cultures, the inscriptions of what constitutes data for description entails particular ways of "seeing" and abstracting from daily life and the partitions of people and events.[15] The historical concern with the reason of schooling, then, might also be viewed as a historical-cultural and political sociology. It is to undo the philosophical dichotomy of nominalism and realism in order to recognize the connection of epistemology and ontology in the materiality of schooling.[16]

---

[13] See, e.g., Nancy Lesko, *Act Your Age: A Cultural Construction of Adolescence* (New York: Routledge, 2001); Catarina Silva Martins, "From Scribbles to Details: The Invention of Stages of Development in Drawing and the Government of the Child," in *A Political Sociology of Educational Knowledge: Studies of Exclusions and Difference*, ed. Thomas S. Popkewitz, Jennifer Diaz, and Christopher Kirchgasler (New York: Routledge, 2017), 105–118; Ó, "The Disciplinary Terrains of Soul and Self-Government."

[14] Ana Luisa Paz, "Can Genius be Taught? Debates in Portuguese Music Education (1868–1930)," *European Educational Research Journal* 16 (2017): 504–516; Ana Laura Godinho Lima, "The Development of the Child and National Progress: Behaviorism and Cultural Deprivation in Brazil," in *The International Emergence of Educational Sciences*, 128–148; Gil, Natália de Lacerda, "The Quantification of an Educational System: Numbers in the Social Differentiation of Brazil," in *The International Emergence of Educational Sciences*, 225–224.

[15] See, e.g., Soraya de Chadarevian and Theodore M. Porter, eds., "Histories of Data and the Database," Special Issue *Historical Studies in the Natural Sciences* 48, 5 (2018); Inés Dussel, "The Visual Turn in the History of Education," in *Rethinking the History of Education*, 29–50; Inés Dussel, "Tactile Pedagogies in the Postwar: Cybernetics, Art, and the Production of a New Educational Rationale," in *The International Emergence of Educational Sciences*, 51–70.

[16] This rethinking of realism is found in Karen Barad, *Meeting the Universe Halfway: Quantum Physics and the Entanglement of Matter and Meaning* (Durham: Duke University Press, 2007). Its articulation in relation to the argument about "reason" is pursued theoretically in the notion of social epistemology. See Thomas S. Popkewitz, "Social Epistemology, the Reason of 'Reason,' and the Curriculum Studies." *Special Issue: Nuevas Perspectivas sobre el Curriculum Escolar. Education Policy Analysis Archives* (2014), accessed April 10, 2020, http://dx.doi.org/10.14507/epaa.v22n22.2014.

Indigenous Foreigner and Traveling Libraries: History as the Ironic Emptying of History

This interest in a History of the Present brings another entry point in my conversations with Depaepe's scholarship. This entrance requires a biographical note.

The note begins with the invitation to participate in multi-year seminar on the history and philosophy of education that Depaepe and (Paul) Smeyers organized at the University of Leuven. The meetings had no agenda other than to engage in substantive conversations with people from these two fields. While I do not have membership in either discipline, I found the conversations continually intellectually fascinating. During these years, I began work on a transnational project in which Depaepe participated, published as *Inventing the Modern Self and John Dewey: Modernities and the traveling of pragmatism in education*.[17] The project was to think historically about how ideas travel transnationally across time/space to think about schooling and modernity.

The challenge of the book was theoretically and methodologically to think historically about the traveling and translation of ideas. The book was to maintain a sensitivity to how fields of thought are inscribed materially in different social and cultural spaces; yet to explore a particular transnational quality of modernity as forms of "reasoning" about society, people, and education. John Dewey was a useful focal point to explore these historical intersections. Dewey embodied a particular American expression of pragmatism that travelled across continents that still continues today. In thinking of Dewey in this manner, I realized that the study could have involved others: Montessori, Deleuze, Foucault, Vygotsky, among others, but few in education are as iconic as Dewey.

The book's historical reasoning required thinking through the intersection of theory and method. That empirical problem of the archive was to read Dewey as neither the autobiographical origin of the texts, nor his texts as stable objects to identify its essential meanings for assessing fealty or transgression as the texts as they travel and are used in other cultural and social spaces. These objectifications of Dewey's writing entail an epistemological romanticizing of the historical archive. The archive becomes the site to find the given words, and how their rendering change over time and space. This reading of documents as "the given word" is ahistorical; it gives the semiotics of the text a transcendental and realist

---

[17] The contributors were: Tom De Coster et al., "Dewey in Belgium: A Libation for Modernity?," in *Inventing the Modern Self and John Dewey: Modernities and the Traveling of Pragmatism in Education*, ed. Thomas S. Popkewitz (New York: Palgrave, 2005), 85–110.

philosophical base. The given words in Dewey's texts become like the medieval Philosopher's Stone: the origin of ideas archived as the basis of what was true and essential.

The problem of the book became a problem of how to unthink the "sightlessness" sight of the romanticism of the archive that takes away the historical complexities.[18] The historical problem undertaken was to think of pragmatism (and Dewey's texts) as intermediary in a complex movement of thought that connected with assemblages of historical lines in different cultural and social spaces to activate aspirations and desires in the modern school.

Initially, I thought about the ironic phrase of "indigenous foreigner" as a method to historicize Dewey. The phrase of indigenous foreigner seems like an oxymoron. It plays with things that do not seem to belong together but do when thought of historically. The indigenous foreigner is to historicize how disciplinary projects travel and are assembled and connected in particular historical spaces as if they "belong" or are felt as "at home" to express one's hopes, desires, and fears. It is to think about the conditions of "Dewey's" arrival in Belgium, Colombia, China, Turkey, and Japan as a local hero but also as appearing in the image of the Anti-Christ who represents everything foreign and threatening.[19] In a sense, Dewey becomes the native and indigenous to the educational expressions of people's hopes, desires, and fears about future.

Thinking of Dewey as an indigenous foreigner across historical spaces and time was to open up a way of thinking and studying, but it was not sufficient. I draw into this conversation Deleuze and Guattari's conceptual personae.[20] The writings of Dewey historically enunciated particular solutions and plans for action that go beyond articulating philosophical ideals or the semantics of texts. The pragmatism embodied particular images and narratives of American Exceptionalism, Protestant reformism and The Social Question about rectifying the dangers of urbanization, industrialization, and immigration. It also embodied the American Enlightenment's faith in science as the apotheosis of reason that Dewey's pragmatism translated into an anthropological psychology for the pedagogy of schools.

---

[18] See, e.g., Melissa Andrade-Molina and Paola Valero, "The Sightless Eyes of Reason: Scientific Objectivism and School Geometry," paper presented at the Ninth Congress of European Research in Mathematics Education, Prague, 2015.

[19] Dewey in Brazil was feared bringing an urbanism of Northern Protestant reformism among Counter-Enlightenment thought. In 1960s/1970s Mexico, Dewey was viewed as an agent of American imperialism.

[20] Gilles Deleuze and Felix Guattari, *What is Philosophy?*, trans. Hugh Tomlinson and Graham Burchell (New York: Columbia University Press, [1991] 1994).

The traveling of pragmatism, however, disconnected from its American Exceptionalism as it became an indigenous foreigner entering the Mexican revolutionary party's discourse and the Village Institutes of the new republican governing of Turkey. In each of these conditions, the translations are part of creative, vibrant historical practices rather than being reductive or additive. The new texts produced phantasma of collective belonging and subjectivity through the interstices of different moving historical lines in which Dewey was assembled.

The joining of the notion of indigenous foreigner with that of conceptual personae served as a theoretical/methodological apparatus to think about the different historical lines that meet and travel with "pragmatism." But I also realized that the ideas needed help. That help occurred in a conversation in a small conference where contributors to the book gathered as part of a Leuven meeting. During the meeting, Depaepe suggested thinking of Dewey in a traveling library. The phrase, I thought, elegantly captured the complexities important to the historical studies that were to form the book. The seemingly stable and transcendental texts of Dewey were not that! They were continually worked on in different cultural landscapes as grids of practices.

Traveling libraries provided the theoretical nuances that connected the indigenous foreigner with the dynamic settlements that occurred in different times/spaces. Dewey never arrived alone. The reasoning was articulated as part of a tapestry of "thought" occurring at the interstices of the collective readings. The texts of Dewey met other texts/authors to form a library. The emergent reason is not merely a copy of any single author; nor is it a replication of the prior spaces of action. Metaphorically, Dewey's texts sat on a desk with other enunciations that are worked on collectively to create a cultural landscape to reason about people, events, and change.

Depaepe's reflective comment about traveling libraries is a strong provocation to the ironic poetics of the historical realism that connects positivism and empiricism in contemporary sciences and the historical romanticizing of archival documents. I have focused on this as the semiotic realism of "the given word" in archival documents. This realism is so deeply embedded as imputed reality of historiography that it appears as its philosophical and theoretical reflections. Gary McCulloch, a productive historian of education and collaborator with the prominent curriculum historian Barry Franklin, writes about the relation of theory, interpretation, and facts as a long-standing canon of the historian's craft.[21]

---

[21] Gary McCulloch, "Historians and Their Facts. Discussion: The Cult of Facts, Romanticizing the Archive, and Ignoring Styles of Reasoning: Delusive Technologies of Conducting Historical Research," *Bildungsgeschichte. International Journal for the Historiography of Education* 8 (2018): 206–207.

The argument draws on Edward Halle Carr's *What is History*.[22] Carr makes the distinction between facts as "facts of the past," on the one hand, and "historical facts" whereby the historian decides which are the important facts to build the interpretive analytics, on the other.

The reference to Carr is to assert that there is nothing new to thinking about theory in the practices of historians as it has been a non-stop trope. Yet to perform this observation in reading Carr's text, McCulloch expresses a semiotic "realism" as its historical claim. Carr's reflection of theory and method, ironically, becomes a transcendental narrative. The text is read as "the given word"; unmitigated and atemporal utterances that are outside of history. Carr's text is seen ahistorically, with the past as evidence of the sameness of the present.

To read there is "nothing new" inscribes a presentism. McCulloch ignores how the historical enunciations, ordering, and classifications of Carr's text require historicizing their intelligibility, something made visible in the introductory notes of the second edition by R.W. Davies and Richard J. Evans. Carr's narrative of historiography enunciates a Cartesian "reasoning" that separates the subjective (bias) and the objective. Carr's differentiation of "facts" was part of mid twentieth century discussion connected with British debates between humanism and empiricism, and liberalism and Marxism in post-War Britain in the ordering of problems and modes of studying.

Carr's reasoning about historical methods is about its regulations of the timeless truth of the archival documents. In Carr's narrative, the historian is the magistrate of the archive in what the conceptual historian Reinhart Koselleck critically called as having "the veto power of the sources" that regulates the archive.[23] But as Koselleck continues, that regulation entails "extra- and prelinguistic factors," and "historical experience and memory" that are not transmitted solely in the language of the text.[24]

Walter Benjamin imaginatively calls this historical realism as "the emptying of history."[25] It can be contrasted with Burke and Grosvenor's creative study of

---

[22] Edward Hallett Carr, *What is History? The George Macaulay Trevelyan Lectures Delivered in the University of Cambridge January–March 1961. Introduction by Richard J. Evans and Notes towards Second Edition by R. W Davies* (London: Penguin Modern Classic, [1961] 2018)

[23] Reinhart Koselleck, *Sediments of Time: On Possible Histories*, ed. and trans. Sean Franzel and Stefan-Ludwig Hoffmann (Stanford: Stanford University Press, [2000] 2018).

[24] Koselleck, *Sediments of Time*, 20–21.

[25] Walter Benjamin, "Theses on the Philosophy of History," trans. Harry Zohn, in *Illuminations: Essays and Reflections*, ed. H. Arendt (New York: Schocken Book, [1955] 1985), 253–264.

biography of a nineteenth century architect.²⁶ In comparison to the reading of Carr, Burke and Grosvenor examine different historical lines embedded in the organizing of the architectural spaces of British schools. This reading of the archive historically is to think of the excesses that are in the archival texts that constitute its historicity. Ann Laura Stoler argues, as well, against the semiotic realism of the archive.²⁷ She argues that archives are sites that pull in some facts, and orders them into qualified knowledge and ways of knowing. Examining the Dutch archives in Indonesia during their colonialization, Stoler argues that the archive is not just there to be read as if its statements are what is true. There is "an archival form, prose style, repetitive refrain, arts of persuasion, affective strains that shape rational responses, categories of confidentiality and classification, and not the least, genres of documentations."²⁸

The politics of the archive is to emanate ways of knowing that collude and collide on the edges of social and racial categories. A document "animates political energies and expertise, that pulls on some 'social facts' and converts them into qualified knowledge, that attends to some ways of knowing while repelling and refusing others."²⁹

The elegance of "traveling libraries" posed by Depaepe works to challenge the emptying of history and rejects the semiotic realism that reads texts as "the given word".³⁰ History is not merely about the processes of the past given as the memory of the present. The French and gender historian Joan Scott explores the limits of semiotic realism through the notion of experience that is often taken as what is natural and real in historical studies.³¹ Scott argues that the personal expressions, meanings, and sense of belonging and emotion are entangled with the production of collective memory that enables the author's experience as "shared". Experience entails the excesses of what is visible and given as possibilities embodied in the enunciations of particular modes of living. This is where historical practices enter into the reading of texts so as not to empty its historicity.

---

26 Catherine Burke and Ian Grosvenor, "The 'Body Parts' of the Victorian School Architect E.R. Robson or an Exploration of the Writing and Reading of a Life," in *Rethinking the History of Education*, 201–220.
27 Ann Laura Stoler, *Along the Archival Grain: Epistemic Anxieties and Colonial Common Sense* (Princeton: Princeton University Press, 2008).
28 Stoler, *Along the Archival Grain*, 31.
29 Stoler, *Along the Archival Grain*, 30.
30 See, e.g., Depaepe, "Why Even Today Educational Historiography."
31 Joan W. Scott, "The Evidence of Experience," *Critical Inquiry* 17 (1991): 773–797.

About Method and the Archive: Social Improvement and Making Kinds of People

Notions of indigenous foreigner and traveling libraries bring into view the relation of theory to historical methods. This entails, ironically, entering a realism but one that Hacking (2004) calls a radical realism or dynamic nominalism. It is the entanglements of nominalism and realism – epistemology and ontology – in contemporary discussions about the new materialism. The history is of descent rather than development. Such study asks about the conditions that make statements possible as objects of reflection and action. The objectifications are taken as "the given word" and theorize as archival events of an historical study. My exemplars are the idea of social improvement and the modern school as a historical project in the making of people. Their connections in a grid of practices are worked on as indigenous foreigner and traveling libraries in a History of the Present.

The idea of social improvement has a prominent place in educational planning and research. Its place is sometimes official in the notion of instructional improvement. Its principles in the reasoning of schooling are often not publicly articulated but signaled with notions of development and/or history that assume a naturalness to the evolution of schooling. The school's history is told through the arrow of time that follows the development of the internal organization and its external relations that identifies, for example, "the rise" of compulsory education and "the increasing" of the age of children leaving school. The talk about the "rise" of schooling inscribes improvement that in turn inscribes a temporality as the natural advance of the institution. This naturalizing of the arrow of time not only occurs in historical studies. Contemporary literature talks about stages of teacher development and the object of the professions as achieving social improvement.

Social improvement connects with other historical lines (traveling libraries) as an author and actor in the processes of change in the nineteenth century. "Social improvement" ordered social affairs in the framing of time in which society and people could be managed to effect change. In many social spheres, life was a manageable process in "the arrow of time." Factories could be organized through rationalizing labor as sequences of production that superseded the older craft knowledges, dreamed of in utopic terms for capitalism, socialism, and, in the twentieth century, communism. It entered into the psychologies of child studies as notions of a life that one can and should live. The conditions of its activation gave the possibility of creating a historical memory of the school as the "rise" of compulsory education and the reasonableness of having children go to school for longer times.

Traveling with Enlightenment thought and human improvement was the idea of social change often given the name of progress. The notion of progress was not only social but inscribed as the making of an autobiography.[32] The managing of life gave the past and present as an arrow of time whose processes can obtain progress; but that arrow continually held fears of decay and degeneration.

The inscriptions of improvement in historical narratives as an arrow of time is not an arrow at all. Its narratives of change are made possible through multiple temporal dimensions that connect the past with its present. This connection is paradoxically as the arrow of social improvement generates desires about the potentialities of society and people. The flow of time articulates the emergence of the universalized humanity.[33] Social improvement activates a here and now oriented to philosophical ideals of a universalized humanity that functions as the memory of the past inscribed as the desires of the present.

My focus on social improvement is not merely "an idea" but can be of an indigenous foreigner – historical agent but different from the human actors such as John Dewey. Thinking of social improvement as an agent is to focus on how its reasoning embodies particular solutions and plans for action about what matters about the world and the self. The complexities of that reasoning are not stable but change in time and space. The inscriptions of improvement in social practices and pedagogical projects, for example, entail a memory of the past that orders time as a regular and irreversible quality of human life. That memory connects with notions of development in the sciences that, paradoxically, brings the past and present into a relation with an anticipated future.[34]

---

32 Burton J. Bledstein, *The Culture of Professionalism, the Middle Class, and the Development of Higher Education in America* (New York: Norton, 1976). Charlies Eliot, an important leader in the nineteenth century formation of the American modern school, spoke of his life as the planning of a career. If I return to the notion of conceptual personae, Eliot's experiences formed at the interstices of theater, literature, newspapers, as well as theories about society in the social and psychological sciences.

33 This quality of science as anticipatory is discussed in Popkewitz, *Impracticality of Practical Research*; for discussion of desires and potentialities, see, e.g., Giorgio Agamben, *Potentialities: Collected Essays in Philosophy*, trans. Daniel Heller-Roazen (Stanford: Stanford University Press, 1999); and Gilles Deleuze and Claire Parnet, *Dialogues*, trans. Hugh Tomlinson and Barbara Habberjam (New York: Columbia University Press, [1977] 1987).

34 Thomas S. Popkewitz, "The Paradoxes of Practical Research: The Good Intentions of Inclusion that Exclude and Abject," *The European Educational Research Journal* 19 (2020): 271–288.

Humanity becomes a history of development that could be acted on to bring its perfection. Improvement expresses desires about the potentialities of society and people that can be activated through the correct mixtures of science, technology, and policy.

This connection of the improvement that attaches the past with the present as desires brings into focus the school. The modern school gives a historical presence to how time and space are connected to produce different kinds of people. One of these kinds of people is the citizen. One does not need to go too far to think about the formation of the Europe and North America republics as giving recognition to education as important for government. That government related to the desire of producing citizens whose mode of living and participation was necessary for the new forms of republican government to operate.[35] The citizen was a very different kind of person from its name in the Greek city states but also different in the French and American Republics, and again different in turn to the twentieth century American Progressive Education, Portuguese education, and German notions of *Bildung*.[36]

When speaking of history as the interstices of past and future in the present, this should not be confused with a presentism that uses its criteria of relevance to judge the past. The present is something else. To study the school as making people is to think about the different historical lines that travel, connect, assemble and disconnect in what earlier I wrote about in different traveling libraries. French and Portuguese pedagogies at the turn of the twentieth century, for example, observed and "registered" the inner physical and moral life in order to map the spirituality of the educated subject ('the human soul') who contributed to social life.[37] This notion of the human soul, however, is not the same as in G. Stanley Hall's Child Studies. Hall's studies of the adolescent were to reconcile faith and reason. The Child Studies inscribed Christian belief and the "Enlightenment's empiricism" in psychic development of the child's "soul" to find "the missing links" that would fulfill human destiny in achieving "the beautiful, and the true social, moral and religious good." The soul of the child embodied

---

[35] Barbara Cruikshank, *The Will to Empower: Democratic Citizens and the Other Subjects* (Ithaca: Cornell University Press, 1999); Gordon S. Wood, *The Radicalism of the American Revolution* (New York: Vintage, 1991).

[36] See, e.g., Ó, "The Disciplinary Terrains of Soul and Self-Government"; Rebekka Horlacher, *The Educated Subject and the German Concept of Bildung: A Comparative Cultural History* (New York: Routledge, 2015).

[37] Jorge Ramos do Ó, Catarina Silva Martins, and Ana Luisa Paz, "Genealogy of History: From Pupil to Artist as the Dynamics of Genius, Status, and Inventiveness in Art Education in Portugal," in *Rethinking the History of Education*, 157–178.

a romantic desire of building the organic values of a pastoral community into an increasingly specialized and mechanized urban, industrial, scientific civilization. Science provided the "laborious method of observation, description, and induction" that would enable "conquering nature" and developing "reason, true morality, religion, sympathy, love, and esthetic enjoyment of the child."[38]

The desire about the potentialities was not only about what a child is to become but also what is not to be – studies that gave attention to "deviant" populations, studies of the turn of the century Social Question, with different sets of relations and a comparativeness to today's Social Questions of urban education and racism. When the objects of classroom planning and research are stripped of their moral entitlements, the anticipatory change embodied in the notion of improvement inscribes the double potentialities. There is the child to-be and the child not-to-be. The creative child, for example, is a particular way of thinking, differentiating, and ordering that simultaneously inscribes distinctions about the characteristics and qualities of the child who also is not "creative." Catarina Martins, for example, explores how the idea of creativity and artists appeared in the nineteenth century as a concept of science that embodies differences. The idea of creativity is also to distinguish and differentiate who is not that kind of child.[39]

The double gestures in the making of kinds of people is historically evident in the formation of school subjects of art, mathematics, music, or science education. The curriculum of the school is like an alchemy, or as translations and transformations in which there are the movements from disciplinary spaces of knowledge production (e.g., physics, art, history) to the spaces of schooling that have different priorities and classificatory systems. The symbols and artifacts of disciplines enter into school as the microscopes of science, music instruments and the notions for Euclidian geometry. But entering the spaces of the schools, the symbols, notational systems, and hardware of the cognitive disciplines are disconnected and re-worked in the school as principles of moral

---

[38] G. [Granville] Stanley Hall, *Adolescence: Its Psychology and its Relation to Physiology, Anthropology, Sociology, Sex, Crime, Religion, and Education, Vol. 1* (New York: Appleton, [1904] 1928), vii.
[39] Catarina Silva Martins, "Disrupting the Consensus: Creativity in European Educational Discourses as a Technology of Government," in *The "Reason" of Schooling: Historicizing Curriculum Studies, Pedagogy, and Teacher Education*, ed. Thomas S. Popkewitz (New York: Routledge, 2015), 99–114; Catarina Silva Martins, "From Scribbles to Details," 105–118; Catarina Silva Martins, "The Alchemies of the Arts in Education: Problematizing Some of the Ingredients of the Recipe," in *Spectra of Transformation*, ed. Benjamin Jörissen et al. (Munster/New York: Waxmann, 2018), 51–67.

order in a comparative style of reasoning about differences in the kinds of people.[40]

This comparativeness was given expression in debates about differences articulated in what is normally labeled "The Quarrel of the Ancients and the Moderns" of the seventeenth century and into the eighteenth century. The human history gave the possibility for The Quarrel to differentiate "the modern" and civilized person through distinctions and rules of politeness, refinement, manners, and decencies between people as a degree of being "civilized" (Passavant 2000). The comparative reasoning stabilized the representations of populations and identities.

The comparativeness is activated as partial folds in the modern school curriculum and research that embodied the hope of making children who will participate in society that simultaneously instantiated fears about threats to the hopes. The fears are of dangerous populations abject from the spaces of belonging: the "backward" child at the turn of the twentieth century who later becomes the unmotivated, lazy child who lacks self-esteem and courage, identified in the US as "grit." The comparative reason and double gestures historically are entangled with issues of racism, eugenics, and what Jill Casid terms "the colonial machinery of dominance."[41]

Critique as Method and Change: Historicizing as "Unthinking"/Thinking

This History of the Present is critical history. The mention of critique, I recognize, is often not seen as positive or important to the social body. American and Western European research tied to professional fields tend to define critical as negative. What is needed and the real challenge, it is said, is knowledge for social improvements that identify the pathways and the impediments for progress. While I have already discussed the limits of this notion of progress, I focus here on the optimism given to research as providing the useful and practical knowledge for change. The search for practical knowledge becomes defined as the true wisdom for activating the future and its potentialities. Historical studies are not immune from this doxa that is expressed as relevance for understanding present issues.

---

[40] Kirchgasler, "Building Bridges and Colonial Residues"; Kirchgasler, "Scientific Americans," 89–104; Popkewitz, "What is 'Really' Taught," 77–89.
[41] Jill H. Casid, *Scenes of Projection: Recasting the Enlightenment Subject* (Minneapolis: University of Minnesota Press, 2015), 122.

Yet if we think historically about this idea of practical knowledge and relevancy through the prior discussions, the doxa of social improvement and experience elides the political of schooling. But as importantly, it erases the significance of a critical historical project. It is often forgotten that the notion of critique was important to Enlightenment traditions concerned with freedom and liberty but somehow got sidelined on the way to the present. The German philosopher/social historian Blumenberg argues that the Enlightenment cosmopolitan concerned with reason, rationality, and progress has two complementary sides.[42] One evolved into social planning and interventions, the strand of research lined with notions of social improvement and schooling as making kinds of people and differences. The other side of "reason" important to the Enlightenment's ideas of progress was a different notion of science, what Blumenberg called "renunciation."

The notion of renunciation situates change as the possibility of refusing what seems self-evident about who people are and can be. Change is not asking about the governing "by institutions, prescribed by ideology, guided by pragmatic circumstances," but about making visible the objectification of social life as having historically "their own specific regularities, logic, strategy, self-evidence and 'reason'."[43] This historicizing continually asks how we arrived at the present and its limits, a method of thinking about who we are and should be and of change. To return to Foucault,

> Criticism is a matter of flushing out that thought and trying to change it: to show that things are not as self-evident as one believed, to see that what is accepted as self-evident will no longer be accepted as such. Practicing criticism is a matter of making facile gestures difficult.[44]

Criticism, then, is an optimism about the possibilities of change. That optimism in change is making unstable what is taken as natural and "bound up more with circumstances than necessities, more arbitrary than self-evident, more a matter

---

42 Hans Blumenberg, *The Legitimacy of the Modern Age*, trans. Robert M. Wallace (Cambridge: Massachusetts Institute of Technology, [1966] 1983). The different epistemes in which the word "critical" is evoked in education are explored in an edited book that I did with Lynn Fendler: Thomas S. Popkewitz, and Lynn Fendler, eds., *Critical Theories in Education: Changing Terrains of Knowledge and Politics* (Routledge: New York/London, 1999).
43 Michel Foucault, "A Question of Method," in *The Foucault Effect: Studies in Governmentality: With Two Lectures by and an Interview with Michel Foucault*, ed. Graham Burchell, Colin Gordon, and Peter Miller (Chicago: University of Chicago Press, 1991), 75.
44 Michel Foucault, *The Care of the Self: The History of Sexuality, Vol. 3* (New York: Vintage House, 1988), 155–156.

of complex, but temporary, historical circumstances than with inevitable anthropological constants."[45] Critical research is "unthinking" what seems as natural in order to think and act with degrees of freedom that requires historical methods in the study of the present. It is to cut into the taken-for-granted and common sense of schooling so as to enable thinking about change outside of the frameworks of its contemporaneity.

The History of the Present is a method to unthink the very structuring of thought and action that organize the present. Such a critical engagement with the present was embodied in the idea of traveling libraries; that is, to question the multitudes of intersecting historical lines that are presupposed and that give intelligibility to what matters in the problem of change.

The notion of the critical embodied in this discussion is to open up possibilities outside of the framework of its contemporaneity. Its humanism is in the "testing of the limits of the present, freeing ourselves from the particular dogma of the present" through a resistance to what seems inevitable and necessary by "modifying the rules of the game, up to a certain point."[46] The sense of hesitation embedded in "up to a certain point" suggests that this freeing-up is without guarantees and a conditionality and incompleteness to what constitutes the past and the present.

The interest in the study of education as historicizing the present as a strategy of change might sound like an oxymoron. The cutting into the necessities and self-evident qualities of everyday life engages a notion of agency and change in a different register than that which relies on the objectification of schooling as the origins for ordering and codifying its development. The good intentions of that ordering of history bring into view a comment made by Albert Einstein. He said that it is not adequate to use the language that got us into the situation with which we live as the language for its understanding; a statement that can be viewed as homologous to the earlier discussion of semiotic realism and Walter Benjamin's notion of emptying of history.

---

45 Foucault, *Care of the Self*, 156.
46 Miichel Foucault, "What is the Enlightenment? Was ist Aufklärung?," in *The Foucault Reader*, ed. Paul Rabinow (New York: Pantheon Books, 1984), 48.

CODA: A Critical Science and the Paradox of the Comparative Reason of Change

I approached schooling as a History of the Present, a way of thinking that connects with discussions in the humanities, social/cultural theories, and the more general field of history that has tended to be removed from the history of education. This latter's attachments to analytical traditions of positivism and realism embody "the givenness of the word."

The History of the Present keeps an Enlightenment's cosmopolitanism as an attitude about reason and science. That attitude is about a disciplined attention to the things of the world that revises the notion of the empirical of the archive. The critical stance is to make visible how the problems, methods, and solutions for rectification of social and personal issues are formed and, paradoxically, differentiate, divide, and exclude in efforts to include.

The theoretical and methodological implications of notions of indigenous foreigner and traveling libraries form in an apparatus to historicize that formation of schooling. It is a scholarship of making fragile what seems as natural and inevitable, and thus to open up alternatives outside of those enclosed within contemporaneous frameworks. As an alternative, it is not to claim the History of the Present as anyone's savior. There are no such guarantees. At best, it is to challenge the imputed realities given in history studies through a mode of study that acknowledges the debt to the conversations with Depaepe.

Bibliography

Agamben, Giorgio. *Potentialities: Collected Essays in Philosophy.* Translated by Daniel Heller-Roazen. Stanford: Stanford University Press, 1999.

Andrade-Molina, Melissa, and Paola Valero. *"The Sightless Eyes of Reason: Scientific Objectivism and School Geometry."* Paper presented at the Ninth Congress of European Research in Mathematics Education, Prague, 2015.

Baker, David P. *The Schooled Society: The Educational Transformation of Global Culture.* Stanford: Stanford University Press, 2014.

Barad, Karen. *Meeting the Universe Halfway: Quantum Physics and the Entanglement of Matter and Meaning.* Durham: Duke University Press, 2007.

Benjamin, Walter. "Theses on the Philosophy of History." Translated by Harry Zohn. In *Illuminations: Essays and Reflections.* Edited by Hannah Arendt, 253–264. New York: Schocken Book, [1955] 1985.

Berger, Peter, Brigitte Berger, and Hans Kellner. *The Homeless Mind: Modernization and Consciousness.* New York: Vintage, 1974.

Bledstein, Burton J. *The Culture of Professionalism, the Middle Class, and the Development of Higher Education in America*. New York: Norton, 1976.

Blumenberg, Hans. *The Legitimacy of the Modern Age*. Translated by Robert M. Wallace. Cambridge: Massachusetts Institute of Technology, [1966] 1983.

Burke, Catherine, and Ian Grosvenor. "The 'Body Parts' of the Victorian School Architect E.R. Robson or an Exploration of the Writing and Reading of a Life." In *Rethinking the History of Education: Transnational Perspectives on its Questions, Methods, and Knowledge*, edited by Thomas S. Popkewitz, 201–220. New York: Palgrave, 2013.

Carr, Edward Hallett. *What is History? The George Macaulay Trevelyan Lectures Delivered in the University of Cambridge January-March 1961. Introduction by Richard J. Evans and Notes towards Second Edition by R.W Davies*. London: Penguin Modern Classic, [1961] 2018.

Casid, Jill H. *Scenes of Projection: Recasting the Enlightenment Subject*. Minneapolis: University of Minnesota Press, 2015.

Chadarevian, Soraya de, and Theodore M. Porter, eds. "Histories of Data and the Database." Special Issue *Historical Studies in the Natural Sciences* 48, no. 5 (2018).

Coster, Tom De, Marc Depaepe, Frank Simon, and Angelo Van Gorp. "Dewey in Belgium: A Libation for Modernity?" In *Inventing the Modern Self and John Dewey: Modernities and the Traveling of Pragmatism in Education*, edited by Thomas S. Popkewitz, 85–110. New York: Palgrave, 2005.

Cruikshank, Barbara. *The Will to Empower: Democratic Citizens and the Other Subjects*. Ithaca: Cornell University Press, 1999.

Deleuze, Gilles, and Felix Guattari. *What is Philosophy?* Translated by Hugh Tomlinson and Graham Burchell. New York: Columbia University Press, [1991] 1994.

Deleuze, Gilles, and Claire Parnet. *Dialogues*. Translated by Hugh Tomlinson and Barbara Habberjam. New York: Columbia University Press, [1977] 1987.

Depaepe, Marc. "Social and Personal Factors in the Inception of Experimental Research in Education (1890–1914)." *History of Education* 16 (1987): 275–298.

Depaepe, Marc. "Differences and Similarities in the Development of Educational Psychology in Germany and the United States before 1945." *Paedagogica Historica* 33 (1997): 69–97.

Depaepe, Marc. "The Practical and the Professional Relevance of Educational Research and Pedagogical Knowledge from the Perspective of History." In *Philosophy and History of the Discipline of Education: Evaluation and Evolution of the Criteria for Educational Research*, edited by Paul Smeyer and Marc Depaepe, 49–72. Leuven: Leuven University Press, 2001.

Depaepe, Marc [in cooperation with Kristof Dams, Maurits De Vroede, Betty Eggermont, Hilde Lauwers, Frank Simon, Roland Vandenberghe, and Jef Verhoeven]. *Order in Progress: Everyday Education Practice in Primary Schools, Belgium 1880–1970*. Leuven: Leuven University Press, 2000.

Depaepe, Marc. "Why Even Today Educational Historiography is not an Unnecessary Luxury: Focusing on four Themes from Forty-Four Years of Research." *Espacio, Tiempo y Educación* 7 (2020): 227–246. Accessed April 10, 2020. http://dx.doi.org/10.14516/ete.335.

Dussel, Inés. "The Visual Turn in the History of Education." In *Rethinking the History of Education: Transnational Perspectives on its Questions, Methods, and Knowledge*, edited by Thomas S. Popkewitz, 29–50. New York: Palgrave, 2013.

Dussel, Inés. "Tactile Pedagogies in the Postwar: Cybernetics, Art, and the Production of a New Educational Rationale." In *The International Emergence of Educational Sciences in the Post-World War Two Years: Quantification, Visualization, and Making Kinds of People*, edited by Thomas S. Popkewitz, Daniel Pettersson, and Kai-Jung Hsiao. New York: Routledge, 2021.

Foucault, Michel. "Governmentality." In *The Foucault Effect: Studies in Governmentality: With Two Lectures by and an Interview with Michel Foucault*, edited by Graham Burchell, Colin Gordon, and Peter Miller, 87–104. Chicago: University of Chicago Press, 1991.

Foucault, Michel. "A Question of Method." In *The Foucault Effect: Studies in governmentality: With Two Lectures by and an Interview with Michel Foucault*, edited by Graham Burchell, Colin Gordon, and Peter Miller, 73–86. Chicago: University of Chicago Press, 1991.

Foucault, Michel. *The Care of the Self: The History of Sexuality, Vol. 3*. New York: Vintage House, 1988.

Foucault, Michel. "What is the Enlightenment? Was ist Aufklärung?" In *The Foucault Reader*, edited by Paul Rabinow, 32–51. New York: Pantheon Books, 1984.

Gil, Natália de Lacerda. "The Quantification of an Educational System: Numbers in the Social Differentiation of Brazil." In *The International Emergence of Educational Sciences in the Post-World War Two Years: Quantification, Visualization, and Making Kinds of People*, edited by Thomas S. Popkewitz, Daniel Pettersson, and Kai-Jung Hsiao, 225–241. New York: Routledge, 2021.

Hacking, Ian. *Historical Ontology*. Cambridge: Harvard University Press, 2004.

Hall, G[ranville] Stanley. *Adolescence: Its Psychology and its Relation to Physiology, Anthropology, Sociology, Sex, Crime, Religion, and Education, Vol. 1*. New York: Appleton, [1904] 1928.

Horlacher, Rebekka. *The Educated Subject and the German Concept of Bildung: A Comparative Cultural History*. New York: Routledge, 2016.

Kirchgasler, Christopher. "Building Bridges and Colonial Residues: Transnational School Reforms and the Making of Human Kinds." PhD diss., University of Wisconsin-Madison, 2017.

Kirchgasler, Kathryn L. "Scientific Americans: Historicizing the Making of Differences in Early 20th-Century US Science Education." In *A Political Sociology of Educational Knowledge: Studies of Exclusions and Difference*, edited by Thomas S. Popkewitz, Jennifer Diaz, and Christopher Kirchgasler, 89–104. New York: Routledge, 2017.

Koselleck, Reinhart. *Sediments of Time: On Possible Histories*. Edited and translated by Sean Franzel and Stefan-Ludwig Hoffmann. Stanford: Stanford University Press, [2000] 2018.

Lesko, Nancy. *Act Your Age: A Cultural Construction of Adolescence*. New York: Routledge, 2001.

Lima, Ana Laura Godinho. "The Development of the Child and National Progress: Behaviorism and Cultural Deprivation in Brazil." In *The International Emergence of Educational Sciences in the Post-World War Two Years: Quantification, Visualization, and Making Kinds of People*, edited by Thomas S. Popkewitz, Daniel Pettersson, and Kai-Jung Hsiao, 128–148. New York: Routledge, 2021.

Madeira, Ana Isabel. "Portuguese, French, and British Discourses on Colonial Education: Church-State Relations, School Expansion, and Missionary Competition in Africa, 1890–1930." *Paedagogica Historica* 41 (2005): 31–60.

Martins, Catarina Silva. "Disrupting the Consensus: Creativity in European Educational Discourses as a Technology of Government." In *The "Reason" of Schooling: Historicizing Curriculum Studies, Pedagogy, and Teacher Education*, edited by Thomas S. Popkewitz, 99–114. New York: Routledge, 2015.

Martins, Catarina Silva. "From Scribbles to Details: The Invention of Stages of Development in Drawing and the Government of the Child." In *A Political Sociology of Educational Knowledge: Studies of Exclusions and Difference*, edited by Thomas S. Popkewitz, Jennifer Diaz, and Christopher Kirchgasler, 105–118. New York: Routledge, 2017.

Martins, Catarina Silva. "The Alchemies of the Arts in Education: Problematizing Some of the Ingredients of the Recipe." In *Spectra of Transformation*, edited by Benjamin Jörissen, Lisa Unterberg, Leopold Klepacki, Juliane Engel, Viktoria Flasche, and Tanja Klepacki, 51–67. Munster/New York: Waxmann, 2018.

McCulloch, Gary. "Historians and Their Facts. Discussion: The Cult of Facts, Romanticizing the Archive, and Ignoring Styles of Reasoning: Delusive Technologies of Conducting Historical Research." *Bildungsgeschichte. International Journal for the Historiography of Education* 8 (2018): 206–207.

Meyer, John W., David H. Kamens, Aaron Benavot, Yun-Kyung Cha, and Suk-Ying Wong. *School Knowledge for the Masses and National Primary Curriculum Categories in the Twentieth Century*. Washington, DC: Falmer Press, 1992.

Ó, Jorge Ramos do. "The Disciplinary Terrains of Soul and Self-Government in the First Map of the Educational Sciences." In *Beyond Empiricism: On Criteria for Educational Research (Studia Paedagogica 34)*, edited by Paul Smeyers and Marc Depaepe, 105–116. Belgium: Leuven University Press, 2003.

Ó, Jorge Ramos do, Catarina Silva Martins, and Ana Luisa Paz. "Genealogy of History: From Pupil to Artist as the Dynamics of Genius, Status, and Inventiveness in Art Education in Portugal." In *Rethinking the History of Education: Transnational Perspectives on its Questions, Methods, and Knowledge*, edited by Thomas S. Popkewitz, 157–178. New York: Palgrave, 2013.

Passavant, Paul A. "The Governmentality of Discussion." In *Cultural Studies and Political Theory* edited by Jodi Dean, 115–131. Ithaca: Cornell University Press, 2000.

Paz, Ana Luisa. "Can Genius be Taught? Debates in Portuguese Music Education (1868–1930)." *European Educational Research Journal* 16 (2017): 504–516.

Popkewitz, Thomas S., ed. *Inventing the Modern Self and John Dewey: Modernities and the Traveling of Pragmatism in Education*. New York: Palgrave Macmillan Press, 2005.

Popkewitz, Thomas S. *Cosmopolitanism and the Age of School Reform: Science, Education, and Making Society by Making the Child*. New York: Routledge, 2008.

Popkewitz, Thomas S. "The Past as the Future of the Social and Educational Sciences." In *Education Systems in Historical, Cultural, and Sociological Perspectives*, edited by Daniel Tröhler and Raghild Barbu, 163–180. Leiden: Brill/Sense, 2011.

Popkewitz, Thomas S. "Social Epistemology, the Reason of 'Reason,' and the Curriculum Studies." Special Issue *Nuevas Perspectivas sobre el Curriculum Escolar. Education Policy Analysis Archives* (2014). Accessed April 10, 2020. http://dx.doi.org/10.14507/epaa.v22n22.2014.

Popkewitz, Thomas S., ed. *The "Reason" of Schooling: Historicizing Curriculum Studies, Pedagogy, and Teacher Education*. New York: Routledge, 2015.

Popkewitz, Thomas S. "What is 'Really' Taught as the Content of School Subjects? Teaching School Subjects as an Alchemy." *High School Journal* 101 (2018): 77–89.

Popkewitz, Thomas S. "How Theory Acts as the Retrieval Apparatus in Methods: Historical Thoughts on Romanticized Intellectual Practices." In *Handbook of Historical Studies in Education: Debates, Tensions and Directions*, edited by Tanya Fitzgerald, 153–169. New York: Springer, 2020.

Popkewitz, Thomas S. *The Impracticality of Practical Research: A History of Sciences of Change that Conserve*. Ann Arbor: University of Michigan Press, 2020.

Popkewitz, Thomas S. "The Paradoxes of Practical Research: The Good Intentions of Inclusion that Exclude and Abject." *The European Educational Research Journal* 19 (2020): 271–288.

Popkewitz, Thomas S., and Lynn Fendler, eds. *Critical Theories in Education: Changing Terrains of Knowledge and Politics*. New York: Routledge, 1999.

Popkewitz, Thomas S., Barry Franklin, and Miguel Pereyra, eds. *Cultural History and Education: Critical Studies on Knowledge and Schooling*. New York: Routledge, 2001.

Popkewitz, Thomas S., Daniel Pettersson, and Kai-Jung Hsiao, eds. *The International Emergence of Educational Sciences in the Post-World War Two Years: Quantification, Visualization, and Making Kinds of People*. New York: Routledge, 2021.

Priem, Karin, and Frederik Herman, eds. *Fabricating Modern Societies. Education, Bodies, and Minds in the Age of Steel*. Leiden: Brill, 2019.

Rancière, Jacques. *The Politics of Aesthetics*. Translated by Gabriel Rockhill. New York: Bloomsbury Academic, 2004.

Scott, Joan W. "The Evidence of Experience." *Critical Inquiry* 17 (1991): 773–797.

Smeyers, Paul, and Marc Depaepe, eds. *Educational Research: The Educationalization of Social Problems*. Dordrecht: Springer, 2008.

Sobe, Noah. *Provincializing the Worldly Citizen: Yugoslav Student and Teacher Travel and Slavic Cosmopolitanism in the Interwar Era*. New York: Peter Lang, 2008.

Sobe, Noah. "Entanglements and Transnationalism in the History of American Education." In *Rethinking the History of Education: An Intercontinental Perspective on the Questions, Methods, and Knowledge of Schools*, edited by Thomas S. Popkewitz, 93–108. New York: Palgrave Macmillan, 2013.

Stoler, Ann Laura. *Along the Archival Grain: Epistemic Anxieties and Colonial Common Sense*. Princeton: Princeton University Press, 2008.

Wood, Gordon S. *The Radicalism of the American Revolution*. New York: Vintage, 1991.

2 The Politics of Diversity: Gender, Culture, and Post-colonial Education

Section editor: Pieter Verstraete

Ian Grosvenor (University of Birmingham, UK)
Engaging with "the Act of Looking Back, [and] of Seeing with Fresh Eyes": the Colonial Experience and Pedagogies of Display

Abstract: In the collection The Colonial Experience in Education (Gent, 1995) Marc Depaepe opened his contribution with the question 'Can art save the world?' He continued, "In my view, this question also applies to our discipline: can history, and particularly the history of education, save the world?" The present essay[1] takes as its focus the informal learning space of the museum and the art gallery, and the emergence of curatorial activism. In doing so it explores the changing discourse and politics around displaying the history of the "colonial experience."

Keywords: colonial; museum; activism; artefact; decolonize

In "An Agenda for the History of Colonial Education" in the collection *The Colonial Experience in Education* (Gent 1995) Marc Depaepe opened his article with the question "Can art save the world?" The question had been used in an advertising campaign in the city of Antwerp as cultural capital of Europe in 1993. He continued, "In my view, this question also applies to our discipline: can history, and particularly the history of education, save the world?" His answer was framed around thinking harder and deeper about the human condition:

> the study of the colonial past can help ... in making us aware of the very different conditions and often smart injustices in which children grew and grow up ... It can also show

---

[1] This essay originated in a presentation at "Looking Back/Moving Forward – Histories of Education in/for the Twentieth Century," A Colloquium in honor of Professor Marc Depaepe, KU Leuven Kulak, November 9, 2018 and a shorter version was published under the title "'Can art save the world?': the Colonial Experience and Pedagogies of Display" in *Paedagogica Historica* 55, no. 4 (2019): 642–649.

https://doi.org/10.1515/9783110623451-009

how western imperialism and racism, in the name of education and civilization, dehistoricized and desocialized autochthonous populations.[2]

The present essay revisits Depaepe's questions by taking as it focus the very spaces where art is presented to the public, the informal learning space of the museum and the art gallery, and the emergence in recent years of curatorial activism. In doing so it seeks to explore the changing discourse and politics around addressing through display the history of the "colonial experience" and its meaning in today's globalized world.

Berlin 1884–85

European rivalry over access to the natural resources of the continent of Africa and the desire to create new markets for European goods led to a conference in Berlin which brought together rival powers. Organized by the German Chancellor Otto von Bismarck, the conference legitimated and formalized the ground rules for European colonization of Africa. The General Act which emerged from the Berlin Conference included the following statement:

> The Signatory Powers exercising sovereign rights or authority in African territories will continue to watch over the preservation of the native populations and to supervise the improvement of the conditions of their moral and material well-being.[3]

At the time of the conference, only the coastal areas of the continent were colonized by the European powers. The Act "legitimated" the appropriation of land without consent and the colonial powers scrambled to gain control over Africa's interior. By 1914 European states had claimed nearly 90 percent of African territory. The borders established were based on the political or administrative needs of the colonial powers, disregarded cultural and linguistic boundaries already established by the indigenous population, and overrode existing African autonomy and self-governance. The greatest beneficiaries of the "scramble for Africa" were Belgium, France, Germany, Great Britain, and Portugal.[4]

---

[2] Marc Depaepe. "An Agenda for the History of Colonial Education," in *The Colonial Experience in Education*, edited by António Nóvoa, Marc Depaepe, and Erwin V. Johanningmeier, *Paedagogica Historica*, Supplementary Series, 1, 15–22 (Gent, 1995).
[3] General Act of the Berlin Conference on West Africa, February 26, 1885.
[4] See Chamberlain, Muriel Evelyn, *The Scramble for Africa* (London: Longman, 2013).

Berlin 2018

Between April and August 2018 the Hamburger Bahnhof-Museum für Gegenwart in Berlin presented the exhibition *Hello World. Revising a Collection*. The exhibition consisted of a series of multilayered narratives, one of which, curated by Sven Beckstette and Azu Nwagbogu, was entitled *Colomental. The Violence of Intimate Histories*. The curators invited three contemporary artists, Peggy Buth, Astrid S. Klein, and Dierk Schmidt, to address the question: "What of our [Germany's] colonial past?" The word *Colomental* was created from the fusion of "colonial" and "mentality" and was used as a metaphor to capture the impact of colonialism on subconscious perceptions and present actions:

> To be "colomental" is a state which describes how our colonial past has become a symptom of an incurable, chronic disease; a still painful particle in our flesh and blood which we have to accept whether we are comfortable with it or not an itchy scar which will bind the two continents, Europe and Africa, together forever.[5]

Schmidt's contribution was a 14-painting series[6] which visualized the brutal consequences of the legal document ratified by the 1884–85 conference which translated into the genocide Germany committed against the Herero and Nama peoples between 1904 and 1908 in what is now Namibia. More recently, the genocide resulted in a legal case against the German state.[7] The legal documents were displayed alongside Schmidt's translation of historical sources and their emotional legacy into his abstract paintings. Other historical sources used by artists in the exhibition included photographs of a ball held by French colonials in 1900 in which Malagasy people are dressed in elaborate costumes to reflect the "colonialists 'ideal' for civilized people who should entertain and complete the gathering but as decoration only" and photographs from the German Colonial

---

5 Sven Beckstette and Azu Nwagbogu, "Sven Beckstette and Azu Nwagbogu in Conversation." In *Hello World. Revising a Collection*, 355–359 (Berlin: Hamburger Bahnhof Museum für Gegenwart, 2018).
6 Dierk Schmidt, *The Division of the Earth- Tableaux on the Legal Synopses of the Berlin Africa Conference*, 2007. *Hello World. Revising a Collection* (Berlin: Hamburger Bahnhof Museum für Gegenwart, 2018).
7 See Jason Burke and Philip Oltermann, "Germany Faces up to African Genocide," *The Guardian*, December 26, 2016; Justin Huggler, "Germany forced to face up to 'forgotten genocide' in Africa." *The Daily Telegraph*, June 18, 2018, 12.

Society photographic archive and the Musée royal de l'Afrique central de Tervuren, Belgium.[8]

London 1924

London 1924 saw the British Empire Exhibition at Wembley.[9] 18 million people visited the exhibition between April and October, including five million children who, according to the Prince of Wales in his closing address, gained from it "a vivid impression of the responsibilities which will come to them in the future as citizens of empire."[10] The exhibition was organized into a series of geographically focused pavilions and zones and one of the most popular attractions was the "Races in Residence" display of people from the Empire in working "villages" showing "daily life".[11] In the Gold Coast Pavilion visitors could see and hear "the mysterious native drum," which as the *Official Guide* pointed out, took "the place of the telephone, telegraph wire and wireless communications in more civilized communities." There were also wooden idols which the *Official Guide* described as of "immense size and unattractive aspect". A Weekly *Bulletin of Empire Study* was produced for circulation to schools and included detailed lesson plans. In the "Notes for Lessons" on Australia, the absence of "black fellows" at the Exhibition was lamented, but was followed by discussion as to whether they were "savages" and the important role of missionary stations.[12] In total some 273 colonized people from Malaya, Burma, Hong Kong, West Africa,

---

8 *Hello World. Revising a Collection*, 355–367. The Musée royal de l'Afrique central de Tervuren, was inaugurated in 1910 and was the beneficiary of an extensive collection of cultural artefacts from the Congo collected via scientific missions, military expeditions, territorial agents, and Christian missionaries. The museum was closed for renovations in 2013 and reopened in 2018 as the Africa Museum with a contemporary and decolonised vision of Africa. See Anon, "Un musée sans pareil," *Tribal Art Magazine*, Special Issue 8 (2018): 12–17.
9 See Ian Grosvenor, "Teaching the Empire: the weekly *Bulletin of Empire Study* and the British Empire Exhibition, London, 1924," in *Modelling the Future. Exhibitions and the Materiality of Education* edited by Martin Lawn, 107–128. Oxford: Symposium, 2009.
10 *The Observer*, November 2, 1924, 14.
11 Grosvenor, "Teaching the Empire," 118–120.
12 *The Weekly Bulletin of Empire Study*, no. 2, February 1, 1924, 9. The *Bulletin* was issued in 24 weekly parts and at least 124,000 were circulated to schools. It was aimed at children between the ages of 11 and 16 and it was estimated by the editors that one and a half million children were learning lessons of Empire (quoted in Grosvenor, "Teaching the Empire," 110–111).

and Palestine were on public display for the duration of the exhibition.[13] The villages, a phenomenon known as "human zoos,"[14] separated the peoples of Empire into a racial hierarchy and asserted the national unity of the "we" and racial superiority.

Melbourne 2018

Colony: Frontier Wars at the National Gallery of Victoria, Melbourne examined through historical and contemporary art by Indigenous and non-Indigenous artists "the immeasurable loss" experienced by Aboriginal peoples and their descendants because of British colonization. Artists challenged accepted accounts of Australian history through:

> re-imaging pre-contact cultural objects, re-configuring nineteenth century photographic representations of unidentified Indigenous people and responding to instances of violence recorded in settler accounts or transmitted in oral histories, which cannot be erased.[15]

As colonists sought to expand control in unceded Indigenous lands violent confrontations both physical and symbolic resulted in the Frontier Wars of the exhibition's title. *Colony: Frontier Wars* addressed the argument of who had control of the past and what counted as "truth" and as one artist curator attested: "It is only through the recognition of what has gone before – however difficult this journey may be – that we can mourn, heal and find some peace within and between ourselves."[16]

---

13 G.C. Lawrence, ed., *Official Guide to the British Empire Exhibition* (London: Fleetway, 1925), 126; Ann Clendinning, "On the British Empire Exhibition, 1924–25," in BRANCH: *Britain, Representation and Nineteenth-Century History*, edited by Dino Franco Felluga, Extension of Romanticism and Victorianism on the Net, accessed October 12, 2018 http://www.branchcollective.org.
14 See Blanchard Pascal, Nicolas Bancel, Gilles Boetsch, Eric Deroo, Sandrine Lemaire, and Charles Forsdick, eds., *Human Zoos. Science and Spectacle in the Age of Colonial Empires* (Liverpool: Liverpool University Press, 2008). A parallel can be drawn between the British Empire exhibition's paternalistic and dehumanizing African "working villages," with the Brussels Expo of 1958 where visitors were presented with "working" Congolese villages; see Matthew Standard, "'Bilan du monde pour un monde plus déshumanisé': The 1958 Brussels World's Fair and Belgian Perceptions of the Congo," *European History Quarterly* 35, no. 2 (2005): 267–298.
15 Cathy Leahy and Judith Ryan, eds., *Colony. Australia 1770–1861/Frontier Wars* (Melbourne: National Gallery of Victoria, 2018), 3.
16 Ibid., viii.

Collections are the foundation of museum work and for many institutions established in the nineteenth century the nature of these collections are directly entangled with the political and cultural legacies of colonialism. Being a colonial power involved both the accumulation of privilege and the production of systemic inequalities. Objects were amassed from colonies as Europeans stole and traded in a desire to understand and classify the world, a world which necessarily was reflective of their own sense of superiority. An obsession with the processes of gathering and classifying also resulted in administrative structures emerging whereby national and metropolitan archives became repositories of colonial information collected in the service of state and empire.[17] Both the Berlin and Melbourne exhibitions drew on objects and archives as they connected past and present, acknowledged and reflected alternative histories, and questioned the assumption of the superiority of one culture over another. Both exhibitions were revisionist and involved, to paraphrase Adrianne Rich, "the act of looking back, of seeing with fresh eyes" so that debate about the connection between present and past could move in new critical directions.[18] The exhibitions were also indicative of an emerging movement "to question the subjects and objects that have been in the custodianship of … archives and ethnological collections … for a long time" and to determine how such institutions could change their narratives in a global postcolonial world.[19] Both exhibitions were the product of partnerships between curators and artists.

Can these exhibitions as creative interventions help save the world? Certainly, "seeing with fresh eyes" is an idea that has political traction. As early as 1947 George Orwell noted "the advantages we [Britain] derive from colonial exploitation," and that "this relationship has never been made clear by official Socialist propaganda, and the British worker, instead of being told that, by world standards, he is living above his income, has been taught to think of himself as an overworked, down-trodden slave." Orwell concluded that "European nations *must* stop being exploiters abroad if they are to build true Socialism at home."[20] More recently, Nils Muizniek, the Council of Europe's Commissioner for Human Rights, was forthright in a statement published in July 2017 under

---

17 See Thomas Richards, *The Imperial Archive: Knowledge and the Fantasy of Empire* (London: Verso, 1993); Ann Stoler, "Colonial Archives and the Arts of Governance," *Archival Science* 2 (2002): 87–109; Sophie Berrebi, *The Shape of Evidence* (Amsterdam: Valiz, 2014).
18 Adrienne Rich, *On Lies, Secrets and Silence* (London: W. W. Norton &Co, 1972), 35.
19 Beckstette and Nwagbogu, *Hello World*, 357.
20 George Orwell, "Toward European Unity," 1947,
   http//: orwell.ru/library/articles/European_Unity/english/e_teu, accessed October 30, 2018.

the heading *Afrophobia: Europe should confront this legacy of colonialism and the slave trade:*

> Colonialism scarred the destiny of millions of men, women and children and left an indelible mark on our world. It shaped European societies for centuries and led to deeply rooted prejudices and inequalities. Its consequences are still largely ignored or denied today ... European states must first come to terms with their own past. To this end, those that have not done so should publicly acknowledge that slavery, the slave trade and colonialism are among the major sources of current discrimination against Black People. This is a *sine qua non* for overcoming Afrophobia.[21]

It is also an idea which can be found in postcolonial literature, as Sisodia in *The Satanic Verses* observed, "the Trouble with the English is that their history happened overseas, so they don't know what it means."[22] However, it is also an idea which today is confronted by a new "normal" in global politics where history has been abandoned in favor of "forgetting, misremembering and mistaking the past,"[23] and where there has generally been an abject failure on the part of former colonial powers to come to terms with their national pasts. David Andress termed this phenomenon "cultural dementia" and he has persuasively documented how in Britain and France, for example, there has been:

> an actively constructed, jealously guarded toxic refusal to engage with facts that are well-known but emotionally and politically inconvenient, and with other experiences that are devastating to the collective self-regard of huge segments of societies that have no visible desire to come to terms with reality.[24]

---

21 Nils Muiznick, http:// www.coe.int/en/web/commissioner/-/afrophobia-europe-should-confront-this-legacy-of-colonialism-and-the-slave-trade, accessed October 4, 2018; Morgan Philip D., and Sean Hawkins, eds., *Black Experience and the Empire* (Oxford: Oxford University Press, 2004).
22 Salman Rushdie, *The Satanic Verses* (London: Vintage Books, 1998), 363. The words are presented as speech in the novels: "The trouble with the Engenglish is that their hiss hiss history happened overseas, so they dodo don't know what it means.". – "The see secret of a dinner party in London is to ow ow outnumber the English. If they're outnumbered they bebehave; otherwise, you're in trouble" – "Go to the Ché Ché Chamber of Horrors and you'll see what's rah rah wrong with the English. That's what they rereally like, caw corpses in bubloodbaths, mad barbers, etc. etc. etera. Their pay papers full of kinky sex and death. But they tell the whir world they're reserved, ist ist istiff upper lip and so on, and we're ist ist istupid enough to believe."
23 David Andress, *Cultural Dementia. How the West has Lost its History, and Risks Losing Everything Else* (London: Head of Zeus, 2018), 47.
24 Ibid., 144.

Further, it has also been documented by Maura Reilly in *Curatorial Activism. Towards an ethics of curating* that exhibitions which do tackle white privilege and western-centrism are generally criticized for being overtly preoccupied with identity-driven social and political issues, "utilizing morality base approaches," denigrated as politically correct or accused of catering for particular audiences and thereby indirectly ghettoizing their subject matter. [25]

Historians have long followed Walter Benjamin's call to brush history against the grain, to engage in an active process of remembering, and to seek out material in the archive which challenges crude reductionism and provides counter-histories. But what happens when, in Andress' words, "people don't want to listen, or learn?" At the end of *Cultural Dementia* Andress directly addresses his readers:

> And now, at the very end, you will want me to tell you how it might be fixed. But I don't know ... Like anyone else stranded at this moment in time I can only hope that there must be a way to get past this ... without collapse into conflict and catastrophe.

He continues, "So I turn back to you and ask, what do *you* think that way could be?".[26] So how indeed might we reconnect with historical reality? And what might our role be in this process as historians of education? Reilly in the final section of *Curatorial Activism* presents "A Call to Arms: Strategies for Change", where she writes:

> How can we elicit sympathy, to the point of action? How can we go about educating disbelievers who contend because there are signs of improvement – that the battle has been won? How do we fight against cognitive dissonance when people's instinct is to rationalize or ignore concepts that they don't agree with? If we present empirical evidence that works against people's core belief, how can we guarantee that this evidence is accepted? How do we denaturalize what is perceived as natural? And in so doing, do we run the risk of encountering backlash anger, denial, or worse, dismissal?[27]

Part of her solution to these problems is for curators to look beyond their own expertise and engage in partnership building which would reflect the ambition of telling "alternate stories of difference, culture, power, and agency,"[28] and

---

25 Maura Reilly, *Curatorial Activism. Towards an Ethics of Curating* (London: Thames and Hudson, 2018), 100.
26 Andress, *Cultural Dementia*, 149.
27 Reilly, *Curatorial Activism*, 217–218.
28 Chandra Talpade Mohanty, *Feminisms Without Borders* (North Carolina: Duke University Press, 2003), 244.

where curators would position themselves as "mediators of cultural exchange" so that there is a critical dialogue which "would allow for an ensemble of perspectives to emerge".²⁹ As historians we should be equally active in looking beyond our own expertise and reaching out to artists and curators to work in partnership to develop exhibitions and other interventions in learning which draw on our knowledge of colonial archives and objects. But we should go further than this.

In "*Feeling* and *Being* at the (Postcolonial) Museum: Presencing the Affective Politics of 'Race' and Culture" Divya P. Tolia-Kelly asked the question of what happens when someone who is the object of racialized cultures in the everyday encounters themselves in the museum:

> The museum cabinet, viewed through a postcolonial lens, exposes the continuities of imperial taxonomies and hierarchies of culture that underpin its use. The result is an encounter with epistemic violence and subjugation, sanctioned in the present. The museum space thus operates as a theatre of pain.³⁰

Following on from Reilly's call for critical dialogue through partnership we should also strive to establish embodied legacies through collaborative research projects focusing on the colonial. In other words, we should work with community partners to co-design and co-produce research projects which brush history against the grain, engage in projects that will utilize community knowledge and skills to provide advice and guidance, broker relationships and convene and facilitate activities so as to reach new audiences through exhibitions and other cultural interventions. Community participants, as Facer and Enright (2016) have shown, can develop new skills, knowledge and understanding, and the confidence to apply them in networks and partnerships beyond a project. ³¹ At the center of such partnership would be a commitment to widening understanding of every part of the historical process.³² However, it has to be recognized at the outset that even where such initiatives achieve success, "the dominant discourse will remain undisturbed"³³ as society is dominated by a particular notion of community, "one that overlooks the fact that representations of reality can

---

29 Reilly, *Curatorial Activism*, 105.
30 Divya P. Tolia-Kelly, "*Feeling* and *Being* at the (Postcolonial) Museum: Presencing the Affective Politics of 'Race' and Culture," *Sociology* 50, no. 5 (2016): 897.
31 Keri Facer, and Bryony Enright, *Creating Living knowledge* (Bristol: University of Bristol, 2016).
32 See Ludmilla Jordanova, *History in Practice* (London: Edward Arnold, 2000), 200–107.
33 Tolia-Kelly, *Feeling* and *Being*, 900.

have powerful effects," and "this discourse shapes reality, both by mystifying and naturalizing existing power relations."[34] As Tolia-Kelly concludes, "there is no value-free act of cultural representation."[35]

The impact of colonialism is global and we should seek to identify and document the rationale, content, participants, and impact of exhibitions and cultural interventions that have used objects and/or archives to challenge "vision[s] of the past" that are "the opposite of a coherent history" and instead have questioned assumptions, countered omissions, inspired debate, and disseminated new knowledge. [36] Museums and art galleries are sites of learning and as such naturally fall within our frame of reference as historians of education. "Traces are not only what is left when something is gone, they can also be marks of a project to come", [37] and as Michael Fielding has argued "our capacity to interrogate the present with any degree of wisdom or any likelihood of creating a more fulfilling future rests significantly on our knowledge and engagement with the past" [38] and he challenged historians "to be active, not merely receptive in our conversations with the past".[39] Such a project would build on the work already begun by Reilly in *Curatorial Activism*[40] and recent exhibitions such as *Racism and Citizenship* (Monument to the Discoveries, Lisbon, 2017); *The Past is Now* (Birmingham Museum and Art Gallery, Birmingham, 2017); *Blind Spots. Images of the Danish West Indies* (Royal Danish Library, Copenhagen, 2017); *John Akomfrah: Signs of Empire* (New Museum, New York, 2018); *Here We are Today* (Bucerius Kunst Forum, Hamburg, 2019); and *Otobong Nkanga: From Where I Stand* (Tate St Ives, 2019). Such a project would, however, inevitably connect with and have to address two other critical agendas: the restitution of cultural artefacts taken as part of the global project of colonialism and the growing demand to decolonize Western epistemic dominance.

---

34 Waterton and Smith, quoted by Tolia-Kelly, *Feeling* and *Being*, 900–901.
35 Ibidem, 901.
36 Andress, *Cultural Dementia*, 32.
37 John Berger, "Giorgio Morandi," in *The Shape of a Pocket*, 139–146 (London: Bloomsbury, 2001), 144.
38 Michael Fielding, "Putting Hands Around the Flame: reclaiming the radical tradition in state education," *Forum* 47, no. 2–3 (2005): 1.
39 Michael Fielding, "Afterword. Anarchism, texts and children: active conversations with the past," *Paedagogica Historica* 50, no. 4 (2014): 460–64.
40 Reilly, *Curatorial Activism*, 98–157. See also Robert R. Janes and Richard Sandell, eds., *Museum Activism* (London: Routledge, 2019).

Discussions about the restitution of cultural property have a long history[41], but the debate was energized in 2017 when French President Macron gave a speech in Ouagadougou, Burkina Faso, and expressed his desire during his term of office to see the temporary or permanent restitution of African cultural artefacts. The previous year Macron had declared:

> Colonization was a significant part of French history. It was a crime, it was crime against humanity, a true example of barbarism. And it is an example of this past history that we must have the courage to confront by earnestly apologizing to those toward whom we have committed these acts.[42]

Following his Ouagadougou declaration Macron commissioned a report by Felwine Sarr and Bénédicte Savoy which was published in 2018 as *The Restitution of African Cultural Heritage. Toward a New Relational Ethics*. Macron marked its publication by announcing the restitution of 26 works of art which had been requested by Benin. Macron's declarations, the report, and his subsequent action elicited "a defensive reflex and a gesture of retreat" within France with cultural institutions expressing concerns about what would happen to their collections as a consequence. French colonizers in Africa had imported cultural acquisitions and these artefacts were slowly integrated into regional and national collections. Outside of France restitution provoked mixed responses. For example, in Germany a joint open letter to Chancellor Merkel from German African diaspora organizations requesting a response to Macron's initiative received no reply.[43] In England, Sarr and Savoy accused the British Museum of behaving "like an ostrich with its head in the sand" over the return of artefacts and that the institution could not "hide any longer on the issue".[44] The Rijksmuseum in the Netherlands declared the failure to return artefacts stolen from former colonies as a disgrace and opened talks with Sri Lanka and Indonesia.[45] Guido Gryseels, the former director, of the Tervuren Museum near Brussels, declared in June 2018: "Africa was a continent that has been pillaged and plundered. We cannot continue to ignore

---

41 See Felwine Sarr and Bénédicte Savoy, *The Restitution of African Cultural Heritage. Toward a New Relational Ethics*, trans. Drew S. Burk (Paris: Ministére de la Culture, 2018), 7–14.
42 Ibid., 1–2.
43 Ibid., 15.
44 Quoted in Lanre Bakare, "British Museum has 'head in the sand' over the return of artefacts," *The Guardian*, June 22, 2019.
45 https://news.artnet.com/art-world/rijksmuseum-may-return-looted-artifacts-1487446 accessed November 2019; David Boffey, "Rijksmuseum says failure to return artefacts is 'disgrace'", *The Guardian*, March 14, 2019.

this situation and we must seek to find solutions."[46] It is clear that the restitution of cultural property cannot be seen in isolation, as an editorial in *The Guardian* newspaper stated last year:

> They must be taken together with an understanding that the imperial past is not dead but is a set of narratives that are still alive, still unresolved, and still bringing real-world consequences.[47]

In this context "to speak of restitution" is, as Sarr and Savoy conclude, "to simultaneously reopen the old colonial machine as well as the file containing the erased memories of both the Europeans and the Africans", with the Europeans having "no idea how to continue to maintain their prestigious museums" while Africans find themselves "struggling to recover the thread of an interrupted memory".[48]

Student led-movements such as *Rhodes Must Fall, Why is my curriculum white? Why isn't my professor Black?, Rhodes Must Fall Oxford,* and *Decolonising our Mind* are symptomatic of this struggle against memory and a rejection of mainstream Western epistemic knowledge in favor of diverse forms of knowledge and diverse concepts of what counts as knowledge, where "Knowledge-as-intervention-in-reality" triumphs over "Knowledge-as-a-representation-of-reality".[49] In short, decolonization is about engaging with "epistemic disobedience"[50] and accepting "other ways of being, thinking, knowing, sensing, feeling, doing and living".[51] It is a challenge to Western knowledge and its "organizing principles of progress, possession, universalism, certainty, and neutralization of differ-

---

[46] Quoted in Sarr and Savoy, *The restitution*, 16. In one section of the report headed 'A Family Affair' the authors provide some figures relating to objects from sub-Saharan Africa held by European museums: British Museum (69,000), Weltmuseum of Vienna (37,000), Musée royal de l'Afrique centrale in Tervuren Belgium (180,000), Musée du quai Branly-Jacques Chirac (70,000), and the proposed Humboldt Forum, Berlin (75,000).
[47] "Restituting objects is also a case of restituting memory," *The Guardian*, September 26, 2018.
[48] Sarr and Savoy, *The restitution*, 16.
[49] Carol Azumah Dennis. "Decolonising Education: A Pedagogic Intervention." In *Decolonising the University*, edited by Gurminder K. Bhambra, Dalia Gebrial, and Kerem Nişancıoğlu, 190–207 (London: Pluto Press, 2018), 201–202
[50] Walter D. Mignolo, "Epistemic Disobedience and the Decolonial Option: A Manifesto," *Transmodernity: Journal of Peripheral Cultural Production of the Luso-Hispanic World* 1, no. 2 (2011): 44.
[51] C.E Walsh, quoted by Dennis, "Decolonising Education," in *Decolonising the University*, ed. Bhambra et al., 199.

ence either through incorporation, erasure, or elimination."⁵² In other words, it is a challenge to those institutions in the contemporary world where the practice of preserving and producing certain types of knowledge is institutionalized, namely the Western University. As Bhambra, Gebrial, and Nişancioğlu have forcefully argued, it is difficult to turn away from the Western university as

> a key site through which colonialism – and colonial knowledge is produced, consecrated, institutionalised and naturalised. It was in the university that colonial intellectuals developed theories of racism, popularised discourses that bolstered support for colonial endeavours and provided ethical and intellectual grounds for the dispossession, oppression and domination of colonised subjects.

Universities provided colonial administrators with "the knowledge of the peoples they would rule over," and "the foundation of European higher education institutions in colonised territories itself became an infrastructure of empire, an institution and actor through which the totalising logic of domination could be extended". The formal end of empires, they conclude, did little to change this logic.⁵³ Indeed, as Robert Gildea has recently written, "the more empire appears to have declined and fallen, the more the fantasy of empire has been conjured up as a model for projecting power onto the world stage' and, in the case of Brexit Britain there is 'a nostalgia for empire'".⁵⁴

Questioning assumptions, countering omissions, inspiring debate, and disseminating new knowledge is at the center of curatorial activism as outlined above and of the project to "decolonize" the museum and art gallery, but what of the discipline of history, of history of education, and the prospect of collaborative research projects focusing on the colonial? Gildea in *Empires of the Mind* (2019) provides a concise overview of how writing "the story of empire" has changed over the last 30 years with the emergence of global and postcolonial histories and "the return of empire to public consciousness" and "passionate public debate".⁵⁵ The publication of *The Colonial Experience in Education* following the International Standing Conference for History of Education [ISCHE] in

---

52 Sharon Stein, "The Persistent Challenges of Addressing Epistemic Dominance in Higher Education: Considering the Case of Curriculum Internationalization," *Comparative Education Review* 61, no. 1 (May 2017 Supplement): 25–50.
53 Gebrial Bhambra and Nişancioğlu, "Introduction: Decolonising the University", in Bhambra et al., *Decolonising the University*, 5.
54 Robert Gildea, *Empires of the Mind. The Colonial Past and the Politics of the Present* (Cambridge: Cambridge University Press, 2019), i. See also, David Reynolds, *Island Stories. Britain and its History in the Age of Brexit* (London: William Collins, 2019).
55 Gildea, *Empires of the Mind*, 7–14.

Lisbon in 1993 was a seminal moment in our field of study even though the editors noted that the state of research into the history of colonial education was "still too incipient".[56] Depaepe's opening essay was complemented by that of his co-editor António Nóvoa who argued that future research on colonial education should include a focus on the experience of educational actors, cultural practices inside schools, the discourse of colonial education, and the redefinition of identities.[57] ISCHE returned to the theme of empire in 1999 when it addressed the issue of "Education and Ethnicity" and it was evident that researchers had responded to Novoa's agenda.[58] The theme of empire and education was the focus of another collection of papers in 2009 commissioned under the heading of "Empires Overseas and Empires at Home". Here the focus was on placing the "metropole and colony" within the same analytical frame and emphasizing how colonialism 'intersected and interacted across frontiers, creating 'Zones of Contact' and elements of interdependence and interconnectedness in social change and education".[59] This shift in focus reflects a broader shift in historical research where emerging lines of domestic resistance and dissent from the imperial project are being documented alongside genealogies of opposition to empire.[60] Given the current debates about restitution and the decolonization of Western epistemic dominance, a new collection of essays on the experience of colonial education would be timely.

However, not everything is rosy in the garden of history. A recent report, *Race, Ethnicity and Equality in UK History: A Report and Resource for Change*, published by the UK's Royal Historical Society, highlighted the racial and ethnic inequalities in the teaching and practice of History in Britain. It drew attention to the under representation of Black and Minority Ethnic (BaME) students and staff in university History departments, the substantial levels of "race-based bias and discrimination" experienced by BaME historians in UK universities, and the negative impact of narrow school and university curriculums on diversity and inclu-

---

56 Nóvoa, Depaepe, and Johanningmeier, *Colonial Experience*, 9.
57 António Nóvoa, "On History, History of Education, and History of Colonial Education," in Nóvoa et al., *Colonial Experience*, 36–52.
58 See *Education and Ethnicity*, ed. Geoffrey Sherington and Craig Campbell, *Paedagogica Historica*, Supplementrary Series, volume V11 (Gent, 2001).
59 Joyce Goodman, Gary McCulloch, and William Richardson, "'Empires overseas' and 'Empires at home': postcolonial and transnational perspectives on social change in the history of education," *Paedagogica Historica* 45, no. 6 (2009): 702–703.
60 See for example Marc Matera, *Black London: The Imperial Metropolis and Decolonization in the 20th Century* (Oakland, CA: University of California Press, 2015); Priyamvada Gopa, *Insurgent Empire. Anticolonial Resistance and British Dissent* (London: Verso, 2019).

sion.⁶¹ Maybe this is a problem unique to the British academy. Whatever the case, effecting change to enrich both academic and public understanding of the past will require substantial structural and cultural change within the discipline. Change which is essential if the partnerships with civic society mediators and communities discussed in this paper are to be sustained.

How to end this exploration of colonial experience and pedagogies of display? The African American author James Baldwin wrote that:

> History is not the past.
> It is the present.
> We carry our history with us,
> We *are* our history.
> If we pretend otherwise, we literally are criminals.⁶²

There are some autobiographical texts from the 1970s and 1990s where adults recalled the impact of the 1924 London Empire exhibition on the child they were. While Eric Pasold was "overwhelmed" by the "colourful, bustling spectacle" and "the more exotic the pavilions the more they thrilled me", Ibrahim Ismaa'il, a Somali from Cardiff, was differently overwhelmed: "It appeared to me as if the world had been made for Europeans, who had only to stretch out their hands to bring before them, as if by magic, all the products of the universe".⁶³

---

61 Hannah Atkinson, Suzanne Bardgett, Adam Budd, Margot Finn, Christopher Kissane, Sadiah Qureshi, Jonathan Saha, John Siblon, and Sujit Sivasundaram, *Race, Ethnicity and Equality in UK History: A Report and Resource for Change* (London: Royal Historical Society, 2018). The report should be read alongside *Common Cause Research. Building Research Collaborations between Universities and Black and Minority Ethnic communities*, by David Bryan, Katherine Dunleavy, Keri Facer, Charles Forsdick, Omar Khan, Mhemooda Malek, Karen Salt, and Kristy Warren (Bristol: University of Bristol and the Arts and Humanities Research Council, 2018).
62 James Baldwin, *I am Not Your* Negro, compiled and edited by Raoul Peck (London: Penguin, 2017).
63 Alexander C.T Geppert, "True Copies: time and space travels at British imperial exhibitions, 1880–1930," in *The Making of Modern Tourism*, edited by Hartmut Bergoff, Barbara Korte, Ralf Schneider, and Christopher Harvie, 223–248 (Basingstoke: Palgrave, 2002, 231).

Bibliography

Websites

https://news.artnet.com/art-world/rijksmuseum-may-return-looted-artifacts-1487446. Accessed November 12, 2019.

The Guardian. https://www.theguardian.com/commentisfree/2018/dec/26/the-guardian-view-on-the-restitution-of-cultural-property. Accessed March 7, 2021.

Secondary Sources

Anon. "Un musée sans pareil." *Tribal Art Magazine*, Special Issue 8 (2018): 12-17.

Atkinson, Hannah, Suzanne Bardgett, Adam Budd, Margot Finn, Christopher Kissane, Sadiah Qureshi, Jonathan Saha, John Siblon, and Sujit Sivasundaram. *Race, Ethnicity and Equality in UK History: A Report and Resource for Change*. London: Royal Historical Society, 2018.

Andress, David. *Cultural Dementia. How the West has Lost its History, and Risks Losing Everything Else*. London: Head of Zeus, 2018.

Bakare, Lanre. "British Museum has 'head in the sand' over the return of artefacts." *The Guardian*, June, 22, 2019.

Baldwin, James. *I am Not Your Negro*. Compiled and edited by Raoul Peck. London: Penguin, 2017.

Bhambra, Gurminder K., Dalia Gebrial, and Kerem Nişancıoğlu. "Introduction: Decolonising the University." In *Decolonising the University*, edited by Gurminder K. Bhambra, Dalia Gebrial, and Kerem Nişancıoğlu, 1–18. London: Pluto Press, 2018.

Beckstette, Sven, and Azu Nwagbogu. "Sven Beckstette and Azu Nwagbogu in Conversation." In *Hello World. Revising a Collection*. 355–359. Berlin: Hamburger Bahnhof Museum für Gegenwart, 2018.

Berger, John. "Giorgio Morandi." In *The Shape of a Pocket*, 139–146. London: Bloomsbury, 2001.

Berrebi, Sophie. *The Shape of Evidence*. Amsterdam: Valiz, 2014.

Boffey, Daniel. "Rijksmuseum says failure to return artefacts is 'disgrace.'" *The Guardian*, March 14, 2019.

Blanchard Pascal, Nicolas Bancel, Gilles Boetsch, Eric Deroo, Sandrine Lemaire, and Charles Forsdick, eds. *Human Zoos. Science and Spectacle in the Age of Colonial Empires*. Liverpool: Liverpool University Press, 2008.

Bryan, David, Katherine Dunleavy, Keri Facer, Charles Forsdick, Omar Khan, Mhemooda Malek, Karen Salt, and Kristy Warren. *Common Cause Research. Building Research Collaborations between Universities and Black and Minority Ethnic communities*. Bristol: University of Bristol and the Arts and Humanities Research Council, 2018.

Burke, Jason, and Philip Oltermann. "Germany Faces up to African Genocide." *The Guardian*, December 26, 2016.

Chamberlain, Muriel Evelyn. *The Scramble for Africa*. London: Longman, 2013.

Clendinning, Anne. "On the British Empire Exhibition, 1924–25." In BRANCH: *Britain, Representation and Nineteenth-Century History*, edited by Dino Franco Felluga, Extension of Romanticism and Victorianism on the Net. Accessed October 12, 2018. http://www.branchcollective.org.

Dennis, Carol Azumah. "Decolonising Education: A Pedagogic Intervention." In *Decolonising the University*, edited by Gurminder K. Bhambra, Dalia Gebrial, and Kerem Nişancıoğlu, 190–207. London: Pluto Press, 2018.

Depaepe, Marc. "An Agenda for the History of Colonial Education." In *The Colonial Experience in Education*, edited by António Nóvoa, Marc Depaepe, and Erwin V. Johanningmeier, *Paedagogica Historica*, Supplementary Series, 1, 15–22. Gent, 1995.

Education and Ethnicity, edited by Geoffrey Sherington and Craig Campbell, Paedagogica Historica Supplementary Series, volume V11. Gent, 2001.

Facer, Keri, and Bryony Enright. *Creating Living knowledge*. Bristol: University of Bristol, 2016.

Fielding, Michael. "Putting Hands Around the Flame: reclaiming the radical tradition in state education." *Forum* 47, no. 2–3 (2005): 1–10.

Fielding, Michael. "Afterword. Anarchism, texts and children: active conversations with the past." *Paedagogica Historica* 50, no. 4 (2014): 460–64.

Geppert, Alexander C.T. "True Copies: time and space travels at British imperial exhibitions, 1880–1930." In *The Making of Modern Tourism*, edited by Hartmut Bergoff, Barbara Korte, Ralf Schneider, and Christopher Harvie, 223–248. Basingstoke: Palgrave, 2002.

Gildea, Robert. *Empires of the Mind. The Colonial Past and the Politics of the Present*. Cambridge: Cambridge University Press, 2019.

Goodman, Joyce, Gary McCulloch, and William Richardson. "'Empires overseas' and 'Empires at home': postcolonial and transnational perspectives on social change in the history of education." *Paedagogica Historica* 45, no. 6 (2009): 702–703.

Gopa, Priyamvada. *Insurgent Empire. Anticolonial Resistance and British Dissent*. London: Verso, 2019.

Grosvenor, Ian. "Teaching the Empire: the weekly *Bulletin of Empire Study* and the British Empire Exhibition, London, 1924." In *Modelling the Future. Exhibitions and the Materiality of Education* edited by Martin Lawn, 107–128. Oxford: Symposium, 2009.

Huggler, Justin. "Germany forced to face up to 'forgotten genocide' in Africa." *The Daily Telegraph*, June 18, 2018.

Janes, Robert R., and Richard Sandell, eds. *Museum Activism*. London: Routledge, 2019.

Jordanova, Ludmilla. *History in Practice*. London: Edward Arnold, 2000.

Lawrence, G.C. ed., *Official Guide to the British Empire Exhibition*. London: Fleetway, 1925.

Leahy, Cathy, and Judith Ryan, eds. *Colony. Australia 1770–1861/Frontier Wars*. Melbourne: National Gallery of Victoria, 2018.

Matera, Marc. *Black London: The Imperial Metropolis and Decolonization in the 20th Century*. Oakland, CA: University of California Press, 2015.

Mignolo, Walter D. "Epistemic Disobedience and the Decolonial Option: A Manifesto." *Transmodernity: Journal of Peripheral Cultural Production of the Luso-Hispanic World* 1, no. 2 (2011): 44–65.

Mohanty, Chandra Talpade. *Feminisms Without Borders*. North Carolina: Duke University Press, 2003.

Morgan Philip D., and Sean Hawkins, eds. *Black Experience and the Empire.* Oxford: Oxford University Press, 2004.

Muizniek, Nils. http://www.coe.int/en/web/commissioner/-/afrophobia-europe-should-confront-this-legacy-of-colonialism-and-the-slave-trade. Accessed October 4, 2018.

Nóvoa, António. "On History, History of Education, and History of Colonial Education." In *The Colonial Experience in Education*, edited by António Nóvoa, Marc Depaepe, and Erwin V. Johanningmeier, *Paedagogica Historica*, Supplementary Series, 1, 23–61. Gent, 1995.

Orwell, George. "Toward European Unity." 1947. http//:orwell.ru/library/articles/European_Unity/english/e_teu. Accessed October 30, 2018.

Rich, Adrienne. *On Lies, Secrets and Silence.* London: W. W. Norton & Co., 1972.

Richards, Thomas. *The Imperial Archive: Knowledge and the Fantasy of Empire.* London: Verso, 1993.

Reilly, Maura. *Curatorial Activism. Towards an Ethics of Curating.* London: Thames and Hudson, 2018.

Reynolds David. *Island Stories. Britain and its History in the Age of Brexit.* London: William Collins, 2019.

Rushdie, Salman. *The Satanic Verses.* London: Vintage Books, 1998.

Sarr, Felwine, and Bénédicte Savoy. T*he Restitution of African Cultural Heritage. Toward a New Relational Ethics.* Translated by Drew S. Burk. Paris: Ministére de la Culture, 2018.

Schmidt, Dierk, *The Division of the Earth¬Tableaux on the Legal Synopses of the Berlin Africa Conference*, 2007. *Hello World. Revising a Collection.* Berlin: Hamburger Bahnhof Museum für Gegenwart, 2018.

Standard, Matthew. "'Bilan du monde pour un monde plus déshumanisé': The 1958 Brussels World's Fair and Belgian Perceptions of the Congo." *European History Quarterly* 35, no. 2 (2005): 267–298.

Stein, Sharon. "The Persistent Challenges of Addressing Epistemic Dominance in Higher Education: Considering the Case of Curriculum Internationalization." *Comparative Education Review* 61, no. 1 (May 2017 Supplement): 25–50.

Stoler, Ann. "Colonial Archives and the Arts of Governance." *Archival Science* 2 (2002): 87–109.

Tolia-Kelly, Divya P. "*Feeling* and *Being* at the (Postcolonial) Museum: Presencing the Affective Politics of 'Race' and Culture." *Sociology* 50, no. 5 (2016): 896–912.

Mathieu Zana Etambala (RMCA/UGent/KU Leuven, Belgium)
A Virtual Visit to the Renovated Royal Museum for Central Africa. Two Major Challenges: Decolonization and Africanization

Abstract: The AfricaMuseum in Tervuren was officially reopened on December 8, 2018. The renovation took more than a decade. Expectations were high because the objective of the new site planning was double: decolonization and Africanization. A visit to the renovated museum shows that in some rooms one has not got any further than cosmetic procedures and in others there is still an exotic walm hanging around. This article proposes a virtual walk through the museum halls, highlighting some missed opportunities for African historical and cultural reality to come into its own.

Keywords: Africa Museum, Renovation, Decolonization, Africanization

Introduction

In the edition of August 2, 1913, *Le Journal du Congo*, a propaganda newspaper of the Belgian Department of Colonies, mentioned that French colonial circles had insisted that they wanted the construction of a colonial museum similar to the Tervuren *Congo Museum* – later called *AfricaMuseum*. Indeed, French colonials had expressed the hope of building a *French Tervuren*. On February 16, 2019, some months after the opening of the renovated *AfricaMuseum* renamed *Royal Museum for Central Africa* (RMCA), the French journalist Philippe Dagen criticized the renovation in *Le Monde*, stating that exotic traces remained tangible in various rooms of the museum.

I enjoy city trips and in most of the cities I regularly visit, I always drop by museums. Thus, in Paris I visited the *Museum National d'Histoire Naturelle* where I learned that for a long period of time in the European past, "the expansionist

---

Note: The author wishes to thank the section editor and the anonymous reviewers of this chapter for their guidance and helpful comments. He also wishes to thank in particular Angelo Van Gorp for initial editing and translation work and Geert Thyssen for the final copy-editing of the chapter.

https://doi.org/10.1515/9783110623451-010

aims are inseparable from scientific objectives".[1] And the objectives of the European museums were, firstly, to constitute or collect, store, and preserve mineral, animal, and vegetal collections. Secondly, plants, beasts, stones etc. were classified and categorized. The exact same approach was adopted when ethnographic museums were created. Yet this archaic way of approaching human groups very easily led to all kinds of evolutionist theories. Classification and categorization were thus at the origin of racist thinking. Black people appeared in the ethnographic and anthropological studies as inferior as they were assumed to be at a lower scale of evolution. Their cultural customs and useful objects were seen as primitive.

I have had a successful career as a researcher at the RMCA, from which I retired in February 2020. I was thus not involved in the renovation project mentioned. Of course, I know that those who conceived the new exhibition had two goals: decolonization and Africanization. And the debate on what those two terms actually mean, which is sometimes a very theoretical one, is still ongoing.

I have explored the renovated RMCA several times, together with friends and colleagues. It is with the eyes of an historian, the heart of a pragmatic (West-Flemish) peasant, and the soul of an old member of Belgium's Congolese diaspora that I walked around in the renewed museal environment.

During these walks I noted down many scientific observations and reflections on the various manmade objects, photographs and paintings, press cuttings, and other documents, some of which are here presented. All these critical remarks are brought together in the present contribution. I firmly believe that some exhibited objects need new interpretations and that the organization of some rooms has not fully succeeded from a museological point of view. Now, I want to invite the reader to accompany me on a virtual visit of the RMCA.

An African Welcome. Why Not?

The former *AfricaMuseum* received a thorough facelift. The new building has been conceived of as a splendid modern architectural project. I am not an expert in architecture but I find that the new *Musée National de la RD Congo* (MNDRC), inaugurated in Kinshasa on November 23, 2020, has a more exquisite modern

---

1 Jean-François Lasnier, "Le Muséum, une histoire, des missions," *Le Muséum National d'Histoire Naturelle* (2016): 8–15.

style.² That said, with regard to its imposing architecture, Jean-Pierre Dikaka, responsible for the Educational Service of the MNRDC, told *Radio France Internationale* (RFI) that it is a modern take on the way Congolese houses, huts, and villages are built.³

African Artistic or Architectural Inspiration

Placed in the RMCA's entrance hall is a colossal wooden block coming from an extremely large tropical tree. It is sad that it was chosen not to place in this hallway for instance a panel representing the marvelous, telling mural paintings of Ekibondo, a Bangba-Mangbetu village in the Niangara territory of the Congolese Uele region, where Ekibondo's Mfumu Palata (ca. 1870–1952), a chief awarded a medal by the colonial administration, encouraged his people to paint the walls of their huts.⁴ Following the funerals of this chief who died on September 26, 1952, his village was abandoned and the huts collapsed.⁵

Another panel could have been dedicated to the beautiful court of justice for natives of Niangara in Upper Uele. In colonial propaganda booklets a visit to "the cemetery of the pioneers and the former bureau of the territory which constitutes one of the vestiges of the beginning of the occupation" was promoted rather than this indigenous tribunal.⁶ Niangara was a very important colonial commercial and industrial center during the colonial period, where several monuments have been erected to honor Europeans. On September 9, 1938, a monument was inaugurated for the Italian explorer Giovanni Miani (1810–1872), the first European to point out the existence of ethnic groups as the Ababua, the Makere, and the Ambarambo and to mention streams like the Tele, the Poko, and the Makongo as tributaries of the Bomokandi river in the Uele region. He died in the village of Nangazizi in the territory of the Mangbetu chief Mbunza (ca. 1830–1875).⁷ Still

---

2 André-Bernard Ergo, "Musées du Congo," *Mémoires du Congo, du Rwanda et du Burundi* 52 (2019): 14–16; Fernand Hessel, "Nouveau Musée National du Congo," *Mémoires du Congo, du Rwanda et du Burundi* 52 (2019): 17–19.
3 Anonymous, "RFI," *Le Musée national inauguré à Kinshasa* (2019), November 19.
4 Benoît Verhaegen, "Ekibondo," *Biographie Belge d'Outre-Mer* Brussels (1977): 135–137; Nzungu Vincke. *La céramique Bakongo* (Brussels: Galérie Congo, 2002).
5 Andry Scohy, *L'Uele secret* (Brussel: Office International de Librairie – La Librairie Congolaise: 1955).
6 Anonymous, *Guide du voyageur au Congo Belge et au Ruanda-Urundi* (Brussels, 1951), 583.
7 Léon Guebels, "Miani Giovanni," *Biographie Coloniale Belge* 1 (1948): 678–685; Marthe Coosemans, "Mbunza," *Biographie Coloniale Belge* 1 (1948): 672–674.

in Niangara the then colonial authorities also intended to immortalize by means of a monument Louis Chaltin (1857–1933), a Belgian lieutenant who played a prominent role in the conquest of the Uele country and the occupation of the Lado Enclave (Sudan).[8]

The Penetration in the Dark Continent

An impressive *prahu* (canoe) welcomes visitors to the RMCA. The renovators' rationale for this is fairly simple: it has to make visitors relate to the Polish-British writer Joseph Conrad (Jozef Teodor Konrad Korzeniowski, 1857–1924), who wrote in his *Heart of Darkness* (1899): "And the canoe leads us to the museum by the Congo river."[9] Maybe Conrad echoed a sense of anticipation of most explorers had who penetrated the tropical Congo basin at the end of the nineteenth century. However, here we must query our understanding. The *prahu* has to provoke the feeling of a heroic adventure through wild nature inhabited by barbarian peoples. The idea of Africa as a *terra incognita* is not far away. Henry Morton Stanley (1841–1904), who was the last great white explorer in the heart of Africa entitled his books *Through the Dark Continent* (1878) and *In Darkest Africa* (1890). Yet, after the period of explorations came that of (military) conquest and occupation of large territories on behalf of the homeland or king.

The Congolese canoe, considered as one of the showpieces of the RMCA, arrived on January 3, 1958 as an ethnographic object. It is 22.5 meters long, at different points more than one meter wide, and it weighs approximatively 3.5 tons. At both extremities, one can observe two hollows wherein outboard motors were attached for canoeing. It was cut from sipo-wood (entandrophragma) by inhabitants of Ubundu. This exceptional acquisition was described as a large canoe resembling the old war vessels of the Walengola ethnic group similar to those then still used by fishermen of the Wagenia population.[10]

The visitor is informed that King Leopold III used this indigenous vessel, which is why hollows were carved out at its extremities. Leopold III did indeed use it on Saturday March 30, 1957 during his journey in Congo, to cross the Congo river in Stanleyville, from the left to the right bank, on which occasion a motor

---

[8] L. Lotar and M. Coosemans, "Chaltin Louis," *Biographie Coloniale Belge* 1 (1948): 229–232 (first names unknown).

[9] Matthias De Groof, "Décolonialisme ou les palimpsestes de l'AfricaMuseum," *L'Art Même* 77 (2019): 26–27.

[10] Anonymous, "Sites, Monuments, Arts indigènes, Archives et Découvertes historiques – Congo Belge," *Touring Club du Congo Belge* 11 (November 30, 1958): 41–42.

was attached to the boat.¹¹ But this is a very Eurocentric account of this Congolese *prahu*, which also needs to be seen from an African viewpoint.

Without a doubt, the *prahu* is not regarded as a romantic artefact in the collective memory of the Walengola. This people will never forget how they were forced for decades to transport materials for the conqueror and occupier. They did not at all enjoy this carrier service. Moreover, until 1913 the *Force Publique* or Colonial Army was entitled to claim local canoes without paying for their military expeditions.

The *prahu* stands within an extremely empty space. The whole, I think, could be transformed in a learning module on mobility. In this corridor, a specimen of *tipoyes* and *pousse-pousses* made by Congolese artists during colonial and the postcolonial times could be exhibited. A *tipoye*, like a sedan chair, is only represented in photographs because, contrary to the canoe, an indigenous exemplar in real life scale was never brought to the RMCA. Even a sedan chair sculptured in bronze or alloy was never acquired.

Sedan chairs are nonetheless significant for the presentation of colonial society since the white colonizer imposed a system of both juxtaposition and superposition which respectively signified segregation and domination. The white dominating minority were assumed superior to the black dominated majority, as is clear from the fact that black porters had to carry white men in such chairs or *tipoyes* for their travels.¹²

Another means of transport was the *pousse-pousse*. It was introduced in Congo after the World Exhibition of Brussels of 1958, where hundreds of Congolese visitors discovered it. After the World Exhibition, the *pousse-pousse* appeared in the streets of Kinshasa. But it was another type which was constructed without a motor and with a kind of bin in the front serving to transport goods instead of passengers.

The reality is that the colonizers introduced new modes of transport in Africa. During colonial domination, the Congolese were introduced to animals and objects previously unknown to them, for instance, in the Uele regions horses and donkeys imported from Sudan (the Nile region) and in Lower Congo by the dominating colonial authorities. So it was that lieutenant Oscar Michaux (1860–1918), who first arrived in Boma on January 6, 1890, ironically wrote in

---

11 Léopold III, *Carnets de voyages 1919–1983* (Brussels: Racine, 2004), 299.
12 Mathieu Zana Etambala, "Le tipoye en Afrique noire," *Carnets de Sciences Humaines* 6 (2011): 7–15 and 7 (2012): 14–22.

his diary about him being made responsible for the royal cavalry of the Colonial Army: he had to command and keep an eye on 17 donkeys and mules.[13]

In his travel story, Constant De Deken (1852–1896), a Belgian missionary explorer, tells how surprised the people of a village at the bank of the Kasaï-river were when they saw a horse transported in his boat:

> While buying provisions, some negroes noticed the horse of the inspector that stood on the steerage. Astounded, they called the others and grabbed by the arms those who were very scared. A general cry of astonishment, a droning clapping, clattering with the lips, so great was their amazement at this large animal eating at the manger. Some thought it was an elephant or a hippopotamus; others declared it was a big European goat the Europeans wanted for diner. Nobody realized it should be ridden because horses, oxen and donkeys were totally unknown in the region. But the most surprising for the poor souls was the tail of the beast. They thought it was something artificial, an ornament that was stitched to it. To show their error, I took the tail with both hands and began to pull strongly. Then the screeching crowd roared with laughter; I invited them to pull the tail as well, but nobody dared to approach the horse.[14]

It is not surprising at all, then, that horses appeared in the art of the peoples in Lower Congo or in the Kasaï. During ethnographic expeditions in the Mayombe region organized by the National Museum of Zaïre in the years 1974–76, some equestrian statues were acquired. These *Mintadi* or *Bitumba* were in soapstone, steatitis or laterite stone and represented couples of cavalrymen (men and women seated as Amazones). One statue represents a notable riding an ox.[15] Horsemen figures, representing people with prestige, can even be found in the funeral ceramics which were popular in some communities in Lower Congo. All these dignitaries riding a horse were seen by the common people as socially Europeanized.[16]

The Rejection of Colonial Art

Upon leaving the long corridor, one finds exhibited on the wall upstairs a painting by the artist Cheri Samba. The canvas dates from June 2002 and is titled *Réorganisation du Musée Royal de l'Afrique Centrale*. In a long comment written in

---

13 Oscar Michau, *Au Congo : carnet de campagne* (Namur: Librairie Dupagne-Counet, 1913), 46; René Cambier, "Michaux Oscar," *Biographie Coloniale Belge* 1 (1948): 685–693.
14 Constant De Deken, *Twee jaar in Congo* (Antwerpen: Uitgeverij De Vlijt, 1952), 83–84.
15 A. Duriaux and H. Bouraly, *Mintadi – Bitumba, témoins de la tradition Bas-Congo (catalogus)*. Kinshasa, s.d. (first names unknown).
16 Nzungu Vincke, *La céramique Bakongo* (Brussels: Galérie Congo, 2002).

Lingala, and translated in French, we learn that the work is about a RMCA's reorganization. Samba presents a scene alongside the stairs, which in earlier times formed the entrance to the museum, featuring a perhaps-tropical forest in the background. Two groups of people, a Congolese and a Belgian one, pull a rope tied around a plasterwork representing a Leopard man or *Aniota*, with the Congolese wanting to pull it outside while the Belgians try to keep it inside and the director of the museum watches the event with desperation. Cheri Samba provided the following comment upon finishing it: "The vision and the perspectives had to be changed. A critical light had to be cast on the works which crystallize the prejudices, the sculptures principally serving a colonial ideology."[17] The message is clear: a rejection of colonial art of the museum, which should be substituted by African art!

The Repository

The visitor enters in a room containing many *oeuvres* which in earlier times served to promote colonialism. This is an effort to neutralize the colonial character of the RMCA. Indeed, it must be interpreted as an act more specifically to decolonize busts and sculptures henceforth considered as representing the wildness, ferocity, and murderous character of the Congolese and their societies. I have to admit that I feel rather sad upon arriving in this "demolition room": the place where old colonial busts and sculptures are kept. In my opinion, colonial art should be respected and deserves a better destiny than to be humped together in an iconoclastic way. It should be studied by art historians.

One of the most impressive works which is sheltered here is the *Aniota* or Leopard men work sculpted by Paul Wissaert (1885–1972). For a long time it was considered as a masterpiece of colonial art, occupying a very central place in the museum. *Aniota* are men who constituted an secret ritual association. Other mysterious groups were formed by *Elephant* or *Crocodile* men.[18]

Stored also in this room are sculptures made by Herbert Ward (1863–1919), an Englishman who worked as a colonial agent and officer in Congo where he first arrived in 1884. After his colonial career, he became a collector, writer, painter, and sculptor. He wrote books with such titles as *Five Years with the Congo*

---

17 Chantal Tombu, *La peinture populaire en héritage: Hommage de JP Mika aux Bula Matari* (Weyrich: Africa Editions, 2018), 70–71.
18 Mathieu Zana Etambala, "Een bezoek aan het oude Museum van Belgisch Congo te Tervuren," *Hermes* March (2019): 30–33.

Cannibals (1890), today considered humiliating for the Africans.[19] Upon his return to Europe, Ward went to live in Paris. He left many photographs, croquis drawings of native types, and objects like musical instruments, weapons, masks, and figures. He was an artist who produced numerous anthropological heads of Africans and sculptures with which he wanted to identify tribes, such as the *Indigène Aruimi – Souvenir de voyage de l'expédition Stanley, 1900–1902* (Emin Pacha relief expedition, Aruwimi Native) and the *Jeune Fille Ba-Kongo*, ca. 1902 (Young Mukongo Girl). The two sculptures, which are in possession of the Musée d'Orsay, were shown in 2019 at the exposition *Le modèle noir: de Géricault à Matisse* in Paris, for they teach visitors a lot about the anthropological thinking of Western voyagers and people at the turn of the nineteenth and twentieth century.[20] Curiously, Ward's sculptures are in no way different from those made by Congolese craftsmen and subsequent artists. Under the influence of European art, though, the canon or rule of proportions changed. In traditional African art, the canon was 1/3, which meant an exaggeration of the limbs (*membrofocalism*), while the European was 1/7. The Congolese craftsmen adopted the white mode of sculpting, but they did not baptize their own works with negative names such as "a cannibal".[21]

This is about colonial heritage, which is always varied, as much so in Belgium as in other former colonizing states. Streets were given colonial names and colonial monuments, and statues are scattered throughout the Belgian urban landscape. Colonization had an influence on art through paintings, sculptures, and so on. Of course, art can be fleeting but it would be a shame if all colonial statues, sculptures, paintings, busts etc. were demolished, because art historians can help to interpret scientifically representations of the colonized populations, and related European stereotypes about primitive and backward African peoples remain vivid today.

Sometimes there is confusion about the colonial aspects of a monument. That is the case with the statue of King Leopold II at the Throne Place in Brussels. The idea for the erection of this monument was conceived immediately after the death of Leopold II on December 17, 1909. But the execution of the project kept Belgians and Congolese waiting for a long time. The massive work of Thomas Vinçotte (1850–1925) was inaugurated on November 15, 1926, the date of

---

19 Jean-Marc Jadot, "Ward Herbert," *Biographie Coloniale Belge* 1 (1948): 956–961.
20 Anonymous, *Le modèle noir: de Géricault à Matisse* (Paris: Éditions Musée d'Orsay/Flammarion, 2019).
21 Pamphile Mabiala Mantuba-Ngoma, "Bula Matari: une création artistique dans Congo colonial," in *La mémoire du Congo. Le temps colonial*, edited by Jean-Luc Vellut (Tervuren: AfricaTervuren-Snoeck, 2005), 89.

Leopold II's patron feast. In the inscription, *Leopoldo II – Regi Belgarum – Patria amor*, is no no reference to the Belgian-Congo, but it was casted by the *Compagnie des Bronzes* of Brussels with cupper and tin imported from Congo and offered by the *Union Minière du Haut-Katanga* (UMHK). The stones of the pedestal were furnished by the *Carrières de Merbes-Sprimont*.[22] More interesting, however, is the reason why Vinçotte made an equestrian statue:

> The horse is the real pedestal of the royal monument. The image of the King on a horse was after all familiar to the inhabitants of Brussels who for so many years had seen him ride a horse each day along the boulevards of the capital.[23]

So, the statue on the Throne Place does not bear a colonial hallmark. The representation of Leopold II on a horse has nothing to do with the way the Congolese saw their Sovereign. But a copy of this monument was inaugurated by King Albert I in Léopoldville (Kinshasa) on July 1, 1928.[24] In the eyes of the Congolese, this monument, a symbol of Belgian domination, was strange; it was not understandable. Like other colonial monuments, it disappeared from the urban landscape of Kinshasa in 1972. There are only a few pictures of the demolishing of colonial statues in Congo.

The Acquisitions of the RMCA

The aim of this section is to show by means of some examples how the RMCA acquired its collections. It goes without saying that Henry Morton Stanley's is very important. Stanley did not obtain his African craftwork by theft; his expedition material was obtained in accordance with official regulations. In the same room as the one devoted to Stanley are also shown the modern Congolese paintings related to the Canadian professor Bogumil Jewsiewick, who worked in Congo. These are works Congolese painters produced on Jewsiewick's request, with him often presenting to them the topics to be painted.[25]

---

22 Edouard Carton de Wiart, "L'histoire du monument de Léopold II à Bruxelles et à Léopoldville," *Les Cahiers Léopoldiens* 4 (1959): 133–140.
23 Ibid., 135.
24 Whyms, *Léopoldville. Son histoire 1881–1956* (Brussels: Office de Publicité, 1956), 104 (first name unknown).
25 See Bogumil Jewsiewick, *Art pictural zaïrois* (Septentrion: Celat, 1992); and Bogumil Jewsiewicki, *A Congo Chronicle: Patrice Lumumba in Urban Art* (New York: Museum for African Art, 1999).

For this room, I wish to stress the different ways objects found their way to the RMCA and suggest three categories through which visitors might critically view it: the looted craftwork; the collections of ethnographic expedition; and the collector's items sent to the museum by colonial agents and missionaries.

The Looted Craftwork

The collection of Commander Charles Lemaire (1863–1925), considered one of the prototypes of white colonial officers, is very interesting. After having headed the Equator district, Lemaire accepted two important missions conceived by Leopold II: one in 1898, to the Katanga, and another in 1902, to the Bahr-el-Ghazal. Lemaire in 1920 was to be appointed Director of the Antwerp Colonial High School by his friend and Minister of the Colonies Louis Franck.[26]

Yet Commander Lemaire was an awful death machine. What he meant by pacification was really a brutal form of subjection of villagers. What he called *palavre* was in fact war. He undertook 13 punitive expeditions which he recorded in detail in his journal. All that which Lemaire gathered and which is now displayed in the RMCA was loot resulting from cruel colonial warfare against indigenous populations.

A Luba mask is lacking in this room. It is considered by Julien Volper as an emblematic mask and a great icon of the museum. This mask, pictured on postcards, national stamps, and posters, was stolen by an officer of the *Force Publique*, Oscar Michaux (1860–1918).[27] It belonged to the loot resulting from a village attack in 1896.

But I want to add another controversial artefact, the statue of Lusinga Tumbwe, which represents an ancestor likewise named Lusinga. It was captured in 1884 as part of a military attack coordinated by Emile Storms against the fighters of chief Lusinga. Storms himself did not participate in the fighting, but writes the following about it in his diary:

> The first shot fired is destined for Lusinga who falls, mortally wounded. He says he is dying but, as the last syllable expires on his lips, his head is severed, which is carried away on a spear while the general attack occurs in the village. It is an indescribable jumble. Most of the *Rougas-Rougas* of Lusinga seeing their *Mtémi* killed do not even try to defend their homes, others defend themselves on the spot. Fire breaks out at all points in the village, everything that is still free seeks to save itself. Three other villages suffer the same fate.

---

[26] Norbert Laude, "Lemaire Charles," *Biographie Coloniale Belge* 2 (1951): 603–608.
[27] René Cambier, "Michaux Oscar," *Biographie Coloniale Belge* 1 (1948): 685–693.

Around noon, there is no more of the full power of Lusinga than four heaps of ash. Large quantities of food fell into the hands of my warriors and a meal is taken on the battlefield itself, the costs of which are provided by the body of the vanquished. Fifty to 60 men died on the battlefield and 125 people fell into our hands. Everything that escaped the flames, became the spoils of our warrior.

Storms' men recovered Lusinga's head, his skull ending up in the collections of the Royal Institute of Natural Sciences in Brussels.

The Ethnographic Mission of Hutereau

After a career of several years in Congo, working mostly in the Uele-region but also a little in the Lower Congo and Equator regions following his arrival in 1896, Captain Armand Hutereau (1875–1914) returned to Brussels in September 1909.[28] In collaboration with Baron de Haulleville, the director of the former Congo Museum, and Maes, an ethnologist, he published a study about the familial and legal customs of the Congolese populations.

In December 1910, he is attached to the Ministry of Colony and charged with a mission of ethnographic studies in regions of the Uele and Ubanghi river. Hutereau left Belgium on February 25, 1911. According to the report he made for the Ministry of Colonies, the actual ethnographic expedition began on May 16, 1911 in Ibembo, on the Itimbiri River in Lower Uele, and ended in Dongo on April 4, 1913 in the vicinity of Libenge, located on the Ubangi river. Back in Belgium, Hutereau published the *Histoire des peuplades de l'Uele et de l'Ubangi*, a book which contains numerous interesting pictures. It is the first book in the series of *Bibliothèque-Congo* under the direction of Victor Denyn and Edouard De Jonghe, both working at the Department of Colony.

The Assistance of Congolese

In one of the display cases, one finds the *Dictionnaire français-lomongo* (Lonkundo) edited in 1952 in the *Annales du Musée royal du Congo belge* by Father Gustaaf Hulstaert (1900–1990), who was later to publish in the *Académie Royale des*

---

28 Armand Engels, "Hutereau Joseph-Armand," *Biographie Coloniale Belge* 3 (1952): 461–463.

Sciences d'Outre-Mer's *Contes Mongo* (1965) and *Fables Mongo* (1970), respectively, and by 1972 had authored 245 articles and books.[29]

I do not believe it would be good to reject and remove this book. However, a colonial museum that aims to Africanize should present, not anonymously but nominatively, the Congolese, without whom it was not possible to compose grammars and dictionaries. The employees of the missions. Another Congolese worth mentioning here is Donzwau M.D. Nlemvo (ca. 1871–1938). In 1978, a biography devoted to Nlemvo – who assisted at W. Holman Bentley's protestant missionary (1855–1905) – was submitted by Father François Bontinck to the edition of one of the best Kikongo dictionaries.[30] He wrote:

> Among Africans who contributed greatly (...) to the preservation of their *Donzwau Nlemvo* people, a *Mukongo* originated from Mbanza Kongo (Angola) doubtlessly has a place of honour."[31]

Since 1882 Nlemvo had been a devoted servant and friend to Bentley, accompanying him to England on several occasions for the publication of a dictionary, a grammar, and a Kikongo bible translation. The presence of Nlemvo and other assistants who deserve to be showcased would help to Africanize this room. Where are the names and portraits of the auxiliaries of the missionaries?

The Individualistic African art

Like other colonizers, Belgian anthropologists of the time long swore by studies of pure tribal art productions. From their point of view, native artists and craftsmen were making traditional household articles and producing ancestral rituals and religious objects. However, several of them quickly became influenced by things brought into their communities from Europe; moreover, white people were sometimes the object of their art productions.

---

[29] Jean Jacobs, "Gustaaf Hulstaert," *Bulletin Séance Académie royale des Sciences d'Outre-Mer* 44 (1998): 77–89.
[30] Lacroix, "Bentley W. Holman," *Biographie Coloniale Belge* 1 (1948): 115–120 (first name unknown).
[31] François Bontinck, "Donzwau M.D. Nlemvo (c. 1871–1938) et la Bible Kikongo," *Revue Africaine de Théologie* 2 (1978): 5–32.

The Bula Matadi

The colonial policy of King Leopold II, and later the Belgian state, was one of indirect rule. It was said in colonial propaganda that this was dictated by respect for the indigenous cultures. Yet in reality, a kind of ethnocracy was inaugurated, obsessed with the classification of ethnic groups. Great effort was put into creating local chieftains or territorial communities governed by chiefs who accepted the Belgian colonial authority. These were called the *mfumu mpalata* or *chefs médaillés*, their medals being clear proof of their communities' subjection.

White domination was based on military superiority. Europeans could conquer and occupy African territories thanks to firearms against which Africans could only use poisoned arrows. Hence, the colonizers were often sculpted carrying guns or rifles, with the missionaries being recognizable by their long beards, clerical garbs, and sometimes bibles held in their hands.

While reproducing the white man and his universe, African artists tried to make visible and tangible the views the dominated held of the dominant. In several cases, the collaborators or auxiliaries of colonizers and missionaries were also represented in sculptures, and these also belong to the category of settler statues which in Congo are called *Bula Matadi*.[32]

This art should receive special attention in the RMCA. It proves that African art is not fixed in its own ancestral and traditional subjects. It too has been subject to change over the years and decades, having been influenced, for example, by Western mastery over African society.

Other Expressions of the Colonial Situation

In Kinshasa I recently found two anthropomorphically shaped pipes. The first, a wooden one, is clearly a female figure. The mouth of the pipe is a piece of bone (of a goat or cow) which is hollowed out and on which a human face is engraved. In the thick and hollow belly, another bone with a human face is inserted. I am sure the artist who sculpted this pipe was inspired by a European pipe model.

---

[32] Werewere Liking, *Statues colons* (Abidjan: Les Nouvelles Éditions Africaines, 1987); Eliane Girard and Brigitte Kernel, *Colons: statuettes habillées d'Afrique de l'Ouest* (Éditions Syros alternative: Paris, 1993); Pamphile Mabiala Mantuba-Ngoma, "Bula Matari: une création artistique dans Congo colonial," in *La mémoire du Congo. Le temps colonial*, edited by Jean-Luc Vellut (Tervuren: AfricaTervuren-Snoeck, 2005), 171–172, and Mathieu Zana Etambala, "À propos d'une statue colon: le président Joseph Kasa-Vubu (1960–1965), l'héritier des anciens Rois Kongo ou du Roi Baudouin?" *Museum Dynasticum* 26 (2015): 45–59.

The second pipe, made in stone, also has a man-like shape. The stem of the pipe, in which a reed stalk is inserted for smoking, resembles a penis shaped as a big European cannon. Guns in colonial times were mostly associated with the power of white colonizers. Perhaps here it symbolizes libido or sexual vigor? When looking at the head of the male figure, one can see how he sticks out his tongue. I am not an art historian, but I suspect it represents a man taking drugs. It is possible, I think, the artist wanted to express two sociological issues characterizing life in the indigenous cities of Léopoldville in the forties and fifties of the past century: prostitution and drug abuse.

In November 1958, on the eve of the great wave of independence of African countries, the review *Touring Club du Congo Belge* reproduced an article on the growth of a new genre of African art. In it, Vaudiau declared traditional black art in decline, unable to regenerate itself, stripped of myths and beliefs at its core. In contrast, he praised the initiative of French artist Pierre Lods, who had been a soldier in an earlier life and come to found the Atelier de Poto-Poto (Brazzaville) in 1951. A year later, that establishment became a successful *École de Peinture*. Vaudiau was convinced that there was nothing more viable for the future than a "negro art" that was desacralized and conserved its most original faculties of expression while adopting European techniques and materials deemed more suitable and resistant and varied respectively.[33]

The inspiration was left completely free, and each African artist developed their own style of sculptures in ivory and wood with incrustations of maroquinerie and was believed to be able to produce real masterpieces. Ceramists and potters had the opportunity to research new shapes. Following Vaudiau, African artists were living a period that saw the future of African art being at stake. One must admit, he wrote, that traditional art had as many chances, if not more, to continue to perish slowly while faced with a Europe at times badly understood as did the best plastic traditions to which the contrary applied. Until then European ethnographic museums had no or little interest for this new African individualistic artistic plastic art. Yet, that does not mean that Africans' ways of feeling and creating were totally Europeanized. The idea existed that a restitution of African cultural treasures could inspire new-born African artists:

> Henceforth, should one aspire to return to Africa of all these treasures which our collectors have foolishly removed? Numerous black intellectuals have not actually failed to underline this compelling necessity for African museums (...). It is but all too right to finally see the Africans getting back their masterpieces. However, henceforth, they have to take care of this

---

[33] M Vaudiau, "À propos de la naissance d'un art individualiste africain," *Touring Club du Congo Belge* 11 (November 30, 1958): 5–15 (first name unknown).

wicked *museomania* – no doubt one of the most contestable finds (*trouvailles*) of our nineteenth century and a disease we are not entirely cured of. Copying Europe, the great drama of the last half century, or the art of the ancestors they no longer understand – one must recognize that these were two imitations that are equal. The [artist's] consciousness of his dignity as a creator of art – equal to all other creators, no matter the power of the country to which they belong – has to be restored ...[34]

Congolese painting is a very recent phenomenon, people generally think. However, in a book published on the occasion of an exhibition organized on the occasion of the eightieth anniversary of the *Belgolaise* bank in 1989, it is nevertheless pointed out that before the arrival of Europeans in certain Congolese villages, residents used to employ the walls of their huts to paint with historical scenes. Yet, because this did not happen on durable materials such as brick walls but on wood and clay, the paintings disappeared very quickly.[35] The RMCA has beautiful collections of paintings that were already made in the thirties of the last century. In my opinion, these are insufficiently exposed in the exhibition.

The Memorial Room

One room, the memorial room, is still very controversial. On one side of this room, the 1508 names of Belgians who died in Congo between 1876 and 1908 are engraved on the wall. It is mentioned in beautiful writing and with allegories that these heroes and patriots died in honor of their country. In the same space are featured some display cases filled with trophies obtained by the *Force Publique* during the nineteenth century Arab Campaign.[36] A visible place is reserved for a bust of Leopold II, the founding father of Congo Free State. Since several years, a wide-ramping movement has emerged in favor of removing the statues of Leopold II from the Belgian landscape. In the RMCA, Leopold II's bust has been removed from the memory hall and placed between said show cases. The bust is now put in a dark display window, together with elephant tusks. Leopold II can easily be associated with ivory and rubber, as he is considered one

---

34 M. Vaudiau, "À propos de la naissance d'un art individualiste africain," *Touring Club du Congo Belge* 11 (November 30, 1958): 5–15.
35 Joseph-Aurélien Cornet, Rémi De Cnodder, and Ivan Dierickx, *60 Ans de peinture au Zaïre* (Les Éditeurs d'Art Associés: Brussels, 1989).
36 See Paul Ceulemans, *La question arabe et le Congo (1883–1892)* (Brussels: Académie Royal des Sciences Coloniales, 1959); Philippe Marechal, *De 'Arabische' campagne in het Maniema-gebied (1892–1894): situering binnen het kolonisatieproces in de onafhankelijke Kongostaat* (Tervuren: Royal Museum for Central Africa, 1992).

of the greatest rubber and ivory magnates of his time. The Congolese, suffering from forced labor and huge rubber taxes, were the victims of horrible atrocities.

The Congolese diaspora strongly protests against the memorial room, as they wanted also the black victims of colonial violence to be remembered.

Belgian colonial historiography comprises different writings glorifying Belgian presence in Congo. As far back as the 1920s and 30s, some authors presented Belgium as a colonial empire.[37] *Congo terre d'héroïsme* and *Trois chapitres de l'épopée congolaise* are titles of books written by a certain Albert François in 1948 and 1949 respectively. Most chapters in the latter work are about *Les conquérants à l'oeuvre, Les rassembleurs de terres, La conquête des frontières, La Campagne Arabe, La Campagne Madhiste, La Campagne du Lomami, La Campagne des Grands Lacs, La Campagne du Katanga, La Campagne de l'Uele, Expédition contre Bokoyo, Campagne contre les Budjas*, etc. Such colonial war chronicles produced representations of the Belgians as winners, victors, conquerors.

It should be noted that at the time Belgians considered anybody who went to Congo a hero. That colonial conviction has to be fully decolonized. Moral thinking has developed since the end of the nineteenth and beginning of the twentieth century. Generalizing about all Belgians who died in Congo being patriots and heroes perhaps was possible in former times but no longer today. Lieutenant Jean Bollen for instance, killed on August 5, 1895 at Kayeye, in the Kasaï region, during a battle against revolting Congolese soldiers, at the beginning of 1895 had murdered tens of Kuba chiefs to avenge the death of lieutenant Gustave Fish by a Kuba poisoned arrow. Another example is that of Lieutenant Willem Van Kerckhoven, known to be one of the most terrible rapists, plunderers, and killers in the history of the Congo Independent State.[38]

It was decided to project artistically the names of the Congolese who died in Belgium during different World Exhibitions. Why did one not do this with the Congolese who were victims of colonial violence in Congo? Why did one not arrange another hall with photographs of Congolese imprisoned, beaten to death, hanged or executed by a firing squad? A good place to show such pictures would have been the room with portraits of Mobutu, Kasa-Vubu, and other renowned Congolese. A picture of Isidore Bakanja here is lacking. This Congolese in early 1909 had been beaten with a *chicote* (whip) containing nails by the commercial agent Van Cauter of the *Société Anonyme Belge*. Bakanja died of his injuries in July that year. The judicial inquiry was a mockery, and Van Cauter could

---

37 Pierre Daye, *L'empire colonial belge* (Brussels: Berger-Levrault, 1923).
38 A. Lacroix, "Croes Jean," *Biographie Coloniale Belge* 2 (1951): 206–207 (first name unknown); A. Lacroix, "Bollen Jean," *Biographie Coloniale Belge* 1 (1948): 141–142 (first name unknown); and René Cambier, "Van Kerckhoven Guillaume," *Biographie Coloniale Belge* 1 (1948): 566–573.

leave the colony a free man. Bakanja was beatificated by pope John-Paul II in 1991, recognizing him as one of numerous victims of colonial violence, but nowhere in the RMCA can visitors see an image of him.[39]

The History Room: The Belgian Human Rights Activists

To me, many important adjustments seem necessary to the history room. That is why I would like to present my observations in two paragraphs. Some attention is paid to a report by the British Consul Roger Casement at the basis of the *Congo Reform Association*, inaugurated by Edmund Dene Morel in 1904. This anti-Congolese campaign was to force Leopold II to surrender his African territory to Belgium in 1908.[40]

The point I want to make here is that in Belgium too, personalities dared to openly criticize the Congolese regime of Leopold II. They took up the defense of the Congolese people and may thus be considered human rights activists. In my view, they should be considered heroes who deserve a place not only in Belgian history manuals but also Congolese ones. I choose here to focus on three such persons: Arthur Vermeersch, Emile Vandervelde, and Stanislas Lefranc.

Father Arthur Vermeersch

Jesuit father Arthur Vermeersch (1858–1936) in 1906 published *La question congolaise*, which trashed Leopold II's colonial regime. The moral theologian was much sharper in his criticisms than Félicien Cattier, a professor at the ULB, who had vetted the king's Congo policy shortly before Vermeersch did. Father Vermeersch's point of view did not please Belgian Catholics, among whom was the new Archbishop Mercier. Catholic journals also refused to promote this book. Vermeersch did not avoid public debates about Leopold's Congo politics. He was really critical, even when faced by Catholic ministers, rabid royal-

---

39 Daniël Vangroenweghe, *Bakanja Isidore: Martyr du Zaïre, battu à mort par un Blanc, béatifié par Jean-Paul II* (Brussels: Éditions Didier Hatier, 1989).
40 Anonymous, "Le Rapport Casement (rapport de R. Casement, consul britannique, sur son voyage dans le Haut-Congo, 1903)," *Enquêtes et Documents d'Histoire Africaine* 6 (1985): 56– 120; Roger Louis and Jean Stengers, *Morel's History of the Congo Reform Movement* (Oxford: Clarendon Press, 1968).

ists, and convinced colonials. At a conference he held in the spring of 1908, he even mocked their ignorance about the traditions and the natural rights of the inland African populations; Leopold II's land and concession policies were taken to pieces by Father Vermeersch. In 1913 he travelled extensively through the Belgian Congo, on which occasion he also visited the British protectorates in East Africa and the Portuguese colony. His travel journal is a wonderful source of information about the early years of the Belgian colony. Unfortunately, he was unable to publish it because the "Great War" erupted, preventing him from doing so.

Emile Vandervelde

In a similar vein, socialist leader Emile Vandervelde (1866–1938) in the July 1907 edition of *La Société Nouvelle* published an article, *La Belgique et le Congo léopoldien*, in which Leopold II was presented as one of the biggest capitalists of Europe. He also declared that "the chore of rubber inevitably led to innumerable abuses and that "our concern must be to help, as effectively as possible, the natives oppressed by the Sovereign of Congo."[41]

Vandervelde made two voyages to Congo. In July 1908, he went there for several months and he published his travel story in 1909. In 1910 he returned to Belgian Congo as a lawyer to defend the Presbyterian missionaries in their conflict with *La Compagnie du Kasai*.[42]

The Colonial Judge Stanislas Lefranc

Stanislas Lefranc, born in Liège, was a judge in Congo from February 1, 1901 to September 25, 1907, when he resigned. He was in attendance in Boma, Equator, Stanley Pool, and Niangara in the Uele-region, and between 1908 and 1910 he published three very critical booklets on *Le Régime Congolais*. In the first he describes himself as a magistrate to the land of rubber, and the Congo Free State as the "Negro State" where martyr populations live. He considered the state and commercial agents as greedy thieves. Magistrate Stanislas Lefranc's voice is of special significance because he was a privileged witness of the oppression and

---

[41] Emile Vandervelde, "La Belgique et le Congo Léopoldien," *La Société Nouvelle* 1 (1907): 54–59.
[42] Emile Vandervelde, *Les derniers jours de l'État du Congo, journal de voyage* (Brussels: Édition de la Société Nouvelle, 1909).

ill-treatment of the Congolese populations. Together with Father Vermeersch and Emile Vandervelde, he should be praised as a human rights activist. Another brave figure in the Congo debate of that time was the progressive liberal Georges Lorand, who took up the moral defense of the colonized Congolese peoples. I am convinced that they deserve to be included as such in Belgian history textbooks and be honored by the Congolese by means of street names and monuments in Congo.

The History Room: the Congolese Perspective

The history room too has weaknesses. A first such weakness is that one has not adopted a longer-term historical perspective. Visitors would understand "Kimbanguism", for example, better if this phenomenon emerging as a religious resistance movement against colonialism was also traced in its development after Congolese independence in 1960. The Kimbanguist church was very dynamic in the postcolonial era. It should be viewed and presented more from a Congolese perspective.

A second weakness constitutes the depiction of Congolese politics in the postcolonial period, which is mainly limited to press clippings and photographs. Yet, the Mobutu era of 1965–1997 was also characterized by the production of all kinds of medals, glasses, cigar bands, pins, special uniforms, and garments that were used on the occasion of major celebrations or birthdays of party events.

The Kimbanguist Church

Take the example of the Kimbanguist Church, which was founded in April 1921 as a non-violent religious movement by a Mukongo, Simon Kimbangu (ca. 1885–1951) at Nkamba, his native village in Lower Congo. Kimbangu only wanted freedom of religion and of association to create a black church independent of European missions. In October 1921, he was arrested and condemned to death as he was accused to have disturbed the colonial order. The sentence was commuted and Kimbangu was relegated to the Prison for Blacks in Elisabethville (Lubumbashi). To humiliate him, he was forced to cook and to serve the other black prisoners. He died in October 1951.[43]

---

43 Mathieu Zana Etambala, "La mort du prophète congolais Simon Kimbangu (12 octobre 1951)

Each kimbanguist manifestation was oppressed and so thousands of his followers were deported to relegation camps in Ekafera and other places which were hardly accessible. The colonial period sent the kimbanguists to the catacombs. However, from 1955 onwards, the movement was tolerated and on December 24, 1959 it obtained full freedom. The three sons of Simon Kimbangu transformed the movement in a modern institutionalized Church – the *Église de Jésus Christ sur la Terre par le Prophète Simon Kimbangu* (EJCSK) – and managed to transfer their father's body from Lubumbashi to Nkamba in April 1960. The kimbanguists perceive the recognition of their Church and the repatriation of Kimbangu body as a victory on the colonial administration and the European missions.

The independence of Congo very much energized the EJCSK. On the one hand, it conquered a very visible place in the Congolese landscape by erecting the first kimbanguist primary schools in January 1960 and a big temple in Kinshasa, which was inaugurated by President Mobutu in December 1966. On August 16, 1969, the Kimbanguist Church was admitted as member of the *World Council of Churches*, and on May 24, 1974 it joined the Conference of the Churches of Africa. On August 26, 1976, the Faculty of Kimbanguist Theology was opened in Kinshasa,[44] and, on April 6, 1981, an immense mausoleum in Nkamba-Jérusalem, Simon Kimbangu's birthplace. Kimbangu was finally rehabilitated by the Zairian Republic on September 12, 1991.

There exist photographs which show the evolution of the Kimbanguist Church. Some of these are plasticized and sold in little markets in Kinshasa. Such pictures should be shown – not in an anecdotal way – in the display window devoted to this movement and Church.

The Mobutu regime

The presentation of the 32-year-long postcolonial Mobutu era is sadly limited to a mass of press cuttings. During the 1970s and 1980s, the regime had a heavy political impact on the daily life of the Congolese. A new national traditional costume was imposed: the *pagne* for women, the *abacost* ("*à bas les costumes*") for men. During national manifestations, activities, and ceremonies, men and women wore *pagnes* and *boubous* (unisex robes) with portraits of the president

---

et la controverse au sujet de sa conversion à la religion catholique," *La Revue Africaine des Sciences Missionnaires*, n° 11–12 (2000): 128–207.

[44] Kuntima Diangienda, *L'Histoire du Kimbanguisme* (Éditions Kimbanguistes: Kinshasa,1984), 311.

as the "*Sauveur du Zaïre*" (Redeemer of Zaïre) or slogans like "*Salongo alingi mosala*" (Salongo likes working).⁴⁵

The regime produced medals at the occasion of the fifth and tenth anniversary of the *Mouvement Populaire de la Révolution* (MPR), Mobutu's party of unity, as monopartism was seen as growth from the Bantu philosophy. Mobutu was presented as a *conditor* (guide). And at the occasion of the national presidential elections of 1984, the very popular Zairian singer Luambo (1938–1989) and his *Tout Puissant O.K.* jazz band recorded the album *Candidat na Biso* (Our candidate) to glorify Mobutu Sese Seko and sustain him as the sole candidate for the Congolese presidency. Official buildings were painted with party slogans like "*Le M.P.R. avant tout – Le reste après*" (The MPR above all – The rest later) or "*Pour nous: souvent! Pour le M.P.R.: Toujours!*" (*For us: often! For the MPR: always*).

The press cuttings come from the Belgian as well as the Zairian press. But the newspapers in opposition to the Mobutu-regime, such as *Miso Gaa*, *Étincelle* and *Lumière*, are completely ignored. Nevertheless, there are a lot of opposition pamphlets and newspapers in the RMCA archives. *Ignorantia*, or did one fail to make an effort to find them?

There is no question as to the way the Mobutu regime dealt with colonial monuments: these disappeared completely from the urban landscape. However, there exist photographs of this Congolese iconoclasm, taken in 1972. In his book entitled *A Plague of Europeans*, published in 1973, the British historian David Killingray integrated two pictures representing Congolese workers demolishing monuments of the explorer Stanley and of King Albert.⁴⁶

Languages and Music

In an article published in the review of the Touring Club of Belgium in 1955, a philosophical observation was made about history. The article claimed that of the recent or contemporary history since the "white occupation" only written documents exist. It recognized, however, that the memories of elderly people, their experiences, and their considerations were equally important. Regularly, testimonials of Congolese were thus recounted.

---

45 Union des Ecrivains Zaïrois, *Authenticité et Développement (Colloque national sur l'Authenticité, Kinshasa 14–21 septembre 1981)* (Kinshasa: Éditions Présence Africaine, 1982).
46 David Killingray, *De Europeanenplaag: De Westerling in Afrika sinds de vijftiende eeuw* (Leiden: A.W. Sijthoff, 1977).

It is obvious that the Europeans behind this article were interested in precolonial time, not in the colonial era of conquest, occupation, and exploitation. It was about tribal history based on unwritten sources and oral tradition, meaning stories told by elderly villagers, about a time during which they preferred for centuries to live quietly on their fields, under palm trees or while fishing. In other oral testimonies they waged wars, undertook migration to new regions, and forged friendships with other tribes. Younger generation of Africans were not interested in genealogies or traditions, and this was the reason why all these stories had to be written down for history. Later it was to become clear that legends, genealogies, languages, place names etc. collected by Europeans had not been a waste of time and effort:

> because these will be the sources of the History of the Negroes. Each civilized people is looking for its history and the negroes are evolving into a civilized people.[47]

In this part of the RMCA great effort is expended to show that the Congolese spread historical and sociological messages through other means such as clothing or everyday artefacts.

The Proverb Emblems

Let us virtually linger for a moment before the display window exhibiting emblems of proverbs. The emblems are sculpted so as to display a central figure and some secondary figures which, together, embody a proverb. It is not easy to interpret these emblems' symbolic meanings.[48] A very interesting exhibition about proverb emblems was organized more than 30 years ago in the Afrika Museum of Berg-en-Dal in the Netherlands. In the exhibition catalogue many figurative languages of the emblems are clearly explained.[49] It shows a central figure of a woman with her hands in a cooking pot, and the following secondary figures: a dog, generally used for hunting; a hatchet, which was used as a farming equipment; maize; and a peanut. These are symbols well understood by men and women of the Bawili or Basolongo societies at the mouth of the Congo-river, as women used it to leave messages to their husbands and friends to in-

---

47 Ibid., 27.
48 Léo Bittremieux, *Symbolisme in de Negerkunst* (Brussel: Vromant, 1937).
49 Jos Vissers, *Spreekwoorden in beeld: een aparte kunst uit Cabinda* (Afrika Museum: Berg-en-Dal, 1985).

form them about specific household problems, such as tensions between husbands and wives.

Probably hundreds of such covers are kept in the archives of European Museums. They are not lacking in the National Museum of the *République Démocratique du Congo*, but they have almost totally disappeared from the Bawili society in Lower Congo. The reason for this is that young girls who went to schools run by missionary sisters received a professional education just like European girls. In these domestic science schools they learned to prepare food with Western cooking utensils.

The proverb emblems disappeared from Basolongo daily life because upon leaving school, the young schoolgirls did not forget the cookery courses given by the female missionaries. They returned to the villages at the mouth of the Congo river converted into modern housewives who rejected the traditional utensils.

The Maputa

But material objects can also speak. Many *pagnes* (or cloths called *maputa* in Congo) with inscriptions are displayed in this room. The accompanying short texts are sometimes written in Swahili, Lingala or other Congolese languages. It is a good thing that these modern clothes of strange origin are shown. However, it is a pity these are not put into historical perspective.

As a matter of fact, these cloths were already imported at the West coast of Africa during the sixteenth century. They were already mentioned in travel stories of that time. At the turn of the nineteenth and twentieth centuries, *pagnes* were worn by men. At that time, elegant Congolese women were dressed in raffia skirts. And so, the RMCA possesses a marvelous painting of Masala, a linguist, and a little chief who was invited to the International Exhibition of 1885, wearing a *pagne*.

The *pagnes* women wore can teach us something of Congolese history. In 1955, when King Baudouin visited Belgian Congo, native women were looking for *pagnes* with a picture of the king. This cloth by that time had been commercialized by Utexléo for over 50 years. In 1948, when Charles De Gaulle visited Brazzaville and delivered a famous speech about the future of the French colonies, heard in Léopoldville, Congolese women had already wanted *pagnes* bearing the image of the French president.

Conclusion

The RMCA's reopening on December 8, 2018 sparked a series of negative reactions. Colonial-minded people and royalists firstly regretted the name change of the former AfricaMuseum: the institute was not only decolonized but also rebaptized!

In the Congolese diaspora, some felt deeply disillusioned, not only because they had been insufficiently consulted in the renovation debates, but also because, in their opinion, the decolonization of the RMCA did not go far enough. According to them, the museum had failed to get rid of the racist features of colonization.[50]

In my view, the RMCA has not sufficiently explored the way in which other museums focusing on ethnographic art from the colonial period attempt to tackle the prejudices and stereotypes Afro-descendants suffer. The new and renovated Rautenstrauch-Joest Museum in Cologne could have served as an example. A space is dedicated to *The Distorted View: Prejudices*. It exhibits more than just photographs from family albums and newspaper clippings and books about the Congolese diaspora. Visitors can discover how black peoples were represented as childlike, cannibalistic, wild, rural, in need of help, servile, and instinct driven. At the same time, they are confronted with the European complex of superiority. On a screen one can see German football supporters making monkey sounds when black players touch the ball. Advertising posters of the Welthungerhilfe, the image of a Sarotti-Moor, cartoons, the book of Agatha Christy entitled *10 Kleine Negerlein* (10 Little Niggers) etc. are shown.[51]

Now that the stormy debate about decolonization and Africanization has somewhat quieted, the discussion about restitution will demand full attention. For those interested in this issue, the section in this article on acquisitions of the RMCA may be of some help.

---

[50] Gratia Pungu, "Une renovation ratée," *Ensemble* 99 (2019): 32–36; Billy Kalonji, "Comprenez notre déception," *Ensemble* 99 (2019): 37–38; and Elikia M'Bokolo, "Un espace de démonstration du génie du colonialisme," *Ensemble* 99 (2019): 49–55.

[51] Anonymous, *People in their Worlds: The New Rautenstrauch-Joest Museum, Cultures of the World. Ethnologica* (Cologne, 2010, 60–67).

Bibliography

Anonymous. "Le Rapport Casement (rapport de R. Casement, consul britannique, sur son voyage dans le Haut-Congo, 1903)." *Enquêtes et Documents d'Histoire Africaine* 6 (1985): 56–120.
Anonymous. "Le ravitaillement des troupes en operation." *Le Journal du Congo* 44 (Saturday 2 August) (1913): 2.
Anonymous. "RFI." *Le Musée national inauguré à Kinshasa* (2019).
Anonymous. "Sites, Monuments, Arts indigènes, Archives et Découvertes historiques – Congo Belge." *Touring Club du Congo Belge* 11 (November 30, 1958): 41–42.
Anonymous. *Guide du voyageur au Congo Belge et au Ruanda-Urundi.* Brussels, 1951.
Anonymous. *Le modèle noir: de Géricault à Matisse.* Paris: Éditions Musée d'Orsay/Flammarion, 2019.
Anonymous. *Panorama des 20 ans du Mouvement Populaire de la Révolution (20 mai 1967–20 mai 1987).* Kinshasa, 1987.
Anonymous. *People in their Worlds: The New Rautenstrauch-Joest Museum, Cultures of the World. Ethnologica.* Cologne, 2010.
Bittremieux, Léo. *Symbolismein de Negerkunst.* Brussel: Vromant, 1937.
Bontinck, François. "Donzwau M.D. Nlemvo (c. 1871–1938) et la Bible Kikongo." *Revue Africaine de Théologie* 2 (1978): 5–32.
Cambier, René. "Michaux Oscar." *Biographie Coloniale Belge* 1 (1948): 685–693.
Cambier, René. "Van Kerckhoven Guillaume." *Biographie Coloniale Belge* 1 (1948): 566–573.
Carton de Wiart, Edouard. "L'histoire du monument de Léopold II à Bruxelles et à Léopoldville." *Les Cahiers Léopoldiens* 4 (1959): 133–140.
Ceulemans, Paul. *La question arabe et le Congo (1883–1892).* Brussels: Academie Royal des Sciences Coloniales, 1959.
Coosemans, Marthe. "Mbunza." *Biographie Coloniale Belge* 1 (1948): 672–674.
Cornet, Joseph-Aurélien, Rémi De Cnodder, and Ivan Dierickx. *60 Ans de peinture au Zaïre.* Les Éditeurs d'Art Associés: Brussels, 1989.
Couttenier, Maarten. *Congo tentoongesteld: Een geschiedenis van de Belgische antropologie en het museum van Tervuren (1882–1925).* Leuven: Acco, 2005.
Daye, Pierre. *L'empire colonial belge.* Brussels: Berger-Levrault, 1923.
De Deken, Constant. *Twee jaar in Congo.* Antwerpen: Uitgeverij De Vlijt, 1952.
De Groof, Matthias. "Décolonialisme ou les palimpsestes de l'AfricaMuseum." *L'Art Même* 77 (2019): 26–27.
De Rop, Albert. *Bibliographie analytique de G. Hulstaert.* Antwerp: M.S.C. Borgerhout, 1972.
Devriese, Robert. "L'Africa Museum!" *Mémoires du Congo, Rwanda et Burundi* 51 (2018): 13–17.
Diangienda, Kuntima. *L'Histoire du Kimbanguisme.* Éditions Kimbanguistes: Kinshasa, 1984.
Duriaux, A., and H. Bouraly. *Mintadi – Bitumba, témoins de la tradition Bas-Congo (catalogus).* Kinshasa, s.d. (first names unknown).
Engels, Armand. "Hutereau Joseph-Armand." *Biographie Coloniale Belge* 3 (1952): 461–463.
Ergo, André-Bernard. "Musées du Congo." *Mémoires du Congo, du Rwanda et du Burundi* 52 (2019): 14–16.
Girard Eliane, and Kernel Brigitte. *Colons: statuettes habillées d'Afrique de l'Ouest.* Éditions Syros alternative: Paris, 1993.

Guebels, Léon. "Miani Giovanni." *Biographie Coloniale Belge* 1 (1948): 678–685.
Hessel, Fernand. "Nouveau Musée National du Congo." *Mémoires du Congo, du Rwanda et du Burundi* 52 (2019): 17–19.
Jacobs, Jean. "Gustaaf Hulstaert." *Bulletin Séance Académie royale des Sciences d'Outre-Mer* 44 (1998): 77–89.
Jadot, Jean-Marc. "Ward Herbert." *Biographie Coloniale Belge* 1 (1948): 956–961.
Jewsiewick, Bogumil. *Art pictural zaïrois*. Septentrion: Celat, 1992.
Jewsiewicki, Bogumil. *A Congo Chronicle: Patrice Lumumba in Urban Art*. New York: Museum for African Art, 1999.
Kalonji, Billy. "Comprenez notre déception." *Ensemble* 99 (2019): 37–38.
Killingray David. *De Europeanenplaag: De Westerling in Afrika sinds de vijftiende eeuw*. Leiden: A.W. Sijthoff, 1977.
Lacroix, A. "Bentley W. Holman." *Biographie Coloniale Belge* 1 (1948): 115–120.
Lacroix, A. "Croes Jean." *Biographie Coloniale Belge* 2 (1951): 206–207.
Lacroix, A., "Bollen Jean." *Biographie Coloniale Belge* 1 (1948): 141–142.
Lasnier Jean-François. "Le Muséum, une histoire, des missions." *Le Muséum National d'Histoire Naturelle* (2016): 8–15.
Laude, Norbert. "Lemaire Charles." *Biographie Coloniale Belge* 2 (1951): 603–608.
Leclère, Constant. *La formation d'un empire colonial belge*. Brussels: Vromant, 1932.
Léopold III. *Carnets de voyages 1919–1983*. Brussels: Racine, 2004.
Liking, Werewere. *Statues colons*. Abidjan: Les Nouvelles Éditions Africaines, 1987.
Lotar, L., and M. Coosemans. "Chaltin Louis." *Biographie Coloniale Belge* 1 (1948): 229–232 (first names unknown).
Louis, Roger, and Jean Stengers. *Morel's History of the Congo Reform Movement*. Oxford: Clarendon Press, 1968.
M'Bokolo, Elikia. "Un espace de démonstration du génie du colonialisme." *Ensemble* 99, Brussels (2019): 49–55.
Mabiala Mantuba-Ngoma, Pamphile. "Bula Matari: une création artistique dans Congo colonial." In *La mémoire du Congo. Le temps colonial*, edited by Jean-Luc Vellut, 171–172. Tervuren: AfricaTervuren-Snoeck, 2005.
Mabiala Mantuba-Ngoma, Pamphile. *L'art au service du culte catholique en République Démocratique du Congo*. Kinshasa: Médiaspaul Editions, 2018.
Marechal, Philippe. *De 'Arabische' campagne in het Maniema-gebied (1892–1894): situering binnen het kolonisatieproces in de onafhankelijke Kongostaat*. Tervuren: Royal Museum for Central Africa, 1992.
Michaux, Oscar. *Au Congo: carnet de campagne*. Namur: Librairie Dupagne-Counet, 1913.
Pungu, Gratia. "Une renovation ratée." *Ensemble* 99 (2019): 32v36.
Scohy, Andry. *L'Uele secret*. Brussel: Office International de Librairie – La Librairie Congolaise: 1955.
Tombu, Chantal. *La peinture populaire en héritage : Hommage de JP Mika aux Bula Matari*. Weyrich: Africa Editions, 2018.
Union des Ecrivains Zaïrois. *Authenticité et Développement (Colloque national sur l'Authenticité, Kinshasa 14–21 septembre 1981)*. Kinshasa: Éditions Présence Africaine, 1982.
Vandervelde, Émile. "La Belgique et le Congo Léopoldien." *La Société Nouvelle* 1 (1907): 54–59.

Vandervelde, Émile. *La Belgique et le Congo.* Paris: Félix Alcan, 1911.
Vandervelde, Émile. *Les derniers jours de l'État du Congo, journal de voyage.* Brussels: Édition de la Société Nouvelle, 1909.
Vangroenweghe, Daniël. *Bakanja Isidore: Martyr du Zaïre, battu à mort par un Blanc, béatifié par Jean-Paul II.* Brussels: Éditions Didier Hatier, 1989.
Vaudiau, M. "À propos de la naissance d'un art individualiste africain." *Touring Club du Congo Belge* 11 (November 30, 1958): 5–15.
Verhaegen, Benoit. "Ekibondo." *Biographie Belge d'Outre-Mer* Brussels (1977): 135–137.
Vincke, M. Nzungu. *La céramique Bakongo.* Brussels: Galérie Congo, 2002.
Vissers, Jos. *Spreekwoordenin beeld: een aparte kunst uit Cabinda.* Afrika Museum: Berg-en-Dal, 1985.
Whyms. *Léopoldville. Son histoire 1881–1956.* Brussels: Office de Publicité, 1956.
Zana Etambala, Mathieu. "À propos d'une statue colon: le président Joseph Kasa-Vubu (1960–1965), l'héritier des anciens Rois Kongo ou du Roi Baudouin?" *Museum Dynasticum* 26 (2015): 45–59.
Zana Etambala, Mathieu. "Een bezoek aan het oude Museum van Belgisch Congo te Tervuren." *Hermes* March (2019): 30–33.
Zana Etambala, Mathieu. "La mort du prophète congolais Simon Kimbangu (12 octobre 1951) et la controverse au sujet de sa conversion à la religion catholique." *La Revue Africaine des Sciences Missionnaires*, n° 11–12 (2000): 128–207.
Zana Etambala, Mathieu. "Le tipoye en Afrique noire." *Carnets de Sciences Humaines* 6 (2011): 7–15 and 7 (2012): 14–22.

Rebecca Rogers (Université de Paris, France)
French Variations on the Educational Civilizing Mission (19th – 20th century). *Cherchez les missionaires, cherchez les femmes!*

Abstract: Scholarship has long recognized the existence of a discourse about the "civilizing mission" in France that encouraged the development of educational initiatives overseas. This scholarship, however, is often highly specialized: specialists of mission study the work of religious teachers; specialists of the Third Republic link educational mission to that of the Republican pedagogical project; specialists of Jewish history track the activities of the Alliance Israélite Universelle throughout the Mediterranean, and specialists of women argue for the need to include women in all of these studies. This essay brings together these different perspectives on the French civilizing mission to highlight the number and variety of educational projects that led so many men and women to cross oceans and seas to spread their vision of what represented "civilization".

Kewords: civilizing mission, female religious teachers, colonies, Alliance Israélite universelle, historiography.

In the spirit of many of Marc Depaepe's exhortations to the community of historians of education, this essay is a call to take fuller account of the activities of missionary organizations in the history of colonial education. Almost 30 years ago, while President of ISCHE, Marc Depaepe delivered an opening address that was published as "An agenda for the history of colonial education". He argued for the "enduring need for a thoroughgoing historical analysis of the history of colonial education" and proposed a series of questions that urged historians to move from an exploration of the education policy of the "motherland" to the analysis of how this policy was carried out and the effects of "civilizing work".[1] Since that initial call to arms, the field of colonial history of education has considerably expanded. More recently, Marc Depaepe has urged historians to explore more carefully the tools of the civilizing mission–notably schoolbooks–in an effort to approach the everyday schooling realities and their effects

---

[1] Marc Depaepe, "An Agenda for the History of Colonial Education," *Paedagogica Historica* 31, sup. 1 (1995): 15–21.

on both individuals and groups.² As always, his suggestions and examples offer powerful stimulus to develop methods and to refine theories that acknowledge the complexity of the educational work accomplished in colonial contexts.

This essay pursues a similar goal to that of Depaepe's agenda, adopting what I might term an educational missionary voice with respect to scholarship on France and its Empire although I do not have "ten commandments" that echo those offered by Marc Depaepe in 2010.³ Rather I have two propositions for historians of education interested in tracing the impact of the European civilizing mission in non-European settings: firstly, historians should *cherchez les missionnaires* and, secondly, *cherchez les femmes*. I am responding to a long tendency within French colonial historiography to privilege studies of educational policies within the colonies without sufficiently acknowledging the weight and the role of religious organizations that often preceded the colonial state on the ground and remained after Independence. The French State was rarely alone in its efforts to establish schools for indigenous pupils. In sub-Saharan Africa, state schools competed for students with French Catholic teaching orders and British missionary organizations. Missionary schools competed amongst each other, with consequences in terms of the policies adopted, the programs developed, and the students who received forms of Western or "adapted" education. Paying attention to the religious actors of the mission is one intellectual goal, the second involves paying attention to the role of women and gender in this process. Until recently, women were neglected when considering the French civilizing mission. Introducing women as both teachers and students directs attention to the gendered characteristics and consequences of educational initiatives in the colonies.⁴ Recognizing the diversity of educational "missionary" agents and bringing these variations of the civilizing mission within the same analytical frame is an important stake in any effort to grapple with the nature of the colonial legacy in education. Like a musical variation, the schools, the textbooks, the

---

[2] Marc Depaepe, "Études des manuels et chansons scolaires dans la perspective de l'Histoire de l'éducation coloniale—une introduction," in *Manuels et chansons scolaires au Congo Belge*, ed. M. Depaepe, J. Briffaerts, P. Kita Kyankenge Masandi, and H. Vinck (Leuven: University Press, 2003), 7–29; M. Depaepe, "Writing histories of Congolese Colonial and Post-Colonial Education: A Historiographical View from Belgium," in *Connecting Histories of Education: Transnational and Cross-cultural Exchanges in (Post-) Colonial Education*, ed. Barnita Bagchi, Eckhardt Fuchs, and Kate Rousmaniere (New York: Berghahn, 2014), 41–60.

[3] Marc Depaepe, "The Ten Commandments of Good Practices in History of Education Research," *Zeitschrift für pädagogische Historiographie* 16, no. 1 (2010): 31–34.

[4] See, for example, Rebecca Rogers, "'*Cherchez la femme*': Women and Gender in French Scholarship on the Empire," *Journal of Women's History*, 28, no. 4 (2016): 124–133.

pedagogical projects, and the students varied but there were important similarities and forms of transfer that deserve our scholarly attention.

After an initial presentation of the Republican agenda in colonial education, this essay explores how recent scholarship has enriched our understanding of this agenda through studies of the actors, associations, and texts that circulated between metropole and colony. It then turns to a separate strand of scholarship that has focused on contributions of religious missionaries to the "civilizing mission". In highlighting the need to "cherchez les femmes" in our histories of mission, the essay draws attention not only to the women who were active proponents of the French civilizing mission, but also to the variety of their initiatives with respect to indigenous women. Finally, the essay concludes with a "new" agenda for the history of colonial education that de-nationalizes and trans-nationalizes the objects we study and the questions we ask. While the focus is on France, the concern here is to expand our vision of the Western European "civilizing mission" and to encourage others to recognize the polyphonic nature of this mission and the variations that developed locally.

A Republican Agenda: Spreading the Universal Values of the French

Jules Ferry is best known in France for the series of educational laws in 1881–82 that introduced obligatory, secular, primary education to all students from the age of six to 13. But he was also Prime Minister in 1884 when he delivered a stirring call for the French to spread their values through colonization. In his oft-cited speech on this topic, he developed the political, economic, strategic, and cultural reasons that justified French expansion overseas. Much like in Rudyard Kipling's "White Man's Burden", the spread of French schools was part of a political project: "the superior races have a right because they have a duty. They have the duty to civilize the inferior races".[5]

The history of French colonization began well before decolonization produced a wave of more critical postcolonial approaches. One finds, for example, detailed studies of the ways the French state organized educational systems and set up schools.[6] These histories, however, remained very centered on colonial ad-

---

[5] Jules Ferry, "Discours du 28 juillet 1885 à la Chambre," *Discours et opinions de Jules Ferry*, ed. Paul Robiquet (Paris: Armand Colin & Cie., 1897), 210.
[6] Pascale Barthélémy, "L'enseignement dans l'Empire colonial français : une vieille histoire?" *Histoire de l'éducation* 128 (2010): 5–28.

ministrator's initiatives, on efforts to track statistical growth, and on the evolution of official doctrines with respect to indigenous education. Were French education officers interested in assimilating indigenous students into a universal French polity, or did they adapt their civilizing efforts to the purported needs of their colonial subjects? How did such policies vary across time and space? While a few dissertations offered in-depth study of how these politics played out in specific regions or in specific schools, the overall tendency of these studies was to approach the spread of colonialism from above. From the 1960s to the 1990s scholars pursued studies on specific colonies that offered insight into a more social history of education that highlighted the complexity of local situations and often noted the interactions between missionary and colonial actors on the ground.[7] In 1997, US scholar Alice Conklin's important book, *A Mission to Civilize*, contributed to a different sort of conversation about the French empire, one that paid closer attention to the circulation of ideas and administrators between the metropole and the colonies.[8] More importantly for the purposes of this essay, she sought to unpack the meanings behind the "mission to civilize", drawing attention to the weight of both mission and civilization in French expansion.

In the past 30 years the field of French colonial history has vastly expanded and increasingly engaged with the trends of a new imperial history that emphasizes circulations and networks, breaking down the top-down interpretations of historical processes. In education this has led to attention being paid to those agents of Empire who sought to spread the Republican civilizing agenda. Studies now examine the educational administrators, such as Georges Hardy whose careers led them around the Empire.[9] Author of *La Conquête morale, l'enseignement en AOF* in 1917, Hardy developed the "classic" argument for the civilizing mission

---

[7] See, in particular, two studies that study colonial politics, missionaries, and both men and women: Denise Bouche, *L'enseignement dans les territoires français de l'Afrique occidentale de 1817 à 1920. Mission civilisatrice ou formation d'une élite*, history dissertation, Université de Paris I, 1975; Yvonne Turin, *Affrontements culturels dans l'Algérie Coloniale. Écoles, médecines, religion, 1830–1880* (Paris: François Maspero, 1971). See, as well, Antoine Léon's early effort to synthesize the relationship between colonialism and education that noted the importance of including missionaries in this story, *Colonisation, Enseignement et éducation. Étude historique et comparative* (Paris: L'Harmattan, 1991), 29–36.

[8] Alice Conklin, *A Mission to Civilize. The Republican Idea of Empire in France and West Africa, 1895–1930* (Stanford: Stanford University Press, 1997).

[9] Carine Eizlini, "Georges Hardy pédagogue et idéologue en Afrique occidentale Française" in *L'école aux colonies, les colonies à l'école*, ed. Gilles Boyer, Pascal Clerc, and Michelle Zancarini-Fournel (Lyon, ENS Editions, 2013), 39–55.

that has long held pride of place in discussions of colonial ideology. Far from advocating the "assimilation" of native students into French culture, his text was among the first of educational administrators to argue for the necessary adaptation of lesson plans and textbooks to local realities and local needs.

Hardy was not just a colonial doctrinaire. He founded the *Bulletin de l'enseignement de l'AOF* in 1912 that chronicled French interventions in education, and even included textbooks designed for indigenous students in history and geography. His career led him from the sprawling federation of Afrique Occidentale Française (AOF) between 1912 and 1919 to a position as Director general in charge of Public Instruction in Morocco, then back to Paris as head of the École Coloniale in Paris. His career came to a forced conclusion in 1943 while Rector of Algiers as the tide of the war made his sympathies for the Vichy government unpalatable.[10] While his writings testify unquestionably to the weight of evolutionary racial thinking during the interwar period, they also demonstrate the "scientific" training of colonial officers, and the impact of the emerging field of ethnography. For Hardy, the characteristics of French "civilization" placed teachers and administrators as the "natural" educators of indigenous people, but he also used the *Bulletin* to urge teachers to send in ethnographic studies of the localities where they taught. The colonial encounter thus brought knowledge back to the metropole as recent scholarship has shown.[11]

Although French administrators established educational doctrines, I would argue that teachers were the critical players in this history; they were the ones who set up schools, gave lessons in French or agriculture, encouraged a sense of French identity or nourished nationalist feelings. Some of the most important scholarship has investigated the creation of teacher training schools, explored the characteristics of schooling in Indochina, Madagascar or Afrique Occidentale Française, questioned the experiences of students, and challenged easy assumptions about the "Frenchness" of knowledge and learning that circulated between France and the colonies.[12] While little work exists on the ways the civilizing mis-

---

10 Jean-François Condette, "HARDY Georges," in *Les recteurs d'académie en France de 1808 à 1940*. Tome II, *Dictionnaire biographique*, ed. J.-F. Condette (Paris: Institut national de recherche pédagogique, 2006), 213–214.
11 See in particular Spencer Segella, "Georges Hardy and Educational Ethnology in French Morocco, 1920–26," *French Colonial History* 4 (2003), 171–90.
12 See, in particular, Fanny Colonna, *Instituteurs algériens, 1883–1939* (Paris, Presses de la Fondation Nationale des Sciences Politiques, 1975); Jean-Hervé Jézéquel, *Les 'mangeurs de craies'. Histoire sociale des instituteurs en Afrique Occidentale Française* (Paris: Karthala, 2008); Pascale Barthélémy, *Africaines et diplômées à l'époque coloniale (1918–1957)* (Rennes: Presses Universitaires de Rennes, 2010); Harry Gamble, *Contesting French West Africa. Battles over Schools and the Colonial Order, 1900–1950* (Lincoln & London: University of Nebraska Press, 2017); Céline

sion impacted schools in France, there is ample evidence for the ways a colonial imaginary attracted teachers to the colonies motivated by a variety of factors, including higher pay. The schoolteacher Pierre Dechamps was particularly instrumental in the creation of the Mission laïque. The Mission's sub-title – Association pour la propagation de l'enseignement laïque au colonies et à l'étranger –, aptly summarizes its goal of spreading secular education to the colonies and abroad. Founded in 1902, the Mission laïque was (and still is) a private structure that carried the ideals of French secular education around the world and notably to the Middle East in the years before World War I.[13] The École normale Jules Ferry (1902–1912), was briefly the educational arm of this enterprise, training male and female schoolteachers who then led colonial careers in Africa, Indochina, the Maghrib or the West Indies.[14] Sosthène Pénot was one such schoolteacher who trained in this colonial normal school in Paris and then had a career in Madagascar. His journal brings to light the lived experiences of this colonial teacher and how the experience of imperial teaching changed individuals.[15]

More recently, interest in understanding the educational legacy in the postcolonial period has drawn attention to those administrators whose careers spanned the tumultuous decades of the mid-twentieth century. Albert Charton, Inspector General of education in AOF from 1929 to 1939 was the promoter of rural schools; after the war he returned to Indochina where he was instrumental in developing both primary and higher education but also accompanied the evolution of the French civilizing mission into one of cultural diplomacy. In 1952 he created the *Mission d'enseignement français et de coopération culturelle* which remained active until 1975.[16] The continued presence of French educational administrators and French teachers thanks to the existence of cooperation agreements

---

Labrune-Badiane and Étienne Smith, *Les hussards noirs de la colonie. Instituteurs africains et "petites patries" en AOF* (Paris: Karthala, 2018); Thuy Phuong Nguyen, *L'école française au Vietnam de 1945 à 1975. De la mission civilisatrice à la diplomatie culturelle* (Amiens: Encrage Editions, 2017).

13 André Thevenin, *La mission laïque française à travers son histoire 1902–2002* (Paris: Mission Laïque Française, 2002).

14 Gérard Vigner, "L'école Jules-Ferry, école normale de l'enseignement colonial: une formation pour apprendre à enseigner dans les colonies (1902–1912)", *Documents pour l'histoire du français langue étrangère ou second* 55 (2015) : 1–17.

15 Simon Duteil, "Un instituteur colonial à Madagascar au début du XXe siècle," *Histoire de l'éducation* 128 (2010): 79–102

16 Thuy Phuong Nguyen, "De la "mission civilisatrice" à la mission culturelle: un discours (post-colonial contrarié (Indochine 1946–1952)," in *Repenser la mission civilisatrice. L'éducation dans le monde colonial et postcolonial au XXe siècle*, ed. Damiano Matasci, Miguel Bandeira Jerónimo, and Hugo Gonçalves Dores (Rennes: Presses universitaires de Rennes, 2020).

has begun to draw attention to the structural as well as pedagogical legacies of colonialism, although unquestionably much remains to be done in this area.[17]

Scholarship has increasingly explored the dense web of relations between the French metropole and colony, but compared to the historiography concerning the British, Dutch or Belgian Empires, it is striking that religious missionaries are relatively marginal in these new histories of Empire. And yet, like in these other imperial contexts, religious missionaries were often at the vanguard of Empire, opening schools and health dispensaries well before the colonial state initiated such measures. Less marked by the secular bias of French historians, US scholars were often the first to analyze together the republican mission to civilize with the Christian missions in the Empire. J.-P. Daughton, in particular, has highlighted the extent to which the political and religious mission interacted, notably on the ground, where schooling, teaching and the moral reform of indigenous societies were integral facets of French cultural polititcs.[18] The edited volume *In God's Empire: French Missionaries and the Modern World* pursues the first of my propositions to include missionaries in the history of empire; schools and education, however, are not the focus of this volume.[19] In what follows, I draw attention to sources and scholarship that bring education into the story of the French religious mission in the colonies.

Proposition I: the History of Education in the Colonies Needs to Consider the Educational Work of French Religious Missionaries

Sources concerning the history of religious mission and its relationship to education are not difficult to locate. From the outset, Catholic, Protestant, and Jewish missionaries understood the need to chronicle or leave visual evidence of

---

[17] Odile Goerg and Marie-Albane de Suremain (dirs), "Coopérants et coopération en Afrique: circulations d'acteurs et recompositions culturelles (des années 1950 à nos jours," *Outre-Mers. Revue d'histoire* (2014). See in particular the article by Françoise Raison-Jourde on the interactions between French "coopérants" and their students in Madagascar, as well as the article by Honoré Ouedraogo based on interviews with former students of secondary schools in Upper Volta (Burkina Faso).
[18] J.-P. Daughton, *An Empire Divided. Religion, Republicanism, and the Making of French Colonialism* (Oxford & New York: Oxford University Press, 2006).
[19] Owen White and J.P. Daughton, eds., *In God's Empire: French Missionaries and the Modern World* (Oxford: Oxford University Press, 2012).

their efforts to civilize or convert indigenous children. The characteristics of the religious mission, however, operated differently for the Christian and Jewish missionaries, since the Alliance Israélite Universelle (founded in 1860) directed its attention to fellow Jews; bringing civilization through instruction was their principal goal. Indeed the activities of the AIU provided a model for later nineteenth-century Republican initiatives, such as the Alliance française or the Mission laïque.

No matter the religion, however, all understood the need to communicate about their activities in France, among their members and with respect to the populations they encountered. In the nineteenth century, as Catholic missionary orders multiplied, they created annals, bulletins, or journals that recounted the histories of their work on the ground. When Pauline Jaricot founded the Oeuvre pour la propagation de la foi in 1822, this lay missionary society used the press to garner support and then to relay the nature of their activities in the *Bulletin des Annales de la propagation de la foi*. Individual congregations quickly adopted some form of regular mode of communication as their activities spread beyond the metropole. Between 1823 and 1919, one study notes the creation of 380 missionary journals, 79 of which were in French.[20] These tales of mission would later serve missionaries and historians in their efforts to trace the success and failures of the schools that emerged virtually everywhere that missionaries settled.[21]

Along the western coast of Africa, where the slave trade had been active, Catholic and Protestant missionaries competed for the souls but also the minds of the populations they encountered. This imperial rivalry had an impact on the educational strategy of the groups involved, as Catholics and Protestants in this area targeted different populations. The British Christian Missionary Society developed an important network of schools including a grammar school in Lagos that responded to indigenous demands for a form of education associated with European elite education, notably the study of Latin and Greek.[22] The fathers of the Société des Missions Africaines, on the other hand, who were from more modest social backgrounds than their Protestant rivals, focused

---

20 Jean Comby, *Deux mille ans d'évangélisation. Histoire de l'expansion chrétienne* (Paris: Desclée 1992), cited in Annie Lenoble-Bart, "Missionnaires catholiques en Afrique, entre information et communication," *Revue des sciences religieuses* 80, no. 2 (2006): 193–204.
21 While these abundant sources await the critical eye of historians of education, it is arguably more urgent to follow the example of our Belgian colleagues with interviews of the now elderly missionary actors living both in the former colonies and the metropole.
22 Bernard Salvaing, *Les missionnaires à l'encontre de l'Afrique au XIXe siècle (Côte des Esclaves et pays Yoruba, 1840–1891* (Paris: L'Harmattan, 1995), 134–137.

their efforts on the poor, orphans, and mixed-race children.[23] A strategy of educating mixed-race children in orphanages is evident in many parts of the French Empire. Owen White, in particular, has shown how the French colonial state capitalized on the early missionary initiatives with respect to orphans. In French West Africa, the Pères du Saint-Esprit, the Père blancs, and the Sœurs de Saint-Joseph de Cluny opened orphanages as early as the mid nineteenth century that evolved into institutions known as écoles-ouvroirs where boys and girls studied the rudiments and learned manual skills.[24] In these colonial settings there is a long history of missionary engagement with the lowest social categories, including the disabled, but we still await the histories, which integrate these analyses into a broader understanding of how the missionary presence affected attitudes to the schooling of the least advantaged.

Studies of missionary schools are more common in histories that address the ways anticlerical legislation was or was not enacted in different colonial settings. The Governor of Côte d'Ivoire, for example, opposed application of the legislation arguing the French should use the free collaboration of Catholic missions to teach the French language, while in neighboring Upper Senegal-Niger, the governor accused the missionaries of focusing far too much on conversion while exploiting students to work in the fields.[25] This top-down presentation of missionary schools offers less insight into the educational work within such institutions, insight that relies on other types of sources. These sources are at the heart of the collection *Lettres d'exil*, which adroitly analyzes what missionary letters can tell us about the effects of the anti-congregational legislation between 1901 and 1904 that set sent thousands of religious teachers into exile.[26] Patrick Cabanel notes

---

[23] Bernard Salvaing, "Missionnaires catholiques français et protestants britanniques face à l'Afrique. le cas de la Côte du Bénin et du pays Yoruba (1841–1891)," *Revue française d'histoire d'Outre-Mer* 262–263 (1984): 31–57; Anne Hugon, *Un protestantisme africain au XIXe siècle. L'implantation du méthodisme en Gold Coast (Ghana), 1837–1874* (Paris: Karthala, 2007).

[24] Owen White, *Children of the French Empire: Miscegenation and Colonial Society in French West Africa, 1895–1960* (Oxford: Oxford University Press, 1999).

[25] Elizabeth Foster, *Faith in Empire: Religion, Politics, and Colonial Rule in French Senegal, 1880–1940* (Stanford: Stanford University Press, 2013), 83–93.

[26] Patrick Cabanel, *Lettres d'exil, 1901–1909. Les congrégations françaises dans le monde après les lois laïques de 1901 et 1904, Anthologie de textes missionnaires* (Turnhout: Brepols, 2008). For information on the characteristics of the religious exile see Patrick Cabanel and Jean-Dominique Durand, ed., *Le grand exil des congrégations religieuses françaises : 1901–1914: actes du colloque international de Lyon, Université Jean-Moulin Lyon III, 12–13 juin 2003* (Paris: Cerf, 2005). For an analysis that brings together both Republican and religious missionaries, see Patrick Cabanel, ed., *Une France en Méditerranée. Écoles, Langue et culture françaises, XIXe–XXe siècles* (Paris: CREAPHIS, 2006).

the attraction of Brazil for a number of French congregations, but neighboring Belgium and Spain also welcomed many female congregations who opened schools and attracted students, notably girls from local elites.[27] Not surprisingly, given the nature of these missionary sources, it is the movement of exile that is analyzed most carefully, rather than the schools and educational works that emerged far from home. Still schooling was essential for the survival of these institutions and this study offers many examples of how political exile led to the creation of French schools around the world.

Historians of the Alliance Israélite Universelle (AIU) have from the outset focused more centrally on schools in their studies, given the founders' expectation that contact with French culture would bring emancipation and modernity to the Jewish populations where they established schools. In the wake of Aron Rodrigue's pioneering studies of the AIU's activities in the Ottoman Empire, many scholars have analyzed the arrival of Alliance teachers and the effect of their schools on Jewish communities from Morocco in Northern Africa to Iraq and Iran in the Middle East. By 1914, the AIU ran 183 schools totaling some 43,700 students.[28] Unlike the literature on Christian missions, which often remains frustratingly elusive about the actual content of the educational program, scholarship on the Alliance offers detailed analyses of the teachers who left Paris with the objective of "regenerating" their Jewish brethren and the nature of the schools they established. The AIU's archives provide exceptional insight into educational realities on the ground, providing opportunity to develop the sort of studies encouraged in Depaepe and Simon's famous "plea".[29] The material on teachers is particularly rich, since the AIU thought seriously about the nature of teacher training, opening in Paris a normal school for boys in 1867 (the École normale Israélite Orientale-ENIO) and the École Normale Israélite Orien-

---

[27] For an analysis of what the study of this movement offers for the transnational history of education, see Rebecca Rogers, "Congregações femininas e difusão de um modelo escolar: uma história transnacional," *Pro-Posições* 25 no.1 Campinas Jan./Apr.014, 55–74. Available in French on-line. http://dx.doi.org/10.1590/S0103-73072014000100004. The very active forum Relins-Europe gives insight into what international comparative research on religious institutes can offer for historians of education: https://kadoc.kuleuven.be/relins/eu/index.htm.

[28] See Aron Rodrigue, *French Jews, Turkish Jews: The Alliance Israélite Universelle and the Politics of Jewish Schooling in Turkey, 1860–1925* (Bloomington: Indiana University Press, 1990). For the figures on teachers see Rodrigue, *Images of Sephardi and Eastern Jewries in Transition. The Teachers of the Alliance Israélite Universelle, 1860–1939* (Seattle: University of Washington Press, 1993), 14.

[29] Marc Depaepe and Frank Simon, "Is there any Place for the History of 'Education' in the 'History of Education'? A Plea for the History of Everyday Educational Reality in- and outside Schools," *Paedagogica Historica* 3, no. 1 (1995): 9–16.

tale pour Jeunes Filles in 1922. And virtually from the outset the AIU included both boys and girls in its educational purview. In seeking to transform Jewish societies through what was termed the "new education" of women, the AIU, like the Catholic missionaries, left a gendered institutional and cultural heritage that has rarely been analyzed in conjunction with studies of other religious missionaries.[30] The final section of this essay turns then to consider what specific attention to women and to the gendered characteristics of the civilizing mission offer for historians of education.

Proposition 2: Histories of Education in Imperial Settings Need to Include Missionary Women

Women were very much a part of religious missions to imperial spaces, although the absence of any overview on the subject makes it difficult to estimate overall figures. In 1934, a statistical survey undertaken by Rome of Catholic missions to foreign countries noted that 57% of a total of 35,996 missionaries were women.[31] Although historians of French missionary activities are well aware that women were very present in efforts to enlighten, civilize or convert other women, the historiography on women and mission has remained strikingly piecemeal and poorly integrated into overviews on the subject, for reasons I have analyzed elsewhere.[32] Here I would like to "chercher les femmes missionnaires" drawing attention to the educational role women played in Christian and Jewish organizations. How does such an approach open perspectives for a gendered social history of educational practices in colonial settings? Paying attention to the religious variations of the civilizing mission with regard to women offers ways of moving into the classrooms and workhouses where indigenous girls and women encountered European women and were given lessons and taught skills about which little has been written. These lessons were, of course, gendered; studying their messages, how they circulated among women of different gener-

---

30 A recent collection has a series of chapters that begin to consider these legacies, Jérôme Boquet, ed., *L'enseignement français en Méditerranée. Les missionnaires et l'Alliance israélite universelle* (Rennes: Presses universitaires de Rennes, 2010).
31 Claude Prudhomme, "Missionnaire," in *Dictionnaire de la colonisation française*, ed. C. Liauzu (Paris: Larousse, 2007), 473.
32 Rogers, Rebecca, "Genre, mission et colonisation," in *Religions et colonisation. Afrique-Asie-Océanie-Amériques (XVIe – XXe siècles)*, ed. Dominique Borne and Benoît Falaize (Paris: L'Atelier, 2009), 93–100. See as well the analyses of Sarah Curtis, "The double invisibility of Missionary Sisters," *Journal of Women's History* 28, no. 4 (2016): 134–143.

ations, different religions, different social groups and within different settings sheds light on the multiple factors that shaped social hierarchies but also empowered individuals to challenge these racial and religious hierarchies in specific contexts.

In terms of numbers Catholic teaching sisters were far more numerous than the Jewish teachers of the Alliance Israélite Universelle or the *demoiselles institutrices* of the Protestant Services des Missions Évangéliques de Paris.[33] They have also garnered far more attention in the scholarly literature beginning with Elisabeth Dufourcq's four volume study of the female missionary "diaspora" and a series of studies around the largest French female missionary order: the Sœurs de Saint-Joseph de Cluny.[34] Most scholars of mission have focused on the phenomenon itself, describing the women, the numbers involved, the locations where they settled, the nature of their encounter with other cultures, etc. These studies pay relatively little attention to the mechanics of schooling, their implicit audience being other historians of (Catholic) missions and not historians of education who would like to know who attended classes, what clothes students wore, whether they wore shoes, what educational material was used in class, what program of study was followed, in what language, and what place physical or manual activities played in the schoolroom.

There are, of course, exceptions, most notably the scholarship of Sarah Curtis, who began her career as a historian of education. Her remarkable study of the "Civilizing Habits" of three Superior Generals who opened schools for girls in a wide range of mission territories (including the United States and the Ottoman Empire) reveals how women religious teachers challenged gendered expecta-

---

[33] To my knowledge there is, as yet, no substantive scholarly work on French Protestant missionary women. One chapter in a recent volume discusses a Protestant family in Zambezia but little is said about the schools they ran. See Émilie Gangnat, Geneviève Granier and Jean-François Zorn, "Une famille missionnaire protestante à la période héroïque de la mission: Les Volla et leurs enfants au Zambèze (1902–1913)" in *Hommes et femmes en mission (XIXe – XXe siècle). Entre partage et confrontation*, Actes de la XXXVIIe session du CREDIC (Paris, 23 août – 27 août 2016), ed. Bernadette Truchet and Jean-François Zorn (Paris: Karthala, 2018), 197–237.

[34] Elisabeth Dufourcq, *Les congrégations religieuses féminines hors d'Europe de Richelieu à nos jours. Histoire naturelle d'une diaspora*, 4 vol. (Paris: Librairie de l'Inde, 1993); E. Dufourcq, *Les aventurières de Dieu. Trois siècles d'histoire missionnaire française* (Paris: Éditions Jean-Claude Lattès, 1993); Geneviève Lecuir-Nemo, *Femmes et vocation missionnaire. Permanence des congrégations féminines au Sénégal de 1819 à 1960: adaptation ou mutation ? Impact et insertion*, thèse d'histoire, Université de Paris I, 1995; Philippe Delisle, "Colonisation, christianisation et émancipation. Les sœurs de Saint-Joseph de Cluny à Mana (Guyane française). 1828–1846," *Revue française d'histoire d'outre-mer* 85, no. 320 (1998): 7–32; Pascale Cornuel, "Anne-Marie Javouhey à Mana – Une mission maternaliste ?", in *Les Conditions matérielles de la mission – Contrainte, dépassement, imaginaires*, ed. M. Cheza and J. Pirotte (Paris: Karthala, 2005).

tions about their behavior.³⁵ Paying careful attention to the schools and work environments in which they labored (the former slave colony of Mana in French Guiana, for example, or on the Aegean island of Siros), Curtis shows as well the importance of evaluating educational interventions in our efforts to understand how religious mission contributed to the diffusion of culture, language, class, and gender norms, as well as to forms of indigenous resistance that often reoriented the mission.³⁶

Recent publications of missionary texts further reveal the tremendous potential of missionary archives to unpack the nature of the educational mission and the ways gender operated in imperial contexts. Chantal Paisant's anthology, *La mission au feminine*, follows the Sœurs de Saint-Joseph de Cluny to Senegal, the Sœurs des Sacrés-Coeurs de Picpus to Chili, Peru, Ecuador, and Bolivia, a Dame du Sacré-Coeur to Santiago du Chili, and the Franciscaines missionnaires de Marie to the Far-East.³⁷ Two other anthologies, edited by Patrick Cabanel and Chantal Verdeil, bring to the fore how French teaching sisters participated in the civilizing mission in areas that would become colonies but also in Latin America and the Middle East. These sources invite cross-cultural comparisons on the capacity of French congregations to adapt their religious goals to different contexts and how schooling played into such adaptations.

The correspondences and journals that religious sisters so scrupulously maintained show how they shared their experiences and responded to the demands of families or the constraints posed by the economic circumstances of the female students they schooled. In Latin America, the journal of Cléonisse Cormier (1803–1868) as well as her letters back to her Superiors in France offer detailed descriptions of the first four houses of the Sœurs de Picpus in Valparaiso (1838), in Santiago du Chili (1841), and in Lima (1849).³⁸ The two schools

---

35 Sarah Curtis, *Civilizing Habits. Women and the Revival of French Empire* (Oxford: Oxford University Press, 2010).
36 This issue of local female resistance to schooling is analyzed in Estelle Pagnon, "'Une œuvre inutile'? La scolarisation des filles par les missionnaires catholiques dans le Sud-Est du Nigéria (1885-1930)," *Clio. Histoire, femmes et sociétés* 6 (1997): 35–59.
37 Chantal Paisant ed., *La mission au féminin. Témoignages de religieuses missionnaires au fil d'un siècle (XIXe-début XXe siècle). Anthologie de textes missionnaires* (Turnhout: Brepols, 2009). See as well the anthologies of Cabanel, note 26, and Chantal Verdeil, ed., *Missions chrétiennes en terre d'Islam. Moyen-Orient Afrique du Nord (XVIIe – XXe siècles)* (Turnhout: Brepols, 2013).
38 Paisant, ed., *La mission au feminine*, as well as Chantal Paisant, "Les sœurs de Picpus en Amérique latine: Les premières missions d'éducation," *Transversalités* 71 (1999): 205–228. This article examines the material, pedagogical, and social dimensions of the schools founded in Latin America.

in Valparaiso, for example, both welcomed boarders but from different social groups. In the "first" school for girls whose husbands were expected to be diplomats or international merchants, the sisters taught in Spanish and offered a range of lessons in the humanities, the sciences (geography, cosmography, physics, natural history, and botany), foreign languages (French and English), and the decorative arts. The "second" school that targeted less affluent families offered a program of study that went beyond primary education in France at the time; preparation for the First Communion juxtaposed lessons in writing, arithmetic, Castillan grammar, geography, and epistolary styles. Within the poor schools, which they opened in both Valparaiso and Santiago, the sisters adopted mutual education practices in the early years when the teachers themselves spoke little Spanish. Older students taught pronunciation in particular. In both the boarding schools and the poor schools the sisters brought from France a penchant for the organization of exams, the distribution of medals, and the conviction of the importance of emulation for students to progress.

Similarly rich studies have emerged from studies using the archives of the Alliance Israélite Universelle, revealing not only the training of future female teachers but also their trajectories within the network of Alliance schools. As early as 1872, three different female institutions in Paris welcomed aspiring women teachers within unusual cosmopolitan settings where "Western" and "Oriental" young women learned their lessons together. This initial Parisian experience informed the vision these women then adopted concerning their role in the transformation of patriarchal Jewish communities elsewhere.

Female Jewish teachers were often at the origin of the first women's schools in the regions where they settled; there they contributed over time to the dissemination of the French language but also to the development of more manual training through the creation of vocational schools.[39] Rachel Béhar, for example, insisted from the outset on the need to found professional workshops for girls. Born in Jerusalem, she was one of the first students to be trained at the École Bischoffsheim in Paris and was part of a familial Alliance dynasty with both her brother as well as her sister. Appointed director of the Moroccan school in Tetuan in 1895, after eight years directing first a school in Constantinople and then another in Andrianople in Turkey, Béhar's reports back to the Central Committee in Paris insisted that teachers coming to Morocco should be better prepared to teach crafts and should learn these skills in Paris before arriving. This emphasis on craft apprenticeship was the product of her experiences in Tur-

---

[39] Frances Malino, "L'émancipation des femmes," in *Histoire de l'Alliance Israélite Universelle de 1860 à nos jours*, éd. André Kaspi (Paris: Armand Colin, 2010), 263–294.

key where workshops for girls were established almost from the outset. Training girls to sew was an important part of the westernizing educational project, and it began with teaching students but also adult women how to sew European clothes that would begin the cultural transformation the Alliance sought to achieve. In Tangiers, where a girls' school was founded as early as 1873, the female director opened sewing workshops and established contracts with local craftsmen to form apprentices. In the 1890s, she also convinced the local Alliance committee to fund the purchase of sewing machines.[40]

Inspection visits, teacher reports, and the Alliance's newspaper *La Revue des écoles* all illustrate the way educational ideals forged in Paris were modified through the experience of living in communities which bore little relationship either to teachers' native homes or to the French boarding school community where they were trained. Women directors learned about others' initiatives through the periodicals of the Alliance, but they also drew on their own experiences as assistant teachers or from personal exchanges with other teachers. The frequency and the intensity of exchanges – between Paris and the school, or between members of this closely-knit community – seem to have encouraged female Alliance teachers to defend educational orientations at times in opposition to local traditions or even in opposition to French colonial authorities following the establishment of the Protectorate.[41] The Benchimol sisters, Hassiba and Claire, for example, were adamant about the need to eradicate child marriage and to educate women to have a sense of self-worth:

> You are no doubt aware of the degrading condition of complete servitude which afflicts the feminine sex here in Fez. The man is master here... A woman is a slave who owes passive obedience to her lord and master. I must confess that as a woman and a feminist, these practices did not fail to revolt me, and I would like to have the power to reform this society, which is deficient in so many respects.[42]

For most of these teachers, women's sense of self-worth came through lessons in French as well as manual lessons that allowed women to escape the tyranny of the home and achieve some form of economic independence.

---

40 Michael Laskier, *The Alliance Israélite Universelle and the Jewish Community of Morocco: 1862–1962* (Albany: SUNY Press, 1983), 127.

41 Frances Malino, "Institutrices in the Metropole and the Maghreb: A Comparative Perspective," *Historical Reflections* 32, no. 1 (Spring 2006): 129–43.

42 Letter of November 25, 1900, translated by Malino in Ibid. For a case study of Claire and Hassiban Benchimol's youngest sister, Alégrina, see Malino, "Alégrina Benchimol Lévy, directrice d'école de l'Alliance israélite universelle (Tétouan, 5 mars 1885– ?)," *Archives juives* 34, no. 1 (2001): 129–132.

Bringing gender and religion into the same analytic vision offers a far more nuanced history of education in the colonies. To paraphrase the title of an issue of *Studia Paedagogica*, the forgotten contribution of the female teaching missionary adds an important dimension to the history of imperial schooling.[43]

Conclusion: A "New" Agenda? De-nationalizing, Trans-nationalizing, and Gendering the Civilizing Mission in Education

In 2009, Bart Hellinckx, Frank Simon and Marc Depaepe's impressive historiographic essay about "The forgotten contribution of the Teaching Sisters" deliberately excluded colonial or missionary education in their 50-page overview and even then their bibliography was almost 40 pages long. This points to the difficulty of a single person being able to master this literature, and the need to develop conversations that introduce scholars to the wealth of studies that exist and that are underway. Paying attention to mission as well as to women's education is not in reality "new" at all; the challenge, however, is in orchestrating the diversity of approaches together. Specialists of Christian mission tend to organize conferences together, to publish in specialist venues together, and to ignore what is written on Jewish missionaries (whose own habits are very similar). Specialists of education in the colonies are often specialized by geographical area, for reasons that are readily comprehensible. French educational initiatives play out very differently in the West Indies, Africa, the Middle East, and Indochina. And yet similarities exist in part because the missionary actors shared similar training and maintained contact through the periodicals, newsletters, and correspondences that have proven to be such rich sources for historians interested in how civilizational discourses are translated into educational programs.[44]

Far from advocating the abandonment of detailed case studies that bring to light these acts of translation, this essay seeks, in the spirit of international cooperation that has so marked the scholarship of Marc Depaepe, to bring these

---

[43] Bart Hellinckx, Frank Simon, and Marc Depaepe, "The Forgotten contribution of the Teaching Sisters. A historiographical essay on the educational work of Catholic Women Religious in the 19th and 20th centuries," *Studia Paedagogica* 44 (Leuven: Leuven University Press, 2009).
[44] See Rebecca Rogers, "French nuns go international: Rereading histories of girls' education through a political and transnational lens," in *Gender, Power and Education in a Transnational World*, ed. Adelina Arredondo and Christine Mayer (New York: Palgrave Macmillan 2020) (ISCHE Global Histories of Education).

case studies together, to urge scholars to look beyond the national, to take seriously the perspectives offered by the transnational, and to never forget that both men and women were part of the vast movement that led Europeans to use schools as a way of transmitting what they considered their "superior civilizing duty" with consequences that deserve our collective attention.

Bibliography

Barthélémy, Pascale. "L'enseignement dans l'Empire colonial français : une vieille histoire?" *Histoire de l'éducation* 128 (2010): 5–28.

Barthélémy, Pascale. *Africaines et diplômées à l'époque coloniale (1918–1957)*. Rennes: Presses Universitaires de Rennes, 2010.

Boquet, Jérôme, ed. *L'enseignement français en Méditerranée. Les missionnaires et l'Alliance israélite universelle*. Rennes: Presses universitaires de Rennes, 2010.

Bouche, Denise. *L'enseignement dans les territoires français de l'Afrique occidentale de 1817 à 1920. Mission civilisatrice ou formation d'une élite*. History dissertation, Université de Paris I, 1975.

Cabanel, Patrick, and Jean-Dominique Durand, ed. *Le grand exil des congrégations religieuses françaises: 1901–1914: actes du colloque international de Lyon, Université Jean-Moulin Lyon III, 12–13 juin 2003*. Paris: Cerf, 2005.

Cabanel, Patrick, ed. *Une France en Méditerranée. Écoles, langue et culture françaises, XIXe-XXe siècles*. Paris: CREAPHIS, 2006.

Cabanel, Patrick. *Lettres d'exil, 1901–1909. Les congrégations françaises dans le monde après les lois laïques de 1901 et 1904, Anthologie de textes missionnaires*. Turnhout: Brepols, 2008.

Colonna, Fanny. *Instituteurs algériens, 1883–1939*. Paris: Presses de la Fondation Nationale des Sciences Politiques, 1975.

Comby, Jean. *Deux mille ans d'évangélisation. Histoire de l'expansion chrétienne*. Paris: Desclée 1992.

Condette, Jean-François. "HARDY Georges." In *Les recteurs d'académie en France de 1808 à 1940. Tome II, Dictionnaire biographique*, edited by J.-F. Condette, 213–214. Paris: Institut national de recherche pédagogique, 2006.

Conklin, Alice. *A Mission to Civilize. The Republican Idea of Empire in France and West Africa, 1895–1930*. Stanford: Stanford University Press, 1997.

Cornuel, Pascale. "Anne-Marie Javouhey à Mana – Une mission maternaliste?" In *Les Conditions matérielles de la mission – Contrainte, dépassement, imaginaires*, edited by M. Cheza and J. Pirotte, 187-207. Paris: Karthala, 2005.

Curtis, Sarah. "The double invisibility of Missionary Sisters." *Journal of Women's History* 28, no. 4 (2016): 134–143.

Curtis, Sarah. *Civilizing Habits. Women and the Revival of French Empire*. Oxford: Oxford University Press, 2010.

Daughton, J.-P. *An Empire Divided. Religion, Republicanism, and the Making of French Colonialism*. Oxford and New York: Oxford University Press, 2006.

Delisle, Philippe. "Colonisation, christianisation et émancipation. Les sœurs de Saint-Joseph de Cluny à Mana (Guyane française). 1828–1846." *Revue française d'histoire d'outre-mer* 85, no. 320 (1998): 7–32.
Depaepe, Marc, and Frank Simon. "Is there any Place for the History of 'Education' in the 'History of Education'? A Plea for the History of Everyday Educational Reality in- and outside Schools." *Paedagogica Historica* 3, no. 1 (1995): 9–16.
Depaepe, Marc. "An Agenda for the History of Colonial Education." *Paedagogica Historica* 31, sup. 1 (1995): 15–21.
Depaepe, Marc. "Études des manuels et chansons scolaires dans la perspective de l'Histoire de l'éducation colonial-une introduction." In *Manuels et chansons scolaires au Congo Belge*, edited by M. Depaepe, J. Briffaerts, P. Kita Kyankenge Masandi, and H. Vinck, 7–29. Leuven: University Press, 2003.
Depaepe, Marc. "The Ten Commandments of Good Practices in History of Education Research." *Zeitschrift für pädagogische Historiographie* 16, no. 1 (2010): 31–34.
Depaepe, Marc. "Writing histories of Congolese Colonial and Post-Colonial Education: A Historiographical View from Belgium." In *Connecting Histories of Education: Transnational and Cross-cultural Exchanges in (Post-) Colonial Education*, edited by Barnita Bagchi, Eckhardt Fuchs, and Kate Rousmaniere, 41–60. New York: Berghahn, 2014.
Dufourcq, Elisabeth. *Les aventurières de Dieu. Trois siècles d'histoire missionnaire française*. Paris: Éditions Jean-Claude Lattès, 1993.
Dufourcq, Elisabeth. *Les congrégations religieuses féminines hors d'Europe de Richelieu à nos jours. Histoire naturelle d'une diaspora*. 4 vol. Paris: Librairie de l'Inde, 1993.
Duteil, Simon. "Un instituteur colonial à Madagascar au début du XXe siècle." *Histoire de l'éducation* 128 (2010): 79–102.
Eizlini, Carine. "Georges Hardy pédagogue et idéologue en Afrique occidentale Française." In *L'école aux colonies, les colonies à l'école*, edited by Gilles Boyer, Pascal Clerc, and Michelle Zancarini-Fournel, 39–55. Lyon: ENS Editions, 2013.
Ferry, Jules. "Discours du 28 juillet 1885 à la chambre." *Discours et opinions de Jules Ferry*, edited by Paul Robiquet. Vol. 5, Discours sur la politique extérieure et coloniale (2e partie): affaires tunisiennes (suite et fin), Congo, Madagascar, Égypte, Tonkin. Trois préfaces, 172–220. Paris: Armand Colin & Cie., 1897.
Foster, Elizabeth. *Faith in Empire: Religion, Politics, and Colonial Rule in French Senegal, 1880–1940*. Stanford: Stanford University Press, 2013.
Gamble, Harry. *Contesting French West Africa. Battles over Schools and the Colonial Order, 1900–1950*. Lincoln and London: University of Nebraska Press, 2017.
Gangnat, *Émilie*, Geneviève Granier, and Jean-François Zorn. "Une famille missionnaire protestante à la période héroïque de la mission: Les Volla et leurs enfants au Zambèze (1902–1913)." In *Hommes et femmes en mission (XIXe-XXe siècle). Entre partage et confrontation*, Actes de la XXXVIIe session du CREDIC, Paris, 23 août–27 août 2016, edited by Bernadette Truchet and Jean-François Zorn, 197–237. Paris: Karthala, 2018.
Goerg, Odile, and Marie-Albane de Suremain, eds. "Coopérants et coopération en Afrique: circulations d'acteurs et recompositions culturelles (des années 1950 à nos jours)." *Outre-Mers. Revue d'histoire* vol. 101, no. 384–385 (2014).

Hellinckx, Bart, Frank Simon, and Marc Depaepe. "The Forgotten contribution of the Teaching Sisters. A historiographical essay on the educational work of Catholic Women Religious in the 19th and 20th centuries." *Studia Paedagogica* 44 (Leuven University Press, 2009).

Hugon, Anne. *Un protestantisme africain au XIXe siècle. L'implantation du méthodisme en Gold Coast (Ghana), 1837–1874.* Paris: Karthala, 2007.

Jézéquel, Jean-Hervé. *Les 'mangeurs de craies'. Histoire sociale des instituteurs en Afrique Occidentale Française.* Paris: Karthala, 2008.

Labrune-Badiane, Céline, and Étienne Smith. *Les hussards noirs de la colonie. Instituteurs africains et petites patries en AOF.* Paris: Karthala, 2018.

Laskier, Michael. *The Alliance Israélite Universelle and the Jewish Community of Morocco: 1862–1962.* Albany: SUNY Press, 1983.

Lecuir-Nemo, Geneviève. *Femmes et vocation missionnaire. Permanence des congrégations féminines au Sénégal de 1819 à 1960: adaptation ou mutation ? Impact et insertion.* History dissertation, Université de Paris I, 1995.

Lenoble-Bart, Annie. "Missionnaires catholiques en Afrique, entre information et communication?" *Revue des sciences religieuses* 80, no. 2 (2006): 193–204.

Léon, Antoine. *Colonisation, Enseignement et éducation. Étude historique et comparative.* Paris: L'Harmattan, 1991.

Malino, Frances. "Alégrina Benchimol Lévy, directrice d'école de l'Alliance israélite universelle (Tétouan, 5 mars 1885–?)." *Archives juives* vol. 34, no. 1 (2001): 129–132.

Malino, Frances. "Institutrices in the Metropole and the Maghreb: A Comparative Perspective." *Historical Reflections* vol. 32, no 1 (Spring 2006): 129–43.

Malino, Frances. "L'émancipation des femmes." In *Histoire de l'Alliance Israélite Universelle de 1860 à nos jours*, edited by André Kaspi, 263–294. Paris: Armand Colin, 2010.

Nguyen, Thuy Phuong. "De la "mission civilisatrice" à la mission culturelle: un discours post-colonial contrarié (Indochine 1946–1952)." In *Repenser la "mission civilisatrice". L'éducation dans le monde colonial et postcolonial au XXe siècle*, edited by Damiano Matasci, Miguel Bandeira Jerónimo, and Hugo Gonçalves Dores, 141–155. Rennes: Presses universitaires de Rennes, 2020.

Nguyen, Thuy Phuong. *L'école française au Vietnam de 1945 à 1975. De la mission civilisatrice à la diplomatie culturelle.* Amiens: Encrage Editions, 2017.

Pagnon, Estelle. "'Une œuvre inutile'? La scolarisation des filles par les missionnaires catholiques dans le Sud-Est du Nigéria (1885-1930)." *Clio. Histoire, femmes et sociétés* 6 (1997): 35–59.

Paisant Chantal, ed. *La mission au féminin. Témoignages de religieuses missionnaires au fil d'un siècle (XIXe-début XXe siècle). Anthologie de textes missionnaires.* Turnhout: Brepols, 2009.

Paisant, Chantal. "Les sœurs de Picpus en Amérique latine: Les premières missions d'éducation." *Tranversalités* 71 (1999): 205–228.

Prudhomme, Claude. "Missionnaire." In *Dictionnaire de la colonisation française*, edited by Claude Liauzu, 473. Paris: Larousse, 2007.

Raison-Jourde, Françoise. *Bible et pouvoir à Madagascar au XIXe siècle. Invention d'une identité chrétienne et construction de l'État.* Paris: Karthala, 1991.

Rodrigue, Aron. *French Jews, Turkish Jews: The Alliance Israélite Universelle and the Politics of Jewish Schooling in Turkey, 1860–1925.* Bloomington: Indiana University Press, 1990.

Rodrigue, Aron. *Images of Sephardi and Eastern Jewries in Transition. The Teachers of the Alliance Israélite Universelle, 1860–1939.* Seattle: University of Washington Press, 1993.

Rogers, Rebecca. "'*Cherchez la femme*': Women and Gender in French Scholarship on the Empire," *Journal of Women's History* 28, no. 4 (2016): 124–133.

Rogers, Rebecca. "Congregações femininas e difusão de um modelo escolar: uma história transnacional." *Pro-Posições* 25, no. 1 Campinas (2014): 55–74.

Rogers, Rebecca. "French nuns go international: Rereading histories of girls' education through a political and transnational lens." In *Gender, Power and Education in a Transnational World*, edited by Adelina Arredondo and Christine Mayer, 69–92. New York: Palgrave Macmillan 2020.

Rogers, Rebecca. "Genre, mission et colonisation." In *Religions et colonisation. Afrique-Asie-Océanie-Amériques (XVIe–XXe siècles)*, edited by Dominique Borne and Benoît Falaize, 93–100. Paris: L'Atelier, 2009.

Salvaing, Bernard. "Missionnaires catholiques français et protestants britanniques face à l'Afrique. Le cas de la Côte du Bénin et du pays Yoruba (1841–1891)." *Revue française d'histoire d'Outre-Mer* no. 262–263 (1984): 31–57.

Salvaing, Bernard. *Les missionnaires à l'encontre de l'Afrique au XIXe siècle (Côte des Esclaves et pays Yoruba, 1840–1891*, 134–137. Paris: L'Harmattan, 1995.

Segella, Spencer. "Georges Hardy and Educational Ethnology in French Morocco, 1920–26." *French Colonial History* 4 (2003): 171–90.

Thevenin, André. *La mission laïque française à travers son histoire 1902–2002*. Paris: Mission Laïque Française, 2002.

Turin, Yvonne. *Affrontements culturels dans l'Algérie Coloniale. Écoles, médecines, religion, 1830–1880*. Paris: François Maspero, 1971.

Verdeil, Chantal, ed. *Missions chrétiennes en terre d'Islam. Moyen-Orient Afrique du Nord (XVIIe-XXe siècles)*. Turnhout: Brepols, 2013.

Vigner, Gérard. "L'école Jules-Ferry, école normale de l'enseignement colonial: une formation pour apprendre à enseigner dans les colonies (1902–1912)." *Documents pour l'histoire du français langue étrangère ou second* 55 (2015): 1–17.

White, Owen, and J.P. Daughton, eds. *In God's Empire: French Missionaries and the Modern World*. Oxford: Oxford University Press, 2012.

White, Owen. *Children of the French Empire: Miscegenation and Colonial Society in French West Africa, 1895–1960*. Oxford: Oxford University Press, 1999.

Eckhardt Fuchs (Technische Universität Braunschweig, Germany)
Textbooks in their Contexts: Textbook Studies Revisited

Abstract: Textbook-orientated research is a broad and multi-disciplinary field that is difficult to gauge or evaluate as there is considerable disparity on many levels between the various approaches. Only recently scholars have started to explore textbooks in relation to society, education policy, academia, educational practice, and the economy. This essay elaborates on some new research perspectives that go beyond mere content analysis by looking at the extent to which constructions of cultural difference can be found in textbooks and on which social contexts these might be based. It also introduces issues that emerge in this new "textbook-related" research – such as the impact and the production of textbooks as well as classroom implementation.

Keywords: Textbooks studies, historiography, diversity, textbook revisions, politics

The content, design, and educational aims and objectives of textbooks have changed over time, as have the manner of their production, their role in the classroom, and the ways in which their users acquire the knowledge canonized in them. Today's textbooks coexist or compete with other forms of educational media and are themselves undergoing a process of transformation in the wake of the digital revolution. These developments notwithstanding, research shows that textbooks remain the most important educational medium in schools worldwide, created in negotiation processes at the societal level and delivering the knowledge these societies deem relevant enough to pass on to the younger generation. Yet, textbooks are more than simply mediators of knowledge. They always contain and enshrine underlying norms and values; they transmit constructions of identity; and they generate specific patterns of perceiving the world. All this means that textbooks are frequently contested, within and between societies, among political, social, religious, and ethnic groups.

Generations of textbook researchers have wrestled with the question of precisely what makes textbooks and their specific methods of analysis so distinctive, without yet reaching consensus on any definition. Yet this lack of delimitation is no reason for disquiet if one views textbooks and their associated research as contingent conditions that are subject to constant change and to wide-ranging definitions.

Only recently scholars have started to explore textbooks in relation to society, education policy, academia, educational practice and the economy, from the perspectives of scholarship, didactics, educationalists, textbook authors, education policy representatives, and publishing houses. Textbook-related research has also responded to current societal developments. Education systems all over the world find themselves faced with the challenge of addressing the increasing cultural, ethnic, and religious diversity of school classrooms in the light of more heterogeneous (im)migration societies. This especially affects curricula as well as teaching and learning materials, which have a particularly crystallizing effect on issues of inclusion and exclusion. Textbook-related research has begun to investigate the extent to which constructions of cultural difference can be found in textbooks and on which social contexts these might be based. Here new issues emerge in textbook-related research – for example, the issue of difference in textbooks, as well as its complex subject matter, classroom implementation, subject orientation, and educational objectives. The following chapter will elaborate on some new research perspectives that go beyond content analysis by putting textbooks in their contexts.

Textbook Research and Textbook Revision

It appears fairly obvious that textbook-orientated research and textbook revision are closely related. Up until today, textbook revision has been dominated by its aim to liberate textbooks from nationalistic, chauvinistic, and biased interpretations in order to contribute towards peace and international understanding. Especially in its early days, textbook-orientated research was deeply influenced by this normative and, in many cases, highly political nature of textbook revision. At the same time, looking over past historiography it is clear that textbook-orientated research has always been subject to significant political and thus normative constraints. Textbook-orientated research has been marked by the tension between normative assumptions (e.g. that the improvement of textbooks has a direct impact on learning outcomes), political expectations (e.g. that a good textbook makes a good citizen), and academic objectivity. This tension has been shaped by comparative textbook analysis from the very beginning, whether by the League of Nations during the interwar period, or by UNESCO, the Council of Europe, and bilateral textbook conferences in the post-war era. Even though the majority of textbook-related research today has distanced itself from this normative and political point of departure, the latter continues to play a key role, particularly in cases of war-affected or post-conflict societies. Here, textbook-orientated research – primarily analyses of stereotyping and enemy images in textbooks and other teaching materials – provides political recommendations for the revision of such materials. In the past decades this has been most relevant for three regions: the Balkans, East Asia, and the Near and Middle East. There is very recent research on all three regions, ultimately serving to support political and social processes of reconciliation and the reification of textbook contents. In the case of the Near and Middle East, research aims both to support the dialogue between the Arab states and, in the context of Israel and Palestine, to contribute to a mutual understanding of different interpretations of history, objectifying their portrayal. East Asia is another region that has been marked by textbook conflicts for a long time. Since 2001 historians and educators have been discussing controversial issues and developed various bi- and multilateral textbooks and teaching materials. East Asian textbook revision activities have caused fierce political debates but have also been a tool to enhance the academic communication between China, Japan, and South Korea. The ways in which textbook activities and academic historical research have contributed to coming to terms with the region's past has been widely analyzed over the last decade.

The highly explosive political nature of textbooks and research pertaining to them is, however, not only relevant for cases of textbook revision in contexts of social conflict. A multitude of textbook conflicts – especially in relation to history textbooks – have resulted in so-called "history wars", waged on a national level within a specific society. These conflicts are essentially disputes over the formation of a national tradition, the securing of legitimization processes, and the construction of national identity. It is no longer the historical profession that exclusively determines the way in which a nation ought to remember its past but a wider public that uses digital media to resonate about controversial historical events well beyond the context of the specialized academic discourse. Over the last decade, there has been a worldwide increase in public disputes of this kind surrounding the interpretation of historical events and the question as to which interpretations should be included in history textbooks. The Armenian genocide in Turkey, the textbook debate in Greece, the colonial past in France, the role of indigenous population in Australia, or the Enola Gay debate in the USA are but a few examples.

As a general rule, it can be said that the experience of the globalizing world and increasing demands to account for the histories of hitherto "unheard voices" from socially, religiously, and ethnically disadvantaged groups have contributed to a questioning of the dominating national narrative. The challenges of the multi-ethnic classroom, as well as attempts to construct supra-national identities, reveal the limitations of a master narrative purely based on national history.

On the other hand, it appears impossible to ignore the neo-conservative trend that seeks to uphold traditional national history and prescribe certain identity constructions with a view to sustaining particular national values. Overall, textbook conflicts are not confined to conflict-affected countries or societies in transition where textbook revision plays an important part in enhancing reconciliation. In addition, globalization has led to a new understanding of the nation, the role of historical scholarship and the public awareness of the political dimension of memory production and, therefore, has a major impact on textbook issues. Textbook-orientated research has started to contextualize the analysis of textbooks and educational media within these developments.

Minorities and Gender

Academic criticism of textbook content, which began in the 1970s, primarily addressed ideological content and the intelligibility of teaching texts.[1] The textbook was now viewed as both a product of and a factor in social processes and as an object of political interest. The most prominent proponent of such an approach in the USA has been Michael W. Apple. The first studies to address themes such as national minorities, race, gender or social class in textbooks were published in the 1960s. The depiction of minorities and issues of race in the USA were included in these early studies and the subject of sexual equality was first explored in the 1980s. However, Apple was the first to consider these themes as relevant factors in the production of legitimate knowledge in textbooks. He worked from the premise that due to both content and format, textbooks represent a specific construction of reality as well as the considered selection and organization of knowledge. Textbook production is the result of complex negotiation processes and power structures and reflects differences in social class, race, gender/sex, and religious affiliation between stakeholders.[2] Béatrice Ziegler, for example, was also able to show in her study of Swiss history textbooks that migration was only ever referred to in the context of migrant labor and of being "swamped" or "overrun" with foreigners, and that pupils from families with a migration background were confronted with a narrative of migration that returned them

---

[1] John W. Meyer, Patricia Bromley, and Francisco O. Ramirez, "Human Rights in Social Science Textbooks: Cross-national Analyses, 1970–2008," *Sociology of Education* 83, no. 2 (2010): 111–134.
[2] Michael W. Apple and Linda K. Christian-Smith, *The Politics of the Textbook* (New York: Routledge, 1991).

to the status of "newcomers" or "strangers".³ Studies from other multicultural countries reveal racist presentations and stereotypical depictions of Black people in textbooks, while the subject of historic "white dominance" is suppressed. Research on this subject includes a study on racism in Brazilian textbooks and the depiction of racist violence against Black Americans in American social studies textbooks.⁴

Despite concerted efforts over many years to develop gender-sensitive textbooks and educational media, an international comparative study conducted by UNESCO in 2008 revealed that although the majority of textbooks are not openly discriminatory, they still convey a wide range of stereotypes.⁵ The UNESCO handbook was based on practical findings and on scientific textbook analysis and documented that the representation of women and girls in textbooks remains biased. They are depicted less frequently than men and boys and are portrayed in gender-typical roles. A quantitative analysis of character representations in Malaysian textbooks supported these findings.⁶ A study of 42 Pakistani textbooks in Urdu, English, and Pashto also showed that outdated gender identities were perpetuated by the dominance of masculine language that consequently reinforced social structures.⁷ Two studies exploring gender representations in Iranian and Ugandan textbooks reached similar conclusions.⁸ Academic studies examining other subjects in the humanities corroborate the above findings. Susanne Knudsen points out that her research into Swedish textbooks

---

3 Béatrice Ziegler, "Politische Bildung im Deutschschweizer Lehrplan (Lehrplan 21)," 2010, https://plone.unige.ch/aref2010/symposiums-longs/coordinateurs-en-h/nouvelles-demandes-sociales-et-valeurs-portees-par-l2019ecole/Politische%20Bildung.pdf.
4 Paulo V. B. da Silva, Rozana Teixeira, and Tânia M. Pacifico, "Políticas de promoção de igualdade racial e programas de distribuição de livros didáticosm," *Educação e Pesquisa* 39, no. 1 (2013): 127–143.
5 Carole Brugeilles and Sylvie Cromer, *Comment promouvoir l'égalité entre les sexes par les manuels scolaires? Guide méthodologique à l'attention des acteurs et actrices de la chaîne du manuel scolaire* (Paris: UNESCO, 2008).
6 Zarina Othman, Bahiya Abdul Hamid, Mohd S. M. Yasin, Yuen Chee Keong, and Azhar Jaludin. "Gender Images in Selected Malaysian School Textbooks. A Frequency Analysis," *International Journal of Learning* 10, no. 18 (2012): 101–126.
7 Qaisar Khan, Sultana Nighat, Bughio Qasim, and Arat Naz, "The Role of Language in Gender Identity Formation in Pakistani School Textbooks," *Indian Journal of Gender Studies* 21, no. 1 (2014): 55–84.
8 Amanda Barton and Lydia N. Sakwa, "The Representation of Gender in English Textbooks in Uganda," *Pedagogy, Culture and Society* 20, no. 2 (2012): 173–190.

found scant representation of female authors, artists or historical figures and advocates more intensive consideration of gender issues within textbook research.[9]

The Nation and Beyond

Conventional research into stereotypes has been complemented since the 1970s by new themes such as multilateralism, Europeanisation, and transnational perspectives. The shifts in global political constellations since 1989, as well as the emergence of new ethnic and political conflicts, particularly in Europe, have provided new subject matter for content analysis, as have processes of Europeanisation and globalization. The majority of current textbook-related research has moved away from the normative political assumptions that dominated the initial periods of textbook revision but these nevertheless continue to play a significant role in post-conflict societies and those still at war. In such instances textbook research comprises the analysis of textbooks and teaching materials for stereotypical representations and images of the enemy with the aim of providing policy-relevant recommendations for the revision of such material. This currently applies predominantly to three regions: the Balkans, the Middle East and, in terms of conflict concerning textbooks, East Asia. Recent research has been conducted into each of these regions with the ultimate goal of supporting political and social reconciliation processes and of improving the objectivity of textbook content.[10] Research in the Middle East has attempted to provide support for the dialogue between Arab states and, in the case of Israel and Palestine, to contribute to the creation of a reciprocal understanding for different interpretations of history and the objective presentation of such interpretations.[11] East Asia on the other hand, while not a post-conflict region, is an area that has been marked by protracted conflict surrounding textbooks. Textbook revision here focuses primarily on academic expertise from historians and educational practitioners

---

9 Susanne Knudsen, "Dancing with and without gender – reflections on gender, textbooks and textbook research," In *"Has past passed?" Textbooks and educational media for the 21st century*, edited by Mike Horsley (Stockholm: Stockholm Institute of Education Press, 2005), 70–81.
10 See for example, Augusta Dimou, *"Transition" and the politics of history education in Southeast Europe* (Göttingen: V&R unipress, 2009); and Jon Dorschner and Thomas Sherlock, "The role of history textbooks in shaping collective identities in India and Pakistan," in *Teaching the violent past: history education and reconciliation*, ed. by Elisabeth A. Cole (Lanham, Md.: Rowman and Littlefield, 2009), 275–315.
11 Ruth Firer and Sami Adwan, *The Israeli-Palestinian conflict in history and civics textbooks of both nations* (Hanover: Hahn, 2004).

rather than on textbook analysis. The latest papers examining the region not only analyze the conflicts surrounding textbooks but also search for solutions.[12]

In the last ten years there has been a worldwide increase in public confrontations where the interpretation of historical events in history books has been questioned, as has the selection of events to be included.[13] In general, it appears that an increased separation of nations from their history acts as a catalyst for such debates. The experiences of an increasingly globalized world and the mounting calls for the "unheard voices" of socially, religiously, and ethnically disadvantaged groups to be heard are leading to some national narratives to be called into question and for other national histories to be contextualized or even abandoned. The limitations of exclusively national historical narratives are being exposed by the challenges of multi-ethnic classrooms and attempts to construct supranational identities.

Textbook research is increasingly drawing on approaches used in European and transnational research. Questions of how textbooks contribute to national constructions of identity are being answered with reference to national identities or to Europe.[14] Although the idea of a uniform and unalterable European historical narrative has been met with skepticism by academics, the plurality of conceptions of Europe appears to exclude a singular, binding historical narrative.[15] Textbook researchers have seized upon this theme and are not only questioning the diversity of representations of Europe and "Europeanness" in current textbooks, they are simultaneously using comparative analyses to study historic shifts in textbooks and therefore to identify convergent or concurrent perceptions

---

[12] Yoshiko Nozaki and Mark Selden, "Historical Memory, International Conflict, and Japanese Textbook Controversies in Three Epochs," *Journal of Educational Media, Memory and Society* 1, no. 1 (2009): 117–144; and Sven Saaler, *Politics, Memory, and Public Opinion. The History Textbook Controversy and Japanese Society* (München: Iudicium, 2005).

[13] Maria Repoussi, "Politics Questions History Education. Debates on Greek History Textbooks," in *Jahrbuch der Internationalen Gesellschaft für Geschichtsdidaktik* (2006/2007): 99–110; Maria Repoussi, "Common Trends in Contemporary Debates on Historical Education," in *Jahrbuch der Internationalen Gesellschaft für Geschichtsdidaktik* (2008/2009): 75–90; and Stuart McIntyre and Anna Clark, *The History Wars* (Melbourne: Melbourne University Press, 2003).

[14] Markus Furrer, *Die Nation im Schulbuch – zwischen Überhöhung und Verdrängung: Leitbilder der Schweizer Nationalgeschichte in Schweizer Geschichtslehrmitteln der Nachkriegszeit und Gegenwart* (Hanover: Hahn, 2004); for a non-European perspective see Mary A. Rojas, "An Examination of U.S. Latino Identities as Constructed in/through Curricular Materials," *Linguistics and Education* 3, no. 24 (2013): 373–380; for an example re the case of Cyprus see Stavroula Philippou, ed., *"Europe" turned local – the local turned European? Constructions of "Europe" in social studies curricula across Europe* (Münster: LIT, 2012).

[15] Eckhardt Fuchs and Simone Lässig, "Europa im Schulbuch," *Geschichte für heute* 2, no. 1 (2009): 66–69.

in textbooks of self and other in relation to Europe.[16] The contextualization of research within the framework of European identity building and within the inconsistencies and diversity of commonly competing representations of Europe is, however, still in its infancy.[17]

Macro-sociological studies also provide explanatory models for global textbook and curriculum development. Such international and comparative studies that examine trends in textbook research and associated theory formation and that are firmly committed to a neo-institutionalist approach have convincingly demonstrated that curricular structures and textbook content align with one another when viewed from a global perspective.[18]

Impact and Reception

A social-science oriented branch of textbook research has been developing since the mid-1980s, which, in connection with American mass-communications research, has found that media content does not have a demonstrable impact upon recipients.[19] In terms of textbook research this means that learning outcomes are not traceable directly to textbook content. Applied research had, until the beginning of the 1990s at least, focused primarily on questions of con-

---

[16] Stephanie Jackson and Sylvie Iris, "Eurogame. Teaching the Geography of Europe and Its Regions through Online Multimedia Games," *Internationale Schulbuchforschung* 24, no. 2 (2002): 175–187; and Eugen Kotte, *"In Räume geschriebene Zeiten": nationale Europabilder im Geschichtsunterricht der Sekundarstufe II* (Idstein: Schulz-Kirchner-Verlag, 2007).
[17] Yasemin Soysal, "Lernziel: Europa. Schulbücher auf dem Prüfstand," *Zeitschrift für Kulturaustausch* 3 (2002).
[18] Patricia Bromley, "Holocaust education and human rights: Holocaust discussions in social science textbooks worldwide, 1970–2008," in *"Holocaust education" als Gegenstand international-vergleichender Erziehungswissenschaft*, edited by Matthias Proske and Wolfgans Meseth (Münster: Waxmann, 2013); and Patricia Bromley, John W. Meyer, and Francisco O. Ramirez, *The worldwide spread of environmental discourse in social science textbooks, 1970–2008: cross-national patterns and hierarchical linear models*, https://worldpolity.files.wordpress.com/2010/08/bromley-meyer-ramirez-environmentalism-in-textbooks-6-2010.pdf; Francisco O. Ramirez, John Boli, and John W. Meyer, "Explaining the origins and expansion of mass education," in *Sociological worlds: comparative and historical readings on society*, ed. by Stephen K. Sanderson (London: Fitzroy & Dearborn, 2000); Francisco O. Ramirez and John W. Meyer, "National Curricula. World Models and Historical Legacies," in *Internationalisierung. Semantik und Bildungssystem in vergleichender Perspektive* ed. by Marcelo Caruso and Heinz-Elmar Tenorth (Frankfurt a. M.: Peter Lang, 2002), 91–108.
[19] Klaus Lange, "Zu Methodologie und Methoden einer sozialwissenschaftlichen Unterrichtsmedienforschung," *Internationale Schulbuchforschung* 3 (1981): 16–28.

tent acquisition and pupils' actual achievements and did not consider the source of disseminated knowledge or the socio-cultural backgrounds of the students and pupils.[20]

Social studies approaches researching the impact and reception of textbooks in classrooms are currently gaining in significance. This field is still in its infancy and studies tend to be integrated into more general investigations related to didactics in history and geography teaching.[21] Nevertheless, there is increasing interest in the way in which textbooks are employed in classrooms and the influence this may have on the development of historical awareness among pupils. Textbook authors and educationalists expect history teaching materials to play a guiding role in classroom teaching and to positively influence teaching quality.[22] However, the concrete effects of this medium are still relatively unknown, particularly in the context of other media and agencies of socialization.

The question of quality occurs frequently in relation to teaching materials and is regularly – and often publicly – discussed, but the relationship between quality and learning outcomes has not to this date attracted intense interest from either academia or education policy makers. An empirical impact study into teaching materials provides answers to the question of how textbook content is transmitted by teachers and received by pupils.[23] Another study examining the introduction of an English textbook in Switzerland concluded that problems experienced were associated more with the reorganization of foreign-language teaching and with the education policy framework in place at that time than with the quality of the material itself.[24] Findings such as these reveal a supplementary layer of mechanisms, in addition to factors related to teaching and to the school system, that influence how teaching materials affect the learning

---

[20] Michael W. Apple and Linda K. Christian-Smith, *The Politics of the Textbook* (New York: Routledge, 1991).
[21] Bodo von Borries, *Schulbuchverständnis, Richtlinienbenutzung und Reflexionsprozesse im Geschichtsunterricht: einequalitativ-quantitative Schüler- und Lehrerbefragung im deutschsprachigen Bildungswesen 2002* (Neuried: Ars Una, 2005); and Peter Gautschi, ed., *Geschichtsunterricht heute: eine empirische Analyse ausgewählter Aspekte* (Bern: hep verlag, 2007).
[22] Bernhard C. Schär and Vera Sperisen, "Zum Eigensinn von Lehrpersonen im Umgang mit Lehrbüchern: das Beispiel 'Hinschauen und Nachfragen'," in *Forschungswerkstatt Geschichtsdidaktik 09: Beiträge zur Tagung "Geschichtsdidaktik Empirisch 09,"* ed. by Jan Hodel and Beatrice Ziegler (Bern: hep verlag, 2011), 124–134.
[23] Werner Wiater, "Lehrplan und Schulbuch. Reflexionen über zwei Instrumente des Staates zur Steuerung des Bildungswesens," in *Das Schulbuch zwischen Lehrplan und Unterrichtspraxis*, ed. by Eva Matthes, and Carsten Heinze (Bad Heilbrunn: Klinkhardt, 2005), 41–64.
[24] Lucien Criblez, Armanda Nägeli, and Rosa Stebler, *Schlussbericht. Begleitung der Einführung des Englischlehrmittels Voices auf der Sekundarstufe I* (Zürich: Universität Zürich, 2010).

process. In order to estimate how the contents of teaching materials influence the attitude and actions of pupils it is necessary to consider socio-political and cultural contexts in addition to the relationship between the pupil and the teaching material. Factors such as social background, membership of social groups and associations as well as individual circumstances play a significant role.[25]

Investigations into the effects of textbooks on learning outcomes, learning success, and motivation have also been moving closer to the spotlight as a result of the current media shift. One of the few studies to examine the relationship between textbooks and learning success looked at American SAT exam results between 1963 and 1979. It found that an incremental deterioration in results could be attributed to reduced complexity in language textbooks and the subsequent negative effect on reading and oral skills.[26] A study of university teaching materials asked whether textbook selection had any influence upon students' comprehension of a particular topic and concluded that there was no correlation.[27]

Existing studies focus almost exclusively on mathematic and scientific subjects. And although they have drawn no conclusions on the contribution of teaching materials to learning success, they have prompted research in this area, which has predominantly focused on the analysis of textbooks in relation to proposed and implemented curricula, thus concentrating less on the realized curricula and more on the opportunities for learning, that is to say learning outcomes and learning successes.[28]

Textbook Production

In many countries textbooks are a commodity produced by commercial publishing houses. The production of textbooks does not only fulfil education policy requirements but also serves an immense market with a high economic value. Pro-

---

[25] Veronika Kalmus, *"What do pupils and textoobks do with each other? Methodological problems of research on socialization through educational media."* Curriculum Studies 36, no. 4 (2004): 469–485.

[26] Donald P. Hayes, Loreen T. Wolfer, and Michael F. Wolfe, *"Schoolbook simplification and its relation to the decine in SAT-verbal scores."* American Educational Research Journal 33, no. 2 (1996): 489–508.

[27] Cheryl Cisero Durwin and William M. Sherman, "Does choice of college textbook make a difference in students' comprehension?" *College teaching* 56, no. 1 (2008): 28–34.

[28] Linda Haggarty and Birgit Pepin, "An investigation of mathematics textbooks and their use in English, French and German classrooms: who gets an opportunity to learn what?", *British Educational Research Journal* 28, no. 4 (2002): 567–590.

duction costs, which include author and consultant fees, editorial, advertising, printing and marketing costs, depend to varying degrees upon the print run and lifespan of the textbook. Such costs are primarily carried by the publishers who also carry the economic risk but within a broken market where buyer and seller are not necessarily on opposite sides of the deal.

In Europe the role of publishers, authors, and other stakeholders in textbook production was not thoroughly investigated by researchers until the 1970s, although in the USA this had been common since the 1930s. The principal reason for this is that in the USA education is the responsibility of the individual states and the textbook market is open to free competition without government regulations. Against this background it was also in the USA that the first studies to investigate textbook selection and application in lessons were conducted. It was not until 30 years later that the first European study was published on this topic. In his dissertation Carl August Schröder, who later became director of Westermann Verlag in Braunschweig, Germany, explored the role taken by national and international stakeholders (both public and private) when textbook revisions are undertaken as a result of international cooperation. Taking examples from the Federal Republic of Germany he illustrated the tasks, possibilities, and also the limitations of textbook revision when confronted with the conflicting priorities of national and inter- or transnational interest groups and stakeholders.[29] His work remained unique in Europe for many years and it was several decades before the production conditions surrounding textbooks were again a subject of interest to researchers.

There is still very little existing research into the history of textbook publishers, their production mechanisms, social and public impact, or into authors and their interaction with educational institutions and practices. Prior studies into the history of textbooks have certainly addressed these aspects, but without systematically analyzing the complex social position of textbooks.[30] These questions were explored in a seminal German study exploring the nineteenth century history of the *Verlag der Buchhandlung des Waisenhauses*, a publishing house

---

[29] Carl A. Schröder, *Die Schulbuchverbesserung durch internationale geistige Zusammenarbeit* (Braunschweig: Georg Westermann Verlag, 1961).
[30] Heinz Rommel, *Das Schulbuch im 18. Jahrhundert* (Wiesbaden: Dt. Fachschriften-Verlag, 1968); Walter Manz, "Der königlich-bayerische Zentralschulbücherverlag 1785 bis 1849 (1905): der Staat als Schulbuchverleger im 19. Jahrhundert," *Archiv für Geschichte des Buchwesens* 6 (1966): 2–312; and John A. Nietz, *Old textbooks: spelling, grammar, reading, arithmetic, geography, American history, civil government, physiology, penmanship, art, music, as taught in the common schools from colonial days to 1900* (Pittsburgh: University of Pittsburgh Press, 1961).

that produced history and geography textbooks.³¹ Ingeborg Jaklin conducted a comparable study for Austria in which she investigated textbook production by two publishing houses in the eighteenth century.³² Caroline Cody's 1990 study provided an initial examination of the subject in the USA.³³ The Swiss education historian Anne Bosche examined the introduction of newly available information and new teaching materials into primary schools in the Zurich canton in the context of the social and cultural changes that took place in the 1960s and 1970s.³⁴

A relatively large number of studies have examined the production and distribution of textbooks and the development of the textbook market, such as the study by Antonio Viñao³⁵ addressing Spain in the early modern era. Emmanuelle Chapron demonstrated that the development of France's textbook market in the eighteenth century was by no means homogenous; that it was shaped, certainly at a regional level, by diverse administrative regulations, family connections, and local retail networks.³⁶ In the nineteenth century the textbook market in various countries was closely regulated by the state and this was compounded by the introduction of approval processes. During the same period powerful text-

---

31 Julia Kreusch, *Der Verlag der Buchhandlung des Waisenhauses als Schulbuchverlag zwischen 1830 und 1918. Die erfolgreichen Geografie- und Geschichtslehrbücher und ihre Autoren* (Tübingen: Verl. der Franckeschen Stiftungen Halle im Max Niemeyer Verlag, 2012).
32 Ingeborg Jaklin, *Das österreichische Schulbuch im 18. Jahrhundert aus dem Wiener Verlag Trattner und dem Schulbuchverlag* (Wien: Praesens, 2003).
33 Caroline Cody, "The Politics of Textbook Publishing, Adoption and Use." In Textbooks and Schooling in the United States. Eight-ninth Yearbook of the National Society for the Study of Education, Part 1, ed. by David L. Elliot and Arthur Woodward, 127–145 (Chicago: University of Chicago Press, 1990).
34 Anne Bosche, *Schulreformen steuern: die Einführung neuer Lehrmittel und Schulfächer an der Volksschule (Kanton Zürich, 1960er- bis 1980er-Jahre)* (Bern: hep verlag, 2013).
35 Antonio Viñao, "Towards a typology of the primers for learning to read (Spain, c. 1496–1825)," *Paedagogica Historica* 38 (2002): 73–94.
36 Emanuelle Chapron, "Das Elementarschulbuch im 18. Jahrhundert: räumliche Ausbreitung und Handelspraktiken zwischen Paris und der Champagne (1680–1730)," in *Schulbücher und Lektüren in der vormodernen Unterrichtspraxis. Zeitschrift für Erziehungswissenschaft. Sonderheft 17*, ed. by Stephanie Hellekamps (Wiesbaden: Springer Fachmedien, 2012), 91–104; and Volker Titel, "Die Marktsituation des Schulbuchhandels im 19. und frühen 20. Jahrhundert," in *Die Rolle von Schulbüchern für Identifikationsprozesse in historischer Perspektive*, ed. by Heinz-Werner Wollersheim (Leipzig: Leipziger Universitäts-Verlag, 2002), 71–86.

book publishing houses established themselves in most Western countries.[37] In Germany these were often closely linked with academic publishers.[38]

The history of textbook publishing houses for the period from 1871 to 1945 is comparatively well documented, particularly for Germany. The German textbook production system was uniquely organized until the early twentieth century: part of the revenue from textbook sales formed a type of social insurance for primary school teachers as the publishers were required to collaborate with teaching associations and with widow and orphan funds. Several existing studies focus on individual publishing companies[39]; some of these works present comprehensive overviews[40] although others are less detailed.[41] Thomas Keiderling[42] investigated the relationship between publishing firms and authors in the nineteenth and twentieth centuries and concluded that the influence of textbook publishers over text drafts gradually increased over this period. Using textbook analysis, Julio Ruiz Berrio examined the hidden political agenda of the influential Spanish publisher Calleja. The firm started publishing textbooks in 1876, which proved highly successful but which subliminally advocated the modernization of the country.[43]

---

37 Volker Titel, "Die Marktsituation des Schulbuchhandels im 19. und frühen 20. Jahrhundert," In *Die Rolle von Schulbüchern für Identifikationsprozesse in historischer Perspektive*. ed. by Heinz-Werner Wollersheim, (Leipzig: Leipziger Universitäts-Verlag, 2002), 71–86.
38 Thomas Keiderling, "Der Schulbuchverleger und sein Autor: zu Spezialisierungs- und Professionalisierungstendenzen im 19. und frühen 20. Jahrhundert," in *Die Rolle von Schulbüchern für Identifikationsprozesse in historischer Perspektive*, ed. by Heinz-Werner Wollersheim (Leipzig: Leipziger Universitäts-Verlag, 2002), 87–95.
39 Daniel Tröhler and Jürgen Oelkers, eds., *Über die Mittel des Lernens: kontextuelle Studien zum staatlichen Lehrmittelwesen im Kanton Zürich des 19. Jahrhunderts* (Zürich: Verlag Pestalozzianum, 2001).
40 Julia Kreusch, "Der Schulbuchverlag: Entwicklungstendenzen, Bildungspolitik und Schulreform, Das Schulbuchzulassungsverfahren, Schulbuchverlag und Schulbuchproduktion," in *Geschichte des deutschen Buchhandels im 19. und 20. Jahrhundert, Bd. 2: Die Weimarer Republik 1918–1933*, ed. by Ernst Fischer (Berlin: de Gruyter, 2012), 219–240.
41 Ingeborg Jaklin, *Das österreichische Schulbuch im 18. Jahrhundert aus dem Wiener Verlag Trattner und dem Schulbuchverlag* (Wien: Praesens, 2003).
42 Thomas Keiderling, *"Der Schulbuchverleger und sein Autor: zu Spezialisierungs- und Professionalisierungstendenzen im 19. und frühen 20. Jahrhundert,"* in *Die Rolle von Schulbüchern für Identifikationsprozesse in historischer Perspektive*, ed. Heinz-Werner Wollersheim (Leipzig: Leipziger Universitäts-Verlag, 2002), 87–95.
43 Julio Ruiz Berrio, *La Editorial Calleja, un agente de modernización educativa en la Restauración* (Madrid: UNED, 2002).

Conclusion

Textbook-orientated research is a broad and multi-disciplinary field that is difficult to gauge or evaluate as there is considerable disparity on many levels between the various approaches. Authors bring many dimensions and questions to the texts written for textbooks, they derive their specialist knowledge from varying theoretical discourses, they position themselves within different disciplinary contexts, and they employ a range of methodological and analytical processes. These many dissimilarities could themselves be used to link typological distinctions. "Textbook research" does not exist as a clearly delineated research field; therefore, the term "textbook-orientated research" is more appropriate to describe this discipline. On the one hand the term emphasizes the field's immense thematic and methodological diversity and on the other it defines the interdisciplinary and multidisciplinary dimension beyond the academic university canon. Textbook-orientated research has neither its own distinct theory nor a specific arsenal of methods; rather it uses approaches from the humanities and from cultural and social studies most appropriate to the issue in question. The prevailing methods remain comparative, hermeneutic, and critical text analyses, which allow textbook content to be systematically analyzed in order to explore a range of diverse questions. Textbook analysis has become progressively embedded within the cultural contexts of textbook production, use, and implementation. This positioning combined with the interrelationship between textbooks and other educational media has forged associations and revealed parallels between textbook-orientated research and current academic, didactic, and social developments. The field increasingly employs discourse-analytical approaches as well as methods from fields such as ethnography, media science, visual studies, and the social sciences, for instance in the evaluation and impact analysis of textbooks in classrooms, or for quantitative analysis. Textbook analysis is distinctive from other research fields in that it operates within the areas of overlap and conflict between academic knowledge production and education policy and practice.

Textbook-related research has distanced itself from textbook revision to minimize the influence of political and normative trends. This is not to deny the numerous points of overlap between the two. Particularly in and about societies marked by violent conflicts and in post-conflict societies, textbook revision still constitutes an important means with which to reify the dialogue. While textbook-orientated research provides the scholarly basis here, as well as politically relevant assessments by experts and recommendations for intervening in education policy, these are not its only objectives. Textbook-orientated research has also been emancipating itself from traditional content analysis, pursuing two new paths with a view to methodological diversity. The first involves locating textbook contents within specific contexts – of society and politics, specialist research and of other educational media – thus gaining access to a wealth of specialized discourses, even while the educational dimension of the textbook nevertheless remains a central aspect. Textbook-orientated research draws on approaches from discourse theory, media studies, the social sciences, and cultural studies, using the tools of conflict-, memory-, or transnational research. Self-reflection on the theory of the textbook and the status of textbook-orientated research, however, remain a rarity. Textbook-related research, on the other hand, is pursuing a promising path, especially as it seeks to fill a gap in the area of empirical research on impact and reception. There are also methodological studies that use methods from textbook-orientated research and subject them to critical self-reflection such as those visualizing the historical dimension of textbooks as educational media that have altered over the centuries. In addition, textbook-related research has recently turned its attention to the impact if textbooks in the classroom, mechanisms of their production and approval, and the role of digital media. Although textbook-orientated research has only taken initial steps in this area thus far, it has succeeded in opening up a new area of research.

Bibliography

Alayan, Samira, and Naseema Al-Khalidi. "Gender and agency in history, civics, and national education textbooks of Jordan and Palestine." *Journal of Educational Media, Memory and Society* 2, no. 1 (2010): 78–96.

Alayan, Samira, Achim Rohde, and Sarhan Dhouib. *The politics of education reform in the Middle East: self and other in textbooks and curricula*. New York: Berghahn Books, 2012.

Apple, Michael W., and Linda K. Christian-Smith. *The Politics of the Textbook*. New York: Routledge, 1991.

Barton, Amanda, and Lydia N. Sakwa. "The Representation of Gender in English Textbooks in Uganda." *Pedagogy, Culture and Society* 20, no. 2 (2012): 173–190.

Bechet, Christophe. "La révision pacifiste des manuels scolaires. Les enjeux de la mémoire de la guerre 14–18 dans l'enseignement belge de l'Entre-deux-guerres." *Cahiers d'Histoire du Temps Présent* 20 (2008): 49–101.

Blänsdorf, Agnes. "Lehrwerke für Geschichtsunterricht an Höheren Schulen 1933–1945: Autoren und Verlage unter den Bedingungen des Nationalsozialismus." In *Nationalsozialismus in den Kulturwissenschaften. Bd. 1: Fächer – Milieus – Karrieren*, edited by Hartmut Lehmann and Otto G. Oexle, 273–370. Göttingen: Vandenhoeck & Ruprecht, 2004.

Borries, Bodo von. *Schulbuchverständnis, Richtlinienbenutzung und Reflexionsprozesse im Geschichtsunterricht: eine qualitativ-quantitative Schüler- und Lehrerbefragung im deutschsprachigen Bildungswesen 2002*. Neuried: Ars Una, 2005.

Bosche, Anne. *Schulreformen steuern: die Einführung neuer Lehrmittel und Schulfächer an der Volksschule (Kanton Zürich, 1960er- bis 1980er-Jahre)*. Bern: hep verlag, 2013.

Bromley, Patricia. "Holocaust education and human rights: Holocaust discussions in social science textbooks worldwide, 1970–2008." In *"Holocaust education" als Gegenstand international-vergleichender Erziehungswissenschaft*, edited by Matthias Proske and Wolfgans Meseth. Münster: Waxmann, 2013.

Bromley, Patricia, John W. Meyer, and Francisco O. Ramirez. *The worldwide spread of environmental discourse in social science textbooks, 1970–2008: cross-national patterns and hierarchical linear models*. https://worldpolity.files.wordpress.com/2010/08/bromley-meyer-ramirez-environmentalism-in-textbooks-6-2010.pdf.

Brown, Anthony L., and Keffrelyn D. Brown. "Strange Fruit Indeed. Interrogating Contemporary Textbooks Representations of Racial Violence Toward African Americans." *Teachers College Record* 112, no. 1 (2010): 31–67.

Brugeilles, Carole, and Sylvie Cromer. *Comment promouvoir l'égalité entre les sexes par les manuels scolaires? Guide méthodologique à l'attention des acteurs et actrices de la chaîne du manuel scolaire*. Paris: UNESCO, 2008.

Chapron, Emanuelle. "Das Elementarschulbuch im 18. Jahrhundert: räumliche Ausbreitung und Handelspraktiken zwischen Paris und der Champagne (1680–1730)." In *Schulbücher und Lektüren in der vormodernen Unterrichtspraxis. Zeitschrift für Erziehungswissenschaft. Sonderheft 17*, edited by Stephanie Hellekamps, 91–104. Wiesbaden: Springer Fachmedien, 2012.

Cody, Caroline. "The Politics of Textbook Publishing, Adoption and Use." In *Textbooks and Schooling in the United States. Eight-ninth Yearbook of the National Society for the Study of Education, Part 1*, edited by David L. Elliot and Arthur Woodward, 127–145. Chicago: University of Chicago Press, 1990.

Criblez, Lucien, Armanda Nägeli, and Rosa Stebler. *Schlussbericht. Begleitung der Einführung des Englischlehrmittels Voices auf der Sekundarstufe I*. Zürich: Universität Zürich, 2010.

da Silva, Paulo V. B., Rozana Teixeira, and Tânia M. Pacifico. "Políticas de promoção de igualdade racial e programas de distribuição de livros didáticos." *Educação e Pesquisa* 39, no. 1 (2013): 127–143.

Dimou, Augusta. *"Transition" and the politics of history education in Southeast Europe*. Göttingen: V&R unipress, 2009.

Dorschner, Jon, and Thomas Sherlock. "The role of history textbooks in shaping collective identities in India and Pakistan." In *Teaching the violent past: history education and reconciliation*, edited by Elisabeth A. Cole, 275–315. Lanham, Md.: Rowman & Littlefield, 2009.

Durwin, Cheryl Cisero, and William M. Sherman. "Does choice of college textbook make a difference in students' comprehension?" *College teaching* 56, no. 1 (2008): 28–34.

Firer, Ruth, and Sami Adwan. *The Israeli-Palestinian conflict in history and civics textbooks of both nations*. Hanover: Hahn, 2004.

Foster, Stuart J., and Keith A. Crawford. *What shall we tell the children? International perspectives on school history textbooks*. Greenwich, Conn.: Information Age Publishing, 2006.

Fuchs, Eckhardt. "Current Trends in History and Social Studies Textbook Research." *Journal of International Cooperation in Education* 14, no. 2 (2011): 17–34.

Fuchs, Eckhardt. "The (hi)story of textbooks: research trends in a field of textbook-related research." *Bildungsgeschichte: international journal for the historiography of education* 4, no. 1 (2014): 63–80.

Fuchs, Eckhardt, and Annekatrin Bock, eds. *The Palgrave Handbook of Textbook Studies*. New York: Palgrave, 2018.

Fuchs, Eckhardt, and Simone Lässig. "Europa im Schulbuch." *Geschichte für heute* 2, no. 1, 2009: 66–69.

Fuchs, Eckhardt, Inga Niehaus, and Almut Stoletzki. *Das Schulbuch in der Forschung. Analysen und Empfehlungen für die Bildungspraxis*. Göttingen: V&R unipress, 2014.

Furrer, Markus. *Die Nation im Schulbuch – zwischen Überhöhung und Verdrängung: Leitbilder der Schweizer Nationalgeschichte in Schweizer Geschichtslehrmitteln der Nachkriegszeit und Gegenwart*. Hanover: Hahn, 2004.

Gautschi, Peter, ed. *Geschichtsunterricht heute: eine empirische Analyse ausgewählter Aspekte*. Bern: hep verlag. 2007.

Haggarty, Linda, and Birgit Pepin. "An investigation of mathematics textbooks and their use in English, French and German classrooms: who gets an opportunity to learn what?" *British Educational Research Journal* 28, no. 4 (2002): 567–590.

Hayes, Donald P., Loreen T. Wolfer, and Michael F. Wolfe. "Schoolbook simplification and its relation to the decine in SAT-verbal scores." *American Educational Research Journal* 33, no. 2 (1996): 489–508.

Jackson, Stephanie, and Sylvie Iris. "Eurogame. Teaching the Geography of Europe and Its Regions through Online Multimedia Games." *Internationale Schulbuchforschung* 24, no. 2 (2002): 175–187.

Jaklin, Ingeborg. *Das österreichische Schulbuch im 18. Jahrhundert aus dem Wiener Verlag Trattner und dem Schulbuchverlag*. Wien: Praesens, 2003.

Kalmus, Veronika. *"What do pupils and textoobks do with each other? Methodological problems of research on socialization through educational media."* Curriculum Studies 36, no. 4 (2004): 469–485.

Keiderling, Thomas. "Der Schulbuchverleger und sein Autor: zu Spezialisierungs- und Professionalisierungstendenzen im 19. und frühen 20. Jahrhundert." In *Die Rolle von Schulbüchern für Identifikationsprozesse in historischer Perspektive*, edited by Heinz-Werner Wollersheim, 87–95. Leipzig: Leipziger Universitäts-Verlag, 2002.

Khan, Qaisar, Nighat Sultana, Qasim Bughio, and Arat Naz. "The Role of Language in Gender Identity Formation in Pakistani School Textbooks." *Indian Journal of Gender Studies* 21, no. 1 (2014): 55–84.

Knudsen, Susanne. "Dancing with and without gender – reflections on gender, textbooks and textbook research." In *"Has past passed?" Textbooks and educational media for the 21st century*, edited by Mike Horsley, 70–81. Stockholm: Stockholm Institute of Education Press, 2005.

Kotte, Eugen. *"In Räume geschriebene Zeiten"*: nationale Europabilder im Geschichtsunterricht der Sekundarstufe II. Idstein: Schulz-Kirchner-Verlag, 2007.

Kreusch, Julia. "Der Schulbuchverlag: Entwicklungstendenzen, Bildungspolitik und Schulreform, Das Schulbuchzulassungsverfahren, Schulbuchverlag und Schulbuchproduktion." In *Geschichte des deutschen Buchhandels im 19. und 20. Jahrhundert, Bd. 2: Die Weimarer Republik 1918–1933*, edited by Ernst Fischer, 219–240. Berlin: de Gruyter, 2012.

Kreusch, Julia. *Der Verlag der Buchhandlung des Waisenhauses als Schulbuchverlag zwischen 1830 und 1918. Die erfolgreichen Geografie- und Geschichtslehrbücher und ihre Autoren.* Tübingen: Verl. der Franckeschen Stiftungen Halle im Max Niemeyer Verlag, 2012.

Lange, Klaus. "Zu Methodologie und Methoden einer sozialwissenschaftlichen Unterrichtsmedienforschung." *Internationale Schulbuchforschung* 3 (1981): 16–28.

Manz, Walter "Der königlich-bayerische Zentralschulbücherverlag 1785 bis 1849 (1905): der Staat als Schulbuchverleger im 19. Jahrhundert." *Archiv für Geschichte des Buchwesens* 6 (1966): 2–312.

McIntyre, Stuart, and Anna Clark. *The History Wars.* Melbourne: Melbourne University Press, 2003.

Meyer, John W., Patricia Bromley, and Francisco O. Ramirez. "Human Rights in Social Science Textbooks: Cross-national Analyses, 1970–2008." *Sociology of Education* 83, no. 2 (2010): 111–134.

Nietz, John A. *Old textbooks: spelling, grammar, reading, arithmetic, geography, American history, civil government, physiology, penmanship, art, music, as taught in the common schools from colonial days to 1900.* Pittsburgh: University of Pittsburgh Press, 1961.

Nozaki, Yoshiko, and Mark Selden. "Historical Memory, International Conflict, and Japanese Textbook Controversies in Three Epochs." *Journal of Educational Media, Memory and Society* 1, no. 1 (2009): 117–144.

Othman, Zarina, Bahiyah Abdul Hamid, Mohd S. M. Yasin, Yuen Chee Keong, and Azhar Jaludin. "Gender Images in Selected Malaysian School Textbooks. A Frequency Analysis." *International Journal of Learning* 10, no. 18 (2012): 101–126.

Philippou, Stravroula, ed. *"Europe" turned local – the local turned European? Constructions of "Europe" in social studies curricula across Europe.* Münster: LIT, 2012.

Ramirez, Francisco O., John Boli, and John W. Meyer. "Explaining the origins and expansion of mass education." In *Sociological worlds: comparative and historical readings on society,* edited by Stephen K. Sanderson. London: Fitzroy Dearborn, 2000.

Ramirez, Francisco O., and John W. Meyer. "National Curricula. World Models and Historical Legacies." In *Internationalisierung. Semantik und Bildungssystem in vergleichender Perspektive,* edited by Marcelo Caruso and Heinz-Elmar Tenorth, 91–108. Frankfurt a. M.: Peter Lang, 2002.

Repoussi, Maria. "Politics Questions History Education. Debates on Greek History Textbooks." In *Jahrbuch der Internationalen Gesellschaft für Geschichtsdidaktik* (2006/2007), 99–110.

Repoussi, Maria. "Common Trends in Contemporary Debates on Historical Education." In *Jahrbuch der Internationalen Gesellschaft für Geschichtsdidaktik* (2008/2009), 75–90.

Rojas, Mary A. "An Examination of U.S. Latino Identities as Constructed in/through Curricular Materials." *Linguistics and Education* 3, no. 24 (2013): 373–380.

Rommel, Heinz. *Das Schulbuch im 18. Jahrhundert.* Wiesbaden: Dt. Fachschriften-Verlag, 1968.

Ruiz Berrio, Julio. *La Editorial Calleja, un agente de modernización educativa en la Restauración.* Madrid: UNED, 2002.

Saaler, Sven. *Politics, Memory, and Public Opinion. The History Textbook Controversy and Japanese Society.* München: Iudicium, 2005.

Schär, Bernhard C., and Vera Sperisen. "Zum Eigensinn von Lehrpersonen im Umgang mit Lehrbüchern: das Beispiel 'Hinschauen und Nachfragen.'" In *Forschungswerkstatt Geschichtsdidaktik 09: Beiträge zur Tagung "Geschichtsdidaktik Empirisch 09"*, edited by Jan Hodel and Béatrice Ziegler, 124–134. Bern: hep verlag, 2011.

Schröder, Carl A. *Die Schulbuchverbesserung durch internationale geistige Zusammenarbeit*. Braunschweig: Georg Westermann Verlag, 1961.

Soysal, Yasemin. "Lernziel: Europa. Schulbücher auf dem Prüfstand." *Zeitschrift für Kulturaustausch* 3 (2002).

Titel, Volker. "Die Marktsituation des Schulbuchhandels im 19. und frühen 20. Jahrhundert." In *Die Rolle von Schulbüchern für Identifikationsprozesse in historischer Perspektive*. edited by Heinz-Werner Wollersheim, 71–86. Leipzig: Leipziger Universitäts-Verlag, 2002.

Tröhler, Daniel, and Jürgen Oelkers, eds. *Über die Mittel des Lernens: kontextuelle Studien zum staatlichen Lehrmittelwesen im Kanton Zürich des 19. Jahrhunderts*. Zürich: Verlag Pestalozzianum, 2001.

Viñao, Antonio. "Towards a typology of the primers for learning to read (Spain, c. 1496–1825)." *Paedagogica Historica* 38 (2002): 73–94.

Wiater, Werner. "Lehrplan und Schulbuch. Reflexionen über zwei Instrumente des Staates zur Steuerung des Bildungswesens." In *Das Schulbuch zwischen Lehrplan und Unterrichtspraxis*, edited by Eva Matthes and Carsten Heinze, 41–64. Bad Heilbrunn: Klinkhardt, 2005.

Ziegler, Béatrice. "Politische Bildung im Deutschschweizer Lehrplan (Lehrplan 21)." 2010. https://plone.unige.ch/aref2010/symposiums-longs/coordinateurs-en-h/nouvelles-demandes-sociales-et-valeurs-portees-par-l2019ecole/Politische%20Bildung.pdf.

3 Flood Lands of Pedagogy: Meanderings between Empiricism, Theory, and Practice

Section editor: Frederik Herman

Eva Matthes (Augsburg University, Germany)
"Geisteswissenschaftliche Pädagogik," Teacher Training and Educational Science – Different Concepts and Attributions of Significance. Germany, 1900–2000

Abstract: In my contribution I look at publications of the so-called *Geisteswissenschaftliche Pädagogen* with regard to questions of teacher education for *Volksschulen* and *Höhere Schulen* [elementary and secondary schools]. In this context, I will deal both with the role which the educational scientists ascribe to educational science in the curriculum for teacher training, and with their own concepts of educational science for teacher training. My theses are that the attributions of significance and the concepts firstly differ referring to the different forms of teacher education for *Volksschulen* and *Höhere Schulen* and that they vary secondly between the individual representatives of *Geisteswissenschaftliche Pädagogik*, who are sometimes – falsely – seen as a monolithic block.[1]

Keywords: teacher education; educational science; pedagogical academy; university; elementary school teachers, secondary school teachers

Introduction

The discussion about the proportion and significance of the school subjects, subject-related didactics, educational science and psychology in teacher training is an ongoing issue.[2] Likewise, over a long period, there have been very different views with regard to the question which content and/or competences and/or attitudes educational science shall convey: general key qualifications, theory of education – derived from examples in the history of education, good teaching competencies, educational knowledge with regard to economy, society and politics, pedagogical attitude/pedagogical ethics, a researcher's habitus, or a combina-

---

[1] For the translation I thank Ileana Weichselgartner and Sylvia Schütze.
[2] This is also confirmed by the contributions in the *Handbuch Lehrerbildung*, ed. Sigrid Blömeke et al. (Bad Heilbrunn: Klinkhardt, 2004), from a national perspective, and by the contributions in *The Sage Handbook of Research on Teacher Education*, ed. Jean Clandinin and Jukka Husu (London: Sage, 2017), from an international perspective.

tion of those?³ In this context, there is a recurring discussion of the role and the orientation, which the history of education have and may give in teacher education – a topic, which the jubilarian of this volume has reflected in many contributions and which plays an important role in the subsequently presented positions. Furthermore, it is a very decisive question – historically and in comparison to other countries – where teacher education shall take place: at teacher seminaries, at separate colleges or academies for teacher training, at universities?⁴

This contribution will attempt to present relevant answers from selected representatives of the so-called *Geisteswissenschaftliche Pädagogik* (GP). It starts from the hypothesis that a) the attributions of significance and the underlying concepts differ, especially depending on whether the authors refer to elementary or to secondary schools, and that b) the positions of the educationalists of the GP (the GPs) vary, being not at all a monolithic block.⁵

But before the positions of the individual GPs are described, this school of thought in the German educational science shall be briefly explained. GP saw itself decidedly in the tradition of the philosopher Wilhelm Dilthey and his definition of the humanities as an independent group of sciences in contrast to the natural sciences. One of the central motives for the emergence of GP was the antagonism against a growing tendency to think about education in categories derived from the natural sciences. Philosophers, who were interested in pedagogical questions, saw this thinking gaining ground, due to the triumphant march and the universal and comprehensive explanatory claim of the natural sciences in the second half of the twentieth century. Against this background, they fiercely criticized the so-called "experimental pedagogy" which demerged from Wilhelm Wundt's experimental psychology.⁶ This criticism characterized also the "Pedagogical Conference" in the year 1917, which was summoned by the Prussian Minister of Cultural Affairs at that time, August von Trott zu Solz, in Berlin; this conference is presumed to be the GP's hour of birth, which was then named "Cultural Pedagogy". Following Dilthey, it was specified as the cen-

---

[3] This is likewise reinforced by the contributions in the two handbooks mentioned above; for relevant international developments from a historical perspective see Wendy Robinson, "Teacher Education: A Historical Overview," in *The Sage Handbook of Research on Teacher Education*, 49–67; for the national developments from a historical perspective cp. Uwe Sandfuchs, "Geschichte der Lehrerbildung in Deutschland," in *Handbuch Lehrerbildung*, 14–37.
[4] See Robinson, "Teacher Education," 49–67.
[5] For the description of the positions from Spranger to Weniger, see also Eva Matthes, *Geisteswissenschaftliche Pädagogik. Ein Lehrbuch* (München: Oldenbourg, 2011), 118–132.
[6] For the international distribution and the importance of the experimental pedagogy see Marc Depaepe, *Zum Wohle des Kindes? Pädologie, pädagogische Psychologie und experimentelle Pädagogik in Europa und den USA, 1890 bis1914* (Weinheim: Deutscher Studien Verlag, 1993).

tral scientific method of GP to understand cultural contexts, in contrast to the natural-scientific explanation of causal relationships. The GPs claimed to understand the particular present cultural situation in its historical having-become and to be able to lead education and its system on this basis, to give it orientation. This was the prevailing opinion of Eduard Spranger (see below) and Theodor Litt (see below) at the "Pedagogical Conference." This scientific positioning corresponded to the aspirations and expectations of the German policy at the end of the First World War. An educational science was to be established at the German universities, which saw itself decidedly as a tradition-conscious science of orientation.

In the Weimar republic, GP became probably the most influential, in retrospect at least the best-known paradigm. During National Socialism, it was marginalized due to its individual-pedagogical perspective, but had its heydays in the early Federal Republic of Germany in the 1950s, as an almost undisputed paradigm of educational science at universities and teacher training colleges. All GPs regarded themselves as advisors of educational politics and took up this position, thus also influencing the development of teacher education.

It shall be mentioned here that GP hat an enormous international reputation, especially in Eastern Europe and in Asia. In the Federal Republic of Germany, GP sank nearly into oblivion from the 1970s until the mid-1980s; but meanwhile it has experienced a kind of renaissance, although a critical one, especially with regard to the GPs' attitudes during National Socialism.[7] At present, however, the rather ahistorical so-called "Empirical Educational Research" dominates in educational science. As mentioned above, when dealing with the GP, it is indispensable to mention or even to elaborate for the first time the content-related differences between the individual representatives, notwithstanding their fundamental commonalities, as will be done in the following text.

The Position of Eduard Spranger (1882–1963)

Training of Elementary School Teachers

In order to understand and to appreciate Spranger's[8] influential and widely received publication *Gedanken über Lehrerbildung* [Thoughts on teacher education]

---

7 Cp. Matthes, *Geisteswissenschaftliche Pädagogik*, esp. 31–41; 184–201.
8 Spranger was born in Berlin and studied at the Friedrich Wilhelm University, with philosophy as his main subject. One of his most important teachers was Wilhelm Dilthey. In 1905, he re-

from the year 1920,⁹ it is necessary to take a brief look at the development of the elementary school teacher training in the Weimar Republic. Since 1918, this training was organized in seminars, i.e., the prospective elementary school teachers, after having visited an elementary school themselves, attended a preparatory school (until the age of 16) and subsequently for two or three years a teacher seminar. It was defined in article 143, para. 2, of the *Weimar Reichsverfassung* (according to the wishes of the elementary school teachers' unions) that the elementary school teacher training should "be uniformly regulated according to the principles, which generally apply to higher education", in the future. Despite the constitutional defaults, however, it didn't come to any German-wide reorganization of teacher training. In Bavaria and Württemberg, the preparatory schools and seminars remained unchanged. In Oldenburg, "pedagogical courses" and in Baden seminar-like teacher training colleges were established. Meanwhile, in Thuringia, Saxony, Hesse, Hamburg, Mecklenburg-Schwerin, and Brunswick, the elementary school teacher training was annexed to the universities and technical colleges. In Prussia, they struggled over the reorganization for a long time until 1926, when independent "Pedagogical Academies"¹⁰ were finally set up.¹¹ The university professors were mostly unanimous towards

---

ceived a doctor's degree from Friedrich Paulsen. In 1908, he habilitated under Dilthey's mentorship with a treatise about "Wilhelm von Humboldt und die Humanitätsidee"; he received the Venia legendi for Philosophy and Pedagogy. In 1911, he received a call to the University of Leipzig; in 1919, he accepted a call to the Chair of Philosophy and Pedagogy at the Friedrich Wilhelm University in Berlin. At this time, he was a close advisor of the Prussian Ministry of Cultural Affairs and exerted an enormous influence on educational politics, especially on the reform of the academic studies of elementary school teachers. In the 1920s, due to his numerous publications, Spranger became a scientist of high international reputation. His behavior during the time of National Socialism is disputed. After the unconditional surrender of Germany, Spranger became temporarily provisional president of the Friedrich Wilhelm University in Berlin. In the following months, he received several calls to West German universities, and in summer 1946, due to his political dissatisfaction in the Soviet occupation zone, he gladly accepted the call to a Chair of Philosophy at the University of Tübingen. Nevertheless, he continued to deal with pedagogical questions and submitted many widely-read educational contributions, until his retirement and beyond. Furthermore, he acted as educational-political advisor, mainly with regard to teacher education. For more details, see Matthes, *Geisteswissenschaftliche Pädagogik*, 13–17.
9 Eduard Spranger, "Gedanken über Lehrerbildung," in *Gesammelte Schriften, vol. III: Schule und Lehrer*, ed. Eduard Spranger (Heidelberg: Quelle & Meyer, 1970/1920), 27–73.
10 See the publication by the Prussian Minister of Culture Carl Heinrich Becker, *Die Pädagogische Akademie im Aufbau unseres nationalen Bildungswesens* (Leipzig: Quelle & Meyer, 1926).
11 See for example Hans-Karl Beckmann, *Lehrerseminar – Akademie – Hochschule. Das Verhältnis von Theorie und Praxis in drei Epochen der Volksschullehrerausbildung* (Weinheim/Basel: Beltz, 1968); Sebastian Müller-Rolli, "Lehrer," in *Handbuch der deutschen Bildungsgeschichte*,

a university education of elementary school teachers. They perceived it as an endangerment to the idea and dignity of the German universities (with its separation of theory and practice).

Already in the preface of his *Gedanken über Lehrerbildung*,[12] Spranger makes clear that he is also against elementary school teacher training at universities, something thoroughly controversial in Prussia: establishing such a new "Pedagogical Faculty" might "comprise only second rate content, being put into the old and unrelinquishable scholarly ideal of university."[13] A university elementary school teacher training, even at the conventional faculty of philosophy,[14] "is a great misunderstanding both of the university and the dignity of the teaching profession."[15] Spranger reproaches elementary school teachers, who strive for a university education, a merely social perspective, i.e., to raise their social status.[16] "The long fights of the teachers should not have been conducted, just to end in a plagiarism" (Spranger refers to the alignment with the university training for secondary school teachers; E. M.).[17] He wants to develop an independent concept for elementary school teacher training. It is based on the following fundamental conviction: the "people's teacher" has the culturally very significant task of bringing up the people's children, according to their diverse learning abilities, thus giving them opportunities to participate actively in culture:

> The teacher of the people must neither be a specialist nor a jack-of-all-trades and a walking encyclopedia: he must primarily be a medium of culture or, what means the same: a *me-*

---

vol. V: *1918–1945. Die Weimarer Republik und die nationalsozialistische Diktatur,* ed. Dieter Langewiesche and Heinz-Elmar Tenorth (München: Beck, 1989), 240–258.
12 It should be noted that Spranger speaks only of "teacher training" as do many of his time when he talks about the elementary school teacher training. The teachers at the higher secondary schools were not considered to be teachers by many, but academics or scholars. The traditional name was "philologists", since the higher secondary teachers at the beginning of the nineteenth century regarded themselves as philologists, and classical philology (not pedagogy!) as their discipline of professional reference. See, for example, Eva Matthes, "Theologe – Philologe – Fachwissenschaftler – Pädagoge? Historisch-systematische Akzentsetzungen zur (Aus)Bildung der Lehrer an höheren Schulen," *Anregung. Zeitschrift für Gymnasialpädagogik* 46 (2000): 328–341; Christoph Führ, "Gelehrter Schulmann – Oberlehrer – Studienrat. Zum sozialen Aufstieg der Philologen," in *Bildungsbürgertum im 19. Jahrhundert,* part 1, 2nd. edn., ed. Werner Conze and Jürgen Kocka (Stuttgart: Klett-Cotta 1992), 417–457.
13 Spranger, "Gedanken über Lehrerbildung," 27.
14 See ibid., 54.
15 Ibid., 28.
16 See ibid., 28, 67.
17 Ibid., 28,67.

dium of education. This, however, requires a special curriculum which differs from the scholarly education, without being in any way inferior.[18]

This must be a *Hochschule für Menschenbildner* [College for educators of men][19] or – as he also puts it – a *Bildnerhochschule* [Educators' College].[20] Spranger highlights continuously that it is not all about "that the teacher of the people shall be cheated out of his share in science under a shiny name."[21] He rather emphasizes "the independence and height of the cultural function", that exists in "educating a *whole* person and not just a scientific mind."[22] An important principle for Spranger's explanations is his concept of science; for him this refers to "the order of our cognitions according to their strictly relevant, objective cohesion."[23] This order is determined by the law of objectivity and does not ask for possibilities to apply the results.[24] Education as an act shall "give birth to all directions of valuation with regard to a developing individual soul's experiences, attitudes and practical behavior, in accordance with the norm of its objectively valuable configuration."[25] This is "a very peculiar task."[26]

For the organization of the studies at the "teacher training colleges" – as he calls these institutions, too –, he makes the following suggestions: the course of studies shall last three years; directly after their admission, each student shall come "into a personal relationship with a child as an educator", "which shall preferably endure throughout the three years of his [her] stay at the college. This is part of the very spirit of this educational institution."[27] The college shall include a "scientific department (to which theoretical pedagogy belongs), a technical and an artistic one, and a practical-pedagogical one."[28] "[...] all these branches of the individual college must be related to the unifying point of self-education and the educational task, which is its center of gravity."[29] The third academic year shall be organized as a "practical year."[30] "The techni-

---

18 Ibid., 53–54.
19 Ibid., 56.
20 Ibid., 53.
21 Ibid.
22 Ibid.
23 Ibid., 28.
24 See Spranger, "Gedanken über Lehrerbildung," 45.
25 Ibid.
26 Ibid.
27 Ibid., 56.
28 Ibid., 57.
29 Ibid.
30 Ibid.

cal-artistic department of the teacher training college" shall be "the place where the spirit of the new education comes to expression most visibly": the detachment from the ideal of a predominantly theoretical person, the commitment to the ideal of an open-minded human being, who has also developed his/her creative abilities."[31]

Spranger warns of an overestimation of the theory of pedagogics:

> It is important, but it does not replace the pedagogical talent and the mental attitude, such as the theory of his art (aesthetics) and the technique of his art cannot replace the artist's talent or assume his role. Theoretical pedagogy is the scientific investigation of education as a peculiar cultural process. It consolidates the educator, but it does not make him.[32]

"Pedagogy on a philosophical basis"[33] is therefore only taught four hours a week, and eight hours a week are added for the subjects (humanities and natural sciences),[34] for *"pedagogy alone just cannot be studied like philosophy alone*, because for both one has to know something before."[35] Further optional subjects, mainly from the technical and the artistic field, shall be added. How does Spranger see the relationship between elementary school teacher training and secondary school teacher training at universities? With the former, "a new type of cultural activity"[36] shall be created:

> Who wants to tell us that he will not – by his inherent values – surpass the corresponding performances of the university graduate? If whole persons and whole educators result from our teacher training college, perhaps a spirit of education will emerge which will eclipse the achievements of the university in this field, some of which are quite contestable. Maybe the teachers of science at the universities will be forced into a defensive position, just as the

---

31 Ibid., 61.
32 Ibid., 47; See also 57–58.
33 Ibid., 59.
34 See ibid.
35 In his (unpublished) memorandum (probably 1946) for President Paul Wandel (President of the Administration for Public Education of the Soviet Occupation Zone), which lies in Theodor Litt's estate (Litt-Nachlass), Litt expresses very similar thoughts to those of Spranger regarding the question of the "Pedagogical Faculties" (newly planned faculties at the universities for teacher training), but in an even sharper diction: "An increase in the [pedagogical] professorships would only be an artificial inflation. The reason why pedagogy, as far as it is science, does not demand further expansion, is that education does not itself produce its material content, but takes it from the totality of cultural activities, the continuation of which it has to provide [...] For this same reason, however, pedagogy is also dependent on the closest cooperation with the totality of those sciences by which it is informed about the above-mentioned cultural functions. Detached from them, it must become idle" (University Archive Leipzig, Litt-Legacy).
36 Ibid., 68.

theologians once had to give way for the philologists[37] and other disciplines of the faculty of philosophy.[38]

He thus suggests that he can also imagine an education of secondary school teachers at the teacher training colleges in the future – but under no circumstances visa-versa an education of elementary school teachers at universities, since as places of science and research, they are unsuitable places for that.[39]

The Training of Secondary School Teachers

It becomes at least doubtful whether Spranger seriously considers that secondary school teachers should also be trained at the teacher training colleges in the intermediate term, if one regards the arguments he puts forth in his 1925 memorandum *Die Ausbildung der höheren Lehrer an der Universität* [The education of secondary school teachers at the university] at the faculty of philosophy of the University of Berlin.[40] As starting point for his arguments he chooses the "view" that "the preparatory education of the secondary school teachers in the faculties of philosophy does not correspond to their future professional tasks; yes, one has claimed occasionally that the university would almost induce

---

37 Spranger alludes to the fact that until the beginning of the nineteenth century, theologians were active as teachers at higher secondary schools (mostly for an interim period, until the takeover of a parish), who were then finally displaced by the philologists (as independent higher teachers).
38 Ibid., 68–69.
39 Detailed studies on Spranger's contributions to the education of elementary school teachers (with expertises even after 1945!) are available from Fritz Hartmut Paffrath, *Eduard Spranger und die Volksschule. Eine historisch-systematische Untersuchung* (Bad Heilbrunn: Klinkhardt 1971), 104–106; Gerhard Meyer-Willner, *Eduard Spranger und die Lehrerbildung. Die notwendige Revision eines Mythos* (Bad Heilbrunn: Klinkhardt, 1986). Both also thought that until the 1950s, Spranger still preferred a seminar-oriented elementary school teacher training; the organizational concept of the "Bildnerhochschule" was rather an emergency solution to prevent the university training of elementary school teachers.
40 The memorandum was published without mentioning the author. However, Meyer-Willner could prove beyond any doubt that the author was Spranger (see Meyer-Willner, *Eduard Spranger und die Lehrerbildung*, 87). The memorandum to which the faculty of philosophy at the University of Berlin had approved without a dissenting vote was submitted to the Prussian Minister of Cultural Affairs, Carl Heinrich Becker. See Spranger, *Die Ausbildung der höheren Lehrer an der Universität* [memorandum of the faculty of philosophy at the Friedrich Wilhelm University of Berlin] (Leipzig: Quelle & Meyer, 1925), 6.

them to a wrong professional stance."[41] Spranger now replies that the majority of university professors are meanwhile well aware that they must not focus their teaching solely on future researchers, but rather take into account the needs of future secondary teachers[42]:

> However, this realization does not mean in any way that the faculty of philosophy could infer thereof a reshaping of itself, which could be described as its 'pedagogization'. It cannot formally orient its own teaching exclusively towards pedagogical principles, nor can it grant such considerable space to pedagogical lectures and exercises in terms of curriculum as is often demanded today.[43]

The core of the university is "science as such".[44] In that, he sees no problem for the secondary school teachers, because at these schools "the pedagogical is only the form", "in which subject content and objective educational assets must be alive, if education shall not perish due to mental anemia."[45] In his memorandum, Spranger deals only briefly with the "special field of pedagogical training."[46] Here he takes up ideas which he already expressed in his (unpublished) memorandum for the Prussian Minister of Cultural Affairs von Trott zu Solz in June 1915 and which he also uttered at the "Pedagogical Conference" in May 1917.[47] This memorandum arose as a reaction to a draft about the reorganization of the exams for the secondary school teachers (which was adopted as such in 1918), in which pedagogy was no longer part of the scientific examination; instead, pedagogical content should be examined at the end of the subsequent two-year practical training. For Spranger, this means a clear devaluation of the educational science, and he points out that due to this decision, the demand for pedagogical courses is also clearly diminishing.[48] He advocates the anchoring of cultural pedagogy in the secondary school teacher training: "Pedagogy [...] in its historical section should comprise a rather all-encompassing, philosophically informed history of education and intellectuality, in its systematic section a cul-

---

41 Ibid., 7. Spranger himself spoke in his *Gedanken über Lehrerbildung* about the "partly quite contestable achievements of the university" (69) in the field of teacher education.
42 See ibid., 8.
43 Ibid.
44 Ibid.
45 Ibid., 9.
46 Ibid., 26.
47 See Eva Matthes, "Die Pädagogik konstituiert sich als universitäres Fach," in *Verlag Julius Klinkhardt. 1834–2009. Verlegerisches Handeln zwischen Pädagogik, Politik und Ökonomie*, ed. Uwe Sandfuchs, Jörg-W. Link, and Andreas Klinkhardt (Bad Heilbrunn: Klinkhardt, 2009), 81–94; 83–85.
48 See ibid., 83–84.

ture-philosophically founded theory of education."⁴⁹ In 1915, Spranger emphasizes that practical pedagogy has no place at the university,⁵⁰ in 1925 (somewhat more moderately) that it might "only be useful under two aspects: as a necessary guide to future professional ethics and as an opportunity to discover one's personal suitability or unsuitability for the profession as educator in time."⁵¹ His rejection of training schools, expressed in 1915, remains the same in principle:

> From the onset, any discussion about the connection between a compulsory training school⁵² and the university must be sharply rejected [...] If there is any lecturer of pedagogy at a university who is constantly close enough to practice to believe that he and his likeminded colleagues can be effective in an exemplary and stimulating way, then he may set the matter in motion on an optional basis.⁵³

At the end, however, Spranger faces the question of "what the university can do to form the right professional ethics in the future teacher"⁵⁴ and comes to the following conclusion: "The theoretical ability has to be provided by pedagogical lecture, the deeper practical ability by the model of the academic teacher, who is fraught with his subject and interested in his students."⁵⁵ Finally, Spranger underlines once again the justification of the training of secondary school teachers at universities, even with its shortcomings, in drastic words: it is still better "that a merely scholarly head comes to the schools than a friend of children who is empty-minded and therefore cannot give more to the children than every playmate of the same age."⁵⁶

---

49 Spranger, *Die Ausbildung der höheren Lehrer an der Universität*, 20–21. Spranger shows great skepticism with regard to didactical courses. He gives the following reasons: "the student has hardly no time for this, but also – as he lacks the practical touch with the problems – usually no understanding" (ibid., 28).
50 See Eva Matthes, "Die Pädagogik konstituiert sich als universitäres Fach," 84.
51 Spranger, *Die Ausbildung der höheren Lehrer an der Universität*, 28–29.
52 See Matthes, "Die Pädagogik konstituiert sich als universitäres Fach," 84.
53 Spranger, *Die Ausbildung der höheren Lehrer an der Universität*, 29.
54 Ibid., 30.
55 Ibid.
56 Ibid.

The Position of Theodor Litt (1880–1962)

Unlike Spranger, Litt[57] has not presented an explicit theory of teacher education, and there is only one explicitly subject-related publication, *Hochschule und Lehrerbildung* [University and teacher education][58], and a series of short, mostly unpublished statements in the Litt legacy at the archives of the University of Leipzig. Like Spranger, however, Litt was passionately in favor of keeping elementary school teacher training away from the university; this is verified by Litt's corresponding activities and statements in the Weimar Republic,[59] his – albeit unsuccessful – struggle against the "Pedagogical Faculties" in the Soviet Occupied Zone,[60] as well as his already mentioned publication in the Federal Republic

---

57 Litt was born in Düsseldorf and studied Ancient Languages, History and Philosophy at the University of Bonn. In 1903, he passed a State Examination; in 1904, he received a doctor's degree in Classical Philology. From 1906 to 1919, he was senior teacher for Ancient Languages and History at a grammar school in Cologne. After his statements at the "Pedagogical Conference" in Berlin in 1917, he worked for half a year as advisor in the Prussian Ministry of Cultural Affairs. He published several contributions about cultural pedagogy. In 1920, he received a call to the Chair of Philosophy and Pedagogy at the University of Leipzig – as successor of Eduard Spranger, who had received a call to the Friedrich Wilhelm University in Berlin. Litt published a lot and reached a high scientific reputation in the 1920s. In 1931/32, he was Rector of the University of Leipzig. His attitude towards the National Socialist regime is recognized in the scientific community as critical, even consequently deprecatory. In 1937 he was retired ahead of schedule at his own request. In 1945, he first took over the Chair of Philosophy and Pedagogy at the University of Leipzig again. But he deeply disapproved the politics of the new rulers; therefore he followed the call to the Chair of Philosophy and Pedagogy at the University of Bonn in October 1947. In the Federal Republic of Germany, he was involved with a democratic orientation of the educational system beyond the time of his retirement – in publications, lectures, and as educational-political advisor. He fiercely criticized the (educational-political) developments in the GDR. For more details, see Matthes, *Geisteswissenschaftliche Pädagogik*, 8–12.
58 Theodor Litt, "Hochschule und Lehrerbildung," in *Überlieferung und Neubeginn. Probleme der Lehrerbildung und Bildung nach zehn Jahren des Aufbaus*, ed. Oskar Hammelsbeck (Ratingen: Henn, 1957), 33–37.
59 See Eva Matthes, "Theodor Litt (1880–1962)," in *Sächsische Lebensbilder*, vol. 5, ed. Gerald Wiemers (Leipzig: Verlag der Sächsischen Akademie der Wissenschaften, 2003), 435–464; 441–442.
60 See ibid., 459–460. On July 12, 1946, the pedagogical faculties were founded by Order No. 205 of the Soviet Military Administration in Germany (SMAD). The "Law on the Democratization of the German School" in May 1946, which provided for an eight year "elementary school for all," had preceded the founding of these faculties. The graduates of the pedagogical faculties received the teaching authorization for this type of school. In an unpublished and unaddressed statement "Zum Plan der Pädagogischen Fakultät," Litt writes: "The comprehensive teacher will

of Germany. He says that the takeover of the elementary school teacher training would lead to the destruction of the faculty of philosophy, since this would hence become a mere teacher-training faculty. The fact that universities are not able to perform the task of teacher training satisfactorily has been shown by previous experiences with secondary school teacher training:

> In too many cases, [there is an enormous gap] between the content of university teaching and the tasks awaiting the future teacher, a gap [...] which the elite of the highly gifted does not bother to overcome, but the dutiful average (without which we simply cannot get along) succeeds only with great difficulty and often fails completely. Tough and abrupt, the world of research and the world of human education exist too often in parallel.[61]

And he adds the (rhetorical) question:

> In view of this fact, should it be advisable to entrust the faculty of philosophy with the training of such educators, who will be led much further away from the fields of scientific research due to the character of their educational activity?[62]

Hence, the problems of secondary school teacher training are for the most part not due to the disinterest, the unwillingness of the professors: "Very often, it is just the case that those who devote themselves to research are too occupied by this issue, as to give enough attendance to the other side of their duty." Only few professors have the gift that "the passion of pursuing truth in research and the passion of human education are coupled."[63] This cannot be made a prerequisite for everyone without harming the university.[64] Like Spranger, Litt sees the pursuit of knowledge as the core of the university. Thus, he pleads for keeping the teacher training colleges as places of elementary school teacher training.

---

have sipped all sorts of things and learned nothing properly. He will neither be an ordinary subject teacher nor an ordinary elementary school teacher [...]."
61 Litt, "Hochschule und Lehrerbildung," 34–35.
62 Ibid., 35.
63 Ibid.
64 See ibid. Despite all agreement in principle Spranger argues – at least in his memorandum of 1925 – more openly/pragmatically than Litt. However, this can also be due to the (compromised) character of the memorandum, especially since the Prussian Minister of Culture, Becker, in his thoughts on higher education published in 1919, spoke out against a pure research orientation of the universities and for "university didactics" (Leipzig: Quelle & Meyer, 24). In addition, the memorandum had to take into account in some way about 50 obtained expert opinions and the previous consultations in the faculty. See Meyer-Willner, *Eduard Spranger und die Lehrerbildung*, 87. Meyer-Willner nevertheless assumes that Spranger "has definitely articulated his own opinion" (ibid.).

He calls them with Spranger's term *Bildnerhochschule*,[65] which subordinates "all of its issues under the chief aspect of human education."[66] "Whatever it adopts from the results of science, must be redesigned, rethought in the way, which subordination under the idea of human education demands."[67] The teacher training college shall draw its identity and self-confidence from the fact that it is shaped by the guiding idea of human education.[68] One shall say good-bye to the idea that "the scientific academy [i.e. the university; E. M.] is the unsurpassable model of academia."[69]

The Position of Herman Nohl (1879 – 1960)

Nohl[70] did not present any theoretical considerations with regard to the education of elementary school teachers; reflections on the education of secondary teacher training can be found in the lecture *Die Ausbildung der wissenschaftlichen Lehrer durch die Universität* [The scientific training of subject teachers at universities], held at the so-called *Göttinger Philologentag* in 1927. In this contribution, there are many parallels to Spranger's ideas in the memorandum from 1925, but also some explicit differences. First of all, Nohl refers to the old com-

---

65 Ibid., 36.
66 Ibid.
67 Ibid.
68 See ibid., 36 – 37.
69 Ibid., 36.
70 Nohl was born in Berlin. He studied History, German Literature, and Philosophy at the Friedrich Wilhelm University in Berlin. Wilhelm Dilthey became his most important academic teacher. In 1904, he received a doctorate in Philosophy, in 1908 a habilitation in Philosophy at the University of Jena. After the First World War, Nohl dealt especially with education-theoretical and education-political issues. In 1920, he received a call to the Chair of Practical Philosophy with special consideration of Pedagogy at the University of Göttingen; this chair was converted into a Chair of Pedagogy in 1922. One of the core topics in his numerous publications was the substantial founding of Pedagogy as science. One of his key issues was – quasi inversely – the professionalization of the educational professions, last but not least in adult education and social work. Nohl's position in the time of National Socialism is disputed; especially in the first phase, there were some approaches; Nohl was, however, forced to retire due to "political unreliability" in 1937. In 1945, Nohl returned to his chair in Göttingen and was both scientifically and education-politically active again, also beyond his retirement, after the end of the war for example through his engagement for the founding of the Teacher Training College (for elementary school teachers) in Göttingen. For more details, see Matthes, *Geisteswissenschaftliche Pädagogik*, 3 – 7.

plaint about the "insufficient training of the secondary school teachers at the university", which was due to the fact

> that the student at the university is trained as a specialist scientist in order to become a researcher – and the better his university teachers are, the stricter –, only to realize at the start of his professional activity, that there are also very different tasks awaiting him than the conveyance of the pure search for truth.[71]

This contradiction is unsolvable and permanently virulent. But there is an additional problem, namely that the contents to be taught by the teachers at school are partly no longer taught at the university:

> The withdrawal from educational research with reference to the scientific character of the teacher can help no longer, because the contents of this scholarliness – not its formal stance – are apparently no longer sufficient with regard to life [...]: with them, the teacher feels no longer secure.[72]

Nohl attributes this to the fact that the sciences are too far from real life and do not sufficiently develop their "meaning for life".[73] Like Spranger and Litt, however, he opposes the pedagogization of science, because "the strongest educational force of science always lies in its unconditional objective energy with which it obeys its own law."[74] The scientific teachers at the university must express this more strongly than has been the case in the past; in doing so, they will also underline the vitality of their science.[75] Like Spranger and Litt, Nohl warns of searching the way out of this disappointment by the specialist sciences in pedagogy: the teacher thinks

> that he is able to flee from this faithlessness with regard to his 'subject' to pedagogy. But it is obvious that one can definitely not teach without faith in the content value of the intellectual world which one conveys. The pedagogy per se remains formal in essence, the teacher's higher strength comes from his intellectual conviction.[76]

---

[71] Herman Nohl, "Die Ausbildung der wissenschaftlichen Lehrer durch die Universität," in *Pädagogische Aufsätze*, 2nd. enlarged ed., ed. Herman Nohl (Langensalza et al.: Beltz, 1929/1927), 183–189.
[72] Nohl, "Die Ausbildung der wissenschaftlichen Lehrer durch die Universität," 184.
[73] Ibid., 184.
[74] Ibid.
[75] See ibid.
[76] Ibid., 184–185.

In the next step, Nohl turns to the role of pedagogy in secondary school teacher training. He firmly advocates scientific studies of pedagogy:

> It is quite impossible to expect the pedagogical introduction of the teacher to the ethics of his profession only in his year of internship and thus to abandon just *at this point* the great task of the university to convey the idea of the profession and to leave this to the practice. The purpose of pedagogical lectures and seminars will therefore not be the introduction to pedagogical technique, but first and foremost the justification of the pedagogical work before oneself, in the context of all intellectual being, so that the university student may know his position in the circle of the whole and become certain of the peculiar character of the pedagogical attitude in face of the strange demands of life.[77]

Therefore, based on his understanding of the relationship between theory and practice, Nohl decisively rejects any pedagogical recipe; he is concerned with the study of a scientific (cultural) pedagogy. In terms of curriculum, he demands lectures about general pedagogy, history of pedagogy, contemporary pedagogy and child psychology, and the establishment of posts for the necessary personnel.[78] Unlike Spranger – and in explicit contrast to his Berlin memorandum –, Nohl considers "*subject-related didacticis*" to be indispensable.[79] There is no question that "the decisive bridge between the scientific subjects and pedagogy lies" in subject-related didactics "and that only these subject-related didactics complete the training of the future teacher at the university."[80] Once again, this does not refer to teaching technology, but

> a basic reflection of the pedagogical forming of the respective science, its educational meaning and the basic attitude it conveys, on the choice of material and the structure of the curriculum, the position of the teacher in the educational process between subject and students, etc.[81]

Nohl emphatically rejects the idea of implementing the pedagogical training of secondary school teachers at Pedagogical Academies.[82] Pedagogy as a science must be embedded in the university and must have an important position within the scientific studies of the secondary school teachers. Like Spranger, Nohl rejects training schools[83] and, like him, advocates "several weeks of observation

---

77 Ibid.
78 See ibid.,186–187.
79 Ibid., 187.
80 Ibid.
81 Ibid, 187.
82 See ibid.
83 See ibid., 188.

during the holidays."[84] Like him, he is also in favor of a final examination in pedagogy at the university and complains its abolition to be a mistake.[85] Wilhelm Flitner and Erich Weniger have dealt far more extensively with teacher training and its contents than their academic teacher Herman Nohl.

The Position of Wilhelm Flitner (1889–1990)

Flitner[86] was professor at the Pedagogical Academy in Kiel from 1926 to 1929. In the context of his professional engagement, he pondered the aims and structure of elementary school teacher studies at academies. In his publication *Das Pädagogikstudium an der Pädagogischen Akademie"* [Studies of pedagogy at the Pedagogical Academy] (1929), he summarizes his key considerations. He points out that

> the academization of the teaching profession [...] is a demand of the teachers themselves, arisen from their professional experience, and even if profession-political motives play a role here, as in the academization of other professions, one must not ignore this deeper motive by referring to this external one.[87]

---

84 Ibid.
85 See ibid., 188–189.
86 Flitner was born in Berka near Weimar. He studied predominantly Philosophy at the University of Jena. His most important academic teacher was Herman Nohl. In 1912, he received a doctorate in Philosophy. In 1914, he passed the State Examination to become a secondary school teacher for German, History, and English. Afterwards, he worked as senior teacher. In 1923, he habilitated under the educational scientist Wilhelm Rein at the University of Jena. In 1926, he received a call to the Pedagogical Academy in Kiel; from this date, he got involved in the reform of (elementary) teacher training. In 1928, he received a call to a Chair of Educational Science at the University of Hamburg; at this university, elementary school teacher training was already integrated. During the time of National Socialism, Flitner kept his chair, but went, however, after short hesitation, into a kind of inner emigration. After the end of the Second World War, Flitner was a very esteemed education-political reference person for the British occupying power. In the Federal Republic of Germany, he acted as educational-political advisor beyond his retirement, last but not least in issues of teacher training, and published numerous relevant contributions. For more information, see Matthes, *Geisteswissenschaftliche Pädagogik*, 17–21.
87 Wilhelm Flitner, "Das Pädagogikstudium an der Pädagogischen Akademie," in *Gesammelte Schriften, vol. 4: Die Pädagogische Bewegung. Beiträge – Berichte – Rückblicke*, ed. Wilhelm Flitner (Paderborn u. a.: Schöningh, 1987/1929), 363–370; 267–268.

"Regarding its intellectual content", the reform of teacher training had arisen "from the progressive education movement."[88] *"The far-reaching goals of the reform* aim at a new German education and at the type of a 'people's teacher' who shall convey this education."[89] Flitner refers explicitly approvingly to the memorandum of the Prussian Minister of Cultural Affairs Becker.[90] As core of the new approach, he envisages an "education which encompasses the whole people" and the acknowledgement of a "pedagogical task of the state."[91] With regard to contents, he sees a major challenge for the pedagogical academy in the fact that its courses of study are limited to two years for economical-political reasons.[92] This requires dense and very concentrated studies.[93] It is paramount that the academic character of the studies is preserved.[94]

Unlike Spranger and Litt, but in agreement with Weniger (see below), Flitner emphasizes that educational theory has to be at the center of the studies.[95] It must offer the prospective teacher a basic orientation which enables him to evaluate his practical experiences and to judge them in a reflective and differentiated manner.[96] In this context, an *"introduction to the pedagogical controversies of the present"* is mandatory.[97] In a second step, it is about a deeper understanding of the disputes and their background.[98] However, the aim of the theoretical education shall not only be related "to the practical situation of the teacher in public schools" at the present.[99] Rather a counterweight is necessary, "by which the whole range of a scientifically orderly and comprehensive reflection can only be achieved."[100] "The whole *inner connectivity of educational science* must be shown, so that those everyday questions lose their episodic character and become discernable as mere momentums in a system."[101] For this, historical-systematic approaches are indispensable.[102]

---

88 Flitner, "Das Pädagogikstudium an der Pädagogischen Akademie," 266–267.
89 Ibid., 267.
90 See Becker, *Die Pädagogische Akademie im Aufbau unseres nationalen Bildungswesens*.
91 Ibid.
92 See ibid., 263.
93 See ibid.
94 Ibid., 264; 265.
95 See ibid., 366–367.
96 See ibid., 269–270.
97 Ibid., 268.
98 Ibid.
99 Ibid., 270.
100 Ibid.
101 Ibid.
102 Ibid.

In 1933, after the National Socialists had gained the power already, Flitner positions himself again in favor of the Pedagogical Academies.[103] He emphasizes that a return to teacher training at seminars is unacceptable. "The task of elementary school teachers is so difficult today that an intellectual education, which is not sovereign, puts the existence of the large school apparatus into question."[104] He then refers to the successes of the Pedagogical Academies[105] and emphasizes once again (now in explicit demarcation from Spranger) "that it is definitely a scholarly education at the Pedagogical Academy, which is acquired through the studies of educational science"[106] – Flitner thus once again declares educational science to be the core professional science for elementary school teachers. The study at the pedagogical academies has therefore to be triannual: "An academic scientific education is impossible without an academic triennium, even if the study is limited to one discipline, to educational science."[107] In addition to the scientific study of pedagogy, "subject-related work" is necessary. This "cannot be organized like scientific studies; there is no time for it. It can only be striven for as an unscholarly, inexpert intrusion into the contents of a popular education, as a 'genuine formation of laity'."[108]

Flitner deals again with the role and the task of educational science at teacher training colleges in his publication *Der Standort der Erziehungswissenschaft* [The position of educational science] from 1964. Here he states once again that educational science should be the scientific core at teacher training colleges, in other words: the scientific necessities of teacher training should be determined by the tasks of education and teaching. In particular, this article is concerned with clarifying the relationship between educational science and its neighboring disciplines. As initial consideration, Flitner formulates – as he emphasizes himself – very pointedly:

> Now, of course, the future teacher cannot be expected to be thoroughly familiar with so many different sciences. For in addition to educational science, which is itself very complex, psychology and sociology, philosophy, civics and the school subjects cannot be taught in such a comprehensive manner as well.

---

103 See Flitner, "Die Entwicklung der Pädagogischen Akademien," 363–370.
104 Ibid., 363.
105 See ibid., 363–364.
106 Ibid., 364.
107 Ibid, 365.
108 Ibid. Flitner refers in parts of his text to the publication of Helmuth Kittel, who worked at the Academy of Altona: *Der Weg zum Volkslehrer. Über die Entwicklung der Pädagogischen Akademie Jena* (Jena: 1933).

I argue rather radically that it must be sufficient, but also possible, that the teacher is thoroughly educated in educational science – which, however, is only possible if he confines himself to a few special fields. Besides this occupation-related key study, at most one further scientific field of his choice can be thoroughly developed.[109]

Important findings for teacher training from psychology and sociology must be integrated into the educational-scientific curriculum; educational science, with its pedagogical-anthropological foundation, serves as an instrument of selection with regard to the findings of the neighboring sciences.[110]

The Position of Erich Weniger (1894–1961)

Not only for biographical reasons – his many appointments to various teacher training institutions –, but also because he felt obliged to a reflected academic teacher training – due to his scientific-theoretical position with regard to the relationship between theory and practice and the relative autonomy of education[111] –, a great part of Weniger's[112] publications deal with corresponding topics.

---

109 Wilhelm Flitner, "Der Standort der Erziehungswissenschaft und Lehrerausbildung um 1970," in *Gesammelte Schriften vol. 3: Theoretische Schriften*, ed. Wilhelm Flitner (Paderborn u.a.: Schöningh, 1964/1989), 422–466; 422–423.
110 See Flitner, "Der Standort der Erziehungswissenschaft und Lehrerausbildung um 1970," 423–425.
111 In accordance with his teacher Herman Nohl, Weniger sees a high responsibility of teachers for their pupils; the teachers have to monitor whether the demands, which are made on the pupils from the outside, do serve their development or unpedagogical objectives. For more details see Matthes, *Geisteswissenschaftliche Pädagogik*, 53–54.
112 Weniger was born in Hannover; he studied Philosophy and History at the University of Göttingen. His most important academic teacher was Herman Nohl. In November 1921, he passed the State Examination for secondary school teachers for the subjects German, History, and Latin; in December 1921, he received a doctor's degree in History. Since January 1923, he worked as scientific assistant at the chair of Herman Nohl. In 1926, he habilitated with a contribution about "Die Grundlagen des Geschichtsunterrichts. Untersuchungen zur geisteswissenschaftlichen Didaktik." In 1929, Weniger was appointed professor at the Pädagogische Akademie in Kiel as Flitner's successor, in 1930 he became director of the newly founded Pädagogische Akademie Altona. After the closing of this Academy due to cost cuts, he was moved to the Pädagogische Akademie in Frankfurt/M. In 1933, he was sent on forced leave due to "political unreliability." Because of his following military-pedagogical activities and publications, however, his attitude towards National Socialism is disputed. In 1946, supported by Nohl, Weniger became director of the newly founded Pädagogische Hochschule in Göttingen and in 1949 Nohl's successor at the Chair of Pedagogy at the University of Göttingen. One focus of his scientific work was teacher training. His activities in the "Deutschen Ausschuss für das Erziehungs- und Bildungs-

His anthology *Die Eigenständigkeit der Erziehung in Theorie und Praxis* [The sovereignty of education in theory and practice] is subtitled *Probleme der akademischen Lehrerbildung* [Problems of academic teacher education]. His preface begins as follows:

> In this book, the author wants to account for his scientific dealing with pedagogy for a quarter of a century, which – since the founding of the first Pedagogical Academies in Prussia in 1926 – could concurrently be theoretical and practical working for the academic education of elementary school teachers and – since Herman Nohl's appeal at the *Göttinger Philologentag* in 1927 – for the educational training of philologists.[113]

The Training of Elementary School Teachers

Weniger demands an academic education of elementary school teachers, whose importance for the cultural and social development he values very highly. He emphatically rejects two views: first, the idea that elementary school teachers "need not know more than what they will have to teach their children afterwards",[114] which shall justify the limited training in teacher seminars; second, the idea that one must be born to become an educator, that the teaching profession is "an art" and therefore not teachable.[115] He contradicts and argues that education is an "intellectual attitude," "which of course cannot be taught mechanically, but which can be illustrated vividly [...]."[116] "And because it is an intellectual attitude, it can be awakened."[117] It is about the "adoption of the educational stance" into the will of the teacher.[118] For Weniger, there is no doubt that the academization of elementary school teacher training in the Weimar Republic

---

wesen," a non-party, cross-national educational-political advisory body, must also be mentioned. For more details, see Matthes, *Geisteswissenschaftliche Pädagogik*, 21–25.
113 Erich Weniger, *Die Eigenständigkeit der Erziehung in Theorie und Praxis* (Weinheim: Beltz, 1952).
114 Erich Weniger, "Die persönlichen Voraussetzungen des Volkslehrers und die Lehrerbildung," in *Die Eigenständigkeit der Erziehung in Theorie und Praxis*, ed. Erich Weniger (Weinheim: Beltz, 1952/1932), 38–44; 39.
115 Weniger, "Die persönlichen Voraussetzungen des Volkslehrers und die Lehrerbildung." In this statement one can also see a certain demarcation of or at least differentiation from Spranger's position, shown above. Weniger attaches more importance to educational science than Spranger.
116 Weniger, "Die persönlichen Voraussetzungen des Volkslehrers und die Lehrerbildung," 41.
117 Ibid., 42.
118 Ibid., 43.

is indispensable, since it requires a new type of "people's teacher," which is wanted by the National Constitution.[119]

The elementary school teacher thus enters "the circle of the leading positions of the public life, which can only be administered with full responsibility, independence, maturity and a clear overview."[120] In addition to his function as "representative of the homogeneous German education", he has to be "the advocate of those classes" who "enter the circle of the national community with new responsibility and independence: the proletariat and the peasantry."[121] In his farewell speech to the Pedagogical Academy in Altona, which he led and which was closed – like seven others – for political and financial reasons in 1932, he even says that it has been their goal to educate people's teachers who regard themselves quasi as "missionaries of a pedagogical ethos, which aims at the whole of life and public education."[122] Weniger is convinced that this specific form of education can neither be taught in teacher seminars nor at universities[123]; he therefore advocates specific academic institutions for the training of elementary school teachers – in the Weimar Republic the "Prussian Academies", the basic concept and goals of which he still favors after 1945, and the revival of which he forces – now named "teacher training college."[124] Which specific tasks does he assign to the pedagogical academies/teacher training colleges?

> The scientific goal of the academy [...] is to regain an elementary public education that makes the fundamental facts of the world and of life accessible again to the youth and to the people without scientification and without popularizing.[125]

On the one hand, the "people's educator" must be prepared for his task to convey the basic knowledge and customs of the people[126], on the other hand, to con-

---

119 See Erich Weniger, "Die neue Lehrerbildung," in *Lehrerbildung, Sozialpädagogik, Militärpädagogik. Politik, Gesellschaft, Erziehung in der geisteswissenschaftlichen Pädagogik*, selected and commented by Helmut Gaßen (Weinheim/Basel: Beltz, 1990/1929), 14–20; 17.
120 Ibid., 18.
121 Ibid., 18.
122 Erich Weniger, "Abschied von der Pädagogischen Akademie," in *Lehrerbildung, Sozialpädagogik, Militärpädagogik* (Weinheim/Basel: Beltz, 1990/1932), 21–28; 24.
123 See Erich Weniger, "Aufgaben und Gestaltung der Lehrerbildung," in *Lehrerbildung, Sozialpädagogik, Militärpädagogik* (Weinheim/Basel: Beltz, 1990/1953), 91–111; 95.
124 Erich Weniger, "Denkschrift über den Wiederaufbau der akademischen Lehrerbildung," in *Lehrerbildung, Sozialpädagogik, Militärpädagogik* (Weinheim/Basel: Beltz, 1990/1945), 47–90.
125 Weniger, "Abschied von der Pädagogischen Akademie," 24.
126 Erich Weniger, "Zur Entwicklungsgeschichte der deutschen Lehrerbildung," in *Lehrerbildung, Sozialpädagogik, Militärpädagogik* (Weinheim/Basel: Beltz, 1990/1933), 29–46; 43; Weniger, "Denkschrift über den Wiederaufbau der akademischen Lehrerbildung," 53, 57.

vey the central cultural achievements of the people.[127] For this purpose, he must learn the art of elementarization.[128] Besides, Weniger regards the "mutual pervasion of theory and practice" as a crucial characteristic of the pedagogical academies/teacher training colleges.[129] It is about various forms of introduction to pedagogical ethics.[130] Finally, he emphasizes the importance of music and arts classes at the pedagogical academies/teacher training colleges.[131] The same applies to civic education: "The college, as long as it is kept small enough [...], has an unprecedented opportunity to represent the genuine democratic, humane existence of our people, which the university can never do."[132] Weniger – unlike Spranger and Litt – attributes a key function to educational science at the teacher training colleges:

> The only subject of scientific efforts at the teacher training colleges is educational science (pedagogy, psychology) [...] In this field the student shall really be educated scientifically. Here he learns the methods of criticism and interpretation all sciences work with. Here he is introduced to the sources and, provided he has the necessary time and rest, can also advance to own scientific work.[133]

With regard to the conveying of cultural contents, however, the teacher training colleges shall refrain from scientific teaching, because corresponding attempts only lead to "dilettantism."[134]

The Training of Secondary School Teachers/"Philologists"

Weniger describes their pedagogical training as the "thorniest problem."[135] Most of them want to be "basically scientists"[136]. They have no "affection" for their

---

127 See Weniger, "Zur Entwicklungsgeschichte der deutschen Lehrerbildung," 44.
128 See ibid., 45; Weniger, "Denkschrift über den Wiederaufbau der akademischen Lehrerbildung," 53.
129 Weniger, "Denkschrift über den Wiederaufbau der akademischen Lehrerbildung," 55.
130 See Weniger, "Denkschrift über den Wiederaufbau der akademischen Lehrerbildung," 55; Weniger, "Zur Entwicklungsgeschichte der deutschen Lehrerbildung," 38–39.
131 See Weniger, "Denkschrift über den Wiederaufbau der akademischen Lehrerbildung," 57; Weniger, "Aufgaben und Gestaltung der Lehrerbildung," 102.
132 Weniger, "Aufgaben und Gestaltung der Lehrerbildung," 102–103.
133 Ibid., 101.
134 Ibid.
135 Ibid., 107.
136 Ibid., 107–108.

profession.[137] This is an unbearable situation: "We must use all our theoretical knowledge to achieve the practical goal of preparing students for their educational profession."[138] A great challenge and still unsolved problem is the "rather early decision about the educational aptitude of the students."[139] The necessary scientific preparation for secondary school teaching requires – besides the subject-related studies – an educational-scientific study. The aim is "to convey a scientific understanding of the educational reality, the educational system, the school organization, and their underlying ideas, theories and objectives."[140]

> This reality of education and of the school system has a structure which one must know if one wants to work in it responsibly and not only like a technician [...] If one does not adopt this knowledge as one's own, one remains – despite all subject-related scientific qualification – at best a craftsman of one's subject, at worst a dilettante and improviser.[141]

He also formulates his criticism very clearly in a publication from 1953: "The fact that the training of secondary school teachers lacks scientific dignity especially in a field which is essential for their later profession, certainly does not benefit them."[142] In addition, Weniger advocates – like Nohl – the integration of general didactics and subject-related didactics into the training of secondary school teachers:[143]

> Unfortunately, one can find just among philologists the grotesque superstition that the scientific discipline always carries the decision about its educational significance in itself; or that teaching is only applied and simplified science; that the subject matter already has an educational effect in itself; that the question of the right teaching method is a purely practical one; and many other hollow, but widespread errors.[144]

---

137 Ibid., 108.
138 Ibid.
139 Erich Weniger, "Pädagogische Ausbildung der Philologen," in *Die Eigenständigkeit der Erziehung in Theorie und Praxis*, ed. Erich Weniger (Weinheim: Beltz, 1952), 475–481, 476; see also Weniger, "Aufgaben und Gestaltung der Lehrerbildung," 109.
140 Ibid., 479.
141 Ibid., 479–480.
142 Erich Weniger, "Aufgaben und Gestaltung der Lehrerbildung," in *Neue Wege für die Schule. Beiträge zur Neuordnung von Schulaufbau, Berufsschule und Lehrerbildung*, ed. Institut zur Förderung öffentlicher Angelegenheiten e. V. (Mannheim: Institut zur Förderung öffentlicher Angelegenheiten, 1953), 85–113; 110.
143 Here, Weniger takes a clear opposite position to Spranger.
144 Weniger, "Pädagogische Ausbildung der Philologen," 480.

Weniger considers it very important that the future secondary school teachers develop "the pedagogical ethos" which they must share with all other teacher students and teachers and which shall awaken in them "the feeling for the inner unity of the educational task of our people."[145]

The Position of Albert Reble (1910–2000)

It was not only Nohl's two academic students Wilhelm Flitner and Erich Weniger who dealt intensively with questions of teacher training, but also Litt's (younger) academic student Albert Reble.[146] In 1954, he became professor of Pedagogy at the Pedagogical Academy in Bielefeld and explained his views regarding the training of elementary school teachers at pedagogical academies in his inaugural lecture. Like Flitner and Weniger, he emphasizes that in elementary school teacher training, educational science is the "core science",[147] since the scientific training at the pedagogical academies refers to educational science – and only to it. Until the 1960s, the view was still widespread in West Germany that the academic training of future elementary school teachers should not take place at the university, but at a teacher training college or a pedagogical academy, and that it could only there be realized in a meaningful way; Reble also emphatically sup-

---

145 Weniger, "Aufgaben und Gestaltung der Lehrerbildung," 111.
146 Reble was born in Magdeburg. He studied to become an elementary teacher at the Pedagogical Academy in Erfurt. After his examination in 1932, he studied Philosophy, German, and History at the University of Jena, since the winter term 1932/33 Philosophy and Pedagogy with Theodor Litt at the University of Leipzig, who became his most important academic teacher. In 1935, he received a doctor's degree from Litt for a dissertation about Schleiermacher's cultural philosophy. Then he passed the examination to become a middle school teacher and in 1939 to become a secondary school teacher for the subjects German, History, and Philosophy. After his military service, he first became a teacher at the Franckeschen Stiftungen in Halle and was then appointed as professor for History of Pedagogy at the University of Halle-Wittenberg. In 1949, Reble went to the Western part of Germany due to political dissent and became a teacher in Düsseldorf and in Lüdenscheid. From 1954 to 1960, he was professor for Pedagogy at the Pedagogical Academy in Bielefeld, in 1961 at the Pedagogical Academy in Münster. He campaigned strongly for enhancements of the pedagogical academies and worked also as advisor of the Ministry of Cultural Affairs in North Rhine-Westphalia. In 1961, he accepted a call to the Chair of Pedagogy at the University of Würzburg. He further campaigned for reforms of teacher education. Last, but not least, he became famous with his important book "Geschichte der Pädagogik" (first edition 1951), which was written mainly for teacher students. For more details, see Eva Matthes, "Zum 100. Geburtstag des Erziehungswissenschaftlers Albert Reble (1910–2000)," *Jahrbuch der Akademie gemeinnütziger Wissenschaften zu Erfurt* (2010): 52–54.
147 Albert Reble, *Lehrerbildung in Deutschland* (Ratingen: Aloys Henn, 1958), 123.

ported this view.[148] The overall atmosphere of the teacher training colleges with their focus on education and teaching in theory and practice and their strong aesthetic and collaborative orientation was seen as a strong foundation for the development of a "pedagogical ethos,"[149] an "educational strength."[150]

It is striking how Reble tries to integrate himself in the tradition of GP by corresponding remarks. Taking the positions of Spranger and Litt, who both warned against an overestimation of educational science and an over-theorization of elementary school teacher training, Reble yet tries to uphold the importance of a scientific dealing with educational science at pedagogical academies. In a way, Reble's position thus seems somewhat arbitrary or – to put it more sharply – maneuvering at some points, especially since he still has clear sympathy for Spranger's concept of the *Bildnerhochschule* in the early 1960s.[151] The following statement, for example, can be read as a reference to Spranger and especially to Litt – and can only be fully understood if one knows their positions:

> If educational science wants to fulfil its task in the whole of teacher training properly, it must also give sufficient room to the other forming forces and explicitly oppose an over-theorizing of teacher training. It must limit itself in the sense of a fruitful interaction and must also decisively reject exaggerated expectations which are shown to it by various sides. Some students and also others have indeed the exaggerated expectation that educational science might be the absolutely reliable guiding force for pedagogical practice – and pedagogy is sometimes even adjudged to be the healing power for the whole social life, especially in times of crisis.[152]

Here Reble apparently takes up a position of his revered teacher Theodor Litt, who repeatedly warned against pedagogization and expectations of salvation through pedagogy, especially in the context of the progressive education movement in the 1920s.[153] At the same time, Reble attributes a key position to educational science with regard to the training of elementary school teachers:

---

148 See Albert Reble, "Um Lehrerbildung und Pädagogische Hochschule," *Pädagogische Arbeitsblätter zur Fortbildung für Lehrer und Erzieher* 9 (1957): 337–352.
149 Albert Reble, "Der Dozent in der Lehrerbildung," *Studentische Rundschau* 2 (1955): 113–115, 113.
150 Reble, *Lehrerbildung in Deutschland*, 134; emphasis in the original version.
151 See Albert Reble, "Eduard Spranger und die Lehrerbildung," *Pädagogische Rundschau* 16 (1962): 553–570.
152 Reble, *Lehrerbildung in Deutschland*, 137.
153 Theodor Litt, "Die gegenwärtige Lage der Pädagogik und ihre Forderungen," in *Pädagogik und Kultur. Kleine pädagogische Schriften 1918–1926*, ed. Friedhelm Nicolin (Bad Heilbrunn: Klinkhardt, 1965/1926), 58–98.

At the teacher training college [used synonymously to "pedagogical academy"; E. M.], one can and one should learn to work scientifically not in English or German or History etc., but *only in the field of educational science*. And in this field the teacher student *must* necessarily learn to work scientifically. Not only the status of teacher training depends on it, but also the performance of the future generation of teachers and of our schools.[154]

Reble is clear on the fact that those who represent educational science at the teacher training colleges and pedagogical academies must also be researchers. He therefore sees no difference in the scientific value between them and the representatives of educational science at the university. In this context, Litt's statements in his previously quoted article *Hochschule und Lehrerbildung* from 1957, in which he emphasizes the different tasks between lecturers at universities – truth seekers – and teacher training colleges – people's educators –[155], cause great problems for Reble. He tries to follow Litt as far as possible – and yet contradicts him at one point. He follows his view that educational science "shall *not* become the autocratic and meaningful center of the whole training"[156] and here distances himself from his colleague Theo Dietrich[157], who in 1955 presented a publication entitled *Die Erziehungswissenschaft als Sinnmittelpunkt einer Pädagogischen Hochschule* [Educational science as center of meaning in teacher training colleges].[158] Reble emphasizes nevertheless the necessity of independent research at the educational professorships of the pedagogical academies/teacher training colleges. But he even cannot bear this contradiction to his teacher Theodor Litt and stresses in a footnote that Litt has meanwhile "principally agreed" with his argumentation in a personal letter. He had "only reservations as to whether enough pedagogical lecturers could be found who were qualified for sci-

---

154 Reble, *Lehrerbildung in Deutschland*, 160.
155 See Litt, "Hochschule und Lehrerbildung," 36.
156 See Reble, *Lehrerbildung in Deutschland*, 185.
157 Dietrich was born in 1917 in Löbichau/Thuringia. He first studied at the teacher training college in Bayreuth, second at the University of Jena and received a doctor's degree there in 1946. His doctoral adviser and most important academic teacher was Peter Petersen, the scientific assistant of whom he was until 1949. After some years' work as teacher, he was called to a Chair of Educational Science at the Teacher Training College of Bremen; this college was integrated into the University of Bremen at the beginning of the 1970s. In 1975, Dietrich changed to a Chair of General Pedagogy at the University of Bayreuth, which he held until his retirement in 1988. The organization of teacher training was one of his central scientific topics. For more details, see Theo Dietrich, "Mein Weg zu einer berufsfeld- und wissenschaftsorientierten universitären Lehrerbildung! –?," in *Geschichte der Lehrerbildung in autobiographischer Sicht*, ed. Dieter P.J. Wynands (Frankfurt/M. u.a.: Peter Lang, 1993), 105–133.
158 See ibid.

entific research."¹⁵⁹ Challenged by Dietrich's criticism of Spranger's concept of the *Bildnerhochschule*, Reble cannot help but notice a certain tension between Spranger's view and his own, but notwithstanding much appreciation for Spranger and relativizing Dietrich's position:

> It is certainly true that this view has played an important role for Spranger: anyone who wants to educate others must first of all be an educated person himself. It also seems irrefutable to us that Spranger himself then, on the basis of this thought, gave pedagogical science only a very modest, even too modest place in the overall education; but more than a reference to his 'cultural pedagogical' attitude [this reference comes from Dietrich; E. M.], his own, but probably justified reference to the situation of the educational science at that time (1920!) may perhaps help us to understand it.¹⁶⁰

Moreover, the negative consequences of this restriction had been missing; but Spranger's great conceptual achievement remains:

> The weak position which the [scientific; E. M.] pedagogy actually occupied in Spranger's own conception – the big success does not lie in his reflections on the precise structure of the studies, but in his general idea of an independent institution for teacher training, differentiated from the old types of higher educational institutions [universities; E. M.] and squarely characterized by teacher training, but fundamentally regarded as equal to those – has however, in our opinion, been *already* corrected to a considerable degree with the foundation of the Prussian Pedagogical Academies.¹⁶¹

Reble also clearly states how he would like educational science to be anchored in the pedagogical academy/teacher training college: The focus shall be on general pedagogy, which he also calls "theoretical pedagogy;"¹⁶² this shall be flanked by school pedagogy, which comprises general didactics, too, and which he also calls "practical pedagogy."¹⁶³ He attributes a key position to general pedagogy inasmuch as it must lay the foundations for learning to judge in a pedagogically reflected manner, to think pedagogically, and to act accordingly.¹⁶⁴ General pedagogy, which he understands as an integrating philosophical-hermeneutic-empirical discipline, must also integrate pedagogically significant in-

---

159 See ibid.; Albert Reble, "Um Lehrerbildung und Pädagogische Hochschule," 337–352; 349.
160 Reble, "Um Lehrerbildung und Pädagogische Hochschule," 351.
161 Ibid., 351–352; see also Albert Reble, "Zur Diskussion der Lehrerbildung," *Pädagogische Rundschau* 12 (1957/58): 391–401; 400–401.
162 Reble, *Lehrerbildung in Deutschland*, 206.
163 Ibid.
164 See ibid., 181–182.

sights from sociology and psychology.¹⁶⁵ Moreover, it is indispensable to have a problem- and social-historical knowledge of education and teaching.¹⁶⁶ The same focus must also apply to educational studies in university teacher training courses.¹⁶⁷

> The general pedagogical views are not only necessary for the teachers of all school subjects, school levels and school types; on closer examination, they even prove to be the central and the superordinate, i.e. the interdisciplinary ones in a deeper sense.¹⁶⁸

All the more painful for him was the marginal position of educational science in the teacher examination regulations of Bavaria, which he could not change – certainly one of the most frustrating experiences in his scientific life.¹⁶⁹ Reble had accepted the integration of the teacher training colleges into the universities at the end of the 70s, or to be more precise: he had considered it to be the best solution at that time.¹⁷⁰

Conclusion

My analyses were able to confirm the theses set out in the introduction: the positions of the presented *Geisteswissenschaftlichen Pädagogen* are indeed related to each other, but can nevertheless, to some extent very definitely, be distinguished from one another.

---

165 See ibid., 146, 180–181.
166 See ibid., 149–151; Albert Reble, *Die historische Dimension der Pädagogik in Wissenschaft und Lehrerbildung*, Schriftenreihe "Reden zur Zeit," ed. Institut für Demokratieforschung Würzburg (Würzburg: [o. V.], 1978), 32.
167 See ibid., 190–191.
168 Albert Reble, "Was fordert die Schule von der Erziehungswissenschaft in der Lehrerausbildung? Betrachtungen zur geschichtlichen Entwicklung und zur Gegenwartslage," in *Pädagogik in geschichtlicher Erfahrung und gegenwärtiger Verantwortung*. Festschrift zum 65. Geburtstag von Karl Ernst Maier, ed. Helmut Heim and Heinz Jürgen Ipfling (Frankfurt/M. u.a.: Peter Lang, 1986), 52–87; 65.
169 See ibid., 68; Albert Reble, "Bewegte Jahre. Hochschule und Schule, Erziehungswissenschaft und Lehrerausbildung um 1970," in *Lehrerbildung, Lehrersein nach 1945 – exemplarisch dargestellt*. Horst-Erich Pohl zum 60. Geburtstag, ed. Wolfgang Hinrichs (Berlin/Vilseck: Tesdorpf, 1987), 13–24; 21; Albert Reble, "Erfahrungen in der Lehrerausbildung 1930–1980," in *Geschichte der Lehrerbildung in autobiographischer Sicht*, ed. Dieter P.J. Wynands (Frankfurt/M. u.a.: Peter Lang, 1993), 293–328, especially 318–320.
170 Reble, "Bewegte Jahre," 19–20.

Many things are striking and worth discussing; I would like to pick out just one aspect: the justification of the particular relevance and value of their respective institutional domains: for Spranger, Litt, and Nohl the universities, demanding an independent (cultural) pedagogy for secondary school teacher training, but not regarding this – very strongly pointed out by Spranger and Litt – to be the central professional science for secondary school teachers; for Flitner, Weniger, and Reble the pedagogical academies/teacher training colleges, conjuring the scientific character of those solely through their own discipline – educational science. As holder of a Chair of Pedagogy at a Bavarian university, where he experienced the ignoring of educational science in the training of secondary school teachers – and thus also the marginalization of his work –, Reble then also advocated the integration of primary and lower secondary school teacher training into the university – which, however, did not lead to the desired upgrading of educational science at the university.

The separation of "higher" and "lower" school teacher training, as it was advocated by the *Geisteswissenschaftlichen Pädagogen* – sometimes very rigidly, even ideologically, profession-politically – has now been largely overcome institutionally in Germany (only in Baden-Württemberg there are still separated *Pädagogische Hochschulen*[171] for the training of primary and lower secondary school teachers); however, the differences – often even claimed as opposites – between the value of scientific research for truth and scholarship/scientific knowledge on the one hand and human education on the other do still exist; corresponding devaluations take place even within the universities. At the same time, an alignment of the remuneration and reputation of elementary and lower secondary school teachers with those of higher secondary school teachers has not yet been attained in Germany to this day; in my opinion, this is a social scandal, which urgently needs to be revised.

Bibliography

Becker, Carl Heinrich. *Gedanken zur Hochschulreform*. Leipzig: Quelle & Meyer, 1919.
Becker, Carl Heinrich. *Die Pädagogische Akademie im Aufbau unseres nationalen Bildungswesens*. Leipzig: Quelle & Meyer, 1926.
Beckmann, Hans-Karl. *Lehrerseminar – Akademie – Hochschule. Das Verhältnis von Theorie und Praxis in drei Epochen der Volksschullehrerausbildung*. Weinheim/Basel: Beltz, 1968.
Blömeke, Sigrid et al., eds. *Handbuch Lehrerbildung*. Bad Heilbrunn: Klinkhardt, 2004.

---

171 Those teacher training colleges are now called "Universities of Education" in English.

Clandinin, Jean, and Jukka Husu, eds. *The Sage Handbook of Research on Teacher Education.* London: SAGE Reference, 2017.

Depaepe, Marc. *Zum Wohle des Kindes? Pädologie, pädagogische Psychologie und experimentelle Pädagogik in Europa und den USA, 1890 bis1914.* Weinheim: Deutscher Studien Verlag, 1993.

Dietrich, Theo. "Mein Weg zu einer berufsfeld- und wissenschaftsorientierten universitären Lehrerbildung! –?." In *Geschichte der Lehrerbildung in autobiographischer Sicht*, edited by Dieter P.J. Wynands, 105–133. Frankfurt/M. u. a.: Peter Lang, 1993.

Flitner, Wilhelm. "Der Standort der Erziehungswissenschaft und Lehrerausbildung um 1970." In *Gesammelte Schriften. vol. 3: Theoretische Schriften*, edited by Wilhelm Flitner, 422–466. Paderborn u. a.: Schöningh, 1989/1964.

Flitner, Wilhelm, ed. *Gesammelte Schriften vol. 3: Theoretische Schriften.* Paderborn u. a.: Schöningh, 1989.

Flitner, Wilhelm. "Das Pädagogikstudium an der Pädagogischen Akademie." In *Gesammelte Schriften, vol. 4: Die Pädagogische Bewegung. Beiträge – Berichte – Rückblicke*, edited by Wilhelm Flitner, 363–370. Paderborn u. a.: Schöningh, 1987/1929.

Flitner, Wilhelm. "Die Entwicklung der Pädagogischen Akademien." In *Gesammelte Schriften, vol. 4: Die Pädagogische Bewegung. Beiträge – Berichte – Rückblicke*, edited by Wilhelm Flitner, 363–370. Paderborn u. a.: Schöningh, 1987/1933.

Flitner, Wilhelm, ed. *Gesammelte Schriften, vol. 4: Die Pädagogische Bewegung. Beiträge – Berichte – Rückblicke.* Paderborn u. a.: Schöningh, 1987.

Führ, Christoph. "Gelehrter Schulmann – Oberlehrer – Studienrat. Zum sozialen Aufstieg der Philologen." In *Bildungsbürgertum im 19. Jahrhundert*, part 1, 2nd. edn., edited by Werner Conze and Jürgen Kocka, 417–457. Stuttgart: Klett-Cotta, 1992.

Kittel, Helmuth. *Der Weg zum Volkslehrer. Über die Entwicklung der Pädagogischen Akademie Jena.* Jena: Diederichs, 1932.

Langewiesche, Dieter, and Heinz-Elmar Tenorth, eds. *Handbuch der deutschen Bildungsgeschichte, vol. V: 1918–1945. Die Weimarer Republik und die nationalsozialistische Diktatur.* München: Beck, 1989.

Litt, Theodor. "Die gegenwärtige Lage der Pädagogik und ihre Forderungen." In *Pädagogik und Kultur. Kleine pädagogische Schriften 1918–1926*, edited by Friedhelm Nicolin, 58–98. Bad Heilbrunn: Klinkhardt, 1965/1926.

Litt, Theodor. "Hochschule und Lehrerbildung." In *Überlieferung und Neubeginn. Probleme der Lehrerbildung und Bildung nach zehn Jahren des Aufbaus*, edited by Oskar Hammelsbeck, 33–37. Ratingen: Henn, 1957.

Litt, Theodor. "Zum Plan der Pädagogischen Fakultät." Unpublished manuscrpt.

Matthes, Eva. "Theologe – Philologe – Fachwissenschaftler – Pädagoge? Historisch-systematische Akzentsetzungen zur (Aus)Bildung der Lehrer an höheren Schulen." *Anregung. Zeitschrift für Gymnasialpädagogik* 46 (2000): 328–341.

Matthes, Eva. "Theodor Litt (1880–1962)." In *Sächsische Lebensbilder*, vol. 5, edited by Gerald Wiemers, 435–464. Leipzig: Verlag der Sächsischen Akademie der Wissenschaften, 2003.

Matthes, Eva. "Die Pädagogik konstituiert sich als universitäres Fach." In *Verlag Julius Klinkhardt. 1834–2009. Verlegerisches Handeln zwischen Pädagogik, Politik und Ökonomie*, edited by Uwe Sandfuchs, Jörg-W. Link, and Andreas Klinkhardt, 81–94. Bad Heilbrunn: Klinkhardt, 2009.

Matthes, Eva. "Zum 100. Geburtstag des Erziehungswissenschaftlers Albert Reble (1910–2000)." In *Jahrbuch der Akademie gemeinnütziger Wissenschaften zu Erfurt* (2010): 52–54.
Matthes, Eva. *Geisteswissenschaftliche Pädagogik. Ein Lehrbuch*. München: Oldenbourg, 2011.
Meyer-Willner, Gerhard. *Eduard Spranger und die Lehrerbildung. Die notwendige Revision eines Mythos*. Bad Heilbrunn: Klinkhardt, 1986.
Müller-Rolli, Sebastian. "Lehrer." In *Handbuch der deutschen Bildungsgeschichte, vol. 5: 1918–1945. Die Weimarer Republik und die nationalsozialistische Diktatur*, edited by Dieter Langewiesche and Heinz-Elmar Tenorth, 240–258. München: Beck, 1989.
Nohl, Herman. "Die Ausbildung der wissenschaftlichen Lehrer durch die Universität." In *Pädagogische Aufsätze*, 2nd. enlarged edn., edited by Herman Nohl, 183–189. Langensalza u. a.: Beltz, 1929/1927.
Nohl, Herman, ed. *Pädagogische Aufsätze*, 2nd. enlarged edn. Langensalza u. a.: Beltz, 1929.
Paffrath, Fritz Hartmut. *Eduard Spranger und die Volksschule. Eine historisch-systematische Untersuchung*. Bad Heilbrunn: Klinkhardt, 1971.
Reble, Albert. "Der Dozent in der Lehrerbildung." *Studentische Rundschau* 2 (1955): 113–115.
Reble, Albert. "Um Lehrerbildung und Pädagogische Hochschule." *Pädagogische Arbeitsblätter zur Fortbildung für Lehrer und Erzieher* 9 (1957): 337–352.
Reble, Albert. "Zur Diskussion der Lehrerbildung." *Pädagogische Rundschau* 12 (1957/58): 391–401.
Reble, Albert. *Lehrerbildung in Deutschland*. Ratingen: Aloys Henn, 1958.
Reble, Albert. "Eduard Spranger und die Lehrerbildung." *Pädagogische Rundschau* 16 (1962): 553–570.
Reble, Albert. *Die historische Dimension der Pädagogik in Wissenschaft und Lehrerbildung*, Schriftenreihe "Reden zur Zeit," edited by Institut für Demokratieforschung Würzburg, Würzburg: [o. V.], 1978.
Reble, Albert. "Was fordert die Schule von der Erziehungswissenschaft in der Lehrerausbildung? Betrachtungen zur geschichtlichen Entwicklung und zur Gegenwartslage." In *Pädagogik in geschichtlicher Erfahrung und gegenwärtiger Verantwortung. Festschrift zum 65. Geburtstag von Karl Ernst Maier*, edited by Helmut Heim and Heinz Jürgen Ipfling, 52–87. Frankfurt/M. u. a.: Peter Lang, 1986.
Reble, Albert. "Bewegte Jahre. Hochschule und Schule, Erziehungswissenschaft und Lehrerausbildung um 1970." In *Lehrerbildung, Lehrersein nach 1945 – exemplarisch dargestellt. Horst-Erich Pohl zum 60. Geburtstag*, edited by Wolfgang Hinrichs, 13–24. Berlin/Vilseck: Tesdorpf, 1987.
Reble, Albert. "Erfahrungen in der Lehrerausbildung 1930–1980." In *Geschichte der Lehrerbildung in autobiographischer Sicht*, edited by Dieter P.J. Wynands, 293–328. Frankfurt/M. u. a.: Peter Lang, 1993.
Robinson, Wendy. "Teacher Education: A Historical Overview." In *The Sage Handbook of Research on Teacher Education*, edited by Jean Clandinin and Jukka Husu, 49–67. London: SAGE Reference, 2017.
Sandfuchs, Uwe. "Geschichte der Lehrerbildung in Deutschland." In *Handbuch Lehrerbildung*, edited by Sigrid Blömeke et al., 14–37. Bad Heilbrunn: Klinkhardt, 2004.
Spranger, Eduard. "Gedanken über Lehrerbildung." In *Gesammelte Schriften, vol. 3: Schule und Lehrer*, edited by Eduard Spranger, 27–73. Heidelberg: Quelle & Meyer, 1970/1920.

Spranger, Eduard, ed. *Gesammelte Schriften, vol. III: Schule und Lehrer.* Heidelberg: Quelle & Meyer, 1970.

Spranger, Eduard. *Die Ausbildung der höheren Lehrer an der Universität* [Memorandum of the Faculty of Philosophy at the Friedrich Wilhelm University of Berlin]. Leipzig: Quelle & Meyer, 1925.

Weniger, Erich. "Die neue Lehrerbildung." In *Lehrerbildung, Sozialpädagogik, Militärpädagogik. Politik, Gesellschaft, Erziehung in der geisteswissenschaftlichen Pädagogik*, selected and commented by Helmut Gaßen, 14–20. Weinheim/Basel: Beltz, 1990/1929.

Weniger, Erich. "Die persönlichen Voraussetzungen des Volkslehrers und die Lehrerbildung." In *Die Eigenständigkeit der Erziehung in Theorie und Praxis*, edited by Erich Weniger, 38–44. Weinheim: Beltz, 1952/1932.

Weniger, Erich. "Abschied von der Pädagogischen Akademie." In *Lehrerbildung, Sozialpädagogik, Militärpädagogik*, selected and commented by Helmut Gaßen, 21–28. Weinheim/Basel: Beltz, 1990/1932.

Weniger, Erich. "Zur Entwicklungsgeschichte der deutschen Lehrerbildung." In *Lehrerbildung, Sozialpädagogik, Militärpädagogik*, selected and commented by Helmut Gaßen, 29–46. Weinheim/Basel: Beltz, 1990/1933.

Weniger, Erich, ed. *Lehrerbildung, Sozialpädagogik, Militärpädagogik*, selected and commented by Helmut Gaßen. Weinheim/Basel: Beltz, 1990.

Weniger, Erich. "Denkschrift über den Wiederaufbau der akademischen Lehrerbildung." In *Lehrerbildung, Sozialpädagogik, Militärpädagogik*, selected and commented by Helmut Gaßen, 47–90. Weinheim/Basel: Beltz, 1990/1945.

Weniger, Erich, ed. *Die Eigenständigkeit der Erziehung in Theorie und Praxis.* Weinheim: Beltz, 1952.

Weniger, Erich. "Pädagogische Ausbildung der Philologen." In *Die Eigenständigkeit der Erziehung in Theorie und Praxis*, edited by Erich Weniger, 475–481. Weinheim: Beltz, 1952.

Weniger, Erich. "Aufgaben und Gestaltung der Lehrerbildung." In *Lehrerbildung, Sozialpädagogik, Militärpädagogik*, selected and commented by Helmut Gaßen, 91–111. Weinheim/Basel: Beltz, 1990/1953.

Weniger, Erich. "Aufgaben und Gestaltung der Lehrerbildung." In *Neue Wege für die Schule. Beiträge zur Neuordnung von Schulaufbau, Berufsschule und Lehrerbildung*, edited by Institut zur Förderung öffentlicher Angelegenheiten e. V., 85–113. Mannheim: Institut zur Förderung öffentlicher Angelegenheiten, 1953.

Wynands, Dieter, P.J., ed. *Geschichte der Lehrerbildung in autobiographischer Sicht.* Frankfurt/M. u. a.: Peter Lang, 1993.

András Németh and Éva Szabolcs (ELTE Eötvös Loránd University, Hungary)
Educational Science as an Academic Discipline in Hungary (1867–1953): Turns and Developmental Phases

Abstract: Our article is based on the results of our research in the field of educational sciences in Hungary from the birth of the Austro-Hungarian Empire until the establishment of the so-called Rákosi dictatorship. The first phase was characterized by the institutionalization of pedagogy as a university discipline in the last third of the nineteenth century. During this period, Herbartianism, which was the academic foundation of education, reached its peak. The second phase continued into the twentieth century. During this period, an educational science movement emerged, which focused on the empirical paradigm of social science research; however, the various approaches of this movement (experimental pedagogy, children's research, etc.) were not yet accepted as established academic fields of educational science. The third phase is characterized by the permanent institutionalization of the educational sciences, with a focus on German *Geisteswissenschaften*. After World War II, Hungary became part of the sphere of interest of the Soviet Union, which led to the fourth stage of development of educational science, which was strongly influenced by the political power shifts and the ideology of Stalinism.

Keywords: history of educational sciences in Hungary; discipline formation; Herbartianism; *Geisteswissenschaft*; educational science under Stalinism

Introduction

Recently, numerous historical anthologies and monographs have been published focusing on the social history approach (discipline formation and development)

Note: This article summarizes our previous research concerning the emergence of educational science in Hungary. Our research group continues to reveal the characteristics of educational science in the 1960s and 90s by analyzing contemporary academic journals and publications. Results of this research process – namely the relationship of ideological pressure and emerging scientific standards – will be published in the near future. We are most grateful to our dear colleague Prof. Marc Depaepe for the many years of inspiring cooperation and his helpful comments and suggestions.

https://doi.org/10.1515/9783110623451-014

of educational sciences – often using Rudolf Stichweh's concept of discipline.¹ Although several general characteristics can be seen in these developmental tendencies, specific lines can be observed in different countries and historical regions.² Accordingly, this article aims to introduce the peculiar developments in Hungary between 1867 and 1953, primarily focusing on the first half of the twentieth century.³ It is generally shown that in the examined period the Hungarian

---

1 See Rudolf Stichweh, *Wissenschaft, Universität, Professionen* (Frankfurt am Main: Suhrkamp, 1994).
2 Wolfgang Brezinka, *Pädagogik in Österreich. Geschichte des Faches an den Universitäten von 18. bis zum Ende des 20. Jahrhunderts*, Band 1 (Wien: ÖAV, 2000); Klaus-Peter Horn, András Németh, Béla Pukánszky, and Heinz-Elmar Tenorth, eds., *Erziehungswissenschaft in Mitteleuropa. Aufklärerische Traditionen – deutscher Einfluß – nationale Eigenständigkeit* (Budapest: Osiris, 2001); Kathleen Anne Cruikshank, "The prelude to education as an academic discipline: American Herbartianism and the emergence of a science of pedagogy," in *History of Educational Studies*, ed. Peter Drewek and Cristoph Lüth, Suppl. Series 3, *Paedagogica Historica*, (Ghent: University of Ghent, 1998), 99–120; Brian Simon, "The study of education as a university subject in Britain," in *The State And Educational Change: Essays In The History Of Education And Pedagogy*, ed. Brian Simon (London: Lawrence and Wishart, 1994), 127–146; Heinz-Elmar Tenorth and Klaus-Peter Horn, "Erziehungswissenschaft in Deutschland in der ersten Hälfte des 20. Jahrhunderts," in *Erziehungswissenschaft in Mitteleuropa*, ed. Klaus-Peter Horn et al. (Budapest: Osiris, 2001), 176–191; András Németh, "Die Entwicklung der Pädagogik zur Universitätsdisziplin, sowie ihre Institutonalisierung an der Universität in Budapest," in *Erziehungswissenschaft in Mitteleuropa*, ed. Klaus-Peter Horn et al. (Budapest: Osiris, 2001), 309–345; Rita Hofstetter and Bernard Schneuwly, eds., *Erziehungswissenschaft(en) in 19.–20. Jahrhundert. Zwischen Profession und Disziplin* (Bern: Lang, 2002); Klaus-Peter Horn, *Erziehungswissenschaft in Deutschland im 20. Jahrhundert* (Bad Heilbrunn: Klinkhardt, 2003); Peter Wagner and Björn Wittrock, "States, institutions and discourses: A comparative perspective on the structuration of the social sciences," in *Discourses on society. The shaping of the social science disciplines*, ed. Peter Wagner, Björn Wittrock, and Richard Whitley (Dordrecht: Kluwer, 1992), 331–358.
3 This paper was supported by the National Research, Development and Innovation Office's NKFIH (OTKA) grant (no. 127937). Our paper has several antecedents, Johanna Hopfner, András Németh, and Éva Szabolcs, eds., *Kindheit, Schule, Erziehungswissenschaft in Mitteleuropa 1948–2008*. (Bern et. al: Peter Lang Verlag, 2009); Éva Szabolcs, "Értékelmélet és kultúrfilozófia a Magyar Paedagogia című folyóiratban. Kornis Gyula és Prohászka Lajos," in *A szellemtudományi pedagógia magyar recepciója*, ed. András Németh (Budapest: Gondolat, 2004), 145–160; András Németh, "The development phases of educational sciences as an academic discipline in Hungary in the first half of the 20th century," *Foro de Educación* 15 (2017): 1–23; András Németh, *Erziehungswissenschaft in Ungarn (1870–1952)* (Budapest: Gondolat, 2013); András Németh, *A magyar neveléstudomány fejlődése. Nemzetközi tudományfejlődés és recepciós hatások, egyetemi tudománnyá válás, középiskolai tanárképzés* (Budapest: Gondolat, 2014); András Németh, "Die Entwicklungsperioden der ungarischen Erziehungswissenschaft im 19. und 20. Jahrhundert," in *University and Universality. The Place and Role of the University of Pécs in Europe from the Middle Ages to Present Day*, ed. Ágnes Fischer-Dárdai, István Lengvári, and Éva Schmelczer-Pohánka

history of pedagogy and educational science is on the one hand a "history of reception", especially of German and Austrian patterns, and on the other hand, it is characterized by great adaptational achievement. The four stages of this development – (1) the foundation of Hungarian educational sciences, (2) the emergence of the empirical approach, (3) the *Geisteswissenschaften*-centered pedagogy, and (4) the reshaping which occurred during Stalinism – are introduced in chronological order.

The Foundation of the Hungarian Educational Sciences

After the 1867 Compromise, Hungary became a nation state within the Austro-Hungarian Monarchy with an almost completely independent domestic policy.[4] The merger to form the *Szabadelvű Párt* (Liberal Party) led by Kálmán Tisza brought about long-lasting political stability in Hungary which was nevertheless based on a restrictive right to vote.[5] Yet this enabled Hungary to expand internally into a modern constitutional state.[6] Thanks to the liberal government, the 1867 Compromise also paved the way for the development of a modern school system. The reorganization of the primary school system was a high priority both in Hungary and in Austria. Accordingly, in 1868 the Hungarian parliament adopted a new public education law (Act 38 of 1868), which for the first time established compulsory schooling for children aged six to 12, followed by a three-year "repeating school".[7] As for the Hungarian secondary school system, it had been radically reformed earlier (in 1849) by the Austrian *Organisationsentwurf*[8] and intro-

---

(Pécs: University Library of Pécs and Centre for Learning, 2017), 309–328. The results and texts of these publications have been used in this article.
4 The 1867 Compromise (or Austro-Hungarian Compromise of 1867) refers to the constitutional agreements by which the Austrian Empire was transformed into the dual monarchy of Austria-Hungary. Among the related regulations, the most important (and the first in order of time) was the Act 12 of 1867.
5 For details, see Friedrich Gottas, *Ungarn im Zeitalter des Hochliberalismus. Studien zur Tisza-Ara (1975–1890)* (Wien: Verlag der österreichische Akademie der Wissenschaften, 1976).
6 Andreas Helmedach and Harald Roth, "Habsburgreich," in *Studienbuch Östliches Europa. Band 1: Geschichte Ostmittel – und Südosteuropas*, ed. Harald Roth (Köln: Böhlau, 1999), 201–202.
7 See also Penka Peykovska, "Literacy and Illiteracy in Austria Hungary. The Case of Bulgarian Migrant Communities", *Hungarian Historical Review* 3 (2014): 704.
8 *Entwurf der Organisation der Gymnasien und Realschulen in Oesterreich*. According to Vetter, the English translation of the title is the following: "Sketch of the organization of grammar

duced a new eight-class gymnasium with a four-class lower and a four-class upper part, as well as a six-year secondary school program ("*Realschule*").[9]

After 1867, a differing pedagogical approach became necessary to fulfil the expectations of the new educational policy. In the background of the uniform national concept of education, the new elements of the educational idea of Hungarian national liberalism can also be found. Its backbone was the literary past, local history, and natural history. The concept set itself the task of replacing religious education in the curriculum with secular ethics. In addition to the Greek and Latin classics, the focus was on historicizing the national literature and history, the natural conditions of the home country, and the emphasis on the unity of national and European culture. It reflected a classicist cult of harmony, propagating a corresponding moral and artistic style that avoided any dissonance.[10]

Herbartianism seemed to be the most suitable way to underpin the theoretical background of this educational concept and the effective work of the new Hungarian school system. The reception of Herbartianism – as can be seen in other Central European countries[11] – became more and more widespread during the modernization of the Hungarian school system and accelerated in the 1870s.[12] The main representative of Hungarian Herbartianism, Mór Kármán (1843–1915), studied philosophy and philology at the University of Vienna and received his doctoral degree from the Faculty of Philosophy at the University of Pest in 1866. József Eötvös, the Minister of Religion and Public Education, commissioned him to study the system of German practical teacher training at

---

schools and 'Realschulen' in Austria". See Eva Vetter, "Hegemonic discourse in the Habsburg Empire: The case of education. A critical discourse analysis of two mid 19th century government documents," in *Diglossia and Power. Language Policies and Practice in the 19th Century Habsburg Empire*, ed. Rosita Rindler Schverje (Berlin, New York: Mouton de Gruyter, 2003), 287. Later this regulation was extended to Hungary.

9 See András Németh, "Die ungarischen Bildungsreformen: Von der theresianisch-josephinischen Reichsreform zur nationalstaatlichen Bildungspolitik (1777–1867)," in *Schule und Reform*, ed. Flavian Imlig, Lukas Lehmann, and Karin Manz (Wiesbaden: Springer, 2018), 112. This latter type of school partly reached the qualification level of the eight-class gymnasium in 1875 and 1883, and fully in 1924.

10 Ibid., 113. László Felkai, *Neveléstörténeti dolgozatok a dualizmus korából* (Budapest: Tankönyvkiadó, 1979), 224; Endre Ballér, *Tantervelméletek Magyarországon a XIX. és XX. században* (Budapest: OPI, 1996), 41.

11 Jürgen Oelkers, *Reformpädagogik: Eine kritische Dogmengeschichte* (Weinheim: Juventa Verlag, 1989); Heinz-Elmar Tenorth, "Erziehungswissenschaft in Mitteleuropa," in *Erziehungswissenschaft in Mitteleuropa*, ed. Horn, Németh, Pukánszky and Tenorth, 23–40.

12 For details see Imre Garai, "Középiskolai tanárképzés intézményei. A tanárvizsgáló bizottság és a tanárképző intézetek működése a fővárosi egyetemen az 1862–1919 közötti időszakban" (habilitation thesis, Eötvös Loránd Tudományegyetem, 2019).

the University of Leipzig, where he studied from 1869 to 1871 in Tuiskon Ziller's pedagogical seminar.[13]

During his study in Leipzig, Mór Kármán became acquainted with Wilhelm Rein. This meeting later developed into a lifelong friendship and intensive scientific cooperation; moreover, their scientific careers developed in parallel. After his return to Hungary in 1871, in 1872 Kármán became a private professor in pedagogy, ethics, and psychology at the University of Pest. In the same year, he was commissioned by the Ministry of Religion and Public Education to set up a model gymnasium for teacher training in Pest-Buda where he held a position of supervisor until 1897. Between 1873 and 1883, Kármán was the secretary of the Hungarian Educational Council, and played an important role in shaping the curriculum for the country's gymnasiums. Between 1873 and 1876, he co-published the magazine *Magyar Tanügy* (Hungarian Education) with Gusztáv Heinrich, and became its sole editor after 1876. Due to serious illness, he withdrew into temporary retirement for several years after 1897. From 1907 onwards, he was responsible for the field of theoretical education at the Ministry of Religion and Public Education. In 1908, he was ennobled and in the following year he was appointed full professor at the University of Budapest.[14]

The institutionalization of Herbartian positions as the fundamental point of departure of university pedagogy and gymnasium teacher education was implemented by Kármán and founded on the model of Ziller's pedagogical seminar. The foundation of the model secondary school mentioned above was also influenced by the pedagogical approaches of Ziller's *Übungsschule* in Leipzig and later Rein's *Pädagogische Universitäts-Seminar* in Jena.[15] The teacher training initiatives introduced by Kármán were completely different from those of Ágost Lubrich, contemporary professor of educational science. In the background of the disagreement was the protest of Lubrich, who rejected the inclusion of Herbartian pedagogy because he believed it endangered the Christian Catholic traditions of the university.[16]

---

13 Ödön Weszely, "Kármán Mór emlékezete," *Magyar Paedagogia* 25 (1916): 517.
14 Ibid., 517–518; András Németh, "Der Einfluss des Herbartianismus an der Budapester Universität und seine Rolle in der Lehrerbildung – eine Fallstudie," in *Herbartianische Konzepte der Lehrerbildung*, ed. Rotraud Coriand (Bad Heilbrunn: Klinkhardt, 2003), 234–235; András Németh, "Herbartische Einflüsse auf ungarische Bildungspolitik nach 1867," in *Erziehung und Unterricht: Neue Perspektiven auf Johann Friedrich Herbarts Allgemeine Pädagogik*, ed. Katja Grundig de Vazquez and Alexandra Schotte (Paderborn: Ferdinand Schöningh Verlag, 2018), 233–245.
15 Ibid., 236–238.
16 Németh, *A magyar neveléstudomány fejlődése*, 211–212.

Due to the growing influence of Herbartian pedagogy, a generation of scientists – recruited almost exclusively from Kármán's pupils – started to work as teachers towards the end of the 1890s. Pedagogues such as Ernő Fináczy, János Waldapfel, László Nagy, and Ödön Weszely significantly contributed to the reception and acceptance of Herbartianism as a foundation of education as a university discipline. Furthermore, beyond influencing secondary education, Herbartianism also played an important role in primary school teacher training and primary school practices.[17]

From the turn of the century onwards the profile of Hungarian university pedagogy was determined by the above-mentioned Ernő Fináczy (1860–1935), professor of the University of Budapest, who represented the Catholic direction of Herbartianism. The core of his scientific work emphasizes the historical-deductive foundations of Catholic-oriented normative pedagogy based on ancient and Christian traditions, the results of which can be traced in an impressive five-volume work on the history of education. In the first decades of the century, he was the chairman of the Hungarian Pedagogical Society and editor of the magazine Magyar Paedagogia.[18] His expertise determined the pedagogical profile of the period.[19] Another influential pedagogue of the period was István Schneller (1847–1939), professor at the other Hungarian university founded in Kolozsvár (Cluj) in the 1870s. He was a Protestant Lutheran theologian and the representative of the theological and pedagogical views of Schleiermacher – and an opponent of Herbartian philosophy and pedagogy that was at that time the mainstream educational philosophy in the Austro-Hungarian Monarchy.[20]

The Emergence of the Empirical Paradigm

The reception of positivism in Hungarian universities at the end of the nineteenth century was linked with the name of Imre Pauer (1845–1930), a professor

---

[17] Ibid., 238.
[18] Éva Szabolcs, "Neveléstudomány és a Magyar Paedagogia 1892–1919," in *Neveléstudománytörténeti tanulmányok*, ed. András Németh and Heinz-Elmar Tenorth (Budapest: Osiris Kiadó, 2000), 229–257.
[19] András Németh and Béla Pukánszky, *A pedagógia problématörténete* (Budapest: Gondolat, 2004), 218–220.
[20] András Németh, *A magyar neveléstudomány fejlődéstörténete* (Budapest: Osiris, 2002), 306–312.

of philosophy who had the necessary qualifications to teach pedagogy.[21] The positivist pedagogy taking place within the university appears in the early works of Ákos Pauler (1876–1933), professor of philosophy. From 1898, he expanded his knowledge of experimental psychology over the course of a year at the institute of Wundt in Leipzig. Later he studied for a year in Paris where he attended Pierre Janet's psychology lectures.[22]

In the reception and later in the dissemination of extracurricular pedagogical issues of the epoch, primary school teachers and teacher training played an important role; one of their representatives, László Nagy (1857–1931) and his colleagues founded the *Magyar Gyermektanulmányi Társaság* (Hungarian Society for Child Study) in 1906.[23] As a result of the dissemination of modern pedagogical-psychological endeavors, the organizers of this society expected the establishment of an experimental basis for the educational sciences.[24] In order to spread the child-centered pedagogical developments, training courses were held for practicing teachers and books and magazines were published on the subject.[25] Besides these, from 1907, the independent journal of the society *A gyermek* (The Child) was published under the editorship of László Nagy. As one of the most outstanding personalities of theoretical pedagogy in Hungary, Ödön Weszely contributed significantly to the diffusion of the ideas of progressive education and pedology, and to the disclosure of these scientific results to teachers.[26]

After the turn of the century, Weszely's efforts in the spirit of experimental pedagogy were particularly notable during his time at the University of Pécs, where he was appointed professor of pedagogy in 1923. His institute included a specialized library with 2,000 volumes, as well as a pedagogical research lab-

---

21 *A budapesti Királyi Magyar Tudományegyetem Almanachja az MCMIX–MCMX. tanévre* (Budapest: M. Kir. Tudományegyetemi Nyomda, 1910), 93.
22 Ágnes Zimányi, "Az abszolútum jelentősége és ismeretének eredete Pauler Ákos bölcseletében" (PhD diss., Pázmány Péter Katolikus Egyetem, 2017), 71–73.
23 Erzsébet Nagy Zoltánné Áment, "Pályakép több olvasatban. Nagy László élettörténete," *Új Pedagógiai Szemle* 57 (2007): 146–163.
24 Marc Depaepe, *Zum Wohl des Kindes? Pädologie, pädagogische Psychologie und experimentelle Pädagogik in Europa und den USA, 1890–1940* (Weinheim, Leuven: Leuven University Press, 1993).
25 Éva Szabolcs, "The emergence of child study ideas in the educational press in Hungary at the turn of the 19th–20th century," in *Pädagogische und kulturelle Strömungen in der k.u.k. Monarchie: Lebensreform, Herbartianismus und reformpädagogische Bewegungen*, ed. Johanna Hopfner and András Németh (Frankfurt am Main: Peter Lang Verlag, 2008), 135–140.
26 Sándor Köte, *Egy útmutató pedagógus. Nagy László élete és munkássága* (Budapest: Tankönyvkiadó, 1983).

oratory and a museum. Weszely's life's work completes the late Herbartianism, above all the most complete reception of the "Pure Conception". Thanks to this, the influence of new pedagogical concepts from the period after the turn of the century, pedology, and new results from modern psychology became noticeable in his theoretical and educational work. The humanities orientation of his systematizing works from the 1920s represents a peculiar bridge, a transition between late Herbartianism and the *Geisteswissenschaft* approach of the 1930s.[27]

The efforts of the mentioned representatives of progressive education and radical intelligentsia converged during the cultural and educational reforms of the liberal mayor of Budapest, István Bárczy, who served as mayor from 1906 to 1918. The Pedagogical Seminar (founded in 1912) educated teachers in the capital, while the journal *Népművelés* (Folk Education), published from 1906, reflected the cultural and educational program of Bárczy.[28] Other progressive journals, like *Huszadik Század* (20th Century) and *Nyugat* (The West) provided opportunities for publishing not only for the representatives of Hungarian pedology and experimental psychology, but also for a variety of target groups, such as the Hungarian life reform movement as well as for anarchist, syndicalist, and the Tolstoyan movement (Ervin Szabó, Jenő Schmidt, Ervin Batthyány) and the Hungarian secession (*art nouveau*). Among those who published in the journal *Népművelés* and among those who held lectures and courses in the Pedagogical Seminar, as well as among the members of the Hungarian Society for Pedology, we can find leading personalities of the artistic community in Gödöllő, who developed new methods of musical and artistic education. With the end of the revolutions in 1918 and 1919, the first exciting phase of the relationship between the Hungarian life reform movement and progressive education came to an end. This phase is characterized by the symbiosis of the two movements.[29]

---

[27] András Németh and Béla Pukánszky, "Paradigmen in der Geschichte der ungarischen Pädagogik," *Paedagogica Historica. International Journal of the History of Education. Supplementary Series* III (1998): 275–276.

[28] András Németh, *Weszely Ödön* (OPKM: Budapest, 1990), 13–17.

[29] András Németh and Béla Pukánszky, "Life reform efforts in the Austro-Hungarian monarchy and their impact on Hungarian cultural and pedagogical reforms," *Paedagogica Historica* 56 (2019): 429–446.

The Broad Institutionalization of Hungarian University Pedagogy as Geisteswissenschaft

A new epoch of economic, social, and political development in Hungary began in 1920 that was primarily determined by the consequences of the peace agreement of the lost war. The Treaty of Trianon (1920) shook all strata of Hungarian society: Hungary had to acknowledge in a binding manner that two thirds of the territory of the historical kingdom fell to various neighboring and successor states according to the international law. Therefore, the intense efforts to develop education were regarded as a strategically important task which, in turn, received exceptional financial support. The background of this cultural policy was the idea of the so-called "cultural superiority", the ideology that came from a prominent cultural politician, the conservative minister of religion and public education Kuno Klebelsberg (1875–1932).[30] His ideas were centering around a Christian-national ideology and neonationalism, with the help of which a highly qualified "intellectual elite" with nationalistic and revisionist thoughts could be created. At the same time, the general raising of the cultural knowledge of the population was urged. In the interest of these goals Klebelsberg organized the country's unified institutional system (museums and archives were united in one organization), continued university foundations that were already under way (such as those in Debrecen, Szeged, and Pécs), initiated a program to build a large number of new elementary schools, and finally started the modernization of secondary schools.[31]

Parallel to these events, teacher education reform also took place in the 1920s. According to a legal regulation passed in 1924, teacher training institutions were established at all Hungarian universities at the philosophical faculties to enable future secondary school teachers to acquire both subject knowledge and pedagogical knowledge within an organized curriculum. Accordingly, only students enrolled in the faculty of philosophy, with two secondary school sub-

---

[30] These educational efforts went parallel with the political intention of changing the consequences of the Treaty of Trianon.
[31] Andor Ladányi, *Magyar felsőoktatás a 20. században* (Budapest: Nemzeti Tankönyvkiadó, 1999), 51; Zoltán András Szabó, "A trifurkáló fiúközépiskola-rendszer kialakulása Magyarországon (1921□–1924)" (PhD diss., Eötvös Loránd Tudományegyetem, 2017); Zoltán András Szabó, "A klebelsbergi középiskola-koncepció fekete doboza." Nemzetközi hatások, oktatáspolitikai aktorok és törvényhozás," in *Tanárképzés és oktatáskutatás*, ed. Tamás Kozma, Virág Ágnes Kiss, Csaba Jancsák, and Katalin Kéri (Debrecen: Magyar Nevelés- és Oktatáskutatók Egyesülete (HERA), 2015), 272–285.

jects as majors, that completed the prescribed lectures and seminars at the teacher training institute could obtain a secondary school teacher qualification.

In the 20s the national idea and the characteristics of the national mentality became an important topic for philosophy. In connection to these tendencies, the hegemony of the direction of the *Geisteswissenschaften* and Neo-Kantianism[32] also began to play an increasingly important role in the spiritual and pedagogical-psychological thinking of the time.[33] After the 20s the scientific content of pedagogy at the University of Budapest was enriched in this spirit. One of the representatives of Neo-Kantianism was Gyula Kornis (1885–1958), a widely recognized politician in the field of culture and education.[34]

Another development of the 1920s was the fact that – due to the teaching of pedagogy at the universities – progressive educational concepts based on modern child psychology and a sociological orientation gained importance. Kornis himself regularly offered lectures in child psychology. Cecil Bognár (1883–1967) was appointed as a private lecturer in child psychology (pedology) in 1923; later he was a professor of pedagogy at the University of Pécs (1938–1941) and Szeged (1941–1950). Elemér Kenyeres (1891–1933), one of the most outstanding representatives of progressive education, was appointed as a private lecturer in child psychology in 1930. He had extensive contacts with leading psychologists including Édouard Claparede and Jean Piaget.

At the beginning of the 1930s *Ernő Fináczy* retired and the next influential professor as head of the Pedagogy Department at the University of Budapest was Lajos Prohászka (1897–1963). As a philosopher, he drew from the thoughts of the famous German thinker Eduard Spranger (1882–1963), with whom he was in personal working contact. With the appointment of Prohászka who represented philosophical pedagogy of the *Geisteswissenschaften*, the humanities gained the upper hand in the teaching of education at the university.[35]

---

[32] Neo-Kantianism is a philosophical movement beginning in the last decades of the nineteenth century and at the beginning of the twentieth century which focuses on the transcendental logic and epistemological writings of Immanuel Kant.
[33] Tibor Hanák, *Az elfelejtett reneszánsz* (Budapest: Göncöl, 1993), 44.
[34] Szabolcs, Értékelmélet és kultúrfilozófia, 145–160.
[35] András Németh and Imre Garai, "Disciplinary Changes in the Hungarian 'Pädagogik' from the second half of the 19th century to the collapse of Stalinist-type dictatorship," in *Education and "Pädagogik" – Philosophical and Historical Reflections: Central, Southern and South-Eastern Europe*, ed. Blanka Kudláčová and Andrej Rajský (Berlin: Peter Lang Verlag, Bratislava: VEDA, 2019), 214–217.

The Sovietization of the Hungarian Higher Education System and Educational Science in the Rákosi-Era

After World War II, the situation in Central and Eastern Europe changed radically. For decades these countries were regarded as part of the Soviet bloc, which experienced significant border shifts and suffered from ethnic cleansing – all of which impacted (in-)directly on the structure of higher education, academic life, and the relationship with the new communist state power and its higher education authorities. All these countries had similar problems to solve in the reconstruction of the war-ravaged universities.[36]

As in other countries of Central and Eastern Europe, Hungarian universities were able to maintain their traditional internal structure, admission and study organization, as well as academic and student self-government until 1947. This obscured the political pragmatism of the newer, not yet stable regime. Thus, the dynamics of development for the establishment of a European constitutional state in Hungary were preserved even in the short democratic transition phase (1945 – 1948). In the years after World War II the perspectives of child research, pedology, and the pedagogical way of thinking emphasizing children's self-activity came more and more to the fore. The popularity of French and Anglo-American empirical pedagogy grew. The emergence of school reforms and the renewal of educational sciences, the democratic way of thinking, and the issues of social justice, social solidarity, and equal opportunities were in focus.[37]

After this short transitional period, the Cold War began. After 1947, Hungary was gradually incorporated into the Soviet zone with the political hegemony of the Hungarian Communist Party. Higher education institutions gradually lost their autonomy, even though their basic internal structures such as chairs, faculties, and senates were retained. In 1948, other countries under communist control in Central and Eastern Europe experienced drastic university reforms that changed the positions and tasks of universities and academic organizations.

The goals and tasks of universities were no longer established in the spirit of meritocratic European scientific ideas, but according to the ideological doctrines

---

[36] Walter Rüegg and Jan Sedlak, "Die Hochschultrager," in *Geschichte der Universität in Europa. Band IV: Vom Zweiten Weltkrieg bis zum Ende des Zwanzigsten Jahrhunderts*, ed. Walter Rüegg (München: Beck Verlag, 2010), 88.
[37] Erzsébet Golnhofer, *Hazai pedagógiai nézetek 1945 – 49* (Pécs: Iskolakultúra könyvek, 2004).

of Marxism-Leninism that were the only accepted way of "scientific" thinking.[38] Universities, regardless of their traditions, had to adapt themselves to the all-encompassing structures of the so-called "people's democracy." The traditional form of democratic and autonomous university and science management was to be guaranteed by various forms of collective representation. As a result, the direct political and administrative interference of the party and the state affected all important university affairs. This included the appointment of rectors, deans, and the academic staff, the composition of student body and the regulations for students, as well as the content for teaching primarily ideologically loaded subjects such as philosophy (Marxism-Leninism), history, pedagogy, law, ecology, and other human sciences. The orientation of these fields of science was above all the task of the party university, which then received a university rank with privileges for teaching and ideology-oriented research.[39]

Another characteristic of these reforms was the adoption of various elements of the Soviet higher education and science management system. The European university system, which had been labelled as liberal-bourgeois, had to be radically overhauled. The new Soviet university model had to focus purely on theoretical research and teaching in the basic fields of science (philosophy, social sciences, mathematics, and natural sciences). Other subjects such as medicine, agricultural science, and sports science were taught at special independent colleges of increased importance. As a result, the importance of traditional universities was lost. The *Magyar Tudományos Akadémia* (Hungarian Academy of Sciences (was reorganized and became the super-coordinator of all non-military scientific activities both within the country and internationally. The Academy functioned as associations of leading scientists, as knowledge centers, as state supervisory authority – controlling the scientific activities of the universities, the applied graduation procedures, and the awarding of all scientific and academic degrees.[40]

A third characteristic of the reforms was the development of the appointment system of the so-called nomenclature. The various positions of power became posts of strategic importance and the appointed cadres fulfilled the assigned positions based on their political reliability. The nomenclature was a body of privileged persons and leading officials of the party and the state apparatus. Most academic and university positions belonged to the nomenclature sys-

---

38 The Marxist doctrine further developed by Lenin according to the new political and social conditions. After his death, Marxism-Leninism – thanks to Stalin – became the official political ideology of the Soviet Union from the 1920s and later also for the Eastern Bloc.
39 Rüegg and Sedlak, "Die Hochschultrager," 90.
40 Ibid., 90–91.

tem, and the candidates for these positions were accepted only after the party organization responsible for education and research had investigated their political loyalty. Thus, a new elite emerged due to the development of the nomenclature system. The professionalism and professional autonomy so typical of the development of the university and academic elite was replaced by the Eastern model with priority given to a politically committed body of experts. External and internal control mechanisms lost their functions, and between 1949 and 1953 the political sub-system and its party-state form succeeded in suppressing the other subsystems of society to such an extent that the functional multidimensionality of society was supplanted by a kind of one-dimensional, politically-based hierarchization.[41]

The above-mentioned developments were part of a longer transformation process, which, in parallel with the increasingly aggressive expansion of the totalitarian dictatorship, meant the gradual elimination of the organizational frameworks and traditional forms of university and academic institutions. The fundamental transformation of the Hungarian Academy of Sciences was carried out by the *Magyar Tudományos Tanács* (Hungarian Scientific Council) founded in 1948 in order to dismiss the former academic elite, to abolish university autonomy, to reinterpret the role of the academy, and to establish the mechanisms of party control. In September 1949, a decision was made regarding the early retirement of 20 professors, among whom internationally recognized names could be found, and the number of members of the academy was reduced. This decision heavily affected the universities with significant losses in quality but gave way to build the new nomenclature. By October 1949 the transformation of the Hungarian Academy of Sciences was completed and soon all important issues of its function were taken by the state party.[42]

Conclusion

In summary, the transformation of university pedagogy into a nomenclature regulated "quasi-discipline" can be characterized by the following:
- alteration of the institutional infrastructure and ideologization of research; scientific autonomy was replaced by political loyalty, while knowledge

---

[41] Tibor Huszár, *Az elittől a nómenklatúráig* (Budapest: Akadémiai Kiadó, 2007), 47–53.
[42] Ibid., 27–28; Erzsébet Golnhofer, "A Magyar Tudományos Tanács és a neveléstudomány," in *Interdiszciplináris pedagógia és az oktatás finanszírozása*, ed. András Buda and Endre Kiss (Debrecen: Kiss Árpád Archívum Könyvtára, 2016), 246–256.

and performance were de-emphasized; uncritical confirmation of the decisions of party organizations;
- hegemony of the centralized communication networks regulated by ideology, independent national scientific journals, and standard works of Soviet pedagogy and psychology;
- scientific performance was replaced by quasi-scientific missionary works to disseminate communist ideology; university education lost much of its scientific character and diversity;
- instead of professional socialization and education of the next generation of academics, ideological indoctrination of young academics took place; bureaucratic regulations marked the new era and a new system of graduation procedures and academic titles was introduced on the basis of Soviet patterns.[43]

Although the years after the dictatorship of *Rákosi Mátyás* (after 1956) were still characterized by Soviet bloc oppression, a slow and gradual change could be observed in political as well as in cultural life. The "quasi-discipline" nature of education met with professional standards in the following decades of the socialist regime, and thus gradually gave way to scientific criteria and attempts to loosen ideological pressure.

Bibliography

A budapesti Királyi Magyar Tudományegyetem Almanachja az MCMIX–MCMX. tanévre.
  Budapest: M. Kir. Tudományegyetemi Nyomda, 1910.
Áment, Erzsébet, and Nagy Zoltánné. "Pályakép több olvasatban. Nagy László élettörténete."
  Új Pedagógiai Szemle 57 (2007): 146–163.
Ballér, Endre. *Tantervelméletek Magyarországon a XIX. és XX. században.* Budapest: OPI, 1996.
Brezinka, Wolfgang. *Pädagogik in Österreich. Geschichte des Faches an den Universitäten von 18. bis zum Ende des 20. Jahrhunderts.* Band 1. Wien: ÖAV, 2000.
Cruikshank, Kathleen Anne. "The prelude to education as an academic discipline: American Herbartianism and the emergence of a science of pedagogy." In *History of Educational Studies, Suppl. Series 3, Paedagogica Historica,* edited by Peter Drewek and Cristoph Lüth, 99–120. Ghent: University of Ghent, 1998.
Depaepe, Marc. *Zum Wohl des Kindes? Pädologie, pädagogische Psychologie und experimentelle Pädagogiek in Europa und den USA, 1890–1940.* Weinheim, Leuven: Leuven University Press, 1993.

---

[43] See in detail Németh and Garai, "Disciplinary Changes," 223–226.

Felkai, László. *Neveléstörténeti dolgozatok a dualizmus korából*. Budapest: Tankönyvkiadó, 1979.
Garai, Imre. "Középiskolai tanárképzés intézményei. A tanárvizsgáló bizottság és a tanárképző intézetek működése a fővárosi egyetemen az 1862–1919 közötti időszakban." Habilitation thesis, Eötvös Loránd Tudományegyetem, 2019.
Golnhofer, Erzsébet. *Hazai pedagógiai nézetek 1945–49*. Pécs: Iskolakultúra könyvek, 2004.
Golnhofer, Erzsébet. "A Magyar Tudományos Tanács és a neveléstudomány." In *Interdiszciplináris pedagógia és az oktatás finanszírozása*, edited by András Buda and Endre Kiss, 246–256. Debrecen: Kiss Árpád Archívum Könyvtára, 2016.
Gottas, Friedrich. *Ungarn im Zeitalter des Hochliberalismus. Studien zur Tisza-Era (1975–1890)*. Wien: Verlag der österreichische Akademie der Wissenschaften, 1976.
Hanák, Tibor. *Az elfelejtett reneszánsz*. Budapest: Göncöl, 1993.
Helmdach, Andreas, and Harald Roth. "Habsburgreich." In *Studienbuch Östliches Europa. Band 1: Geschichte Ostmittel – und Südosteuropas*, edited by Harald Roth, 201–202. Köln: Böhlau Verlag, 1999.
Hofstetter, Rita, and Bernard Schneuwly, eds. *Erziehungswissenschaft(en) in 19.–20. Jahrhundert. Zwischen Profession und Disziplin*. Bern: Lang Verlag, 2002.
Hopfner, Johanna, András Németh, and Éva Szabolcs, eds. *Kindheit, Schule, Erziehungswissenschaft in Mitteleuropa 1948–2008*. Bern u. a.: Peter Lang Verlag, 2009.
Horn, Klaus-Peter et al., eds. *Erziehungswissenschaft in Mitteleuropa. Aufklärerische Traditionen – deutscher Einfluß – nationale Eigenständigkeit*. Budapest: Osiris, 2001.
Horn, Klaus-Peter. *Erziehungswissenschaft in Deutschland im 20. Jahrhundert*. Bad Heilbrunn: Klinkhardt, 2003.
Huszár, Tibor. *Az elittől a nómenklatúráig*. Budapest: Akadémiai Kiadó, 2007.
Köte, Sándor. *Egy útmutató pedagógus. Nagy László élete és munkássága*. Budapest: Tankönyvkiadó, 1983.
Ladányi, Andor. *Magyar felsőoktatás a 20. században*. Budapest: Nemzeti Tankönyvkiadó, 1999.
Németh, András, and Béla Pukánszky. "Life reform efforts in the Austro-Hungarian monarchy and their impact on Hungarian cultural and pedagogical reforms." *Paedagogica Historica* 56 (2019): 429–446.
Németh, András. "Die Entwicklungsperioden der ungarischen Erziehungswissenschaft im 19. und 20. Jahrhundert." In *University and Universality. The Place and Role of the University of Pécs in Europe from the Middle Ages to Present Day*, edited by Ágnes Fischer-Dárdai, István Lengvári, and Éva Schmelczer-Pohánka, 309–328. Pécs: University Library of Pécs and Centre for Learning, 2017.
Németh, András. "The development phases of educational sciences as an academic discipline in Hungary in the first half of the 20th century." *Foro de Educación* 15 (2017): 1–23.
Németh, András. "Der Einfluss des Herbartianismus an der Budapester Universität und seine Rolle in der Lehrerbildung – eine Fallstudie." In *Herbartianische Konzepte der Lehrerbildung*, edited by Rotraud Coriand, 234–235. Bad Heilbrunn: Klinkhardt, 2003.
Németh, András. *A magyar neveléstudomány fejlődése. Nemzetközi tudományfejlődési és recepciós hatások, egyetemi tudománnyá válás, középiskolai tanárképzés*. Budapest: Gondolat, 2014.
Németh, András. *A magyar neveléstudomány fejlődéstörténete*. Budapest: Osiris, 2002.

Németh, András, and Imre Garai. "Disciplinary Changes in the Hungarian 'Pädagogik' from the second half of the 19th century to the collapse of Stalinist-type dictatorship." In *Education and "Pädagogik"– Philosophical and Historical Reflections : Central, Southern and South-Eastern Europe,* edited by Blanka Kudláčová and Andrej Rajský, 214–217. Berlin: Peter Lang Verlag and Bratislava: VEDA, 2019.

Németh, András, and Béla Pukánszky. "Paradigmen in der Geschichte der ungarischen Pädagogik." *Paedagogica Historica.* Supplementary Series Volume III (1998): 265–276.

Németh, András, and Béla Pukánszky. *A pedagógia problématörténete.* Budapest: Gondolat, 2004.

Németh, András. *Erziehungswissenschaft in Ungarn (1870–1952).* Budapest: Gondolat, 2013.

Németh, András. *Weszely Ödön.* OPKM: Budapest, 1990.

Németh, András. "Die Entwicklung der Pädagogik zur Universitätsdisziplin, sowie ihre Institutonalisierung an der Universität in Budapest." In *Erziehungswissenschaft in Mitteleuropa,* edited by Peter Horn et al., 309–45. Budapest: Osiris, 2001.

Németh, András. "Die ungarischen Bildungsreformen: Von der theresianisch-josephinischen Reichsreform zur nationalstaatlichen Bildungspolitik (1777–1867)." In *Schule und Reform,* edited by Flavian Imlig, Lukas Lehmann, and Karin Manz, 86–116. Wiesbaden: Springer, 2018.

Németh, András. "Herbartische Einflüsse auf ungarische Bildungspolitik nach 1867." In *Erziehung und Unterricht: Neue Perspektiven auf Johann Friedrich Herbarts Allgemeine Pädagogik,* edited by Katja Grundig de Vazquez and Alexandra Schotte, 233–245. Paderborn: Ferdinand Schöningh Verlag, 2018.

Oelkers, Jürgen. *Reformpädagogik: Eine kritische Dogmengeschichte.* Weinheim: Juventa Verlag, 1989.

Peykovska, Penka. "Literacy and Illiteracy in Austria–Hungary. The Case of Bulgarian Migrant Communities." *Hungarian Historical Review* 3 (2014): 683–711.

Rüegg, Walter, and Jan Sedlak. "Die Hochschultrager." In *Geschichte der Universität in Europa. Band IV: Vom Zweiten Weltkrieg bis zum Ende des Zwanzigsten Jahrhunderts,* edited by Walter Rüegg, 75–114. München: Beck Verlag, 2010.

Simon, Brian. "The study of education as a university subject in Britain." In *The State And Educational Change: Essays In The History Of Education And Pedagogy,* edited by Brian Simon, 127–146. London: Lawrence and Wishart, 1994.

Stichweh, Rudolf. *Wissenschaft, Universität, Professionen.* Frankfurt am Main: Suhrkamp, 1994.

Szabó, Zoltán András. "A klebelsbergi középiskola-koncepció fekete doboza. Nemzetközi hatások, oktatáspolitikai aktorok és törvényhozás." In *Tanárképzés és oktatáskutatás,* edited by Tamás Kozma et al., 272–285. Debrecen: Magyar Nevelés- és Oktatáskutatók Egyesülete (HERA), 2015.

Szabó, Zoltán András. "A trifurkáló fiúközépiskola-rendszer kialakulása Magyarországon (1921–1924)." PhD diss., Eötvös Loránd Tudományegyetem, 2017.

Szabolcs, Éva. "Értékelmélet és kultúrfilozófia a Magyar Paedagogia című folyóiratban. Kornis Gyula és Prohászka Lajos." In *A szellemtudományi pedagógia magyar recepciója,* edited by András Németh, 145–160. Budapest: Gondolat, 2004.

Szabolcs, Éva. "The emergence of child study ideas in the educational press in Hungary at the turn of the 19th–20th century." In *Pädagogische und kulturelle Strömungen in der k.u.k. Monarchie: Lebensreform, Herbartianismus und reformpädagogische Bewegungen,* edited by Johanna Hopfner and András Németh, 135–140. Frankfurt am Main: Peter Lang Verlag, 2008.

Szabolcs, Éva. "Neveléstudomány és a Magyar Paedagogia 1892–1919." In *Neveléstudomány-történeti tanulmányok*, edited by András Németh and Heinz-Elmar Tenorth, 229–257. Budapest: Osiris Kiadó, 2000.

Tenorth, Heinz-Elmar, and Klaus-Peter Horn. "Erziehungswissenschaft in Deutschland in der ersten Hälfte des 20. Jahrhunderts." In *Erziehungswissenschaft in Mitteleuropa*, edited by Klaus Peter Horn et al., 176–191. Budapest: Osiris Kiadó, 2001.

Vetter, Eva. "Hegemonic discourse in the Habsburg Empire: The case of education. A critical discourse analysis of two mid 19th century government documents." In *Diglossia and Power. Language Policies and Practice in the 19th Century Habsburg Empire*, edited by Rosita Rindler Schverje, 275–292. Berlin, New York: Mouton de Gruyter, 2003.

Wagner, Peter, and Björn Wittrock. "States, institutions and discourses: A comparative perspective on the structuration of the social sciences." In *Discourses on society. The shaping of the social science disciplines*, edited by Peter Wagner, Björn Wittrock, and Richard Whitley, 331–358. Dordrecht: Kluwer, 1992.

Weszely, Ödön. "Kármán Mór emlékezete." *Magyar Paedagogia* 25 (1916): 517–519.

Zimányi, Ágnes. "Az abszolútum jelentősége és ismeretének eredete Pauler Ákos bölcseletében." PhD diss., Pázmány Péter Katolikus Egyetem, 2017.

Iveta Kestere, Zanda Rubene and Iveta Ozola (University of Latvia, Latvia)
Educational Sciences Between "Real" Moscow and the "Imaginary" West: The Case of Latvia (1989–1999)

Abstract: The study brings into focus the "zero hour" of late 1980s and 1990s, the time when Eastern Europe had disposed of the Soviet dictatorship and was searching for ways to return to the space of Western democracy. Thus, the aim of the study is to explore educational sciences in transition and answer the following questions: (1) When searching for "emancipation" and a new paradigm of educational sciences, how was the "old" Soviet model rooted out? (2) What role did the West play in these processes as a symbolic opposite? The changes of educational sciences are analyzed four-dimensionally, that is: from institutional, socialization, methodological, and communicative perspectives. Using insiders' experiences, we discovered illusions, celebration of freedom, the rebirth of academy and pedagogy, and the gradual introduction of a new "order" of national and global power in the field of educational sciences.

Keywords: educational sciences; academic community; Westernization

Introduction

Our study focuses on the "zero hour" of the late 1980s and 1990s, a time when Eastern Europe had disposed of the dictatorship of the Soviet Union and was searching for ways to join the democratic fold of Europe. Political and intellectual liberation took place simultaneously, and both of these turbulent processes had an immediate effect on the academic community, forcing social sciences and humanities to search for a new pattern in dissociation from its old reputation. In the Soviet Union, educational sciences, known as "Pedagogy",[1] became a pillar of the authoritarian system with a significant role in propagandizing communist ideology. Becher notes that "[t]he main currency for the academic is not power,

---
[1] Hereafter, we use "pedagogical sciences," 'pedagogy", and "educational sciences" as synonyms due to the fact that since 1939, doctorates in Latvia have been awarded in Pedagogical Sciences and even today the name of the field is being under discussion.

https://doi.org/10.1515/9783110623451-015

as it is for the politician, or wealth, as it is for the businessman, but reputation."[2] So, to restore and secure their academic reputation, pedagogy as a research discipline as well as its scholars were in desperate need of change, required for survival in the new conditions of market economy and educational transformation.[3] According to Kuhn's meanwhile classical theory, the field of science as a self-evolving system develops through crises that can be solved by a paradigm shift.[4] In the 1990s, the crisis of pedagogy was not a result of its internal development, but a consequence of political change – the crisis was "imported." The answer to such a crisis is radical transformation: with fast, effective, and inconvenient methods the useless present has to be changed.[5] Celebrated as a liberalization from the experience of Soviet domination, "emancipation" became a cornerstone in the process of change in educational sciences. Erasing the Soviet past, emancipation signified the interruption of the existing order with potential for transformation, escape from determination, and pluralization of truth.[6] Another pillar of change, closely linked to the first, was the West as a model and an emancipator: "Claims to belong to an imaginary 'West' were widespread in post-Soviet national states as a means to distance themselves from Russia."[7] Despite Soviet propaganda, in Latvian public consciousness, the West was associated with freedom, democracy, and prosperity: "The symbols of the Imaginary West did not necessarily represent the "real" West and its "bourgeois" values; rather, they introduced into Soviet reality a new imaginary dimension..."[8] From the post-Soviet perspective of the 1990s, the West was a homogeneous, more ideological than geographical space,[9] the space in which liberalism (also

---

[2] Tony Becher and Paul R. Trowler, *Academic Tribes and Territories: Intellectual Inquiry and the Cultures of Disciplines* (Milton Keynes: SRHE/OUP, 1989), 52.

[3] See Maia Chankseliani and Iveta Silova, "Reconfiguring Education Purposes, Policies and Practices during Post-Socialist Transformations: Setting the Stage," in *Comparing Post-socialist Transformations*, ed. Maia Chankseliani and Iveta Silova (Oxford: Symposium Books, 2018), 7–25.

[4] Thomas S. Kuhn, *The Structure of Scientific Revolutions* (Chicago, London: The University of Chicago Press, 1970).

[5] See Bernard Hemetsberger, "Burbunkologie oder: Zur Bearbeitung von Bildungskrisen," *Pädagogische Korrespondenz* 57 (2018): 110.

[6] See Gert Biesta, "Doing Emancipation Differently: Transgression, Equality and the Politics of Learning," *Civitas Educationis. Education, Politics and Culture* 1 (2012): 8, 11, 14.

[7] Stefan Berger, *The Past as History. National Identity and Historical Consciousness in Modern Europe* (Basingstoke: Palgrave Macmillan, 2015), 330.

[8] Alexei Yurchak, *Everything Was Forever, Until It Was No More. The Last Soviet Generation* (Princeton and Oxford: Princeton University Press, 2005), 203.

[9] "What I call ... the Imaginary West was ... a kind of space that was both internal and external to the Soviet reality. This space was neither explicitly outlined nor described in the Soviet Union

in education) was one of the preconditions for leading society onto the path towards prosperity. The legacy of Soviet authoritarianism and Western *fata morgana* created a dichotomy in the public space, the duality forming the context of the "zero hour" in Latvia. Thus, the aim of our study is to reveal changes in the institutional, socialization, methodological, and communicative dimensions of educational sciences,[10] and answer the following research questions: 1) When searching for "emancipation" and a new paradigm of educational sciences, how was the "old" Soviet model rooted out?; 2) What role did the West play in these processes as a symbolic opposite? In Latvia, pedagogy as an academic discipline started its development with the establishment of the University of Latvia in 1919, and the University became the only institution where all four aforementioned dimensions of the science were developing in the following years,[11] thus making it a center for the development of educational sciences in the country. Therefore, the experience of the University of Latvia is used as a case study in this article.

The study also puts the personal experience of its authors to good use. I, Iveta Kestere, defended my dissertation in pedagogy in 1989, at the culmination of *perestroika*, when scientific works, however, still had to be written and defended in Russian and attested in Moscow. My degree was subjected to nostrification after the restoration of Latvia's independence. I, Zanda Rubene, defended my dissertation in pedagogy in 2004 and used Western critical pedagogy theories for the first time in Latvia. I, Iveta Ozola, defended my dissertation in the history of education as recently as seven years ago, in 2014, and can thus reconstruct the events from 1989 to 1999 only from historical sources. Our doctoral studies and dissertation defenses took place at the University of Latvia. None

---

as a coherent "territory" or "object"... However, a diverse array of discourses, statements, products, objects, visual images, musical expressions, and linguistic constructions that were linked to [the] West ... and circulated widely in late socialism, gradually shaped a coherent and shared object of imagination – the Imaginary West." Yurchak, *Everything Was Forever*, 161.

10 Based on Rita Hofstetter and Bernard Schneuwly, *Zur Geschichte der Erziehungswissenschaften in der Schweiz. Vom Ende des 19. bis zur Mitte des 20. Jahrhunderts* (Bern: hep Verlag AG, 2011).

11 Iveta Ozola and Iveta Ķestere, "Pedagoģijas kā zinātnes ģenēze Eiropā (18. gadsimts – 20. gaddsimta 20. – 30. gadi): historiogrāfiskais aspects" [The genesis of pedagogy as a science in Europe (18th century – 1920 – 30s): historiographic aspect], in *Pedagoģijas vēsture. 15 jautājumi* [History of pedagogy. 15 questions], ed. Aīda Krūze and Iveta Ķestere (Rīga: RaKa, 2010), 78 – 105; Alīda Zigmunde and Iveta Ķestere, "Latvijas Universitātes Pedagoģijas nodaļas pirmsākumi, studiju process, mācībspēki un studenti (1919 – 1944)" [The beginnings of the Department of Pedagogy of the University of Latvia, its study process, teaching staff and students (1919 – 1944)], in *Pedagoģijas vēsture. 15 jautājumi* [History of pedagogy. 15 questions], ed. Aīda Krūze and Iveta Ķestere (Rīga: RaKa, 2010), 176 – 203.

of us participated in decision-making processes in the academic field in the 1990s, but our scientific and professional careers were shaped and supported by professors who were key actors in the transformation of educational sciences after the liberation from the Soviet dictatorship. Therefore, the following narrative will be colored by our personal memories and their subjective insiders' experiences. We as authors are aware of this "breach", but in our recent history research we have learned and argued on many an occasion that in history nothing is neutral and everything is under constant discussion, so we embrace subjectivity as part and parcel of any historical study.[12]

Freedom and New Models of Educational Sciences – the Institutional Dimension

With the onset of institutional changes during the advent of independence, the first things to be abolished were the blatantly ideologized and militarized structures of the University of Latvia: in October 1989, the Department of Scientific Communism was transformed into the Department of Political Science; in June 1991, the Department of Civil Defense was dissolved and military training was removed from the curriculum.[13] Founded in 1947, The Department of Pedagogy and Psychology continued its functioning,[14] but, as mentioned, pedagogy, like all social sciences and humanities in the post-Soviet space, went through a deep crisis.

Following the restoration of Latvia's independence, professors of pedagogy were no longer under the control of Moscow, which until then had given clear instructions and closely monitored their execution. Like their counterparts else-

---

[12] See also Ericka L. Tucke, "The Subject of History: Historical Subjectivity and Historical Science," *Journal of the Philosophy of History* 7 (2013): 205–229; Vita Fortunati and Elena Lamberti, "Cultural Memory: An European Perspective," in *Cultural Memory Studies. An International and Interdisciplinary Handbook*, ed. Astrid Erll and Ansgar Nünning (Berlin, New York: Walter de Gruyter, 2008), 129.

[13] Alberts Varslavāns, ed., *Latvijas Universitāte 75* [University of Latvia at 75] (Rīga, Latvijas Universitāte, 1994); Henrihs Strods, ed., *Latvijas Valsts Universitātes vēsture. 1940–1990* [History of the State University of Latvia. 1940–1990] (Rīga: Latvijas Universitāte), 1999.

[14] In 1996, the Department of Pedagogy and Psychology became the Institute of Pedagogy and Psychology at the University of Latvia, which later, in 2004, merged with the Faculty of Pedagogy and Psychology of the University of Latvia. Aīda Krūze, "Pedagoģijas nodaļa" [Pedagogy Department], in *LU Pedagoģijas, psiholoģijas un mākslas fakultāte zinātnei un izglītībai* [University of Latvia, Faculty of Education, Psychology and Art for science and education], ed. Aīda Krūze, Ērika Lanka, and Jānis Aizpurs (Rīga: LU Akadēmiskais apgāds, 2013), 89–121.

where in Eastern Europe, Latvian academics "were forced to confront the [new] reality."[15] The same scholars who had been educated in the spirit of communist ideology and had diligently served the USSR academic elite with its headquarters in Moscow had to deal with the creation of new educational sciences.[16] There were literally no other professionals in the field. Recruiting specialists from abroad was not possible both due to the lack of knowledge of foreign languages in Latvia,[17] and because of lack of funding all sciences had to struggle with after the disappearance of centralized funding from Moscow.

Figuratively speaking, Soviet pedagogy, its textbooks translated from Russian, and the associated curricula became obsolete overnight. New content for educational sciences was sought in two ways: by reading works of Latvian pedagogues banned during the Soviet era and by trying to obtain books from the West, the latter being hindered by both the lack of knowledge of foreign languages mentioned and that of finances.

A helping hand in updating reading lists was lent by Latvians in exile[18] as well as new foreign partners. An active translation of Western books into Latvian took place, supported, for example, by the Soros Foundation, one of the first Western institutions to implement "the politics of giving" [19] in the intellectual

---

15 See Axel Fair-Schulz and Mario Kessler, "Conclusion. A Note on Research Directions and Literature," in *East German Historians since Reunification. A Discipline Transformed*, ed. Axel Fair-Schulz and Mario Kessler (Albany, NY: State University of New York Press, 2017),'232.

16 In the USSR, anyone who chose an academic career in social sciences or humanities obeyed the canons established by the state and prescribing a monolithic, anti-plural theory of science, a supercritical attitude towards the West, and an optional but desirable membership in the Communist party. Nevertheless, the Soviet academic community was not ideologically monolithic, and the degree of internal freedom of its members and their latent resistance to the political power are the subject of a separate study. Our story presented here reveals that after the restoration of independence, the transformation of the educational scholarly community took place rapidly and steadily. That, in turn, allows us to make a conclusion about the instability of the Soviet academia in Latvia at least from the 1960s, with the generation of scientists who became the main actors in the transformation processes initiated by the regained independence.

17 Although in the Soviet Union, English, German, or French were taught at school and university, without any possibility to practice foreign languages behind the Iron Curtain, language learning was a formality. Latvian academia was governed by the Russian language, and all dissertations had to be defended in Russian.

18 Jānis Stradiņš, "Ceļavārdi II Pasaules latviešu zinātnieku kongresam" [Welcome speech for the second world congress of Latvian scientists], in *II Pasaules latviešu zinātnieku kongress. Rīga, 2001. gada 14–15. augusts. Tēžu krājums* [The Second World Congress of Latvian Scientists. Riga, 14–15 August 2001. Congress proceedings], ed. Juris Ekmanis (Rīga: Latvijas Zinātņu akadēmija, 2001), xxxv.

19 Myriam Southwell and Marc Depaepe, "The Relation between Education and Emancipation: Something Like Water and Oil? Introducing the special issue," *Paedagogica Historica* 55 (2019):

space. The first book in educational sciences to be translated into Latvian was *Basics of Pedagogy* by Professor Herbert Gudjons from the University of Hamburg,[20] but the first book on the history of education published in the West[21] was delivered to Latvia by Professor Günther Böhme from the Goethe University, Frankfurt.

The popularity of German scholarly works confirms the efforts of Latvian educators to re-establish the cultural bond with Germany, which had been severed by the Soviet authorities. German research in the theory of pedagogy was almost unanimously respected in the Latvian academic community. One model for the restoration of educational sciences was thus found; yet a relatively chaotic search through the practices of other Western countries continued – for example, those of the United States.[22] In fact, academics, unlike practitioners, did not think highly of the contribution of the United States and commented behind the scenes that with regard to pedagogy the US offered only practical recipes without theoretical foundation, underpinnings valued highly since Soviet times.

The importance of classic German pedagogical theory in the transformation processes is also recognized by other scholars of post-Soviet countries, such as Blanka Kudláčova and Andrej Rajský, who edited a voluminous study on the educational sciences in Central, Southern, and South-Eastern Europe.[23]

Gradually, local educators began to put their newly acquired knowledge on paper. Book printing was no longer under Moscow's control and censorship, and Riga publishers awoke to the financial profitability of textbooks. As a result, the process of printing books took on unusual speed: all one had to do was find time to write and arrange financing. A blind eye was turned to plagiarism (mostly affecting authors published in the inter-war period) – after all, everyone needed new literature.

As a result, educational sciences enjoyed absolute freedom – each lecturer could develop their own curriculum of pedagogy courses which did not yet have to be approved by any authorities, and they could teach them based on

---

3. For more on the Soros Foundation, see Gita Steiner-Khamsi, "Donor Logic in the Era of Gates, Buffett, and Soros," *Current Issues in Comparative Education* 10 (2008): 10–15.

20 Herberts Gudjons, *Pedagoģijas pamatatziņas* [Basics of Pedagogy] (Rīga: Zvaigzne ABC, 1989).

21 Günther Böhme and Heinz-Elmar Tenorth, *Einführung in die Historische Pädagogik* (Darmstadt: Wbg Academic, 1990).

22 Indra Dedze and Zanda Rubene, "Universities in Latvia – from the Soviet to European Higher Education Area," *Foro de Educación* 14 (2016): 13–38.

23 Blanka Kudláčová and Andrej Rajský, eds., *Education and "Pädagogik." Philosophical and Historical Reflections. Central, Southern and South-Eastern Europe* (Berlin: VEDA/Peter Lang, 2019), 321.

books that were accessible, understandable or self-written. The quality criterion was denial of Soviet-era pedagogy, highlighting inter-war research and (chaotic borrowing of) Western pedagogical ideas. Nostalgia for the development of a national pedagogy, which was disrupted by the Soviet occupation, mixed with a sincere belief in the superiority of all things Western. Secretly cherished during the Soviet era, this belief was grounded in the apparent prosperity and freedom of the West, as seen from the perspective of poor and oppressed Soviet society. The first thing that Soviet scholars escaping from the monolithic Marxist dogma heard in Western educational theories was the permission of pluralism and diversity. Horizons opened up by postmodernism, where "no theory was considered more valid than [an]other" and "thinking correctly" was not among the requirements,[24] were enthusiastically received. The call for deconstruction and demythologization[25] was translated in Latvia into a permission to dispel the myths of Soviet education, an agenda still ignoring the need of self-critical revision of the narratives of national education history.[26]

The dissociation from Russian cultural and scientific traditions in essence produced a new kind of one-sidedness in the development of academic knowledge.[27] The replacement of "heroes", for instance, is well reflected in the pedagogy curriculum. Thus, Latvian educators became fascinated with the Rudolf Steiner Waldorf School and the Montessori system. Both had been known in Latvia during the interwar period, but the mere mention of them was forbidden during the Soviet era. In the 1990s, the Waldorf School and Montessori system received the common label of "alternative pedagogy"[28] and stood in stark contrast to the unified system of education in Soviet schools. The names of Carl Rogers, Robert Slavin, Brian Simon, and Jean Piaget stood next to Latvian and Ger-

---

24 Mariam Meynert, *Conceptualizations of Childhood, Pedagogy and Educational Research in the Postmodern. A Critical Interpretation* (Department of Sociology, Lund University, 2013), 27, 29.
25 See Marc Depaepe, "Demythologizing the Educational Past: An Endless Task in History of Education," in *Between Educationalization and Appropriation. Selected Writings on the History of Modern Educational Systems*, ed. Marc Depaepe (Leuven University Press, 2012), 435–450.
26 Iveta Kestere, Irena Stonkuviene, and Veronika Varik, "History of Education as a Changing Research Field," in *Pedagogy and Educational Sciences in the Post-Soviet Baltic States, 1990–2004: Changes and Challenges*, ed. Iveta Kestere, Ene-Silvia Sarv, and Irena Stonkuviene (Riga: University of Latvia Press, 2020), 271.
27 Zanda Rubene, "Geisteswissenschaften und akademische Bildung in Lettland," in *Wissenschaft und akademische Bildung. Ist Theodor Litt für die gegenwärtige Hochschulpolitik aktuell?*, ed. P. Gutjahr-Löser, D. Schulz und H.W. Wollersheim (Leipzig: Leipziger Universitätsverlag, 2010), 57–73.
28 Inārs Beļickis, *Izglītības alternatīvās teorijas* [Alternative theories of education] (Rīga: Raka, 1997).

man classics of pedagogy (e. g., Georg Kerschensteiner), with books in Russian gradually disappearing from the arena of educational sciences.[29]

The entrance of the market economy into academia also left its mark on the reorganization of educational sciences. Thus, in 1992, the University of Latvia introduced a Master's degree study program in pedagogy, whereby tuition fees were partly paid by students.[30] The student request for a modern curriculum received in part at their own expense, along with professional enthusiasm of academic staff, became the true incentive to change educational sciences. The Master's program became an important place for professors to present and discuss newly acquired knowledge with experienced practitioners, who *en masse* went in quest of new ideas at the University of Latvia. The renewed popularity of pedagogy as a study field and the dialogue established between education practitioners and theoreticians opened up the possibility to restore the reputation of educational sciences in the eyes of Latvian society in general and decision makers in particular. The latter factor, in turn, spurred an influx of financing for educational sciences.

Changes of Educational Sciences – the Socialization Dimension: Old and New Generations

As a new pattern of educational sciences was very much sought after in the West, there emerged an urgent need to align academic degrees with the Western model.[31] In the early 1990s, researchers in social sciences and humanities were subjected to the process of nostrification, where they had to prove that their doctoral or habilitation theses defended during the Soviet era complied to the new

---

29 Oskars Zīds, comp., *Vispārējā pedagoģija. Darba programma akadēmiskajām studijām pedagoģijā un psiholoģijā* [General pedagogy. Work program for academic studies in pedagogy and psychology] (Rīga: Latvijas Universitāte, 1991); Maija Pļaveniece and Iveta Ķestere, *Autorprogramma kursam "Pedagoģija"* [Author program for the course "Pedagogy"] (unpublished manuscript, 1991, handwritten); Maija Pļaveniece and Iveta Ķestere, *Darba programma kursam "Pedagoģija"* [Work program for the course "Pedagogy"] (unpublished manuscript, 1991, handwritten).
30 During the Soviet era, higher education was free of charge and full-time students were paid a study allowance by the state.
31 OECD centrs sadarbībā ar nedalībvalstīm, *Nacionālo izglītības politiku analīze. Latvija* [Analysis of national education policies. Latvia] (Rīga: Profesionālās izglītības attīstības programmas aģentūra, 2000).

scientific requirements.³² On October 1, 1991, the University of Latvia approved of the "Regulations on Granting Scientific Degrees" and established a Habilitation and Promotion Council carrying out the nostrification or the process of recognizing degrees acquired during the Soviet era. The Council of Pedagogical Sciences comprised of the same professors who had obtained their doctoral degrees during the Soviet times for, again, no other people were available. Thus, the result was easy to predict, which is that almost everyone who had applied for nostrification received a doctorate. By June 1999, in Latvia 123 scholars had applied for nostrification and had been awarded a degree of Doctor of Pedagogy or a Habilitation in Pedagogy.³³

However, nostrification was an emotionally difficult process, especially for senior staff. Some academics even refused to resubmit their doctoral dissertations, thus excluding themselves from further research activities in the independent Latvia.³⁴ Yet, there were not many of them, and their number was reduced by a favorable process of nostrification, which unconsciously performed a kind of political function: the authors of dissertations written in the spirit of Soviet ideology were also given the opportunity to integrate into the renewed academic community, thereby sublimating the nostalgia for the "golden years" of the Soviet Union and increasing the ranks of supporters of Latvia's independence. Nostrification remained the only official³⁵ "cleansing" in the field of educational sciences.

It should be noted that although dissertations defended during the Soviet era clearly gave their due to the communist ideology and were written without access to Western research, they were well-grounded in theory and quite applicable in Soviet educational practice. Mediocrity did not work in Moscow institu-

---

32 During the Soviet era, Latvia introduced a two-tier scientific degree system: first, the candidate's degree in pedagogy and, second, the doctoral degree in pedagogy. After the nostrification, candidates received a doctorate (Dr. paed.), and doctors became habilitated doctors (Dr. habil. paed.). In 1998, the two-tier system was abolished and further only a doctoral degree became awarded (Dr. paed.). Yet, the habilitated doctor degree is still used and respected in Latvia as denoting special achievements in the theory of educational sciences.
33 Former Collection of the University of Latvia Pedagogy Museum.
34 Zanda Rubene and Iveta Ozola, "Democratisation of Educational Sciences (Pedagogy) in the Context of the Shift in Political Power of Latvia," in *Pedagogy and Educational Sciences in the Post-Soviet Baltic States, 1990–2004: Changes and Challenges*, ed. Iveta Kestere, Ene-Silvia Sarv, and Irena Stonkuviene (Riga: University of Latvia Press, 2020), 231.
35 A small number of lecturers chose to leave the University of Latvia, feeling responsible for the propaganda of Soviet ideology or, sometimes, because they did not want to lecture in Latvian instead of Russian. In the educational sciences, we are aware of two such cases.

tions, where all doctoral degrees, including those obtained in Latvia, had to be approved and evaluation of dissertations defended in "provinces" was strict.

In parallel with the nostrification process, the training of young researchers continued. The Promotion Council of Pedagogical Sciences of the University of Latvia was approved in 1992, but awarding of degrees according to the new requirements began in 1993. Doctoral theses were no longer evaluated by Moscow but left to the local Promotion Council made up of the professors who had obtained their degree in the Soviet times, which carried out the nostrification process and continued to dominate the field of educational sciences for years to come. It is of notice that the generational change has only recently ended.

The Promotion Council operated without external supervision until 1999, when the Cabinet of Ministers adopted "Regulations on the Procedure and Criteria for Promotion".[36] In place of Moscow's central power, the amendments introduced a national centralization. To assess doctoral dissertations submitted for defense, the Latvian Academy of Sciences established a Qualification Commission, so that henceforth not only professors in pedagogy but also scientists from other fields could evaluate dissertations in education. Scholars from "hard" sciences often made pedagogy suffer for its past "sins", that is: for its ideologized content during the Soviet era. Often, they were moreover neither interested nor qualified to understand research in humanities and social sciences.

Statistics of the Promotion Council's work between 1993 and 1999 speak for themselves[37]: during this period, an average of eight to 10 dissertations per year were successfully defended, but in 2000, when the Qualification Commission was introduced, only one was accepted, and in subsequent years the number of dissertations in pedagogy remained low. Thus, the outside supervision of educational sciences brought discipline.

---

36 Diāna Paukšēna and Ilga Rampāne, comp., *Latvijas Universitātē izstrādātās vai aizstāvētās disertācijas (1996–2005)* [Dissertations prepared or defended at the University of Latvia (1996–2005)] (Rīga: LU Akadēmiskais apgāds, 2008).

37 It should be noted that information on dissertations defended in the first half of the 1990s is not easy to obtain because there were no strict rules on submitting a copy of the dissertation to libraries, as well as the requirement to publish the announcement of defenses in the *Journal of Science* was not always met. See Vija Medne, comp., *Latvijas Universitātes aspiranti un doktoranti. I. daļa. Aspirantūras un doktorantūras personāliju, aizstāvēto disertāciju un iegūto zinātnisko grādu apkopojums (1945–2005)* [Compilation of University of Latvia graduate students and graduates, their dissertations and degrees, part 1. (1945–2005)] (Rīga: LU Akadēmiskais apgāds, 2009); Diāna Paukšēna and Ilga Rampāne, comp., *Latvijas Universitātē izstrādātās vai aizstāvētās disertācijas (1996–2005)* [Dissertations prepared or defended at the University of Latvia (1996–2005)] (Rīga: LU Akadēmiskais apgāds, 2008).

Nevertheless, the large number of dissertations defended in the 1990s also conveyed a positive message about the old Soviet academic elite – they threw the door open to young researchers and supported their entrance into the academic community. Unfortunately, many of the new doctors turned out to be only passers-by in science and chose a more rewarding job or career development in the West instead of poorly paid academic work in Latvia.

Confusion of Educational Sciences – the Methodological Dimension

Here, we must return to the period before World War II. Educational sciences in Latvia developed in the tradition of the liberal arts (*Geisteswissenschaften*) following the example of Germany – a tradition diametrically opposite to the dialectical materialism proclaimed in the Soviet Union as the only correct and scientific view of the world. In 1940, following the incorporation of Latvia into the Soviet Union, the legacy of pre-war pedagogues was described as hostile to the Soviet rule and any mention of it threatened with severe punishment. The intellectual heritage of the "bourgeois" state, as the Soviets called independent Latvia, was hidden away in special library collections and access to it required a written permit. "Idealism" became an unforgivable sin. Pedagogy of the liberal arts was replaced by trivialized Marxism based on social theories, which was imported to Latvia from the Soviet Union after World War II. Professors educated in the Soviet Union were dispatched to the University of Latvia, where they introduced pedagogical curricula and textbooks prepared in the Soviet Union and published translations of articles on the Soviet theory of pedagogy.[38]

The interrupted continuity of scientific development through political interference[39] and 50 years of isolation behind the Iron Curtain had created a situation where post-Soviet scholars knew neither the background of their subject in the global context nor the diversity of theories in their field of research. In the 1990s, the concepts of postmodernism and critical pedagogy were yet foreign to them. Here it is worth to mention Depaepe stating that "not knowing the in-

---
38 On the development of pedagogical science in Latvia during the Soviet occupation, see Aīda Krūze and Iveta Ozola, "Pedagogy as a Science in Latvia," in *History of Pedagogy and Educational Sciences in the Baltic Countries from 1940 to 1990: An Overview*, ed. Iveta Ķestere and Aīda Kruze (Rīga: RaKa, 2013), 234–242.
39 Iveta Ozola, "Pedagoģijas zinātnes ģenēze Latvijā no 20. gadsimta 20. gadiem līdz 60. gadu sākumam. Promocijas darbs" [Genesis of pedagogical science in Latvia from the 1920s to the early 1960s. Doctoral dissertation] (Rīga: Latvijas Universitāte, 2013).

tellectual, social and historical roots of the educational sciences is undoubtedly the best breeding ground for professional incompetence."[40] In fact, the academic field had to be re-educated at a rapid pace.

Throughout the 1990s, research in educational sciences continued in the empirical tradition developed during the Soviet era; that is: theoretical findings were demonstrated during "experiments" with such methods as observation, questionnaires, and analysis of children's activities.[41] Paradoxically, this type of methodology was welcomed in academia: leading scientific institutions in which the main role had been usurped by the ideologically "innocent" representatives of "hard" sciences passionately supported "strong" evidence-based positivist research. In their turn, professors of pedagogy brought up in the Soviet era simply did not know any different. However, the return to a pedagogy as applied philosophy dominating in 1920s and 1930s would have been a step back as well.[42] So, it was methodology that proved to be the most tenacious of the Soviet heritage.

The first dissertations in educational sciences free from the Soviet normativism, positivism and schematism, and developed in the style of postmodernism, using qualitative methods and contextualization and acknowledging the relativity of empirical data,[43] were defended in Latvia only in the beginning of the twenty-first century.[44] After the "allowed ease" of postmodernism, today the methodology of educational sciences has returned to "evidence-based" research, which is welcomed and well received among the politicians and therefore generously funded.

---

40 Marc Depaepe, "Why Even Today Educational Historiography is not an Unnecessary Luxury. Focusing on Four Themes from Forty-four Years of Research," *Espacio, Tiempo y Educación* 7 (2020): 242.
41 I.A. Kairov, ed., *Pedagogika* [Pedagogy] (Moskva: Gosudarstvennoje uchebno – pedagogiceskoje izdatelstvo ministerstva prosvescenija RSFSR, 1956), 17–18.
42 Rubene and Ozola, "Democratisation of Educational Sciences," 233.
43 For research on postmodernism, see Meynert, *Conceptualizations of Childhood*, 133–139.
44 Rubene and Ozola, "Democratisation of Educational Sciences," 234.

Changes of Educational Sciences – the Communicative Dimension: The West in Latvia and Latvia in the West

We can safely say that along with the institutional dimension, the communicative dimension of educational sciences saw the most rapid changes. The fall of the Iron Curtain initiated a breakthrough of post-Soviet scholars to the West and the rapid entry of the West into the post-Soviet space where, until then, international communications meant limited networking of the strictly isolated Soviet academic community. Post-Soviet researchers emerged in the neoliberal, postmodern, and "post-national" world where such global institutions as the UN, World Bank, and OECD had begun their triumphant march.[45]

The intellectual "joining" of the West was seen as a continuation of political liberation. One of the tasks was to remove the Soviet stigma, which, in turn, led to the West being drawn in as an unquestionable argument in every discussion and as a model copied quite uncritically. The attitude towards the West sheds light on the (in)equality of the emancipation process, where the emancipator usurps the leading role in the emancipation and dictates the conditions with the promise of equality in the future.[46] Researchers from Latvia became aware of their unequal position in the Western world and came to terms with it, because Western dominance seemed less humiliating – the Western development path was self-chosen and recognized as a model, unlike the violent incorporation into the USSR. Western fetishization was further nurtured when comparing scientists having grown up in the Soviet Union with their foreign colleagues possessing all the necessary research equipment or resources that had not been available in the USSR, namely: systematic and, most importantly, versatile education, language skills, travel and publishing opportunities, approbation of scientific concepts in an intellectually open professional network.[47] From the per-

---

45 Stefan Thomas Hopmann, "No Child, no School, no State Left Behind: Schooling in the Age of Accountability," *Journal of Curriculum Studies* 40 (2008): 419. See Biesta, "Doing Emancipation," 15–30.
46 Stefan Gross, "Inequality and Emancipation: An Educational Approach," *Journal of Education and Research* 2 (2010): 9–16; Meynert, *Conceptualizations of Childhood*, 138.
47 Depaepe mentions the advantages of Westerners in research, linking those to the theory of social Darwinism ("the strongest survives"). See Marc Depaepe, "It's a Long Way to ... an International Social History of Education: in Search of Brian Simon's Legacy in Today's Educational Historiography," *History of Education* 33 (2004): 540.

spective of the 1990s, the way of life of the Western academic community seemed to be an example of freedom and prosperity and inspired views on the possibility of full political and ideological freedom after the liberation from the Soviet dictatorship. The claim of critics of Western capitalism that education systems across the world are part of the ideological and policy offensive by neoliberal capital, leading to selection, exclusion, and national and international inequalities,[48] was ignored or perceived with suspicion, because it strongly reminded of the traditional slogans of Soviet propaganda. The strict etiquette of Western political correctness was also acquired only gradually.

Researchers in the post-Soviet space became aspiring students, Western educational sciences gained new outlets in the post-Soviet space, and Western researchers acquired the status of teachers and "virgin territories" for their research. Thus, the westernization and globalization of post-Soviet educational sciences began.

To establish contacts with the West, one of the priorities in the 1990s became intensive English and German language learning as the "civilizing mission"[49] of post-Soviet scholars. At the cutting edge were graduates of the Faculty of Foreign Languages, who formed the first wave of post-Soviet scholars in the West. The decisive factor was not research capabilities but the ability to communicate in a foreign language, which became a springboard for a successful career.[50] Scholarships from various foundations (e.g. the Nordic Council, the British Council) opened the doors of Western universities to post-graduate students from Eastern Europe, some of whom faithfully returned to bring their newly acquired knowledge to their homeland, but some spent their time establishing professional (or private) contacts to build their own careers in the West. And they could hardly be blamed, for in the 1990s, Latvia offered neither well-organized possibilities for professional development nor financial security.[51]

---

[48] Dave Hill, "Educational Perversion and Global Neoliberalism," in *Neoliberalism and Education Reform*, ed. E. Wayne Ross and Rich Gibson (Cresskill, New Jersey: Hampton Press, 2006), 107–108.

[49] For language politics in the context of colonization, see Eckhardt Fuchs, "Transnational Perspectives in Historical Educational Research," in *Transnationalizing the History of Education*, ed. Eckhardt Fuchs (Leipzig: Leipziger Universitätsverlag, 2012), 13.

[50] Rubene, "Geisteswissenschaften," 57–73.

[51] Moving to the West reveals the "in-betweenness" of academic identity in the transformation between East and West. Iveta Silova, who started her academic career in Latvia in the 1990s, relates: "As I moved "West" to become a university professor in the United States, my previous academic and professional experiences were quickly discounted as not "Western enough" so my tenure clock had to start from zero and my academic identity had to be rebuilt from scratch. Shifting between these different roles has been both fascinating and complicated. I always

The poverty of the 1990s also put a stamp of "academic tourism" on international cooperation: apart from intellectual hunger, the West quenched material hunger, and along with knowledge and teaching materials, household goods thus travelled back home as well. Since the issue of academic tourism has never been publicly discussed, as it does not fit into the "beautiful" story of international cooperation, we can only imagine what Western intellectuals thought of post-Soviet professors who preferred shopping to academic discussions. However, we should hardly judge those weaknesses from today's perspective – Latvian professors were ordinary humans living in extremely modest conditions. Social solidarity of Western professors deserves a special mention in this context: in addition to books, parcels contained packets of coffee, sugar and other groceries, which in 1990 were in short supply in Latvian stores. This fact is still remembered as a touching example of not only intellectual but also material care on the part of Western professors for their colleagues. So, on encountering the conspicuous "riches" of the West, researchers from a poor Soviet background became increasingly convinced that their choice of the Western path was correct.

In establishing first extensive contacts with Western educators, the academic staff of the University of Latvia were assisted by Latvian diaspora,[52] comprised of World War II refugees and their descendants. They had maintained their Latvian identity and, along with "Soviet Latvians," heartily celebrated Latvia's liberation from the Soviet dictatorship. There was no language barrier, for all could communicate in Latvian. At the same time, however, the wish of Western Latvians to teach local scholars how to develop research in the new democratic conditions was gingerly received, as the memory of Moscow's "colonizers" with their strong, impudent belief in their cultural superiority was too fresh. However, the desire to get to the West and learn previously hidden knowledge prevailed; professionalism was stronger than the feeling of humiliation. The World Conference of Latvian Educators was first held in 1991, and in subsequent years, it took place alternately in Münster (Germany) and Latvia. The conferences were governed by the joy of experimentation shared by both practitioners and theoreticians of education.

The absence of Moscow research funding and the establishment of contacts with Western colleagues also led to the discovery of such a novelty as project work. The first academic grant received by the University of Latvia researchers was to join the project "International Learning" (*Internationales Lernen*) initiated

---

felt fortunate to be a part of the different "worlds" even though I knew that I never fully belonged to any of them. I always have been and continue to be at the "borders." Silova, Millei, and Piattoeva, "Interrupting the Coloniality," 5.
52 Stradiņš, "Ceļavārdi," 35.

by Professor Josef Held from the University of Tübingen (Germany). Latvia became one of eight participating countries and from 1991 to 2007 worked together with Germany, Greece, Croatia, the Netherlands, Spain, Poland, and Switzerland.[53] This project was perfectly attuned to the growing tendency in Western societies to "educationalize" social problems,[54] which given the socially unstable situation of Latvia offered scholars a broad field of study and increased the practical significance of their research, thus raising their prestige in the public eye.

"International Learning" provided an opportunity not only to open the Iron Curtain for the few researchers who had been given the "privilege" to work on the project,[55] but also to bring cooperation partners to Latvia, thus benefitting the entire academic community as well as educational practitioners. Four monographs were published as part of this project and the invitation for Latvian researchers to become co-authors was often (but not always!) a nice "gift" from Westerners for Latvian hospitality and an act of charity, knowing how important a step any publication abroad was for career development in the post-Soviet space. However, referring to Bourdieu, Southwell and Depaepe have rightly warned that the "politics of giving" can turn gifts into debts.[56]

Massive academic cooperation with one particular Western institution was dwindling as a new generation of researchers became more and more demanding to cooperation partners abroad – the West "in general" and welcoming attitude were no longer the most attractive criteria for collaboration. What became important was the prestige of a partner university in the global community and valuable learning offerings in a specific field.

In the following years, Latvian academia became part of the "global-centric" circulation of academic knowledge, or "lending and borrowing"[57] processes. Researchers from Ukraine, Kazakhstan, and Georgia began to study ideas of West-

---

[53] Rubene and Ozola, "Democratisation of Educational Sciences," 236.
[54] See Marc Depaepe and Paul Smeyers, "Educationalization as an Ongoing Modernization Process," in *Between Educationalization and Appropriation. Selected Writings on the History of Modern Educational Systems*, ed. Marc Depaepe (Leuven: University Press, 2012), 167–175.
[55] The issue of corporate links in organizing a team for such a rare and prestigious international project at the time deserves a separate study.
[56] Southwell and Depaepe, "The Relation between Education and Emancipation," 3.
[57] On the concepts of "lending and borrowing" and "cultural transfer," see Gita Steiner-Khamsi and Florian Waldow, eds., *World Yearbook of Education 2012: Policy Borrowing and Lending in Education* (London: Routledge, 2012); Eugenia Roldán Vera and Eckhardt Fuchs, "Introduction: The Transnational in the History of Education," in *The Transnational in the History of Education. Concepts and Perspectives*, ed. Eugenia Roldán Vera and Eckhardt Fuchs (s.l.: Palgrave Macmillan, 2019), 1–48, 16–18; Berger, *The Past as History*, 352.

ern pedagogy in Latvia. With a certain degree of self-irony, we can say that Latvia took on the role of the "new" West.

Conclusion

In the 1990s, as with the Soviet occupation 50 years earlier, the change of political power interrupted the continuity of the development of educational sciences in Latvia for the second time in the twentieth century. Whereas the Soviet government had changed the then paradigm of educational sciences with political orders and repression, in the 1990s it were public pressure and the market economy which changed the model. If in the Soviet Union the choices were strictly limited, then after the restoration of Latvia's independence the number of possible directions for development were unlimited, but only one was recognized as real: that towards the West, which during all those years under the Soviet dictatorship had stood as a symbol of freedom, democracy, security, and prosperity. No matter how skeptical we might be today of the illusions of the 1990s, the "West" created by post-Soviet professors served well as a bearing point among the ruins of the Berlin Wall.

To all four dimensions of educational sciences transformation between Moscow and the West occurred as a breaking of ties with the dictatorship and a rooting out of the dictatorship from people's minds, with the latter task taking much longer time than the former. Limited human resources and finances left no choice but to create a "new (corp)us" out of Soviet-educated academics who in the field of education undertook to free themselves from Moscow's dictate and create "new" educational sciences. The search for a new pattern firstly went in two directions, namely: as a reflection on the pedagogical heritage banned during the Soviet era and excavated later from the collections of libraries, archives, and museums, and as a search, in the West, for an educational model. The first direction quickly disappeared, as "paradise" stored in the collective memory of the independent state of the 1920s–1930s appeared to be old-fashioned and soon became a mere object of curiosity for historians and those lacking proficiency in foreign languages.

The entrance of post-Soviet scholars into West and their ensuing comparison with Western counterparts were hard, as lack of knowledge of contemporary methodologies and theories that had remained hidden behind the Iron Curtain put previously respected Soviet professors in the position of students and "poor relatives." This part of "emancipation" brought along inequality, with the privileged group dictating the conditions of emancipation.[58] It was necessary to learn another world order, other languages, and another "dictionary" of educational sciences. However, "New is exciting. New is cool. New is unprecedented."[59] The new opportunities were tempting, Soviet educators were enthusiasts in their field, and market conditions were pressing.

Gradually, the transfer of "best practices" and "international standards"[60] from the West became a daily routine and material for continuous discussion about whose "policies" and which "standards" counted. Consequently, the pattern of educational sciences in Latvia still depends on each researcher's own considerations. In other words, each post-Soviet academic has gradually discovered their "own" West, both geographically and conceptually. Only the market economy has remained one for all.

Indeed, for those who perceived the "new" with suspicion, the market economy became a harsh stimulus for swift restructuring, where the loss of funding made one learn fast, reviewing the educational content in line with new "customer-centered"[61] demands, seeking resources for international cooperation, and initiating research projects. However, in the 1990s, in Latvia the market economy had not yet gained total control over education as a global "salable good."[62] It is only today that the language of education has been replaced by the language of the market and de-theorized education of new teachers,[63] with many supporters among educational researchers and policymakers.

The field of education has always been subject to self-produced rigorous benchmarking of success, comparison, rankings, and hierarchies;[64] therefore, freedom in education is sooner or later christened "anarchy" and brought to a common standard. That is exactly what happened with educational sciences in Latvia. After the destruction of Moscow's model and the ensuing orgy of freedom, education was arranged under the supervision of new or renewed local in-

---

58 Meynert, *Conceptualizations of Childhood*, 138.
59 Nicholas C. Burbules, "Technology, Education, and the Fetishization of the 'New'," in *Educational Research: Discourses of Change and Changes of Discourse*, ed. Paul Smeyers and Marc Depaepe (Cham: Springer International Publishing, 2016), 9.
60 See Steiner-Khamsi's research, e.g., Steiner-Khamsi and Waldow, *World Yearbook of Education 2012*.
61 Hopmann, "No Child, No School," 419.
62 Nick Grant, "Foreword," in *Global Neoliberalism and Education and Its Consequences*, ed. Dave Hill and Ravi Kumar (New York, London: Routledge, 2009), xii.
63 Hill, "Educational Perversion," 117, 119, 120.
64 Thomas S. Popkewitz, "Culture, Pedagogy, and Power: Issues in the Production of Values and Colonization," *Journal of Education* 170 (1988): 80; Peter Abbs, *Against the Flow: Education, the Arts and Postmodern Culture* (London, New York: RoutledgeFalmer, 2003), 59.

stitutions, the control gradually fortified by the requirements of "global players" (OECD, EU, World Bank) for a single educational space. The awareness that "capitalism is not kind" and autonomous thoughts are subject to ideology in the West also[65] came later. In the 1990s, criticism of the West was not on the agenda, as Moscow was still the main enemy and Western capitalism was not yet fully felt. Even later, the fact that one could publicly complain about capitalism-induced problems seemed an invaluable treasure to academics who had experienced Soviet censorship, the gift unappreciated by their colleagues brought up in democracy.

To free oneself from Moscow was to break the shackles of dictatorship and foreign ideology, but governments, regimes, and the elite always strive "to centralize the conduct and impose their criteria,"[66] thus, making the search for emancipation a "continuous and unfinished process" which interrupts the existing order and at the same time constantly creates hierarchies and disagreements,[67] to the same effect in educational sciences.

Bibliography

Abbs, Peter. *Against the Flow: Education, the Arts and Postmodern Culture*. London, New York: Routledge, 2003.
Becher, Tony, and Paul R. Trowler. *Academic Tribes and Territories: Intellectual Inquiry and the Cultures of Disciplines*. Milton Keynes: SRHE/OUP, 1989.
Beļickis, Inārs. *Izglītības alternatīvās teorijas* [Alternative theories of education]. Rīga: Raka, 1997.
Berger, Stefan. *The Past as History. National Identity and Historical Consciousness in Modern Europe*. Basingstoke: Palgrave Macmillan, 2015.
Biesta, Gert. "Doing Emancipation Differently: Transgression, Equality and the Politics of Learning." *Civitas Educationis. Education, Politics and Culture* 1 (2012): 15–30.
Böhme, Günther, and Heinz-Elmar Tenorth. *Einführung in die Historische Pädagogik*. Darmstadt: Wissenschaftliche Buchgesellschaft, 1990.
Burbules, Nicholas C. "Technology, Education, and the Fetishization of the 'New'." In *Educational Research: Discourses of Change and Changes of Discourse*, edited by Paul Smeyers and Marc Depaepe, 9–16. Cham: Springer, 2016.
Chankseliani, Maia, and Iveta Silova. "Reconfiguring Education Purposes, Policies and Practices during Post-Socialist Transformations: Setting the Stage." In *Comparing Post-socialist Transformations*, edited by Maia Chankseliani and Iveta Silova, 7–25. Oxford: Symposium Books, 2018.

---

65 Hill, "Educational Perversion," 109, 111.
66 Southwell and Depaepe, "The Relation Between Education and Emancipation," 1.
67 Ibid.

Dedze, Indra, and Zanda Rubene. "Universities in Latvia – from the Soviet to European Higher Education Area." *Foro de Educación* 14 (2016): 13–38.

Depaepe, Marc. "Demythologizing the Educational Past: An Endless Task in History of Education." In *Between Educationalization and Appropriation. Selected Writings on the History of Modern Educational Systems*, by Marc Depaepe, 435–450. Leuven University Press, 2012.

Depaepe, Marc. "It's a Long Way to ... an International Social History of Education: in Search of Brian Simon's Legacy in Today's Educational Historiography." *History of Education* 33 (2004): 531–544.

Depaepe, Marc. "Why Even Today Educational Historiography is not an Unnecessary Luxury. Focusing on Four Themes from Forty-four Years of Research." *Espacio, Tiempo y Educación* 7 (2020): 227–246.

Depaepe, Mark, and Paul Smeyers. "Educationalization as an Ongoing Modernization Process." In *Between Educationalization and Appropriation: Selected Writings on the History of Modern Educational Systems*, edited by Marc Depaepe, 167–175. Leuven: Leuven University Press, 2012.

Fair-Schulz, Axel, and Mario Kessler. "Conclusion: A Note on Research Directions and Literature." In *East German Historians since Reunification. A Discipline Transformed*, edited by Axel Fair-Schulz and Mario Kessler, 231–237. Albany, NY: State University of New York Press, 2017.

Fortunati, Vita, and Elena Lamberti. "Cultural Memory: An European Perspective." In *Cultural Memory Studies: An International and Interdisciplinary Handbook*, edited by Astrid Erll and Ansgar Nünning, 127–137. Berlin, New York: Walter de Gruyter, 2008.

Fuchs, Eckhardt. "Transnational Perspectives in Historical Educational Research." *Comparative* 21 (2012): 7–14.

Grant, Nick. "Foreword." In *Global Neoliberalism and Education and Its Consequences*, edited by Dave Hill and Ravi Kumar, vii–xvii. New York, London: Routledge, 2009.

Gross, Stefan. "Inequality and Emancipation: An Educational Approach." *Journal of Education and Research* 2 (2010): 9–16.

Gudjons, Herberts. *Pedagoģijas pamatatziņas* [Pedagogy basics]. Rīga: Zvaigzne ABC, 1989.

Hemetsberger, Bernard. "Burbunkologie oder: Zur Bearbeitung von Bildungskrisen." *Pädagogische Korrespondenz* 57 (2018): 101–113.

Hill, Dave. "Educational Perversion and Global Neoliberalism." In *Neoliberalism and Education Reform*, edited by E. Wayne Ross and Rich Gibson, 107–160. Cresskill, New Jersey: Hampton Press, 2006.

Hofstetter, Rita, and Bernard Schneuwly. *Zur Geschichte der Erziehungswissenschaften in der Schweiz. Vom Ende des 19. bis zur Mitte des 20. Jahrhunderts*. Bern: hep Verlag AG, 2011.

Hopmann, Stefan Thomas. "No Child, no School, no State Left Behind: Schooling in the Age of Accountability." *Journal of Curriculum Studies* 40 (2008): 417–456.

Kairov, Ivan, ed. *Pedagogika* [Pedagogy]. Moskva: Gosudarstvennoje učebno – pedagogičeskoje izdateļstvo miņisterstva prosveščenija RSFSR, 1956.

Kestere, Iveta, Irena Stonkuviene, and Veronika Varik "History of Education as a Changing Research Field." In *Pedagogy and Educational Sciences in the Post-Soviet Baltic States, 1990–2004: Changes and Challenges*, edited by Iveta Kestere, Ene-Silvia Sarv, and Irena Stonkuviene, 261–275. Riga: University of Latvia Press, 2020.

Krūze, Aīda, and Iveta Ozola. "Pedagogy as a Science in Latvia." In *History of Pedagogy and Educational Sciences in the Baltic Countries from 1940 to 1990: An Overview*, edited by Iveta Ķestere and Aīda Krūze, 234–242. Rīga: RaKa, 2013.

Krūze, Aīda. "Pedagoģijas nodaļa" [Pedagogy Department]. In *LU Pedagoģijas, psiholoģijas un mākslas fakultāte zinātnei un izglītībai* [University of Latvia, Faculty of Education, Psychology and Art for science and education], edited by Aīda Krūze, Ērika Lanka, and Jānis Aizpurs, 89–121. Rīga: LU Akadēmiskais apgāds, 2013.

Kudláčová, Blanka, and Andrej Rajský, eds. *Education and "Pädagogik." Philosophical and Historical Reflections. Central, Southern and South-Eastern Europe*. Berlin: VEDA/Peter Lang, 2019.

Kuhn, Thomas S. *The Structure of Scientific Revolutions*. Chicago, London: The University of Chicago Press, 1970.

Medne, Vija, comp. *Latvijas Universitātes aspiranti un doktoranti. I. daļa. Aspirantūras un doktorantūras personāliju, aizstāvēto disertāciju un iegūto zinātnisko grādu apkopojums (1945–2005)* [Compilation of University of Latvia Graduate Students and Graduates, their dissertations and degrees, part I. (1945–2005)]. Rīga: LU Akadēmiskais apgāds, 2009.

Meynert, Mariam. *Conceptualizations of Childhood, Pedagogy and Educational Research in the Postmodern. A Critical Interpretation*. Lund: Lund University, 2013.

OECD centrs sadarbībai ar nedalībvalstīm. *Nacionālo izglītības politiku analīze. Latvija* [Analysis of national education policies. Latvia]. Rīga: Profesionālās izglītības attīstības programmas aģentūra, 2000.

Ozola, Iveta, and Iveta Ķestere. "Pedagoģijas kā zinātnes ģenēze Eiropā (18. gadsimts–20. gadsimta 20.–30. gadi): historiogrāfiskais aspekts" [The Genesis of Pedagogy as a Science in Europe (18th century – 1920s–30s): Historiographic Aspect]. In *Pedagoģijas vēsture: 15 jautājumi* [History of pedagogy. 15 questions], edited by Aīda Krūze and Iveta Ķestere, 78–105. Rīga: RaKa, 2010.

Ozola, Iveta. "Pedagoģijas zinātnes ģenēze Latvijā no 20. gadsimta 20. gadiem līdz 60. gadu sākumam. Promocijas darbs" [Genesis of pedagogical science in Latvia from the 1920s to the early 1960s. Doctoral dissertation]. PhD diss., University of Latvia, 2013.

Paukšēna, Diāna, and Ilga Rampāne, comp. *Latvijas Universitātē izstrādātās vai aizstāvētās disertācijas (1996–2005)* [Dissertations prepared or defended at the University of Latvia (1996–2005)]. Rīga: LU Akadēmiskais apgāds, 2008.

Pļaveniece, Maija, and Iveta Ķestere. "Autorprogramma kursam 'Pedagoģija'." [Author program for the course "Pedagogy"]. Unpublished manuscript, 1991, handwritten.

Pļaveniece, Maija, and Iveta Ķestere. "Darba programma kursam 'Pedagoģija'." [Work program for course "Pedagogy"]. Unpublished manuscript, after 1991, handwritten.

Popkewitz, Thomas S. "Culture, Pedagogy, and Power: Issues in the Production of Values and Colonization." *Journal of Education* 170 (1988): 77–90.

Roldán Vera, Eugenia, and Eckhardt Fuchs. "Introduction: The Transnational in the History of Education." In *The Transnational in the History of Education. Concepts and Perspectives*, edited by Eugenia Roldán Vera and Eckhardt Fuchs, 1–47. S. l.: Palgrave Macmillan, 2019.

Rubene, Zanda, and Iveta Ozola. "Democratisation of Educational Sciences (Pedagogy) in the Context of the Shift in Political Power of Latvia." In *Pedagogy and Educational Sciences in the Post-Soviet Baltic States, 1990–2004: Changes and Challenges*, edited by Iveta

Kestere, Ene-Silvia Sarv, and Irena Stonkuviene, 224–237. Riga: University of Latvia Press, 2020.

Rubene, Zanda. "Geisteswissenschaften und akademische Bildung in Lettland." In *Wissenschaft und akademische Bildung. Ist Theodor Litt für die gegenwärtige Hochschulpolitik aktuell?*, edited by P. Gutjahr-Löser, D. Schulz, und H.W. Wollersheim, 57–73. Leipzig: Leipziger Universitätsverlag, 2010.

Southwell, Myriam, and Marc Depaepe. "The Relation Between Education and Emancipation: Something like Water and Oil? Introducing the Special Issue." *Paedagogica Historica* 55 (2019): 1–7.

Steiner-Khamsi, Gita, and Florian Waldow, eds. *World Yearbook of Education 2012: Policy Borrowing and Lending in Education*. London: Routledge, 2012.

Steiner-Khamsi, Gita. "Donor Logic in the Era of Gates, Buffett, and Soros." *Current Issues in Comparative Education* 10 (2008): 10–15.

Stradiņš, Jānis. "Ceļavārdi II Pasaules latviešu zinātnieku kongresam" [Words for the Second World Congress of Latvian Scientists]. In *II Pasaules latviešu zinātnieku kongress. Rīga, 2001. gada 14.–15. augusts. Tēžu krājums* [Second World Congress of Latvian Scientists. Riga, 14–15 August 2001. Congress proceedings], compiled by Juris Ekmanis, xxxv. Rīga: Latvijas Zinātņu akadēmija, 2001.

Strods, Henrihs, ed. *Latvijas Valsts Universitātes vēsture, 1940–1990* [History of the State University of Latvia, 1940–1990]. Rīga: Latvijas Universitāte, 1999.

Tucke, Ericka L. "The Subject of History: Historical Subjectivity and Historical Science." *Journal of the Philosophy of History* 7 (2013): 205–229.

Varslavāns, Alberts, ed. *Latvijas Universitāte, 75* [University of Latvia at 75]. Rīga: Latvijas Universitāte, 1994.

Yurchak, Alexei. *Everything Was Forever, Until It Was No More. The Last Soviet Generation*. Princeton and Oxford: Princeton University Press, 2005.

Zīds, Oskars, comp. *Vispārējā pedagoģija. Darba programma akadēmiskajām studijām pedagoģijā un psiholoģijā psiholoģijā* [General pedagogy. Work program for academic studies in pedagogy and psychology]. Rīga: Latvijas Universitāte, 1991.

Zigmunde, Alīda, and Iveta Ķestere. "Latvijas Universitātes Pedagoģijas nodaļas pirmsākumi, studiju process, mācībspēki un studenti (1919–1944)" [The beginning of the Department of Pedagogy, University of Latvia, study process, teaching staff and students (1919–1944)]. In *Pedagoģijas vēsture. 15 jautājumi.* [History of pedagogy. 15 questions], edited by Aīda Krūze and Iveta Ķestere, 176–203. Rīga: RaKa, 2010.

Marcelo Caruso, Daniel Przygoda and Friedrich Schollmayer
(Humboldt-Universität zu Berlin, Germany)

"Pedagogic" – A Preliminary Thesis on a Lexical Innovation during the European Enlightenment

Abstract: In many European languages, the use of the adjective "pedagogic" / "pedagogical" has become widespread. In this contribution, the authors look into the historical emergence and varying meanings of this powerful adjective. This development took different shapes in different European languages. The article[1] shows early meanings attached to the adjective, its variations, and uses. Following analytical insights from the historiography of concepts, selected early developments in the diverging German, French, and English lexicographies of defining, on the one side, pedagogy and the pedagogue and, on the other, as a derivative, the adjective "pedagogic/pedagogical" are in focus. This tentative exploration identifies the time of the Enlightenment as the critical period in history for the emergence of this wording.

Keywords: history of concepts; pedagogical; pedagogy; Europe, Enlightenment

Introduction

In the city of Munich in 1877, a rift within the regional school commission for Upper Bavaria led to delicate consultations. It was the time of the Bavarian *Kulturkampf*. District and local clerical inspectors for primary schools feared they would be marginalized from the regular inspection of schools. Indeed, a regulation issued by the Bavarian Ministry of Education on November 16, 1876 could be interpreted as an extension of the competencies of newly appointed professional school inspectors in the regional governments. The school commission proved not to be so radical and decided to uphold the regular clerical inspection of the schools. Yet the commission also recommended the integration of the new

---

[1] Research for this contribution has been carried out as a result of the generous financial support of the German Research Community (DFG) for the project: "Pädagogisch. Emergenz, Durchsetzung, Varianz und Transformation eines modernen Begriffsfeldes (deutsche Staaten, ca. 1750–1850)" (Pedagogic. Emergence, implementations, variations and transformation of a modern conceptual field, German States 1750–1850).

https://doi.org/10.1515/9783110623451-016

professional inspectors into the regular work of the clerical inspectors, because "they do not always enjoy the necessary educational preparation."[2] The actual German term, "pädagogische Bildung", not just general *Bildung*, but a specific "pädagogische" one, points to a decisive criterium in the distributing of power and competencies in this contested situation. This exchange was by no means an exception: teachers, educators, and liberal politicians all positioned the real, "pädagogische" inspection against the bureaucratic and formal one of the churchmen.[3] Almost 70 years later, in another country and in the opposite direction, the power of using this adjective – "pedagógico" in Spanish – came to the fore. The central commission for the admission of children's literature in the Spanish Ministry of Education under dictator Francisco Franco made swift decisions about the prohibition of many different works. The reasons for censure were manifold, but censors repeatedly used "poco pedagógico" – here meaning as being inconvenient from the perspective of Pedagogy – as a knockout criterion.[4] In the Bavarian case, the use of "pädagogisch" aimed to delegitimize the role of Catholics in the school system. In Spain, the use of "pedagógico" shows that this language has become widespread and multipurpose and could work in the opposite direction. In different times and places, the use of this adjective was anything but naïve: it deployed a legitimating force.

In many Western European languages, the adjective "pedagogic," also "pedagogical," referring to actions, persons, materials, and situations, has become increasingly usual. Beyond the more restricted meaning associated with it in English – where teaching is still definitory – this adjective has a broader field of application. In many other European languages, it has acquired a strong evaluative and not only descriptive value. Moreover, "pedagogic" has become a word in everyday language. This has not always been the case. In French, Spanish, German, and other languages, you may praise a good way of teaching when you term it "très pédagogique", "muy pedagógico/a", or "sehr pädagogisch."

---

[2] Copy of the protocol from the meeting of the regional school commission of Upper Bavaria to the Ministry of Education, March 31, 1877. State Archives Munich, RA 53666.
[3] This is a main point in Michael Geiss, *Der Pädagogenstaat. Behördenkommunikation und Organisationspraxis in der badischen Unterrichtsverwaltung, 1860–1912* (Bielefeld: transcript, 2014). For a further discussion of the issue see: Marcelo Caruso, *Biopolitik im Klassenzimmer. Zur Ordnung der Führungspraktiken in den Bayerischen Volksschulen (1869–1918)* (Weinheim, Basel, Berlin: Beltz, 2003). A brief introduction to this controversy in English in: Marcelo Caruso, "Policing validity and reliability. Expertise, data accumulation and data parallelization in Bavaria (1873–1919)," in *The rise of data in education Systems. Collection, visualization and use*, ed. Martin Lawn (Oxford: Symposium books, 2013).
[4] Pedro C. Cerrillo and Ma Victoria Sotomayor, *Censuras y LIJ en el siglo XX (En España y 7 países latinoamericanos)* (Cuenca: Ediciones de la Universidad de Castilla-La Mancha, 2016), 67.

This would also extend to persons, institutions, materials, situations, etc. Additionally, one sure way of delegitimizing an educational approach, a certain teaching method, an individual teaching person, or a specific educational setting would be to call it the contrary to "pedagogic" ("peu pédagogique," "poco pedagógico/a," "unpädagogisch"). It is certainly a broad and powerful semantic field, including descriptive and evaluative modes of coding, that is associated with this adjective.

For historians of education willingly accepting the so-called "Ten Commandments" of the profession,[5] two insights are in focus. First, the development of this vocabulary in the major Western languages (and its probable introduction and transformation in non-European languages) may constitute a major field for analyzing the growth and consolidation of modern ways of speaking about, looking to, and acting upon education. Since when has the adjective "pedagogic" been in circulation, shaping meanings, and orientating all kind of educators? Second, the pervasive use of the adjective seems to be particularly challenging to address. Whereas "Pedagogy" as a discipline may be adequately reconstructed in its past developments and institutionalizations, and the very figure of the Pedagogue and his/her avatars may also be analyzed in its historical and changing shape and attributions, the analytical problem with the adjective form is of an enhanced complexity. In this article, we focus on the historical emergence and varying meanings of this powerful adjective. The adjective itself hints at the emergence of a new field of meaning. As we will show, this took different shapes in different European languages. Beyond "pedagogy" and the "pedagogue", we will focus on the early meanings attached to the adjective, its variations, and uses. Historians, particularly those working in the field of the history of concepts, have advanced valuable insights about the historicity of major concepts. Yet could we capture the effects and pervasiveness of the adjectival use of this semantic field through the lens of a history of concepts hitherto focused only on substantives?

In the following, we will explore the emergence of this specific form of speaking about education following analytical insights from the historiography of concepts. We will briefly characterize this approach and argue for its expansion to words other than nouns (1). Following this, we will briefly argue for a treatment of "pedagogic" as a concept and sketch some central meanings attached to it (2). Then we will present some early developments in the diverging lexicographies of defining, on the one side, pedagogy and the pedagogue and, on

---

[5] Marc Depaepe, "The Ten Commandments of Good Practices in History of Education Research," *Zeitschrift für pädagogische Historiographie* 16 (2010): 31–34.

the other, as a derivative, the adjective "pedagogic/pedagogical" in some major European languages. This exploration, admittedly incomplete and tentative, will focus on the time of the Enlightenment as the critical period in history for the emergence of this wording (3). In the final section, we will briefly discuss the temporality and function of this emerging mode of conceiving of and qualifying education (4).

The History of the Concepts within the History of Education

One major historiographical innovation of the second half of the twentieth century was the emergence of a field of research called the history of concepts. Rather German in its origins and theoretical preferences,[6] it has increasingly become an analytical approach appealing to broader geographical and cultural scholarly communities.[7] Still, questions of its differentiation from discourse analysis or historical semantics are not completely resolved, and probably never will be. Yet the specific approach of reconstructing and analyzing the changing constellations of meaning attached to one particular word has advanced significant insights into both the dynamic and the rather slow pace of historical change.[8] Although the original program of historicizing concepts was by no means limited to political concepts, works systematically addressing the history of concepts are either focused mainly on politics,[9] or still emphasize political concepts within a more comprehensive approach.[10]

---

6 Hans Ulrich Gumbrecht, *Dimensionen und Grenzen der Begriffsgeschichte* (Munich: Fink, 2006).
7 Margrit Pernau and Dominic Sachsenmaier, eds., *Global Conceptual History. A Reader* (London et al.: Bloomsbury, 2016); Jani Marjanen, "Undermining Methodological Nationalism: Histoire Croisée of Concepts as Transnational History," in *Transnational Political Spaces: Agents – Structures – Encounters*, ed. Matthias Albert et al. (Frankfurt/M.: Campus, 2009); Hans Erich Bödeker, "Concept – Meaning – Discourse. Begriffsgeschichte reconsidered," in *History of Concepts. Comparative Perspectives*, ed. Iain Hampsher-Monk et al. (Amsterdam: Amsterdam University Press, 1998).
8 For a recent overview, see *Ernst Müller and Falko Schmieder, Begriffsgeschichte und historische Semantik. Ein kritisches Kompendium* (Frankfurt/M.: Suhrkamp, 2016).
9 Javier Fernández Sebastián and Juan Francisco Fuentes, eds., *Diccionario político y social del siglo XIX español* (Madrid: Alianza, 2002).
10 Hans-Jürgen Lüsebrink, Rolf Reichardt, and Eberhard Schmitt, eds., *Handbuch politisch-sozialer Grundbegriffe in Frankreich 1680–1820* (München: Oldenbourg, 1985).

The comprehensive pioneering work in nine volumes, the *Geschichtliche Grundbegriffe*, inspired and co-edited by Reinhard Koselleck (1923–2006), did include some major educational concepts such as "Bildung"[11] und "Pädagogik."[12] These two seminal contributions in the field of the history of concepts shared at least two central insights. First, apart from occasional mentions, particular communities of knowledge consistently used both concepts only from the second half of the eighteenth century onwards. This insight fitted quite well into the one central comprehensive hypothesis of the *Geschichtliche Grundbegriffe*: the existence of the so-called "saddle period" (*Sattelzeit*). This hypothesis affirmed that the most crucial semantic inventions in the political and social vocabulary mostly occurred in the time between 1750 and 1850. These semantic innovations could imply the reinterpretation of old words or the introduction of new ones. Both "Bildung" and "Pädagogik" were neologisms,[13] although older (Bildung) or Latinized (Pädagogik) forms of these words had existed. Second, both analyses confirmed that under a particular word very different meanings had been subsumed. Clearly, these concepts, while showing a flexibility of meaning, appealed to very different communities with different, sometimes even antagonistic interests and intentions.

Probably due to its well-known cultural and idiosyncratic framing, "Bildung" remained the concept that attracted most of the scholarly attention.[14] For instance, it was almost the only concept included in other "historical" dictionaries, for example in the field of philosophy.[15] Moreover, the international interest on this central concept somewhat confirms its special status in the modern educational imagination.[16] Other central modern concepts in the field of educa-

---

11 Rudolf Vierhaus, "Bildung," in *Geschichtliche Grundbegriffe. Historisches Lexikon zur politisch-sozialen Sprache in Deutschland*, ed. Otto Brunner et al. (Stuttgart: Klett-Cotta, 1972).
12 Wilhelm Rössler, "Pädagogik," in *Geschichtliche Grundbegriffe. Historisches Lexikon zur politisch-sozialen Sprache in Deutschland*, ed. Otto Brunner et al. (Stuttgart: Klett-Cotta, 1978).
13 For Bildung see, for instance, how Shaftesbury's considerations about "formation" had been translated: Rebekka Horlacher, *Bildung* (Bern: Haupt/UTB, 2011), 29–30.
14 Georg Bollenbeck, *Bildung und Kultur. Glanz und Elend eines deutschen Deutungsmusters* (Frankfurt/M.: Suhrkamp, 1996). Even Koselleck himself published a rather systematic approach to the concept of Bildung supported by historical approaches. See Reinhart Koselleck, "Zur anthropologischen und semantischen Struktur der Bildung," in *Begriffsgeschichten – Studien zur Semantik und Pragmatik der politischen und sozialen Sprache*, ed. Reinhart Koselleck (Frankfurt/M.: Suhrkamp, 2006).
15 Ernst Liechtenstein, "Bildung," in *Historisches Wörterbuch der Philosophie*, ed. Joachim Ritter (Basel, Stuttgart: Schwabe, 1971).
16 Susan Cocalis, "The Transformation of 'Bildung' from an Image to an Ideal," *Monatshefte* 70 (1987): 399–414; Michel Espagne and Barbara Cassin, "Bildung," in *Vocabulaire Européen des*

tion have rarely been addressed from the perspective of a history of concepts. For instance, specific attention has been paid to concepts like "generation",[17] or "Bildsamkeit"[18] without motivating a strong and diverse historiography. Research in the history of education has also repeatedly addressed the changing constellations of "Childhood" as a crucial concept for modern education.[19] Other prominent concepts, particularly that of "Pedagogy" as a discipline (Pädagogik, Pedagogía, Pédagogie) have been the focus of important works, particularly in the German educational historiography.[20] But these works rarely referred to the history of concepts as a methodological perspective. Although major works have been published in recent decades analyzing a process of "educationalization" of the modern world, something that in other languages is also conveyed as "Pädagogisierung", this analysis has addressed a social dynamic more than the actual concept.[21] It is not unexpected that the rather elusive, less concrete concept of "pedagogic" has rarely been addressed in historical works, if at all. Even works on educational terminology in a more traditional

---

Philosophies – Dictionnaire des Intraduisibles, ed. *Barbara Cassin* (Paris: Le Seuil, 2004); Stefano Fabbri Bertoletti, *Impulso, formazione e organismo. Per una storia del concetto di Bildungstrieb nella cultura tedesca* (Florence: La Colombaria, 1990).

17 Jutta Ecarius, "Semantiken von Generation. Eine Begriffsgeschichte um Bildung und Erziehung," in *Lebensbilder. Streifzüge in Kunst und Pädagogik*, ed. Eckart Liebau (Oberhausen: Athena, 2009).

18 Heinz-Elmar Tenorth, "Bildsamkeit und Behinderung – Anspruch, Wirksamkeit und Selbstdestruktion einer Idee," in *Ideen als gesellschaftliche Gestaltungskraft im Europa der Neuzeit: Beiträge für eine erneuerte Geistesgeschichte*, ed. Lutz Raphael et al. (Munich: Oldenbourg, 2006).

19 Dietrich Benner, "Die Konstitution des Begriffs moderner Kindheit bei Rousseau, im Philanthropismus und in der deutschen Klassik," in *Das Kind in Pietismus und Aufklärung*, ed. Josef N. Neumann et al. (Tübingen: Max-Niemeyer-Verlag, 2000); Marcelo Caruso, "Learning and new sociability: schooling and the concept of the child in the Spanish Enlightenment," *Paedagogica Historica* 48 (2012): 85–98; C. James Sommerville, *The Discovery of Childhood in Puritan England* (Athens: University of Georgia Press, 1992).

20 Winfried Böhm, "Pädagogik," in *Historisches Wörterbuch der Pädagogik*, ed. Dietrich Benner et al. (Weinheim, Basel: Beltz, 2004); Juliane Jacobi, "Der Blick auf das Kind. Zur Entstehung der Pädagogik in den Schulen des Halleschen Waisenhauses," in *Das Kind in Pietismus und Aufklärung*, ed. Josef N. Neumann et al. (Tübingen: Max-Niemeyer-Verlag, 2000); Christa Kersting, *Die Genese der Pädagogik im 18. Jahrhundert. Campes "Allgemeine Revision" im Kontext der neuzeitlichen Wissenschaft* (Weinheim: Deutscher Studien-Verlag, 1992); Fritz Osterwalder, "Die Geburt der deutschsprachigen Pädagogik aus dem Geist des evangelischen Dogmas," *Vierteljahrsschrift für wissenschaftliche Pädagogik* 68 (1992): 426–454.

21 Marc Depaepe, *Between Educationalization and Appropriation: Selected Writings on the History of Modern Educational Systems* (Leuven: Leuven University Press, 2012); Daniel Tröhler, *Pestalozzi and the Educationalization of the World* (New York: palgrave, 2013).

vein are rare.²² This scarce analytical interest contrasts sharply with the frequent and pervasive use of the adjective. This class of words has been largely neglected in historical research, in all probability because an analytical tradition focused on adjective qualifications as conceptual framing is still weak.²³

The Conceptual Character of "Pedagogic"

Does the frequent and differentiated use of the word pedagogic justify its characterization as a concept or, at least, as a conceptual field? After all, the history of concepts as a distinct historiography of education emphasized nouns in its research record.²⁴ Adjectives are not completely absent from historical research. At least, they are also part of research designs more related to historical semantics, strongly associated with historical linguistics.²⁵ But, are adjectives not too dispersed in their use and too imprecise in their meanings to be treated as concepts?

A discussion about the conceptual character of adjectives directs the attention to the fact that even nouns are not concepts per se. Concepts are semantic and not linguistic units. Reinhart Koselleck addressed this difficulty in the introduction to the first volume about political and social vocabulary in German, published in 1972. There, he differentiated between words with a more unified and clear content, possible of definition, and concepts as plurivalent, even ambiguous units of meaning.²⁶ With regard to methodology, Koselleck recommended sticking to the word but cautioned against reducing conceptual content to just the possibilities of the word. A concept can be described as an "abstract synopsis" (*abstrahierende Zusammenschau*) of meaning.²⁷ Normally, concepts merge incompletely with one word, but they have to be produced with words and the

---

22 For the German educational terminology, see Radoslaw Lis, *Der sprachgeschichtliche Wandel der deutschen Schulterminologie als Resultat der Bildungsreformen im 19. Jahrhundert* (Hamburg: Diplomica, 2013); Solmu Nyström, *Die deutsche Schulterminologie in der Periode 1300–1740* (Helsinki: Druckerei der finnischen Literaturgesellschaft, 1915).
23 In some works, the meanings of the "mechanical" and the "organic" in the history of technological discussions in education played a role. See Caruso, *Biopolitik im Klassenzimmer*; Marcelo Caruso, *Geist oder Mechanik. Unterrichtsordnungen als kulturelle Konstruktionen in Preußen, Dänemark (Schleswig-Holstein) und Spanien 1810–1870* (Frankfurt/M.: Peter Lang, 2010).
24 Müller and Schmieder, *Begriffsgeschichte und historische Semantik*, 278.
25 Gerd Fritz, *Historische Semantik* (Stuttgart: Metzler, 1998), 133–147.
26 Reinhart Koselleck, Introduction to *Geschichtliche Grundbegriffe. Historisches Lexikon zur politisch-sozialen Sprache in Deutschland*, ed. Otto Brunner et al. (Stuttgart: Klett-Cotta, 1972), XXII.
27 Dietrich Busse, *Historische Semantik* (Stuttgart: Klett-Cotta, 1987), 83–84.

word conveying the main contents of a given concept remains the leading indicator for conceptual workings. We argue that adjectives may be conceived of as concepts. The possibility of producing a noun out of an adjective – for instance "true" → "truth" – is an indication that adjectives are also capable of abstraction.[28] These abstractions are not normally related to a particular set of objects, but they are precisely abstractions. In this sense, adjectives may also convey abstract, plurivalent, and ambiguous meanings. Although this may suffice for a characterization of the adjective "pedagogic" as a concept or a conceptual field, it does not relieve us of the methodological problems attached to the historical analysis of adjectives.

The semantic field conveyed by "pedagogic" in European languages other than English is considerably broader. In some of them, this adjective is mainly seen as a relational word, meaning that the adjective links with one noun. For instance, a "pedagogic work" (*pädagogisches Werk*) may indicate that this particular work belongs to the discipline of education/pedagogy. But this relational reference may also express that the "work" has been written by an educator (pedagogue). The decision – whether the relational function alludes to the discipline (pedagogy) or to the person (pedagogue) – can only be reasoned contextually. In this first, relational function, adjectives do not characterize; rather they classify something, for instance, as pertaining to the discipline or to the group of professionals of education. But "pedagogic" as an adjective is even more complicated. Pure relational adjectives in languages such as German, Spanish, and French can be put neither in a comparative ("more pedagogic than") or negative form ("not pedagogic"), nor be combined with other adjectives ("pedagogically acceptable").[29] Yet "pedagogic" may also be used in these other forms, sometimes as a plain adjective like in German (*pädagogischer, unpädagogisch, pädagogisch günstig*), sometimes with adverbial and comparative constructions (Spanish: *más pedagógico que, poco pedagógico, pedagógicamente conveniente*; French: *plus pédagogique que, peu pédagogique, pédagogiquement convenable*). These possibilities point at the fact that "pedagogic" in many languages is not only a relational adjective, but also a qualifying one, capable of also communicating characterizations and evaluations of actions, objects, persons, and situations. The plurivalent and ambivalent meanings of this adjective are partly rooted in the oscillating character of this particular word.

---

28 Ingerid Dal and Hans-Werner Eroms, *Kurze deutsche Syntax auf historischer Grundlage*, 4. ed. (Berlin: de Gruyter, 2014), 72.
29 We follow here the characterization in Igor Trost, *Das deutsche Adjektiv: Untersuchungen zur Semantik, Komparation, Wortbildung und Syntax* (Hamburg: Buske, 2006), 15, for the German language.

Throughout history, both groups of meanings – relations and characterizations – are present in the sources. Yet this very brief introduction shows that the emergence of an educational language, in which this kind of relating and characterizing plays a significant role, did not affect all European languages in a similar way or at the same time. In the following section, starting from a research project focused solely on developments in German, we will sketch some very early developments and transitions in German and in other major European languages.

Unearthing "Pedagogic": German, French, and English Developments

The family of words in focus was beyond doubt well-known in the Western tradition. The old Greek word for the slave that accompanied young boys through the streets of the *polis*, charged with their care, had a long history. In the Hellenistic time it expanded its meaning to include free teachers and instructors.[30] And it famously entered classic Christian literature thanks to Clemens of Alexandria's work, Paedagogus.[31] The term was also widely used in printed books in the early modern period both in Latin and vernacular works. Yet this traditional use referred only to the person or group of persons. The use of the adjective "pedagogic" was virtually unknown. In the following, we will only explore the development of this vocabulary in three main languages of Western Europe – English, French, and German – at the very early stage of the emergence of these words and meanings. As a caveat, a systematic inquiry is currently being conducted for the German case. For the other cases, however, the possibilities and shortcomings of the growing entanglement between transnational history and the availability of text-searchable digitized sources applies.[32] Hypotheses, no more and no less, will be advanced. These hypotheses focus rather on the pace and different paths of the emergence of the new vocabulary and do not intend to provide an in-depth analysis of the conveyed meanings.

---

30 Raffaella Cribiore, *Gymnastics of the Mind. Greek Education in Hellenistic and Roman Egypt* (Princeton, Oxford: Princeton University Press, 2001), 47–50.
31 Clemens von Alexandrien, "Paidagogos," in *Des Clemens von Alexandreia ausgewählte Schriften*, ed. Otto Stählin (München: J. Kösel & F. Pustet, 1934), www.unifr.ch/bkv/rtf/bkv198.rtf.
32 Lara Putnam, "The Transnational and the Text-Searchable: Digitized Sources and the Shadows They Cast," *American Historical Review* 121 (2016): 377–402.

Early emergence of the adjective "pädagogisch" is related to the milieus, institutions, and discourse of the German Pietists. The founder of this second wave of stricter piety, Philipp Jacob Spener (1635–1705), spoke of "pädagogische Operas" – meaning educational works – in his famous *Pia Desideria*.[33] Although evidence is still fragmentary, a pattern emerges for this milieu. For instance, the preacher Joachim Lange (1670–1744) in his work *Des Apostolischen Lichts und Rechts* (1729) wrote about "all kind of educational means" (allerhand paedagogische Mittel). Moreover, the leading Pietist of the early eighteenth century, the person who sealed the alliance of this powerful group with the expanding Prussian Kingdom, August Herrmann Francke (1663–1727), named some of his schools in his caritative complex in the city of Halle "Paedagogio" or "Paedagogii Regii."[34] However, the adjective form of pedagogue was still not a common or frequently used word. References to the word are scant and unsystematic.

This situation changes noticeably after 1760. In the context of a growing interest in all things educational and pedagogical, a more frequent use with a major variation of references and meanings becomes evident. This emergence should not be considered in isolation. At that time, the whole field of educational knowledge expanded, and subjects related to education gained momentum and a decidedly public status. A growing body of specialized journals in German became a distinct phenomenon within Western and Central Europe.[35] In this context, the adjective "pedagogic" consistently emerged at the same time as a cautious but clear push for the secularization of the discussion about education took place.[36] A crucial moment in the consolidation of this new kind of wording included the short process, through which one of the most important educational journals of that time came to have their name. Two reputed names of the educational scene in the German Enlightenment, Johann Bernhard Basedow (1724–1790) and Joachim Heinrich Campe (1746–1818), published the *Pädagogische Unterhandlungen* (Educational negotiations) in the city of Dessau between

---

33 Philipp Jacob Spener, *Pia Desidearia oder Herzliches Verlangen nach gottgefälliger Besserung der wahren Evangelischen Kirchen* (Frankfurt/M.: Zunner, Fritgen, 1676), 343.
34 August Herrmann Francke, *Ordnung und Lehrart / Wie selbige in dem Paedagogio zu Glaucha an Halle eingeführet ist* (Halle: Waisenhaus, 1702); August Herrmann Francke, *Kurzer Bericht von der gegenwärtigen Verfassung des PAEDAGOGII REGII zu Glaucha vor Halle aus der vormals schon edirten, nunmehro aber in vielen Stücken nach und nach verbesserten Ordnung und Lehramt herausgezogen und wiederholet* (Halle: Waisenhaus, 1713).
35 Jens Brachmann, *Der pädagogische Diskurs der Sattelzeit. Eine Kommunikationsgeschichte* (Bad Heilbrunn/Obb.: Klinkhardt, 2008).
36 Walter Sparn, "Religiöse und theologische Aspekte der Bildungsgeschichte im Zeitalter der Aufklärung," in *Handbuch der deutschen Bildungsgeschichte*, ed. Notker Hammerstein et al. (Munich: Beck, 2005).

1777 and 1784. There, their innovative elite school with experimental character, the Philanthropinum, provoked both strong support and opposition. In the first issue of the journal, they explained why the new publication had adopted its title. They wrote that they had not the time "to think about these unimportant insignificancies." Without "any further thinking", they decided to name the new journal Pädagogische Unterhandlungen.[37] This episode shows that the use and, to a certain extent, the meaning of the adjective "pedagogic" was consolidated. For this specific group at least, the term was familiar enough that it could easily become the main title of a journal. Further qualitative and quantitative evidence from the 1770s supports this insight.

We should briefly mention one interesting contrasting aspect that shows that lexicography and discursive evidence may sometimes be at odds with one another. We have explained that a certain implicitness attached to the meaning of the adjective "pedagogic" resounded in Campe's and Basedow's decision to use a rather new adjective in the main title of their newly named educational journal. This contrasts with the absence of this word in the main German dictionary of that time, Johann Christoph Adelung's (1732–1805) *Grammatisch-kritisches Wörterbuch der hochdeutschen Mundart* (1774–1786). Even later editions of this work did not include the new adjective. In contrast, in the French context, where the meaning of this adjective was still in the making, it was at least recorded and fixed in the central lexicographic works of the time. This point is a cautionary tale about the differences between encyclopaedical and lexicographical works, on the one hand, and the actual uses of vocabulary and expressions, on the other.

Processes of revision and secularization of educational notions were not only occurring in the German-speaking countries. In France, Spain, the Italian States, England, etc. a sincere interest in all things educational was also expanding. This interest was gradually departing from a singular emphasis on its religious roots and purposes. Were there similar lexical innovations underway? We will only attempt to put together some fragmentary lexicographical and discursive evidence for France and England for the purpose of contrasting the pace and dynamic of relatively quick and consistent developments in German.

One of the earliest uses of the adjective *pédagogique* in French is present in a book about a "perfect friendship" written by one of the most prolific authors of the seventeenth century, the Catholic Bishop Jean-Pierre Camus (1584–1652). The text was about a religious discussion, where two theologians were talking about Lutherans and Calvinists. The more arrogant of the two, "almost mocking the

---

[37] C., "Plan der pädagogischen Unterhandlungen," *Pädagogische Unterhandlungen* 1 (1777): 10.

simplicity" of his interlocutor, asked, "Are these not the same?" He asked this in a "pedagogic and schoolmasterly tone."[38] This shows us a lead that we will willingly follow further: references to the "pedagogic" character of something are quite negative.

This association of negative meaning to the new adjective was not an outlier. Since 1762, the dictionary of the Royal French Academy (4th edition, the first one being from 1692) included the whole semantic complex. *Pédagogie* did not stand for a systematic knowledge, as in later times, but for the task of "instructing and educating children", which is a considerable departure from the simultaneously emerging word in German. The adjective appeared to have neutral connotations only when it "related to the education of children." Yet in the definition of the pedagogue, the institutionalized negative connotation was clear. The pedagogue was a person "who teaches children and takes care of their education." But, the dictionary explicitly cautioned that, "this person is almost always called pedagogue as a way of scorning or mocking him" ("il ne se dit guère que par derision").[39] Against the background of the mostly positive connotations of pädagogisch, pedagógico, pédagogique, we should bear in mind that this negative connotation was by no means a secondary one. We see this negative meaning as a quite dominant one, referring to the person of an educator. Only in very special materials, such as the translation of the dictionary by the English schoolmaster Thomas Dyche (d. 1733), does the term "pedagogic" appear as the usual adjective ("appartient à la Pédagogie"). Having been authored by a schoolmaster, all traces of meaning that related to pedantry and arrogant scholarly tone were conveniently absent in this dictionary.[40]

Certainly, uses that would become dominant in later times were also present. When an author in the *Mercure de France* discussed "questions Elémentaires et Pédagogiques" (sic), he addressed problems of children's learning and discussed books and methods as well.[41] The adjective "pedagogic" repeatedly appeared in

---

[38] "Mon Docteur en riant en vray Monsieur nostre Maistres, & comme se mocquant de ma simplicité, me repartit d'un ton Pédagogique & Magisterial, & n'est-ce pas la mesme chose?", Jean-Pierre Camus, *Le Cléoroste de monseigneur de Belley, vol. 2* (Lyon: A. Chard, 1626), 131.
[39] *Dictionnaire de l'Académie Française*, 4th ed., vol. 2 (Paris: Chez la Veuve de Bernard Brunet, 1762), 334.
[40] Thomas Dyche, *Nouveau dicionnaire universel des arts ete des sciences* (Avignon: Chez la Veuve de Fr. Girard, 1756), 197.
[41] "Suite des Questions Elémentaires et Pédagogiques, tirées de la Biliotheque des Enfans, contenant le Système du Bureau Typographique," *Mercure de France* 2 (1734): 2145. Further indications about a "pedagogical duty" (*devoir pédagogique*) in "Lettre en réponse à celle d'un Principal du College de Province, sur la Méthode de la Version et de la Composition d'une langue en l'autre," *Mercure de France* 1 (1736): 84.

the *Mercure de France* when discussing a technological innovation for teaching: Louis Dumas' (1676–1744) machine for teaching children to read and to write. This machine, called *bureau typographique*, promised an acceleration of learning. The approach tried to apply Lockean ideas of associative and experiential learning.[42] This rather descriptive usage coincided with the meanings recorded in other publications of the time. For instance, Felbiger's travels from Silesia to Berlin were called "mission pédagogique,"[43] and the biography of a professor of the College Royal de France explains that he only took studies in medicine when he was "fatigué des exercices pédagogiques", i.e. teaching.[44]

Although still rare, the adjective was present in some of the main journals and publications in France at the time. This included the famous *Encyclopédie*, where another variation was introduced: the substantive was adopted in the identical form as the adjective. For instance, in the article about the "science de l'homme" la *Paedagogique* was defined as a part of the "art de transmetre," particularly concerned with "the selection of studies and the way of teaching."[45] This is by no means the only case of taking the adjective form for the substantive one. Still, the rather new adjective could not have been used as a matter of course as it was by Basedow and Campe when they christened their new journal in Dessau. For instance, in a book for autodidactic learning discussed in the *Journal encyclopédique* in 1781, the reviewer referred to a "systême pédagogique" and added, "if it is possible to put it like that" ("si l'on peut parler ainsi").[46]

Even though over the course of time more nouns were combined with the adjective "pédagogique", following the main meanings recorded in dictionaries, the negative undertone was still heavily in use even after the French Revolution. Referring to the old order that the Revolution of 1789 had destroyed, the Abbott Nicolas Halma (1755–1828) spoke of "empires pédagogiques" to describe the old types of school and education and associated them with fear, serfdom, intolerance, and the corruption of costumes.[47] In these political discourses the negative and pedantic meaning of "pedagogic" repeatedly merged with evocation of the

---

42 Paola Bertucci, *Artisanal Enlightenment. Science and the Mechanical Arts in Old Regime France* (New Haven/CT: The Yale University Press, 2017).
43 "Allemagne," *Journal de politique et de littérature* 1 (1775).
44 Joseph-François Carrere, *Bibliotheque littéraire, historique et critique de la médecine ancienne et moderne, vol. 1* (Paris: Chez Ruault, 1776), 146.
45 "La Philosophie," in *Encyclopédie, our dictionnaire raisonné des sciences, des arts et des métiers* (Paris: Briasson, David, Le Breton & Durant, 1751), 8.
46 "Moyen de se préserver des erreurs de l'usage danls l'institution de la jeunesse," *Journal encyclopédique* 8 (1781): 215.
47 Nicolas Halma, *De l'éducation* (Bouillon: Trécourt, 1791), 44.

ancien régime. A member of the French National Assembly, Antoine Claire Thibaudeau (1765–1854), adamantly opposed the educational projects advanced by the Jacobins. He did not hesitate to evoke this negative connotation in his published reply against these projects. He summarized the Jacobin project as being "a kind of educational/pedagogic government that is intended to be established here within a republican government; it is about a new kind of clergy that would replace, in a more calamitous way, the ministries of superstition."[48] Even in those fields where the adjective seemed to be related to a more descriptive use, the negative connotation still worked. Commenting on a manual about good companions, the anonymous reviewer emphasized that the successful combination of instruction and amusement was partly due to the fact that the author had avoided "the pedagogic tone, instead adopting that of sentiment and reason."[49]

The persistence of rather negative connotations for all things associated with the pedagogue was also widely present in English. In a French-English dictionary of 1721 we already find that the French word "pedagogie" meant "pedagogy, discipline" and the Pedagogue was "a pedant."[50] Lexicography for the eighteenth century is quite consistent even for the emergence of the adjective. In John Ash's (1724–1779) dictionary – where for pedagogue the definition of "schoolmaster" or "pedant" is given – a new verb "to pedagogue" as in "to teach with the airs of a pedant" emerged together with the adjective "pedagogical", defined as "belonging to a pedagogue, suited to a schoolmaster."[51] Lastly, Samuel Johnson's (1709–1784) dictionary, probably the most influential English dictionary before the Oxford dictionary in the twentieth century, defined "Pedagogue" as someone "who teaches boys; a schoolmaster; a pedant." The adjective "pedagogical" remains "belonging to a schoolmaster" and also the verb "to ped-

---

48 "C'est un gouvernement pédagogique que l'on veut fonder dans un gouvernement républicaine, une nouvelle espèce de clergé qui remplacerait d'une manière funeste encore les ministres de la superstition." Representative Thibaudeau in his opinions on public instruction (1793), quoted in: Hans-Christian Harten, *Elementarschule und Pädagogik in der Französischen Revolution* (München: Oldenbourg, 1990), 44.
49 "(...) Le ton pédagogique pour prendre celui du sentiment et de la raison (...)." "Manuel de la Bonne Compagnie," *Journal typographque et bibliographique* 9 (1805): 43.
50 Abel Boyer, *The Royal dictionary abridge in two parts* (London: Printed for J. and K. Knapton et al., 1728), n.p.
51 John Ash, *The new and complete dictionary of the English language, vol. II* (London: Printed for Edward and Charles Dilly, 1775), n.p.

agogue" – "to teach with superciliousness" – shows a continuity in its definition.[52]

One peculiarity of the English discussion lies in the relatively frequent use of "pedagogy" for theological discussions. At the end of the seventeenth century, discussing controversies around the Ancient Gospel, one theologian cautioned that in judging the Jews "we must always consider the Pedagogy that they were under (...)."[53] In a comparison between the ancient liturgy and the English one following St. James, a "Pedagogy of the Prophets" is mentioned.[54] In a lengthy discussion about the doctrine of sanctification from the 1770s, the Calvinist theologian James Fraser (1700–1769) defined a "pedagogy of the law" attributed to the Mosaic tradition and seen rather as a legal "pedagogy" addressing only the outward aspects of sin.[55] Clearly, "pedagogy" here depicted a kind of discipline, a regime, similar to the definition mentioned in the French-English dictionary.

Both the verb "to pedagogue" and this particular use of "pedagogy" may also have influenced the quite distinctive path of the English word where both the reference to a scholarly discipline and the adjective with positive connotations for many things educational is, if at all, rare. Moreover, the idea of a pedagogue as a schoolmaster "especially, a pedantic narrow-minded teacher"[56] may have blocked a more widespread and positive use of the adjective "pedagogic". The negative undertone of the substantive also affected the related adjective. "Pedagogic", even to the present day, is defined as both something "pertaining to the science or art of teaching" and as something "affected with a conceit of learning."[57]

As a simple additional test for the possible effect of negative meanings of words associated with the pedagogue, Spanish is an interesting case in point. In the first comprehensive dictionary of the Spanish language, the so-called *Diccionario de Autoridades* (1726–1739), the word *pedagogo*, meaning a person "car-

---

[52] Samuel Johnson, *A dictionary of the English language: in which the words are deduced from their originals*, 11th ed. (Edimburgh: Printed for Thom. Brown, R. Ross, and J. Symington, 1797), n.p.
[53] Isaac Chauncy, *Ancient Gospel pleaded, against the other, called The New Law* (London: Printed for H. Barnard, 1693), 162.
[54] *The ancient liturgy of the Church of Jerusalem, being the liturgy of St. James, freed from all latter additions and interpolations* (London: Printed by James Bettenham, 1744), 20.
[55] James Fraser, *The Scripture Doctrine of Sanctification* (Edinburgh: Printed by John Gray, 1774), 93, 174–175, 97–98.
[56] *The New International Webster's Comprehensive Dictionary of the English Language* (Naples/FL: Trident, 1996), 929.
[57] Ibid.

ing and directing a young man", is already present (Vol. V, 1737). As an "extension" of this basic meaning, the Diccionario also uses the word to mean "all those who accompany another one and lead him to the places they choose and tell him what he has to do."[58] Here we do not have a teacher, but clearly a pedantic and rather intrusive person. For a long time, the evolution of a modern educational vocabulary in Spanish largely ignored this family of words. It was only in the middle of the nineteenth century that the emergence of the adjective *pedagógico* obtained a lexicographical basis. In the "lexicography treasure," the *Real Academia Española*, where the major dictionaries of the language are recorded, the first one alluding to "pedagogic" was that of Salvá in 1846. The definition given was "what it pertains to the teaching of children."[59] Whether the emergence of the Spanish adjective was the result of the close relationship between France and Spain in the field of education,[60] or rather a trace of a broader transfer of educational knowledge from Germany,[61] is not easy to assess. But, here again, the negative connotations of "pedagogic" seem to have blocked the further development of a vocabulary about education associated with the figure of the pedagogue.

"Pedagogic": Semantic Legacies and Semantic Openings

This succinct exploration into the emergence of an adjective could not have been conducted in isolation from the family of words attached to it. Specifically, the eighteenth century seems to be the time of the differentiation and more frequent use of this adjective, which is why we referred back to the existing meanings attached to this word group. On the whole, in the knowledge that crucial languag-

---

58 "Diccionario de Autoridades," accessed March 23, 2019, www.rae.es/recursos/diccionarios/diccionarios-anteriores-1726-1996/diccionario-de-autoridades.
59 "Tesoro lexicográfico de la lengua Española," accessed March 23, 2019, http://ntlle.rae.es/ntlle/SrvltGUILoginNtlle.
60 Alfonso Capitán Díaz, "Dos versiones de la presencia francesa en la realidad educativa española de principios del siglo XIX. El informe de instrucción pública. Los catecismos políticos," *Revista española de pedagogía* XXII (1974): 457–468; Juan Francisco Fuentes, "Aproximación al vocabulario socio-político del primer liberalismo español (1792–1823)," in *La imagen de Francia en España (1808–1850)*, ed. Jean-René Aymes et al. (Bilbao: Universidad del Pais vasco, 1997).
61 Marcelo Caruso, "El fin del sensualismo. La pedagogía alemana en el primer normalismo español (1840–1860)," in *La pedagogía alemana en España e Iberoamérica (1810–2010)*, ed. José María Hernández Díaz (Valladolid: Castilla Ediciones, 2011).

es such as Dutch or Italian may also have played a significant role in this story, we can affirm that this adjective only emerged in the vocabularies of many Western European languages in the eighteenth century. "Pedagogic" became a distinctive word with a partially recursive and frequent use in the early Enlightenment – at least for German – before relatively frequent use of it accompanied the increasing interest in education and schooling in the last decades of the century. In other languages, the meanings attached to the new adjective were quite limited and were, if not outright negative, more strongly related to the schoolmaster.

What we learn about these lexical innovations is that semantic legacies may have played a considerable role in this account. For German, we did not find older strongly negative meanings of the word "pedagogic", pointing towards pedantry, a too scholarly tone, or overly infatuated behavior. Indeed, the name Paedagogium for an institution lost some prestige over the course of time. Whereas in the sixteenth century it designated a school attached to or responsible for preparation for university, in later times it stood instead for lower Latin schools, and this provoked many of the most prestigious Latin Schools to adopt the name Gymnasium.[62] Related to a person, it referred sometimes to poor or younger teachers; but it was also the name of teaching persons in a broader, and not subaltern position.[63] These words may have varied in their meaning and the prestige of the persons and institutions they denoted. The relatively consistent use of the term in a negative manner, associated with the word pedantic, was rare in German.

It is possible to hypothesize that, on the one hand, negative connotations in English and French (and maybe in Spanish) have prevented this word from developing as a consistent qualification for situations, persons, objects, and knowledge related to education. In French and Spanish, the adjective "pedagogic" became a powerful element in the vocabulary of education during the nineteenth century, probably mirroring the cultural ascendancy of Germany/Prussia at that time; the English diverging semantic development, where "pedagogic" lacks many of the normative and evaluative components of its French, German, and Spanish counterparts, may also have resulted from the rather strong tradition of a negative meaning associated to the pedagogue.

Yet, if in all cases semantic traditions have played a major role, it should not be surprising that on the other side of the coin are the semantic openings. In particular the German language, in the absence of a consistent tradition of the Pedagogue as a negative figure, began to use this field of meaning in a more pro-

---

62 Nyström, *Die deutsche Schulterminologie*, 19–21, 249–250.
63 Ibid., 113–115.

spective and positive way. This may have facilitated the development of new meanings related to the secularization and the reinterpretation of educational things. This conceptual shift may have found in this word family an empty, or, at least, not negatively biased, semantic field. Meanings associated with the educational revolution looming on the continent found an expression of their newness in this vocabulary and, in so doing, circumvented the limits of the available vocabulary for things educational. In this sense, the fabric of the Enlightenment not only brought about substantial new ideas and representations about schools, learning, and education, but also new forms of naming and characterizing them.

Bibliography

"Allemagne." *Journal de politique et de littérature* 1 (1775): 4.
Ash, John. *The new and complete dictionary of the English language*. Vol. 2. London: Printed for Edward and Charles Dilly, 1775.
Basedow, Johann Bernhard, and Joachim Heinrich Campe. "Plan der pädagogischen Unterhandlungen." *Pädagogische Unterhandlungen* 1 (1777): 3–14.
Benner, Dietrich. "Die Konstitution des Begriffs moderner Kindheit bei Rousseau, im Philanthropismus und in der deutschen Klassik." In *Das Kind in Pietismus und Aufklärung*, edited by Josef N. Neumann and Udo Sträter, 225–244. Tübingen: Max-Niemeyer-Verlag, 2000.
Bertucci, Paola. *Artisanal Enlightenment. Science and the Mechanical Arts in Old Regime France*. New Haven/CT: The Yale University Press, 2017.
Bödeker, Hans Erich. "Concept – Meaning – Discourse. Begriffsgeschichte reconsidered." In *History of Concepts. Comparative Perspectives*, edited by Iain Hampsher-Monk, Karin Tilmans, and Frank van Vree, 51–64. Amsterdam: Amsterdam University Press, 1998.
Böhm, Winfried. "Pädagogik." In *Historisches Wörterbuch der Pädagogik*, edited by Dietrich Benner and Jürgen Oelkers, 750–782. Weinheim, Basel: Beltz, 2004.
Bollenbeck, Georg. *Bildung und Kultur. Glanz und Elend eines deutschen Deutungsmusters*. Frankfurt/M.: Suhrkamp, 1996.
Boyer, Abel. *The Royal dictionary abridge in two parts*. London: Printed for J. and K. Knapton et al., 1728.
Brachmann, Jens. *Der pädagogische Diskurs der Sattelzeit. Eine Kommunikationsgeschichte*. Bad Heilbrunn/Obb.: Klinkhardt, 2008.
Busse, Dietrich. *Historische Semantik*. Stuttgart: Klett-Cotta, 1987.
Camus, Jean-Pierre. *Le Cléoroste de monseigneur de Belley*. Vol. 2. Lyon: A. Chard, 1626.
Capitán Díaz, Alfonso. "Dos versiones de la presencia francesa en la realidad educativa española de principios del siglo XIX. El informe de instrucción pública. Los catecismos políticos." *Revista española de pedagogía* XXII (1974): 457–468.
Carrere, Joseph-François. *Bibliotheque littéraire, historique et critique de la médecine ancienne et moderne*. Vol. 1. Paris: Chez Ruault, 1776.
Caruso, Marcelo. *Biopolitik im Klassenzimmer. Zur Ordnung der Führungspraktiken in den Bayerischen Volksschulen (1869–1918)*. Weinheim, Basel, Berlin: Beltz, 2003.

Caruso, Marcelo. "El fin del sensualismo. La pedagogía alemana en el primer normalismo español (1840–1860)." In *La pedagogía alemana en España e Iberoamérica (1810–2010)*, edited by José María Hernández Díaz, 31–56. Valladolid: Castilla Ediciones, 2011.

Caruso, Marcelo. *Geist oder Mechanik. Unterrichtsordnungen als kulturelle Konstruktionen in Preußen, Dänemark (Schleswig-Holstein) und Spanien 1810–1870*. Frankfurt/M.: Peter Lang, 2010.

Caruso, Marcelo. "Learning and new sociability: Schooling and the concept of the child in the Spanish Enlightenment." *Paedagogica Historica* 48 (2012): 85–98.

Caruso, Marcelo. "Policing validity and reliability. Expertise, data accumulation and data parallelization in Bavaria (1873–1919)." In *The rise of data in education Systems: Collection, visualization and use*, edited by Martin Lawn, 27–39. Oxford: Symposium books, 2013.

Cerrillo, Pedro C., and Ma Victoria Sotomayor. *Censuras y LIJ en el siglo XX (En España y 7 países latinoamericanos)*. Cuenca: Ediciones de la Universidad de Castilla-La Mancha, 2016.

Chauncy, Isaac. *Ancient Gospel pleaded, agist the other, called The New Law*. London: Printed for H. Barnard, 1693.

Clemens von Alexandrien. "Paidagogos." In *Des Clemens von Alexandreia ausgewählte Schriften*, edited by Otto Stählin. Munich: J. Kösel & F. Pustet, 1934.

Cocalis, Susan. "The Transformation of 'Bildung' from an Image to an Ideal." *Monatshefte* 70 (1987): 399–414.

Cribiore, Raffaella. *Gymnastics of the Mind. Greek Education in Hellenistic and Roman Egypt*. Princeton, Oxford: Princeton University Press, 2001.

Dal, Ingerid, and Hans-Werner Eroms. *Kurze deutsche Syntax auf historischer Grundlage*. Berlin: de Gruyter, 2014.

Depaepe, Marc. *Between Educationalization and Appropriation: Selected Writings on the History of Modern Educational Systems*. Leuven: Leuven University Press, 2012.

Depaepe, Marc. "The Ten Commandments of Good Practices in History of Education Research." *Zeitschrift für pädagogische Historiographie* 16 (2010): 31–34.

Dictionnaire de l'Académie Française. 4th ed. Vol. 2. Paris: Chez la Veuve de Bernard Brunet, 1762.

Dyche, Thomas. *Nouveau dictionnaire universel des arts ete des sciences*. Avignon: Chez la Veuve de Fr. Girard, 1756.

Ecarius, Jutta. "Semantiken von Generation. Eine Begriffsgeschichte um Bildung und Erziehung." In *Lebensbilder. Streifzüge in Kunst und Pädagogik*, edited by Eckart Liebau, 111–129. Oberhausen: Athena, 2009.

Espagne, Michel, and Barbara Cassin. "Bildung." In *Vocabulaire Européen des Philosophies – Dictionnaire des Intraduisibles*, edited by Barbara Cassin, 195–204. Paris: Le Seuil, 2004.

Fabbri Bertoletti, Stefano. *Impulso, formazione e organismo. Per una storia del concetto di Bildungstrieb nella cultura tedesca*. Florence: La Colombaria, 1990.

Fernández Sebastián, Javier, and Juan Francisco Fuentes, eds. *Diccionario político y social del siglo XIX español*. Madrid: Alianza, 2002.

Francke, August Herrmann. *Kurzer Bericht von der gegenwärtigen Verfassung des PAEDAGOGII REGII zu Glaucha vor Halle aus der vormals schon edirten, nunmehro aber in vielen*

Stücken nach und nach verbesserten Ordnung und Lehramt herausgezogen und wiederholet. Halle: Waisenhaus, 1713.

Francke, August Herrmann. *Ordnung und Lehrart / Wie selbige in dem Paedagogio zu Glaucha an Halle eingeführet ist*. Halle: Waisenhaus, 1702.

Fraser, James. *The Scripture Doctrine of Sanctification*. Edinburgh: Printed by John Gray, 1774.

Fritz, Gerd. *Historische Semantik*. Stuttgart: Metzler, 1998.

Fuentes, Juan Francisco. "Aproximación al vocabulario socio-político del primer liberalismo español (1792–1823)." In *La imagen de Francia en España (1808–1850)*, edited by Jean-René Aymes and Javier Fernández Sebastián, 51–62. Bilbao: Universidad del Pais vasco, 1997.

Geiss, Michael. *Der Pädagogenstaat. Behördenkommunikation und Organisationspraxis in der badischen Unterrichtsverwaltung, 1860–1912*. Bielefeld: transcript, 2014.

Gumbrecht, Hans Ulrich. *Dimensionen und Grenzen der Begriffsgeschichte*. Munich: Fink, 2006.

Halma, Nicolas. *De l'éducation*. Bouillon: Trécourt, 1791.

Harten, Hans-Christian. *Elementarschule und Pädagogik in der Französischen Revolution*. Munich: Oldenbourg, 1990.

Horlacher, Rebekka. *Bildung*. Bern: Haupt/UTB, 2011.

Jacobi, Juliane. "Der Blick auf das Kind. Zur Entstehung der Pädagogik in den Schulen des Halleschen Waisenhauses." In *Das Kind in Pietismus und Aufklärung*, edited by Josef N. Neumann and Udo Sträter, 47–60. Tübingen: Max-Niemeyer-Verlag, 2000.

Johnson, Samuel. *A dictionary of the English language: in which the words are deduced from their originals*. 11th ed. Edinburgh: Printed for Thom. Brown, R. Ross, and J. Symington, 1797.

Kersting, Christa. *Die Genese der Pädagogik im 18. Jahrhundert. Campes "Allgemeine Revision" im Kontext der neuzeitlichen Wissenschaft*. Weinheim: Deutscher Studien-Verlag, 1992.

Koselleck, Reinhart. Introduction to *Geschichtliche Grundbegriffe. Historisches Lexikon zur politisch-sozialen Sprache in Deutschland*, edited by Otto Brunner, Werner Conze, and Reinhart Koselleck, XIII–XXVIII. Stuttgart: Klett-Cotta, 1972.

Koselleck, Reinhart. "Zur anthropologischen und semantischen Struktur der Bildung." In *Begriffsgeschichten – Studien zur Semantik und Pragmatik der politischen und sozialen Sprache*, edited by Reinhart Koselleck, 105–158. Frankfurt/M.: Suhrkamp, 2006.

"La Philosophie." In *Encyclopédie, our dictionnaire raisonné des sciences, des arts et des métiers*, 8–10. Paris: Briasson, David, Le Breton & Durant, 1751.

"Lettre en réponse à celle d'un Principal du College de Province, sur la Méthode de la Version et de la Composition d'une langue en l'autre." *Mercure de France* 1 (1736): 81–94.

Liechtenstein, Ernst. "Bildung." In *Historisches Wörterbuch der Philosophie*, edited by Joachim Ritter, 921–937. Basel, Stuttgart: Schwabe, 1971.

Lis, Radoslaw. *Der sprachgeschichtliche Wandel der deutschen Schulterminologie als Resultat der Bildungsreformen im 19. Jahrhundert*. Hamburg: Diplomica, 2013.

Lüsebrink, Hans-Jürgen, Rolf Reichardt, and Eberhard Schmitt, eds. *Handbuch politisch-sozialer Grundbegriffe in Frankreich 1680–1820*. München: Oldenbourg, 1985.

"Manuel de la Bonne Compagnie." *Journal typographique et bibliographique* 9 (1805): 43.

Marjanen, Jani. "Undermining Methodological Nationalism: *Histoire Croisée* of Concepts as Transnational History." In *Transnational Political Spaces: Agents – Structures – Encounters*, edited by Matthias Albert, Gesa Bluhm, Jan Helmig, Andreas Leutzsch, and Jochen Walter, 239–263. Frankfurt/M.: Campus, 2009.

"Moyen de se préserver des erreurs de l'usage danls l'institution de la jeunesse." *Journal encyclopédique* 8 (1781): 210–219.

Müller, Ernst, and Falko Schmieder. *Begriffsgeschichte und historische Semantik. Ein kritisches Kompendium*. Frankfurt/M.: Suhrkamp, 2016.

Nyström, Solmu. *Die deutsche Schulterminologie in der Periode 1300–1740*. Helsinki: Druckerei der finnischen Literaturgesellschaft, 1915.

Osterwalder, Fritz. "Die Geburt der deutschsprachigen Pädagogik aus dem Geist des evangelischen Dogmas." *Vierteljahrsschrift für wissenschaftliche Pädagogik* 68 (1992): 426–454.

Pernau, Margrit, and Dominic Sachsenmaier, eds. *Global Conceptual History. A Reader*. London et al.: Bloomsbury, 2016.

Putnam, Lara. "The Transnational and the Text-Searchable: Digitized Sources and the Shadows They Cast." *American Historical Review* 121 (2016): 377–402.

Rössler, Wilhelm. "Pädagogik." In *Geschichtliche Grundbegriffe. Historisches Lexikon zur politisch-sozialen Sprache in Deutschland*, edited by Otto Brunner, Werner Conze, and Reinhart Koselleck, 623–647. Stuttgart: Klett-Cotta, 1978.

Sommerville, C. James. *The Discovery of Childhood in Puritan England*. Athens: University of Georgia Press, 1992.

Sparn, Walter. "Religiöse und theologische Aspekte der Bildungsgeschichte im Zeitalter der Aufklärung." In *Handbuch der deutschen Bildungsgeschichte*, edited by Notker Hammerstein and Ulrich Herrmann, 134–168. München: Beck, 2005.

Spener, Philipp Jacob. *Pia Desidearia oder Herzliches Verlangen nach gottgefälliger Besserung der wahren Evangelischen Kirchen*. Frankfurt/M.: Zunner, Fritgen, 1676.

"Suite des Questions Elémentaires et Pédagogiques, tirées de la Biliotheque des Enfans, contenant le Systême du Bureau Typographique." *Mercure de France* 2 (1734): 2145–2152.

Tenorth, Heinz-Elmar. "Bildsamkeit und Behinderung – Anspruch, Wirksamkeit und Selbstdestruktion einer Idee." In *Ideen als gesellschaftliche Gestaltungskraft im Europa der Neuzeit: Beiträge für eine erneuerte Geistesgeschichte*, edited by Lutz Raphael and Heinz-Elmar Tenorth, 497–520. Munich: Oldenbourg, 2006.

The ancient liturgy of the Church of Jerusalem, being the liturgy of St. James, freed from all latter additions and interpolations. London: Printed by James Bettenham, 1744.

The New International Webster's Comprehensive Dictionary of the English Language. Naples/FL: Trident, 1996.

Tröhler, Daniel. *Pestalozzi and the Educationalization of the World*. New York: Palgrave, 2013.

Trost, Igor. *Das deutsche Adjektiv: Untersuchungen zur Semantik, Komparation, Wortbildung und Syntax*. Hamburg: Buske, 2006.

Vierhaus, Rudolf. "Bildung." In *Geschichtliche Grundbegriffe. Historisches Lexikon zur politisch-sozialen Sprache in Deutschland*, edited by Otto Brunner, Werner Conze, and Reinhart Koselleck, 508–551. Stuttgart: Klett-Cotta, 1972.

4 Walking the Line: The Attraction of Psychology and Medicine in Educational Theory and Practice

Section editor: Angelo Van Gorp

Jürgen Oelkers (University of Zürich, Switzerland)
From Herbart to Dewey: On the Historical Irresistibility of Learning Psychology

Abstract: Since ancient times, the term "learning" has been closely connected to the tasks of education without much philosophical consideration, with the exception of Francis Bacòn. At the beginning of modern educational theory, the term has also led a shadowy existence, which can be seen, for example, in Herbart's pedagogy and philosophy. This essay thus addresses the question as of how – not even 50 years after Herbart's death – "learning" became a focus of psychological enquiry, and why it became irresistible for educational theory.

Keywords: teaching; learning; problem-solving; behaviorism

Introduction

In modern psychology and educational theory, "learning" is considered to be so fundamental that recently even the history of philosophy could be interpreted as a "learning process" without any further consideration of Platonic ideas, human nature or the Protestant spirit. Philosophers simply learn like everybody, and this is not what differentiates them, but rather what they learn and what they accept as a problem.[1] Learning is often understood as cognitive "problem solving". Learning is driven by problems that trigger the search for solutions without ever reaching a final end. Whatever the solutions may be, they can only persuade, be developed or rejected. A "solution" does not mean that the problem itself disappears; it can only be placated, calmed down or placed into the background, which then suggests new learning. But, how did cognitive learning psychology become so irresistible that it is hardly challenged anymore? And, how was it able to free itself from the claim that it is based on nothing more than crude behaviorism, which would surely not have earned it any philosophical dignity?

Both questions refer to an interdisciplinary history, which does not start with behaviorism, but rather with its decisive introduction into psychology. It dealt with the question of what psychology should be following the success of phys-

---

[1] Jürgen Habermas, *Auch eine Geschichte der Philosophie, Band I/II* (Berlin: Suhrkamp Verlag, 2019).

iology. The description of the change of "behavior" requires no ψυχή (psyche as the Greek breath of life) and thus the question was what will be left of psychology without psyche or the human soul and the inner faculties of man. During the scientific nineteenth century, "learning" had no initial importance in and of itself, and thus was not represented as a basic term in any contemporary branch of psychology. A key reason was that "learning" was neither related to "thinking" nor associated with "development." Both of these notions would have had to reference children, but in the nineteenth century, psychology did not pay much attention to children and how they learn.

One might expect that this did not apply to pedagogy, which is, of course, concerned with the education and development of children. But, even in one of the most elaborate educational theories of the nineteenth century, put forward by philosopher Johann Friedrich Herbart (1776–1841), there is no mention of learning as a basic human skill, and development is only briefly touched upon without any categorical acuity. This was not an anomaly, but can also be seen through comparison. In many regards, Friedrich Eduard Beneke (1798–1854) was Herbart's opponent and rival, and worked on similar topics. However, in the 1877 fourth edition of Beneke's *Lehrbuch der Psychologie als Naturwissenschaft* (Textbook of Psychology as a Science), edited by Johann Gottlieb Dressler,[2] there is no reference to learning or problem solving. The same applies to Herbart's own *Lehrbuch zur Psychologie* (Textbook of Psychology), published in 1834 in its second edition. In addition, there is no place for the category of learning in scientific psychology for one of his other critics, Theodor Waitz (1849), although there the human "course of development" was emphasized, albeit subject to laws of nature and not to learning processes.[3]

There were no attempts yet made to discover any laws of learning, as later on in behaviorism. "Psychology" was the study of the psyche of adults, which presupposed an inner space with which – according to post-Christian versions – substances, forces or faculties were associated. In practice, these were faced with experiences, but they did not, in the modern sense, "learn"; that is, they did not cause any change between two points in time or were themselves changeable. In its outlines, the psyche could only be constant. In this sense, it could only be an object of "influence," i.e. an external factor known as "educa-

---

[2] Eduard Beneke, *Lehrbuch der Psychologie als Naturwissenschaft. Vierte Auflage. Neu bearbeitet und mit einem Anhange über Beneke's sämmtliche Schriften versehen von Johann Gottlieb Dressler* (Berlin: Ernst Siegfried Mittler und Sohn, 1877). Theologian Johann Gottlieb Dressler (1799–1867) was Director of the *evangelisches Landständisches Seminar Bautzen* from 1831 to 1858.
[3] Theodor Waitz, *Lehrbuch der Psychologie als Naturwissenschaft* (Braunschweig: Friedrich Vieweg und Sohn, 1849), 12.

tion." If a psyche is flexible, that is, if it constructs itself and is in a state of constant change, and can thus absorb or reject what it achieves, then, presumably, Herbart's problem was the definition of education, though this did not lead to a psychology of learning.

Herbart's Pedagogy and Philosophy

Herbart presented the final version of his pedagogy in the second edition of *Umriss pädagogischer Vorlesungen* (Outlines of Educational Doctrines).[4] The outlines begin with a setting: pedagogy has one and only one "basic concept," namely the "plasticity of the pupil." This does not refer simply to "plasticity" in the sense of organic life, but to the "plasticity of the will to be moral."[5] Plasticity itself represents the "transition from uncertainty to stability," and this applies to children who must first acquire internal stability, while "[t]he stability of adults continues to develop and becomes unattainable for the educator."[6] However, pedagogy must not assume any "undefined plasticity" in the child; that is, no arbitrary influence of the educator as is the case in sensualism.

Psychology – that of Herbart – "will prevent this error." A clear boundary is drawn in the prevention of this error: "The plasticity of the child is limited by their individuality. The determinability of education is furthermore constrained by the conditions of place and time."[7] The concept of "individuality" is not further elucidated, but the child has always been considered to be not determined and formable at the same time. As a science, pedagogy should "depend" on practical philosophy and psychology; the first shows the aim of education, the other shows the way, the means, and the obstacles.[8] This is explained as follows: "Herein also lies the dependence of pedagogy on experience, in the sense that in part, practical philosophy already assimilates the application to experience, and

---

4 Johann Friedrich Herbart, *Allgemeine Metaphsyik, nebst den Anfängen der philosophischen Naturlehre. Zweyter systematischer Theil* (Königsberg: In Commission bei August Wilhelm Unzer, 1829), 1. English translation: John Frederick Herbart, *Outlines of Educational Doctrine*, transl. Alexis F. Lange; annot. Charles de Garmo (New York/London: The Macmillan Company, 1904).
5 Herbart, *Outlines of Educational Doctrine*, 1: "Plasticity, or educability." Not in the German original.
6 Herbart, *Outlines of Educational Doctrine*, 3.
7 Herbart, *Outlines of Educational Doctrine*, 2.
8 Herbart, *Outlines of Educational Doctrine*, 1.

in part that psychology is not merely grounded in metaphysics, but rather in the experience correctly understood by metaphysics."⁹

Herbart did not envisage scientific disciplines with different methods and approaches, but rather his own theories. The *Allgemeine praktische Philosophie* (General Practical Philosophy) was published in 1808, the first edition of the *Lehrbuch zur Psychologie* (Textbook of Psychology) was released in 1816, followed by the publication of the two-volume *Allgemeine Metaphysik* (General Metaphysics) (1828/1829). The *Umriss* on the pedagogic lectures presumes the basic assumptions of these works, though it does not represent a derivation. This is primarily due to the way in which Herbart arrived at his pedagogy. "Plasticity" was not yet the single basic concept of pedagogy in the *Allgemeine Pädagogik* (General Pedagogy) of 1806, but only became this following the completion of the *Metaphysik*, though only in the sense of an organic dimension that comprises all of life and thus also that of the child.

Herbart considered metaphysics to be the study of the link between the concepts in relation to experience and thus as the one fundamental science in the Aristotelian sense. Herbart presented his first "Introduction to Metaphysics" in 1813, in the first edition of his *Lehrbuch zur Einleitung in die Philosophie* (Textbook on the Introduction to Philosophy). Here, there is already mention of the "inner education" of the psyche, which can be transferred to all beings and which is based on the "irritability of the organism."[10] In its systematic parts, Herbart's *Allgemeine Metaphysik* comprises five sections: methodology; ontology, or the nature of being; *synechology*, or the assessment of space and time; furthermore *eidology*, or the possibility of knowledge; and finally, "outlines of natural philosophy."[11]

In his natural philosophy, Herbart discussed the "plasticity of matter."[12] "Matter" was previously generally understood to be a "real being," which preserves itself and is held together by its own forces.[13] These two forces are "attraction" and "repulsion."[14] According to Herbart, there were two principles for this. The first one briefly states that "[a]ll matter is necessarily elastic."[15] The second principle is somewhat more detailed: all matter is based on the fact that "the ex-

---

9 Herbart, *Outlines of Educational Doctrine*, 2.
10 Johan Friedrich Herbart, *Lehrbuch zur Einleitung in die Philosophie* (Königsberg: Bey August Wilhelm Unzer, 1813), 165.
11 Herbart, *Allgemeine Metaphsyik*.
12 Herbart, *Allgemeine* Metaphsyik, 482–498.
13 Herbart, *Allgemeine* Metaphsyik, 273–274.
14 Herbart, *Allgemeine* Metaphsyik, 276.
15 Herbart, *Allgemeine* Metaphsyik, 279. Letter-spacing in the text is omitted.

ternal state must conform to the internal state, in order to correspond as closely as possible hereto."[16] "Internal education" occurs "in passage through a membrane" or a compression,[17] depending on the "surrounding medium" (the environment), which can excite or inhibit inner growth. An "internally growing body" can be resistant or flexible vis-à-vis the exterior; in the case of flexibility, however, the "whole peculiarity" of the body is never affected.[18]

"Assimilation" refers to the flexibility, and "irritability" to the resistance of growth. A third system, known as "sensitivity," acts as a mediator between these two systems, and ensures "manifold impressions," to the extent that it is not prevented from doing so by the self-preservation of elements, the uniformity of affection or sensation denial.[19] Within the meaning of these terms, "plasticity" represents the foundation of all matter and every life form. But, with regard to the education of children, this merely infers that they are "plastic" in the sense of *bildsam* (educable). Herbart never referred to children or "pupils" of education (*Zöglinge*) as "material", and never presented his own psychology of children.

Central categories used in pedagogy can be found neither in Herbart's metaphysics nor previously in psychology and practical philosophy. These are "local terms" (*Einheimische Begriffe*), that is, terms he used only in education theories. The theoretical framework, however, allows for a link to be established, as can be shown with regard to psychology. Herbart's psychology differentiated itself from its predecessors by the assumption of flexible ideas (*Vorstellungen*) that are acquired and consolidated. The aim of psychology was to explain how this occurs without using the concept of "learning." This applies to the entire Herbart school of thought, including where psychology is offered "according to a genetic method,"[20] which could still be clearly delineated from the rapidly developing discipline of physiology.

In the second volume of Herbart's *Psychologie als Wissenschaft* (Psychology as a Science) it is stated: "The long time of childhood alone (makes) regular ed-

---

16 Herbart, *Allgemeine* Metaphsyik, 483.
17 Herbart, *Allgemeine* Metaphsyik, 491.
18 Herbart, *Allgemeine* Metaphsyik, 492.
19 Herbart, *Allgemeine* Metaphsyik, 496.
20 Wilhelm Volkmann Ritter von Volkmar, *Lehrbuch der Psychologie vom Standpunkte des Realismus und nach genetischer Methode. Des Grundrisses der Psychologie zweite sehr vermehrte Auflage. Erster Band* (Cöthen: Verlag von Otto Schulze, 1875).

ucation possible."²¹ Learning appears in this psychology as a descriptive term, but is not central to the theory. For Herbart's pedagogy, the question of how the stability of will can be achieved through education is decisive. No being, including the psyche, can "contain an original diversity of predispositions."²² The perception of our own conditions and ideas is not based on a "particular disposition," but must "like all else" first come into being in the psyche, and it reaches so far and not further as how it has become.²³ That which "comes into being" are ideas that form solid masses, yet which are also constantly enriched.

Consequently, the "inner apperception" is the psychic mechanism of plasticity, which is triggered by attention, willful or not, i.e. the ability of "generating growth of the imagination."²⁴ Masses of ideas effect apperception; the more structured mass there is, the better apperception will be. "In earlier years of childhood" masses of ideas "have not yet been formed; thus, the simplest, rawest mechanism of hardly acquired ideas is left to its own devices." For the young child "there is no thread available" on which to raise the "accidental excitements" of the yet existing ideas.²⁵ Only a lengthy childhood can change this. Herbart speaks of a "complexion," which "continuously receives new additions,"²⁶ i.e. it must enrich itself, "[f]or there is always something new to see, to hear and to learn; and everything that has been seen, heard and learned is added to the supply of images" and ideas, which have their place in the interior, in opposition to all on the exterior.²⁷

"Learning" is not further specified. What has to be explained is the stability acquired during the educational process. Man views his own self as a "complexion," and the one requirement that stands out above all others is "that this self is capable of imagination, knowledge and perception; and the predominance of this requirement always grows alongside educational progress." Yet the mass of inner perceptions does not grow "in direct proportion to the mass of ideas of one's own actions,"²⁸ that is, it does not depend on busyness (*Geschäftigkeit*), but rather aims at self-awareness in a state of "peaceful existence."²⁹ On the

---

21 Johann Friedrich Herbart, *Psychologie als Wissenschaft, neu gegründet auf Erfahrung, Metaphysik, und Mathematik. Zweyter, analytischer Theil* (Königsberg: In Commission bey August Wilhelm Unzer, 1825), 237.
22 Herbart, *Psychologie als Wissenschaft*, 210.
23 Herbart, *Psychologie als Wissenschaft*, 211.
24 Herbart, *Psychologie als Wissenschaft*, 223–224.
25 Herbart, *Psychologie als Wissenschaft*, 221.
26 Herbart, *Psychologie als Wissenschaft*, 273.
27 Herbart, *Psychologie als Wissenschaft*, 274.
28 Herbart, *Psychologie als Wissenschaft*, 274.
29 Herbart, *Psychologie als Wissenschaft*, 247, 275.

other hand, the self or the I is always in company, and here, the I will obtain "a different shade."[30] For Herbart, the I was considered to be "immediate known and looked through," but in company, it is more of "a wonderful riddle": "Even for a child, others are constant riddles; he asks them as often as he may. He is also asked, and realizes all too well that he can conceal things (...). Thus, in comparison to the other, the I is known, autonomous, and whole."[31]

However, it is not stable in society, because society makes something out of people. It subjects them to the "opinions and prejudices" and offers them images of that to which they should comply. The ego as a "complexion" is thus highly changeable, and is not, strictly speaking, "the same at any moment." The complexion is also never complete, "because it is subject to a fair amount of inconsistency."[32] The will to be moral, by contrast, must attain stability and must also be able to take a stand against society if education is to be successful. Education must utilize plasticity for its own purposes, yet it is not the task of pedagogy to show – in terms of a general theory – how this stability comes about and also how it can be gained, but rather that of psychology. It is stated here that "the general will must come about in a similar way as general thought." Many similar ideas that are in a "state of desire" (*Begehren*) must become "fused," and then this fusion must "be specified and limited by means of judgement." The aim was to let "persistent maxims" arise.[33]

Aesthetic judgements are used to accomplish this.[34] The listener must create morality within themselves with full evidence, and does not merely follow the categorical imperative, as claimed by Kant.[35] The moral maxims must acquire inner authority and must, before all other maxims, "be elevated to the highest level before they can be revered as strict laws." If they have attained this level, they are no longer a matter of choice, but rather acquire an "enduring" apperceptive position and are transformed "into the permanent observer of everything else that stirs within the consciousness." By achieving a "fixed fusion with self-awareness," they become "characteristics of a personality" and serve to provide the inner sense with "its real, permanent foundation." Herbart added: "The question of how moral maxims can achieve this is certainly the most important

---

30 Herbart, *Psychologie als Wissenschaft*, 284.
31 Herbart, *Psychologie als Wissenschaft*, 284–285.
32 Herbart, *Psychologie als Wissenschaft*, 284–285.
33 Herbart, *Psychologie als Wissenschaft*, 409.
34 Herbart, *Psychologie als Wissenschaft*, 414.
35 Herbart, *Psychologie als Wissenschaft*, 416.

in all of psychology."³⁶ The "how," however, was not answered in more detail in psychology, but rather relegated to pedagogy.³⁷

Here, the formation of character was a matter of *Zucht* (guidance),³⁸ indirectly through teaching and directly through influencing the mind. It remained open, however, how exactly "calm-clear, firm and specific judgement" developed,³⁹ and the "aesthetic force of moral prudence" did not go beyond what is later set forth in psychology.⁴⁰ This leaves disciplinary measures.⁴¹ Here, guidance is recommended using pleasure and displeasure, which comes close to what is later assigned to behaviorism. Pleasure is triggered by stimulation; displeasure is generated by pressure: "A particular act of stimulation or pressure, which is motivated by a particular pupil action, and should be viewed as the corresponding response, is called reward, or punishment."⁴² This depends on the "emphasis of guidance" and also on the "childish belief in the benevolent intention and power of the educator."⁴³ Discipline in the sense of guidance only occurs to the extent that "an inner experience can coax the subject to enjoy it." To put it differently: the "power of discipline" only goes so far as "the forthcoming insight of the pupil."⁴⁴ If this was lacking, there was no positive effect.

This, however, had to be avoided. The means of education should correspond to the moral aims, and instruction should even be judged by "whether it makes people better or worse."⁴⁵ This was by no means guaranteed and was even less likely, because successful education – not discipline in the sense of repression – could only be an art in combination with "the finest spirit of observation" and practiced in "the closest adherence to the individual."⁴⁶ If education was to be organized, it should be done as a communal service similar to medi-

---

36 Herbart, *Psychologie als Wissenschaft*, 240. Letter-spacing in the text is omitted.
37 Herbart, *Psychologie als Wissenschaft*, 425.
38 *Zucht* is a central term in Herbart's pedagogy, which is hard to translate. It is not "discipline" in the sense of repression, but implies to form the character in a way of direct guidance. Johann Friedrich Herbart, *Allgemeine Pädagogik aus dem Zweck der Erziehung abgeleitet* (Göttingen: Bey Johann Gottfried Röwer, 1806), 379.
39 Herbart, *Allgemeine Pädagogik*, 316. Letter-spacing in the text is omitted.
40 Herbart, *Allgemeine Pädagogik*, 321.
41 Herbart, *Allgemeine Pädagogik*, 385–410.
42 Herbart, *Allgemeine Pädagogik*, 396. Letter-spacing in the text is omitted.
43 Herbart, *Allgemeine Pädagogik*, 391–392.
44 Herbart, *Allgemeine Pädagogik*, 391.
45 Johann Friedrich Herbart, *Umriss pädagogischer Vorlesungen. Zweyte vermehrte Ausgabe* (Göttingen: Druck und Verlag der Dieterichschen Buchhandlung, 1841), 36.
46 Johann Friedrich Herbart, *Pädagogische Schriften in chronologischer Reihenfolge herausgegeben von Otto Willmann. Zweiter Band* (Leipzig: Verlag von Otto Voss, 1875), 42.

cine,⁴⁷ but not as a large-scale state system with binding standards. As such, the technological use of pedagogy and psychology was precluded. The "mechanics of the mind" should be regarded purely in descriptive terms and not as the foundation for a methodological management of instruction.⁴⁸

In every lesson, instruction had to presume "the compliance of children."⁴⁹ If "learning hurts," then one could conclude physical resistance against mental activity.⁵⁰ On the other hand there exists a popular "healing method" for "every mistake by pupils," which was thought to work like a prescription but did not require medicine and was therefore only popular.⁵¹ This could only be remedied if the "old psychology" was overcome and the new psychology – his – would be accepted.⁵² At the end of the nineteenth century, however, it was Herbart's teachings of increasing and decreasing masses of ideas and their mathematical calculations themselves that seemed to belong to old psychology. From there, there was no route to a psychology of learning, at least not a direct one.

The "New" Psychology

Herbert Spencer's (1820–1903) influential *Principles of Psychology* were not yet concerned with "learning." Psychology referred to the link between inner and external relations; it was unclear how that should happen, and what "inner relations" were, which of course would assume a category such as the "mind" or an inner space. The basic process of psychology was simply stated like this: "A relation in the environment rises into co-ordinate importance with a relation in the organism."⁵³ "Learning" only became a fundamental category within psychology when experimental methods were established and physiology became a fundamental science. This helped shape the relationship between stimulus and response that was used by early behaviorists in the theory of learning. Herbart's "cycle of teaching and learning" was no longer authoritative.⁵⁴ Put differently:

---

47 Herbart, *Pädagogische Schriften*, 42–47.
48 Johann Friedrich Herbart, *Psychologie als Wissenschaft, neu gegründet auf Erfahrung, Metaphysik, und Mathematik. Erster, synthetischer Theil* (Königsberg: In Commission bey August Wilhelm Unzer, 1824), third section.
49 Herbart, *Pädagogische Schriften*, 335.
50 Herbart, *Pädagogische Schriften*, 337.
51 Herbart, *Pädagogische Schriften*, 343.
52 Herbart, *Pädagogische Schriften*, 354.
53 Herbert Spencer, *The Principles of Psychology. Vol. I* (New York: D. Appleton and Company, 1873), 132.
54 Herbart, *Pädagogische Schriften*, 396.

learning became independent of instruction, and psychology became independent of morality.

The history of the theory of learning is older than physiology and behaviorism. It has ancient roots, and its modern version begins with Francis Bacon's *The Advancement of Learning* (1605).[55] The question was as to how knowledge could be improved and acquire practical use. As such, "learning" was synonymous with "research" or "inquiry". Bacon was interested in "distempers of learning,"[56] in other words false attitudes and methods, which led to a kind of learning that only served the imagination and ended in magic, or learning that culminated in disputes over words, or learning that merely served the affectations of authors. These forms of learning were to be replaced by experimental methods and a relationship between trial and error, as is known from legal proceedings. For this reason alone, "learning" was not understood as psychological and was thus neither ability nor disposition or the movement of ideas.

In the English association psychology of the eighteenth century, the term "learning" first appeared in the sense of connections, without already distinguishing between stimulus and response. The basic movements of experience were "pleasure" and "pain," i.e. the pursuit of pleasure and the avoidance of pain. This would explain children's literacy, for example.[57] In Friedrich Schleiermacher's (1768–1834) psychology,[58] pleasure and pain were the "opposing moments of affections of self-awareness," which withstand one another so that one of the two must decrease while the other increases. In the religious feelings of men, for which Schleiermacher's theology is famous, the contrast between pleasure and pain disappeared entirely "in submission to the absolute unit of life."[59] These teachings were invalidated the moment the concept of "soul" lost its Christian reference, which in the mid-nineteenth century was still self-evident in German psychology.[60] What was established instead was a psychology without ψυχή, i.e. an empirical understanding of learning and behavior that should

---

[55] Later extended to *De augmentis scientiarum* (1623).
[56] Francis Bacon, *The Tvvoo Bookes of the Proficience and Aduancement of Learning, Diuine and Humane* (London: Printed for Henrie Tomes, 1605), 17.
[57] Joseph Priestley, *Hartley's Theory of the Human Mind on the Principles of the Association of Ideas; with Essays Relating to the Subject of it* (London: Printed for J. Johnson, 1775), 152–155.
[58] Friedrich Schleiermacher, *Sämmtliche Werke. Dritte Abtheilung. Zur Philosophie. Sechster Band: Psychologie. Aus Schleiermacher's handschriftlichem Nachlasse und nachgeschriebenen Vorlesungen herausgegeben von Leopold George* (Berlin: G. Reimer, 1862), 187.
[59] Schleiermacher, *Sämmtliche Werke*, 461.
[60] Leopold George, *Lehrbuch der Psychologie* (Berlin: Verlag von Georg Reimer, 1854). Leopold George (1811–1873) was a direct pupil of Schleiermacher. George was a grammar school teacher and became a professor of philosophy at the University of Greifswald in 1858.

directly affect school and education. The theoretical architecture of the "soul," as developed between Christian Wolff (1679–1754) and Friedrich Schleiermacher, did not survive this transition.

Wolff was, like Leibniz, a main influence on Herbart's psychology. For Wolff the soul has two components, ideas and images.[61] The soul is considered to be a real being that forms ideas while perceiving and imagining. The basic faculty of the soul is perception and its force is to generate ideas.[62] This is not called "learning" because "soul" was not thought to be individual.[63] "Laws of irritability" were already described in the early eighteenth century in medical physiology, for example in the first volume of Ferdinand Autenrieth's *Handbuch der empirischen menschlichen Physiologie* (Textbook of Empirical Human Physiology).[64] Here, the response of the body's muscles was already viewed as being dependent on the strength of the stimulus, which was also thought to apply to the perceptions of the soul.[65] Without the inner space of the soul, the relationship between stimulus and response could be reconciled and related directly to one another. What was presupposed is the neural system and the reaction of nerves to irritations and, as Helmholtz stated in his *Optics*, the characteristics of nerve fibers are not only irritability (*Reizbarkeit*) but also conductivity (*Leitungsfähigkeit*) or the capability to learn.[66]

"Learning," however, in the sense of physiology could hardly be the basis of teaching. In 1906, Edward Lee Thorndike (1874–1949) described the "art of teaching," i.e. Herbart's topic, as follows: "Using psychological terms the art of teaching may be defined as the art of giving and withholding stimuli with the result of producing or preventing certain responses." This "art" would be reduced to the correct or incorrect application of learning incentives, depending on the response that was achieved. Instruction, however, could not be contingent; it follows a purpose and is intended to achieve an effect, i.e. to transform the "ought" into an "is": "To change what is into what ought to be, we need to

---

61 Christian Wolff, *Anmerckungen über die vernünfftige Gedancken von Gott, der Welt und der Seele des Menschen, auch allen Dingen überhaupt...* (Franckfurt am Mayn: In der Andräischen Buchhandlung, 1724), 403.
62 Wolff, *Anmerckungen*, 408.
63 Wolff, *Anmerckungen*, 433.
64 Johann Heinrich Ferdinand Autenrieth, *Handbuch der empirischen menschlichen Physiologie: Zum Gebrauche seiner Vorlesungen herausgegeben. Erster Theil* (Tübingen: Bey Jakob Friedrich Heerbrandt, 1801), 98–106. Johann Heinrich Ferdinand Autenrieth (1772–1835) was professor of physiology at the University of Tübingen from 1797.
65 Autenrieth, *Handbuch der empirischen menschlichen Physiologie*, 98.
66 Hermann Helmholtz, *Handbuch der physiologischen Optik* (Leipzig: Leopold Voss, 1867), 192.

know the laws by which the changes occur."⁶⁷ The first or general law was that of apperception, so still a reference to Herbart: "The general law of association and its supplement, the law of analogy or assimilation, teach what any pupil thinks or feels or does on any occasion depends upon what he has thought and felt and done in the past and upon the present 'set' or tendency in his mind."⁶⁸

Everything that is assimilated must refer to that which already exists, and nothing is assimilated where there is no willingness. Thorndike's bibliography also indicates the reference to Herbart,⁶⁹ as does the teaching of interests, which should simultaneously be the means and the end, that is, it should be used educationally and motivationally.⁷⁰ The key of Herbartian didactics, the theory of "formal stages," was also still present.⁷¹ The differences become visible when Thorndike discusses the control of learning processes. Here, two further laws are applicable, namely the law of exercise and the law of effect. They refer directly to learning that is generally considered to be a "capacity for permanent modifiability."⁷² An ability responds to stimuli, which describes everything that affects perception that cannot be ignored. Learning does not depend on teaching, but belongs, like Helmholtz stated, to human nature.

The law of exercise has two parts, use and disuse. The law of use states: "To the situation 'a modifiable connection being made by him between a situation S and a response R' man responds originally, other things being equal, by an increase of that connection." The strength of a connection refers to the probability with which it will reoccur in the same situation. The law of disuse states: "To the situation 'a modifiable connection not being made by him between a situation S and a response R, during a length of time T,' man responds originally, other things being equal, by a decrease of that connection." Taken together, both parts form the law of exercise. If a connection is repeated, it is strengthened; if not, it is weakened. The law of effect was of great consequence for pedagogic use: "To the situation 'a modifiable connection being made by him between an S and an R and being accompanied or followed by satisfying state of affairs,' man responds originally by an increase of that connection." The opposite happens when the connection is accompanied or followed by an "*annoying* state of af-

---

[67] Edward Lee Thorndike, *The Principles of Teaching Based on Psychology* (New York: A.G. Seiler, 1906), 7.
[68] Thorndike, *The Principles of Teaching*, 42.
[69] Thorndike, *The Principles of Teaching*, 50.
[70] Thorndike, *The Principles of Teaching*, 5.
[71] Thorndike, *The Principles of Teaching*, 159–160.
[72] Edward Lee Thorndike, *Educational Psychology Vol. I: The Original Nature of Man* (New York: Teachers College, Columbia University, 1913), 171.

fairs."[73] There are limits to the modifiability of connections,[74] but these vary widely, and range between, for example, the laws of gravity and human wariness. The first are immutable, the others change rapidly. The vast majority of connections "can or cannot be regulated by use, disuse, satisfyingness, and discomfort."[75] "Regulation" means control, i.e. the technical application of the psychological law of learning. Satisfaction with a learning process must be strengthened, discomfort must be avoided, if the intended effect is to be achieved. This could only be brought about by the learner who fulfils one of Herbart's criteria, namely that it must be "enjoyable," otherwise he would not be satisfied.

Thorndike's laws are a world away from real situations, and they misappropriate their flexibility. No two consecutive situations are exactly the same, while on the other hand every pedagogic intention is transparent to those affected and can be undermined. However, this led to the use of the law being promoted rather than impeded. Thorndike's starting point was the Theory of Evolution and thus the adaptation of organisms to the environment, which was applied to human behavior and not to biological processes. Adaptation occurs through learning, and what Herbart still called education can be fully absorbed by learning psychology. "Strength of character" would simply be the reinforcement of desired behavioral traits.

Thorndike and Dewey

The Theory of Evolution was also the starting point for John Dewey (1859–1952), who also posed the question of adaptation, but came to very different conclusions. What differentiates him from Thorndike was the role of intelligence in the process of adaptation, or the self-will of human thought and, thus, the science that could be considered for education.[76] John Dewey opposed the idea that reflection or thinking were pure responses to stimuli. For him, reflection very much had a physiological basis; thinking is of a neuronal nature and always moves within an environment of stimuli. However, the responses are never merely singular reflexes, which could also be said of the stimuli: "Neither mere sen-

---

73 Thorndike, *Educational Psychology*, 171.
74 Thorndike, *Educational Psychology*, 173–174.
75 Thorndike, *Educational Psychology*, 174.
76 Stephen Tomlinson, "Edward Lee Thorndike and John Dewey on the Science of Education," *Oxford Review of Education* 23 (1997): 365–383.

sation, nor mere movement, can ever be either stimulus or response; only an act can be that."[77]

In his major work, *How We Think* (1910), Dewey shows what constitutes an act of thinking, namely that it is more than a link between two points in time that can be observed in behavior or not. Thinking is stimulated by problems, and Dewey speaks of a "felt difficulty" that must be accepted emotionally before a thinking process is triggered. This does not refer to a self-referential mental act, as in classical philosophy, but rather to the use of thinking to solve problems, and in this sense it refers to learning. There was a fundamental conflict underlying this theory. Despite all the recognition of Thorndike's groundbreaking research on reinforcing learning, Dewey was more reserved about a reduction of learning to behavior. If "learning" is only considered a change of behavior, then it would be unnecessary to make cognitive demands, or every behavioral change could be understood to be "problem solving". Behavior can be observed, but thinking cannot. For this reason, early behaviorists presumed an inspection ban intended to avoid speculation on the psyche.[78] Yet, even if it is the case that no experimental situation can access the interior of a subject in any way, one cannot deduce that thinking is not occurring, that learning could be delineated from thinking and would then be solely about behavior.

If this were the case, one could not speak of instruction, because learning in behaviorism does not refer to problems that are unknown or unfamiliar to the learner, those which cannot be avoided, or whose solving would lead to growth. Stimuli can appear repeatedly and be associated with the same responses. By contrast, teaching begins with new tasks and problems one does not "respond" to, but to which one opens oneself up. In this regard, teaching opens up the opportunity for future growth by making problems available.[79] However, not every problem is suitable, and not every solution promotes growth. Dewey makes intelligence a decisive factor in the processing of problems. The development of intelligence can be influenced, namely through problem solving that is good or not as good. The individual can see by the results whether the solution was better or

---

[77] John Dewey, "The Reflex Arc Concept in Psychology," *Psychological Review* 3 (1896): 367.
[78] Ontological behaviorism denies the existence of "mind" or "mental" while evidential behaviorism holds the view that behavior provides the only evidence we have for mental or mind. See Dagfinn Follesdal, "Developments in Quine's Behaviorism," *American Philosophical Quarterly* 48 (2011): 273.
[79] John Dewey, *The Middle Works 1899–1924, Vol. 6: How We Think and Selected Essays, 1910–1911*, edited by Jo Ann Boydston; introduced by Horace Standish Thayer/Vivian Throw Thayer (Carbondale/Edwardsville: Southern Illinois University Press, 1985), 83–84.

worse. Actions also have consequences if they have no effect. In this sense, one can learn by doing, which also includes doing nothing.

This does not require inspection. If an individual acts, he or she interacts with others and is under public observation. Social interactions demand coordination, they have to respond to expectations and presume a minimum of commonality, but they are not like in Herbart's psychology based on knowledge of the soul. Learning is triggered by difficulties that would not arise at all if the psyche were transparent. Only a lack of transparency creates problems. Problems can happen or not. Otherwise said, the problems cannot be anticipated when using laws of learning. In 1937, Dewey defined "learning" as follows: "Learning is the product of the exercise of powers needed to meet the demands of the activity in operation." The learner is not merely active externally, that is, he or she merely behaves, but rather can only act if he or she perceives problems and responds in a practiced way: "His faculties are always on the alert, sharpened by constant use, and that he is constantly enlarging his information."[80]

In *How We Think*, "thinking" is an ordered form of problem solving, which occurs over five logically separate phases. It begins, as mentioned, with a felt difficulty, which focuses attention onto a specific point. The whole (whatever it may be) can never appear to be problematic. The difficulty is always a single one and must be emotionally acceptable. Then, it is localized and identified as a "problem". In a third phase, possible solutions must be suggested, which are fourthly thought through and assessed with regard to their conceivable bearing. In the end, there are further observations and experiments, which decide on which of the possible solutions are accepted and which are rejected.[81] What Dewey calls "belief" or "disbelief" could be challenged with new difficulties without having more at one's disposal than habits.[82] As such, experience could be considered a constant reconstruction, but only under the condition that stable habits exist and life is not equated with continuous problem solving. In a learning process problems as well as solutions could only be single and specific.

In the second edition of *How We Think*, published in 1933, Dewey specified "movement of thought" as a way from a doubtful to a settled situation.[83] As in the first edition, movement has five "phases" or "aspects," whose order is not determined, but which must be realized in their entirety if reflective action is

---

[80] John Dewey, *The Later Works, Volume 11: 1935–1937*, ed. Jo Ann Boydston; introd. John J. McDermott (Carbondale: Southern Illinois University Press, 2008), 238.
[81] Dewey, *How We Think and Selected Essays*, 236–237.
[82] John Dewey, *How We Think and Selected Essays*, 237.
[83] John Dewey, *The Later Works, 1925–1953. Vol. 8: Essays and How We Think 1933*, ed. Jo Ann Boydston (Carbondale/Edwardsville: Southern Illinois University Press, 1986), 193.

to be fully completed.[84] The theory of problem solving has its realm of experience in didactics, so it was not the invention of Dewey. Schooling is not possible without learning tasks, and the quality of tasks is a key factor for the success of academic education. This was observed very early on, for example in the criticism of catechistic instruction, but did not define the theories of teaching for a long time.

The type of drill at schools following the Reformation, i.e. the prompting and repetition of words and sentences individually or as a group, was widespread and no chimera of criticism. In the nineteenth century, this practice came under renewed criticism, and unlike the schools of humanism, it was also long-lasting against the backdrop of the developing educational system. The recipient of the criticism of conventional teaching and rote learning then was a communicating profession and not the didactically limited schoolmaster of earlier centuries. What was done in schools was no longer only a topic for a local community. School inspections complained regularly about the lack of skills and the "mechanical" responses by pupils in public examinations.[85] Progress in teaching was described as "lamentably small" and this raised the question of the causes, and there was every reason to suspect that it is the fault of teaching, and more specifically the consistent practice of rote learning, which teachers considered an effective method.[86]

This was especially true in cases where pupils took public examinations and it thereby became obvious what they were unable to master. Both good and poor pupil achievements enabled conclusions to be drawn regarding teaching methods and thus the competence of teaching staff. A teaching sequence used to be completed by examination and examinations in public presupposed rote learning, even if this was generally disputed by the teachers. But the expectations of what was regarded as success of schooling forced teachers to use drill methods. Alternatives were discussed first in teacher education and then in educational psychology.

The Success of "Problem Solving"

In 1877, the geology lecturer George Ferdinand Becker (1847–1919) stated in a memorandum for the new-established University of California:

---

[84] Dewey, *Essays and How We Think 1933*, 199–201.
[85] *Extracts from the Reports of Her Majesty's Inspectors of Schools* (London: Longman, Brown, Green and Longmans, 1832), 48.
[86] *Extracts from the Reports*, 49.

If children are drilled in lessons, line for line, rule for rule, then this is a wrong method of learning. At best, this trains memory, but not the mind or the understanding of facts. (...) The purpose of education being to develop men and women, capable of solving for themselves the problems presented by life, a main object to be kept in view, is (...) to teach them to think. But they can learn to think only by thinking.[87]

Applied to school education, the method of problem solving was termed "thinking under guidance."[88] For Becker, William George Spencer's (1860) textbook *Inventional Geometry* is an example of problem-related teaching that is guided by questions, which leads from the concrete to the abstract and is intended to stimulate independent thought.[89] Refined problem-oriented instruction determines teaching practice today, albeit never alone, also not solely in combination with "projects," and always characterized by major differences. But, there is no longer any doubt in didactics, that learning arises from problems, or that they should be true to life and shape the culture of tasks in schools. This suggests a comprehensive change, which is reflected in the fact that teachers no longer consider rote learning, and by extension cramming, the most effective method. Debates between teachers and in teacher education ensured new convictions. In the nineteenth century, "problem solving" was not a part of school vocabulary and the term was only used within narrow bounds.

For a long time, "solving a problem" only referred to mathematical problems. Apart from that, the use of the term was merely trivial and could be used free from theoretical context. Also in textbooks for teachers "teaching" had only one regular meaning, i.e. "to adjust the subject-matter to be learned to the mind that is to learn it."[90] This was not an argument for rote-learning but instead for a careful planning of the teaching process, yet only on the side of "subject-matter."[91] "Cramming," as was said in March 1868 in another official document, "means the process whereby a man endeavours to acquire a superficial appearance of knowing subjects of which he is really ignorant, by committing to memory a number of disconnected facts of which he does not see the

---

[87] George Ferdinand Becker, *Education: Its Relations to the State and to the Individual, and its Methods. A Series of Lectures Delivered Before the General Assembly of the Students, University of California. Berkeley, Cal.* (Bulletin of the University of California, December 1877), 37–38.
[88] Becker, *Education*, 39.
[89] Becker, *Education*, 2. William George Spencer (1790–1866) was a mathematics teacher and Tutor in Derby. His famous son Herbert Spencer wrote the preface for the American edition of *Inventional Geometry*, published in New York in 1877.
[90] James H. Hoose, *On the Province of Teaching. A Professional Study. With an Introduction by Charles W. Bennett* (Syracuse/New York: Davis, Bardeen & Co./Baker, Pratt & Co., 1879), 83.
[91] Hoose, *On the Province of Teaching*, 83–84.

bearing, by learning by rote the answers to expected questions."[92] A quarter of a century later James Patrick wrote for purposes of teacher training: "Cramming is a mistake for it assumes that learning is everything, and forgets that knowledge must be classified to be helpful."[93] Knowledge in teaching, however, is not a problem of classifications alone but what is learned if learning is no longer committed to learning by heart. Today, we notice that a collection of essays by Karl Popper is entitled *All Life is Problem Solving.*[94] This change can be explained in didactic terms independently of Popper, with the gradual turning away from schematic learning, which had to be implemented in opposition to firm convictions.

The removal of recitation as a teaching standard and the disengagement from catechesis were presumably the key events of an inner school reform, which took longer than a century to fundamentally change a pupil's learning. A prerequisite was that theory itself also changed fundamentally.[95] "Learning" was no longer synonymous with fixed answers to suggestive questions, not even with the controlled development of retrievable habits, but rather was gradually linked in didactics to autonomy, problem solving, and thus with independent thinking. As early as 1871, German teacher educator Friedrich Wilhelm Dörpfeld (1824–1893) had already come to a final judgement on "memory materialism," but this did not lead to any major changes because for a long time, the advantages of the method outweighed the disadvantages for many teachers. In the light of class sizes, the diversity of tasks, constant disciplining, and limited time, there did not seem to be any alternative. It was only the material shift to more resources that enabled developments in the classroom, which on the other hand would never have been possible without a reorientation of the theory, and would least of all have changed social convictions. The fact that "learning" became a fundamental and broadly accepted category is due to its links to school experience and thus also to the change of this experience.

However, it is also more than that. George Herbert Mead (1863–1931) in particular showed that the theory of problem solving could also be understood in social and historical terms. His variant assumes that "problem solving" can be

---

[92] Schools Inquiry Commission, *Schools Inquiry Commission. Vol. V. Minutes of Evidence Taken Before the Commissioners, Part. II* (London: Printed by George E. Eyre and William Spottiswoode, 1868), 650.
[93] James N. Patrick, *Psychology for Teachers with Suggestions on Method. For Use in High Schools and Teachers' Institute* (Boston/New York: Educational Publishing Company, 1901), 46.
[94] Karl Popper, *All Life is Problem Solving* (London: Taylor & Francis, 2001).
[95] The parameters would be the first theory of autonomous learning by Chr. G. W. Ritter (1798) and John Dewey's *How We Think* (1910).

applied not only to those who learn, but also to their institutions, that is, to schools and lessons, for example. In this view, the optics of the theory are twofold; it focuses on the series of problem solutions that characterize the school as an institution, and it identifies new problems or new solutions options. It is fundamental that the zone of the problem must be strictly limited. The problem zone, according to Mead,[96] must be attainable if it is to be processed. The problem within one's own field of experience is "the problem at hand", and only this can be processed.[97] Solved problems are the prerequisite that instruction can take place and school does not have to be continuously re-invented. It is exactly this issue, the persistence of solutions or the "grammar of schooling," that invited criticism.[98] There are no recent didactics that adapt to the historic structure of school and are satisfied with it. One driver is its own theory: whoever presumes "solutions" can imagine better ones and thus give criticism a perspective, i.e. limiting hopelessness.

Today, the theory of problem solving is applied to many pedagogic fields of action. In actual terms, there is no area in didactics that does not attribute learning to problem solving, thus linking it to the assurance that no problem must be left standing alone. The theory is optimistic and has, for this reason, a strong appeal. It has penetrated public discourse and is used on all possible occasions, similar to behaviorist "incentives" or "stimuli," just not for the same control-related purpose. "Problem solving" presupposes thinking, and cannot be a mere "response." This is also complied with. Round tables in politics, for example, work on the solution of problems and not on sales strategies. However, the theory also has clear limitations, in epistemological, sociological, and pedagogical regard. If life is meant to consist entirely of problem solving, then by no means continuously or permanently, nor inexorably or necessarily successfully. "Problems" can be deceiving and "solutions" can be misleading, without simply self-correcting.

If learning and thinking cannot be differentiated and are both concerned with problem solving, then the question arises as to when a problem is solved, and more specifically, what exactly characterizes the solution to a problem? Dewey did not answer this problem, except for his assumption that solutions

---

96 George Herbert Mead, *The Philosophy of the Act. Edited by Charles W. Morris* (Chicago/London: The University of Chicago Press, 1938), 26–44.
97 Mead, *The Philosophy of the Act*, 35.
98 On the grammar of schooling, see also Marc Depaepe, "Dealing with Paradoxes of Educationalization: Beyond the Limits of "New" Cultural History of Education?," *Revista Educação & Cidadania* 7 (2008): 11–31, who borrowed the concept from the American educational historians Larry Cuban, David Tyack, and William Tobin.

are reflected in habits. Habits, however, do not provide a firm foundation, which is exactly the prerequisite for the continual correction of experience. There are problems that cannot be solved, even though – or perhaps even because – "learning" has taken place. The fit between the solution and the problem cannot be taken for granted. Learning can fail as a result of the problem, and problems can resist learning. This applies, for example, to complex pedagogical problems, which are recognized as such but cannot be effectively solved despite the greatest efforts.

The problem is thus: what is considered a solution, and how satisfied is one with this solution? This does not lead to the creation of a different psychology, but the naïve trust in a permanent solution dwindles and the flexibility of problems and solutions is assumed, which should even apply to mathematics. Thinking at any rate, which includes thinking at school, is never concluded, which does not really accommodate the way in which schooling is organized. Educational goals or intentions cannot simply be applied to class settings, and one cannot view the chain of settings as a path to reach a goal. In addition, intentions always incorporate both aspects, and both aspects can use their intentions for or against the learning process. Children can turn a deaf ear and simply ignore what is required of them. They can respond to repetitions with refusal, exploit weak sanctions and use the most empathetic motivation against the educational goal. Children can also experience a lack of success of the best intention, that despite all their efforts, they do not reach the goal, and that ultimately, they fail to make progress despite a high level of motivation if they run out of steam along the way, or if they lack the ability to complete a task.

Attempts to unite or divide cognitive and stimulus-response theories of learning in order to make one appear without value have never succeeded, and the reason for this is not the irreconcilability of humanists and behaviorists.[99] The difference lies in the benefit. Some of them can be used for the control of behavior, the others cannot. This shows the success of behaviorism in economics, but also in new media, that is, the modern attention industry. Everywhere the reaction to a stimulus is intended and the thinking through of problems does not play a role. Whoever expects this, just as in any didactics, has to assume a field of action that demands reflection and cannot be solved with "likes" and "dislikes."

---

[99] See Spence, K.W. "Cognitive vs. Stimulus-Response Theories of Learning." *Psychological Review* 57 (1950): 159–172; and various others, most recently Peter C. Holland, "Cognitive versus Stimulus-response Theories of Learning." *Learning Behavior* 36 (2008): 227–241.

Bibliography

Published sources

Autenrieth, Johann Heinrich Ferdinand. *Handbuch der empirischen menschlichen Physiologie: Zum Gebrauche seiner Vorlesungen herausgegeben. Erster Theil.* Tübingen: Bey Jakob Friedrich Heerbrandt, 1801.

Bacon, Francis. *The Tvvoo Bookes of the Proficience and Aduancement of Learning, Diuine and Humane.* London: Printed for Henrie Tomes, 1605.

Becker, George Ferdinand. *Education: Its Relations to the State and to the Individual, and its Methods. A Series of Lectures Delivered Before the General Assembly of the Students, University of California. Berkeley, Cal.* Bulletin of the University of California, December 1877.

Beneke, Eduard. *Lehrbuch der Psychologie als Naturwissenschaft. Vierte Auflage. Neu bearbeitet und mit einem Anhange über Beneke's sämmtliche Schriften versehen von Johann Gottlieb Dressler.* Berlin: Ernst Siegfried Mittler und Sohn, 1877.

Dewey, John. "The Reflex Arc Concept in Psychology." *Psychological Review* 3 (1896): 357–370.

Dewey, John. *The Middle Works 1899–1924, Vol. 6: How We Think and Selected Essays, 1910–1911,* edited by Jo Ann Boydston; introduced by Horace Standish Thayer/Vivian Throw Thayer. Carbondale/Edwardsville: Southern Illinois University Press, 1985.

Dewey, John. *The Later Works, 1925–1953. Vol. 8: Essays and How We Think 1933,* edited by Jo Ann Boydston. Carbondale/Edwardsville: Southern Illinois University Press, 1986.

Dewey, John. *The Later Works, Volume 11: 1935–1937,* edited by Jo Ann Boydston. With an Introduction by John J. McDermott. Carbondale: Southern Illinois University Press, 2008.

Dörpfeld, Friedrich Wilhelm. "Zur nochmaligen Auseinandersetzung mit dem Memorier-Materialismus." *Evangelisches Schulblatt* 15 (1871): 145–159.

Extracts from the Reports of Her Majesty's Inspectors of Schools. London: Longman, Brown, Green and Longmans, 1832.

George, Leopold. *Lehrbuch der Psychologie.* Berlin: Verlag von Georg Reimer, 1854.

Helmholtz, Hermann. *Handbuch der physiologischen Optik.* Leipzig: Leopold Voss, 1867.

Herbart, Johann Friedrich. *Allgemeine Pädagogik aus dem Zweck der Erziehung abgeleitet.* Göttingen: Bey Johann Gottfried Röwer, 1806.

Herbart, Johan Friedrich. *Lehrbuch zur Einleitung in die Philosophie.* Königsberg: Bey August Wilhelm Unzer, 1813.

Herbart, Johann Friedrich. *Psychologie als Wissenschaft, neu gegründet auf Erfahrung, Metaphysik, und Mathematik. Erster, synthetischer Theil.* Königsberg: In Commission bey August Wilhelm Unzer. 1824.

Herbart, Johann Friedrich. *Psychologie als Wissenschaft, neu gegründet auf Erfahrung, Metaphysik, und Mathematik. Zweyter, analytischer Theil.* Königsberg: In Commission bey August Wilhelm Unzer, 1825.

Herbart, Johann Friedrich. *Allgemeine Metaphsyik, nebst den Anfängen der philosophischen Naturlehre. Zweyter systematischer Theil.* Königsberg: In Commission bei August Wilhelm Unzer, 1829.

Herbart, Johann Friedrich. *Lehrbuch zur Psychologie. Zweyte verbesserte Auflage.* Königsberg: Bei August Wilhelm Unzer, 1834.

Herbart, Johann Friedrich. *Umriss pädagogischer Vorlesungen. Zweyte vermehrte Ausgabe.* Göttingen: Druck und Verlag der Dieterichschen Buchhandlung, 1841.

Herbart, Johann Friedrich. *Pädagogische Schriften in chronologischer Reihenfolge herausgegeben von Otto Willmann. Zweiter Band.* Leipzig: Verlag von Otto Voss, 1875.

Herbart, John Frederick. *Outlines of Educational Doctrine.* Translated by Alexis F. Lange; annotated by Charles de Garmo. New York/London: The Macmillan Company, 1904.

Hoose, James H. *On the Province of Teaching. A Professional Study. With an Introduction by Charles W. Bennett.* Syracuse/New York: Davis, Bardeen &Co./Baker, Pratt&Co., 1879.

Mead, George Herbert. *The Philosophy of the Act. Edited by Charles W. Morris.* Chicago/London: The University of Chicago Press, 1938.

Patrick, James N. *Psychology for Teachers with Suggestions on Method. For Use in High Schools and Teachers' Institute.* Boston/New York: Educational Publishing Company, 1901.

Priestley, Joseph. *Hartley's Theory of the Human Mind on the Principles of the Association of Ideas; with Essays Relating to the Subject of it.* London: Printed for J. Johnson, 1775.

Ritter, Christoph Gerhard Wilhelm. "Philosophische Ideen zu einer allgemeinen Theorie des Lehrens und Lernens als Einleitung in die allgemeine ErziehungsWissenschaft." *Philosophisches Journal* Band 8 (1798): 303–357.

Schleiermacher, Friedrich. *Sämmtliche Werke. Dritte Abtheilung. Zur Philosophie. Sechster Band: Psychologie. Aus Schleiermacher's handschriftlichem Nachlasse und nachgeschriebenen Vorlesungen herausgegeben von Leopold George.* Berlin: G. Reimer, 1862.

Schools Inquiry Commission. *Schools Inquiry Commission. Vol. V. Minutes of Evidence Taken Before the Commissioners, Part. II.* London: Printed by George E. Eyre and William Spottiswoode, 1868.

Spencer, Herbert. *The Principles of Psychology. Vol. I.* New York: D. Appleton and Company, 1873.

Thorndike, Edward Lee. *The Principles of Teaching Based on Psychology.* New York: A.G. Seiler, 1906.

Thorndike, Edward Lee. *Educational Psychology Vol. I: The Original Nature of Man.* New York: Teachers College, Columbia University, 1913.

Volkmann Ritter von Volkmar, Wilhelm. *Lehrbuch der Psychologie vom Standpunkte des Realismus und nach genetischer Methode. Des Grundrisses der Psychologie zweite sehr vermehrte Auflage. Erster Band.* Cöthen: Verlag von Otto Schulze, 1875.

Waitz, Theodor. *Lehrbuch der Psychologie als Naturwissenschaft.* Braunschweig: Friedrich Vieweg und Sohn, 1849.

Wolff, Christian. *Anmerckungen über die vernünfftige Gedancken von Gott, der Welt und der Seele des Menschen, auch allen Dingen überhaupt ...* Franckfurt am Mayn: In der Andräischen Buchhandlung, 1724.

Secondary literatures

Depaepe, Marc. "Dealing with Paradoxes of Educationalization: Beyond the Limits of "New" Cultural History of Education?" *Revista Educação & Cidadania* 7 (2008): 11–31.
Follesdal, Dagfinn. "Developments in Quine's Behaviorism." *American Philosophical Quarterly* 48 (2011): 273–282.
Habermas, Jürgen. *Auch eine Geschichte der Philosophie, Band I/II*. Berlin: Suhrkamp Verlag, 2019.
Holland, Peter C. "Cognitive versus Stimulus-response Theories of Learning." *Learning Behavior* 36 (2008): 227–241.
Popper, Karl. *All Life is Problem Solving*. London: Taylor & Francis, 2001.
Spence, K.W. "Cognitive vs. Stimulus-Response Theories of Learning." *Psychological Review* 57 (1950): 159–172.
Tomlinson, Stephen. "Edward Lee Thorndike and John Dewey on the Science of Education." *Oxford Review of Education* 23 (1997): 365–383.

Kaat Wils (KU Leuven, Belgium)
The Promises of Suggestion. Hypnosis, Education, and the Dangers of Modernity in Belgium around 1900

Abstract: As of 1890, educationalists in Belgium, like elsewhere in Europe, became intrigued by the role of suggestion in education. Interest in the topic remained lively until at least the First World War. Alongside a medical approach in which hypnosis and suggestion functioned as therapeutic tools to cure behavioral problems in children, a much broader interpretation of suggestion as a specific way to communicate with students gained interest as well. Both approaches echoed broader cultural concerns about the societal dangers and promises of hypnosis and suggestion. Indeed, hypnotism and suggestion were in a sense "domesticated" into tools of disciplining as a response to hypnosis' attraction within popular culture. The first approach reinforced the entanglement between (psycho)medical and educational expertise, and strengthened the role of experts in the creation of differences between normal and abnormal, healthy and unhealthy, "vicious" behavior in children that needed correction. The second approach was part of a broader reformulation of modes of thinking about educational interaction. By investigating the workings of the mind and the power of suggestion, medical practitioners demonstrated ways in which one person could exert power over others to make them speak, act, think, and even feel as (s)he wished. Transported to the classroom, this sounded like a recipe that would allow disciplining students without having to resort to openly coercive or punitive teaching methods.

Keywords: suggestion; therapeutic hypnosis; education; Belgium; modernity

Introduction

As of 1890, educationalists in Belgium, like elsewhere in Europe, became intrigued by the role of suggestion in education. Interest in the topic remained lively until at least the First World War. In 1911, for instance, at the International Conference of Pedology in Brussels – a conference studied by Marc Depaepe as part of the broader scientific movement of "pedology" – two contributions were devoted to suggestion and hypnosis.[1] The Russian neurologist Vladimir Bekhterev explained in his paper how problems as diverse as laziness, anxiety, bedwetting, masturbation or kleptomania could successfully be cured by using hypnosis or suggestion in a psychotherapeutic treatment.[2] The Hungarian educator Charles Pekri-Pekár attributed a much broader role to suggestion in matters of education. He explained how education should fundamentally be interpreted as an exercise in "natural" or "normal" suggestion. Through verbal instructions and body language, "the teacher [...] suggests students by developing in them new knowledge, new habits."[3] Each lecture represented one of the two main strands of interpretation that had developed since about 1890 with regard to the role of suggestion in education. Indeed, alongside a medical approach in which hypnosis and suggestion functioned as therapeutic tools to cure behavioral problems in children, a much broader interpretation of suggestion as a specific way to communicate with students had gained interest as well. Both approaches had found fertile ground in Belgian educational and medical intellectual networks. They also echoed broader cultural concerns about the societal dangers and promises of hypnosis and suggestion.

The first, medical approach was fostered by the work of the French doctor Edgar Bérillon. In the mid-1880s, Bérillon had started to experiment with the use of hypnotism with children, in parallel with the broader contemporary development of hypnotherapy as a medical tool. Patients were brought into a sleeplike state of consciousness to create focused attention and increased suggestibility. The therapy mainly consisted of direct suggestion of symptom removal. Hypnotherapists also successfully experimented with suggestion in a waking state, with those patients who were not easily put to sleep. Bérillon specialized in the pedagogical treatment of children with diverse behavioral problems such as deceitfulness or disobedience, "bad habits" such as tics or excessive nail-biting or functional complaints such as mutism. While the method rested either on the use of hypnotic sleep or on suggestion in an awakened state, Bérillon stressed the non-coercive character of the therapy, the success of which depended on the extent to

---

[1] See, for instance, Marc Depaepe, "Le premier (et dernier) congrès international de pédologie à Bruxelles en 1911," *Bulletin de la Société Alfred Binet et Théodore Simon* 87 (1987): 28–54.

[2] W. Bechterew [sic], "L'éducation et la suggestion," in *Premier Congrès International de Pédologie tenu à Bruxelles, du 12 au 18 août 1911*, ed. I. Ioteyko (Brussels, 1912), vol. 1 [discussion]: 42–44, vol. 2: 372–384.

[3] "Le maître, le professeur, l'éducateur en général suggestionne les élèves en développant en eux des connaissances nouvelles, des habitudes nouvelles." See Charles Pekri-Pekár, "La suggestion comme moyen éducatif," in *Premier Congrès International de Pédologie* 1: 392.

which the child itself wanted to be cured.⁴ As early as 1891, the method was implemented by the Brussels doctor Louis Peeters in his private clinic in psychotherapy. Peeters' work with youngsters with behavioral problems at school was positively reported upon in educational circles through the *Revue pédagogique belge*.⁵ The work of other Belgian doctors who specialized in hypnotherapy with children was also noticed by educators. It nurtured expectations for more systematic collaborations between teachers and doctors, in an era in which school medicine was in full development in Belgium's main cities.⁶

The belief in the benefits of integrating insights from medicine into education also fostered educationalists' more broad interest in suggestion as a teaching method. Suggestion was then presented as an extension of the intensive individual therapy that doctors provided. Referring to Alfred Binet's *La suggestibilité* (1900), an experimental study on the different degrees of suggestibility among schoolchildren, educationalists explored the potential of suggestion as a modern alternative to authoritarian teaching styles based on threats of punishments and promises of rewards. Disciplining children remained an important goal, but encouragement and consistent confirmation were now presented as the teachers' main tools. In a 1907 treatise on suggestion and education, a Brussels school director argued as follows: "A mark of esteem, however slight, at the most feeble symptom of improvement will be the most effective suggestion." The secret of successful teaching, he continued, was to be found in a reciprocal affective relationship: "The child obeys best to whoever succeeds best in gaining his

---

4 See, for instance, Edgar Bérillon, *De la suggestion envisagée au point de vue pédagogique* (Paris: Bureau de la Revue de l'hypnotisme, 1886). For a discussion of his work among doctors in Belgium, see for instance "L'hypnotisme envisagé comme adjuvant à l'orthopédie mentale," in *Premier Congrès belge de Neurologie et de Psychiatrie tenu à Liège, du 28 au 30 septembre 1905. Rapports & Comptes rendus*, ed. J. Massaut (Brussels: Severeyns, 1906), 114–116. On Bérillon, see Alan Gauld, *A History of Hypnotism* (Cambridge: Cambridge University Press, 1992), 492–494.
5 Alfred Mabille, "De la suggestion et de ses applications à la pédagogie," *Revue Pédagogique Belge* 4 (1891): 346–349. See also Louis Peeters, *De l'application de la suggestion hypnotique à la pédagogie* (Brussels: Imprimerie Mendes da Costa, 1893).
6 See, for instance, Pol Anri, *De fouten der kinderen: Opvoedkundige nota's* (Ghent: Hoste, 1900), 132–140, referring to the therapeutic work with children of Dr. Leopold Castelain. On the development of school medicine in Belgium, see Karel Velle, "De schoolgeneeskunde in België (1850–1940)," *Geschiedenis der Geneeskunde* 5 (1998): 354–366; Joris Vandendriessche, "Medische expertise en politieke strijd: De dienst medisch schooltoezicht in Antwerpen, 1860–1900," *Stadsgeschiedenis* 6 (2011): 113–128. On the broader medicalization of educational thought in Belgium, see Marc Depaepe, "De markt van het kind: Over de medicalisering van opvoeding en onderwijs," in *De zieke natie: Over de medicalisering van de samenleving, 1860–1914*, ed. L. Nys et al. (Groningen: Historische Uitgeverij, 2002), 260–278.

trust and affection, through kindness and righteousness and by submitting him to his suggestion."[7]

The belief in the beneficial effects of suggestion shared by these educators and doctors was however paralleled by a common anxiety about the negative role of suggestion in contemporary society. At an international medical conference in Brussels, the Belgian neurologist Leopold Castelain, after having extensively praised the benefits of hypnosis in the treatment of psychological and functional problems among children, insisted for instance on the negative power of suggestion. He warned his colleagues against "the power of suggestion that spreads out in the open in licentious newspapers and leaflets, obscene books, in the theatre or elsewhere under the pretext of art, in the streets in the form of examples, direct excitements to debauchery which permeate the brains with images and visions, with motor and sexual incentives that only want to become realities."[8] Medical suggestion had to be used as an antidote to the omnipresent suggestion that characterized modern culture, it seemed. Concern about the dangers of suggestion in an era of rising mass consumption and political democratization was no monopoly of educationalists or doctors. At the Brussels Institute of Sociology, for instance, interest in the role of suggestion in group behavior was outspoken. The work of authors such as Gabriel Tarde, Gustave Le Bon, and also Sigmund Freud was discussed in this perspective. According to one of its members, the later German psycholinguist Paul Menzerath, suggestion even constituted the fundament of social life and the central problem of sociology.[9]

Suggestibility had made its entrance into late-nineteenth century social theory in the slipstream of the popularity of hypnosis as both a therapeutic practice and a form of public entertainment. Not unlike its predecessor, mesmerism

---

[7] "Une marque d'estime, aussi légère qu'elle soit, au moindre symptôme d'amélioration sera la plus efficace des suggestions" and "L'enfant obéit le mieux à qui sait le mieux, par sa bonté et sa justice, le soumettant à sa suggestion, gagner sa confiance et son affection." See Arthur Rombouts, "La suggestion et l'éducation," *La Revue Psychologique* 3 (1910): 156, 159.
[8] "La puissance d'entraînement de la suggestion qui s'étale au grand jour dans les journaux et prospectus licentieux, les livres obscènes, au théâtre ou ailleurs sous prétexte d'art, dans les rues sous forme d'exemples, d'excitations directes à la débauche, qui imprègnent les cerveaux d'images et de visions, d'incitations motrices et sexuelles qui ne demandent qu'à devenir des réalités." See Leopold Castelain, "La suggestion de tous les jours et la puissance physiologique de l'idée avec quelques considérations sur le traitement psychique," in *Congrès International de Neurologie, de Psychiatrie, d'Electricité Médicale et d'Hypnologie. Première session tenue à Bruxelles du 14 au 21 septembre 1897*, vol 2: *Communications*, ed. Jean Crocq (Paris: Alcan, 1898), 224.
[9] Paul Menzerath, "On W.D. Scott, Review of *Personal Differences in Suggestibility*," *Archives Sociologiques*, 1910, Review nr. 54.

or animal magnetism, hypnosis attracted quite some public attention and uneasiness. It not only questioned the boundaries between health and illness and between orthodox medicine and charlatanism, it also seemed to address some key problems of modern mass society and to undermine traditional conceptions of a stable self.[10] In what follows, I will focus on the birth of the paradox that would also reverberate in the field of education: hypnosis and suggestion were perceived as both a disease and a cure, both a danger and a solution for a society whose members were considered to suffer from new, modern illnesses. In the heated public debate of the 1880s, relegating hypnosis to the strictly medical domain appeared to be an elegant way out of this paradox.[11]

Enslaved Subjects in a Modern Mass Society

Animal magnetism was an umbrella term for beliefs and practices (originally introduced under this name by the late-eighteenth century Viennese doctor Franz Mesmer) which involved the physical or mental influence a magnetizer could exert on a subject by using an invisible force or "magnetic fluid," a force that was sometimes likened to an electric current or a nervous fluid. By the use of certain techniques such as fixing the gaze and performing passes upon or close to the subject's body, he or she was brought in a particular state, often a state of somnambulism, which created a remarkable susceptibility for the magnetizer's influence. From the late-eighteenth century on, magnetism gave rise to a culture of spectacular demonstrations of this influence, but also to a strong tradition of curing of mostly physical and sometimes also mental ailments with adults and children. In the 1830s and 1840s, in particular in combination with

---

10 On the public visibility of hypnosis in the period 1880–1900, see, for instance, Ruth Harris, *Murders and Madness: Medicine, Law and Society in the Fin de Siècle* (Oxford: Oxford University Press, 1989), 155–207; Jacqueline Carroy, *Hypnose, Suggestion et Psychologie: L'invention de Sujets* (Paris: Presses Universitaires de France, 1991), 48–64, 89–96; Gauld, *A history of Hypnotism*, 297–362; Stefan Andriopoulos, *Possessed: Hypnotic Crimes, Corporate Fiction, and the Invention of Cinema* (Chicago: The University of Chicago Press, 2008), 19–41; Heather Wolffram, *The Stepchildren of Science: Psychical Research and Parapsychology in Germany, c. 1870–1939* (Amsterdam: Rodopi, 2009), 83–130; Andreas Mayer, *Sites of the Unconscious: Hypnosis and the Emergence of the Psychoanalytic Setting* (Chicago: University of Chicago Press, 2013), 93–107.
11 The text which follows, is largely based on Kaat Wils, "Medical Hypnosis, Self and Society in Fin de Siècle Belgium," *Sartoniana* 31 (2018), 245–257.

phrenology, magnetism also nourished speculations on educational reform and self-help.[12]

In Belgium, medical interest in the therapeutic potential of magnetism was rather marginal in the early and mid-nineteenth century.[13] The handful of doctors who published on the topic were open about the fact that no satisfactory scientific explanation existed as yet for the remarkable influence a magnetizer could have on a subject. They were careful to distance themselves from professional magnetizers, both lay healers and stage performers, who were said to be solely inspired by commercial motives and hence to threaten the dignity of the medical profession.[14] While the therapeutic effectiveness of magnetism was recognized, potential dangers were also identified. In a presentation in 1858 for the Royal Academy of Medicine, the Ghent professor Adolphe Burggraeve for instance concluded that, despite his own positive experience with magnetism as an anaesthetic tool, he had to advise against its use. Ultimately, magnetism was dependent on a perturbation of the nervous system that should not be further provoked. It affected people who were from the start already delicate and in the process became all the more vulnerable. In the end, "they are no longer free human beings, but slaves," Burggraeve argued.[15] The potential moral and more specifically sexual dangers of magnetizers' excessive influence on their subjects were soon also defined in a more collective fashion. In 1863, in a small treatise meant to establish magnetism's alleviating and curative medical effects, the Brussels surgeon Henri Van Holsbeek pointed to the risk that magnetism would

---

[12] See, for instance, Alison Winter, *Mesmerized: Powers of Mind in Victorian Britain* (Chicago: University of Chicago Press, 2000); Joost Vijselaar, *De magnetische geest: Het dierlijk magnetisme, 1770–1830* (Nijmegen: SUN, 2001).

[13] The history of magnetism in Belgium constitutes almost unexplored terrain, except for G. Zorab, "Belgium," in *Abnormal hypnotic phenomena: A survey of nineteenth-century cases*, ed. Eric J. Dingwall, vol. 2 (London: J. London & A. Churchill, 1967), 3–50; Marijke De Sadeleer, "*Druk uw handen op mijn zieke ledematen:* een lichamelijke benadering van het magnetisme in het negentiende-eeuwse België," *Tijd-Schrift. Heemkunde en Lokaal-erfgoed Praktijk in Vlaanderen* 5 (2015): 35–47.

[14] See, for instance, "Observation d'un cas d'hystérie, caractérisé par des symptômes extraordinaires, par M. Le docteur A. Sotteau," *Annales de la Société de Médecine de Gand* 14 (1850): 177–228.

[15] "Ce ne sont plus des êtres libres, mais des esclaves." See Adolphe Burggraeve, "Du magnétisme animal et de ses applications à l'art de guérir," *Bulletin de l'Académie Royale de Médecine de Belgique*, 2nd series, 2 (1858–1859): 155.

"disturb the tranquility of societies and families." To anticipate this, the government should prohibit its non-medical use, Van Holsbeek advised.[16]

It would take another 15 years before calls such as Van Holsbeek's would gain a wider audience. From the early 1880s on, the well-reputed French neurologist Jean-Martin Charcot conferred modern hypnotism scientific legitimacy, a legitimacy it had missed until then, due to its relationship with older forms of animal magnetism. In his public lessons, Charcot experimented on female patients who had been diagnosed with hysteria and whom he believed to be easily hypnotized, as part of their pathological condition. Charcot's belief that hypnosis was essentially a pathological condition, rather than a state akin to sleep, nurtured ideas on the possibly harmful effect of the frequent or unskilled administration of hypnotism, in particular on subjects who were considered to be mentally "delicate". In 1887, Charcot himself publicly stated that medicine had rightly taken possession of hypnotism and should never again leave it in the hands of laymen, hinting in the first place at the popularity of public performances by magnetizers.[17]

In the midst of what became a transnational wave of moral panic on the popularity of itinerant magnetizers' shows, the Belgian government decided to act against the perceived dangers of magnetism, which now also came to be referred to as "hypnotism." In 1888, the Catholic Minister of Justice Jules Lejeune, interpellated in Parliament by a professor of medicine and Academy member, proposed to vote a law which would ban public shows of hypnosis and restrict its medical use on minors and mentally ill to doctors. The issue was brought up a few weeks after a series of popular performances had been held in Brussels. In these shows, a French magnetizer had put his young female subject on stage in a cage with three lions. Anxiety about the excesses of stage hypnotism now seemed justified. During the four years of public debate which followed (and which would lead to the adoption of a slightly altered text of the law), the potential dangers to which Burggraeve and Van Holsbeek had referred stood center

---

16 "Les gouvernements devraient interdire la pratique du magnétisme dans tout autre but que celui de guérir les maladies; nous avons démontré qu'elle était dangereuse, immorale et qu'elle troublait le repos des sociétés et des familles." See Henri Van Holsbeek, *Lettres sur le magnétisme animal* (Brussels: De Tircher et Monceaux, 1863), 26.

17 Jean-Martin Charcot, "Des dangers des représentations publiques des magnétiseurs; nécessité de leur interdiction", in *Œuvres Complètes*, vol. 9, *Hémorragie et ramollissement du cerveau. Métallothérapie et hypnotisme. Electrothérapie*, ed. Jean-Martin Charcot (Paris: Lecrosnier et Babé, 1890), 480. The literature on Charcot is vast. On Charcot's lessons, see Jonathan W. Marshall, *Performing Neurology. The Dramaturgy of Dr Jean-Martin Charcot* (New York: Palgrave Macmillan, 2016).

stage. The main arguments that were used in favor of a ban on shows referred to the moral dangers involved. Hypnotism was said to destroy the free will of its subjects, and hence their moral capacities. Modern city life, it was suggested, added to a general increased nervous sensibility. Women, adolescents, and other "impressionable" or "nervous" people would constitute the first victims of hypnotism's debasing effects on human dignity. It was an argument that could be merged into the new, late-nineteenth century organicist political discourse on the need to protect weak members of society, a discourse that sounded all the more convincing as the dangers of hypnotism were represented in terms of disease, and its success as a new form of epidemic.[18]

Arguments of a more explicitly political nature were equally used. Hypnosis, so it was argued, killed the free will, the foundation of modern citizenship. In the Academy of Medicine, which was requested to formulate an advice on the question, a comparison was made with the importance of the liberty of the nation, a cherished romantic topos in the relatively young and liberal state of Belgium. The effects of hypnotism were also compared with those of ancient slavery.[19] In Parliament, representatives referred to the comparisons that were made in France between individual criminal suggestibility and the suggestibility of the masses in the political demonstrations of French Boulangism, a popular nationalist and anti-parliamentary movement.[20] In a context of recent large scale and violent workers' protest and of an upcoming Socialist Party that strived for universal suffrage, Belgian members of Parliament associated the dangers of hypnotism with their political concern for the crowd, and for mass insurrection. Soon, this association would be made explicit by popular writers on crowd psychology such as Gustave Le Bon, who claimed that a crowd, just like a hypnotizer, made individuals into automatons without a personal will.[21]

---

[18] On this debate, see more extensively Kaat Wils, "From Transnational to Regional Magnetic Fevers. The Making of a Law on Hypnotism in Late Nineteenth Century Belgium," *Notes and Records: The Royal Society Journal of the History of Science* 71 (2017): 179–196.

[19] For the debate in the Academy, see *Bulletin de l'Académie Royale de Médecine de Belgique*, 4th series, 2 (1888): 19, 95–140 (with on page 113 the political references), 225–250, 312–377, 405–438, 503–557, 582–607, 633–644, 664–678, 838–897; 4th series, 5 (1891): 774–777.

[20] For the parliamentary debate, see *Annales Parlementaires. Chambre des Représentants*, Sessions of January 24 and 25, 1888, April 27, 1888, December 3 and 4, 1891, and May 11 and 12, 1892 (with the reference to the Boulangist movement on December 3, 1891); *Annales Parlementaires. Sénat*, Sessions of December 17 and 18, 1891 and May 19, 1892; *Documents Parlementaires. Chambre des Représentants*, April 15, 1890, April 24, 1891, March 10, 1892; *Documents Parlementaires. Sénat*, December 15, 1891.

[21] There exists a wealth of older literature on the connections between hypnotism and early popular crowd psychology. See, for instance, Robert Nye, *The Origins of Crowd Psychology: Gus-*

Hostility towards public shows of hypnosis was probably also informed by gendered concerns. While Charcot experimented exclusively on female patients diagnosed with neurological disorders, Europe's most famous itinerant magnetizer, the Belgian born Donato, performed on young and healthy men.[22] Part of the attraction of his shows consisted precisely in his subjecting even the most disbelieving and resisting men, by preference men of higher social standing, and to force them literally on their knees.[23] Donato was well aware of the way in which his performances destabilized gender (and social) hierarchies, while he kept at the same time heterosexual normativity intact. "In matters of magnetism, it is like in matters of love", he explained, "Magnetizers are seducers. [...] Our subjects, men no less than women, are quite feminine in this respect."[24] In an era in which strength of character constituted an important element of the bourgeois male self, the "loss" of character and masculinity could easily be considered dangerous.

Even though Donato's experiments with healthy men had been successfully replicated by the French doctor Paul Brémaud in 1884, most Belgian doctors who were involved in the debate on the necessity of a law adhered to a more pathological interpretation in line with Charcot's "Parisian school." They associated hypnosis in some way or another with a nervous sensibility close to illness, a position that could fuel the conviction that in particular young people had to be protected.[25] It was a line of thought that allowed for a pessimistic reading of

---

tave Le Bon and the Crisis of Mass Democracy in the Third Republic (London: Sage Publications, 1975); Susannah Barrows, *Distorting Mirrors: Visions of the Crowd in Late Nineteenth-Century France* (New Haven: Yale University Press, 1981); Serge Moscovici, *L'âge des foules, Un traité historique de psychologie des masses* (Paris: Fayard, 1981); Jacqueline Carroy, "Le peuple, le magnétisme et l'hypnose. De l'invention du peuple à celle des foules," in *L'invention du peuple*, ed. Rose Goetz and Alain Trognon (Nancy: Presses Universitaires de Nancy, 1993), 137–148.

22 On Donato's international career and the reception of his shows in Belgium, see Kaat Wils, "Tussen wetenschap en spektakel: Hypnose op de Belgische theaterscène, 1875–1900," *Tijdschrift voor Mediageschiedenis* 20 (2017): 54–73. On his role in the French medical debate on hypnotism, see Harris, *Murders and Madness*, 200–201.

23 See, for instance, a press report in *La Meuse*, November 2, 1877.

24 "Il est en magnétisme comme en amour. Les magnétiseurs sont des séducteurs. [...] Nos sujets, hommes autant que femmes, sont bien féminins sous ce rapport." See Donato, "Examen du livre *Le somnambulisme provoqué. Etudes physiologiques et psychologiques* par le Docteur H. Beaunis, professeur de Physiologie à la Faculté de Médecine de Nancy," *Le Magnétisme* (1886): 220. On the gendered and political significance of Donato's performances in Italy, see Suzanne Stewart-Steinberg, *The Pinocchio Effect: On Making Italians (1860–1920)* (Chicago: Chicago University Press, 2007), 70–73.

25 Paul Brémaud, *Des différentes phases de l'hypnotisme et en particulier de la fascination* (Paris: Cerf, 1884). See also Gauld, *A History of Hypnotism*, 328.

the state of modern society. It also facilitated pleas for a medical monopoly on the use of hypnosis, often with a strong focus on the dangers of public shows. Traces of this interpretation could later also be found in the skepticism of some doctors about the use of hypnosis or suggestion with children. In Belgium, this position was, among others, represented by the famous doctor and educationalist Ovide Decroly, who insisted in a critique of Bérillon on the potentially dangerous character of hypnosis. His colleague Jean Crocq, a psychiatrist who in the late 1890s specialized in the therapeutic use of hypnosis, held a similar skeptical view with regard to children, although he admitted that it could be useful in cases of extreme practices of masturbation or uncorrectable laziness.[26]

During the 1880s, the school of Paris had been confronted with an alternative interpretation of hypnosis, soon cast as "the school of Nancy," an interpretation which would form the basis of most subsequent therapeutic uses of hypnosis and suggestion, including the belief in suggestions' educational potential. In his private clinic in Nancy, the French doctor and university professor Hippolyte Bernheim specialized in hypnosis and suggestion as therapeutic tools to treat patients with a diversity of psychological or functional complaints. Bernheim and a few colleagues in Nancy were inspired by the work of the country doctor Auguste Ambroise Liébeault, who since the 1860s successfully treated patients, among them children, through hypnosis. Liébeault cured for instance children with incontinence, by suggesting them under hypnosis that they would physically sense and, during the night, wake up whenever their bladder would be full.[27] According to the mentioned Belgian psychotherapist Peeters, who was one of Liébeault's loyal students, it was also Liébeault who "discovered" the educational potential of suggestion with perfectly healthy but undisciplined, "lazy" youngsters.[28]

---

[26] See Decroly's intervention in "L'hypnotisme envisagé comme adjuvant à l'orthopédie mentale", 114–115, where he also questioned the positive results that Bérillon presented and called into question the difference between suggestion and the severe language of an authorative person; Angelo Van Gorp, *Tussen mythe en wetenschap. Ovide Decroly (1871–1932)* (Acco: Leuven/Voorburg, 2005), 74–75. Thanks to Angelo Van Gorp for this reference. Jean Crocq Fils, *L'hypnotisme scientifique. Rapport à M. le Ministre de l'Intérieur et de l'Instruction publique* (Paris: Société d'éditions scientifiques, 1900²), 574.
[27] Ambroise Liébeault, "Traitement par suggestion hypnotique de l'incontinence d'urine chez les adultes et les enfants au dessus de 3 ans", *Revue de l'Hypnotisme* 1 (1886–1887): 71–77. On the Nancy school, see Alexandre Klein, "Nouveau regard sur l'Ecole hypnologique de Nancy à partir d'archives inédites," *Le Pays Lorrain* 107 (2010): 337–348.
[28] Peeters, *De l'application de la suggestion*, 11, referred to this discovery of Liébeault.

While proponents of the Nancy school did not associate hypnosis or suggestibility with a dangerous mental state, most of them were nevertheless in favor of a medical monopoly on its practice. This position could be informed by a concern on the possibility of criminal suggestion, the act of instructing subjects under hypnosis to perform criminal acts. It could also be informed by the conviction that hypnosis simply constituted one of the tools that a doctor disposed of, alongside medication or the prescription of hygienic measures. Among hypnosis' proponents who believed in its educational value, however, there was no consensus on whether the practice should be limited to doctors. In 1886, the question was debated at the conference of the French Association for the Advancement of the Sciences. Some participants advocated a medical monopoly, while others suggested that educationalists, who were after all "doctors of the soul," should be allowed to use it as a curative tool to be applied in particular to "vicious natures."[29]

Engaging the Subject to Cure Society

The Belgian debate on the regulation of the practice of hypnotism took place at a time when doctors were looking for ways to strengthen their (still very much contested) authority through legal claims towards a monopoly. In the case of hypnotism, doctors in Belgium succeeded in a very efficient way to have the state defend their interests (albeit with a measure which did not cost anything to the state). The relative ease with which the law came into being testifies of the strength of the wave of moral panic surrounding the phenomenon of hypnosis. When the issue was first raised in Parliament, hypnotism had barely been on the medical research agenda. Medical expertise was hardly developed and there were no testified cases of crimes committed under hypnosis.

Dissident voices who had opposed Lejeune's bill did not fail to notice this. Lay magnetizers pointed to the fact that doctors regularly entrusted patients with chronic complaints to them, as hypnotism was a very time consuming activity that required specific skills. They also pointed to the growing academic consensus on hypnosis' educational potential.[30] The two Academy members

---

29 Edgar Bérillon, "De la suggestion envisagée au point de vue pédagogique", *Revue de l'Hypnotisme* 1 (1886–1887): 84–88 (quotation on p. 88: Félix Hément, a participant in the discussion which followed upon Bérillon's presentation).
30 Albert Bonjean, *L'Hypnotisme, ses rapports avec le droit et la thérapeutique, la suggestion mentale* (Paris: Alcan, 1890); Astère Denis, *La voie naturelle et l'utilité de l'hypnotisme* (Paris-Verviers: Gilon, 1891); Léon Lobet, *L'Hypnotisme en Belgique et le projet de loi soumis aux Cham-*

who did oppose a ban on public performances pointed to the fact that its defenders were unable to name problems that had resulted from performances in Belgium. They merely seemed to reiterate foreign complaints, such as the ones by the Italian doctor Cesare Lombroso against Donato.[31] The sharpest opposition against the bill came from the psychologist Joseph Delboeuf, Belgium's sole hypnosis scholar with international renown around 1890. An old-style liberal, Delboeuf defended the freedom to organize and to assist at hypnosis shows, which he considered both instructive and innocent. The new trend to persecute stage magnetizers in the name of public health and morality was closely intertwined, according to Delboeuf, with the desire of doctors to claim the benefits of these magnetizers' discoveries. Delboeuf also questioned the dangers of criminal suggestion, underlining the amount of role-playing which was at stake in most experiments where hypnotized subjects were incited to commit crimes. As a philosopher, he had invested a lot of his intellectual energy in reconciling scientific determinism with his belief in free will. His interpretation of hypnotism left this belief intact: he saw the patient and his willpower to which the therapist appealed as the active party in hypnosis.[32]

Stressing the societal dangers of a free practice of hypnosis and thereby positing the subject's loss of willpower had served the goal of relocating hypnotism within the confines of established medicine quite efficiently. But it surely was not a very relevant frame of reference when it came to the therapeutic practice of hypnosis. Subjects turned out not to be mere "slaves" of the hypnotizer. Even Donato, who was famous for transforming strong men instantly into unresisting automatons, explained to fellow magnetizers: "magnetism is made of

---

bres législatives (Verviers: Massin, 1891); L. Lobet, L'Hypnotisme devant les Chambres belges: Lettre ouverte à Monsieur le Sénateur (Verviers: Massin, 1891).

31 On the Italian reception of Donato, see Patrizia Guarnieri, "Theatre and Laboratory: Medical Attitudes to Animal Magnetism in Late-Nineteenth-Century Italy," in Studies in Alternative Medicine, ed. Roger Cooter (London: Macmillan, 1988), 118–139; Maria Teresa Brancaccio, "Between Charcot and Bernheim: The Debate on Hypnotism in Fin-de-Siècle Italy," Notes and Records: The Royal Society Journal of the History of Science 71 (2017): 157–177.

32 On Delboeuf's role in the Belgian debate, see Wils, "From transnational to regional magnetic fevers." On Delboeuf's scholarly work on hypnosis, see François Duyckaerts, Joseph Delboeuf, philosophe et hypnotiseur (Le Plessis-Robinson: Laboratoires Delagrange-Synthélabo, 1992); Jacqueline Carroy and Pierre-Henri Castel, eds., Delboeuf et Bernheim entre hypnose et suggestion, special issue Corpus. Revue de Philosophie 32 (1997); Alan Gauld, "Joseph Delboeuf (1831–1896): a forerunner of modern ideas on hypnosis," Contemporary Hypnosis 14 (1997): 216–225; André Leblanc, "Thirteen Days: Joseph Delboeuf versus Pierre Janet on the Nature of Hypnotic Suggestions," Journal of the History of the Behavioral Sciences 40 (2004): 123–147; Jacqueline Carroy, Nuits savantes. Une histoire des rêves (1800–1945) (Paris: Editions de l'EHESS, 2012), 183–202.

sympathy and trust."[33] The few Belgian doctors who had already trained themselves around 1890 in the therapeutic practice of hypnotism or hypnotic suggestion stressed the active role of the subject, without whom a therapy could simply not succeed. Looking back on three years of experience, a doctor from Liege for instance concluded that when he did not succeed in hypnotizing a subject, this was most often the result of the unwillingness of the subject, his lack of attention or his obstinacy in trying to analyze all the acts and words of the hypnotist.[34] Clearly, there were many ways in which a subject could resist.

Throughout the 1890s, medical interest in the practice of hypnotism increased. The newly established Belgian Society for Neurology, and its journal, the *Journal de Neurologie et d'Hypnologie*, explicitly welcomed work on hypnosis and suggestion.[35] When in 1897, the society organized an International Conference, hypnosis – including its therapeutic use with children[36] – was also on the agenda. The theme of criminal suggestion, which had gained quite some attention in Belgium over the past few years, was discussed, in particular in relation to Delboeuf's famous refutation of it. The French lawyer from Nancy Jules Liégeois reiterated his point of view that four to five percent of the population was so impressionable that they could become the unknowing instrument or victim of criminal suggestion. As a means of prevention, Liégeois proposed that the population as a whole would be tested, and that impressionable persons would yearly receive an antidote against malicious suggestion through benevolent suggestion, a kind of moral vaccination, as he called it.[37] In the discussion that fol-

---

33 "Le magnétisme est fait de sympathie et de confiance." See Donato, "La sujétion persistante et la suggestion à échéance," *Le Magnétisme* (1886): 188.
34 "Les insuccès constatés dans le civil sont généralement le résultat du mauvais vouloir du sujet, du peu d'attention apportée par celui-ci ou de son obstination à vouloir analyser tous les actes, toutes les paroles de l'hypnotiseur." See Dr. Ernould, "Hypnotisme ou suggestion hypnotique," *Gazette Médicale de Liège* 4 (1891–1892): 316–317.
35 The journal was launched in 1896 as *Journal de Neurologie & d'Hypnologie: Neurologie, Hypnologie, Psychiatrie, Psychologie*. In 1898, the title was changed into *Journal de Neurologie. Neurologie, Psychiatrie, Psychologie, Hypnologie*. The reference to hypnosis would disappear from the title as of 1907.
36 Leopold Castelain, "La suggestion de tous les jours et la puissance physiologique de l'idée avec quelques considérations sur le traitement psychique," in *Congrès International de Neurologie, de Psychiatrie, d'Electricité Médicale et d'Hypnologie. Première session tenue à Bruxelles du 14 au 21 septembre 1897*, vol 2: *Communications*, ed. Jean Crocq (Paris: Alcan, 1898), 224.
37 "Résumé du Rapport de M. le professeur Liégeois de Nancy. Les suggestions criminelles," *Journal de Neurologie et d'Hypnologie* 2 (1897): 371–376; Jules Liégeois, "La question des suggestions criminelles. Ses origines–son état actuel," *Journal de Neurologie* 3 (1898): 22–49. On the debates on criminal suggestion, see, for instance, Ruth Harris, "Murder under Hypnosis in the Case of Gabrielle Bompard: Psychiatry in the Court-Room in Belle Epoque Paris," *Psychological*

lowed upon Liégeois' lecture, the earlier mentioned doctor Castelain, while not denying the possibility of criminal suggestion, relativized its real danger, and insisted instead on the need to teach people to resist harmful suggestions:

> What is more important in our eyes is to highlight the responsibility of society as a whole in terms of crimes [...] and [...] to develop, through education, especially in cases of mental inferiority, the power of resistance to harmful suggestions. Education, which is a slow, methodical and persevering day-to-day suggestion, will succeed much more surely than somnambulizing with a simple preventive suggestion, even prolonged.[38]

If society offered many dangers indeed, education as a form of everyday suggestion was the best answer to empower vulnerable individuals.

At the same conference, the British doctor Milne Bramwell revealed himself as the main defender of the late Delboeuf. Starting from his clinical experiences, he stressed that the will of the subject should never be underestimated, and that this also applied to the experimental setting of so-called laboratory crimes.[39] It was a point of view that was shared by clinicians who presented their therapeutic work to their peers. Doctor Prosper Van Velsen, for instance, who since 1890 ran a private institute for hypnotherapy in Brussels where he also treated children with behavioral problems, insisted on this point: "One still claims that hypnosis takes away the will; the opposite is the case."[40] Not surprisingly then, Van

---

Medicine 15 (1985): 477–505; Heather Wolffram, "Crime and Hypnosis in Fin-de-Siècle Germany: The Czynski Case," *Notes and Records: The Royal Society Journal of the History of Science* 71 (2017): 213–226; Anthony Kauders, "Negotiating free will: Hypnosis and Crime in early twentieth-century Germany," *The Historical Journal* 60 (2017): 1047–1069.

38 "Ce qui est plus important à nos yeux, c'est de faire ressortir surtout la responsabilité de la société toute entière en matière de crimes [...] et [...] de développer, par l'éducation, surtout dans les cas d'infériorité mentale, la puissance de la résistance aux suggestions malfaisantes. L'éducation, qui est une suggestion lente, méthodique et persévérante de tous les jours, réussira bien plus sûrement que la mise en somnambulisme, avec simple suggestion préventive, même prolongée." Discussion on Jules Liégeois, "L'hypnotisme et les suggestions criminelles," in *Congrès international de neurologie*, vol 1: *Rapports* (Paris: Alcan, 1898), 223–224.

39 "Résumé du rapport de M. le docteur Milne Bramwell de Londres, La valeur thérapeutique de l'hypnotisme et de la suggestion," *Journal de Neurologie & d'Hypnologie* 2 (1897): 378–382. On Milne Bramwell, see Teri Chettiar, "'Looking as Little Like Patients as Persons Well Could': Hypnotism, Medicine and the Problem of the Suggestible Subject in Late Nineteenth-Century Britain," *Medical History* 56 (2012): 335–354.

40 "On dit encore que l'hypnotisme enlève la volonté; c'est le contraire qui se produit, réserve faite aux abus de l'hypnotisme." "Résumé de la communication de M. le docteur Van Velsen, *La suggestion thérapeutique*," *Journal de Neurologie* 2 (1897): 419. With the "abuses," Van Velsen probably alluded to public performances, against which he had publicly taken a stance as

Velsen would also support the pleas of the earlier mentioned school director to make natural suggestion the main educational tool in schools.[41] At the 1897 conference, he expressed his regret that hypnosis was barely taught at Belgian universities – to his knowledge, it was only in Brussels and in Louvain that medical students had the possibility to take a clinical course. His suggestion seemed to be that the only way to fight misconceptions on hypnotism as a dangerous tool that could enslave subjects against their will was to train doctors in its use.

The reports of the meetings of the Belgian Society of Neurology show that even without much formal training, doctors experimented with different forms of hypnosis and suggestion when trying to cure or soften physical symptoms of neurological or mental disorders, such as spasms or forms of paralysis. In order to succeed, they often had to start by overcoming patients' resistance against hypnotism. The anxiety to lose one's free will through hypnosis was indeed reported on as a widespread "superstition" among patients.[42] Complaints about patients' superstitions were nothing new, they were part of a long tradition within the Belgian medical community.[43] The efforts to overcome patients' resistance by persuasion, in turn, testify of the negotiated character of the medical encounter in an era characterized by both medical paternalism and the tentative introduction of medical consent as a legal principle.[44] In the case of hypnotism, a more radical evolution in the doctor-patient relationship seemed to take place. Indeed, the question of the patients' own will was not confined to issues of consent. Doctors described the therapeutic process of suggestion itself as a "reeducation of the will."[45] In order for this reeducation to be successful, a balanced

---

early as 1888, as a student in medicine. See Prosper Van Velsen, "Hypnotisme," *Journal de Bruxelles*, January 15, 1888.
41 Prosper Van Velsen, *Hypnotisme. Suggestion. Psychothérapie* (Brussels: Albert Dewit, 1912), 170–174.
42 Jean Crocq, "Trois cas de Pollakiurie psychopathique, guéris par suggestion," *Revue de Neurologie* 3 (1898): 479.
43 On complaints about superstition, see, for instance, Carl Havelange, *Les figures de la guérison (XVIIIe-XIXe siècles): Une histoire sociale et culturelle des professions médicales au pays de Liège* (Paris: Belles Lettres, 1990), 345–398.
44 The literature on the negotiated character of the medical encounter in the nineteenth century is vast. See, for instance, Nancy Theriot, "Negotiating Illness: Doctors, Patients, and Families in the Nineteenth Century," *Journal of the History of the Behavioral Sciences* 37 (2001): 349–368. For the hospital context in Belgium, see Valérie Leclercq, "Langue de bois et vérités divines: Pratiques de l'information à l'ère du paternalisme médical, Bruxelles, 1870–1930," *Gesnerus. Swiss Journal of the History of Medicine and Sciences* 73 (2016): 123–147.
45 Emile Spehl, "Un cas de tic traité par suggestion," *Journal de Neurologie* 4 (1899): 247. Spehl was one of the two doctors (alongside Jean Crocq) who offered a clinical course in hypnosis at the University of Brussels.

affective relationship between patient and doctor was needed, based on respect, trust, and hope.[46] Differently from other medical disciplines, the patient's trust and confidence were more than merely ethical questions concerning the doctor-patient relationship: they were also a prerequisite for a successful therapy. Similarly, educationalists who believed in the power of suggestion as an educational tool stressed the need to engage in a reciprocal (albeit not egalitarian) relationship with students, in order to make the suggestion work.

While exploring the therapeutic possibilities of hypnotism, members of the Belgian Society of Neurology did not seem to be overly concerned by the social dangers that had been associated with hypnotism. Foreign controversies on criminal suggestion or work on the relationship between suggestion and politics were reported on, but in a rather distant fashion.[47] Doctors were clearly much more interested in concrete ways to cure specific pathologies. These pathologies, however, were not unrelated to the perceived "nervous" state of modern society and its specific public health problems. Addiction to tobacco, alcohol, morphine or cocaine, kleptomania, agoraphobia, sexual inversion (homosexuality), masturbation, neurasthenia, and of course hysteria: for all these conditions – most of them having been medicalized recently – hypnosis had the potential to offer recovery, or at least alleviation.[48] Rather than constituting a danger for society, hypnotism seemed to promise a cure for some of its illnesses, on the condition that the subjects of these illnesses were willing to actively participate in a therapeutic trajectory that would strengthen their will.

---

46 See, for instance, "Revue d'hypnologie", *Journal de Neurologie* 3 (1898): 391.

47 See, for instance, Camille Moreau, "L'hypnotisme dans ses rapports avec la criminalité. Congrès International de Médecine Légale, Bruxelles, 2 au 7 août 1897," *Journal de Neurologie* 2 (1897): 298–300.

48 See, for instance, Otto Wetterstrand, "Le traitement de la morphinomanie, du cocaïnisme et du chloralisme par la suggestion et l'hypnose," *Journal de Neurologie & d'Hypnologie* 1 (1896): 133–134; E. Régis, "Kleptomanie et hypnothérapie" and C. Lloyd-Tuckey, "Quelques cas d'inversion sexuelle traités par la suggestion," *Journal de Neurologie & d'Hypnologie* 2 (1897): 57; Jean Crocq, "Un cas de paraplégie hystérique ayant simulé, pendant seize ans, une sclérose latérale–Guérison par suggestion (Présentation de la malade)," *Journal de Neurologie* 3 (1898): 63–66; Lépinay, "Phobies neurasthéniques traitées par auto-suggestion," *Journal de Neurologie* 4 (1899): 317; Edgar Bérillon, "L'onanisme et son traitement psychothérapique," *Journal de Neurologie* 4 (1899): 318; Dr. Bourdon, "Tabagisme et alcoolisme guéris par la suggestion hypnotique," *Journal de Neurologie* 4 (1899): 318; Vlaviano, "Agoraphobie traitée par la suggestion hypnotique", *Journal de Neurologie* 4 (1899): 400.

Conclusion

In a thought-provoking 2007 article in *Curriculum Inquiry*, Bernadette Baker pointed to the massive but mostly overlooked impact of animal magnetism and hypnosis in the formation of (American) pedagogical "ideas-practices". Debates over the validity of magnetism and hypnosis, she claimed, directly and indirectly shaped education's domain as a field, including its interpenetration of behavior management practices, the contouring of expertise and authority, and the role of will in intelligence testing and child development theories.[49] While this history still awaits writing, both in the United States and elsewhere, my contribution confirms that, indeed, hypnosis and suggestion deserve a place within the history of education. Both interpretations with which this essay started – a medical approach in which hypnosis and suggestion functioned as therapeutic tools to cure behavioral problems in children and a much broader interpretation of suggestion as a specific way to communicate with students – contributed to fundamental transformations of the educational field around 1900. The first approach reinforced the entanglement between (psycho)medical and educational expertise, and strengthened the role of experts in the creation of differences between normal and abnormal, healthy and unhealthy, "vicious" behavior in children that needed correction. The second approach was part of a broader reformulation of modes of thinking about educational interaction. By investigating the workings of the mind and the power of suggestion, medical practitioners demonstrated ways in which one person could exert power over others to make them speak, act, think, and even feel as (s)he wished. Transported to the classroom, this sounded like a recipe that would allow disciplining students without having to resort to openly coercive or punitive teaching methods.

What Baker did not take into account, however, is that hypnotism and suggestion were in a sense "domesticated" into tools of disciplining as a response to hypnosis' role within popular culture. Middle-class anxieties on the alleged uncontrollable effects of spectacular forms of magnetism and hypnosis were strong. In Belgium, they resulted in the law of 1892, a law that was, from an international perspective, quite unique in combining a ban on public shows and a regulation of medical practice, prohibiting its use on minors. Opposition against the law by lay magnetizers stimulated and legitimized medical and educational interest in the topic of hypnosis and suggestion. Anxieties on enslaved subjects and unhealthy mass-behavior were now, so to speak, turned upside down: in

---

49 Bernadette Baker, "Animal Magnetism and Curriculum History," *Curriculum Inquiry* 37 (2007): 123–158.

a doctor's or medically trained educator's hands, hypnotism allowed to actively engage the patient in curing society. Medical hypnosis could, in other words, liberate society from problems that in other, more public contexts had been associated with the dangers of hypnosis and suggestion. The same held true in matters of education. Resistance against the pernicious suggestions of a new, sexualized consumer culture should be trained in schools on a daily basis through natural suggestion. Education constituted, in the end, a form of moral vaccination of the students' will against the many temptations and threats of modernity.

Bibliography

Andriopoulos, Stefan. *Possessed: Hypnotic Crimes, Corporate Fiction, and the Invention of Cinema*. Chicago: The University of Chicago Press, 2008.

Annales Parlementaires. Chambre des Représentants. Brussels: Chambre des Représentants de Belgique, 1888, 1891 and 1892.

Annales Parlementaires. Sénat. Brussels: Sénat de Belgique, 1891 and 1892.

Anri, Pol. *De fouten der kinderen: Opvoedkundige nota's*. Ghent: Hoste, 1900.

Baker, Bernadette. "Animal Magnetism and Curriculum History." *Curriculum Inquiry* 37 (2007): 123–158.

Barrows, Susannah. *Distorting Mirrors: Visions of the Crowd in Late Nineteenth-Century France*. New Haven: Yale University Press, 1981.

Bechterew, Wladimir. "L'éducation et la suggestion." In *Premier Congrès International de Pédologie tenu à Bruxelles, du 12 au 18 août 1911*, edited by Iosefa Ioteyko (Brussels: Misch et Thron, 1912), vol. 1: 42–44, vol. 2: 372–384.

Bérillon, Edgar. *De la suggestion envisagée au point de vue pédagogique*. Paris: Bureau de la *Revue de l'hypnotisme*, 1886.

Bérillon, Edgar. "De la suggestion envisagée au point de vue pédagogique." *Revue de l'Hypnotisme* 1 (1886–1887): 84–88.

Bérillon, Edgar. "L'onanisme et son traitement psychothérapique." *Journal de Neurologie* 4 (1899): 318.

Bonjean, Albert. *L'Hypnotisme, ses rapports avec le droit et la thérapeutique, la suggestion mentale*. Paris: Alcan, 1890.

Bourdon, Dr. "Tabagisme et alcoolisme guéris par la suggestion hypnotique." *Journal de Neurologie* 4 (1899): 318.

Brancaccio, Maria Teresa. "Between Charcot and Bernheim: The Debate on Hypnotism in Fin-de-Siècle Italy." *Notes and Records: The Royal Society Journal of the History of Science* 71 (2017): 157–177.

Brémaud, Paul. *Des différents phases de l'hypnotisme et en particulier de la fascination*. Paris: Cerf, 1884.

Bulletin de l'Académie Royale de Médecine de Belgique. 4th series, 2 (1888) and 5 (1891).

Burggraeve, Adolphe. "Du magnétisme animal et de ses applications à l'art de guérir." *Bulletin de l'Académie Royale de Médecine de Belgique* 2nd series, 2 (1858–1859): 147–165.

Carroy, Jacqueline. "Le peuple, le magnétisme et l'hypnose. De l'invention du peuple à celle des foules." In *L'invention du peuple*, edited by Rose Goetz and Alain Trognon, 137–148. Nancy: Presses Universitaires de Nancy, 1993.
Carroy, Jacqueline. *Hypnose, Suggestion et Psychologie: L'invention de Sujets*. Paris: Presses Universitaires de France, 1991.
Carroy, Jacqueline, and Pierre-Henri Castel, eds. *Delboeuf et Bernheim entre hypnose et suggestion*, special issue *Corpus. Revue de Philosophie* 32 (1997).
Carroy, Jacqueline. *Nuits savantes: Une histoire des rêves (1800–1945)*. Paris: Editions de l'EHESS, 2012.
Castelain, Leopold. "La suggestion de tous les jours et la puissance physiologique de l'idée avec quelques considérations sur le traitement psychique." In *Congrès International de Neurologie, de Psychiatrie, d'Electricité Médicale et d'Hypnologie. Première session tenue à Bruxelles du 14 au 21 septembre 1897*, vol 2: *Communications*, edited by Jean Crocq, 213–224. Paris: Alcan, 1898.
Charcot, Jean-Martin. "Des dangers des représentations publiques des magnétiseurs; nécessité de leur interdiction." In *Œuvres Complètes*, vol. 9: *Hémorragie et ramollissement du cerveau. Métallothérapie et hypnotisme. Electrothérapie*, 479–480. Paris: Lecrosnier et Babé, 1890.
Chettiar, Teri. "'Looking as Little Like Patients as Persons Well Could': Hypnotism, Medicine and the Problem of the Suggestible Subject in Late Nineteenth-Century Britain." *Medical History* 56 (2012): 335–354.
Crocq, Jean. "Trois cas de Pollakiurie psychopathique, guéris par suggestion." *Revue de Neurologie* 3 (1898): 473–482.
Crocq, Jean. "Un cas de paraplégie hystérique ayant simulé, pendant seize ans, une sclérose latérale – guérison par suggestion (Présentation de la malade)." *Journal de Neurologie* 3 (1898): 363–365.
Crocq, Jean. *L'hypnotisme scientifique. Rapport à M. le Ministre de l'Intérieur et de l'Instruction publique*. Paris: Société d'éditions scientifiques, 1900, 2nd edition.
Denis, Astère. *La voie naturelle et l'utilité de l'hypnotisme*. Paris-Verviers: Gilon, 1891.
Depaepe, Marc. "Le premier (et dernier) congrès international de pédologie à Bruxelles en 1911." *Bulletin de la Société Alfred Binet et Théodore Simon* 87 (1987): 28–54.
Depaepe, Marc. "De markt van het kind: Over de medicalisering van opvoeding en onderwijs." In *De zieke natie. Over de medicalisering van de samenleving, 1860–1914*, edited by Liesbet Nys, Henk De Smaele, Jo Tollebeek, and Kaat Wils, 260–278. Groningen: Historische Uitgeverij, 2002.
De Sadeleer, Marijke. "Druk uw handen op mijn zieke ledematen: een lichamelijke benadering van het magnetisme in het negentiende-eeuwse België." *Tijd-Schrift. Heemkunde en Lokaal-erfgoed Praktijk in Vlaanderen* 5 (2015): 35–47.
Documents Parlementaires. Chambre des Représentants. Brussels: Chambre des Représentants de Belgique, 1890, 1891 and 1892.
Documents Parlementaires. Sénat. Brussels: Sénat de Belgique, 1891.
Donato. "Examen du livre *Le somnambulisme provoqué. Etudes physiologiques et psychologiques* par le Docteur H. Beaunis, professeur de Physiologie à la Faculté de Médecine de Nancy." *Le Magnétisme* 1 (1886): 214–220.
Donato. "La sujétion persistante et la suggestion à échéance." *Le Magnétisme* 1 (1886): 131–137, 180–190.

Duyckaerts, François. *Joseph Delboeuf, philosophe et hypnotiseur.* Le Plessis-Robinson: Laboratoires Delagrange-Synthélabo, 1992.
Ernould, Dr. "Hypnotisme ou suggestion hypnotique." *Gazette Médicale de Liège* 4 (1891–1892): 316–317.
Gauld, Alan. *A History of Hypnotism.* Cambridge: Cambridge University Press, 1992.
Gauld, Alan. "Joseph Delboeuf (1831–1896): A Forerunner of Modern Ideas on Hypnosis." *Contemporary Hypnosis* 14 (1997): 216–225.
Guarnieri, Patrizia. "Theatre and Laboratory: Medical Attitudes to Animal Magnetism in Late-Nineteenth-Century Italy." In *Studies in Alternative Medicine*, edited by Roger Cooter, 118–139. London: Macmillan, 1988.
Harris, Ruth. "Murder under Hypnosis in the Case of Gabrielle Bompard: Psychiatry in the Court-Room in Belle Epoque Paris." *Psychological Medicine* 15 (1985): 477–505.
Harris, Ruth. *Murders and Madness: Medicine, Law and Society in the Fin de Siècle.* Oxford: Oxford University Press, 1989.
Havelange, Carl. *Les figures de la guérison (XVIIIe-XIXe siècles): Une histoire sociale et culturelle des professions médicales au pays de Liège.* Paris: Belles Lettres, 1990.
Kauders, Anthony. "Negotiating Free Will: Hypnosis and Crime in Early Twentieth-Century Germany." *The Historical Journal* 60 (2017): 1047–1069.
Klein, Alexandre. "Nouveau regard sur l'Ecole hypnologique de Nancy à partir d'archives inédites." *Le Pays Lorrain* 107 (2010): 337–348.
Leblanc, André. "Thirteen Days: Joseph Delboeuf versus Pierre Janet on the Nature of Hypnotic Suggestions." *Journal of the History of the Behavioral Sciences* 40 (2004): 123–147.
Leclercq, Valérie. "Langue de bois et vérités divines: Pratiques de l'information à l'ère du paternalisme médical, Bruxelles, 1870–1930." *Gesnerus. Swiss Journal of the History of Medicine and Sciences* 73 (2016): 123–147.
Lépinay, "Phobies neurasthéniques traitées par auto-suggestion." *Journal de Neurologie* 4 (1899): 317.
Liébeault, Ambroise. "Traitement par suggestion hypnotique de l'incontinence d'urine chez les adultes et les enfants au-dessus de 3 ans." *Revue de l'Hypnotisme* 1 (1886–1887): 71–77.
Liégeois, Jules. "La question des suggestions criminelles. Ses origines–son état actuel." *Journal de Neurologie* 3 (1898): 22–49.
Lloyd-Tuckey, Charles. "Quelques cas d'inversion sexuelle traités par la suggestion." *Journal de Neurologie & d'Hypnologie* 2 (1897): 57.
Lobet, Léon. *L'Hypnotisme en Belgique et le projet de loi soumis aux Chambres législatives.* Verviers: Massin, 1891.
Lobet, Léon. *L'Hypnotisme devant les Chambres belges. Lettre ouverte à Monsieur le Sénateur.* Verviers: Massin, 1891.
"L'hypnotisme envisagé comme adjuvant à l'orthopédie mentale." In *Premier Congrès belge de Neurologie et de Psychiatrie tenu à Liège, du 28 au 30 septembre 1905. Rapports & Comptes rendus*, edited by J. Massaut, 114–116. Brussels: Severeyns, 1906.
Mabille, Alfred. "De la suggestion et de ses applications à la pédagogie." *Revue Pédagogique Belge* 4 (1891): 346–349.
Marshall, Jonathan W. *Performing Neurology: The Dramaturgy of Dr Jean-Martin Charcot.* New York: Palgrave Macmillan, 2016.

Mayer, Andreas. *Sites of the Unconscious: Hypnosis and the Emergence of the Psychoanalytic Setting*. Chicago: University of Chicago Press, 2013.
Menzerath, Paul. "On W.D. Scott, *Personal Differences in Suggestibility*." *Archives Sociologiques*, 1910: Review nr. 54.
Moreau, Camille. "L'hypnotisme dans ses rapports avec la criminalité: Congrès International de Médecine Légale, Bruxelles, 2 au 7 août 1897." *Journal de Neurologie* 2 (1897): 298–300.
Moscovici, Serge. *L'âge des foules, Un traité historique de psychologie des masses*. Paris: Fayard, 1981.
Nye, Robert. *The Origins of Crowd Psychology: Gustave Le Bon and the Crisis of Mass Democracy in the Third Republic*. London: Sage Publications, 1975.
"Observation d'un cas d'hystérie, caractérisé par des symptômes extraordinaires, par M. Le docteur A. Sotteau." *Annales de la Société de Médecine de Gand* 14 (1850): 177–228.
Peeters, Louis. *De l'application de la suggestion hypnotique à la pédagogie*. Brussels: Imprimerie Mendes da Costa, 1893.
Pekri-Pekár, Charles. "La suggestion comme moyen éducatif." In *Premier Congrès International de Pédologie tenu à Bruxelles, du 12 au 18 août 1911*, edited by Iosefa Ioteyko, vol. 1: 391–400. Brussels: Misch et Thron, 1912.
Régis, E. "Kleptomanie et hypnothérapie." *Journal de Neurologie & d'Hypnologie* 2 (1897): 57.
"Résumé de la communication de M. le docteur Van Velsen, *La suggestion thérapeutique*." *Journal de Neurologie* 2 (1897): 419.
"Résumé du rapport de M. le docteur Milne Bramwell de Londres, *La valeur thérapeutique de l'hypnotisme et de la suggestion*." *Journal de Neurologie & d'Hypnologie* 2 (1897): 378–382.
"Résumé du Rapport de M. le professeur Liégeois de Nancy. Les suggestions criminelles." *Journal de Neurologie et d'Hypnologie* 2 (1897): 371–376.
"Revue d'hypnologie." *Journal de Neurologie* 3 (1898): 391.
Rombouts, Arthur. "La suggestion et l'éducation." *La Revue Psychologique* 3 (1910): 113–163.
Spehl, Emile. "Un cas de tic traité par suggestion." *Journal de Neurologie* 4 (1899): 246–247, 251–252.
Stewart-Steinberg, Suzanne. *The Pinocchio Effect: On Making Italians (1860–1920)*. Chicago: Chicago University Press, 2007.
Theriot, Nancy. "Negotiating Illness: Doctors, Patients, and Families in the Nineteenth Century." *Journal of the History of the Behavioral Sciences* 37 (2001): 349–368.
Vandendriessche, Joris. "Medische expertise en politieke strijd: De dienst medisch schooltoezicht in Antwerpen, 1860–1900." *Stadsgeschiedenis* 6 (2011): 113–128.
Van Holsbeek, Henri. *Lettres sur le magnétisme animal*. Brussels: De Tircher et Monceaux, 1863.
Van Gorp, Angelo. *Tussen mythe en wetenschap. Ovide Decroly (1871–1932)*. Acco: Leuven/Voorburg, 2005.
Van Velsen, Prosper. "Hypnotisme." *Journal de Bruxelles* 15 (January 1888).
Van Velsen, Prosper. *Hypnotisme. Suggestion. Psychothérapie*. Brussels: Albert Dewit, 1912.
Velle, Karel. "De schoolgeneeskunde in België (1850–1940)." *Geschiedenis der Geneeskunde* 5 (1998): 354–366.
Vijselaar, Joost. *De magnetische geest: Het dierlijk magnetisme, 1770–1830*. Nijmegen: SUN, 2001.

Vlaviano. "Agoraphobie traitée par la suggestion hypnotique." *Journal de Neurologie* 4 (1899): 400.

Wetterstrand, Otto. "Le traitement de la morphinomanie, du cocaïnisme et du chloralisme par la suggestion et l'hypnose." *Journal de Neurologie & d'Hypnologie* 1 (1896): 133–134.

Wils, Kaat. "From Transnational to Regional Magnetic Fevers. The Making of a Law on Hypnotism in Late Nineteenth Century Belgium." *Notes and Records: The Royal Society Journal of the History of Science* 71 (2017): 179–196.

Wils, Kaat. "Tussen wetenschap en spektakel: Hypnose op de Belgische theaterscène, 1875–1900." *Tijdschrift voor Mediageschiedenis* 20 (2017): 54–73.

Wils, Kaat. "Medical Hypnosis, Self and Society in Fin de Siècle Belgium." *Sartoniana* 31 (2018): 245–257.

Winter, Alison. *Mesmerized: Powers of Mind in Victorian Britain*. Chicago: University of Chicago Press, 2000.

Wolffram, Heather. *The Stepchildren of Science: Psychical Research and Parapsychology in Germany, c. 1870–1939*. Amsterdam: Rodopi, 2009.

Wolffram, Heather. "Crime and Hypnosis in Fin-de-Siècle Germany: The Czynski Case." *Notes and Records: The Royal Society Journal of the History of Science* 71 (2017): 213–226.

Zorab, George. "Belgium." In *Abnormal hypnotic phenomena: A survey of nineteenth-century cases*, edited by Eric J. Dingwall, vol. 2, 3–50. London: J. London & A. Churchill, 1967.

Nelleke Bakker (University of Groningen, the Netherlands)
MBD and De-educationalization: a Countertendency in the pre-ADHD Era

Abstract: This essay explores the possibility of a process of de-educationalization as opposed to the continuing educationalization that is considered to be a key aspect of western societies. It examines the way school-based children's problems, such as inattention and overactivity, were perceived and treated in the 1960s to 1980s, the pre-ADHD era. The focus is on the Netherlands, where the most prominent forerunner of ADHD, Minimal Brain Damage/Dysfunction (MBD), was diagnosed frequently. Its popularity among the larger public was based on individualized remedial teaching in special schools with small classes, claiming success while removing blame from parents and teachers. These conditions have created fertile ground for a positive reception of ADHD and large-scale use of medication as a quick and cheap fixer of school problems. Therefore, it is concluded that MBD has played a significant role in preparing the way for biomedicalization and de-educationalization of these problems.

Keywords: de-educationalization; neurologization (of causes of behavior); biomedicalization (of treatment of behavior); minimal brain damage/dysfunction; learning disabilities

Introduction

In close cooperation with other Flemish researchers Marc Depaepe has enriched the study of the history of education with the concept of "educationalization."[1] It refers to the process of extension and intensification of education in children's lives and the progressively important role of education and educational expertise in society at large across the West since the age of Enlightenment. Once started, educationalization turned increasing numbers of children into pupils. Unlike Mi-

---

[1] Marc Depaepe, *De pedagogisering achterna: Aanzet tot een genealogie van de pedagogische mentaliteit in de voorbije 250 jaar* (Leuven/Amersfoort: Acco, 1998); Marc Depaepe, Frank Simon and Angelo Van Gorp, eds., *Paradoxen van pedagogisering: Handboek pedagogische historiografie* (Leuven/Voorburg: Acco, 2005); Marc Depaepe, *Between Educationalization and Appropriation: Selected Writings on the History of Modern Educational Systems* (Leuven: Leuven University Press, 2012). Next to "educationalization," the authors also use "pedagogization" as a synonym.

chel Foucault's critical interpretation of the enlightened disciplinary "knowledge–power" that regulates and controls human life, Depaepe's "educationalization" does not refer to dehumanizing aspects of the power of educational institutions exclusively. Though it allows for the normalizing power of school discipline, "educationalization" focuses on the provision of increasing opportunities to children by the school system and on educationists promoting child-focused knowledge of teaching and learning. For Depaepe there is no "master plan" of duty and discipline in an "imprisoned society" but a balanced understanding of "the subtle paradox of educationalisation: the pastoral compulsion of the educator (…) and the liberating experience of the learning, knowledge-acquiring individual."[2] Neither is there a single engine behind the ongoing process. Like individuals, societies profit from more and better education and they promote the teaching of national, civic or religious cultural values to be appropriated. Despite criticism that focuses on the limited explanatory power of the concept as regards the powerful and all but liberating "teaching apparatus" of neo-liberal modern states,[3] this nuanced perspective has inspired many researchers across the international community of historians of education.

However useful the concept of educationalization may be for the interpretation of historical developments in education, the process to which it refers seems in more recent years to be confronted with a countertendency that manifests itself especially in the English-speaking world. After the 1970s witnessed the replacement of the last remnants of forced disciplining with more gentle and subtle kinds of psychological influencing of children, the 1980s and 1990s saw a considerable decrease in the belief in the power of child-rearing and education in bringing about certain behavior in children. This went together with the regeneration of a romantic focus on a child's inborn talent that should develop itself with the help of a supportive environment. By consequence, this developmentalism leaves little room for the educator's molding hands. Today, development instead of child-rearing governs educational studies. This new romanticism has engaged with a new belief in organic or "natural" causes of behavior, assumingly located in the brain, which reduces adult nurturing largely to optimizing the de-

---

[2] Marc Depaepe, "Educationalisation: A Key Concept in Understanding the Basic Processes in the History of Western Education," in Marc Depaepe, *Between Educationalization*, 138.

[3] Critical reflexion on the use of the concept for understanding modern societies can be found in the volume *Educational Research: the Educationalization of Social Problems*, ed. Paul Smeyers and Marc Depaepe (New York etc.: Springer, 2008). See for educationalization and neo-liberalism: Maarten Simons and Jan Masschelein, "'It Makes Us Believe That It Is About Our Freedom': Notes on the Irony of the Learning Apparatus," in *Educationalization of Social Problems*, ed. Smeyers and Depaepe, 191–204.

velopment of the child's brain through a healthy lifestyle and effective teaching.[4] If the unfolding of a child's talent does not run smoothly, psychiatric diagnoses implicating a neurological dysfunction such as Attention Deficit Hyperactivity Disorder (ADHD) are sought for and given more easily than ever before.[5] At the same time psychodynamic theory has made way for neuropsychology as predominant explanatory paradigm for educationists. Therefore, we may interpret this shift of focus from nurture to nature as a process of psychopathologization of children's behavior and of neurologization of the assumed causes of unwanted behaviors. Was the growing belief in the etiological key-role of the brain paralleled by a decreasing belief in the role of education as "treatment" of school-based children's problems? In other words, do we also notice "de-educationalization"? And if so, which forces were driving it forward?

To answer this question this essay discusses the history of the present obsession with the child's brain by focusing on the most prominent forerunner of ADHD, which was literally held to be an illness of the brain: Minimal Brain Damage and later Minimal Brain Dysfunction (MBD), after neuroscientists had admitted in the 1960s that in most cases no proof of brain damage could be found. Like ADHD, the label had its origin in the United States. It was used in the 1960s to 1980s for children with only mild ("minimal") symptoms such as overactivity and inattention at school. Provided that these were the heydays of antipsychiatry and belief in nurturing approaches, it was remarkably popular among teachers and parents.[6] Claims have been made that, as compared to ADHD, MBD was much less frequently diagnosed and was a much more serious illness with "clear signs of a cerebral disorder".[7] Some authors maintain that in Europe MBD was as a rule not treated in the way ADHD is, with medication, because of a "taboo" on the prescription of psychotropic medicine among child psychiatrists.[8]

---
4 Dick Swaab, *We Are Our Brains: From the Womb to Alzheimer's* (Amsterdam: Contact, 2010); Sheryl Feinstein, *Inside the Teenage Brain* (London: Rowmer & Littlefield, 2009).
5 Laura Batstra, *Hoe voorkom je ADHD? Door de diagnose niet te stellen* (Amsterdam: Nieuwezijds, 2012); Sanne Bloemink, *Diagnosedrift: Hoe onze labelcultuur kinderen tekort doet* (Amsterdam: Amsterdam University Press, 2018).
6 Russell A. Barkley, *Attention-Deficit Hyperactivity Disorder: A Handbook for Diagnosis and Treatment* (New York/London: The Guilded Press, 2006, 3rd ed.), 9; Russell J. Schachar, "Hyperkinetic Syndrome: Historical Development of the Concept," in *The Overactive Child*, ed. Eric A. Taylor (Oxford/Philadelphia: Blackwell/Lippincott, 1986), 19–40; Jane W. Kessler, "History of Minimal Brain Dysfunctions", in *Handbook of Minimal Brain Dysfunctions*, ed. Herbert E. Rie and Ellen D. Rie (New York etc.: Wiley & Sons, 1980), 18–51.
7 Timo Bolt, *Van zenuwachtig tot hyperactief: Andere kijk op ADHD* (Amsterdam: SWP, 2010), 69; Schachar, "Hyperkinetic Syndrome"; Kessler, "History".
8 Bolt, *Van zenuwachtig*, 92; Schachar, "Hyperkinetic Syndrome"; Kessler, "History".

But how was MBD treated in the decades before biological psychiatry[9] took over from the mid-1980s? How serious were the symptoms of the children diagnosed with it and how uncommon was the condition? And, most importantly, what did parents, teachers, and society gain from a neurological diagnosis in times of an overwhelming belief in the forces of child-rearing and education? MBD seems a good case to search for traces of de-educationalization.

In the literature many indications can to be found that non-medical professions have for a long time been involved with the study and treatment of children demonstrating the behavioral symptoms that are now labelled as ADHD. Before Ritalin and pharmaceutical companies established their monopoly on the treatment of inattention and restlessness and these behaviors became symptoms of mental illness, child psychologists, neuropsychologists, and special educationists contributed significantly to the study and treatment of these school-based problems.[10] Some authors even maintain that by the mid-1960s child psychiatrists lost their key-role in mental health care for children, as both institutions for the mentally disabled and outpatient clinics were invaded by psychologists, special educationists, and social workers who introduced new cognitive and behavioral therapies, and promoted the training of communicative and social skills instead of medical treatment.[11] This warns us that the pre-ADHD era, despite similarities between MBD and ADHD, cannot simply be conceived as a prelude to the age of Ritalin, but must be considered in its own terms.

Across the West the 1960s to 1980s have, moreover, been the years in which each of the child-related research areas succeeded in establishing itself as an academic field of study with chairs and laboratories.[12] Besides, special education grew and diversified in these years, before integration became the keyword in

---

[9] Edward Shorter, *A History of Psychiatry: From the Era of the Asylum to the Age of Prozac* (New York etc.: Wiley & Sons, 1997), 239–328; Timo Bolt and Leonie de Goei, *Kinderen van hun tijd: Zestig jaar kinder- en jeugdpsychiatrie* (Van Gorcum: Assen, 2008).

[10] Gerald Coles, *The Learning Mystique: A Critical Look at "Learning disabilities"* (New York: Fawcett Columbine, 1987); James M. Kauffman and Timothy J. Landrum, *Children and Youth with Emotional and Behavioral Disorders* (Austin: Pro-ed, 2006).

[11] Kauffman and Landrum, *Children and Youth*; Ido Weijers, "Zestig jaar kinder- en jeugdpsychiatrie in Nederland (1920–1980)," *Kind en Adolescent* 23 (2002): 82–96.

[12] Helmut Remschmidt, Herman van Engeland and Jorma Piha, eds., *Child and Adolescent Psychiatry: Historical Development, Current Situation, Future Perspectives* (Darmstadt: Steinkopff Verlag, 1999). Barbara Beatty, Emily Cahan and Julia Grant, eds., *When Child Science Encounters the Child: Education, Parenting, and Child Welfare in 20th-Century America* (New York/London: Teachers College Press, 2006); Rita Hofstetter and Bernard Schneuwly, eds., "History of Educational Sciences," *Paedagogica Historica* 40 (2004): 569–784.

the schooling of special-needs pupils.[13] Next to the older schools for the "feeble-minded," new schools and classes were for example established and teaching strategies developed for normally intelligent children with "specific" learning disabilities such as dyslexia, a development that seems to indicate further educationalization, but may also be related to an increased medical interventionism expressed in diagnosing children with neurological dysfunctions.[14]

This essay focuses on the unexplored ground of de-educationalization and searches for signs of it in the expert discourse on brain-related illness of schoolchildren in the decades when MBD was used as a label for "difficult" children. It discusses the case of the Netherlands as part of a developing international scientific community in which scientists from the English-speaking world figured already prominently, but did not yet set the standard as regard definitions and approaches in the way they do today. It will be argued that MBD has played a significant role in preparing the way for bio-medicalization and de-educationalization of school-based children's problems.

Brain Injury and Learning Problems

In the Netherlands the concept of MBD was not used until the 1970s, but a number of other brain-related labels were used from the 1950s, mostly for children with learning problems. In 1949 in Amsterdam at the Second International Congress on Orthopedagogics the recent founder of the first Dutch special school for normally intelligent children with learning and behavioral problems (*leer- en opvoedingsmoeilijkheden*, LOM) discussed these in terms of "partial defects." This child psychologist who would become professor of special education studies, Wilhelmina Bladergroen, related the story of her successful treatment of a young woman with serious learning problems which she diagnosed as effects of "brain paralysis," a story she would endlessly repeat during her career.[15] According to the psychiatrist who wrote the report on the conference's section on

---

13 I.M. Abbring, C.J.W. Meijer and J. Rispens, eds., *Landenstudies. Het onderwijs aan leerlingen met problemen in internationaal perspectief* (Groningen: RION, 1989), 2 vols.
14 This is suggested for example by Coles, *The learning mystique*.
15 Mineke van Essen, *Wilhelmina Bladergroen: Vrouw in de eeuw van het kind* (Amsterdam: Boom, 2012).

partial defects, the psychiatrist and leader of the Amsterdam child guidance clinic Nelly Tibout, pupils struggling with these problems were all "brain-injured."[16]

Having travelled to the United States in the 1920s for her training in child guidance work,[17] this psychiatrist was probably well-informed about the neurologist Alfred Strauss's work. From the 1940s he and Laura Lehtinen had studied mentally retarded pupils and attributed the learning problems of children without a family history of mental deficiency to "brain injury."[18] In the 1950s Strauss and his team expanded their research to include children with normal intelligence who showed similar disturbances in perception, thinking, and emotional behavior. The ensuing heterogeneity of the category of "brain-injured" children stimulated the use of the label "minimal brain damage" for normally intelligent children with only mild symptoms and "specific" instead of general learning disabilities.[19]

The first Dutch expert involved in the study of learning disabilities who discussed brain trauma as a possible cause of learning problems of pupils with normal intelligence in the professional journal on special education was school doctor Dirk Herderschêe, who was responsible for the selection of children for the Amsterdam special schools. In 1955 he deliberately discarded the Freudian reference to parental neglect as cause of these children's learning problems.[20] His contribution was a response to an essay by the first university professor of child psychiatry, Theo Hart de Ruyter, a psychoanalyst who believed in affective neglect as a causative factor of all kinds of children's problems.[21] According to the school doctor heredity and the sequelae of birth trauma or inflammation of the brain were much more likely causes.

---

16 P.H.C. Tibout, "Report of the section partial defects," in *Proceedings of the Second International Congress on Orthopedagogics*, ed. I.C. van Houte and B. Stokvis (Amsterdam: Systemen Keesing, 1950), 384.
17 Nelleke Bakker, "The Discovery of Childhood Mental Illness: The Case of the Netherlands," *Bildungsgeschichte. International Journal for the Historiography of Education* 7 (2017): 191–204.
18 A.A. Strauss and L.E. Lehtinen, *Psychopathology and Education of the Brain-injured Child* (Grune & Stratton: New York, 1947), 4.
19 Barry M. Franklin, *From "Backwardness" to "At-Risk": Childhood Learning Difficulties and the Contradictions of School Reform* (Albany: State University of New York Press, 1994), 49–70; A.A. Strauss and N.C. Kephart, *Psychopathology and Education of the Brain Injured Child* (Grune & Stratton: New York, 1955), 2 Vols.; Schachar, "Hyperkinetic syndrome"; Kessler, "History".
20 D. Herderschêe, "De prophylaxis der oligophrenie," *Tijdschrift voor Buitengewoon Onderwijs en Orthopaedagogiek* 35 (1955): 4–9, 21–26, 65–71.
21 Th. Hart de Ruyter, "De betekenis der psycho-analytische paedagogie voor de opvoeding van kinderen met aanpassingsstoornissen," *Tijdschrift voor Buitengewoon Onderwijs en Orthopaedagogiek* 34 (1954): 38–42, 216–221.

Freudianism dominated the work of the first generation of child psychiatrists and the institutions where they trained and practiced, the child guidance clinics. It also dominated the appointments at the first academic chairs in child psychiatry of the 1950s and 1960s. Like Hart de Ruyter, they looked for causes of childhood problems in the environment, particularly parent-child interaction. The Freudian dominance of the developing academic field would be broken only by the early 1980s, after psychiatry had gone through a revival of bio-psychiatry, a new generation of child psychiatrists had occupied chairs, and a plethora of psychotherapies (such as system therapy and behavioral therapy) had been imported from the United States.[22]

Therefore, it is not a coincidence that the first child-psychiatric handbook that described mental deficiency and learning problems as symptoms of children having suffered "brain infection" was authored by one of the few academic child psychiatrists of his generation who had not trained as a psychoanalyst, Arnold van Krevelen.[23] And it is certainly not a coincidence that another one, Frank Grewel, was the one who started to promote brain injury or "encephalopathy" as alternative to neurosis as cause of learning problems. He also was the first Dutch child neurologist to use the electroencephalogram (EEG). From 1959 onward Grewel reported on his research into "partial learning defects" of children whose school performance did not match their IQ. Together with a special educationist he described for instance a "restless, difficult, and uncontrolled" eight-year-old boy, attending a LOM-school with small classes, who was easily distracted, had no friends, and had reading and speaking problems and an uncontrolled locomotion. Because his EEG was "a little instable", they drew the conclusion that the boy "probably" suffered from "a delay in the development of the brain stem."[24]

Gradually Grewel included more serious cases of "cerebral patients" in his research and indicated "encephalopathy" as the cause of more or less serious learning problems. Primary abnormalities were almost always "organic," he maintained.[25] This made him emphasize the importance of extensive neurological diagnostics of all learning-disabled children, including an EEG, testing of all

---

22 Bolt and De Goei, *Kinderen*, 15–61.
23 D. Arn. van Krevelen, *Nederlands leerboek der speciële kinderpsychiatrie* (Leiden: Stenvert Kroese, 1952), 75–83.
24 F. Grewel and E. Magadant-Mainz, "Partiële defecten: Analyse van een geval en aanwijzingen voor een paedagogisch-therapeutische behandeling," *Tijdschrift voor Buitengewoon Onderwijs en Orthopaedagogiek* 39 (1959): 66–67.
25 F. Grewel, "Terug naar het gewone lager onderwijs," *Tijdschrift voor Orthopedagogiek* 3 (1964): 2–11.

senses and locomotion, and an analysis of perinatal conditions. Next to psychological testing, special educationists had to draw up an individual school prognosis for each child, he insisted in his inaugural lecture as professor of special education studies in 1965.[26] He consistently warned against choosing psychotherapy without having ruled out encephalopathy. Reading problems were, for example, often caused by brain injury, he explained. Psychotherapy could only reduce secondary symptoms, he explained: "Enough mothers of wrongly diagnosed children had been subjected to frustrating psychotherapy or child-rearing advice."[27]

More fundamental research into "cerebral malfunctioning" caused by pre- or perinatal injury to the brain was particularly stimulated by the establishment of the Department of Neuropsychology at the University of Groningen, led by H.F.R. Prechtl.[28] In 1963 he estimated the prevalence of the less serious variety of overactivity, which he labelled the "choreatiform syndrome," to be an alarming 20 percent for school-aged boys and eight percent for girls,[29] numbers that approximated those found for "brain injury" by Strauss and his colleagues in 1955: 15 to 20 percent of all school children.[30] In the next year one of Prechtl's PhD students presented an even higher prevalence: 24 percent of six-year old boys and nine percent of girls of that age suffered from the syndrome.[31]

Behavior modification

By the early 1960s in the Anglo-American world the use of the etiological label "brain damage" for children with learning problems came under attack. Neurologists had come to the conclusion that children with the behavioral symptoms of "brain damage" very often had no history of trauma to or inflammation of their brain, whereas children who did have this history in many cases did not show the symptoms. In 1962, therefore, the Oxford International Study Group

---

26 F. Grewel, *Orthopedagogiek in ontwikkeling* (Groningen: Wolters, 1965).
27 F. Grewel, "Partiële defecten: Pariëtaal syndroom," *Tijdschrift voor Orthopedagogiek* 3 (1964): 254–258.
28 His research into perinatal trauma and diagnosis was reported for example in: H.F.R. Prechtl and J. Dijkstra, *Neurological Diagnosis of Cerebral Injury in the New Born* (Groningen: Noordhoff, 1960). J. Dijkstra pointed at hypoxia as predictor of neurological abnormality: J. Dijkstra, "De prognostische betekenis van neurologische afwijkingen bij pasgeboren kinderen" (PhD diss., University of Groningen, 1960).
29 H.F.R. Prechtl, *Het cerebraal gestoorde kind* (Groningen: Wolters, 1963), 13.
30 Strauss and Kephart, *Psychopathology*.
31 Christina J. Stemmer, *Choreatiforme bewegingsonrust* (Groningen: Van Denderen, 1964), 11.

on Child Neurology held a conference which addressed mainly the problems of definition and diagnosis. The term "minimal cerebral dysfunction" was recommended in place of "minimal brain damage," primarily on the basis of a consensus that brain damage should not be inferred from behavioral signs alone. In the next year in the United States three task forces were established, sponsored by the federal United States Public Health Service Division of Chronic Diseases. In 1966 Task Force I reported on identification and terminology. The monograph mentions 38 terms used to describe or distinguish the conditions grouped as minimal brain dysfunction. Task Force III, reporting in 1969, listed a total of 99 signs and symptoms exhibited by children with minimal cerebral dysfunction and recommended that an effort was made to identify more homogeneous subcategories.[32]

American child psychologists and other experts also held a seminar assembled by one of Strauss' co-workers, the psychologist William Cruickshank, to discuss problems of definition. This topic, more than any other, revealed differences of opinion and provoked heated controversy. Looking backward at this 1965 seminar, the conveners stated: "A child in Michigan would be called perceptually handicapped; in New York, brain injured; in California, neurologically impaired or educationally handicapped. In Florida or Maryland, he would be said to have special learning disabilities."[33] This conference reflects the decreasing concern with etiology, as the general disposition of the conferees was toward an exclusively behavioral definition, like the one that was added to the American psychiatric handbook DSM-II (1968), the "hyperkinetic reaction of childhood," which replaced the "chronic brain syndrome associated with birth trauma" of DSM-I (1952).

As late as 1972 a conference in New York sponsored by the National Institute of Child Health and Human Development showed a parting of ways between physicians on the one hand and educationists on the other hand. The medical group concerned itself with comprehensive diagnosis and the role of medical treatment, such as drug therapy. Educationists focused primarily on the assessment of learning problems and techniques of remedial teaching, which had become urgent because the 1969 federal Children with Learning Disabilities Act dictated the establishment of programs for "learning disability" pupils. The preparation for this Act had stimulated teachers in this field to organize themselves in the Association for Children with Learning Disabilities, which focused on children with disorders in the development of "language, speech, reading, and as-

---

32 Kessler, "History", 42–43; Franklin, *From "Backwardness"*, 65.
33 Quoted in: Kessler, "History", 43.

sociated communication skills," later referred to as "special learning disabilities" of children "with a discrepancy between (his) performance and potential ability."[34]

In the Netherlands these developments resonated and stimulated research, though not yet of a critical kind. In 1971 the decades-old Society for Teachers and Physicians working in Special Education (*Vereniging O. en A.*) organized a conference on "Children with minimal organic-cerebral damage" (*Kinderen met lichte organisch-cerebrale beschadigingen*), which brought together the Dutch researchers in this field. About 100 scientists listened to the opening speech of Bladergroen, who promoted a fundamental senso-motoric re-education of children diagnosed with "choreatiform syndrome" or "minimal brain damage," 90 percent of whom had to cope with serious learning problems, mostly of the hyperkinetic and "attention lability" type, she claimed. As cause of the trouble she pointed at pre- or perinatal hypoxia (a shortage of oxygen), a research finding of one of Prechtl's PhD students.[35]

After the lecture some 20 groups or institutions briefly introduced their programs. The research themes, as well as the labels that were used, varied greatly. Some were university institutions like the Institute for Developmental Neurology in Groningen led by Prechtl, who focused on neurological examinations of newborn babies and follow-up studies, whereas the newer group of special educationists of the same university led by Bladergroen studied the learning and behavioral problems of children diagnosed with "choreatiform syndrome". Others were residential institutions, like the Protestant Heldring Reformatory for girls in Zetten. Its psychiatrist was testing the use of "medicine" and the hypothesis that the girls had been neglected by their parents because of their "minimal brain dysfunction." Another research focus, in the recently established Roman-Catholic residential Roelant Stichting for children with "minimal brain damage" in Ubbergen, likewise shows that we have reasons to doubt if European psychiatrists did in those days as a rule refrain from administering drug therapy. A multidisciplinary team compared the effects of educational treatment and amphetamine. The team also tried to find out about the biochemical and neurological causes of the behavioral disorders of their patients, whom the special educationist called "structopathic" and the neurologist victims of "minimal brain dysfunction."

---

[34] Kessler, "History", 43–44.
[35] Wilhelmina J. Bladergroen, "De orthopedagoog en kinderen met lichte organisch-cerebrale stoornissen," *Tijdschrift voor Orthopedagogiek* 10 (1971): 292–303.

Some institutions focused on diagnostics, like the Child-psychiatric Centre in Amstelveen, which studied the value of a trampoline as a diagnostic instrument for the assessment of "neurological dysfunction" from a kinetic or locomotory perspective. Others focused on the improvement of a particular treatment, like the Leiden University Pedological Institute, which pioneered in systematic observation, computer-assisted instruction, and the use of headphones to improve children's concentration and attention span. Not surprisingly, at the conference no consensus was reached as to the definition of the disorder or a combined research effort. Even in the same institution two researchers sometimes used different terminology.[36] Nevertheless, the conference marks the higher aspirations of the developing field of academic study of learning disabilities and behavioral disorders. In the wake of the conference these topics started to play a more important role in the debate on brain injury or dysfunction as cause of learning problems.

In this climate one of the organizers of the conference and president of the professional society of special educationists, the neurologist J. Valk, introduced Cruickshank's method of dealing with *The brain-injured child in home, school, and community* (1967).[37] The translation of the manual was given a different title: *Buitenbeentjes. Kinderen met hersenbeschadigingen thuis, op school en in de groep* (Outsiders: brain-injured children at home, at school and among their peers, 1970). It was an immediate success.[38] The label "outsiders" even got a life of its own, as it became a common name for hyperactive children in pre-ADHD years. Cruickshank propagated a method of maximum structuring of the learning process of MBD-children in a minimal stimulation environment. It was based on behavioristic conditioning and the training of stimulus control in uncontrolled children.[39] Cruickshank, who refused to treat children undergoing drug therapy, was invited to the Netherlands in 1972. When, after his lecture, he was confronted with critique of the concept of "brain damage" from a psychologist, blaming it of obscuring social and cultural deprivation, to the surprise of the panel of experts he replicated that he could do without it. Adequate training programs for MBD-children could be developed without knowing the exact

---

[36] "Symposion Zetten mei 1971. Verslagen van verschillende onderzoekingen," *Tijdschrift voor Orthopedagogiek* 10 (1971): 304–307.
[37] William M. Cruickshank, *The Brain-Injured Child in Home, School, and Community* (New York: Syracuse University Press, 1967).
[38] Between 1970 and 1975 four editions appeared: William M. Cruickshank, *Buitenbeentjes: Kinderen met hersenbeschadigingen thuis, op school en in de groep. Vertaald en bewerkt voor Nederland door J. Valk* (Rotterdam: Lemniscaat, 1975), fourth edition.
[39] Cruickshank, *The Brain-Injured Child*.

neurological base of the disorder, he claimed. The Dutch panel of recently appointed university professors of special education studies, however, did not yet want to let go of the "damage" from their vocabulary.[40] In the meantime, a "structured" approach and behavior modification techniques were widely introduced in special schools.[41]

In 1973 a co-researcher of Prechtl at the University of Groningen, the neurologist B.C.L. Touwen, issued a translation of another popular product of Strauss' research group, authored by Strauss, Lehtinen, and a journalist and father of an MBD-child. The book was titled *The Other Child. The Brain-injured Child* and it was first published in 1960. We learn from this book that the Other Child (with capitals) showed five conspicuous difficulties: "hyperkinesis (hyperactivity), distractibility (short attention span), disinhibition (impulsivity), inflexibility (including perseveration), and emotional instability."[42] The authors promoted an approach to the vulnerable Other Child, which focused on the need to "structure" their environment and emphasized good old order and regularity. Awareness of developments in the Anglo-American scientific world made the Dutch translator systematically replace "brain-injured child" with "a child with a functional disorder of the brain." What an Other Child needed most was understanding and acceptance of his "otherness" from his family, teachers, and environment. Unlike Cruickshank, Strauss and his co-authors emphasized the need to conceive of the Other Child as unique and entitled to not only a small class at a special school but an individual development program and personal guidance as well. Teachers and parents, likewise, needed expert guidance to prevent secondary effects of the child's "otherness" from disturbing their relationship.[43]

In the early 1970s child psychiatrists authoring manuals for professionals working with "problem" children easily added the neurological concepts and brain-related etiology to their texts. A new introduction to child psychiatry authored by two psychoanalysts, for example, included a chapter on "organicity," which explained both minimal brain dysfunction and minimal brain damage along the lines of their many possible symptoms, next to more serious damage to the brain. Choreatiform and hyperkinetic restlessness were mentioned only as

---

[40] "Toespraak van prof.dr. W.M. Cruickshank," *Tijdschrift voor Orthopedagogiek* 11 (1972): 265–271; "Slotbijeenkomst werkbezoek," *Tijdschrift voor Orthopedagogiek* 11 (1972): 280–282.
[41] J. Valk, "De structurerende benadering als opvoedkundig beginsel," *Tijdschrift voor Orthopedagogiek* 9 (1970): 222–229.
[42] Richard S. Lewis et al., *The Other Child. The Brain-Injured Child* (New York/London: Grune & Stratton, 1960), 61.
[43] R.S. Lewis et al., *Het andere kind: Herkennen en begrijpen van het kind met lichte hersenfunctiestoornis* (Wageningen: Ouders van Nu, 1973).

symptoms of MBD.[44] To a manual for teachers and welfare workers on children with learning and behavioral problems a chapter was added on encephalopathies such as hyperkinesis and minimal brain damage, which was said to be usually caused by hypoxia. The author of the manual presented MBD prevalence numbers higher than those reported in the 1960s. He reported researchers like Prechtl to have found neurological abnormalities with 20 percent of school-aged boys and the German psychiatrist R. Lempp to have claimed that 40 percent of children's behavioral disorders were "certainly" caused by brain injury. However, the advice was double edged. Drug therapy might "sometimes" be helpful, but love, understanding, and "firm and consequent control" were always needed to support an MBD-child.[45]

Handbooks on learning disabilities for teachers authored by the first generation of university professors of special education studies gave by comparison hardly any attention to brain injury as cause of learning problems. Bladergroen, for example, preferred "choreatiform syndrome" as a label for overactive children and mentioned "light cerebral derangement" next to other organic conditions producing the problems of children she treated in LOM-schools.[46] Another founder of the academic study of learning and behavioral disabilities, a former member of the Ubbergen-team, J.F.W. Kok, briefly discussed children with brain-related impairment as a heterogeneous category, which included those with the "choreatiform syndrome" who could be handled in normal schools, those with a "weak structure" for whom a LOM-school and "structuring group therapy" were indicated, and the more serious cases of "structopathic" children to be treated with cognitive and behavioral therapy in institutions.[47] All of these authors emphasized that no two learning-disabled children were the same and that treatment always had to be individualized.

---

44 Th. Hart de Ruyter and L.N.J. Kamp, *Kinderpsychiatrie* (Deventer: Van Loghum Slaterus, 1972), 123–134.
45 Vedder, *Kinderen met leer- en gedragsmoeilijkheden* (Groningen: Wolters, 1970), eighth edition, 183–199.
46 W. Bladergroen, *Scholen voor kinderen met leer- en opvoedingsmoeilijkheden (L.O.M.-scholen)* (s.l.: s.n., 1970), 7.
47 J.F.W. Kok, *Struktopathische kinderen, een orthopedagogisch behandelingstype* ('s-Hertogenbosch: Malmberg, 1970); J.F.W. Kok, *Opvoeding en hulpverlening in behandelingstehuizen* (Rotterdam: Lemniscaat, 1970).

Criticism of MBD

Whereas during the 1970s the larger public in the Netherlands got used to MBD as a label for children with learning and behavioral problems, scientists doubted more and more the reality of a childhood syndrome of brain dysfunction. This became particularly manifest when in 1977 the international Society of Biological Psychiatry devoted its annual conference in Amsterdam to "Minimal Brain Dysfunction: fact or fiction." None of the lectures by international experts in the field was optimistic about the future of MBD as a diagnostic entity. The president of the Society criticized the label as "ill-defined," "vague," and therefore open to multiple interpretation. As causes of this vagueness he mentioned the mixing up of symptomatological and etiological meanings of the label, the non-specificity of the behavioral disorders commonly associated with MBD, all of which could just as well be due to causative factors of a different kind, and the ambivalence of the results of drug therapy.[48] After years of research into the influence of several kinds of drugs on MBD-children's behavior two Flemish child neurologists warned their co-researchers that stimulant drug therapy should be used only when hyperactivity and distractibility were the main problems. In other cases Cruickshank's "Minimal Stimulation Program" or behavior modification techniques like Kok's residential therapy for "structopathic" children were advised.[49]

At the Amsterdam conference an American child psychiatrist criticized not only the ambiguous title of MBD, the speculative notions about etiology, the heterogeneity and non-specificity of its manifestations, but also the practice of diagnosing, based on parents' and teachers' reports. These were subjective by nature, he insisted.[50] A British colleague stated frankly that he conceived of the very loose concept of MBD as "so overinclusive as to be more harmful than helpful in clinical practice." He also criticized the taking for granted of so-called "soft neurological signs" or slightly deviant neurological functions observed as EEG-irregularities. According to him, these were proof of a "diagnostic of soft thinking." Likewise, he criticized the neglect of development by researchers in the field. Children outgrew many symptoms and the plasticity of their central nerv-

---

[48] H.M. van Praag, "Introduction," in *Minimal Brain Dysfunction: Fact or Fiction*, ed. A.F. Kalverboer, H.M. van Praag and J. Mendlewicz (Basel etc.: Karger, 1978), 2–4.
[49] K. Pyck and P. Baines, "The Influence of Drugs on Minimal Brain Dysfunction," in *Minimal Brain Dysfunction*, 68–83.
[50] D. Shaffer, "Longitudinal Research and the Minimal Brain Damage Syndrome," in *Minimal Brain Dysfunction*, 18–34.

ous system had turned out to be much greater than was commonly assumed.[51] This plasticity was the subject of new research of Prechtl, who reported on recent publications in this field. As other neurologists he had shifted his focus away from the brain and toward the highly integrated and differentiated central nervous system as a whole.[52]

The lecture by a psychologist of the University of Groningen, Alex Kalverboer, was most critical of MBD as a label for a syndrome. Based on a review of the research literature he drew the conclusion that, despite the wide interest, progress in the field was slow. He attributed this to differences in refinement and standardization between disciplines. Although meaningful relationships between neurology and behavior were found, intra- and inter-individual variability turned out to be the main research finding. Therefore, he agreed with researchers who had drawn the conclusion that there was no scientific evidence linking behavioral disorders and independent signs of neurological dysfunction in children that would justify including them all in one syndrome. Labels like MBD were referring to heterogeneous groups of children and should therefore not be used. Further study of neurobehavioral relationships, however, was urgently needed, as was the development of relevant sub-classifications, he insisted.[53]

The rising interest in MBD, as well as the many mysteries surrounding the label, indeed stimulated research. Neurologists and neuropsychologists continued to look for causes of problem behavior, whereas special educationists focused on methods of remedial teaching. More centers of study were established, including residential institutions. Kok, Touwen, and Kalverboer continued to be involved in this research, which turned out to produce only more fuel for those who criticized the label as too unspecific.[54] Theoretically, special educationists exchanged the neurological model for social learning models based on empirical research and observation in classrooms,[55] and gradually also for models that shifted the focus away from the child toward the influence of the environment

---

51 W. Yule, "Diagnosis: Developmental Psychological Assessment," in *Minimal Brain Dysfunction*, 35–54.
52 H.F.R. Prechtl, "Minimal Brain Dysfunction Syndrome and the Plasticity of the Nervous System," in *Minimal Brain Dysfunction*, 96–105.
53 A.F. Kalverboer, "MBD: Discussion of the Concept," in *Minimal Brain Dysfunction*, 5–17.
54 For example a PhD tutored by Kalverboer: J.J. van der Meere, "Attentional Deficit Disorder with Hyperactivity: a Misconception" (PhD diss., University of Groningen, 1988).
55 For example: J.J. Dumont, *Leerstoornissen 3: Controversen en perspectieven* (Rotterdam: Lemniscaat, 1982).

on their cognitive and emotional development.[56] A shift of focus in the opposite direction of what the biologizing of psychiatry would soon bring.

In 1982 the professional journal on special education studies devoted a special issue to MBD to compensate for the many oversimplified stories released by the press.[57] Suggestions had been made that ten to 20 percent of the schoolchildren suffered from MBD.[58] Numbers of children sent to MBD-consulting hours to be tested had risen to an unprecedented level, whereas scientists' confidence in the use of the label had fallen to an all-times low. The vagueness of the popular label was underlined by the fact that in hardly any case of a tested child traces of a neurological dysfunction were found.[59] The EEG, moreover, was now discredited by experts as a diagnostic tool. MBD, a neurologist claimed, provided children with "a license for their behavior and parents with a license for failure."[60] In the meantime, parents' associations had been established, including a foundation to promote the integration of "outsiders".[61] Books, pamphlets, and magazines spread the message about the neurological background of learning and behavioral problems.[62] Neither children nor parents or teachers were to blame, the brain was.

The rising number of MBD diagnoses had significant effect. When government expenditure on LOM-schools and institutional care for "neurologically impaired" children continued to grow, the National Health Council (*Gezondheidsraad*) installed a committee of experts in 1979 to advice on this matter. Neurologists, such as Touwen, and psychologists, such as Kalverboer, were among its members, as was one special educationist, Kok. The committee did not report until 1985. Consistent with the international scientific consensus the report unanimously discarded the MBD label as "inadequate and unjustifiable." However, because the use of the term was so widespread and established in the lit-

---

56 J.F.W. Kok, "Structuurzwakte door opvoeding," *Tijdschrift voor Orthopedagogiek en Kinderpsychiatrie* 3 (1978): 21–29; H. Baartman, "Ontwikkelingen in de theoretische orthopedagogiek," in *Orthopedagogiek: Inzicht, uitzicht, overzicht*, ed. R. de Groot and J. van Weelden (Groningen: Wolters-Noordhoff, 1992), 46–73.
57 R. de Groot, "Redactioneel," *Tijdschrift voor Orthopedagogiek* 21 (1982): 203–204.
58 J. Troost, "MBD en de rol van de kinderneuroloog," *Tijdschrift voor Orthopedagogiek* 21 (1982): 239–243.
59 M. de Feijter, E. Lelieveld and A.F.M.M. Verdonck, "Minimal Brain Dysfunction?," *Tijdschrift voor Orthopedagogiek* 21 (1982): 205–218.
60 Troost, "MBD", 243.
61 Landelijke Stichting Integratie Buitenbeentjes, *Meer begrip voor buitenbeentjes* (Lochem/Poperinge: De Tijdstroom, 1979).
62 For example: Elisabeth Lockhorn, *Mijn kind is anders: Ouders en specialisten over Minimal Brain Dysfunction (MBD)* (Amsterdam: Meulenhoff Informatief, 1981).

erature and in common speech, the committee did not recommend throwing it away. The experts emphasized that they used it only to indicate "certain symptoms of a group of behavioral and learning disorders" and explained that the international literature had already got rid of MBD and replaced it with "hyperactivity" and "attention deficit disorder." In line with Kalverboer's earlier conclusion, the experts moreover insisted that rather than referring to a syndrome, "the use of the term MBD should be regarded as a signal to commence investigations in various directions for the purpose of drawing up a diagnostic profile of the child in question."[63] The Dutch experts disapproved of the use of drug therapy as there was no proof that a biochemical defect caused the problems of MBD-children. Categorical facilities or rehabilitation centers were no longer needed, as the individual child's learning problems had become pivotal. More research into these problems and their treatment, however, was an urgent need, according to the committee.[64] In a second report, published in 1987, the prevalence of MBD-symptoms (without specific learning disabilities such as dyslexia) was estimated to be some five percent of schoolchildren,[65] a number comparable to modern ADHD's prevalence in the Netherlands.[66]

By that time the committee's researchers were by and large the only academics who still used the label MBD. Psychiatrists began to use the American handbook DSM, which never included it. Special educationists continued their research into much more specific fields under the umbrella of learning disabilities, such as dyslexia and dyscalculia. Child-psychiatric manuals for school doctors and professionals in special education and youth care replaced the label MBD with the new DSM-III (1980) label ADD with or without Hyperactivity, and later with DSM-III-R (1987)'s label ADHD.[67] At the same time LOM-schools were seriously criticized as too expensive and promoting separation instead of integration of children with only minor problems. Pupils with special needs were to receive educational support within the regular school, the new consensus taught.[68] With the help of the media parents and their associations needed

---

[63] Gezondheidsraad, *Eerste deeladvies inzake Minimal Brain Dysfunction (MBD)* ('s-Gravenhage: Gezondheidsraad, 1985), 13–14.
[64] Gezondheidsraad, *Eerste deeladvies*, 115–32.
[65] Gezondheidsraad, *Minimal Brain Dysfunction (MBD): Tweede Deeladvies* ('s-Gravenhage: Gezondheidsraad, 1987).
[66] Batstra, *Hoe voorkom je ADHD?*
[67] F.C. Verhulst and J.A.R. Sanders-Woudstra, *Kinderpsychiatrie voor de praktijk* (Alphen aan den Rijn/Brussel: Samsom Stafleu, 1987), 100–106.
[68] K. van Rijswijk and E. Kool, "De ontwikkeling van het speciaal onderwijs in de tweede helft van de 20ᵉ eeuw" in *Het kind van de eeuw: het kind van de rekening?* ed. R. de Groot and J.D. van der Ploeg (Houten: Bohn StafleuVan Loghum, 1999), 131–155.

only a little more time to exchange the overinclusive, etiological label MBD for the symptoms describing one ADHD and to submit to Ritalin's regime.

Conclusion

In search of signs of de-educationalization, the history of the use of MBD as label for assumingly brain-related learning and behavioral problems of schoolchildren in the decades preceding the ADHD era shows that the label has never been uncontroversial. Neurologists and neuropsychologists were the first scientists who expressed their objections, calling it vague, non-specific, and overinclusive. Special educationists were, on the other hand, as a rule positive about "brain injury" as explanation for school problems. They used a variety of apparently "hardcore" neurological labels to successfully promote the study of learning disabilities and methods of individual remedial teaching as an academic discipline. By focusing on treatment rather than etiology, they managed to get round disputed matters such as causation, prevalence, and the use of medication.

The learning and behavioral problems that were labelled with MBD were neither rare – estimations in the Netherlands ran up to 20 percent of schoolchildren – nor more serious than the symptoms of ADHD. They were, however, too differentiated and unspecific to establish a causal link with neurological trauma or any particular brain dysfunction. Dutch researchers recognized these limits of the psychiatric label MBD relatively late. In 1971 none of the experts researching children with "minimal organic-cerebral damage" expressed as yet doubts as to the validity of the diagnosis and the assumed etiology. In the next years neurological and educational research parted ways. The latter focused on the development of American style treatment of overactive or easily distracted children with structuring behavior modification therapy and on remedial teaching of learning-disabled children. It shows that brain-related diagnosing and educational therapy went together well. This combination continued even after Dutch neuroscientists lost confidence in MBD as a label for low-achieving children, while special education studies seem to have gained prestige from the association with neurological trouble.

MBD's popularity among the larger public was based on individualized remedial teaching in special schools with small classes, claiming success while removing blame from parents and teachers. These conditions, next to the high number of MBD-diagnoses, have lengthened the use of the label well into the 1980s and created fertile ground for a positive reception of ADHD and large-scale use of medication as a quick and cheap fixer of school problems. Once more child scientists embraced an overinclusive label with a speculative etiology.

However, our search for signs of de-educationalization shows that it was the attractiveness of the neurological label that provided a much wanted explanation for otherwise unexplainable learning problems, and the sheer volume of the diagnosing of MBD that in the end discredited the didactic and behavioristic treatment of school-based children's problems. Ritalin's regime frames educational intervention as less cost-effective and more time-consuming than medication.

Bibliography

Baartman, H. "Ontwikkelingen in de theoretische orthopedagogiek." In *Orthopedagogiek: Inzicht, uitzicht, overzicht*, edited by R. de Groot and J. van Weelden, 46–73. Groningen: Wolters-Noordhoff, 1992.
Bakker, Nelleke. "The Discovery of Childhood Mental Illness: The Case of the Netherlands." *Bildungsgeschichte. International Journal for the Historiography of Education* 7 (2017): 191–204.
Barkley, Russell A. *Attention-Deficit Hyperactivity Disorder: A Handbook for Diagnosis and Treatment*. New York/London: The Guilded Press, 2006, third edition.
Batstra, Laura. *Hoe voorkom je ADHD? Door de diagnose niet te stellen*. Amsterdam: Nieuwezijds, 2012.
Beatty, Barbara, Emily Cahan, and Julia Grant, eds., *When Child Science Encounters the Child: Education, Parenting, and Child Welfare in 20th-Century America*. New York: Teachers College Press, 2006.
Bladergroen, Wilhelmina. *Scholen voor kinderen met leer- en opvoedingsmoeilijkheden (L.O.M.-scholen)*. s.l.: s.n., 1970.
Bladergroen, Wilhelmina J. "De orthopedagoog en kinderen met lichte organisch-cerebrale stoornissen." *Tijdschrift voor Orthopedagogiek* 10 (1971): 292–303.
Bloemink, Sanne. *Diagnosedrift: Hoe onze labelcultuur kinderen tekort doet*. Amsterdam: Amsterdam University Press, 2018.
Bolt, Timo. *Van zenuwachtig tot hyperactief: Andere kijk op ADHD*. Amsterdam: SWP, 2010.
Bolt, Timo, and Leonie de Goei. *Kinderen van hun tijd: Zestig jaar kinder- en jeugdpsychiatrie*. Van Gorcum: Assen, 2008.
Coles, Gerald. *The Learning Mystique: A Critical Look at "Learning Disabilities."* New York: Fawcett Columbine, 1987.
Cruickshank, William M. *The Brain-injured Child in Home, School, and Community*. New York: Syracuse University Press, 1967.
Cruickshank, William M. *Buitenbeentjes. Kinderen met hersenbeschadigingen thuis, op school en in de groep. Vertaald en bewerkt voor Nederland door J. Valk*. Rotterdam: Lemniscaat, 1975, fourth edition.
Depaepe, Marc. *De pedagogisering achterna: Aanzet tot een genealogie van de pedagogische mentaliteit in de voorbije 250 jaar*. Leuven/Amersfoort: Acco, 1998.
Depaepe, Marc, Frank Simon, and Angelo Van Gorp, eds. *Paradoxen van pedagogisering: Handboek pedagogische historiografie*. Leuven/Voorburg: Acco, 2005.
Depaepe, Marc. *Between Educationalization and Appropriation: Selected Writings on the History of Modern Educational Systems*. Leuven: Leuven University Press, 2012.

De Feijter, M., E. Lelieveld, and A.F.M.M. Verdonck. "Minimal Brain Dysfunction?" *Tijdschrift voor Orthopedagogiek* 21 (1982): 205–218.

De Groot, R. "Redactioneel." *Tijdschrift voor Orthopedagogiek* 21 (1982): 203–204.

Dijkstra, J. "De prognostische betekenis van neurologische afwijkingen bij pasgeboren kinderen." PhD diss., University of Groningen, 1960.

Dumont, J.J., *Leerstoornissen* 3: *Controversen en perspectieven*. Rotterdam: Lemniscaat, 1982.

Feinstein, Sheryl. *Inside the teenage brain*. London: Rowmer & Littlefield, 2009.

Franklin, Barry M. *From "Backwardness" to "At-Risk": Childhood Learning Difficulties and the Contradictions of School Reform*. Albany: State University of New York Press, 1994.

Gezondheidsraad. *Eerste deeladvies inzake Minimal Brain Dysfunction (MBD)*. 's-Gravenhage: Gezondheidsraad, 1985.

Gezondheidsraad. *Minimal Brain Dysfunction (MBD): Tweede Deeladvies*. 's-Gravenhage: Gezondheidsraad, 1987.

Grewel, F. "Terug naar het gewone lager onderwijs." *Tijdschrift voor Orthopedagogiek* 3 (1964): 2–11.

Grewel, F. "Partiële defecten: Pariëtaal syndroom." *Tijdschrift voor Orthopedagogiek* 3 (1964): 254–258.

Grewel, F. *Orthopedagogiek in ontwikkeling*. Groningen: Wolters, 1965.

Grewel, F., and E. Magadant-Mainz. "Partiële defecten: Analyse van een geval en aanwijzingen voor een paedagogisch-therapeutische behandeling." *Tijdschrift voor Buitengewoon Onderwijs en Orthopaedagogiek* 39 (1959): 66–74.

Hart de Ruyter, Th. "De betekenis der psycho-analytische paedagogie voor de opvoeding van kinderen met aanpassingsstoornissen." *Tijdschrift voor Buitengewoon Onderwijs en Orthopaedagogiek* 34 (1954): 38–42, 216–21.

Hart de Ruyter, Th., and L.N.J. Kamp. *Kinderpsychiatrie*. Deventer: Van Loghum Slaterus, 1972.

Hart de Ruyter, Th., and L.N.J. Kamp. *Kinderpsychiatrie*. Deventer, Van Loghum Slaterus, 1978, third edition.

Herderschêe, D. "De prophylaxis der oligophrenie." *Tijdschrift voor Buitengewoon Onderwijs en Orthopaedagogiek* 35 (1955): 4–9, 21–6, 65–71.

Hofstetter, Rita, and Bernard Schneuwly, eds. "History of Educational Sciences." *Paedagogica Historica* 40 (2004): 569–784.

Kalverboer, A.F. "MBD: discussion of the concept." In *Minimal Brain Dysfunction: Fact or Fiction*, edited by A.F. Kalverboer, H.M. van Praag, and J. Mendlewicz, 5–17. Basel etc.: Karger, 1978.

Kauffman, James M., and Timothy J. Landrum. *Children and Youth with Emotional and Behavioral Disorders*. Austin: Pro-ed, 2006.

Kessler, Jane W. "History of Minimal Brain Dysfunctions." In *Handbook of Minimal Brain Dysfunctions*, edited by Herbert E. Rie and Ellen D. Rie, 18–51. New York etc.: Wiley & Sons, 1980.

Kok, J.F.W. *Struktopathische kinderen, een orthopedagogisch behandelingstype*. 's-Hertogenbosch: Malmberg, 1970.

Kok, J.F.W. *Opvoeding en hulpverlening in behandelingstehuizen*. Rotterdam: Lemniscaat, 1970.

Kok, J.F.W. "Structuurzwakte door opvoeding." *Tijdschrift voor Orthopedagogiek en Kinderpsychiatrie* 3 (1978): 21–29.

Landelijke Stichting Integratie Buitenbeentjes. *Meer begrip voor buitenbeentjes.* Lochem/Poperinge: De Tijdstroom, 1979.

Landenstudies. Het onderwijs aan leerlingen met problemen in internationaal perspectief, edited by I.M. Abbring, C.J.W. Meijer, and J. Rispens. Groningen: RION, 1989. 2 Vols.

Lewis, Richard S., Alfred A. Strauss, and Laura E. Lehtinen, *The Other Child: The Brain-injured Child.* New York/London: Grune & Stratton, 1960.

Lewis, R.S., A.A. Strauss, and L.E. Lehtinen. *Het andere kind: Herkennen en begrijpen van het kind met lichte hersenfunctiestoornis.* Wageningen: Ouders van Nu, 1973.

Lockhorn, Elisabeth. *Mijn kind is anders: Ouders en specialisten over Minimal Brain Dysfunction (MBD).* Amsterdam: Meulenhoff Informatief, 1981.

Prechtl, H.F.R. *Het cerebraal gestoorde kind.* Groningen: Wolters, 1963.

Prechtl, H.F.R. "Minimal Brain Dysfunction Syndrome and the Plasticity of the Nervous System." In *Minimal Brain Dysfunction: Fact or Fiction,* edited by A.F. Kalverboer, H.M. van Praag, and J. Mendlewicz, 96–105. Basel etc.: Karger, 1978.

Prechtl, H.F.R., and J. Dijkstra. *Neurological Diagnosis of Cerebral Injury in the New Born.* Groningen: Noordhoff, 1960.

Pyck, K., and P. Baines. "The Influence of Drugs on Minimal Brain Dysfunction." In *Minimal Brain Dysfunction: Fact or Fiction,* edited by A.F. Kalverboer, H.M. van Praag, and J. Mendlewicz, 68–83. Basel etc.: Karger, 1978.

Remschmidt, Helmut Herman van Engeland and Jorma Piha, eds. *Child and Adolescent Psychiatry: Historical Development, Current Situation, Future Perspectives.* Darmstadt: Steinkopff Verlag, 1999.

Schachar, Russell J. "Hyperkinetic Syndrome: Historical Development of the Concept." In *The Overactive Child,* edited by Eric A. Taylor, 19–40. Oxford/Philadelphia: Blackwell/Lippincott, 1986.

Shaffer, D. "Longitudinal Research and the Minimal Brain Damage Syndrome." In *Minimal Brain Dysfunction: Fact or Fiction,* edited by A.F. Kalverboer, H.M. van Praag, and J. Mendlewicz, 18–34. Basel etc.: Karger, 1978.

Shorter, Edward, *A History of Psychiatry: From the Era of the Asylum to the Age of Prozac.* New York etc.: Wiley & Sons, 1997.

Simons, Maarten, and Jan Masschelein. "'It Makes Us Believe That It Is About Our Freedom': Notes on the Irony of the Learning Apparatus." In *Educational Research: The Educationalization of Social Problems,* edited by Paul Smeyers and Marc Depaepe, 191–204. New York etc.: Springer, 2008.

"Slotbijeenkomst werkbezoek." *Tijdschrift voor Orthopedagogiek* 11 (1972): 280–282.

Stemmer, Christina J. *Choreatiforme bewegingsonrust.* Groningen: Van Denderen, 1964.

Strauss, A.A., and N.C. Kephart. *Psychopathology and Education of the Brain Injured Child.* Grune & Stratton: New York, 1955. 2 Vols.

Strauss, A.A., and L.E. Lehtinen. *Psychopathology and Education of the Brain-injured Child.* Grune & Stratton: New York, 1947.

Swaab, Dick. *We Are Our Brains: From the Womb to Alzheimer's.* Amsterdam: Contact, 2010.

"Symposion Zetten mei 1971. Verslagen van verschillende onderzoekingen." *Tijdschrift voor Orthopedagogiek* 10 (1971): 304–307.

Tibout, P.H.C. "Report of the Section Partial Defects." In *Proceedings of the Second International Congress on Orthopedagogics,* edited by I.C. van Houte and B. Stokvis, 380–385. Amsterdam: Systemen Keesing, 1950.

"Toespraak van prof.dr. W.M. Cruickshank." *Tijdschrift voor Orthopedagogiek* 11 (1972): 265–271.

Troost, J. "MBD en de rol van de kinderneuroloog." *Tijdschrift voor Orthopedagogiek* 21 (1982): 239–243.

Valk, J. "De structurerende benadering als opvoedkundig beginsel." *Tijdschrift voor Orthopedagogiek* 9 (1970): 222–229.

Van der Meere, J.J. *Attentional Deficit Disorder with Hyperactivity: A Misconception.* Groningen: Universiteitsdrukkerij, 1988.

Van Essen, Mineke. *Wilhelmina Bladergroen: Vrouw in de eeuw van het kind.* Amsterdam: Boom, 2012.

Van Krevelen, D. And. *Nederlands leerboek der speciële kinderpsychiatrie.* Leiden: Stenvert Kroese, 1952.

Van Praag, H.M. "Introduction." In *Minimal Brain Dysfunction: Fact or Fiction,* edited by A.F. Kalverboer, H.M. van Praag, and J. Mendlewicz, 2–4. Basel etc.: Karger, 1978.

Van Rijswijk, K., and E. Kool. "De ontwikkeling van het speciaal onderwijs in de tweede helft van de 20^e eeuw." In *Het kind van de eeuw: Het kind van de rekening?,* edited by R. de Groot and J.D. van der Ploeg, 131–155. Houten: Bohn StafleuVan Loghum, 1999.

Vedder, R. *Kinderen met leer- en gedragsmoeilijkheden.* Groningen: Wolters, 1970, eighth edition.

Verhulst, F.C., and J.A.R. Sanders-Woudstra. *Kinderpsychiatrie voor de praktijk.* Alphen aan den Rijn/Brussel: Samsom Stafleu, 1987.

Weijers, Ido. "Zestig jaar kinder- en jeugdpsychiatrie in Nederland (1920–1980)." *Kind en Adolescent* 23 (2002): 82–96.

Yule, W. "Diagnosis: developmental psychological assessment." In *Minimal Brain Dysfunction: Fact or Fiction,* edited by A.F. Kalverboer, H.M. van Praag, and J. Mendlewicz, 35–54. Basel etc.: Karger, 1978.

5 Turns Taking Turns: Concepts, Approaches, and Methodologies in the Making

Section editor: Sarah Van Ruyskensvelde

Jeroen J.H. Dekker (Rijksuniversiteit Groningen, the Netherlands)
Dangerous, Seductive, and Innovative. Visual Sources for the History of Education

Abstract: This chapter focuses on images as sources for the history of education. Those sources could be scientifically dangerous – do they provide strong enough evidence? -, seductive – with their potential of bringing the researcher almost face to face with people in the past -, and innovative in adding new evidence and new insight to the history of education. After a discussion of the sources' dangerous and seductive aspects because of its complex relationship with educational reality, we concentrate on seventeenth-century emblematic books with educational and moral messages for parents and adolescents. Some emblems, consisting of text and image, are analyzed and interpreted with classic historic source criticism and with an educational variant of the iconographic method. It could indeed be concluded that also those visual sources could be dangerous and seductive. They, however, may shed new light on important issues in the history of education such as parenting and moral education, and also, if approached by historical source criticism, they do not differ in evidential value and strength from the traditional sources for the history of education and childhood.

Keywords: Visual sources, Emblems, Early modern Europe, Parenting, Historical sensation.

"Imagine"

In 1998, the twentieth ISCHE (International Standing Conference for the History of Education) conference in Kortrijk / Leuven was entitled "Imagine, All the Education. The Visual in the Making of the Educational Space through History". For this title, Marc Depaepe, the organizer of the conference, referred to the famous 1971 song *Imagine* by John Lennon. While Lennon imagined an ideal world of brotherhood and world peace, it was the intention of the conference organization that the participants would imagine education by focusing on the visual in the history of education. This was new for ISCHE. Never before had an ISCHE conference focused on the visual and, therefore, it was not a matter of fact that enough supply of good presentations would be available for the conference organizer's demand or that enough good material would be produced to make a volume fitting the scholarly standard. After all, not only within ISCHE conferences, but also in the study of the history of education more generally, most research focused on texts. Images, if used at all, were mostly treated as illustrations and not as primary sources; this, with the exception of a few national conferences and some publications of individual authors. One of them was the French historian Philippe Ariès (1914–1984), also one of the founding fathers of the cultural history of education with his *L'Enfant et la vie familiale sous l'Ancien Régime* from 1960, a study with groundbreaking and frequently debated theses on schooling and discipline and on childhood in history, yet long neglected because of its innovative and pioneering use of images. While the innovative French Annales School opened a new approach of topics and sources, visual sources remained neglected also by them for a long time. This was with the exception of Ariès who can be considered an outsider because only during the very last part of his career, he connected to the Annales's Powerhouse the *École des Hautes Études en Sciences Sociales*.[1] About his use of visual sources, art historian Francis Haskell wrote: "Philippe Ariès was far more aware than any of the *Annales* historians of the significance of figurative sources".[2] For the rest, this pioneering book was neither mentioned nor referred to in the introduction to and the contributions of the publication of the selected conference contributions.

Those contributions, published in the 505 page long special issue of *Paedagogica Historica* entitled *The Challenge of the Visual in the History of Education*, showed that something had changed in the study of the history of education with contributions on images as sources in a great variety and over several epochs.[3] This varied from religious iconography to Jesuit emblems in the sixteenth and seventeenth centuries, from Comenius's famous seventeenth-century *Orbis Sen-*

---

1 Philippe Ariès, *L'Enfant et la vie familiale sous l'Ancien Régime* (Paris: Librairie Plon, 1960). See Jeroen J.H. Dekker and Leendert F. Groenendijk, "Philippe Ariès's Discovery of Childhood after Fifty Years: The Impact of a Classic Study on Educational Research," *Oxford Review of Education* 38 (2012): 134.

2 Francis Haskell, *History and its images. Art and the Interpretation of the Past* (New Haven & London: Yale University Press, 1993): 496–497: "Philippe Aries was far more aware than any of the Annales historians of the significance of figurative sources." Haitsma Mulier, "Kunsthistorici en de geschiedenis. Een verslag van enkele ontwikkelingen," *Bijdragen en Mededelingen betreffende de geschiedenis der Nederlanden* 101 (1986): 202–214; a special issue on 'Historische beeldcultuur' [Historical image culture] of *Tijdschrift voor geschiedenis* 117 (2004); Merlijn Schoonenboom, "De verbeelde geschiedenis. Congresverslag "Kunst als historische bron,"" *Skript historisch tijdschrift* 19 (1997): 34–46.

3 Marc Depaepe and Bregt Henkens, "The History of Education and the Challenge of the Visual," in *The Challenge of the Visual in the History of Education*, ed. Marc Depaepe and Bregt Henkens, in co-operation with James C. Albisetti, Jeroen J.H. Dekker, Mark D'hoker, Frank Simon, and Jo Tollebeek (Gent: C.S.H.P., 2000), *Paedagogica Historica Supplementary Series* 6; also published in *Paedagogica Historica* 36 (2000): 11–17.

sualium Pictus to cigarette cards with ideological messages for youngsters in Nazi-Germany, from wall charts to images in nineteenth-century textbooks, from cartoons to colonial exhibitions, and from architecture to twentieth-century photographs and films. In sum, almost the entire educational technology available before the Internet Age was present. Moreover, in two introductory texts Hans-Ulrich Grunder addressed the negative image of images as dangerous for children and youngsters and António Nóvoa put the visual in the context of the new cultural history of education. After the conference and the publication of the special issue of *Paedagogica Historica*, the use of the visual in the study of the history of education increased and contributed substantially to the variety of sources now used within the new social and cultural history of education.[4] This was, apart from developments within the history of education, due to a variety of developments in various other academic disciplines such as art history, iconography,[5] cultural history, and cultural anthropology. Also, the enormous impact of the Internet and social media in particular after the year 2000 should not be underestimated. In other words, next to the cultural turn, history of education also underwent a visual turn.[6]

Within this visual turn, several approaches of images developed, two of them present during the ISCHE conference and in the special issue.[7] Those

---

[4] On social and cultural history of education, cf. António Nóvoa, "On History, History of Education, and History of Colonial Education," in *The Colonial Experience in Education. Historical Issues and Perspectives*, ed. António Nóvoa, Marc Depaepe, and Erwin V. Johanningmeier (Gent: C.S.H.P., 1995), *Paedagogica Historica Supplementary Series* 1: 23–61. On the use of images in history of education, see for example Jody Crutchley, Stephen G. Parker, and Sian Roberts, "Sight, sound and text in the history of education," *History of Education* 47 (2018): 143–147. An introduction to the special issue of the same title: Karin Priem and Inés Dussel, "The visual in histories of education: a reappraisal," *Paedagogica Historica* 53 (2017): 641–649. An introduction to the special issue of the same title: Kate Rousmanière, "Questioning the visual in the history of education," *History of Education* 30 (2001): 109–116; Jeroen J.H. Dekker, "Images as representations. Visual sources on education and childhood in the past," in *Paedagogica Historica* 51 (2015): 706–709; Jeroen J.H. Dekker, *Het verlangen naar opvoeden. Over de groei van de pedagogische ruimte in Nederland sinds de Gouden Eeuw tot omstreeks 1900* (Amsterdam: Bert Bakker, 2006).
[5] Cf. António Viñao, "Iconology and Education: Notes on the Iconographic Representation of Education and Related Terms," in *The Challenge of the Visual*, ed. Marc Depaepe et al., 75–91.
[6] Cf. Ulrike Mietzner, Kevin Myers, and Nick Peim, *Visual History. Images of Education* (Oxford: Peter Lang, 2005).
[7] Apart from images, also objects in general recently received more attention in cultural history and history of education; see for example Annette Caroline Cremer and Martin Mulsow, ed. *Objekte als Quellen der historischen Kulturwissenschaften. Stand und Perspektiven der Forschung*

two approaches are in the words of Franz Pöggeler *Bildung durch Bilder,* or education by images, and *Bildung in Bildern,* or education in images.⁸ *Bildung durch Bilder* is about the positive and negative educational power of images and originated in educational studies. *Bildung in Bildern* uses images as sources for the history of education and this approach originated mainly from outside the educational sciences in the fields of cultural history, art history, iconography, and cultural anthropology. While this distinction seems to be clear, research practice turns out to be more complex with, for example, also the historical study of images apart from contributing to their role in the educational process in the past also contributing to the history of education as such.⁹

That being said, this chapter focuses on *Bildung in Bildern,* or on the use of images as sources for the history of education, but this does not mean that the sources could not also have an educational intention as such; quite on the contrary, as we will see below in section three. The chapter's title suggests that visual sources could be dangerous, seductive, and innovative. This happened earlier with other new sources. In 1946, personal documents were characterized as "the most dangerous of all sources" by the Amsterdam professor of history Jan Romein in a reaction to his Amsterdam colleague Jacques Presser, who applauded such sources and coined the term "ego-documents".¹⁰ New sources that try to join the party of the traditional written sources are initially considered suspect, or at least considered as less strong in providing evidence, and, as a result, scientifically dangerous. But eventually, they could be innovative, adding new evidence and new insight to the history of education.

In section two, we will turn to the dangerous – do they provide strong enough evidence? – and seductive – through their potential of bringing the re-

---

(Köln: Böhlau, 2017), with a suggestion to approach objects in four ways, as illustration, argument, theme, and source (see pages 17–19).

8 Franz Pöggeler, "Bildung in Bildern. Versuch einer Typologie pädagogische relevanter Bildformen," in *Bild und Bildung. Beiträge zur Grundlegung einer pädagogischen Ikonologie und Ikonographie,* ed. Franz Pöggeler (Frankfurt a. M.: Peter Lang, 1992), 11–52. See recently Rita Hofstetter and Bernard Schneuwly, "Teaching culture and emotions. The function of art in Vygotsky's theory of child development (1920–1934)," in *Images of education. Cultuuroverdracht in historisch perspectief,* Hilda Amsing et. al. (Groningen: Uitgeverij Passage, 2018), 182–194; and Ian Grosvenor, ""A joyful idea reborn". Aesthetic education in a time of crisis," in *Images of education,* 208–219.

9 Cf. the *micro storia* by Noah W. Sobe, "Illustrating American progressive education. The cover illustration of John Dewey's 1899 *School and Society,*" in *Images of education,* 141–154.

10 Jan Romein, *De biografie* (Amsterdam: Ploegsma, 1946), 204, quoted by Arianne Baggerman and Rudolf Dekker, ""De gevaarlijkste van alle bronnen". Egodocumenten: nieuwe wegen en perspectieven," *Tijdschrift voor Sociale en Economische Geschiedenis* 1 (2004): 8–9.

searcher almost face to face with people in the past – aspects of visual sources by looking at their complex relationship with educational reality. In section three, we will concentrate on seventeenth-century emblematic books as examples of dangerous, seductive, and innovative visual sources. In section four, it will be concluded that visual sources could be dangerous, seductive, and innovative, but that those aspects could apply to most sources for the history of education and childhood.

Imaging Educational Reality

It is only via sources that we can come closer to the past. By indirect observation of the past, sources deliver clues or traces that refer to aspects of reality. It is true that for contemporary history, oral history interviews seem to deliver a more direct observation of the past. While such interviews could give us important information about the historical actor's individual experience of what once happened, it should, however, be realized that those interviews were not produced in the past but in the present with the interviewee no longer in the situation and the position, for example as a child, of the past. Hence, oral history can never be the voice of the past as sometimes promised, but only a voice from the present about the past with individual reflections and memories on past behavior, experiences, and events.[11]

Contact with the past will mostly be realized by looking at sources produced in that very past. Such sources could roughly be divided into categories such as written sources, visual sources, and material objects (among them those from archaeological research). Looking at those sources, and sometimes even touching them, brings the historian closer to people in the past. Research about the *Ancien Régime* cannot rely on visual sources such as photographs, films, radio, TV, and finally the Internet; hence looking at the faces of people is only possible by studying pictures, such as paintings, drawings, and emblems. Such sources could draw you in another time, could suggest direct contact with people and

---

[11] Paul R. Thompson, *The Voice of the Past. Oral History* (Oxford: Oxford University Press, 1978). See for the value of oral history interviews for historical child abuse and violence against children Christiaan Ruppert, Catrien Bijleveld, Mariëlle Bruning, Jeroen J.H. Dekker, Jan Hendriks, Trudy Mooren, Carol van Nijnatten, Wim Slot, and Micha de Winter, *Onvoldoende beschermd. Geweld in de Nederlandse jeugdzorg van 1945 tot heden* (Den Haag: Commissie Onderzoek naar Geweld in de Jeugdzorg, 2019).

patterns of behavior of that time, and so cause the experience of historical sensation.[12]

According to the Dutch historian Johan Huizinga (1872–1945) in his essay *The task of the history of culture*, historical sensation resulted from "what happens between the historian and the past". It could also be formulated as historical contact, which "can be provoked by a line from a chronicle, by an engraving, a few sounds from an old song."[13] Although historical sensation could be caused by various sources, Huizinga himself experienced it in its strongest way while looking at art by Jan Van Ecyk, Rogier Van der Weijden, and Hugo Van der Goes in an exhibition in Bruges in 1902.[14] The use of such master pieces of art for direct contact with the past could be complex because of the existence of published interpretations. Yet, according to Ankersmit, experiencing them "as if a whole civilization saw it for the first time" remains possible.[15] As a matter of fact, getting contact with the past should not be taken literally. This is not about a time machine available for historians but about a methodological habitus that could make it easier to get insight in the past.

No doubt this historical sensation could be realized easier through the seduction of visual sources. When doing this with seventeenth-century Dutch images, the researcher has to cope with radically changing interpretations of art historians about the relationship of these sources in particular (family) portraits and genre painting, with reality.[16] Dutch painting and drawing from the second half of the sixteenth century began to focus more on aspects of daily life, partly due to the Calvinistic Reformation and its 1566 iconoclastic outbreak, known in Dutch as the *Beeldenstorm*. As a result, genre painting, in particular, flourished according to Wayne Franits "on the prodigious scale that one finds in the Neth-

---

12 Cf. Bram Kempers, "De verleiding van het beeld. Het visuele als blijvende bron van inspiratie in het werk van Huizinga," *Tijdschift voor Geschiedenis* 105 (1992): 30–50.
13 Huizinga translated by Frank R. Ankersmit, *Sublime Historical Experience* (Stanford: Stanford University Press, 2005), 120–121.
14 Ankersmit, *Sublime*, 126.
15 Ankersmit, *Sublime*, 127. The paragraph on historical sensation is based on Jeroen J.H. Dekker, "Mirrors of reality? Material culture, Historical Sensation, and the Significance of Images for Research into Long-Term Educational Processes," in *Educational Research: Material culture and its representation*, ed. Paul Smeyers and Marc Depaepe (Dordrecht: Springer, 2014), 35–36.
16 This paragraph is based on Jeroen J.H. Dekker, "The Restrained Child. Imaging the Regulation of Children's Behaviour and Emotions in Early Modern Europe: The Dutch Golden Age," in *Images of the European Child*, ed. María del Mar del Pozo Andrés and Bernat Sureda García, Special Issue of *History of Education and Children's Literature* 13 (2018): 21–24.

erlands".[17] Becoming "more true-to-life",[18] those pictures did have for many art historians an "ostensible capacity to proffer unmediated access to the past", or, in Huizinga's words, historical sensation. They were "direct transcriptions of the mundane experiences of contemporary Netherlanders"[19] and were considered as almost mirrors of reality.

In the twentieth century, this paradigm of interpretation of Dutch genre paintings became weaker and, instead another paradigm, the iconological approach inspired by Erwin Panofsky's *Studies in Iconology* from 1939, gained significance. The images now evolved from reality mirroring pictures to puzzles of complex messages.[20] Art historian Francis Haskell even wrote that "even images formerly assumed to depict only what could have been seen by an 'innocent eye' were in fact the products of conscious or unconscious manipulation: Dutch genre scenes and still lives, for instance".[21] From the 1980s, however, this paradigm was also contested. It was argued that the strong emphasis on complex symbols was incompatible with "the realistic look of Dutch art".[22] This new paradigm was strongly advocated by the art historian Jan Baptist Bedaux, in his contribution, *The Reality of Symbols*, in which he, just as usual prior to the iconological turn, pointed to the realistic aspects of Dutch painting and drawing.[23]

While this debate was often technical, methodical, and addressed the relationship between emblems and paintings, the meaning of symbols and their seemingly decreasing influence during the seventeenth century, it also was a debate about the fundamental issue of the relationship between source and reality. Were the images mirroring reality, or puzzles of complex symbols, or perhaps ref-

---

17 Wayne Franits, *Dutch Seventeenth Century Genre Painting* (New Haven & London: Yale University Press, 2008 or 2004), 261; note 3 on secular painting.
18 Josua Bruyn, "A Turning-Point in the History of Dutch Art," in *Dawn of the Golden Age, Northern Netherlandish Art 1580–1620*, ed. Ger Luijten et. al. (Amsterdam/Zwolle: Rijksmuseum/Waanders, 1993), 112–121.
19 Franits, *Dutch Seventeenth Century*, 1.
20 Franits, *Dutch Seventeenth Century*, 4.
21 Haskell, *History and its Images*, 5. Erwin Panofsky, *Studies in Iconology. Humanistic Themes in the Art of the Renaissance* (New York: Harper and Row, 1972 or 1939).
22 Franits, *Dutch Seventeenth Century*, 5.
23 Jean Baptist Bedaux, *The Reality of Symbols. Studies in the Iconology of Netherlandish Art 1400–1800* ('s-Gravenhage/Maarssen: Gary Schwarz/SDU, 1990), 112–113. Cf. Willem Th.M. Frijhoff and Marijke Spies, *1650. Bevochten eendracht* (The Hague: SDU, 1999); Jean Baptist Bedaux, "Introduction," in *Pride and Joy. Children's portraits in the Netherlands 1500–1700*, ed. Jan Baptist Bedaux and Rudolf E.O. Ekkart (Gent/Amsterdam/New York: Ludion and Abrams, 2000), 19–22; Jeroen J.H. Dekker, Leendert F. Groenendijk, and Johan Verberckmoes, "Proudly raising vulnerable youngsters. The scope for education in the Netherlands," in *Pride and Joy*, 43–60; Dekker, "Mirrors of reality?," 38–40.

erences to the reality of symbols? It seems that the theory of representation could help in this issue.[24] In the interpretation of philosopher and historian Frank Ankersmit,[25] a representation of reality does not mean mirroring reality, but refers to various aspects of reality.[26] This means that both real people, among them children, parents, and educators, and ideas and messages on patterns of behavior belong to historic realities. Thus, both visual sources about real people and genre paintings and prints about messages on patterns of behavior could enable the historian of education to engage in a closer contact with the realities studied, not by mirroring those realities but by referring to aspects of them.[27]

The Evaluation of Visual Sources: Emblems on Parenting and Education

In this section, danger, seduction, and the innovative value of visual sources are shown by evaluating two seventeenth-century emblems through three source characteristics: 1) its strength, 2) its educational meaning, and 3) its relationship with educational reality. This evaluation is inspired by the stages of a classic iconographical analysis of a) the image's authenticity, date, and the artist's identity, b) the image's main elements, c) the image's subject-matter and meaning, and d) the relationship of the image to the cultural context. Stating the meaning of the image, stage c, involves knowledge of the symbol language of the specific period, to be found in contemporary art theory publications, such as Cesare Ripa's popular painter's guide and texts by the French painter Charles Le Brun (1619–1690), explaining to the reader how to interpret the expression of the pas-

---

[24] See for the following Jeroen J.H. Dekker, "Images as representations. Visual sources on education and childhood in the past," *Paedagogica Historica* 51 (2015): 706–709.

[25] See Frank R. Ankersmit, *Meaning, truth, and reference in historical representation* (Ithaca, New York: Cornell University Press, 2012); Frank R. Ankersmit, "Representatie als cognitief instrument," *Algemeen Nederlands Tijdschrift voor Wijsbegeerte* 103 (2011): 243–262; and Frank R. Ankersmit, *De navel van de geschiedenis. Over interpretatie, representatie en historische realiteit* (Groningen: Historische Uitgeverij Groningen, 1990). Cf. P.B.M. Blaas, "Op zoek naar een glimp van het verleden. De geschiedfilosofie van Frank Ankersmit," *Tijdschrift voor Geschiedenis* 119 (2006): 377–386.

[26] Ankersmit, "Representatie," 246–249 and 250–252.

[27] See Eddy de Jongh and Gert Luijten, *Mirror of everyday life. Genreprints in the Netherlands 1550–1700* (Amsterdam/Gent: Rijksmuseum/Snoeck-Ducaju & Zoon, 1986). Cf. Joseph Wachelder, "Chardins *Touch*. De kunst van het spelen," in *Images of education*, 30–32.

sions in the face, in general, and in the eyebrows, in particular.[28] For the remainder, the meaning of symbols should not be over-interpreted for becoming less crucial and more an addition to the painting during the seventeenth century, while being crucial for the meaning's interpretation in sixteenth century paintings.[29]

The above proposed three-fold evaluation of emblem characteristics is an educational application of this iconographical method. The first characteristic, the source's strength and usefulness, is about the results of iconographical research into a series of topics: its authenticity to assure that we do not have to do with a forgery, its date, and the author's or artist's identity, so that the source can be related to a period of history, and, if possible, to an artist, the identity of the people represented in the image, so that we know with whom we could come face to face – not an issue with genre paintings and emblems as sources on patterns of behavior –, the artist's educational intentions, and finally the source's public reception. The strength and usefulness of a source depends on the outcome of those criteria, but is not simply adding up, for e.g. a popular source with thus major impact could be evaluated as strong even if scoring low on the other criteria with the exception of authenticity. The source's second characteristic, its educational meaning, forms the educational application of the iconographical investigation into subject-matter and meaning of the image and includes the enumeration of the main elements of the source. The source's relationship with educational reality, its third characteristic, is the educational application of relating the source to its cultural context. Below follows the presentation of the source and its evaluation by those three criteria.

---

28 See Dekker, "The Restrained Child," 25–27. On Le Brun see Peter Harrison, "Reading the passions: The fall, the passions, and dominion over nature," in *The soft underbelly of reason: The passions in the seventeenth century*, ed. Stephen Gaukroger (London and New York: Routledge, 1998), 49–78 (see page 61); Hugh Honour and John Fleming, *A World History of Art* (London: Laurence King Publishing, 2009, 7th edition), 604. According to Jan Plamper, *The History of Emotions. An Introduction* (Oxford: Oxford University Press, 2015), 19, Le Brun's "taxonomy of facial expression" was used until the nineteenth century.
29 Cf. Jeroen J.H. Dekker, *De pedagogische ruimte in de tijd* (Groningen: Rijksuniversiteit Groningen, 2019), 5–8.

The Source: Mirror from the Ancient and Modern Time by Jacob Cats

Emblem books differ fundamentally from paintings, as they combine text with image, and because of their large readership. The topics in both sources are often based on the same popular proverbs, and then contain the same educational meaning. Jacob Cats (1581–1660) authored most popular Dutch emblem books on moral and educational issues. He wrote them by adopting and adapting the existing and very popular *ars amatoria* style. One of his emblem books, *Spiegel Van den Ouden ende Nieuwen Tijdt* [Mirror of the Ancient and Modern Time, further abridged as *Mirror*] was published in 1632, and contained texts written by Cats and pictures made by Adriaan van de Venne. Moreover, it contains more than 1,600 proverbs in various languages.[30] Each emblem is entitled after a proverb, and its meaning is extensively explained in a text full of quotes in several languages, including many quotes from the Bible and Ovid's *Metamorphoses*. Part I of *Mirror* consists of seven emblems mentioned by Cats *Opvoedinghe van kinderen* [Child rearing] and 45 emblems on *Eerlicke Vryage* [Fair courtship]. For the evaluation of the source, emblems IV and VII on, respectively, child rearing and courtship were selected. Together they represent the main educational message of Cats: educating young children and instructing them at the right time in a context of parental and marital love as parental duties; and finding a partner by avoiding the moral dangers and pitfalls of courtship.[31] Courtship was also treated extensively in the emblem book *Sinne- and minnebeelden*.[32] After the five emblems in *Mirror* on parenting and child rearing, two emblems form the transition to the second topic of courtship and its dangers. Emblem VI, "Es musz ein ieder ein par narren Schuhen vertretten, wo nicht mer" [One must wear a pair of shoes from a jester, before one is truly wise] is about the *sui generis* character of youth as a phase of enjoying life, of learning, and of making mistakes, also in matters of

---

30 Jacob Cats, *Spiegel Van den Ouden ende Nieuwen Tijdt, Bestaende uyt Spreeck-woorden ende Sin-Spreucken, ontleent van de voorige ende tegenwoordige Eeuwe, verlustigt door menigte van Sinne-Beelden, met Gedichten en Prenten daer op passende; Dienstigh tot bericht van alle gedeelten des levens; beginnende van de Kintsheyt, ende eyndigende met het eynde alles vleech* ('s Gravenhage: Isaac Burchoorn, Boeck-drucker, 1632); a facsimile edition similar in appearance and format is available (Amsterdam: Facsimile Uitgaven Nederland NV, 1968).
31 See Jeroen J.H. Dekker and Inge J.M. Wichgers, "The Embodiment of Teaching the Regulation of Emotions in Early Modern Europe," *Paedagogica Historica* 54 (2018): 58–65.
32 See Jeroen J.H. Dekker, *Educational Ambitions in History. Childhood and Education in an Expanding Educational Space from the Seventeenth to the Twentieth Century* (Frankfurt am Main /Berlin/Bern/Brussels/New York/Oxford/Vienna: Peter Lang, 2010), 59–64.

love.³³ Emblem VII, *Amor docet Musicam* [Love teaches Music] not only emphasizes Amor's necessity, but also anticipates, as we will see below, Amor's risks and pitfalls, the main topic of the next emblems of part one of *Mirror*.

The Source's Strengths and Weaknesses

Historians inspired by the positivistic criteria proclaimed by the famous nineteenth-century German historian Leopold von Ranke would probably decide about the strength of sources by measuring their distance to reality. As a result, sources, among them *belles-lettres*, hagiographies, and later on also ego-documents and visual sources, were neglected or evaluated as weak sources, as they were unable to tell "*Wie es eigentlich gewesen*". However, as argued above, the complex relationship between sources and reality makes that, on the one hand, no source mirrors reality, while, on the other hand, all sources have a relationship with aspects of reality. Source criticism works out differently for different sources like written and visual ones. Moreover, the strength of a source depends on its potential to answer research questions.³⁴ This point of view will guide my evaluation of the strengths and weaknesses of the two selected emblems from *Mirror* by Jacob Cats.

Determining authenticity, date, and identity of the artist is no problem for this source, in contrast to many paintings with date, name of the artist, and sometimes also the people represented remaining unknown.³⁵ This source was a bestseller and was distributed in large numbers with the name of author, artist of the images, publishing house, and year of publication on the title page. It is true that in editions after the seventeenth century, some changes could be observed, both in text and images. While important for research in the development of the source across historical time, this issue is not treated in this chapter, which focuses on the seventeenth century.³⁶

---

33 Cf. Dekker, "The Restrained Child," 37–38.
34 According to Marc Bloch, *Apologie pour l'histoire ou métier d'historien* (Paris: Armand Colin, 1975 or 1941), 66: "C'est une des tâches les plus difficile de l'historien que de rassembler les documents dont il estime avoir besoin".
35 Cf. the anonymous *Portrait of a Family*, c.1668, see Dekker, *Educational Ambitions*, 50–51.
36 A complete list of editions of the works of Cats is Jan Bos and J.A. Gruys, ed. *Cats Catalogus. De werken van Jacob Cats in the Short-Title Catalogue, Netherlands* (The Hague: Royal Library of the Netherlands, 1996). For the historical change of an image see María del Mar del Pozo Andrés and Sjaak Braster, "An image travelling across Europe. The transformation of "The school in an uproar" into "Le désordre dans l'école"(1809–1855)," in *Images of education*, 84–97.

Not only the author's identity, but also his intentions are clear. Jacob Cats, one of the richest and most powerful men of the Dutch Republic and, for a long time, *Raadspensionaris* [Grand Pensionary] of the States of Holland and Zeeland (which could be considered a "prime minister" of the Dutch Republic), was a politician and no philosopher or theologian. He wrote his emblem books next to his function in politics and not for profit, although his emblem books turned out to become profitable. A faithful Christian, he was an educational moralist with a mission to tell people about an active and adequate parenting style that revolved around having patience with children and with their temporal weaknesses, but never drifting away from the Christian foundations of his educational advices.

His educational ideas and advices were shared with an impressive readership. His emblem books became best and long sellers: ranked third on the seventeenth century bestseller list after the Bible and *De Imitatione Christi* by Thomas à Kempis. By reading those books and by trying to decode the meaning of image and text, it becomes possible to put ourselves into the position of this massive seventeenth-century readership. The books were popular as a result of several reasons: the combination of text and image made them attractive, because of the foundation of his advices on the Christian virtues of faith, hope and love, and the cardinal virtues of wisdom, justice, fortitude, and temperance (instead of on specific church bound principles) the emblem books were also sold outside of the Calvinist community, of which he was a devoted member, and finally the use of easy-to-learn rhymes.[37]

The combination of text and image made the emblem books more attractive for the contemporary readers but also makes it stronger as a source. The image represents only a part of the meaning of the emblem, with the text providing extra and essential information. This makes the interpretation of the image of the emblem less speculative than the interpretation of genre paintings or drawings that come without complementary texts. The strength of emblem books, such as *Mirror*, while primarily intended for a Dutch readership, is its transnational and even European scope.[38] As mentioned before, *Mirror* contains more than 1,600 proverbs in several languages and numerous quotes from the Bible and from classic texts, such as Ovid's *Metamorphoses*.

---

[37] See Jeroen J.H. Dekker, "Woord en beeld: Jacob Cats en de pedagogische cultuuroverdracht in de zeventiende eeuw," in *De gereformeerden en hun vormingsoffensief door de eeuwen heen*, ed. Jan W. Steutel, Doret J. de Ruyter, and Siebren Miedema (Zoetermeer: Meinema, 2009), 47–65.
[38] Another popular emblem book by Cats, *Houwelick* [Marriage] from 1625 was written in Dutch only and intended for mothers.

It therefore seems that emblems from *Mirror* are a strong source for answers on questions about the educational discourse, and how this discourse, originally starting in philosophical texts in Greek and Latin and in mostly Latin written theological texts, in an almost playful form reached the broad middle class in the seventeenth-century Dutch Republic.

The Emblem's Educational Meaning

The iconographic method could help historians when using emblems with images, often containing a hidden meaning.[39] This meaning could be reconstructed by first looking precisely to the image's elements and then to the accompanying text. In the words of James Hall: "the elements of a picture make not only a unity of design but contain a unity of meaning, sometimes not immediately recognizable."[40]

In the middle of the image of emblem IV (Figure 1) stands a man caressing a swine that goes lying in the manure. Right behind him stand two women who look at him and at the swine. The younger woman, the arms crossed, is watching full of attention. An older woman, also watching full of attention, shows a look of disapproval, to be seen in the expression of her face. Her strained mouth and lowered eyebrows express abomination, so Le Brun would interpret it with his seventeenth-century way of looking. Moreover, she points with her right hand and a piercing index finger to the man and the swine. She clearly disagrees with man's behavior. At the background is a farmhouse. Outside are two other people, a woman also looking at the man and the swine but in the image without an expression on her face, and another person, probably a man who looks to the other side and therefore cannot see the man caressing the swine. The German title of the emblem (in the image below is also a Dutch translation), *"Wann man die Sauer kutzelt, so legt sie sich im dreck"*, which means "When the swine is pampered, she goes lying in the manure". Still the emblem's image and caption together are not giving enough information to clarify its meaning. To interpret its meaning, the complementary text is needed. After reading this text, it turns out that the image is about bad education: the swine represents the child and the man is the parent. The emblem's message is that parents should, in their love for their children, not caress them too much, as pampering children is not educating them but, according to Cats, making children lazy, as is the swine. More disci-

---

39 See further Dekker, "The restrained child," 25–27. See Franits, *Dutch Seventeenth Century*, 4.
40 James Hall, *Dictionary of subjects and symbols in art* (London: John Murray, 1991 or 1974), x.

Figure 1: Emblem IV, "Wann man die Sauer kutzelt, so legt sie sich im dreck" [When the swine is pampered, she goes lying in the manure], Jacob Cats, *Spiegel Van den Ouden ende Nieuwen Tyt*, 1657 (Special Collections, University Library, University of Groningen).

pline and educational activism are necessary for children's adequate development. The meaning of the emblem – the necessity of active parenting – becomes

Figure 2: Emblem VII, Amor docent Musicam [Love teaches music], Jacob Cats, *Spiegel Van den Ouden ende Nieuwen Tyt*, 1657 (Special Collections, University Library, University of Groningen).

clear when combining the, initially perhaps funny, encoded image with the accompanying text.[41]

Also the meaning of emblem VII, *Amor docet Musicam* (Figure 2) is not immediately clear. The first impression of the emblem's image leads to the conclu-

---

41 Cats, *Spiegel*, Emblem IV, 10–11. Cf. Dekker and Wichgers, "The Embodiment," 60–61.

sion that it is a representation of the Merry Family such as those by Jan Steen, who always depicted people playing on music instruments. Those images represent, however, the proverb *As the Old Sing, so Pipe the Young* on the impact of parental behavior on children. Emblem VII represents another proverb, namely *Amor docet Musicam*.[42]

The image of this emblem tells about the fruitful working of love, in the text represented by Amor, son of Venus. In the image, he is mentioned with his name Eros, put in the Greek alphabet, and he sits prominently in the middle of the emblem behind a table, looking concentrated to a music book that is in front of him. On the table is another, closed book, which is perhaps a music book. In his left hand, Amor has an arrow; his other main attribute, the bow, is invisible. His right hand lays in the left hand of an older woman. This woman also looks concentrated at the music book. She does not play an instrument in contrast to the other four people in the main part of the image, who together form a music company of two boys and one girl playing music instruments and another girl singing. On her lap is the text of a song. When using Le Brun's seventeenth-century method of interpreting their emotional state by looking at the lifted mouth and cheeks and the widely opened eyes in their faces, we could conclude this is happiness. For the rest, in this case of making music faces also do show an expression related to efforts to play a specific instrument as for example with the boy playing the pan flute, which influences the position of his cheeks. Still, the youngsters seem to look rather happy, with one exception, that of the singing girl. Her eyes and mouth are widely open, but not only because she sings. Her facial expression seems to refer rather to fear, not because of not being able to properly sing, but of fear for Amor's arrow. Before her feet is a rose in little pieces and another closed book. Amor and the singing girl do look rather sensual when compared with the other people in the emblem. Moreover, if Amor's arrow should be raised and thrown, it should hit the singing girl. Through a window, we can see in the background another group of people. A young man or somewhat older boy, leaning on something that looks like a lance, looks longingly at an older girl or young woman lying on the floor, seemingly asleep before a small fountain. On top of it is a small cupid.

The image seems to communicate a double message. The inside main part of the image emphasizes the fruitful effects of Amor who does not use the disciplinary methods common at school but only love, as it is formulated in the accompanying text. Indeed, everything goes smoothly, as the children are seemingly

---

[42] See Dekker and Wichgers, "The Embodiment," 62–63.

happy.⁴³ The unhappy singing girl is the first counterpart to this message. This counterpart is enforced in the outside part of the image that seems to refer to the dangers and pitfalls of love. That is the main subject of the next emblems of part I of *Mirror*. The double message characterizes the emblem as a transition emblem from rather optimistic to mainly warning messages.

The Emblem's Relationship to Educational Reality

The emblems have a twofold relationship with reality. First, their content refers to desired patterns of educational behavior and to parents, children, and youngsters with their specific roles in the educational process. Secondly, the emblems represent educational ideas present in the heads of many parents and future parents who read them and looked at them as a result of their great popularity. Historians of education can only catch a glimpse of the educational reality when using a single source. Therefore, it is better to use multiple sources for answering the same research questions. The historian of education should operate in those matters like a detective or a journalist. Within the social sciences, using various sources became a methodically accepted research method, which goes by the name of triangulation, only recently. Yet, it was already established in the historical sciences, especially for historians of education and childhood who are confronted with a serious problem of scarcity of sources.⁴⁴

The relationship of a specific source with reality is different in perspective, intention, and often also in interest.⁴⁵ Emblems as a source are special, in that they are a triple source consisting of a caption with information on the meaning, an image showing part of the emblem's story, and finally a text telling the story as a whole. In the case of *Mirror*, it also provides quotations from other sources onto which the emblem has been based. However, it remains wise to confront emblems with other sources, in particular with genre painting. The emblems in *Mirror* are about a specific proverb, mostly shown in the emblem's caption. Part of genre painting of the late sixteenth and seventeenth centuries is also based on proverbs, often even the same ones. In the 1970s and 1980s, art historians even stated that genre paintings, such as those by Jan Steen, should be interpreted mainly from the meanings of emblems, such as those by Cats. This ap-

---

[43] Cats, *Spiegel*, Emblem VII, 19–22.
[44] Cf. Peter Stearns, "Challenges in the History of Childhood," *The Journal of the History of Childhood and Youth* 1 (2008): 35–42; Paula S. Fass, "Childhood and Memory," *The Journal of the History of Childhood and Youth* 3 (2010): 155–164.
[45] Dekker, "The Restrained Child," 32–33.

proach was criticized strongly by art historians, such as Jean Baptiste Bedaux, who in *The reality of symbols* warned that historians cannot neglect the reference to the reality of those paintings, and should not exaggerate the complexity of the symbols in paintings and emblems. It still remains that genre painting and emblems often do cover the same educational themes. For example, active education, a fundamental theme in the emblem books by Cats and present in emblem IV, is also prominent in many genre paintings. This makes the emblem as a source even stronger, as representations of broadly shared ideas of the necessity of education and parental responsibility. Indeed, emblem books as sources in connection with genre painting show even more strongly that consciousness of the necessity of education was a central issue in the educational discourse of the sixteenth and seventeenth centuries among philosophers, theologians, and in popular books and emblem books, such as those by the educational moralist Cats.

Conclusion

In drawing up a balance, it seems that all sources for the history of education and childhood, including written ones, could potentially be dangerous and seductive. Indeed, all sources represent only a segment of historical reality, or show one perspective. "New" sources are often initially considered as less strong and more dangerous than traditional and "tested" source materials. This has been the case with for example personal documents or ego documents that have a seductive dimension because of seemingly opening an intimate and private world, which was initially considered as dangerous because of not fitting the most important criterium for historical sources as stated in the nineteenth century by Leopold von Ranke, namely objectiveness. Eventually, personal documents became accepted as sources for historical research and that happened with visual sources too. Also those sources were initially neglected, even by the innovative historians of the Annales School that shifted many boundaries in historical research, but not this one. If used, visual sources in the history of education were mostly sources with the intention of *Bildung durch Bilder*, such as the famous *Orbis Sensualium Pictus* by Comenius and many illustrations in textbooks. Starting with the publication in 1960 by Philippe Ariès, the innovative outsider in French cultural history, visual sources became, although initially very slowly, part of the history of education too, now both for *Bildung durch Bilder* and for *Bildung in Bildern*. The last 20 years saw a fast acceleration of this process. The conference *Imagine* from 1998 in Kortrijk / Leuven stimulated this development through its great audience of historians of education. As with all sources, including digital images in this digital age, the emblems studied in this chapter could also be potentially dangerous if interpreted wrongly because of the sometimes complex puzzles present in the image. But they are also seductive for seemingly bringing the researcher face to face with patterns of behavior in the past. Therefore, as with all sources for the history of education, those emblems should also be evaluated by the criteria of source criticism so that it becomes clear that they would fit the research questions asked of them.

Bibliography

Amsing, Hilda, et al. *Images of education. Cultuuroverdracht in historisch perspectief.* Groningen: Uitgeverij Passage, 2018.
Ankersmit, Frank R. "Representatie als cognitief instrument." *Algemeen Nederlands Tijdschrift voor Wijsbegeerte* 103 (2011): 243–262.
Ankersmit, Frank R. *De navel van de geschiedenis. Over interpretatie, representatie en historische realiteit.* Groningen: Historische Uitgeverij Groningen, 1990.
Ankersmit, Frank R. *Sublime Historical Experience.* Stanford: Stanford University Press, 2005.
Ariès, Philippe. *L'Enfant et la vie familiale sous l'Ancien Régime.* Paris: Librairie Plon, 1960.
Baggerman, Arianne, and Rudolf Dekker. ""De gevaarlijkste van alle bronnen". Egodocumenten: nieuwe wegen en perspectieven." *Tijdschrift voor Sociale en Economische Geschiedenis* 1 (2004): 3–22.
Bedaux, Jan Baptist, and Rudolf E.O. Ekkart, eds. *Pride and Joy. Children's portraits in the Netherlands 1500–1700.* Gent/Amsterdam/New York: Ludion and Abrams, 2000.
Bedaux, Jean Baptist. "Introduction." In *Pride and Joy*, edited by Jan Baptist Bedaux and Rudolf E.O. Ekkart, 11–31. Gent/Amsterdam/New York: Ludion and Abrams, 2000.
Bedaux, Jean Baptist. *The Reality of Symbols. Studies in the Iconology of Netherlandish Art 1400–1800.* 's-Gravenhage/Maarssen: Gary Schwarz/SDU, 1990.
Blaas, P.B.M. "Op zoek naar een glimp van het verleden. De geschiedfilosofie van Frank Ankersmit." *Tijdschrift voor Geschiedenis* 119 (2006): 377–386.
Bloch, Marc. *Apologie pour l'histoire ou métier d'historien.* Paris: Armand Colin, 1975 or 1941.
Bos, Jan, and J.A. Gruys, eds. *Cats Catalogus. De werken van Jacob Cats in the Short-Title Catalogue, Netherlands.* The Hague: Royal Library of the Netherlands, 1996.
Bruyn, Josua. "A Turning-Point in the History of Dutch Art." In *Dawn of the Golden Age, Northern Netherlandish Art 1580–1620*, edited by Ger Luijten et al., 112–121. Amsterdam/Zwolle: Rijksmuseum/Waanders, 1993.
Cats, Jacob. *Spiegel Van den Ouden ende Nieuwen Tijdt, Bestaende uyt Spreeck-woorden ende Sin-Spreucken, ontleent van de voorige ende tegenwoordige Eeuwe, verlustigt door menigte van Sinne-Beelden, met Gedichten en Prenten daer op passende; Dienstigh tot bericht van alle gedeelten des levens; beginnende van de Kintsheyt, ende eyndigende met het eynde alles vleech.* 's Graven-Hage: Isaac Burchoorn, Boeck-drucker, 1632 [a facsimile edition similar in appearance and format: Amsterdam: Facsimile Uitgaven Nederland NV, 1968].
Cremer, Annette Caroline, and Martin Mulsow, eds. *Objekte als Quellen der historischen Kulturwissenschaften. Stand und Perspektiven der Forschung.* Köln: Böhlau, 2017.

Crutchley, Jody, Stephen G. Parker, and Sian Roberts. "Sight, sound and text in the history of education." *History of Education* 47 (2018): 143–147.

Dekker, Jeroen J.H. "Images as representations. Visual sources on education and childhood in the past." *Paedagogica Historica* 51 (2015): 706–709.

Dekker, Jeroen J.H. "Mirrors of reality? Material culture, Historical Sensation, and the Significance of Images for Research into Long-Term Educational Processes." In *Educational Research: Material culture and its representation*, edited by Paul Smeyers and Marc Depaepe, 31–51. Dordrecht: Springer, 2014.

Dekker, Jeroen J.H. "The Restrained Child. Imaging the Regulation of Children's Behaviour and Emotions in Early Modern Europe: The Dutch Golden Age." *History of Education and Children's Literature* 13 (2018): 21–24 [Special Issue 'Images of the European Child' edited by María del Mar del Pozo Andrés and Bernat Sureda García].

Dekker, Jeroen J.H. "Woord en beeld: Jacob Cats en de pedagogische cultuuroverdracht in de zeventiende eeuw." In *De gereformeerden en hun vormingsoffensief door de eeuwen heen*, edited by Jan W. Steutel, Doret J. de Ruyter, and Siebren Miedema, 47–65. Zoetermeer: Meinema, 2009.

Dekker, Jeroen J.H., and Inge J.M. Wichgers. "The Embodiment of Teaching the Regulation of Emotions in Early Modern Europe." *Paedagogica Historica* 54 (2018): 58–65.

Dekker, Jeroen J.H., and Leendert F. Groenendijk. "Philippe Ariès's Discovery of Childhood after Fifty Years: The Impact of a Classic Study on Educational Research." *Oxford Review of Education* 38 (2012): 133–147.

Dekker, Jeroen J.H. *De pedagogische ruimte in de tijd*. Groningen: Rijksuniversiteit Groningen, 2019.

Dekker, Jeroen J.H. *Educational Ambitions in History. Childhood and Education in an Expanding Educational Space from the Seventeenth to the Twentieth Century*. Frankfurt am Main/Berlin/Bern/Brussels/New York/Oxford/Vienna: Peter Lang, 2010.

Dekker, Jeroen J.H. *Het verlangen naar opvoeden. Over de groei van de pedagogische ruimte in Nederland sinds de Gouden Eeuw tot omstreeks 1900*. Amsterdam: Bert Bakker, 2006.

Dekker, Jeroen J.H., Leendert F. Groenendijk, and Johan Verberckmoes. "Proudly raising vulnerable youngsters. The scope for education in the Netherlands." In *Pride and Joy*, edited by Jan Baptist Bedaux and Rudolf E.O. Ekkart, 43–60. Gent/Amsterdam/New York: Ludion and Abrams, 2000.

Del Mar del Pozo Andrés, María, and Sjaak Braster. "An image travelling across Europe. The transformation of "The school in an uproar" into "Le désordre dans l'école" (1809–1855)." In *Images of education. Cultuuroverdracht in historisch perspectief*, edited by Hilda Amsing et al., 84–97. Groningen: Uitgeverij Passage, 2018.

Depaepe, Marc, and Bregt Henkens, editors in co-operation with James C. Albisetti, Jeroen J.H. Dekker, Mark D'hoker, Frank Simon, and Jo Tollebeek. *The Challenge of the Visual in the History of Education. Paedagogica Historica Supplementary Series* 6. Gent: C.S.H.P., 2000 (also published in *Paedagogica Historica* 36 (2000)).

Depaepe, Marc, and Bregt Henkens. "The History of Education and the Challenge of the Visual." In *The Challenge of the Visual in the History of Education. Paedagogica Historica Supplementary Series* 6, edited by Marc Depaepe et al., 11–17. Gent: C.S.H.P., 2000.

Fass, Paula S. "Childhood and Memory." *The Journal of the History of Childhood and Youth* 3 (2010): 155–164.

Franits, Wayne. *Dutch Seventeenth Century Genre Painting*. New Haven & London: Yale University Press, 2008 or 2004.
Frijhoff, Willem Th. M., and Marijke Spies. *1650. Bevochten eendracht*. The Hague: SDU, 1999.
Grosvenor, Ian. ""A joyful idea reborn". Aesthetic education in a time of crisis." In *Images of education. Cultuuroverdracht in historisch perspectief*, edited by Hilda Amsing et al., 208–219. Groningen: Uitgeverij Passage, 2018.
Haitsma Mulier, Eco. "Kunsthistorici en de geschiedenis. Een verslag van enkele ontwikkelingen." *Bijdragen en Mededelingen betreffende de geschiedenis der Nederlanden* 101 (1986): 202–214.
Hall, James. *Dictionary of subjects and symbols in art*. London: John Murray, 1991 or 1974.
Harrison, Peter. "Reading the passions: The fall, the passions, and dominion over nature." In *The soft underbelly of reason: The passions in the seventeenth century*, edited by Stephen Gaukroger, 49–78. London and New York: Routledge, 1998.
Haskell, Francis. *History and its images. Art and the Interpretation of the Past*. New Haven & London: Yale University Press, 1993.
Hofstetter, Rita, and Bernard Schneuwly. "Teaching culture and emotions. The function of art in Vygotsky's theory of child development (1920–1934)." In *Images of education. Cultuuroverdracht in historisch perspectief*, edited by Hilda Amsing et al., 182–194. Groningen: Uitgeverij Passage, 2018.
Honour, Hugh, and John Fleming. *A World History of Art*. London: Laurence King Publishing, 2009, 7th edition.
Jongh, Eddy de, and Gert Luijten. *Mirror of everyday life. Genreprints in the Netherlands 1550–1700*. Amsterdam/Gent: Rijksmuseum/Snoeck-Ducaju & Zoon, 1986.
Kempers, Bram. "De verleiding van het beeld. Het visuele als blijvende bron van inspiratie in het werk van Huizinga." *Tijdschift voor Geschiedenis* 105 (1992): 30–50.
Mietzner, Ulrike, Kevin Myers, and Nick Peim. *Visual History. Images of Education*. Oxford: Peter Lang, 2005.
Nóvoa, António. "On History, History of Education, and History of Colonial Education." In *The Colonial Experience in Education. Historical Issues and Perspectives. Paedagogica Historica Supplementary Series* 1, edited by António Nóvoa, Marc Depaepe, and Erwin V. Johanningmeier, 23–61. Gent: C.S.H.P., 1995.
Panofsky, Erwin. *Studies in Iconology. Humanistic Themes in the Art of the Renaissance*. New York: Harper and Row, 1972 or 1939.
Plamper, Jan. *The History of Emotions. An Introduction*. Oxford: Oxford University Press, 2015.
Pöggeler, Franz. "Bildung in Bildern. Versuch einer Typologie pädagogische relevanter Bildformen." In *Bild und Bildung. Beiträge zur Grundlegung einer pädagogischen Ikonologie und Ikonographie*, edited by Franz Pöggeler, 11–52. Frankfurt a. M.: Peter Lang, 1992.
Priem, Karin, and Inés Dussel. "The visual in histories of education: a reappraisal." *Paedagogica Historica* 53 (2017): 641–649.
Romein, Jan. *De biografie*. Amsterdam: Ploegsma, 1946.
Rousmanière, Kate. "Questioning the visual in the history of education." *History of Education* 30 (2001): 109–116.
Ruppert, Christiaan, Catrien Bijleveld, Mariëlle Bruning, Jeroen J.H. Dekker, Jan Hendriks, Trudy Mooren, Carol van Nijnatten, Wim Slot, and Micha de Winter. *Onvoldoende*

beschermd. Geweld in de Nederlandse jeugdzorg van 1945 tot heden. Den Haag: Commissie Onderzoek naar Geweld in de Jeugdzorg, 2019.

Schoonenboom, Merlijn. "De verbeelde geschiedenis. Congresverslag "Kunst als historische bron." *Skript historisch tijdschrift* 19 (1997): 34–46.

Sobe, Noah W. "Illustrating American progressive education. The cover illustration of John Dewey's 1899 *School and Society.*" In *Images of education. Cultuuroverdracht in historisch perspectief*, edited by Hilda Amsing et. al., 141–154. Groningen: Uitgeverij Passage, 2018.

Stearns, Peter. "Challenges in the History of Childhood." *The Journal of the History of Childhood and Youth* 1 (2008): 35–42.

Thompson, Paul R. *The Voice of the Past. Oral History.* Oxford: Oxford University Press, 1978.

Viñao, António. "Iconology and Education: Notes on the Iconographic Representation of Education and Related Terms." In *The Challenge of the Visual in the history of education. Paedagogica Historica Supplementary Series* 6, edited by Marc Depaepe et al., 75–91. Gent: C.S.H.P., 2000.

Wachelder, Joseph. "Chardins *Touch*. De kunst van het spelen." In *Images of education. Cultuuroverdracht in historisch perspectief*, edited by Hilda Amsing et al., 30–32. Groningen: Uitgeverij Passage, 2018.

María del Mar del Pozo Andrés (University of Alcalá, Spain) and Sjaak Braster (Erasmus University of Rotterdam, The Netherlands)

Teachers Acting as Photographers: The Progressive Image of the Cervantes School of Madrid (1918–1936)

Abstract: In the twenty-first century, historians, in general, and historians of education, in particular, have been under the spell of the visual turn. Images are no longer illustrations to brighten up texts, but rather they have become objects of in-depth social semiotic analysis. The seeds for the use of images in historical research, however, were already planted at the beginning of the twentieth century. In this article, we go back to the roots of the attraction for images felt by historians. Furthermore, we will link this academic interest with the fascination of amateur photographers for creating new ways of giving visibility to their world and their daily activities. But what happens if these amateur photographers are professional teachers? In order to answer this question, we will specifically focus on the photographs taken by the headmaster and teachers of an experimental public school in Madrid, the Cervantes School, in the 1920s and 1930s. For this purpose we have built a photographic archive of all the existing pictures (N=431) that were taken in this "new school" where, contrary to other internationally well-known institutions that were inspired by the New Education movement, children from lower income families were educated. We then raise the question as to what sort of image of this anonymous school in Madrid is conveyed via this photographic archive, and more specifically, what differences we can find between the image of this unknown public school and the so-called "progressive image" of education that was exhibited through the official channel of the New Education movement, the British journal *The New Era?* We conclude with some remarks about the usefulness of our pictorial archive for drawing conclusions about the Cervantes School that could not have been reached if we were solely to rely on the textual material that was previously collected by one of the authors of this article.

Note: This work forms part of the Project *School Culture and Practices in the 20th Century.* EDU2017–82485-P. Funded by the Ministry of Science, Innovation and Universities (MCIU); Spanish State Research Agency (AEI); European Regional Development Fund (ERDF, EU).

Keywords: visual turn; teachers; amateur photography; photographic archive; progressive education.

The Origin of the "New" Cultural History and the Quest for the Visible

In the 1920s and 1930s, an extraordinarily innovative North American historian, Caroline Farrar Ware, undertook various research projects on subjects that for the most part had been ignored. Whereas traditional historiography tended to focus on intellectual leaders and politicians, Farrar Ware believed that "history should concern itself with the inarticulate masses, their lives, languages, loves, etc.", and that historians should make an effort to understand the "processes of change that affected the multitude".[1] In order to promote her bottom-up vision of history, she organized several panels and seminars during the conference of the American Historical Association of December 1939, of which the proceedings were published in 1940. The sixth section of the book, "Sources and Materials for the Study of Cultural History", included a chapter about "Documentary Photographs".[2]

The primary author of this work, Roy Emerson Stryker, was an economist and photographer in charge of the Information Division of the Farm Security Administration, where he was given the task of creating a narrative of the Great Depression. For his chronicle, Stryker relied on hundreds of thousands of photographs taken between 1935 and 1943 by professionals such as Dorothea Lange, Walker Evans, and Gordon Parks. These photographers were unknown at the time but would become world famous thanks to the many iconic images that they produced for this project.[3] Stryker himself acknowledged in an interview that his co-author actually wrote most of the article.[4] The co-author he was re-

---

1 James W. Cook and Lawrence B. Glickman, "Twelve Propositions for a History of U.S. Cultural History," in *The Cultural Turn in U.S. History. Past, Present, and Future*, ed. James W. Cook et al. (Chicago: University of Chicago Press, 2008), 6.
2 Roy E. Stryker and Paul H. Johnstone, "Documentary Photographs," in *The cultural approach to History*, ed. Caroline F. Ware (New York: Columbia University Press, 1940), 324–330.
3 Colleen McDannell, *Picturing Faith: Photography and the Great Depression* (New Haven CT: Yale University Press, 2004), 6.
4 "Oral History Interview with Roy Emerson Stryker, 1963–1965." Tape recorded interview on January 23, 1965, Archives of American Art, Smithsonian Institution, accessed October 10, 2019, https://www.aaa.si.edu/collections/interviews/oral-history-interview-roy-emerson-stryker-12480.

ferring to, Paul H. Johnstone, was an authority on agricultural history. In addition to using photographic archives from the Farm Security Administration to illustrate his conferences, Johnstone participated as a photographer in the creation of these collections of images. One of his colleagues defined him as a historian who "belongs to the school that approaches history from the standpoint of the cultural patterns of common people".[5] This approach is more than evident in the 1940 article. In the text, classic images like "drawings and paintings" – that is, works produced by "the formal arts" – are described as sources of traditional historiography, due to their having always served to document the lives of "those who have so frequently been assumed to be the elite". However, the modern historiographic tendencies – so goes the article – seek to scrutinize "the mass of people", and for this purpose they require a new iconographic source, namely, photography, which "can easily reach the vast number of human beings whose lives ordinarily are unrecorded, either in literary sources or in formal graphic sources".[6]

Bringing back Ware's edited volume, and the chapter of Stryker and Johnstone, into the spotlight serves to contextualize our work from various perspectives. Firstly, we acknowledge the fact that cultural history constituted a historiographic tradition for much of the twentieth century and that the cultural turn of the 1970s and 1980s was oblivious to the antecedents that emerged in the 1920s and 1930s. The connection between these two stages lies in the way that both sought to fashion a history "from below", a history of the lay people, the common populace, and not just that of the leaders or the rich and famous. Secondly, we can see how in both instances this cultural historiographic approach sought novel primary sources of information, ultimately opting for photography as a medium more suited than the written text for documenting working class life. And finally, these photographers and historians had already come to realize, in the first decades of the twentieth century, the value of photography as historical evidence. They were, of course, aware of the medium's potential perversions, similar to those of any other document: "For the moment that a photographer selects a subject, he is working upon the basis of a bias that is parallel to the bias expressed by an historian when he selects his subject, his angle of approach, or his materials".[7]

---

5 Gove Hambidge, *The Prime of Life* (New York: Doubleday, Doran & Co, 1942), 179.
6 Stryker and Johnstone, "Documentary Photographs," 327.
7 Stryker and Johnstone, "Documentary Photographs," 327.

The methodological turn involved in going from written to iconographic sources implied a revolutionary change in the historian's mental processes.[8] One cannot scrutinize photographs with the objective of finding in them information that will confirm or corroborate something already known; this serves no purpose, as it leads to a saturation of historiographic analysis and the perpetuation of the merely illustrative use of images. Nor should images be considered as an objective/subjective form of interpreting and analyzing a historical reality, as evidence of something that happened and that helps to recreate or reconstruct (depending on the historiographic paradigm we are aligned with) the past. We propose a holistic approach that integrates other types of documentary sources, all of which will help to resituate and gain a global understanding of the historical object. We have adapted into pedagogic culture the concept of "visibility", considered in the classic studies of sociology and mass-media as a sociological category.[9] The visible constitutes a "prolongation of the visual *impregnated with the symbolic*" and symbols (gestures and representations) "are no more or less than whatever *renders* things visible".[10] From this perspective, images give visibility to the occult discourses of the school institution, those discourses that are not visualized in texts, either due to their triviality, to the fact that they make up part of a pedagogical tradition that is known and shared by all of the current actors (though not by historians)[11] or because of the complexity of the message; while such a message may be difficult to express concisely in written form, the image allows for its total absorption. The audiences of expert educators enjoyed a sort of "pedagogical gaze"— similar to the "medical gaze" described by Foucault – that enabled them to "see" in a photograph aspects that were invisible to a public untrained in educational matters. Our experience as historians of

---

8 The following article presents an overview of the work done by historians of education in relation to the recent visual turn, with the ISCHE organized by Marc Depaepe in Kortrijk as a turning point. See: María del Mar del Pozo Andrés and Sjaak Braster, "The visual turn in history of education: Origins, methodologies, and examples," in *Handbook of historical studies in education: Debates, tensions, and directions*, ed. Tanya Fitzgerald (Singapore: Springer, 2020), 893–908.
9 Andrea Mubi Brighenti, "Visibility: a category for the social sciences," *Current Sociology* 55 (2007): 323–342; Andrea Mubi Brighenti, "Visual, visible, ethnographic," *Etnografia e Ricerca Qualitativa* 1 (2008): 91–113; and Andrea Mubi Brighenti, *Visibility in Social Theory and Social Research* (Basingstoke: Palgrave Macmillan, 2010).
10 Brighenti, *Visibility in Social Theory*, 32 (Italics in the original).
11 María del Mar del Pozo Andrés and Teresa Rabazas Romero, "Las imágenes fotográficas como fuente para el estudio de la cultura escolar: precisiones conceptuales y metodológicas," *Revista de Ciencias de la Educación* 231–232 (2012): 406–407.

education allows us to reconstruct these images from the gaze of the teachers who first saw them.

The Building of a Photographic Archive: A New Challenge for the Historian

Photography's power for capturing and representing social realities and transmitting messages to large audiences was a well-known fact in 1889, when the medium was already being used in a myriad of domains by intellectuals, scientists, scholars, politicians, and pedagogues.[12] Much as the first wave of cultural history embraced photography as one of its most valued resources, the same could be said of the simultaneous pedagogical trend represented by the New Education movement or progressive education. In her international courses and conferences, Maria Montessori showed, starting in the second decade of the century, a series of photographs and films that she had carefully selected, using them to construct a consistent iconography of her method that was widely reproduced.[13] Many educators, including Ovide Decroly and Adolphe Ferrière, followed her example. Albums with photographs of innovative schools and educational experiments were shown regularly at the New Education Fellowship congresses, where they served to illustrate and better portray the plenary conferences. Two of the three most important journals of the movement, *The New Era* and *Progressive Education*, published hundreds of photographs that illustrated for their readers the main features of the New Education movement.[14] Some of the well-known inno-

---

[12] Many countries sent wonderful photographic albums to the Paris World Exhibitions of 1889 and 1900, some of these going on to constitute the basis of National School Museums. The photographs were not only of educational buildings, as in previous World Exhibitions; there were images of school interiors, children in schoolyards and in classrooms, and of the daily life in schools, the so-called *"Scènes de la vie scolaire"*. See, i.e., Vesna Rapo, *Croatian School Museum. The Paris Room. Achievements of Croatian Education at Exhibitions of the Second Half of 19th Century* (Zagreb: Croatian School Museum, 2006), 541–660 and Inés Dussel, "The Spectacle of Schooling and the Construction of the Nation in Argentina's Participation in World Exhibitions (1867–1889)," in *Modelling the Future. Exhibitions and the Materiality of Education*, ed. Martin Lawn (Oxford: Symposium Books, 2009), 143–148.

[13] Francesca Comas Rubí and Bernat Sureda García, "The photography and propaganda of the Maria Montessori method in Spain (1911–1931)," *Paedagogica Historica* 48 (2012): 571–587.

[14] Sjaak Braster, "The progressive child: images of new education in the New Era (1920–1939)," *History of Education & Children's Literature* XIII (2018): 215–250; Sjaak Braster and María del Mar del Pozo Andrés, "Picturing the Progressive Education: Images and Propaganda in *The New Era* (1920–1939)," *Historia y Memoria de la Educación* 8 (2018): 147–193; and Sjaak Braster and

vative institutions developed and commercialized collections of postcards that were sold on a massive scale to visitors and admirers. These objects offered an image of the institution that had been painstakingly prepared for the public. Many experimental schools, some well-known and others practically obscure, put considerable effort into constructing an institutional archive that remained part of the center, a guarantor of the school's progressive memory.[15]

In this article, we will be studying the photographic archive of the Cervantes School of Madrid, one of the unknown experimental schools that, despite its exclusion from the list of progressive schools that was periodically compiled by Ferrière, was part of the New Education movement. The Swiss pedagogue did in fact visit the school in November 1930, and while he stated in public that he considered it an "active" school,[16] he privately (in the pages of his personal diary) declared it "a marvel" of organization, praising in particular the classes of manual work.[17] He considered the school's headmaster, Ángel Llorca y García, to be "*un des pionniers de l'Éducation nouvelle en Espagne*".[18] The Cervantes school was also paid a visit by representatives of the Jean Jacques Rousseau Institute, Pierre Bovet and Edouard Claparède, who praised it in the Swiss and German press. It was the Belgian pedagogue Alexis Sluys who had first declared the center "new" in 1922, a mere four years after its creation.[19] Three factors in particular drew the attention of these visitors. Firstly, unlike most of the new schools in Europe, the Cervantes was a public center, financed by the state and situated in a poor suburb of Madrid. Secondly, the state had made the Cervantes school an experimental center where pedagogical innovations could be tested and then implemented in other public schools. To this end, the school was given its own normative guidelines, a special budget and the freedom to choose its own teachers and to introduce new methods. As a prominent experimental center, thousands of Spanish and foreign educators visited the school, observing teaching practices that they would then apply in their own classrooms. In affording rural Spanish schoolteachers a glimpse of Europe, it is not surprising that

---

María del Mar del Pozo Andrés, "From savages to capitalists: Progressive images of education in the UK and the USA (1920–1939)," *History of Education* 49 (2020): 571–595.

15 Catherine Burke and Ian Grosvenor, "The progressive image in the history of education: stories of two schools," *Visual Studies* 22 (2007): 155–168.

16 "Breves nouvelles de divers pays. Espagne," *Pour l'Ère Nouvelle* 36 (1928): 91.

17 *Petit Journal de Ferrière*, 1930, Vols. I and II. Quoted in María del Mar del Pozo Andrés, "La Escuela Nueva en España: Crónica y semblanza de un mito," *Historia de la Educación. Revista Interuniversitaria* 22–23 (2003–2004): 318.

18 "L'École Cervantes à Madrid," *Pour l'Ère Nouvelle* 63 (1930): 272.

19 Alexis Sluys, *Réformes Pédagogiques en Espagne* (Bruxelles: Ligue de l'Enseignement, 1923), 44–47.

some of them stated that "The 'Cervantes' School has been the best teacher-training college in Spain".[20] And finally, a crucial part of this experiment had to do with the relationship with families and with the community; because the school was meant to serve as an agent of a neighborhood's social transformation, and many of the pedagogical experiments had a markedly social component.

Much has been written about the features that made the Cervantes School one of Spain's most important progressive schools. The principal source of documentation is the collection of professional journals in which the principal, Ángel Llorca y García, published dozens of articles as well as chronicles about all of the center's activities. The periodicals also featured reports written by some of the school's many visitors. The documentary legacy benefitted enormously when, in 2004, Ángel Llorca's personal archive -consisting of some 20,000 manuscripts– was digitalized and made available to the public at the same time that his heirs donated this trove of information to the Ángel Llorca Foundation. In 2005–2010 the personal archives of three other teachers from the Cervantes School, Justa Freire Méndez, Elisa López Velasco, and Manuel Alonso Zapata, were also donated by their families, some of them going to the library of the *Residencia de Estudiantes* and others to the Ángel Llorca Foundation. Among these documentary riches are many photographs that have never been used for anything beyond illustrating books and articles. On the contrary, the written sources, published or unpublished, have been the basis of much research.[21] In this article we intend to contrast these known written sources with the unknown iconographical ones.

Starting in 2008, photographs began to appear, but they were scattered over different centers of documentation. Our first task as historians was to construct a single virtual archive of images from the Cervantes School. The collection we have managed to put together thus far consists of 431 photographs of school-re-

---

20 "La heroica historia de la escuela "Cervantes" de Madrid," *Escuelas de España* 21 (1935): 434.
21 María del Mar del Pozo Andrés, *Urbanismo y Educación. Política Educativa y Expansión Escolar en Madrid (1900–1931)* (Madrid: Universidad de Alcalá, 1999), 194–200; María del Mar del Pozo Andrés, "Las "fundaciones" de Ángel Llorca," Introduction to *Comunidades Familiares de Educación. Un modelo de renovación pedagógica en la Guerra Civil*, Ángel Llorca y García (Barcelona: Octaedro, 2008), 15–151; María del Mar del Pozo Andrés, "Un emblema de la renovación pedagógica española: el Grupo escolar Cervantes de Madrid (1918–1936)," in *La Nueva Educación. En el Centenario del Instituto-Escuela*, ed. Almudena de la Cueva (Madrid: Fundación Francisco Giner de los Ríos and Institución Libre de Enseñanza, 2019), 326–355; and María del Mar del Pozo Andrés, "Madrid, a showcase for national pedagogical renovation (1898/1936)," in *Madrid, ciudad educadora 1898/1938. Memoria de la Escuela Pública*, ed. María del Mar del Pozo Andrés (Madrid: Ayuntamiento de Madrid, 2019), 297–325.

lated subjects that unquestionably refer to the Cervantes School (we eliminated the pictures of the teachers' pedagogic travels throughout Spain and Europe and of their educational activities in other centers). The conservation sites of these photographs are:

1) The archive of the Cervantes School, which preserves the greatest part of the collection. The material is kept in loose envelopes and in two albums put together in the 1970s and 1980s by some of the school's teachers.

2) The archives of the *Residencia de Estudiantes* and of the Ángel Llorca Foundation, which hold the documentary and photographic legacy of the principal, Ángel Llorca, and of three teachers, Manuel Alonso Zapata, Elisa López Velasco, and Justa Freire Méndez. Between 1990 and 2010, the heirs of these educators bequeathed various collections to these two institutions.

3) The private archive of Antonio Moreno, which contains a photographic album from the Cervantes School that was put together around 1925 and was offered as a gift in the 1980s by Ángel Llorca's heirs.

4) The Spanish National Library and the Museum of History of Madrid, where two photography collections of Madrid schools from the first third of the twentieth century include several pictures of the Cervantes School taken by a professional photographer, specialized in emblematic buildings in Madrid, Jesús García Férriz (1900–1988).[22]

5) Photographs published in the national press and discovered in the collections of the Digital Repository of the National Library and the Virtual Library of Historical Press of the Ministry of Culture.

6) The archive of the photographic studio "Alfonso", situated within the State Archives, where thousands of negatives and photographic plates were kept of photographs that had been acquired by the periodicals, as well as those of images that had been discarded or never published.

7) Ministerial reports elaborated in the 1920s for the purpose of divulging government initiatives for improving primary education in Madrid. These images portray modern school buildings, innovative educational activities and experiments in arts and crafts and trade-oriented activities promoted by the public schooling system.[23]

---

[22] Iñaki Bergera and Cristina Jiménez, "Férriz y Cabrero: Lecciones de una desconocida y paradigmática colaboración entre fotógrafo y arquitecto," *Revista de Arquitectura* 18 (2016): 53–66 and Cristina Jiménez Izquierdo, "Férriz y Cabrero, el valor del legado fotográfico" (paper presented at the Congreso Internacional sobre Fotografía, Valencia, Spain, October 5–6, 2017).

[23] Ministerio de Instrucción Pública y Bellas Artes, *La primera enseñanza en Madrid. 1924* (Madrid: Talleres del Instituto Geográfico y Estadístico, 1925) and Ministerio de Instrucción Pública y

8) The memoirs published by the principal of the Cervantes for each academic year. These records, which appeared yearly between 1923 and 1936, gave a detailed account of the school's activities. Only two of these accounts are accompanied by photographs.[24]

9) Photograms from the film *Grupo escolar Cervantes de Madrid*, kept in several of the archives mentioned above. This film was part of the longer movie titled *¿Qué es España?* (What is Spain?), filmed between 1926 and 1929, which sought to portray scientific and pedagogical modernization in Spain in the 1920s. Designed by the socialist intellectual Luis de Araquistáin and directed by filmmaker César Coll y Cuchí, the film sought to divulge, especially in Latin American countries, the progress of Spanish culture in the three previous decades.[25] This was in fact the way it was used, being shown in several conferences given in Latin America by liberal and socialist politicians. One section of the film, devoted to "school organization", showed an average day at the Cervantes School, including the activities that took place during each session, and was narrated in the same style as other films from the same time dealing with New Education initiatives, such as the Swiss film *Home Chez Nous*, inspired by Ferrière.

Who Constructs the Image of an Educational Institution? *Chercher le Photographe*

It is possible that the Cervantes School, with the 431 photographs from a relatively short period (1922–1936), was the Spanish school with the largest collection of images of itself at the time. Of these pictures, 63 were published either in the press or in the memoirs mentioned above, some of them even appearing in different media and multiple times. Only 19 were produced by a known author, a professional photographer whose name figured in the caption or on the back

---

Bellas Artes, *Un ensayo de clases complementarias. Estado actual de la enseñanza en España* (Madrid: Imp. de "La Enseñanza", 1928).
24 Ángel Llorca y García, *Grupo escolar "Cervantes". Madrid. La labor de un año (15 de julio de 1925 al 15 de julio de 1926)* (Madrid: Imp. de la Librería y Casa Editorial Hernando, 1926); and Ángel Llorca y García, *El Grupo escolar "Cervantes". Madrid (1933 a 1934)* (Madrid: Establecimiento Tipográfico, 1934).
25 Juan Francisco Fuentes, "La arboleda encontrada. ¿Qué es España? Un documental atribuido a Luis Araquistáin," in *El Laboratorio de España 1907–1939. La Junta para Ampliación de Estudios e Investigaciones Científicas*, ed. José Manuel Sánchez Ron et al. (Madrid: Sociedad Estatal de Conmemoraciones Culturales/Residencia de Estudiantes, 2007), 251–261; and *¿Qué es España? Imatges Rescatades*. DVD (València: IVAC, 2012).

of the image. It is likely that others were taken by professional photographers too, given the technical expertise apparent in the composition, framing, and development, along with their publication in the postcard format. Most of these photographs, however, come from the portable cameras of amateur photographers, a fact denoted by the small format, technical imperfections, and by the dialogue that is apparent between the takers of the pictures and their subjects. Nor is there anything surprising about this; after the first Kodak camera was commercialized in the United States in 1888, photographic culture became accessible to thousands of people – those in Spain being known as *Kodakistas*. Those who took the activity seriously considered themselves true innovators, "like free creators (...), able to experiment with new forms and procedures and activities".[26]

One of these committed *Kodakistas* was Ángel Llorca himself (Figures 1 and 2). In 2006, when the local archivist of Orxeta, Alicante, his birthplace, took to cataloguing all of the photographic material referring to the town in the private archives – much of which was gathering dust in the residents' attics – the author of most of these pictures turned out to be none other than the Cervantes director himself. With his Kodak Brownie camera, commercialized by Eastman Kodak beginning in February 1900, Llorca captured the life of his neighbors at the turn of the century. He shows a predilection for images having to do with progress, for artistic compositions that bring Goya's paintings to mind, for the typical characters and customs of his village town, and, above all, for the humble workers and peasants and town folk. Developing the photographs himself with materials and plates imported from France, he assembled a documentary collection known today as the *Colección Maestro D. Ángel Llorca*.[27]

Llorca never relinquished this hobby, and it was he who took charge of the photographic chronicles of the trips abroad with the other teachers from the Cervantes. We still have the negatives to many of these images. He also seems to have transmitted his passion for this activity to several of his close collaborators, particularly to Elisa López Velasco and Justa Freire. Given that the great majority of the extant images come from the personal archives of these three teachers and from the Cervantes School itself, together with the photos showing them using a camera, we can conclude that the amateur photographers who documented the life of the Cervantes School were none other than Ángel Llorca, Elisa López Ve-

---

26 Carmelo Vega, *Fotografía en España (1839–2015). Historia, tendencias, estéticas* (Madrid: Cátedra, 2017), 257.
27 Sergio Llorens Campello, *Orxeta en los albores del siglo XX. Proyecto de recuperación de la memoria gráfica y el patrimonio cultural orchetano* (Villajoyosa: Ajuntament d'Orxeta, 2013), XXVII.

Figure 1 and 2: Ángel Llorca holding his camera, Orxeta, 1905–1906. *Colección Maestro D. Ángel Llorca*, Local Archive, Orxeta.

lasco, and Justa Freire (Figures 3 and 4). The themes of the photographs and the sites of conservation suggest that on some occasions they were taken as keepsakes, as personal memories for the participants of the experience. Many others, however, were clearly meant to document the school activities for the purpose of either showing them to families and visitors or for building a collective memory that could be transmitted to future generations. Ángel Llorca and Justa Freire kept their "old papers" in their personal archives and in that of the Cervantes School, suggesting that they perceived themselves as being at the vanguard and that they wished "for their experience to be known and to serve as an example and a stimulus for the younger generations".[28] They also evidenced, as many other amateur photographers over the world,[29] an unquestionable historical consciousness, stressing "the importance of building one's own image, one that they hope will remain in the collective memory".[30] Many other teachers in many coun-

---

28 María del Mar del Pozo Andrés, "Mujer, autoridad y educación: El caso singular de la maestra Justa Freire," in *Autoridad, Poder e Influencia. Mujeres que hacen historia*, ed. Henar Gallego Franco and María del Carmen García Herrero (Barcelona: Icaria, 2017), 164.
29 Elizabeth Edwards, *The Camera as Historian. Amateur Photographers and Historical Imagination, 1885–1918* (Durham & London: Duke University Press, 2012), 13.
30 del Pozo, "Mujer, autoridad y educación," 165.

Figure 3: Ángel Llorca, Justa Freire and Elisa López Velasco on a trip through Europe. Summer of 1925. Legacy Elisa López Velasco, Ángel Llorca Foundation.

tries who were involved in the New Education movement did the same thing, "keeping among their 'old papers' that which they wished to immortalize".[31]

Ángel Llorca attended four congresses of the New Education Fellowship (in 1923, 1925, 1927, and 1929), both on his own and accompanied by other teachers from the Cervantes School. His presence at these events, where he went virtually unnoticed in the midst of the more prominent figures, was marginal; he was not mentioned in the records of the sessions and barely appeared in the background of the photos taken (Figure 5). In his private diaries, and in a letter to Ferrière that we are not certain was ever sent, we can see Llorca's misgivings about these experiences. The conclusion that he expressed most frequently upon visiting the exhibits and attending the conferences was that he was not seeing or hearing anything new. And yet, he compiled lengthy lists of ideas that he planned to apply in the Cervantes School. Whereas in his letter to Ferrière he asserts that "I have never gone abroad for the purpose of explaining what we do here",

---

31 Ana Chrystina Venancio Mignot, "Editando o legado pioneiro: o arquivo de uma educadora," in *Refúgios do eu. Educacão, história, escrita autobiográfica*, ed. Ana Chrystina Venancio Mignot, Maria Helena Camara Bastos, and Maria Teresa Santos Cunha (Florianópolis: Mulheres, 2000), 125.

Figure 4: Justa Freire taking a photograph of Cervantes students during an excursion. 1926/1930. Archive Cervantes School.

he also expresses resentment at the failure of the journal, *Pour l'Ère Nouvelle*, to acknowledge the participation of the Cervantes Schools' teachers in the Heidelberg congress (1925). He also complains in his letters that this same journal paid no attention whatsoever to Spanish pedagogical innovations. Yet, Llorca never did get up the nerve to send an article about the Cervantes School; it seems that the dreary conferences he had attended, coupled with his own insecurity, led him to conclude that it was not worth expounding on experiences that may well have been of no interest to anyone.[32] Llorca was thoroughly familiar with the latest pedagogical writings of the New Education movement, even those that were barely known in Spain, and he did not hesitate to pay out of his own pocket the considerable travel expenses so as to see first-hand the cutting-edge initiatives, with the idea of adapting them to his own school. Yet, he

---

32 María del Mar del Pozo Andrés, Introduction to *Desde la escuela y para la escuela. Escritos pedagógicos y diarios escolares*, Ángel Llorca (Madrid: Biblioteca Nueva, 2008), 40–46.

found it irksome if a visitor suggested that the influence of these experiences could be seen in the educational activities of the Cervantes School.³³

At this point in the article we cannot help but wonder if these internal contradictions of Ángel Llorca that we find in the written texts are also visible in the photographs taken at the Cervantes School. What progressive image of the school do the existing photographs convey? What differences can we find between the progressive image portrayed by an anonymous new school, such as the Cervantes School, and that exhibited through the official channel of the journal *The New Era*?

Figure 5: Group photograph taken at the Fourth Conference of the New Education Fellowship (Locarno, 1927). In the first row of chairs on the left: Decroly, Ferrière, Bovet, and Ensor, and on the right: Claparède. In the back, marked by a circle, is Ángel Llorca. *Pour l'Ère Nouvelle* 31 (1927): n.p.

---

33 María del Mar del Pozo Andrés, "Community and the myth of the ideal school: Circulation and appropriation of the Hamburg *Gemeinschaftsschulen* in Spain (1922–1933)," *Paedagogica Historica* 50 (2014): 605–606; and María del Mar del Pozo Andrés and Sjaak Braster, "The Dalton Plan in Spain: Reception and Appropriation," *Revista de Educación* 377 (2017): 129.

The Visibilization of Progressive Education: From *The New Era* to the Madrid Suburbs

In a previous article based on an analysis of all the visual images published in *The New Era* between 1920 and 1939, we developed a coding scheme with seven variables: gender composition, happiness, nudity, body posture of the teacher, individuality, space, and activity of the child.[34] On the one hand, this scheme was theoretically informed by the work of Burke and Grosvenor, who constructed a progressive image in the history of education after exploring two collections of photographs found in the archives of two progressive schools in the UK.[35] On the other hand, the scheme with variables and categories was informed by the open and axial coding we have done following the principles of the Grounded Theory Method.[36] Our objective was to see if these variables gave visibility to six of the ideas that are universally accepted as characteristics of the New Education movement: pedocentrism, activity of the child, freedom, contact with nature, co-education, and individualization versus socialization. The hypothesis was that the image of the New Education movement, as it was emerging from the visual sources published in the journal *The New Era*, would correspond with the principles of the New Education movement that could be found in non-visual sources. In the end, we detected this correspondence (albeit with a few exceptions), and we also discovered proof that the idea of a progressive image of education, a concept coined by Burke and Grosvenor, could be successfully applied (again, with some minor exceptions) to describe the images found in *The New Era*.

Starting from the 431 photographs of the Cervantes School, we performed the same analytical procedure in order to compare them with the 944 photographs published in *The New Era*. The leading question was if the image of this experimental public school coincided with the progressive image of education conveyed by the archives of two progressive British schools, and by the imagery published in one of the loudspeakers of the New Education Fellowship, their international journal *The New Era*. The simple fact that most of the images in the Cervantes School were made by its teachers in their role as amateur photographers could well result in an adjustment of the elements that constitute a progressive image of education.

---

34 Braster and del Pozo, "Picturing the Progressive Education," 156–157.
35 Burke and Grosvenor, "The progressive image in the history of education," 155–168.
36 Anselm Strauss and Juliet Corbin, "Grounded theory methodology: An overview," in *Handbook of qualitative research*, ed. Norman K. Denzin and Yvonna S. Lincoln (Thousand Oaks: Sage, 1994), 273–285.

In a preliminary approximation we can see the iconographic contents that appear in both series (Table 5.4.1). In *The New Era*, 8.6% of the images were portraits of heroes of the New Education movement. In 6.3% of the images of adults from the Cervantes School we find photographs of teachers as well as of important pedagogical figures (such as Claparède) and politicians (such as the President of the Spanish Second Republic). Remarkably, however, there is not a single picture of Llorca posing with any of them. The central theme of these images is undoubtedly the children, whose preponderance is far greater than in the photos from *The New Era*. If half of the photographs in said journal were of toddlers (and this led us to conclude that this represented an effort to convey the pedocentric message of the New Education), the figure of 81.7% in the pictures from the Cervantes School leave no doubt as to its emphasis on pedocentrism. There is another difference: whereas *The New Era* shows many more products and results of the children's activities, the Cervantes School offers more images of children engaged in educational activities. At this point we can also find a subtle contradiction between the written texts and the iconographical sources. Ángel Llorca elaborated a discourse in which the activity of the teacher was linked to the activity of the pupil. In other words, the teacher was going to do things in order to make the child do things. The iconographic discourse of the Cervantes School, however, shows numerous images of children, without any adults present. As a result, the idea of the cooperation between children and adults is rather lost in the visual sources.

Table 5.4.1: Subjects of all images in *The New Era* (1920–1939) and the Cervantes School (1922–1936).

		Data source	
		The New Era	Cervantes School
Subjects of the images	Buildings	6.0%	5.3%
	Landscapes	1.4%	0.2%
	Portraits of adults only	8.6%	6.3%
	Objects and art made by children	34.5%	6.5%
	Children (with or without adults)	49.5%	81.7%
		100.0%	100.0%

The first variable that we analyzed was the gender of the children shown (Table 5.4.2). In *The New Era* approximately half of the photos show boys and girls together, leading us to conclude that coeducation was an idea that New Education advocates wished to stress as an important feature of their movement.

Photographs of the two sexes together at the Cervantes are practically non-existent, simply because it was a boys' school; it was only after 1931 that the Republican government authorized the gradual introduction of coeducation, a fact that is hinted at in the collection. Pictures of boys or girls on their own are rare, as was the case in *The New Era*. Burke and Grosvenor concluded that this representation was characteristic of the "progressive image" in history of education, because of how it served to diminish the tension between individualism and collectivism.[37] The amateur photographers from the Cervantes School, however, came up with a photographic composition that highlighted the individual; these consisted of well-defined close-ups of children on their own looking directly at the camera with a less defined – even unrecognizable – group of children in the background (Figure 6).

Table 5.4.2: Gender composition shown in the images with children in *The New Era* (1920–1939) and the Cervantes School (1922–1936).

		Data source	
		The New Era	Cervantes School
Gender composition	Boys and girls	55.2%	5.7%
	One single boy	3.2%	1.1%
	Only boys	20.6%	91.2%
	One single girl	4.1%	0.3%
	Only girls	17.0%	1.7%
		100.0%	100.0%

Table 5.4.3: Contentment shown in the images with children in *The New Era* (1920–1939) and the Cervantes School (1922–1936).

		Data source	
		The New Era	Cervantes School
Happiness	Laughing	1.7%	4.4%
	Smiling	7.3%	13.2%
	Serious	91.0%	82.4%
		100.0%	100.0%

---

37 Burke and Grosvenor, "The progressive image in the history of education," 160.

Figure 6: Children in the courtyard of the Cervantes School. 1926/1930. Archive Cervantes School.

The second variable that we analyzed was contentment or happiness (Table 5.4.3), which seemed to be one of the most obvious characteristics of the New Education experiences, as well as one of the most easily objectifiable, through facial expressions. And yet, in the photographs published in *The New Era* we see children who, far from laughing or even smiling, bear serious, concentrated expressions. While we find much the same thing in the Cervantes photographs, there is a greater percentage of happy faces, though many of these seem to be the result of a complicity between the teacher-photographers and the student-subjects.

Figure 7: Naked pupils on the rooftop of the school. 1929/1930. Archive Cervantes School.

We take nakedness, the third variable analyzed (Table 5.4.4), to be an iconographic symbol of the idea of freedom.[38] Although the Cervantes School had both a swimming pool and a rooftop where children habitually went without clothing, nakedness is a not a feature that is commonly represented in its photographs. Nor was it in *The New Era*. The explicit message appearing in the memoirs of the school was that the activities at the pool and on the rooftop were of an exclusively hygienic nature (swimming and sunbathing). The photographs attest to the spontaneity, autonomy, free play, and joy that the children felt in these spaces (Figure 7).

The fourth variable analyzed was the body posture/position of the teachers in the photos (Table 5.4.5). In general, the progressive image of education is incompatible with that of a teacher in a central position or situated above the children. The Cervantes collection shows a greater percentage of teacher-centered photographs than *The New Era*, but all of these images are from the first schooling stage, with the pupils' desks facing the blackboard in a traditional classroom

---

38 Braster and del Pozo, "Picturing the Progressive Education," 170–174.

Table 5.4.4: Nakedness shown in the images with children in *The New Era* (1920–1939) and the Cervantes School (1922–1936).

		Data source	
		The New Era	Cervantes School
Nakedness	Fully naked	2.6%	3.1%
	Bare feet, chest, limbs	15.0%	4.8%
	Dressed	82.4%	92.0%
		100.0%	100.0%

configuration. The introduction of moveable tables and chairs allowed for new possibilities of group work and led to a change in the teacher's position. Here we come across one of the big differences between the photos of *The New Era* and those of the Cervantes School. *The New Era* opted for the invisibility of the teacher, who in 78.4% of cases was not in the picture at all, a clear way of advocating for the non-interventionist role of the instructor. The Cervantes teachers, on the other hand, tended to figure in a tangential position (60.6%). This was a way of making visible their role in guiding and helping with the maturing process of the children, who were of course situated at the center of the teaching-learning activity (Figure 8).

Table 5.4.5: Body posture of the teacher shown in the images with children in *The New Era* (1920–1939) and the Cervantes School (1922–1936).

		Data source	
		The New Era	Cervantes School
Body posture of the teacher	Dominant	6.2%	12.0%
	Tangential	15.4%	60.6%
	Absence	78.4%	27.4%
		100.0%	100.0%

The fifth variable analyzed was the dialectic between the principles of individualization and socialization (Table 5.4.6), which required a very precise definition of the categories "individual" and "social". Here we have applied the same descriptions used in the previous article.[39] In general, the images associated with

---

[39] Braster and del Pozo, "Picturing the Progressive Education," 180.

Figure 8: Open-air drawing class with teachers in tangential positions. 1930s. Archive Cervantes School.

socialization easily outnumber those of individualization in both series of pictures. This difference is even more significant in the photographs from the Cervantes School due to the number of pictures taken during the excursions. However, several of the Cervantes pictures classified as individual show an iconography similar to that of images considered representative of the Dalton Plan in many countries (children working on their own, books within easy reach, teachers in a tangential position, and writing in the center of the image – represented by the students' notebooks).[40] The global choreography of the Dalton Plan that is visible in these symbols attests to the tension inherent in the innovative discourse of Ángel Llorca, that is, his reticence to acknowledge the fact that his colleagues expressed unequivocally: that the method used in the Cervantes School was very similar to the Dalton Plan. The photographs show that this assertion is true (Figure 9).

---

40 Del Pozo and Braster, "The Dalton Plan in Spain," 116.

Figure 9: A class at the Cervantes School, c. 1925/1926. Archive Cervantes School.

Table 5.4.6: Individuality shown in the images with children in *The New Era* (1920–1939) and the Cervantes School (1922–1936).

		Data source	
		The New Era	Cervantes School
Individuality	Individual	24.8%	15.8%
	Social	75.2%	84.2%
		100.0%	100.0%

The sixth variable that we analyzed was the space in which educational activities took place, which we labelled as "inside" or "outside" of the school (Table 5.4.7). The latter category refers to the idea of education in contact with nature. Although the differences in this respect are not statistically significant between the two sets of photographs, the Cervantes School does have more images taken outside of the classroom than *The New Era*, either in the playground or on excursions around Madrid. These photographs complemented the unpublished memoirs of the school and allowed us to identify and better interpret some

Figure 10: Excursion to El Escorial. 1922. Archive Justa Freire, Foundation Ángel Llorca.

outdoor activities, i.e. the first excursion to *El Escorial* organized by the Cervantes School in 1922 (Figure 10).

Table 5.4.7: The use of space shown in the images with children in *The New Era* (1920–1939) and the Cervantes School (1922–1936).

		Data source	
		The New Era	Cervantes School
Space	Inside buildings, classrooms, etc.	50.5%	44.0%
	Outside in nature, or school yard	49.5%	56.0%
		100.0%	100.0%

The seventh variable analyzed (Table 5.4.8) could be said to be the essence of the New Education; there was a reason that the French-speaking version of the movement used the term "*l'école active*". This idea of the active school appears in many of the different educational activities portrayed in the photographs of *The New Era* and the Cervantes School. Most of the activities shown in *The*

New Era have to do with art, crafts, and free play. These last two activities are abundant in the Cervantes images, although artistic ones are scarce and are essentially reduced to drawing or musical activities, as none of the children are engaged in dance or theatre. The iconography of this school is centered more on sporting activities and on the dining hall. But the outstanding difference – in comparison with *The New Era* – is the considerable number of photographs in which children and teachers are simply posing, capturing the moment for posterity as it were, which reinforces the idea that many of those taking the photos were from the school's teaching staff (Figure 11).

Figure 11: Crafts: woodwork. 1925/1930. Archive Cervantes School.

Table 5.4.8: Activities shown in the images with children in *The New Era* (1920–1939) and the Cervantes School (1922–1936).

		Data source	
		The New Era	Cervantes School
Activity	3 Rs	12.9%	4.8%
	Crafts	32.0%	13.1%
	Dance, theatre, or music	17.2%	2.6%
	Free play	17.0%	15.3%
	Posing	1.3%	44.3%
	Science	6.2%	0.6%
	Gymnastics, sport, etc.	2.6%	8.0%
	Eating	1.7%	7.1%
	Washing	2.6%	0.9%
	Gardening, animals	6.2%	0.6%
	Domestic activities	0.0%	2.6%
	Political or administrative activities	0.4%	0.3%
		100.0%	100.0%

Conclusions

We began this article with the observation that the visual turn at the beginning of the twenty-first century had roots in the early twentieth century. In order to understand school photography in those early days, we must take into account the gaze of the teacher and his role as an amateur photographer. The teachers of progressive schools were very aware of their "avant-garde" image, which they wanted to preserve and transmit to future generations in the same way that they wished to make their personal archive – their "old papers", as they liked to call them – accessible to their successors.

Therefore, if we want to reconstruct the historical image of a school, we have no choice but to engage in the painstaking activity of bringing together all the photographic material, which is all too often scattered among various personal and institutional collections, into one photographic archive. In the case of the Cervantes School in Madrid, assembling this photographic archive resulted in an image of a school that is (literally) seen through the lenses of teachers in their role of amateur photographers. The image offered is even more pedocentric than the progressive image constructed by the propagandists of the New Education movement. If the teachers of an internationally unknown "new school" in Madrid are in charge of making pictures of their institution, then they seem to express with images an even stronger passion for child-centered education than the images in the official publications of the New Education movement.

Finally, we conclude that our previous work in telling the story of an experimental public school in the suburbs of Madrid, based upon textual materials, needs to be complemented by visual sources. In other words, we need a holistic approach, one that includes a triangulation of textual and visual data, for telling new stories that could not be told by relying solely on texts. Adding a visual archive to existing textual archives is a necessary step for achieving a deeper understanding of school histories. The time when images were used as mere illustrations is over. As is the stance that images constitute an unreliable, dangerous, and inferior source in historical research.

Bibliography

Bergera, Iñaki, and Cristina Jiménez. "Férriz y Cabrero: Lecciones de una desconocida y paradigmática colaboración entre fotógrafo y arquitecto." *Revista de Arquitectura* 18 (2016): 53–66.

Braster, Sjaak. "The progressive child: images of new education in the New Era (1920–1939)." *History of Education & Children's Literature* XIII (2018): 215–250.

Braster, Sjaak, and María del Mar del Pozo Andrés. "From savages to capitalists: Progressive images of education in the UK and the USA (1920–1939)." *History of Education* 49 (2020): 571–595.

Braster, Sjaak, and María del Mar del Pozo Andrés. "Picturing the Progressive Education: Images and Propaganda in *The New Era* (1920–1939)." *Historia y Memoria de la Educación* 8 (2018): 147–193.

Burke, Catherine, and Ian Grosvenor. "The progressive image in the history of education: stories of two schools." *Visual Studies* 22 (2007): 155–168.

Chrystina Venancio Mignot, Ana. "Editando o legado pioneiro: o arquivo de uma educadora." In *Refúgios do eu. Educacão, história, escrita autobiográfica*, edited by Ana Chrystina Venancio Mignot, Maria Helena Camara Bastos, and Maria Teresa Santos Cunha, 123–143. Florianópolis: Mulheres, 2000.

Comas Rubí, Francesca, and Bernat Sureda García. "The photography and propaganda of the Maria Montessori method in Spain (1911–1931)." *Paedagogica Historica* 48 (2012): 571–587.

Cook, James W., and Lawrence B. Glickman. "Twelve Propositions for a History of U.S. Cultural History." In *The Cultural Turn in U.S. History. Past, Present, and Future*, edited by James W. Cook et al., 3–57. Chicago: University of Chicago Press, 2008.

Dussel, Inés. "The Spectacle of Schooling and the Construction of the Nation in Argentina's Participation in World Exhibitions (1867–1889)." In *Modelling the Future. Exhibitions and the Materiality of Education*, edited by Martin Lawn, 129–152. Oxford: Symposium Books, 2009.

Edwards, Elizabeth. *The Camera as Historian. Amateur Photographers and Historical Imagination, 1885–1918*. Durham & London: Duke University Press, 2012.

Fuentes, Juan Francisco. "La arboleda encontrada. ¿Qué es España? Un documental atribuido a Luis Araquistáin." In *El Laboratorio de España 1907–1939. La Junta para Ampliación de Estudios e Investigaciones Científicas*, edited by José Manuel Sánchez Ron et al., 251–261. Madrid: Sociedad Estatal de Conmemoraciones Culturales/Residencia de Estudiantes, 2007.
Hambidge, Gove. *The Prime of Life*. New York: Doubleday, Doran & Co, 1942.
Jiménez Izquierdo, Cristina. "Férriz y Cabrero, el valor del legado fotográfico." Paper presented at the Congreso Internacional sobre Fotografía, Valencia, Spain, October 5–6, 2017.
Llorca y García, Ángel. *Grupo escolar "Cervantes". Madrid. La labor de un año (15 de julio de 1925 al 15 de julio de 1926)*. Madrid: Imp. de la Librería y Casa Editorial Hernando, 1926.
Llorca y García, Ángel. *El Grupo escolar "Cervantes". Madrid (1933 a 1934)*. Madrid: Establecimiento Tipográfico, 1934.
Llorens Campello, Sergio. *Orxeta en los albores del siglo XX. Proyecto de recuperación de la memoria gráfica y el patrimonio cultural orchetano*. Villajoyosa: Ajuntament d'Orxeta, 2013.
McDannell, Colleen. *Picturing Faith: Photography and the Great Depression*. New Haven, CT: Yale University Press, 2004.
Ministerio de Instrucción Pública y Bellas Artes. *La primera enseñanza en Madrid. 1924*. Madrid: Talleres del Instituto Geográfico y Estadístico, 1925.
Ministerio de Instrucción Pública y Bellas Artes. *Un ensayo de clases complementarias. Estado actual de la enseñanza en España*. Madrid: Imp. de "La Enseñanza", 1928.
Mubi Brighenti, Andrea. "Visibility: a category for the social sciences." *Current Sociology* 55 (2007): 323–342.
Mubi Brighenti, Andrea. "Visual, visible, ethnographic." *Etnografia e Ricerca Qualitativa* 1 (2008): 91–113.
Mubi Brighenti, Andrea. *Visibility in Social Theory and Social Research*. Basingstoke: Palgrave Macmillan, 2010.
Pozo Andrés, María del Mar del. *Urbanismo y Educación. Política Educativa y Expansión Escolar en Madrid (1900–1931)*. Madrid: Universidad de Alcalá, 1999.
Pozo Andrés, María del Mar del. "La Escuela Nueva en España: Crónica y semblanza de un mito." *Historia de la Educación. Revista Interuniversitaria* 22–23 (2003–2004): 317–346.
Pozo Andrés, María del Mar del. "Las "fundaciones" de Ángel Llorca." Introduction to *Comunidades Familiares de Educación. Un modelo de renovación pedagógica en la Guerra Civil*, Ángel Llorca y García, 15–151. Barcelona: Octaedro, 2008.
Pozo Andrés, María del Mar del. Introduction to *Desde la escuela y para la escuela. Escritos pedagógicos y diarios escolares*, Ángel Llorca, 11–55. Madrid: Biblioteca Nueva, 2008.
Pozo Andrés, María del Mar del, and Teresa Rabazas Romero. "Las imágenes fotográficas como fuente para el estudio de la cultura escolar: precisiones conceptuales y metodológicas." *Revista de Ciencias de la Educación* 231–232 (2012): 401–414.
Pozo Andrés, María del Mar del. "Community and the myth of the ideal school: Circulation and appropriation of the Hamburg *Gemeinschaftsschulen* in Spain (1922–1933)." *Paedagogica Historica* 50 (2014): 599–614.
Pozo Andrés, María del Mar del, and Sjaak Braster. "The Dalton Plan in Spain: Reception and Appropriation." *Revista de Educación* 377 (2017): 113–134.

Pozo Andrés, María del Mar del. "Mujer, autoridad y educación: El caso singular de la maestra Justa Freire." In *Autoridad, Poder e Influencia. Mujeres que hacen historia*, edited by Henar Gallego Franco, and María del Carmen García Herrero, 159–183. Barcelona: Icaria, 2017.

Pozo Andrés, María del Mar del. "Madrid, a showcase for national pedagogical renovation (1898/1936)." In *Madrid, ciudad educadora 1898/1938. Memoria de la Escuela Pública*, edited by María del Mar del Pozo Andrés, 297–325. Madrid: Ayuntamiento de Madrid, 2019.

Pozo Andrés, María del Mar del. "Un emblema de la renovación pedagógica española: el Grupo escolar Cervantes de Madrid (1918–1936)." In *La Nueva Educación. En el Centenario del Instituto-Escuela*, edited by Almudena de la Cueva, 326–355. Madrid: Fundación Francisco Giner de los Ríos and Institución Libre de Enseñanza, 2019.

Pozo Andrés, María del Mar del, and Sjaak Braster. "The visual turn in history of education: Origins, methodologies, and examples." In *Handbook of historical studies in education: Debates, tensions, and directions*, edited by Tanya Fitzgerald, 893–908. Singapore: Springer, 2020.

Rapo, Vesna. *Croatian School Museum. The Paris Room. Achievements of Croatian Education at Exhibitions of the Second Half of 19th Century*. Zagreb: Croatian School Museum, 2006.

Sluys, Alexis. *Réformes Pédagogiques en Espagne*. Bruxelles: Ligue de l'Enseignement, 1923.

Strauss, Anselm, and Juliet Corbin. "Grounded theory methodology: An overview." In *Handbook of qualitative research*, edited by Norman K. Denzin and Yvonna S. Lincoln, 273–285. Thousand Oaks: Sage, 1994.

Stryker, Roy E., and Paul H. Johnstone. "Documentary Photographs." In *The cultural approach to History*, edited by Caroline F. Ware, 324–330. New York: Columbia University Press, 1940.

Vega, Carmelo. *Fotografía en España (1839–2015). Historia, tendencias, estéticas*. Madrid: Cátedra, 2017.

Nele Reyniers (KU Leuven, Belgium)
Sound as an Archival Source in the History of Education for Children with Mental Disabilities.

Abstract: In this chapter, a relatively new perspective in the history of education is introduced, namely the sound studies perspective. This approach focuses on sounds and silences in scientific research. By means of a case study of the first Belgian institutions with specialized treatment and education – so-called asylums –, the history of children with mental disabilities is analyzed from this sound studies perspective. The main question is how these mentally disabled children were defined along acoustic lines. The analysis of the children's personal files pointed towards the importance of vocalization and language in the admission procedures of children with mental disabilities to specialized institutions in nineteenth century Belgium.

Keywords: sound studies; mental disability; asylum; special education; noise

Introduction

"It is the language that characterizes the human being",[1] Sister Gerarda stresses in her publication on the mother tongue instruction for children with disabilities.[2] Born Gerarda Beun, Sister Gerarda joined the Belgian Order of the Sisters of Charity in 1904. These Sisters of Charity took care of the poor, the sick, and the elderly.[3] They were also the first to establish a specialized institution for girls with mental disabilities in Belgium: the Saint Benedict institute which was founded in 1884. Due to administrative difficulties, it was not until 1887 that the first girls were admitted to receive specialized treatment and education.[4]

---

1 Heritage Centre of the Sisters of Charity, O.L.V. Ten Doorn Eeklo, Sister Gerarda Beun, inv. no. 350/2, Article on mother-tongue instruction for children with disabilities, June 17, 1950. "*C'est le langage qui caractérise l'être humain*" (translated by the author).
2 In the original French text the terms "*les enfants déficients*" are used, here translated as children with disabilities.
3 Heritage Centre of the Sisters of Charity, "Sister of Charity SJM," http://heritagecentre-scjm.org/about-us/sisters-of-charity-scjm/.
4 Xaverina De Waepenaere, *Zuster Gerarda Beun achteraf bekeken 1886–1971* (Eeklo: Pauwels N.V., 1985), 13.

From the 1910s onwards, Sister Gerarda was involved in the teacher training of the sisters in the order's various institutes, including Saint Benedict.[5] One of her main areas of expertise in this teacher training was the importance of language, i.e. spoken language education. The underlying idea, as the above quotation suggests, was that spoken language is one of the most important characteristics of "normal" human beings and hence should play an important role in the education of so-called abnormal children. Therefore, children with disabilities were required to learn to speak properly: that is to say, to produce the right sounds. Thus, this chapter will focus on the importance of sonic aspects in the first initiatives for mentally disabled children, and it will be looked at through the prism of the interdisciplinary field of sound studies.

Initiated by Murray Schafer's seminal work on soundscapes[6] – another word for acoustic landscapes –, the aim of sound studies is to incorporate sounds and silences into human scientific research. In disciplines such as music studies, anthropology, and sociology, a substantial body of research exists on the acoustics and the spatial, power structures, noise, and technology.[7] The contribution of sound studies to scientific research is twofold. Their first aim is to provide alternative insights about issues that have been studied already. Sound studies have shown, for example, how an acoustic perspective might shed some new light on issues such as power, agency, discipline, and surveillance. Michael Gallagher, a lecturer in digital education, aims at contesting the dominant view on discipline and surveillance in schools taking place through vision, by pointing out the value of sound in the exercise of power in schools. One of the examples he refers to is the importance of quietness in schools: how teachers emphasize the need of being silent and attempt to regulate noise levels. He even stresses the advantage of the ear over the eye in surveillance situations, since the eyes are directional whereas the ears have the capacity to capture information from all around. [8] Tom Rice, a social anthropologist, analyzes what he calls the acoustical agency of prisoners. By highlighting actions such as window-to-window communication, shouting between cells, eavesdropping, and the use of music, he contests the idea of prisoners as a "captive audience to the sonic environment" and pris-

---

[5] De Waepenaere, *Zuster Gerarda Beun*, 28.
[6] Raymond Murray Schafer, *The tuning of the world* (New York: Knopf, 1977).
[7] Trevor Pinch and Karin Bijsterveld, *The oxford handbook of sound studies* (Oxford: University Press, 2012); Mark M. Smith, *Hearing history, a reader* (London: The University of Georgia Press, 2004); Veit Erlmann, *Hearing cultures: essays on sound, listening, and modernity* (Oxford: Berg, 2004).
[8] Michael Gallagher, "Sound, space and power in a primary school," *Social and Cultural Geography* 12 (2011): 51.

ons "as dominated and determined solely by prison authorities".[9] Hence, his sonic perspective and the insights gained from it lead him to construct a counter-narrative of the acoustical agency of the prisoners themselves instead. The second contribution of sound studies to scientific research is their attempt to hear the voices of subordinate populations in historiography, such as the prisoners in Rice's studies. The essay "Listening to the mind" discusses how sound can be used to give a voice to those previously silenced in the history of mental health. By making use of sound recordings it is possible to gain access to the voices of the patients in mental health institutions, which are often neglected in the existing historiography.[10]

Scholars within the history of education have also started to apply the sound studies approaches to their research.[11] This is not surprising considering the prevalence of sounds and silences in education as claimed by Jody Crutchley and others: "sounds, random and ordered, are part of every contemporary culture; in education, the composed and performed sounds of music in music lessons and related practices in schools, the technologically-generated sounds of radio, television and digital media, even the voices of children and teachers are but some of the examples of the sonic culture of school life".[12] Janice Schroeder, for example, examines the vocalizations of teachers and schoolchildren in nineteenth century English education discourse.[13] Josephine Hoegaerts studies the paradox of the silent classroom and the speaking citizen in her article "Silence as Borderland".[14] As Pieter Verstraete points out in his work on the educationalization of silence throughout history, silence can be a research topic just as well as sound or voice can.[15] This chapter builds on the alliance between these two disciplines – sound studies on the one hand and the history of educa-

---

9 Tom Rice, "Sounds inside: prison, prisoners and acoustical agency," *Sound Studies* 2 (2016): 6.
10 Carolyn Birdsall, Manon Parry and Viktoria Tkaczyk, "Listening to the mind: tracing the auditory history of mental illness in archives and exhibitions," *The Public Historian* 37 (2015): 47.
11 Special issue *Paedagogica Historica:* Pieter Verstraete and Josephine Hoegaerts, "Educational soundscapes: tuning in to sounds and silences in the history of education," *Paedagogica Historica* 53 (2017): 491–497; Special issue *History of Education:* Jody Crutchley, Stephen G. Parker, and Siân Roberts, "Sight, sound and text in the history of education," *History of Education* 47 (2018): 144.
12 Crutchley, Parker and Roberts, "Sight, sound and text," 144.
13 Janice Schroeder, "The schooled voice: sound and sense in the Victorian schoolroom," *Zeitschrift fur Anglistik und Amerikanistik* 63 (2015): 31.
14 Josephine Hoegaerts, "Silence as borderland: a semiotic approach to the 'silent' pupil in nineteenth-century vocal education," *Paedagogica Historica* 53 (2017): 514.
15 Pieter Verstraete, "Silence or the sound of limpid water: disability, power, and the educationalisation of silence," *Paedagogica Historica* 53 (2017): 498.

tion on the other – to provide an alternative perspective on how people define "otherness" – in this case, "mental disability" – in an educational setting. According to the literature, mental disability was often characterized as a lack of intellectual capacity, and the diagnosis of mentally disabled children was largely dependent upon the measure of children's intellectual capacities. With the introduction of intelligence testing in the late nineteenth and early twentieth century, things such as IQ-tests, these measurements assumed to be objective.[16] This chapter will show that mental (dis)ability was not (only) a natural phenomenon that could objectively be measured, but that it was also a social construct. At a certain moment in time, at a certain place definitions of mental (ab)normality were based upon societal norms. Several sound studies have already pointed out how sonic aspects play a role in the definition processes of the "self" and the "other".

A notable example to illustrate this is the book *Noise, a human history of sound and listening* by David Hendy.[17] He demonstrates how sounds have played a role throughout human history in enabling people to distinguish between "the self" and "the other". He points towards the human tendency to make sonic distinctions between "us" and "them" with a sense of superiority among the "us" and a sense of inferiority among "the other". One of his most striking examples is the story of the colonizers versus the colonized and how the colonizers tried to legitimize their colonization process by referring to the colonized as inferior and wild. They mentioned, for example, the "shouts and grunts", "dreadful shrieks", "hideous shouts" or "loud and inharmonious cries" of the colonized which stood in sharp contrast with the godly sounds the civilized colonizers made themselves.[18] For that reason, they urged the need to civilize these "others" and thus justified their conquests by problematizing the sounds of the colonized. Hendy defines noise – after Peter Bailey[19] – as sound that is determined to be "out of place" according to time and place-related societal norms.[20] So, people distinguish between "us" and "them" and this perception of the others' sounds as noises, sounds out of place, is subjective and culturally determined.[21] This is

---

[16] Special issue in *Paedagogica Historica:* Antonio Fco. Canales and Simonetta Polenghi, "Classifying children: a historical perspective on testing and measurement," *Paedagogica Historica* 55 (2019): 343–352.
[17] David Hendy, *Noise. A Human History of Sound and Listening* (London: Profile books, 2013).
[18] Hendy, *Noise*, 162–164.
[19] Peter Bailey, "Breaking the sound barrier," in *Hearing history, a reader*, ed. Mark M. Smith (London: University of Georgia Press, 2004), 23.
[20] Hendy, *Noise*, ix–x.
[21] Bailey, "Breaking the sound barrier," 27.

also the case in the definition of (in)sanity and thus in the distinction between sane and insane people, as demonstrated by Dolly MacKinnon in her article "Hearing madness and sounding cures: recovering historical soundscapes of the asylum". Sounds produced by the inmates in her study were interpreted by others as signs of madness. Her main argument is that "nineteenth and early twentieth-century medical and lay communities not only knew what madness looked like, but also they knew what madness sounded like".[22] Moreover, this "cultural specificity of language, sound, noise and silence, and the psychological variability of hearing, diagnosing and understanding those sounds (…), is an area yet to be fully explored".[23] In this chapter, this demand for further exploration is met by applying this idea of the cultural specificity of sound and its perception to the case study of children with mental disabilities. Hence, the research question is: how was mental disability defined along acoustic lines in the first Belgian asylums for children with mental disabilities?

Listening to Sound in the Sources: a Methodological Reflection

The source material needed for this case study, i.e. the personal files of the children in the asylums, confronted me as a researcher with two methodological issues; what Vehkalahti called "the institutional gaze"[24] on the one hand and "schizophonia" – a concept introduced by Murray Schafer[25] – on the other.

As Annemieke Van Drenth pointed out in her study on the "School for idiots" established in 1855 in the Netherlands by Reverend Van Koetsveld, the sources we need to rely on are "more or less official data".[26] These data were collected with the specific aim of justifying the (legal) admission of a child to an asylum for children with mental disabilities, in her case Van Koetsveld's School for idiots. Van Drenth published two articles about her study on this school in which a methodological evolution can be observed. As she describes herself,

---

22 Dolly MacKinnon, "Hearing madness and sounding cures: recovering historical soundscapes of the asylum," *Politiques de communication* 1 (2018): 79.
23 MacKinnon, "Hearing madness," 80.
24 Kaisa Vehkalahti, "Dusting the archives of childhood: child welfare records as historical sources," *History of education* 45 (2016): 430–445.
25 Raymond Murray Schafer, *Our sonic environment and the soundscape. The tuning of the world* (Vermont: Destiny Books, 1994), 88.
26 Annemieke Van Drenth, "The 'truth' about idiocy: revisiting files of children in the Dutch 'School for Idiots' in the nineteenth century," *History of Education* 45 (2016): 480.

the first study in 2007 was "strongly framed by the empirical question of what was represented in and through these data".[27] The data was considered as evidence waiting to be grasped by a researcher. Thus, Van Drenth herself was unable to escape the institutional gaze. Kaisa Vehkalahti introduces this term in her article "Dusting the archives of childhood"[28] and she uses it to denote a strong research focus on the structure and organization of institutions and emphasize the dominant voices in the sources which effectively prevents minorities from having a voice. In the international studies on the history of asylums for children with mental disabilities, this "institutional gaze" is dominant since mainly the organizational structure of the institutions and the life and working conditions inside the asylums are outlined.[29] Vehkalahti explains this focus on the institutional gaze by pointing towards the sources themselves: "the primary aim of institutional and authoritative documentation is to provide information for decision-making" and therefore "contains information selected based on this point of departure".[30] The archives of the institutions are organized explicitly to enable historical research on the institution itself and its organization and structure. As a consequence, they force the researcher to adopt an institutional perspective and hence limit research agendas.

So how then can we make use of the official documents – often the only sources available – but simultaneously reach beyond this institutional gaze? Vehkalahti herself considers this possible as long as researchers dealing with administrative sources are aware of the institutional gaze. She claims that it even allows us to unravel underlying power relations, untangle administrative practices and professional developments, and uncover discourses of childhood.[31] In 2016, Van Drenth wrote a second article based on her data about the "School for idiots", in which she reconsidered her previous analysis and re-analyzed her data from another theoretical and methodological point of view. She adopted a praxeographic approach with a focus on the disentanglement of the practices and procedures in a similar way as the second solution offered by Vehkalahti. By doing so, Van Drenth sheds some light on the logic that guided the early form of diagnosis of children's idiocy. She concludes that the practices involved, namely an observation questionnaire and the rules, procedures, and practicalities that

---

27 Van Drenth, "The 'truth' about idiocy," 481.
28 Vehkalahti, "Dusting the archives," 430–445.
29 Some examples are: James W. Trent, *Inventing the Feeble Mind: a history of mental retardation in the United States* (Berkeley: University of California press, 1995); Steven Taylor, *Child Insanity in England, 1845–1907* (London: Palgrave Macmillan, 2017).
30 Vehkalahti, "Dusting the archives," 438.
31 Vehkalahti, "Dusting the archives," 437.

governed the life within the asylum, both helped shape this logic: "the modus of care and education gradually took over the traditional medical and psychiatric dispositive with its strong focus on pathology of body and mind".[32] Like Van Drenth's study, this chapter also draws on official, administrative documents justifying the admission procedure of a child to the Belgian asylums for children with mental disabilities. Instead of a praxeographic approach, this study uses a sound studies approach to overcome the methodological issue of the institutional gaze. The official documents are considered to be the written account of the official discourse about idiocy of the persons involved in diagnosing children with mental disability. This chapter hence elaborates on the third solution proposed by Vehkalahti: to uncover the discourses of childhood. Within our analysis of the official discourse about idiocy the focus therefore lies on sounds and silences mentioned in the documents.

This brings us to the second methodological issue, namely schizophonia. Murray Schafer, who is widely regarded as the founding father of sound studies, introduced the term in the 1970s to point towards the extracting of sound from its original context.[33] Although Schafer uses this concept in the specific context of electroacoustic transmission techniques, this idea also applies to historical research with a sound studies approach. Given the ephemeral nature of sound, a medium is always needed to transfer the sounds from the past to the present: historians cannot make use of the original sounds of the past but are forced to rely on representations of these sounds, either electronic recordings or written accounts.[34] In both cases, the sound itself has vanished but is represented via media and left to the researcher to interpret. In this study, this issue is avoided since the aim is not to reproduce the actual acoustic reality of the past, but rather to examine the discourse on mental disability and analyze how the sounds and silences produced by the children were part of the argumentation. In this way, the focus is on how these sounds and silences were heard and interpreted by physicians, parents, and religious institutions as signs of mental disability and hence part of the definition and the diagnosis of mental disability. In order to operationalize this approach, the sections of the personal files of the children dealing with the argumentation pro mental disability were examined for accounts of sounds and silences produced by the children, such as screaming, laughing, and mutism.

---

32 Van Drenth, "The 'truth' about idiocy," 490.
33 Schafer, *Our sonic environment and the soundscape*, 88.
34 Jan-Friedrich Missfelder, "Period Ear. Perspektiven einer Klanggeschichte der Neuzeit," *Geschichte und Gesellschaft*, 38 (2012): 33.

Disability as Sound Out of Place

The first Belgian institutes with specialized treatment and education for children with mental disabilities were established by the Catholic Order of Sisters and Brothers of Charity: the Saint Benedict institute for girls (1884) and the Saint Joseph institute for boys (1901).[35] For children to be admitted to these so-called asylums, they needed to be "defined" as mentally disabled. A judgement was to be formed about "abnormal" children (meaning children in need of special treatment and education) by determining criteria to define children with mental disability. The archives of these institutions reveal what these definitions consisted of. For this study, the personal files of the girls and boys in these institutes were analyzed. Due to the large amount of personal files in the archives, a selection of these files of both the Saint Benedict institute and the Saint Joseph institute was made on a five-yearly basis. Consequentially, 374 personal files of the Saint Benedict institute and 322 personal files of the Saint Joseph institute were studied. The analysis ended in 1920 as, in that year, a law was enacted that legally separated children with mental disabilities from insane children, which ushered in a "new" period in the history of children with mental disabilities.[36] These personal files consisted of several documents in which doctors, parents, and neighbors testified about the behavior of the child and why he/she had to be admitted to an asylum for children with mental disabilities. One of these documents was a report of a physician who recommended that the child be admitted to the asylums based on several symptoms he considered to be distinguishable for children with mental disabilities. Another document was a standardized two-page entry form completed when the child was admitted to the institute, with general information about the child, its family, the mental disability, and its causes etc. These questionnaires were similar to the ones studied by Van Drenth in her second study on the Dutch "School for idiots". In addition to the questionnaire, observation notes were added to the personal files. Before the staff of the asylum decided whether or not a child would be admitted, he or she was subjected to observation for five days. During this period all observations were meticulously noted. They formed the basis for the decision of whether

---

35 The archive of the Saint Joseph institute is preserved in both the archive of the Brothers of Charity and the Museum of Dr. Ghuislain. The archive of the Saint Benedict institute is preserved in the heritage center of the Sisters of Charity.
36 Fanny Claeys and Lies Vanovenacker, "'Da's ene van achter de kerk zeker?' Een historisch pedagogisch onderzoek naar het opvoedingsproject voor meisjes in het medischpedagogisch instituut Sint-Benedictus te Lokeren (1921–1970)" (master's thesis, University of Gent, 2012), 45.

the child was to be sent home or admitted to the asylum. Also after admission, the child was subjected to monthly observations about his/her behavior, attitudes, and progress. The purpose of all these documents was to legitimate the removal of a child out of his/her domestic sphere to an asylum, thus these observation notes contain arguments for or against the "diagnosis" of mental disability. As a result, these documents provide a wealth of information on how people – i.e. doctors, parents, medical staff, the community – defined mental disabilities, the criteria they used for it, and thus the discourse about mental disability. In the analysis of this discourse, the focus was on the sounds and silences produced by the children and how these were interpreted as signs of mental disability. In 47% of the selected personal files of children admitted to the Saint Benedict and the Saint Joseph institute, at least one of the symptoms was related to these sounds, as shown by the following reports of girls[37] in the Saint Benedict institute:

> In that same year, Mona was admitted to the Saint Benedict institute, because she, according to a doctor in Leuven, "screams and sings in an incoherent way and without motive in the streets."[38]
> Five-year-old Holly was admitted to the institute in 1900. One of the symptoms of her mental disability noted down in her personal file was "savage screams".[39]
> Lucy was the fourth girl admitted to the Saint Benedict institute. She entered the institute on 8 January 1887. The physician certified that he had observed that Lucy had a mental illness and one of the symptoms mentioned is "a screaming noise all day long."[40]

By making use of the word "noise", the physician clearly problematizes the sounds produced by the child. As Hendy pointed out for the colonizers, here the physician defines these sounds as inferior by equating them with noise and therefore considers them as signs of mentally disabled. Apart from the screams and singing, language was also a frequently mentioned problem. The language problems referred to were unarticulated language, poor use of language, and an unintelligible language.[41] These language problems accounted

---

[37] The names used to refer to the children are pseudonyms due to privacy rules.
[38] Heritage Centre of the Sisters of Charity, Lokeren, Saint Benedict, inv. no. 357/1, personal file, M.P. "*elle crie et chante d'une manière incohérente et sans motifs dans les rues*" (translated by the author).
[39] Heritage Centre of the Sisters of Charity, Lokeren, Saint Benedict, inv. no. 367/2, personal file, H.W. "*cries sauvages*" (translated by the author).
[40] Heritage Centre of the Sisters of Charity, Lokeren, Saint Benedict, inv. no. 357/1, personal file, L.D.B. "*criant tapage le long du jour*" (translated by the author).
[41] In the original text the following terms were used: "*articulation des sons difficile*", "*langage défectueux*", "*articulent des mots incompréhensibles*".

for 93% of all the sound-related symptoms, i.e. sounds produced by the children, mentioned in the personal files.

The importance of sound and language in particular when defining mentally disabled children was not only a Belgian phenomenon. Similar findings are observed in other countries such as England. In his work about asylums in England between 1845 and 1907, Steven Taylor states the following: "a theme that is recurrent in all our institutions when describing harmless congenital cases of idiocy; that is the (in)ability to speak and converse. [...] Evidently, not all children with a diagnosis of idiocy were admitted with an inability to converse, for those who could speak their linguistic dexterity was still used to determine their condition."[42]

This focus on speech and language not only transcends national borders but also transcends the boundaries between different types of disabilities. When looking at the history of children with aural disabilities, referred to as deaf children in the nineteenth and twentieth century, the same issue arises. Jonathan Rée describes this history clearly in his book *I see a voice. Deafness, language and the senses – a philosophical history*.[43] A very famous debate in this area involved the importance of speech and language for humanity: the manualism versus oralism debate. Whereas the advocates of the first group supported sign language for deaf people, the latter stressed the importance of spoken language and hence stimulated deaf children to learn lip-reading and speech production.[44] Especially in the arguments of this last group, spoken language and speech are stressed as one of the key characteristics of human beings. Jonathan Rée refers to the theory of Johann Gottfried von Herder, who saw speech as a precondition for human consciousness and not just as an expression of it.[45] Herder even made the distinction between vocality and speech: "speech being what happens when the voice takes on the artificial inflections of a human institution, whilst the voice in itself was simply the medium for the spontaneous exuberance of shouts (...) It was not the sounds of voices, but the words of language, that were the essence of humanity."[46] This view on speech as the "the source of civilization"[47] is

---

[42] Taylor, *Child Insanity in England*, 48.
[43] Jonathan Rée, *I see a voice. Deafness, language and the senses – a philosophical history* (New York: Metropolitan Books, 1999).
[44] Rée, *I see a voice*, 9.
[45] Rée, *I see a voice*, 66.
[46] Rée, *I see a voice*, 66–67.
[47] Rée, *I see a voice*, 93.

also to be found in the reasoning of the Brothers and Sisters of Charity in this case study. The quote of Sister Gerarda at the beginning of this chapter already pointed this out: "It is the language that characterizes the human being".[48] In both the Saint Joseph and the Saint Benedict institutes, children with mental disabilities thus had to learn to speak correctly (or as correctly as possible) in order to be seen as "true humans". This also explains the negative connotation of symptoms such as "savage screams", since they were considered noise in contrast to language and speech as the most articulated and intelligible sounds.[49] Speech and language were not only criteria used to define mental disability but were also part of the solution offered in the institutions. Hence, speech and language training played a very important role in the specialized education for children with mental disabilities. Again, Sister Gerarda can be cited as an example, since in one of her publications concerning child language, she claims that "a very important point in the upbringing of children is language instruction, which starts with learning to speak".[50] Moreover, she stresses the importance of language learning, in particular of the mother tongue, in the education of children with disabilities, since, "language is the social link and vehicle for information par excellence."[51]

Because of the focus on speech and language, the absence of speech was considered equally problematic, if not more. Or as Peter Bailey pointed out: "the potential for disturbance and disorder in noise is eloquently registered in its significant absence".[52] Hence, mutism was also a criterion to define a child as mentally disabled and admit him/her to an asylum, as the following case of Tina makes clear: "In 1891 a young girl of thirteen years old, Tina, was admitted to the institute. In her information file provided by parents, guardians and especially by the physicians, one of the signals which "proved" her mental disability, was complete mutism."[53]

---

48 Heritage Centre of the Sisters of Charity, O.L.V. Ten Doorn Eeklo, Sister Gerarda Beun, inv. no. 350/2, article on mother-tongue instruction for children with disabilities, June 17, 1950. "*C'est le langage qui caractérise l'être humain*" (translated by the author).
49 Bailey, "Breaking the sound barrier," 23–24.
50 Heritage Centre of the Sisters of Charity, O.L.V. Ten Doorn Eeklo, Sister Gerarda Beun, inv. no. 350, Article on child language, 1922. "*Een zeer belangrijk punt in de opvoeding der kinderen is het taalonderwijs, dat begint met leeren (sic) spreken*" (translated by the author).
51 Heritage Centre of the Sisters of Charity, O.L.V. Ten Doorn Eeklo, Sister Gerarda Beun, inv. no. 350/2, article on mother-tongue instruction for children with disabilities, June 17, 1950. "*Le langage est par excellence le lien social et le véhicule d'information*" (translated by the author).
52 Bailey, "Breaking the sound barrier", 53.
53 Heritage Centre of the Sisters of Charity, Lokeren, Saint Benedict, inv. no. 358, personal file, T.B.

In his aforementioned book, Jonathan Rée describes the accounts of incurably mute people in the archives of anthropology and natural history. He claims that these congenital mutes were always considered unattractive: idiotic, ugly, inert, atheistic, and amoral.[54] He explains this by referring again to Herder who maintained that the mute were doomed to remain "like children, or human animals". Lacking any words to organize their experience, he said, they had no chance of raising themselves above their "brutal state", and becoming capable of "ordinary humanity or morality".[55] Also in the study of the Saint Joseph and Saint Benedict institute these ideas might have been part of the reasoning of the staff, since mutism was perceived negatively and actively contested by means of the adapted education for these mentally disabled children.

The Psychopathologization of Sounds and Silences

In this chapter, the sound studies approach was used as a way to study the history of education, i.e. the case study of two Belgian asylums for children with mental disabilities, the Saint Benedict and Saint Joseph institutes. By adopting this approach for the analysis of the discourse about mental disability, this study was able to look beyond the institutional gaze omnipresent in the historiography on asylums for mentally disabled children. It claims that the sounds and silences produced by the children, such as vocality, speech, and language, were a substantial part of the definition of mental disability in nineteenth century Belgium. In that sense, this chapter demonstrates that the labeling of children as mentally disabled was partly a result of the perception of the children's sounds and silences by the so-called experts: the physicians and Brothers and Sisters of Charity. These experts problematized the sounds as signs of mental disability according to their own and societal norms. Consequentially, these sonic symptoms are subjective and culturally determined and thus hearing, diagnosing, and understanding sounds is variable in time and place.[56] Apart from the intellectual capacity of the children measured by intelligence testing, these sounds were also part of the diagnostic process. This chapter therefore adds to the existing literature on the origins of mental disability in showing that subjective factors such as sonic signals were also part of the definition and diagnosis of chil-

---

54 Rée, *I see a voice*, 92.
55 Rée, *I see a voice*, 93.
56 Rée, *I see a voice*, 80.

dren with mental disability. I would like to further reflect on the matter by making use of the concept "psychopathologization" that Nelleke Bakker operationalizes in her article "The discovery of childhood mental illness".[57] She witnesses a shift from a moral disapproval of the children's behavior towards a medical treatment of their unhealthy emotions. She refers to this evolution as the psychopathologization of the emotions by turning them into a mental illness in need of medical treatment. This same concept can also be applied to the case study at hand wherein sounds were interpreted as signs of mental disability. In this way, one can argue that sounds and also silences produced by the children were psychopathologized in the late nineteenth and early twentieth century in the context of the definition of "mental disability" in the educational setting of the asylum.

Bibliography

Primary sources

Heritage Centre of the Sisters of Charity, O.L.V. Ten Doorn Eeklo, Sister Gerarda Beun, inv. no. 350, article on child language, 1922.

Heritage Centre of the Sisters of Charity, O.L.V. Ten Doorn Eeklo, Sister Gerarda Beun, inv. no. 350/2, article on mother-tongue instruction for children with disabilities, 17th of June 1950.

Heritage Centre of the Sisters of Charity, Lokeren, Saint Benedict, inv. no. 357/1, personal file, L.DB.

Heritage Centre of the Sisters of Charity, Lokeren, Saint Benedict, inv. no. 357/1, personal file, M.P.

Heritage Centre of the Sisters of Charity, Lokeren, Saint Benedict, inv. no. 358, personal file, T.B.

Heritage Centre of the Sisters of Charity, Lokeren, Saint Benedict, inv. no. 367/2, personal file, H.W.

---

57 Nelleke Bakker, "The discovery of childhood mental illness: the case of the Netherlands (1920–1940)," *Bildungsgeschichte. International Journal for the Historiography of Education* 7, no. 2) (2017): 192.

Secondary literatures

Bailey, Peter. "Breaking the sound barrier." In *Hearing history a reader*, edited by Mark M. Smith, 23–35. London: University of Georgia Press, 2004.
Bakker, Nelleke. "The discovery of childhood mental illness: the case of the Netherlands (1920–1940)." *Bildungsgeschichte. International Journal for the Historiography of Education* 7 (2017): 191–204.
Birdsall, Carolyn, Manon Parry, and Viktoria Tkaczyk. "Listening to the mind: tracing the auditory history of mental illness in archives and exhibitions." *The Public Historian* 37 (2015): 47–72.
Canales, Antonio Fco., and Simonetta Polenghi. "Classifying children: a historical perspective on testing and measurement." *Paedagogica Historica* 55 (2019): 343–352.
Claeys, Fanny, and Lies Vanovenacker. "'Da's ene van achter de kerk zeker?' Een historisch pedagogisch onderzoek naar het opvoedingsproject voor meisjes in het medischpedagogisch instituut Sint-Benedictus te Lokeren (1921–1970)." Master's thesis, University of Gent, 2012.
Crutchley, Jody, Stephen G. Parker, and Siân Roberts. "Sight, sound and text in the history of education." *History of Education* 47 (2018): 143–147.
De Waepenaere, Xaverina. *Zuster Gerarda Beun achteraf bekeken 1886–1971*. Eeklo: Pauwels N.V., 1985.
Erlmann, Veit. *Hearing cultures: essays on sound, listening, and modernity*. Oxford: Berg, 2004.
Gallagher, Michael. "Sound, space and power in a primary school." *Social and Cultural Geography* 12 (2011): 47–61.
Hendy, David. *Noise. A Human History of Sound and Listening*. London: Profile books, 2013.
Heritage Centre of the Sisters of Charity. "Sister of Charity SJM." Accessed March 10, 2021. http://heritagecentre-scjm.org/about-us/sisters-of-charity-scjm/.
Hoegaerts, Josephine. "Silence as borderland: a semiotic approach to the 'silent' pupil in nineteenth-century vocal education." *Paedagogica Historica* 53 (2017): 514–527.
MacKinnon, Dolly. "Hearing madness and sounding cures: recovering historical soundscapes of the asylum." *Politiques de communication* 1 (2018): 77–106.
Missfelder, Jan-Friedrich. "Period Ear. Perspektiven einer Klanggeschichte der Neuzeit." *Geschichte und Gesellschaft* 38 (2012): 21–47.
Pinch, Trevor, and Karin Bijsterveld. *The Oxford handbook of sound studies*. Oxford: University Press, 2012.
Rée, Jonathan. *I see a voice. Deafness, language and the senses – a philosophical history*. New York: Metropolitan Books, 1999.
Rice, Tom. "Sounds inside: prison, prisoners and acoustical agency." *Sound Studies* 2 (2016): 6–20.
Schafer, Raymond, M. *Our sonic environment and the soundscape. The tuning of the world*. Rochester: Destiny, 1994.
Schafer, Raymond M. *The tuning of the world*. New York: Knopf, 1977.
Schroeder, Janice. "The schooled voice: sound and sense in the Victorian schoolroom." *Zeitschrift fur Anglistik und Amerikanistik* 63 (2015): 31–49.
Smith, Mark M. *Hearing history, a reader*. London: The University of Georgia Press, 2004.
Taylor, Steven. *Child Insanity in England, 1845–1907*. London: Palgrave Macmillan, 2017.

Trent, James W. *Inventing the Feeble Mind: a history of mental retardation in the United States*. Berkeley: University of California Press, 1995.

Van Drenth, Annemieke. "The 'truth' about idiocy: revisiting files of children in the Dutch 'School for Idiots' in the nineteenth century." *History of Education* 45 (2016): 477–491.

Vehkalahti, Kaisa. "Dusting the archives of childhood: child welfare records as historical sources." *History of education* 45 (2016): 430–445.

Verstraete, Pieter. "Silence or the sound of limpid water: disability, power, and the educationalisation of silence." *Paedagogica Historica* 53 (2017): 498–513.

Verstraete, Pieter, and Josephine Hoegaerts. "Educational soundscapes: tuning in to sounds and silences in the history of education." *Paedagogica Historica* 53 (2017): 491–497.

Inés Dussel (DIE-CINVESTAV, México)
What Might a Material Turn to Educational Histories Add to the History of Education? Proof-eating the Pudding

Abstract: In this chapter, I discuss the implications of the material turn for the historiography of education. In dialogue with Marc Depaepe's historiographical arguments and his work on the material culture of education, I present some reflections that follow the thread of my own research on school uniforms in the last two decades. Having started with some grand theoretical claims about the role of these school artefacts in broader power/knowledge regimes, the subsequent steps of my research led me to consider the relevance of the materiality of uniforms, their materials, styles, and textures, their color and visibility, and some patterns of their circulation between home and school and their commodification. The research required the development of a multisensorial approach that paid much more attention to the details and minutiae of schools. In the last section, I reflect on two short essays by Walter Benjamin and Michel Foucault, pointing to their contributions to not only rethinking but also remaking historical studies of educational material culture.

Keywords: material turn; historiography of education; school objects; school uniforms; Marc Depaepe

Introduction

Education takes place through the interaction of human beings as well as through the connections to objects and spaces that give shape and content to educational processes.[1] Take, for example, the involvement of education with tables and caves as referred to by Jan Masschelein: education needs tables, real or metaphorical, on which people gather to work, making this work with knowledge a public issue (a space for communing), and caves that organize an "other space" for education, suspended from daily life.[2]

---

[1] I want to thank Sarah van Ruyskensvelde for her generous comments to earlier versions of this chapter, as well as the suggestions made by the two anonymous reviewers.
[2] Jan Masschelein, "Making the school: stories of caves and tables," in *Old School/Nieuwe Klas*, ed. Wim Lambrecht and Nancy Vansieleghem (Ghent: LUCA School for the Arts, 2014), 43–53.

https://doi.org/10.1515/9783110623451-023

Despite the relevance of objects and spaces for educational matters, for the most part educational histories have been more concerned about human activity and participation, including the debates on whom was visible and how in this history, than about their material configuration. This situation started to change in the last 20 years. I will argue that discussing how this material turn is taking place in the field of educational history is a way to engage with important historiographical reflections about our own work as researchers in education.[3]

In the following chapter, I present some reflections on the contributions, actual and potential ones, afforded by a material turn in educational historiography. I start discussing some recent work that acknowledges the need to look more closely at the materiality of schooling, and some of its theoretical and methodological implications. Heeding Marc Depaepe's advice to study particular contexts and cases instead of producing detached theorizations,[4] in the next section I use my own research work on school uniforms from the last two decades as a thread to analyze some shifts in how objects are conceptualized and studied. I also underline how much of this shift has implied a new sensibility towards the material in education; this is discussed in the concluding pages, with the help of important scholars on the materiality of culture: Walter Benjamin and Michel Foucault.

The Material Turn: Implications for Educational Historiography

At a theoretical and historiographic level, what is known as the "material turn" in social theory has given way to a historiographical change in histories of education. Among the multiple and heterogeneous strands that supported it, each

---

Masschelein notes that caves have appeared in significant ways in educational history, not only through Plato's myth but also in the rock paintings that can be considered as the first inscriptions explicitly made to record and circulate human culture. Metaphorically, they mark a place of shelter and storage, archive and transmission, imagination and recording. Tables and desks will be discussed in the last section of this chapter.

3 See Marc Depaepe, "Why Even Today Educational Historiography is not an Unnecessary Luxury. Focusing on four Themes from Forty-four Years of Research," *Espacio, Tiempo y Educación* 7 (2020): 227–246.

4 Karl Catteeuw, Kristof Dams, Marc Depaepe, and Frank Simon, "Filming the Black Box: Primary Schools on Film in Belgium, 1880–1960: A First Assessment of Unused Sources," in *Visual History. Images of Education*, ed. Ulrike Mietzner, Kevind Myers, and Nick Peim (Bern: Peter Lang, 2005), 203–232.

with its theoretical and methodological assumptions, one could name the social history of objects,[5] the Foucaultian approach to the microphysics of power,[6] Actor-Network Theory,[7] as well as a sensitivity towards culture's textures and details inspired by Walter Benjamin's works[8] and by sensorial histories of education.[9] While the concept of "turn" might be too dramatic and tends to simplify complex strands of theories that share not much more than a particular attention to a specific field of practice,[10] I would like to argue that it is nonetheless helpful to analyze heuristically the ways in which educational historiography has shifted towards new topics and approaches.

Thus, using the lens of the "material turn" it is possible to see that in the last decades historical research in education has been increasingly concerned with the materiality of education, looking at buildings, classrooms, school desks, blackboards, notebooks, visual aids or uniforms and clothing in schools, and other educational spaces. This materiality is considered first as a source for the understanding of broader educational processes, such as the studies on written culture that analyze the production and circulation of school textbooks, school notebooks, illustrated journals or public libraries,[11] and the research

---

5 Arjun Appadurai, ed. *The social life of things. Commodities in cultural perspective* (Cambridge, UK: Cambridge University Press, 1986).
6 Michel Foucault, *Discipline and Punish. The Birth of the Modern Prison*. Translated by A. Sheridan (New York: Pantheon Books, 1977).
7 Bruno Latour, *Reassembling the social. An introduction to Actor-Network Theory* (Oxford, UK: Oxford University Press, 2005).
8 Walter Benjamin, *The Arcades Project*, translated by H. Eiland and K. McLaughlin (Cambridge, MA: The Belknap Press/Harvard University Press, 1999).
9 Ian Grosvenor, "Back to the future or towards a sensory history of schooling," *History of Education* 41 (2012): 675–687; Geert Thyssen and Ian Grosvenor, "Learning to make sense: interdisciplinary perspectives on sensory education and embodied enculturation," *The Senses and Society* 14 (2019): 119–130.
10 Catteeuw, Dams, Depaepe, and Simon, "Filming the Black Box," 229.
11 Among many others, see Anne-Marie Chartier, *Enseñar a leer y escribir. Una aproximación histórica* (México: Fondo de Cultura Económica, 2004); Frederik Herman, Mélanie Surmont, Marc Depaepe, Angelo van Gorp, and Frank Simon, "Remembering the Schoolmaster's Blood-Red Pen. The Story of the Exercise Book and the Story of 'the Children of the Time' (1950–1970)," *History of Education* 3 (2008): 351–375; Marc Depaepe et al., *Order in Progress. Everyday Educational Practice in Primary Schools. Belgium, 1880–1970* (Leuven: Leuven University Press, 2000); Marc Depaepe and Frank Simon, "Is there any Place for the History of 'Education' in the 'History of Education'? A plea for the History of Everyday Educational Reality in- and outside Schools," *Paedagogica Historica* XXX (1995): 9–16. In Latin America, a region where Marc Depaepe's work has been well known for decades, see particularly Héctor Cucuzza and Pablo Pineau, *Para una Historia de la Enseñanza de la Lectura y Escritura en Argentina. Del catecismo colonial a La Razón de mi Vida* (Buenos Aires: Miño y Dávila Editores, 2002); Silvina

done on the history of educational films or aesthetic education that take into account the materiality of the objects and spaces in which these practices take place. [12] But it has also been an object of study in itself, such as Valdenira Barra's study of the blackboard[13] or the history of school desk undertaken by Pedro Moreno Martínez and Marc Depaepe, among several others.[14]

What are the implications for the history of education research of a rigorous study of the material dimension of social life? And how to approach this research avoiding the risks of the fetishization of the material or the antiquarian's gaze?[15] The novelty of this material turn is not its consideration of objects – already present in the work of archeologists and museum specialists –, but how they are conceived and brought into historical research.[16] In what follows, I would like to stress two main implications of this material turn for historical studies.

In the first place, this theoretical and methodological shift implies including objects and things as full participants in social networks – as actors or actants,

---

Gvirtz, *El discurso escolar a través de los cuadernos de clase. Argentina (1930–1970)* (Buenos Aires: EUDEBA, 1999); Sandra Szir, *Infancia y cultura visual. Los periódicos ilustrados para niños (1880–1910)* (Buenos Aires: Miño y Dávila editors, 2007); Nicolás Arata, *La escolarización de la ciudad de Buenos Aires (1880–1910)* (PhD Diss., Departamento de Investigaciones Educativas del CINVESTAV, 2016).

12 Catteeuw, Dams, Depaepe, and Simon, "Filming the Black Box."; Silvia Serra, *Cine, escuela y discurso pedagógico. Articulaciones, inclusiones y objeciones en el siglo XX en Argentina* (Buenos Aires: Editorial Teseo, 2011); Pablo Pineau, ed., *Escolarizar lo sensible* (Buenos Aires: Ed. Teseo, 2014).

13 Valdenira M. Lopes de Barra, *Da pedra ao pó. O itinerário da lousa na escolar pública paulista do século XIX* (Goiânia: Gráfica Universidade Federal de Goiânia, 2016).

14 Marc Depaepe, Frank Simon, and Pieter Verstraete, "Valorising the Cultural Heritage of the School Desk Through Historical Research," in *Educational Research: Material Culture and Its Representation*, ed. Marc Depaepe and Paul Smeyers (Dordrecht: Springer, 2014), 13–30; Pedro Moreno Martínez, "The History of School Desk Development in Terms of Hygiene and Pedagogy in Spain (1838–1936)," in *Materialities of schooling. Design, Technology, Objects, Routines*, ed. Martin Lawn and Ian Grosvenor (Oxford, UK: Symposium Books, 2005), 71–95; Rosa de Souza Castro and Vera Gaspar da Silva, "Cultura material da escola: entram em cena as carteiras," in *Objetos da Escola. Espaços e lugares de constituiçao de uma cultura material escolar (Santa Catarina – Séculos XIX e XX)*, ed. Vera G. da Silva and Marilia G. Petry (Florianópolis: Editora Insular, 2012), 169–186; Juri Meda, *Mezzi di Educazione di Massa. Saggi di storia della cultura materiale della scuola tra XIX e XX secolo* (Milan: Franco Angeli, 2016).

15 Agustín Escolano, "Las materialidades de la escuela (a modo de prefacio)," in *Objetos da Escola*, 11–18.

16 Marc Depaepe, and Paul Smeyers, eds., *Educational Research: Material Culture and Its Representation* (Dordrecht: Springer, 2014).

as Bruno Latour calls them[17] –, which are not only and not mainly a reflection of humans' actions but that also incite actions, emotions, or change courses. While this shift or turn is far from homogeneous, and there are several strands and debates among its referents in relation to inter- or intra-activity, the symmetry between human and non-human actors as an epistemic principle, or language as representation or presentational,[18] most scholars involved in the material turn agree on dismantling the idea that the history of an artefact depends on the uses and meanings that we confer to these objects. Instead, there is a renewed concern on the network of humans and non-humans that are created by the presence of objects or material things; this does not mean animating the inanimate ("objects come alive"), but recognizing things have a density and capacity to act that, while devoid of intentions, still effect actions and affections in the historical trajectories of social beings, as, for example, in the notion of "agential realism" of things.[19] Humans are such because of their interactions with things, as much as things are what they are because of human interventions.[20]

The second implication I would like to point out brings these considerations closer to historiography, and it is related to the reconceptualization of the tem-

---

[17] Bruno Latour, *Reassembling the social. An introduction to Actor-Network Theory* (Oxford, UK: Oxford University Press, 2005).

[18] See for example Tim Ingold, *Making: Anthropology, archeology, art and architecture* (New York/London: Routledge, 2013); William E. Connolly, "The 'New Materialism' and the Fragility of Things," *Millennium: Journal of International Studies* 41 (2013): 399–412. In educational history, important debates about materiality have been advanced by Lynn Fendler and Joyce Goodman, who take up Karen Barad's and Ingold's conceptualizations to argue in favor of a non-representational approach that allow a new imagination for/on materiality. See Lynn Fendler, "The Ethics of Materiality: Some Insights from Non-representational Theory," in *Educational Research: Material Culture and Its Representation*, ed. Marc Depaepe and Paul Smeyers (Dordrecht: Springer, 2014), 115–132; Joyce Goodman, "Circulating Objects and (Vernacular) Cosmopolitan Subjectivities," *Bildungsgeschichte – International journal for the historiography of education* 17 (2017): 115–126.

[19] Joyce Goodman, "Circulating Objects."

[20] This perspective can be traced back to Marxist historical materialism, even though its conceptualization of objects is quite different from what is presented in this text. As an example, Vygotsky underlined the relevance of material and symbolic tools (including linguistic signs) in humanization, pointing that the activity with purposefully constructed objects is central to becoming humans. See, for example, Guillermo Blanck, *El problema del desarrollo cultural del niño y otros textos inéditos* (Buenos Aires: Editorial Almagesto, 1998). But for Marxism, objects are external tools that are subjected to the control of human beings. The new materialisms open the relationships between humans and artefacts in directions that are more plural than traditional Marxism, as can be seen in Deleuze, Manuel de Landa, Rosi Braidotti, among others. See Warren Montag and Ted Stolze, *The New Spinoza* (Minneapolis: The University of Minnesota Press, 1998); William E. Connolly, "The 'New Materialism' and the Fragility of Things."

porality of objects. In contemporary studies of the presence and action of things, objects do not acquire meaning after their material being, but meaning is constrained by matter as much as matter is constrained by meaning.[21] Instead of seeing objects or things as fixed entities, most theories aligned in the material turn consider them as becomings, things always in the making. This becoming is not sequential, as in when it is said that first there were humans that allocate design and meaning, and then, as a mirror reflection, objects that are merely surfaces on which external intentions are inscribed.

This leads to a rethinking of the links between form and matter, not in terms of container and content or surface and interior but as a continuum of life that is interwoven and mutually defined. Tim Ingold's analysis of the movement and becomings of archeological vestiges might clarify this reconsideration. He takes the example of ceramic, which "breathes" and continues to change as it interacts with sand or mud in wherein it is buried. Thus, changes are not only related to its form (as when it stops being a vessel in use and starts being a buried fragment or an object displayed in a museum) but also on its matter.[22] For Ingold, researchers have to take an ecological turn: culture is not a weave of meanings that occurs in a space that has nature as a static background. Meaning is produced through "the engagement and immersion of human subjects" in worlds of experience that are material.[23] This process is in permanent flux, and the borders between the human and non-human are provisional and unstable.[24]

From this standpoint, educational histories are starting to shift from questions about the being of things, defined in static and fixed ways (inter-activity), to questions about becoming that do not take for granted what artefacts are or can do (intra-activity). Following the grain of materials, research has to pay attention to the presence and making of objects as co-constitutive of its weaving. Thus, if things are to be considered sources in the history of education, they can-

---

[21] I am paraphrasing the expression coined by Lorraine Daston, *Things That Talk. Object Lessons from Art and Science* (New York: Zone Books, 2006), 17. See also Daniel Miller, ed. *Materiality* (Durham & London: Duke University Press, 2005); Tim Ingold, "Toward an Ecology of Materials," *Annual Review of Anthropology* 41 (2012): 427–442.

[22] Ingold, *Making*.

[23] Carlos Steil and Isabel de Moura Carvalho, "Diálogos imaginados entre Thomas Csordas y Tim Ingold," in *Cuerpos y corporalidades en las culturas de las Américas,* ed. Silvia Citro, Jose Bezerril, and Yanina Mennelli (Buenos Aires: Biblos, 2015), 43–58 (quote on p. 50).

[24] These theories have complex philosophical assumptions, which exceed the scope of this text but that can be synthetically referred to a series of thinkers that goes from Spinoza to Marx, Heidegger, Merleau-Ponty, and Deleuze. While they have lots of disagreements, all stress the centrality of the material in human experience. For a contemporary discussion, see Steil and de Moura Carvalho, "Diálogos impensados."

not be regarded as complete and finished stories but as "stories caught halfway-through: the middle of things, discontinuities."[25] In their becoming, objects travel through different contexts and are transformed and adapted; they also transform the networks in which they are inscribed. In writing their biography of artefacts, researchers have to take into account their specificities as well as their local and global significance;[26] it is equally important to investigate what things are made of, what are the possibilities of these materials, the history of their design and engineering of their making, their interaction with particular environments as well as their transformations.

The theoretical and methodological assumptions of the material turn are thus more complex than a naïve materialism or a lineal interactionism between predefined entities; they are also distant from the hermeneutical questions of the meanings constructed by humans on inert objects. The material turn has implied setting the objects in movement not as an external action performed by humans but as a means to listen or be attentive to the movement of things, their becomings, their "spillings" into the social weave.[27] In this vein, educational histories adopt an ethnographic sensitivity that intends to map or document the experiences that involved people and objects through their material traces, taken as matter that continues to change in their contact with researchers.

The Study of School Uniforms: Proofing the Pudding

How do you write a material history of education that takes into account the heterogeneous trajectories of artefacts and the multiple possibilities that they open up? As Marc Depaepe suggests "the proof of the pudding is still in the eating",[28] it is better to discuss historiographical reflections in reference to research cases. Thus, in this section I would like to consider my own research on school uniforms, which spans two decades during which scholarship has roughly shifted towards the material, as an analytical thread to follow the changing questions

---

25 Carolyn Steedman, *Dust. The Archive and Cultural History* (New Brunswick, NJ: Rutgers University Press, 2002), 45.
26 Martin Lawn and Ian Grosvenor, "Introduction: The Materiality of Schooling," in *Materialities of schooling*, 1–15.
27 Ingold, *Making*.
28 Depaepe, "Why Even Today Educational Historiography," 228.

and methods with which historians of education have approached the materiality of schooling.[29]

In my own work, the study of material culture was a consequence of adopting a Foucaultian perspective that was interested in how power was materially affected on school bodies and spaces.[30] While in previous research I have approached curriculum history as part of the production of cultural authority through the debates around which knowledge was valuable and have worked mainly through textual documents,[31] in the research on school uniforms my preoccupation shifted towards how this cultural authority was made concrete in the regulation of bodies. In my investigation, the study of how appearances were regulated in schools initially had a central political motivation: to understand what, in this appearance, could account for the power/ knowledge regimes that constituted particular visibilities (modes of seeing and being seen) for children's bodies in Argentina at the turn of the twentieth century.[32] As will be shown, this scope was largely expanded in the next stages of my research, including other timeframes and geographies.

Once I started working in the archives, the corpus grew bigger and bigger, and went from an early interest in disciplinary rules and school hygiene treatises to include descriptions of school daily life, educational journals, series of photographs to compare how the white smocks spread in different localities, and also advertisements in newspapers to analyze the style of uniforms, prices, and materials, and their intertwining with the commodification of children's clothes and school artefacts.[33]

---

[29] In this section I expand some of the arguments presented in a forthcoming chapter focused on memory as a research tool: Inés Dussel, "Research memories and memories as research in the history of education: Historicizing the material and visual culture of schooling," in *Critical Methodologies for Researching Teaching and Learning*, ed. Ch. Siry, C. Schreiber, R. Gomez Fernandez, and R. Reuter (Amsterdam: Sense Publishers, Series *Bold Visions in Educational Research*), in press.

[30] In a way, this earlier approach could be criticized as a search for a "grand theory" to explain education. See, again, Depaepe, "Why Even Today Educational Historiography," 240.

[31] Inés Dussel, *Curriculum, Humanismo y Democracia en la Enseñanza Media (1863–1920)* (Buenos Aires: Oficina de Publicaciones del CBC-UBA/FLACSO, 1997).

[32] Inés Dussel, "The shaping of a citizenship with style: A history of uniforms and vestimentary codes in Argentinean public schools," in *Materialities of Schooling*, 97–124.

[33] The study of the commodification of school objects has been developed more recently by Diana Vidal and Vera Gaspar da Silva, "Por uma história sensorial da escola e da escolarizaçao," in *Cultura material escolar: a escola e seus artefatos (MA, SP, PR, SC e RS), 1870–1925*, ed. César A. Castro (Sao Luis: EDUFMA/Café & Lápis, 2011), 19–41; Juri Meda, *Mezzi di Educazione di Massa. Saggi di storia della cultura materiale della scuola tra XIX e XX secolo* (Milan: Franco Angeli, 2016).

In this history, the interest in the materiality of uniforms increasingly gained center-stage. If at the beginning of this research project I considered uniforms as a neutral surface on which rules and regulations were inscribed, my own questions started to turn towards the specificities of the white smock, which started to look less flat and became more densely crossed by multiple threads that led the research in different directions.

Among its specific traits, a significant line of research was the whiteness of the smocks. Here, my own school memories worked as a trigger for further inquiries.[34] Having attended public schools, I knew that the whiteness of the uniforms obliged to all sorts of care and prevented rough play or running in order to avoid stains or tears. In fact, the best way to keep it clean was to move slowly or, even better, stay still. In line with what Phil Corrigan wrote about what school made with, to and, for his body[35], my point of departure was the violence that uniforms effected on my school experience, most of which took place during the last military dictatorship in Argentina (1976–1983). In my schooling, there were very concrete punishments when stains or tears were detected on or in the white smocks, such as sending back home the deviant students, not being allowed to honor the flag, and even going through some forms of public humiliation in front of the whole school. In school parlance, "dirtiness" carried all the multiple meanings of the (in)appropriate/d other,[36] a sign that denoted (denounced in those authoritarian times) a family that failed to comply with the norm – in my case, evidence of a young, working mother who did not have time to take care of the smock but who also wanted for her daughters the freedom and rebellion of the feminist authors she so much liked. That these decisions were channeled through the carelessness of uniforms is a great hint about what was (and is) at stake with school objects.

My memories of school uniforms, then, showed that their white color was indeed a relevant trait in how this regime of appearances was enacted in Argentinean educational history. Tracing back its discursive equivalences and material proximities, I could observe that the association between whiteness, tidiness, and virtue or moral probity to classify children had a long history.[37] In the ar-

---

34 The relevance of memories in school histories has been poignantly analyzed in Cristina Yanes-Cabrera, Juri Meda, and Antonio Viñao, ed. *School Memories. New Trends in the History of Education* (Cham: Springer, 2017).
35 Philip Corrigan, "The Making of the Boy: Meditations on what Grammar School did with, to, and for my body," *Journal of Education* 170 (1988): 142–161.
36 Trinh T. Minh-ha, "Introduction: She, The Inappropriate/d Other," *Discourse* 8 (1987): 3–9.
37 Georges Vigarello, *Concepts of Cleanliness. Changing Attitudes in France since the Middle Ages* (Cambridge/París: Cambridge University Press/Maison des Sciences de l'Homme, 1988).

chives, I found a poem published in the official journal of the Ministry of Education, *El Monitor de la Educación Común*, in 1902, which made these equivalences very patent:

> Never dress carelessly,
> because in society it is as dishonorable
> a stain in your honor
> as a stain in your dress.[38]

In trying to find out whether these traits were similar to other school experiences, I ended up making a comparative history of the regulation of clothing in schools in various countries and across four centuries.[39] I could see that uniforms started to be donned in orphans' schools in England in the sixteenth century, and were written down as mandatory in the rules of French Lasallean schools in the eighteenth century. They were symbols of negative distinction that singled out poor or orphan children, who were more often than not obliged to wear badges that represented a tribute to the patrons of the orphanage. But uniforms also implied introducing sumptuary textiles (such as linen) in popular milieus as well as cleaning practices that produced cultural and social mobility.[40]

The French Revolution implied a turning point, which led to a twisting of surrounding uniforms. In opposition to luxury clothing, and to the effect of equivalence between uniforms and poverty, uniforms were posited as symbols of egalitarianism and took the form of austere garments, in line with Calvinist ideals of moderate sensibilities.[41] In some cases, uniforms were similar to Roman togas, as part of the turn towards Classical Antiquity that the Jacobins took in their search for references for the new republican order. It is remarkable

---

38 In Spanish: *"Nunca vistas con descuido,/ Que en la sociedad deshonra,/Como una mancha en la honra,/Una mancha en el vestido."* Poem written by "Plaza" and quoted by G. Groff, "La salud del niño. El cuidado de la ropa," *El Monitor de la Educación Común* 22, no. 352 (June 1902): 960–962 (quote on p. 961).
39 In this journey, important references were given by works from Australian scholars, for example Colin Symes and Daphne Meadmore, "Force of Habit: The school uniform as a body of knowledge," in *Pedagogy, Technology, and the Body*, ed. Erica McWilliam and Peter Taylor (New York: Peter Lang, 1996), 171–191; John Synott and Colin Symes, "The Genealogy of the School: An iconography of badges and mottoes," *British Journal of Sociology of Education* 16 (1995): 139–153.
40 Dussel, "The shaping of a citizenship with style."
41 Philippe Perrot, "La richesse cachée: Pour une généalogie de l'austerité des apparences," *Communications* 46 (1987) : 157–179.

that the discursive equivalence between social equality and uniformization that was forged at that time is still powerful in current debates on school uniforms.

A second equivalence emerged in this period of bourgeois revolutions: the uniforms and vestimentary codes had to be part of healthy, scientific policies. In the late eighteenth century, medical doctors appeared as legitimate actors that defended uniforms as the healthiest clothing for children because they enhanced good breathing and blood circulation; these criteria also became relevant in the discussions about military uniforms.[42] By the end of the nineteenth century, Pasteurianism would add the war against microbes as a leitmotiv to the uniformization of children's bodies, in this case following the medical gown.[43] This medical-hygienic model dominated in France, Italy, Spain, and Argentina, even though the colors they adopted were different. While in the European nations dark colors and home-made garments were the norm, in Argentina the option was to don white smocks that became part and parcel of an "aesthetics of wash-ability" that shaped public architecture as a strong imprint of the hygienic movement.[44] It is thus not surprising that the uniforms resembled the medical gowns, which had abandoned their black shades at least one decade before the white smocks were adopted as mandatory in Argentinean schools.

By the late nineteenth century, uniforms became part of the traveling technologies that shaped the expansion of schooling across the globe. Great Britain and Australia prescribed the use of hats and blazers, following the code of elite public schools. In France, New Zealand, and many South American countries, smocks, either white, blue or grey, were adopted, that were used on top of street clothes. The uniforms made the school population easily distinguishable and helped both to enforce the mandatory school laws and to create a school identity in each local community.

In historiographical terms, it is interesting that as objects, uniforms cannot be traced back to a single creator. Instead, their emergence can be pinned to a "choral invention."[45] Symptomatically, all those who claimed authorship were

---

[42] Alain Ehrenberg, *Le corps militaire. Politique et pédagogie en démocratie* (Paris: Editions Aubier, 1983).

[43] Bruno Latour, *The Pasteurization of France*, translated by A. Sheridan and J. Law (Cambridge, MA and London: Harvard University Press, 1988).

[44] Francisco Liernur, "La construcción del país urbano," in *Nueva Historia Argentina. El progreso, la modernización y sus límites (1880–1916)*, ed. Mirta Lobato (Buenos Aires: Editorial Sudamericana, 2000), 409–463; Jorge Salessi, *Médicos, maleantes y maricas. Higiene, criminología y homosexualidad en la construcción de la Nación Argentina (Buenos Aires, 1871–1914)* (Rosario: Beatriz Viterbo Editora, 1995).

[45] Dussel, "The shaping of a citizenship with style," 107.

either schoolteachers or inspectors, most of them male but with two female teachers figuring prominently on these accounts. This speaks to the enormous role that teachers had as producers of "vernacular technologies," as Agustín Escolano calls the technical answers created in the daily grind of schools.[46] It also gives another hint to historians as to the role of human intentions in designing the artefacts, which in this case was quickly superseded by what was added through its inscription in diverse practices and strategies that ended up being more relevant to the social biography of uniforms.

In subsequent approaches to this topic, I started to become interested in the details that did not fit into the Foucaultian-inspired disciplinarian hypothesis of uniforms as key pieces for the regulation of bodies. Why did uniforms take on different colors in different countries? Why in some cases did uniforms in public schools adopt the style of private elite schools, and not in others? Why in some cases were they quickly thrown into the circuits of commodification and consumption, industrially manufactured, as in Argentina, while in other cases such as France they continued to be made within the families and were kept as distinctive objects, with personalized styles? Which histories do these objects tell us, and how to look at it through its textures, materials, design, aesthetics, its physical presence in coming and going from home to school, its circulation or marginalization from the commodities market? In other words, how to take into account their quality of traveling technologies, of mobile objects? How to pay attention to their liminal character, sign of the blurring borders between the domestic and the public spaces? How to study their transformations in the interactions with schools, children, and teachers?

These are questions that I still pursue, attentive to any trace that I find in the archives and to any new story I hear or read. But also I have become much more aware that the history of this artefact is still open, and is being rewritten by contemporary interactions, in its circulation as a symbol of public schooling against neoliberal threats, in each hand that makes it ready to be taken into the school, more or less clean or tidy, and also in the rites of passage of every child that starts its schooling proudly wearing the uniform and also of those who, at the other end, desecrate it as a liberation ritual. Through looking at its openness, I have become much more aware that the uniforms and myself are both part of a muddy history, despite all the efforts of my primary schoolteachers to impose a clean and starched smock, a quiet body, protected from the stains of play – and of history.

---

46 Escolano, "Las materialidades de la escuela (a modo de prefacio)," 15.

Developing Material Sensibilities

Throughout the reflection on my own research project on a material object, I mentioned that I learned to become more attentive to details and textures and adopted more of an ethnographic sensitivity towards the meshworks in which objects were inscribed. Resisting the fetishization of and fascination with objects, I searched nonetheless for a certain loving attitude towards them, that is, an intimate approach so as to listen to their becomings. I had to develop new research questions in order to be able to pay attention to the details and minutiae of their making and keeping up, their visual appearance but also the aural and the tactile involved in their interactions.

In this shift, there were two readings that helped me adopt a sensorial approach to the materiality of schooling, which were written before the material turn but whose approach to objects and affects deeply affected contemporary theorizations. I believe these texts can also contribute to rethink the materiality of our digital present, in which the material, in its concrete finitude, appears to be superseded by virtual entities of seemingly infinite possibilities, shaping a technopolitical horizon that carries new problems and dangers.[47]

The first reading comes from Walter Benjamin, and it is a short piece about the child's desk, an object that for some contemporary educators and designers who are fascinated by digital technologies should be condemned to museums because of its static quality and old-fashioned pedagogy. The text, written around 1932–1938, when he was already exiled from Berlin, starts with this paragraph:

> The doctor determined that I was nearsighted. And he prescribed for me not only glasses but also a desk. It was very cleverly made. The seat could be adjusted so as to be closer or further away from the desktop, which in turn was tilted and served as a writing surface, and there was also a horizontal strut in the seat back that gave you support, not to mention a little book rack that crowned the whole thing and was moveable. The desk by the window was soon my favorite spot. A small cabinet tucked away under its seat contained not only the volumes I needed for school but my stamp album and three more taken with my collection of postcards. [...] Upon getting out of school, often the first thing I did was celebrate reunion with my desk, making it the showplace of one or another of my favorite pursuits – for example, decoupage.[48]

---

[47] Quentin Meillassoux, *Après la finitude. Essai sur la nécessité de la contingence* (Paris: Ed. Du Seuil, 2012).
[48] Walter Benjamin, *Berlin Childhood circa 1900.* Translated and with commentary and afterword by C. Skoggard (Portland, OR: Publication Studio, 2010), 153–154.

The desk was for Benjamin his refuge, his stock, his place for play and learning, his own cave; there he could connect the images of the sheets and fascicles he collected with medieval manuscripts, and read Dickens and Freytag, traveling to Babylon, Baghdad, Alaska, Cairo or Detroit, as the short text states. In his desk he created, with the doctor's permission, his own jurisdiction, and could peruse school notebooks that he had successfully kept out of his teachers' claims. In relation to the materiality of the object, Benjamin valued that it had a surface to read and write, a rack, a cabinet, and a support for his back. It was also important that it was taken away from its habitual circulation, subjected to his own rules, even though these seem to have been nurtured by school codes and practices, for example in relation to writing and reading practices. Benjamin wrote that "[m]y desk and I joined forces against the [school] bench",[49] in order to reclaim his own pace, his own journey towards other countries and knowledges. Would it have been the same if this object were a chair or a table without nooks? Would it have caused the same effect had it not been the desk so close to a school object, in which the transgression of "rendering their [the school's instruments] claims null and void"[50], subtracting the object from the school rules, made it much more appealing as a space of his own? For Benjamin, it was clear that the political experience of knowledge and reading was revealed and deployed in such details, and his writings remain a powerful inspiration for those seeking to develop an attentive, multisensorial listening to the materiality of schooling.

The second reading is from Michel Foucault, and it is another short essay, "Of Other Spaces,"[51] which was originally a conference given in 1967 to the Circle of Architectural Studies and written during a trip to Tunisia. It is a text rich in images and plays with words, in which space appears as a privileged lens to look at contemporary experience, defined by simultaneity, juxtaposition, proximity, and distance, as opposed to the nineteenth century obsession with grand historical narratives. Space is, for Foucault, an entry point to analyze the heterogeneous and multiple dimensions of the social, and to look at that which goes by

---

[49] Benjamin, *Berlin Childhood*, 156. The confrontation with the school bench is clearer in the German version (where there is reference to the *Schulbank*). Interestingly, in the Spanish version the piece is titled "The school desk" [*El Pupitre*], probably leading to overstating the closeness between both types of desks and underplaying the confrontative stance that Benjamin took towards school rules and journeys of knowledge. See Walter Benjamin, "Das Pult," in *Berliner Kindheit um neunhundertzeit* (Frankfurt am Main: Suhrkamp, 1987), 106–108; Walter Benjamin, "El pupitre," in *Infancia en Berlin hacia 1900* (Madrid: Alfaguara, 1987), 95–98.
[50] Benjamin, *Berlin Childhood*, 157.
[51] Michel Foucault, "Of Other Spaces" (translated by J. Miskowiec) *Diacritics* 16: 22–27.

foot in disperse ways, in a direction that would be fully developed by Michel de Certeau. His main interest is on "other spaces" that are for him not utopias (no real places) but heterotopias, concrete placements that contest or subvert common places. Foucault exemplifies these spaces with heterotopias of crisis and passage (boarding schools, honeymoon trips, military service, Jesuit missions) and deviation (prisons, rest homes, asylums); he also analyzes cemeteries, movie theatres, gardens, and carpets as other spaces that condense, as some sort of phantasmatic mirror, contemporary urban life.

In the last paragraph, Foucault speaks about ships as heterotopias, and this is a particularly telling image because education has quite frequently been considered under the metaphor of the journey, the ship or the adventure.[52] Foucault claims that ships have not only been a major tool of economic development but also "the greatest reserve of the imagination."[53] And he closes the essay with these words: "The ship is the heterotopia par excellence. In civilizations without boats, dreams dry up, espionage takes the place of adventure, and the police take the place of pirates."[54]

In civilizations without boats, dreams dry up: this is a statement that should be left resonating for a while. Thinking about our digital present, the risk of dreams drying up, without real ships and desks, is ever more present in a techno-capitalism oriented towards automation, immediacy, and instantaneity. Caves and desks are not held in (high) esteem in a society that claims transparency as a major political and ethical goal,[55] that seeks to turn everything into visible data, predictable and controllable, without bodies, stored in a cloud. And even though the navigation metaphor is probably the dominant in contemporary experience, our explorations are increasingly less autonomous, guided by algorithms that seek to anticipate our desires and organize our movements in efficient, economic ways. In the era of total surveillance, nothing is more real that the saying that spying substitutes for adventure.[56]

These cautions, however, should not be used to feed a nostalgic or apocalyptic approach to the past or the future. Who knows if cellphones or joysticks will

---

52 Nanine Charbonnel, *Les aventures de la métaphore* (Strasbourg: Presses Universitaires de Strasbourg, 1991).
53 Foucault, "Of Other Spaces," 27.
54 Foucault, "Of Other Spaces," 27.
55 Byung-Chul Han, *The Transparency Society* (Palo Alto, CA: Stanford University Press, 2015).
56 See Shoshana Zuboff, *The Age of Surveillance Capitalism: The Fight for a Human Future at the New Frontier of Power* (New York: Public Affairs, 2019); and Evgeny Morozov's critique, "Capitalism's New Clothes," *The Baffler*, February 4, 2019, available at: https://thebaffler.com/latest/capitalisms-new-clothes-morozov.

also act as ships or doorways to other spaces, making room for adventure and for continuity as well as for change in the educational realm. It comes to us, educational researchers and particularly as historians, to remain attentive and open to what humans and non-humans have and might yet become.

Bibliography

Appadurai, Arjun, ed. *The social life of things. Commodities in cultural perspective.* Cambridge, UK: Cambridge University Press, 1986.

Arata, Nicolás. "La escolarización de la ciudad de Buenos Aires (1880–1910)." PhD Diss., Departamento de Investigaciones Educativas del CINVESTAV, 2016.

Benjamin, Walter. *Berlin Childhood circa 1900* (translated and with commentary and afterword by C. Skoggard). Portland, OR: Publication Studio, 2010.

Benjamin, Walter. *The Arcades Project* (translated by H Eiland and K McLaughlin). Cambridge, MA: The Belknap Press/Harvard University Press, 1999.

Barra, Valdenira M. Lopes de. *Da pedra ao pó. O itinerário da lousa na escolar pública paulista do século XIX.* Goiânia: Gráfica Universidade Federal de Goiânia, 2016.

Blanck, Guillermo. *El problema del desarrollo cultural del niño y otros textos inéditos.* Buenos Aires: Editorial Almagesto, 1998.

Castro, Rosa de Souza, and Vera Gaspar da Silva. "Cultura material da escola: entram em cena as carteiras." In *Objetos da Escola. Espaços e lugares de constituiçao de uma cultura material escolar (Santa Catarina – Séculos XIX e XX)*, edited by Vera G. da Silva and Marilia Petry, 169–189. Florianópolis: Editora Insular, 2012.

Catteeuw, Karl, Kristof Dams, Marc Depaepe, and Frank Simon. "Filming the Black Box: Primary Schools on Film in Belgium, 1880–1960: A First Assessment of Unused Sources." In *Visual History. Images of Education,* edited by Ulrike Mietzner, Kevin Myers, and Nick Peim, 203–232. Bern: Peter Lang, 2015.

Charbonnel, Nanine. *Les aventures de la métaphore.* Strasbourg: Presses Universitaires de Strasbourg, 1991.

Chartier, Anne-Marie. *Enseñar a leer y escribir. Una aproximación histórica.* México: Fondo de Cultura Económica, 2004.

Connolly, William E. "The 'New Materialism' and the Fragility of Things." *Millennium: Journal of International Studies* 41 (2013): 399–412.

Corrigan, Philip. "The Making of the Boy: Meditations on what Grammar School did with, to, and for my body." *Journal of Education* 170 (1988): 142–161.

Cucuzza, Héctor, and Pablo Pineau. *Para una Historia de la Enseñanza de la Lectura y Escritura en Argentina. Del catecismo colonial a La Razón de mi Vida.* Buenos Aires: Miño y Dávila Editoresv, 2002.

Daston, Lorraine. *Things That Talk. Object Lessons from Art and Science.* New York: Zone Books, 2006.

Depaepe, Marc. "Why Even Today Educational Historiography is not an Unnecessary Luxury. Focusing on four Themes from Forty-four Years of Research." *Espacio, Tiempo y Educación* 7 (2020): 227–246.

Depaepe, Marc, et al. *Order in Progress. Everyday Educational Practice in Primary Schools. Belgium, 1880–1970.* Leuven: Leuven University Press, 2000.

Depaepe, Marc, and Bregt Henkens. "The Challenge of the Visual in the History of Education." *Paedagogica Historica Supplementary Series VI.* Gent: CSHP, 2000.

Depaepe, Marc, Frank Simon, and Pieter Verstraete. "Valorising the Cultural Heritage of the School Desk Through Historical Research." In *Educational Research: Material Culture and Its Representation*, edited by Marc Depaepe and Paul Smeyers, 13–30. Dordrecht: Springer, 2014.

Depaepe, Marc, and Frank Simon. "Is there any Place for the History of 'Education' in the 'History of Education'? A plea for the History of Everyday Educational Reality in-and outside Schools." *Paedagogica Historica* XXX (1995): 9–16.

Depaepe, Marc, and Paul Smeyers, eds. *Educational Research: Material Culture and Its Representation.* Dordrecht: Springer, 2014.

Dussel, Inés. "Research memories and memories as research in the history of education: Historicizing the material and visual culture of schooling." In *Critical Methodologies for Researching Teaching and Learning*, edited by Christina Siry, Catherine Schreiber, Roberto Gómez Fernández, and Robert Reuter. Amsterdam: Sense Publishers, Series *Bold Visions in Educational Research*, forthcoming.

Dussel, Inés. "The shaping of a citizenship with style: A history of uniforms and vestimentary codes in Argentinean public schools." In *Materialities of Schooling. Design, Technology, Objects, Routines*, edited by Martin Lawn and Ian Grosvenor, 97–124. Oxford, UK: Symposium Books, 2005.

Dussel, Inés. *Curriculum, Humanismo y Democracia en la Enseñanza Media (1863–1920).* Buenos Aires: Oficina de Publicaciones del CBC-UBA/FLACSO, 1997.

Ehrenberg, Alain. *Le corps militaire. Politique et pédagogie en démocratie.* Paris: Editions Aubier, 1983.

Escolano, Agustín. "Las materialidades de la escuela (a modo de prefacio)." In *Objetos da Escola. Espaços e lugares de constituiçao de uma cultura material escolar (Santa Catarina – Séculos XIX e XX)*, edited by Vera G. da Silva and Marilia Petry, 11–18. Florianópolis: Editora Insular, 2012.

Fendler, Lynn. "The Ethics of Materiality: Some Insights from Non-representational Theory." In *Educational Research: Material Culture and Its Representation*, edited by Marc Depaepe and Paul Smeyers, 115–132. Dordrecht: Springer, 2014.

Foucault, Michel. "Of Other Spaces." Translated by J. Miskowiec. *Diacritics* 16 (1986): 22–27.

Foucault, Michel. *Discipline and Punish. The Birth of the Modern Prison.* Translated by A Sheridan. New York: Pantheon Books; 1977.

Goodman, Joyce. "Circulating Objects and (Vernacular) Cosmopolitan Subjectivities," *Bildungsgeschichte – International journal for the historiography of education: IJHE* 17: 115–126.

Groff, G. "La salud del niño. El cuidado de la ropa." *El Monitor de la Educación Común* 22, 352 (June 1902): 960–963.

Grosvenor, Ian. "Back to the future or towards a sensory history of schooling." *History of Education* 41 (2012): 675–687.

Gvirtz, Silvina. *El discurso escolar a través de los cuadernos de clase. Argentina (1930–1970).* Buenos Aires: EUDEBA, 1999.

Han, Byung-Chul. *The Transparency Society.* Palo Alto, CA: Stanford University Press, 2015.

Herman, Frederik, Mélanie Surmont, Marc Depaepe, Angelo van Gorp, and Frank Simon. "Remembering the Schoolmaster's Blood-Red Pen. The Story of the Exercise Book and the Story of 'the Children of the Time' (1950–1970)." *History of Education* 3 (2008): 351–375.

Ingold, Tim. *Making: Anthropology, archeology, art and architecture.* New York/ London: Routledge, 2013.

Ingold, Tim. "Toward an Ecology of Materials." *Annual Review of Anthropology* 41 (2012): 427–442.

Latour, Bruno. *Reassembling the social. An introduction to Actor-Network Theory.* Oxford, UK: Oxford University Press, 2005.

Latour, Bruno. *The Pasteurization of France.* Translated by A. Sheridan and J. Law. Cambridge, MA/London: Harvard University Press, 1998.

Lawn, Martin, and Ian Grosvenor. "Introduction: The Materiality of Schooling." In *Materialities of schooling. Design, Technology, Objects, Routines,* edited by Martin Lawn and Ian Grosvenor, 1–15. Oxford, UK: Symposium Books, 2005.

Liernur, Francisco. "La construcción del país urbano." In *Nueva Historia Argentina. El progreso, la modernización y sus límites (1880–1916),* edited by Mirta Lobato, 409–463. Buenos Aires: Editorial Sudamericana, 2000.

Masschelein, Jan. "Making the school: stories of caves and tables." In *Old School/Nieuwe Klas,* edited by Wim Lambrecht and Nancy Vansieleghem, 43–53. Ghent: LUCA School for the Arts, 2014.

Meda, Juri. *Mezzi di Educazione di Massa. Saggi di storia della cultura materiale della scuola tra XIX e XX secolo.* Milan: Franco Angeli, 2016.

Meillassoux, Quentin. *Après la finitude. Essai sur la nécessité de la contingence.* Paris: Ed. Du Seuil, 2012.

Miller, Daniel, ed. *Materiality.* Durham and London: Duke University Press, 2005.

Montag, Warren, and Ted Stolze. *The New Spinoza.* Minneapolis: The University of Minnesota Press, 1998.

Moreno Martínez, Pedro. "The History of School Desk Development in Terms of Hygiene and Pedagogy in Spain (1838–1936)." In *Materialities of schooling. Design, Technology, Objects, Routines,* edited by Martin Lawn and Ian Grosvenor, 71–95. Oxford, UK: Symposium Books, 2005.

Morozov, Evgeny. "Capitalism's New Clothes." *The Baffler,* February 4, 2019. https://thebaffler.com/latest/capitalisms-new-clothes-morozov.

Perrot, Philippe. "La richesse cachée: Pour une généalogie de l'austerité des apparences." *Communications* 46 (1987): 157–179.

Pineau, Pablo, ed. *Escolarizar lo sensible.* Buenos Aires: Ed. Teseo, 2014.

Salessi, Jorge. *Médicos, maleantes y maricas. Higiene, criminología y homosexualidad en la construcción de la Nación Argentina (Buenos Aires, 1871–1914).* Rosario: Beatriz Viterbo Editora, 1995.

Serra, María Silvia. *Cine, escuela y discurso pedagógico. Articulaciones, inclusiones y objeciones en el siglo XX en Argentina.* Buenos Aires: Editorial Teseo, 2011.

Steedman, Carolyn. *Dust. The Archive and Cultural History.* New Brunswick, NJ: Rutgers University Press, 2002.

Steil, Carlos, and Isabel de Moura Carvalho. "Diálogos imaginados entre Thomas Csordas y Tim Ingold." In *Cuerpos y corporalidades en las culturas de las Américas,* edited by Silvia Citro, Jose Bezerril, and Yanina Mennelli, 43–58. Buenos Aires: Biblos, 2015.

Symes, Colin, and Daphne Meadmore. "Force of Habit: The school uniform as a body of knowledge." In *Pedagogy, Technology, and the Body,* edited by Erica McWilliam and Peter Taylor, 171–191. New York: Peter Lang, 1996.

Synott, John, and Colin Symes. "The Genealogy of the School: An iconography of badges and mottoes." *British Journal of Sociology of Education* 16 (1995): 139–153.

Szir, Sandra. *Infancia y cultura visual. Los periódicos ilustrados para niños (1880–1910).* Buenos Aires: Miño y Dávila editores, 2007.

Thyssen, Geert, and Ian Grosvenor. "Learning to make sense: interdisciplinary perspectives on sensory education and embodied enculturation." *The Senses and Society* 14 (2019): 119–130.

Trinh T, Minh-ha. "Introduction: She, The Inappropriate/d Other." *Discourse* 8 (1987): 3–9.

Vidal, Diana, and Vera Gaspar da Silva. "Por uma história sensorial da escola e da escolarizaçao." In *Cultura material escolar: a escola e seus artefatos (MA, SP, PR, SC e RS), 1870–1925,* edited by Carlos A. Castro, 19–41. Sao Luis: EDUFMA/Café & Lápis, 2011.

Vigarello, Georges. *Concepts of Cleanliness. Changing Attitudes in France since the Middle Ages.* Cambridge/Paris: Cambridge University Press/Maison des Sciences de l'Homme, 1988.

Yanes-Cabrera, Cristina, Juri Meda, and Antonio Viñao, eds. *School Memories. New Trends in the History of Education.* Cham: Springer, 2017.

Zuboff, Shoshana. *The Age of Surveillance Capitalism: The Fight for a Human Future at the New Frontier of Power.* New York: Public Affairs, 2019.

Antonio Viñao (University of Murcia, Spain)
School culture(s): Historiography of a Polysemic Concept

Abstract: The expression "school culture" has been and continues to be widely used ever since in the mid-1990s a number of historians of education began to use it – along with other similar terms – in ways that were by no means consistent. This study attempts to identify the different meanings of the term and evaluate its usefulness in the face of the disparate and often indiscriminate use made of it.

Keywords: School cultures, Educational reforms, Cultural studies, Sociocultural history, School memory.

Genesis and Initial Use of a Concept

The expression "school culture" was introduced in the historical-educational field in the second half of the 1990s by education historians, for the most part Europeans working in the field of cultural history, who resorted to it as a way to refer to systems of school or curricular organization. The meanings and intentions with which they employed it, however, varied.

One of the first historians to use the expression was Dominique Julia, in a work published in 1995 about "school culture as an historical object". In this study, Julia characterized school culture as "a set of *norms* that defines the knowledge that is to be taught and the behavior to be instilled, together with a set of *practices* that will facilitate the transmission of this knowledge and the incorporation of this behavior; norms and practices directed at achieving objectives that may vary in accordance with different epochs." These ways of thinking and acting have been spread or adopted widely in other realms of our

---

Note: Study carried out as part of the National Research Project "La frontera entre ciencia y política y la ciencia en la frontera: la ciencia española (1907 – 1975)," FFI2015 – 64529-P (MIMECO-FEDER).
In this section I partially follow and expand upon Antonio Viñao, *Sistemas educativos, culturas escolares y reformas* (Madrid: Morata, 2002), 70 – 81.

https://doi.org/10.1515/9783110623451-024

"schooled society" and they have come to constitute a "new religion, with its rites and its myths."[1]

We do come across prior uses of the term. In Spain, for example, we find it used in relation to the birth and propagation of the graded school at the start of the twentieth century. In 1990, what we characterize as "a culture or way of life" that is specifically tied to the "school" refers to the organization of space, of schoolwork, of rhythms and schedules, of the classification of teachers and students, among other aspects of the model of school organization.[2] It is in this sense that Aida Terrón and Ángel Mato used the expression "school culture" in 1995 in analyzing the differences between the single classroom school and the graded school and explaining the mechanisms for the transmission of school practices used in the latter. These authors defined "institutionalized school culture" as "the set of theories and practices that has been cemented and consolidated in a school institution over time." The "appropriation" and assimilation of such practices help to understand, in these authors' view, the inertia of teachers who "reproduce what they have seen mechanically and by imitation, with no critical input." "It is from this 'culture' – they hold – together with their formation and their pedagogical experience, whether academic or self-taught, that the teacher organizes his or her daily skirmish with the class and works towards the school's pedagogical objectives, thus demonstrating the usefulness and the true efficacy of the institutional tradition."[3]

The idea of a school culture as a set of norms and practices, of ways of thinking and performing that are peculiar to an institution created specifically for the purpose of transmitting knowledge and inculcating behavior, implies a capacity or power for producing and generating. This, in turn, implies a relative autonomy with regard to other, external cultures, ones with which the school maintains, at each historical moment, a relationship that may be more or less harmonious or conflictive, more or less independent or subordinated, particularly with regard to religious, political or popular aspects of the culture. An example of this creative, productive power can be found in school subjects or disciplines, products of a more or less systematic and accumulative pedagogical mediation – others

---

[1] Dominique Julia, "La culture scolaire comme objet historique," in *Colonial Experience in Education. Historical Issues and Perspectives*, ed. António Nóvoa, Marc Depaepe, and Erwin V. Johanningmeier (Gent: Paedagogica Historica. Supplementary Series (I), 1995), 354.

[2] Antonio Viñao, *Innovación pedagógica y racionalidad científica. La escuela graduada pública en España (1898–1936)* (Madrid: Akal, 1990), 7.

[3] Aida Terrón and Ángel Mato, "Modifications des programmes et inertie institutionnelle: tradition et changement dans le modèle scolaire des classes homogènes," *Paedagogica Historica* XXXI (1995): 129.

might consider it a "didactic transposition" – in a specific field of knowledge.[4] In this case, the notion of a school culture does not refer to culture that is acquired in the school but rather to a culture that is born, configured, and then acquired in the school.[5]

The union of these two aspects – of school culture as the institutionalized set of ways of thinking and acting elaborated on the basis of practical situations and tasks and passed down from one generation of teachers and students to the next, and the concept of a social space which generates its own products – immediately led to the need to study the internal history of the school institution, of the "black box of schooling". The day to day inner workings of the school center, of what went on inside and outside of the classroom had, for the most part, been ignored by historians of education.[6] From this perspective, school culture could be observed and analyzed in these daily activities and rituals and in myriad factors including class schedules; the division of the school calendar into academic and vacation periods; the distribution and uses of school spaces and of furniture and classroom objects; the ways in which students were classified by age and by having fulfilled requirements in certain subjects; how internal hierarchies were established; the systems of incentives, rewards and punishments; systems of evaluation; the structure of class lessons etc.

Another motive for resorting increasingly to the expression school culture has to do with the realization and acknowledgement of the relative failure of one school reform after another, reforms that barely touch the surface of what goes on within the classrooms and teaching centers or that generate, at best, hybrid situations and changes that are merely formal. The failure to achieve mean-

---

[4] The paternity of the idea of "didactic transposition" is usually attributed to a sociologist, Michel Verret, who affirmed that "the teaching of an object always presupposes [...] its prior transformation into an object of teaching"; cf. Michel Verret, *Le temps des études* (Paris: Librairie Honoré Champion, 1975), 140. The concept was first used in the field of didactics of mathematics by Yves Chevallard, *La transposition didactique* (Paris: La Pensée Sauvage, 1985) and later adopted in the didactics of science, before eventually being applied to all of the specific didactics of any given field. For more on this, and for a critical perspective, see Miguel Ángel Gómez García, "La transposición didáctica: historia de un concepto," *Revista Latinoamericana de Estudios Educativos* 1 (2005): 83–111.

[5] André Chervel, *La culture scolaire. Une approche historique* (Paris: Belin, 1998), 5–6 ; and André Chervel, "Des disciplines scolaires à la culture scolaire", in *Education and Cultural Transmission*, ed. Johan Sturm, Jeroen Dekker, Richard Aldrich, and Frank Simon (Gent: Paedagogica Historica. Supplementary Series (II), 1996), 181–195.

[6] Marc Depaepe and Frank Simon, "Is there any place for the History of 'education' in the 'History of Education'? A plea for the history of every day educational reality in-and outside schools," *Paedagogica Historica* XXX (1995): 9–16.

ingful reform has, among other causes, been attributed to the generalized presence in all of these attempts of an a-historical "presentism", that is, an obliviousness of the existence of school cultures made up of traditions and rites that govern the practice and organization of teaching and learning and that, as such, constitute an historic product.[7] In this sense, the concept of school culture aligns closely with that of the "grammar of schooling" coined by Tyack, Tobin, and Cuban in their studies of educational reforms carried out in the United States in the past century,[8] with that of "basic structures of schooling" used by Kliebard,[9] and with the "school form" as a particular historical configuration and a form of dominant socialization in industrialized societies, as expressed by Vincent.[10]

From this perspective, the distinction, opposition, and interaction between the culture of expert, scientific knowledge about education, the culture of policies, reforms, and legal issues involving teaching, and the practical-empirical knowledge of teachers in the practice of their profession – i.e., between theories or proposals, legality, and practice – has itself become an object of analysis for historians of education.[11] This triple distinction owes a considerable debt, at least in my case, to the work done by Sarason on school culture and the problem

---

[7] Antonio Viñao, "Culturas escolares, reformas e innovaciones: entre la tradición y el cambio," in *La construcción de una nueva cultura en los centros docentes* (Murcia: Fórum Europeo de Administradores de la Educación, 1996), 17–29; Antonio Viñao, "Por una historia de la cultura escolar: cuestiones, enfoques, fuentes," in *Culturas y civilizaciones. III Congreso de la Asociación de Historia Contemporánea* (Valladolid: Universidad de Valladolid, 1998), 167–183; Antonio Viñao, "Culturas escolares, reformas e innovaciones educativas," *Con-Ciencia Social* 5 (2001): 27–45, and especially Antonio Viñao, "Do education reforms fail? A historian's response," *Encounters on Education* 2 (2002): 27–47, and Antonio Viñao, "El éxito o fracaso de las reformas educativas: condicionantes, limitaciones, posibilidades," in *La reforma necesaria: entre la política educativa y la práctica escolar*, ed. José Gimeno (Madrid: Morata, 2006), 43–60.

[8] David Tyack and William Tobin, "The 'grammar' of schooling. Why has it been so hard to change?," *American Educational Research Journal* XXXI (1994): 453–479; David Tyack and Larry Cuban, *Tinkering toward Utopia. A Century of Public School Reform* (Cambridge Mss.: Harvard University Press, 1995).

[9] Herbert M. Kliebard, *Changing Course. American Curriculum Reform in the 20th Century* (New York: Teacher College Press, 2002), 5.

[10] Guy Vincent, Bernard Lahire, and Daniel Thin, "Sur l'histoire et la théorie de la forme scolaire," in *L'éducation prisonnière de la forme scolaire? Scolarisation et socialisation dans les sociétés industrielles*, ed. Guy Vincent (Lyon: Presses Universitaires de Lyon, 1994), 11–48.

[11] Agustín Escolano, "Las culturas escolares del siglo. Encuentros y desencuentros," *Revista de Educación*, monographic issue on "La educación en España en el siglo XX" (2000), 201–218; and Viñao, *Sistemas educativos, culturas escolares y reformas*, 90–99.

of change in teaching.[12] In today's world of educational pseudo-markets and the massive infusion of capital into education, I would add to the above distinctions that of the market or business culture, with its vision of education as a business. In the words of Stephen Ball, in the current scenario of global educational policies you've got to "follow the money" if you want to see and understand what is happening.[13]

In summary, school culture could be said to be constituted by a series of theories, ideas, principles, norms, guidelines, rituals, inertias, habits, and practices (ways of doing and thinking, mentalities and conducts), consolidated and cemented over time in the form of traditions, customs, and unquestioned rules, all of which are assumed and shared by the different players in the context of an educational institution. These traditions and "regular, ceremonialized actions", which may be at times "alien to the rationality of their origins", these "myths",[14] are transmitted down through the generations and ultimately provide strategies for:

1) Integrating into or interacting with these institutions.
2) Carrying out, particularly in the classroom, the daily tasks expected of each individual, as well as facing up to the requirements and limitations implicit to these tasks.
3) Surviving through the successive reforms as well as reinterpreting and adapting them — from the school culture — to a given context and needs.

The defining features of school culture can be found in its continuity and permanence over time, its institutionalization and its relative independence, which allows it to generate its own specific products, such as, among others, school subjects. School culture could be described, then, as a sediment formed over time by layers, mixed more than superimposed, which, as in an archeological exploration, can be dug up and separated.

---

12 Seymour B. Sarason, *The Culture of the School and the Problem of Change* (Boston: Allyn and Bacon, 1971), and *Revisiting "The Culture of the School and the Problem of Change"* (New York: Teacher College Press, 1996).
13 Stephen Ball, *Global Education Policy: Austerity and Profit* (La Laguna: Universidad de La Laguna, 2012), 20.
14 Aida Terrón and Violeta Álvarez, "Sobre la cultura escolar y los mitos en nuestra escuela," *Cultura y Educación* 14 (2002): 244–245. In this sense, the "ceremony" would be "an operative, sequential, regulated activity whose units or segments of conduct obey known, temporal limits".

Limitations and Pitfalls of the Expression School Culture

Resorting to the expressions school culture or the grammar of schooling, as explained above, does not come without its risks and limitations. As Robert L. Hampel pointed out in the debate offered in the pages of the journal *History of Education Quarterly* about the work of David Tyack and Larry Cuban in which they coined the expression grammar of schooling, changes in education are hard to "see and quantify, especially if the historian only examines institutional regularities and policy talk."[15] Indeed, if we focus exclusively, or primarily, on continuities and perpetuations, we may be missing the changes, even those changes that a reform has brought about in the school culture, or the compromises and give-and-take that typically result. What we are lacking, then, is a theory, an historical explanation for the change and innovation in education – of its discontinuities – that can be integrated into and combined with the analysis of the continuities and perpetuations. These two aspects of the question are inseparable, among other reasons, because, although change cannot be ordered – this being one of the lessons we learn from the analysis of the interaction between school cultures and educational reforms – neither can it be stopped.

From an anthropological point of view, Elsie Rockwell has shown how educational institutions, for as much as they strive to project an appearance of "cultural coherence" – internal consistency, precise limits, resistance to change – are in fact "riddled with contradictions, consisting of sedimented layers and subject to multiple external cultural currents". As a result,

> It's hard to speak of a "school culture" that corresponds to a circumscribed and universal institution. A school's cultural fabric is an historical construction and as such it evidences links and transformations over time. It is subject to cultural cross-currents from different realms, to which its degree of permeability and absorption varies.[16]

The school practices of teachers, she goes on to say, "include more or less conventional ways of acting, speaking, working, disciplining, treating students, presenting material, conveying knowledge, all of which are reproduced in a way that often goes beyond the planned actions or conscious intentions of the teach-

---

[15] Robert Hampel, William Johnson, David Plank, Diane Ravitch, David Tyack, and Larry Cuban, "History and Educational Reform," *History of Education Quarterly* 36 (1996): 476.
[16] Elsie Rockwell, "Huellas del pasado en las culturas escolares," *Revista de Antropología Social*, 16 (2007): 177–178.

er." It is by "using this cultural fabric as a starting point" that "the teachers integrate their diverse pedagogical approaches in a selective way over the course of their careers", while "continuously incorporating ways of speaking and presenting knowledge that were never prescribed or dictated by the school but that became interwoven with the center's pedagogical tradition."[17]

As a result, the expression "school culture", and other similar terms, unless they are employed paying careful attention to changes and typology in their use, can hardly help us to grasp:

- Other aspects that also condition the relative success or failure of educational reforms: cultural, social and political contexts, support and opposition, internal contradictions, financing, etc.
- The effect and influence on school culture brought about by these reforms and by the change and adaptation to diverse realities and contexts, or vice-versa.
- The mid and long-term changes in the school culture itself. School cultures are not eternal. They constitute a combination – one among many possible combinations – of tradition or continuities and changes, of formations from the past and seeds of possible futures.

On the other hand, the expression school culture suggests, as we have pointed out, a unique construction or structure. Are we right to speak of one single culture? Wouldn't it be more instructive to speak in the plural, of school cultures? From a broader perspective of educational systems, we have already shown how they comprise in fact a compendium, an interaction of three cultures: that of the scientists and experts in education; that of the politicians and administrators who push their reforms 'from above'; and that of the empirical-practical activity of the teachers as they apply their teaching methods and skills. However, from the point of view of these actors, we really ought to make a distinction between the different ways of thinking and doing that are particular to the craft of teaching and those of the student, which have received less attention. And with regard to teachers, we also need to make a distinction among the different subcultures specific to each type of teaching – preschool, primary school, secondary school, higher education, professional-technical formation, adult education, etc. –, to each teaching category – full professor, associate or assistant professor, etc. – and to each field or position – inspector, director, etc. –, existing within the educational system and its institutions. We find yet more subcultures if we focus on the teaching centers themselves, which may be public, private, confessional or secular, large or small, to say nothing of the social groups or class origins of the students themselves.

---

17 Rockwell, "Huellas del pasado en las culturas escolares," 178.

School Culture and Cultural History

The affirmation from 1976 in *Keywords. A Vocabulary of Culture and Society* by Raymond Williams, one of the founding fathers of "Cultural Studies", about the polysemic nature of the term culture in the English language, is perfectly applicable, as he himself recognized, to other European languages:

> Culture is one of the two or three most complicated words in the English language. This is so partly because of its intricate historical development, in several European languages, but mainly because it has now to be used for important concepts in several distinct intellectual disciplines and in several distinct and incompatible systems of thought.[18]

Not only has this situation not changed over time; it has, if anything, become more complex and diverse. In 1999, Andrew Edgar, referring to the term culture and to other related terms in *Key Concepts in Cultural Theory*, acknowledges that the concept "is not easily defined, not least because it can be different meanings in different contexts". Nonetheless, he goes on to define it, affirming that

> it entails recognition that human beings live in a world that is created by human beings, and in which they find meaning. Culture is the complex everyday world we all encounter and through which we all move. Culture begins at the point at which humans surpass whatever is simply given in their natural inheritance.[19]

This indiscriminate use of the concept of culture and its application to any field, situation or aspect of human action only devaluates its heuristic-comprehensive potential, making it necessary to then explain in what sense it is being used and just what is trying to be said. If everything is culture the concept does not serve to understand reality; it becomes meaningless. The same is true when talking about the concept of school culture.

Earlier we looked at some of the objectives and reasons for which a number of education historians began to popularize this term – and other similar ones – in the second half of the 1990s and the first decade of our current century. The prior and simultaneous emergence and upswing of cultural history – a sundry

---

[18] Raymond Williams, *Keywords. A Vocabulary of Culture and Society* (Hammersmith: Fontana Press, 1988), 87.

[19] Andrew Edgar, "Culture," in *Key Concepts in Cultural Theory*, ed. Andrew Edgar and Peter Sedgwick (London: Routledge, 1999), 101–102. As "key concepts" derived from "Culture", the book also deals with those of "Cultural anthropology", "Cultural capital", "Cultural relativism", "Cultural reproduction", "Cultural studies", and "Culture industry".

group of subjects, objects, methodologies, and sources –, and of the new social and cultural history,[20] together with the history of material culture and its relationship with patrimony and memory, have only served to diversify even further the use of the concept of culture and, in particular, that of school culture.

In a strict anthropological sense, the paragraph by Edgar cited above adds an additional aspect to the already broad understanding of the term culture. Not only is it "the complex everyday world we all encounter and through which we all move", one which "begins at the point at which humans surpass whatever is simply given in their natural inheritance", but in this world, "created by human beings", these human beings, he is telling us, need to find "meaning". And this concept, "meaning", goes beyond mere human actions. Anthropologically speaking, what is relevant here is not the action nor even its consequences – material or otherwise – but rather the "meanings" which, consciously or not, are attached to the actions carried out by human beings.

It is in this sense that Clifford Geertz speaks of the textual analogy, or the consideration of social and material reality as a symbolic ritual or a semiotic code, a text or discourse in which we can find meanings inscribed along with the representations of those living in this reality. "The culture of a people is an ensemble of texts, themselves ensembles, which the anthropologist strains to read over the shoulders of those to whom they properly belong".[21] He goes on to affirm in various pages that if culture "consists of socially established structures of meaning", if it is "essentially" a "semiotic" concept and not "an experimental science in search of law but an interpretive one in search of meaning", if, "in short, anthropological writings are themselves interpretations, and second and third order ones to boot. (By definition, only a 'native' makes first order ones: it's *his* culture.)",[22] then practicing ethnography – or history – is ultimately a way of deconstructing reality as if it were a text. This is especially true if this ritual and symbolic reality, full of meanings and interpretations, consists of

> a multiplicity of complex conceptual structures, many of them superimposed upon or knotted into one another, which are at once strange, irregular, and inexplicit, and which he must contrive somehow first to grasp and then to render. [...] Doing ethnography is like trying to read (in the sense of "construct a reading of") a manuscript —foreign, faded, full of ellipses, incoherencies, suspicious emendations, and tendentious commentaries, but writ-

---

20 Sasha Handley, Rohan McWilliam, and Lucy Noakes, eds., *New Directions in Social and Cultural History* (London: Bloomsbury Academic, 2018).
21 Clifford Geertz, *The Interpretation of Cultures. Selected Essays* (New York: Basic Books, 1973), 452.
22 Geertz, *The Interpretation of Cultures*, 12, 5, and 15, following the order of the quotes.

ten not in conventionalized graphs of sound but in transient examples of shaped behavior.[23]

In this way, what is real dissolves into symbolic codes, into signs that must be read and interpreted, into constructions of meanings and representations. "The relationship thus established is not one of dependence of the mental structures on their material determinations", but rather the reverse: "the representations of the social world themselves are the constituents of social reality".[24] Furthermore, these elements cannot be recovered historically; they must be retrieved by means of a reality that is of a second order, i.e., one that is documentary and textual. "The real then takes a new meaning: what is real, in fact, is not (or is not only) the reality aimed at by the text, but the very manner in which the text aims at it in the historicity of its production and the strategy of its writing",[25] in other words, in the representation of the representation. This is why it is not the least bit surprising that a cockfight in Bali[26] or a massacre of cats in eighteenth century France[27] should be analyzed as purely symbolic rituals, conducts or practices. Underlying such studies we find, beyond the logical interest in ritual and symbolic acts, the treatment of political, institutional, and social practices – including education – as a discursive series of symbolic codes and systems that conditions not only the representations configured by those who have created or participated directly or indirectly in them, but also, at another stage, their ulterior representations.

From this anthropological perspective, school culture, for as much coherence, internal consistency, and precise limits as it may feature at a given moment, is always situated – socially and materially – in a particular context and is therefore open, as we have pointed out, to multiple external cultural currents and influences. In other words, notwithstanding the numerous general features that we may attribute to it, it has no choice but to become integrated into and operate within a setting, a milieu to which it must adapt to a greater or lesser degree. This process of adaptation or accommodation to the setting may take myriad forms – from boarding schools in itinerant teachers, from urban graded

---

23 Geertz, *The Interpretation of Cultures*, 10.
24 Roger Chartier, "Intellectual history or sociocultural history? The French trajectories," in *Modern European Intellectual History. Reappraisals & New Perspectives*, ed. Dominick La Capra and Steven L. Kaplan (Ithaca, New York: Cornell University Press, 1982), 40–41.
25 Chartier, "Intellectual history or sociocultural history?," 40.
26 Geertz, *The Interpretation of Cultures*, 412–453.
27 Robert Darnton, *La gran matanza de gatos y otros episodios de la historia cultural francesa* (México D. F.: Fondo de Cultura Económica, 1987), 81–108.

schools to modest rural schoolhouses with a single teacher, from ghetto schools to open-air institutions, to name just a few examples. As a result of this variety/ diversity, it becomes difficult to see their basic elements – their way of doing and thinking, of organizing and using their space, time, material and objects, the interactions taking place in the center and in the classroom – as forming part of a single, broader, general culture. It becomes more daunting yet if we are speaking of representations and meanings, of rituals, symbols, and myths.

School Culture and Recent Trends in Social and Cultural History

It is worth taking a look at a recent book on "key concepts" in the field of "educational studies". Naturally, under the heading "Power" – the others being "Personal", "Philosophy", and "Practice" – we find terms such as class, equality, hegemony, power or politics, but we also come across others – gender, identity, neuroscience, race, sexuality, diversity, pastoral welfare – that would have been very unlikely to appear in a similar sort of book from 20 or 30 years ago. It is even more improbable that in dealing with a concept such as class, this term would have been considered a "zombie" category: "dead of its usefulness for analysis, but still hanging around in sociological textbooks". Today, in contrast to when Marx and Weber were writing, "we live in more individualised ways and have a much less developed sense of class identity". We could even go so far as to say, Broterton adds, that we live in a "classless society", in the sense that, although inequalities have not diminished or disappeared, the concept of "class is now less useful as a way of explaining educational or other forms of inequality and that therefore we need more complex ways of thinking about these issues". It is, ultimately, another form of identity experience, akin to those offered by, among others, the concepts of gender, ethnicity, race, disability or sexuality.[28] As Katrina Navickas puts it,

> Within the framework of representation, class is individualized; it is relegated to one part of the individual identity. Cultural history has focused on individual and group identities outside political or economic structures. Where cultural historians consider class, they see it as a collective identity; but often class is equated to another form of symbolism or represen-

---

[28] Graham Broterton, "Key concept: Class," in *Education Studies. The Key Concepts*, ed. Dave Trotman, Helen E. Lees, and Roger Willoughby (Abingdon, Oxfordshire: Routledge, 2018), 234.

tative experience. They argue that agency is individual rather than collective through class. Economic and social structures are underplayed.[29]

This is not to say that in the social history that prevailed in the historiography of the 1960s and 70s we do not find aspects and elements that linked it to the cultural history that would take its place in the 1980s and 90s. The emphasis that the earlier school placed on "history from below", which focused more on the common, everyday folk, people "without history", than on leaders or prominent public figures, already implied an approximation to the subjective and individual. The history of mentalities itself could well have derived – as we proposed in another work, with inauspicious results – towards a history of the mind and of the modes and technologies of communication[30] or, as Peter Burke has so fittingly suggested, towards a social history of knowledge.[31] But it seems evident that a greater focus was placed on quantitative elements, on the structures and determinisms of social forces and means of production than on personal or subjective aspects. All of this was further upended by the different ways of viewing reality that came about with the advent of women's history, postmodernism, post-Foucaultianism, the return of the subject, or the different turns – cultural, linguistic, visual, emotional, sensorial, corporal, material, spatial, transnational, environmental, contextual, animal, memorialistic, patrimonial – that have emerged and jostled for their place in the last three decades.

Changes in ways of seeing, in where we look from and what we look for, can also be due, consciously or unconsciously, to the

> process through which history has been made to conform to neo-liberal market culture by replacing the categories that privilege power struggles, production and stratification with those that foreground consumption, globalization and individualism.[32]

---

[29] Katrina Navickas, "A return to materialism? Putting social history back into place," in *New Directions in Social and Cultural History*, ed. Sasha Handley, Rohan McWilliam, and Lucy Noakes (London: Bloomsbury Academic, 2018), 88.

[30] Antonio Viñao, "History of education and cultural history. Possibilities, problems and questions," in *Cultural History and Education. Critical Essays on Knowledge and Schooling*, ed. Thomas S. Popkewitz, Barry M. Franklin, and Miguel A. Pereyra (New York: RoutledgeFalmer, 2001), 139–145.

[31] Peter Burke, *A Social History of Knowledge* (Cambridge: Polity Press–Blackwell, 2000); and Asa Brigss and Peter Burke, *A social History of the Media. From Gutenberg to the Internet* (Cambridge: Polity Press, 2002).

[32] Donna Loftus, "Markets and Culture," in *New Directions in Social and Cultural History*, 110.

In one way or another, and in keeping with the times, the focus has been shifting from production to consumption,[33] from the quantitative to the qualitative, from social and economic structures and determinism to the individual subject, from class consciousness to consciousness of one's self, a self made up of diverse identities. These include the processes and experiences of identity involving one's self, others, and one's self as another – "the process of othering"[34] –, concepts or expressions such as selfhood, subjectivity, sense of self, relational self, agency – "the power to change their own history"[35] –, ego-documents, experiences, and narratives of life, personal testimonies and technologies of the self, or matters like emotions, feelings,[36] the body or the senses.[37] And from here, inevitably, to neuroscience and the relationship between human beings and animals – the animal turn – and the ecological or environmental turn. This is to say, a socio-cultural history without limits that encompasses all of existence, but from a single perspective.

Examples of these new tendencies and successive turns in the realm of education history in the last few years are abundant, although the scope of this study precludes their exposition here. However, due to their surge in the historical-educational field and to the expansion that they have brought to school culture as an object of study, I would like to focus specifically on two turns – the material and memorial turns – and their relationship with the material culture of the school, with the school memory and patrimony and with the surge of pedagogical museums.

---

[33] Sasha Handley, Rohan McWilliam, and Lucy Noakes, "Introduction. Toward new social and cultural histories," in *New Directions in Social and Cultural History*, 11.
[34] Penny Summerfield, "Subjectivity, the self and historical practice," in *New Directions in Social and Cultural History*, 29–32.
[35] Navickas, "A return to materialism?," 88.
[36] Rob Boddice, "The history of emotions," in *New Directions in Social and Cultural History*, 45–63.
[37] Judith A. Allen, "The body and the senses," in *New Directions in Social and Cultural History*, 65–83.

Antonio Viñao (University of Murcia, Spain)

The Material Culture of Educational Institutions: School Memory and Patrimony and the Pedagogical Museum Boom

In 2004, in an international symposium held in Brescia and titled "Bilancio e prospettive della storia dell'educazione in Europa", I was entrusted with the subject of "school memory". In my work, after some reflections on the cause of the "memorial turn" in general and the history of education in particular, and of the different types of memory and oblivion, I undertook a synopsis of the state of research regarding the memory and recollections of students – their positive and negative experiences –, the teachers – types of texts and auto-referential testimony – and of the material objects: material culture, school patrimony, and the conspicuous surge of pedagogical museums.[38] Fifteen years have gone by since the event, and I can think of at least two considerations that are worth sharing.

One, which is fundamental, has to do with the clarification of the concept of school memory and to the uses that have been given to this term. I can think of no better way of illustrating this than by transcribing a text that appeared in the introduction of a book from 2017 that brought together a selection of studies from an international symposium that had been held in Seville two years earlier titled "School Memories. New Trends in Historical Research into Education. Heuristic Perspectives and Methodological Issues":

> So, what exactly is understood by "school memory"? While there is no univocal definition we believe that we can state that school memory can be basically understood in two different ways: first as an individual way of reflection about one's own school experience, as in the reconstruction of the self; and then as an individual, collective or public commemoration of a common school past [...].
>
> [...] we wish to clarify that when we speak of "school memory" we are not referring to the memory transmitted by the school but to memory related to the school, school times and teaching, i.e. the memory that individuals, communities and society have built up about the school world and the educational process [...].
>
> Historians of education [...] are more interested in a conception of memory [...] as a practice of individual remembrance or collective and public commemoration of a common school past, based on the analysis of the self-representation of themselves provided by the teachers and students in their individual memoirs and on the representation of the school

---

[38] Antonio Viñao, "La memoria escolar: restos y huellas, recuerdos y olvidos," *Annali di Storia dell'Educazione e delle Istituzione Scholastiche* 12 (2005): 19–33. I did not go into that other kind of school memory, that of educational institutions, a topic I have since gone back to on a number of occasions.

and the teaching offered by the cultural industry, and by the world of information and communication, along with that developed by official commemorations promoted by public institutions in accordance with a specific memory policy and the public use of the past.

This last research perspective in particular enables a deep analysis of an aspect whose historical reach has yet to be correctly situated by historians: how the perception of the public status of education has evolved within a larger or smaller community and the public image of the school and the national education system.[39]

What concerns us here, then, is not so much the memory produced by the school as the memory built individually and socially around schooling and the school. This change of focus transforms the memory of those who spent a certain number of years of their lives – whether few or many – in the classroom or had a close relationship with it, into an immaterial patrimony. At the same time, it converts into material patrimony the school spaces and objects and features of all sorts – didactic or not – that made the teaching and learning processes possible, or that were a product of these processes. This is because both spaces and objects harbor memory and contain their history. This history stretches from the moment they were conceived and created until their physical disappearance, and includes their production, commercialization, acquisition, and the use – scholarly or not – made of them. As Hamilton and Meda have shown, their study requires, among other things, combining economic history with education history.[40]

In recent years we find numerous references, – in books, articles, symposiums and seminars – to the material culture of education or the materiality of schooling.[41] This abundance corresponds to a boom in this period of pedagogical

---

[39] Juri Meda and Antonio Viñao, "School memory: Historiographical balance and heuristic perspectives," in *School Memories. New Trends in the History of Education*, ed. Cristina Yanes-Cabrera, Juri Meda, and Antonio Viñao (Cham: Switzerland, 2017), 1–3.

[40] David Hamilton, "Patents: a neglected source in the History of Education," *History of Education* 38 (2009): 303–310; and Juri Meda, *Mezzi di educazione di massa. Saggi di storia della cultura material della scuola tra XIX e XX secolo* (Milano: Franco Angeli, 2016).

[41] Five significant samples suffice (four books and one congress): Martin Lawn and Ian Grosvenor, eds., *Materialities of Schooling. Design – Technology – Objects – Routines* (Oxford: Symposium Books, 2005); Martin Lawn, ed., *Modelling the Future. Exhibitions and the Materiality of Education* (Oxford: Symposium Books, 2009); Agustín Escolano, ed., *La cultura material de la escuela* (Berlanga de Duero: 2007), and "Education et culture materielle. En France et en Europe du XVIe siècle à nos jours," International colloquium organized by the University of Bordeaux on April 29 and 30, 2014. Of course there are other books, collective or not, that, while not resorting to the term "material culture of the school", deal almost exclusively with issues considered to be from this domain. For example, Sjaak Braster, Ian Grosvenor, and María del Mar del Pozo Andres, eds., *The Black Box of Schooling. A Cultural History of the Classroom* (Brussels: Peter

museums, or centers for the study of educational memory, the emergence of societies for the conservation and study of the historical–educational patrimony (in Spain, Brazil, Portugal, Italy) and the subsequent celebration of annual or biannual colloquiums, meetings, and expositions focused on the subject. It has also led to the formation of research groups that focus almost exclusively on aspects and elements of this material culture, be they objects produced and commercialized outside of the school – textbooks, furniture, desks, blackboards, teaching material for each subject, uniforms, posters, etc. –, objects created in the school – notebooks, exams, notes, etc. – or elements that contribute to the school surroundings: school spaces and schedules, settings, environs, decorations, murals, lighting, odors, etc. Such elements can be readily studied together with aspects of the immaterial culture available in egodocuments, interviews, and life histories, or with the distribution and movement of bodies – the choreography – of those who together inhabited these school spaces.[42]

There are several causes for this boom in museum-patrimony-memorialistic research. One is the increased availability of public and private financing for "curating" and studying cultural patrimony, in our case that of education. Another is the greater audience and increased social dissemination that this type of research and activity enjoys in comparison to the rest of subjects that are commonly studied by historians of education. Another cause, related to the previous one, has to do with the diversity of uses that this type of research and activities lends itself to: nostalgic, therapeutic, commemorative, didactic, academic-scientific, etc.[43] Having acknowledged this trend, we would do well to point out some of the pitfalls and temptations facing those of us involved with it.

Fetishism and antiquarianism with regard to objects are two omni-present temptations in all historical research, particularly when dealing with cultural patrimony. The peril of elaborating a history that is reduced to repeating "this occurred" or "that existed", or of compiling a list or collection of details and variations regarding certain objects runs the risk of converting a supposedly historical operation into an infinite, limitless task, replete with "superfluous" annotations, making no sense at all but aimed at producing in the reader a kind of

---

Lang, 2011), whose title takes us back to the classic 1995 article by Marc Depaepe and Frank Simon referred to in note 7.
42 Betty Eggermont, "The choreography of schooling as site of struggle: Belgian primary schools, 1880–1940," *History of Education* 30 (2001): 129–140.
43 For more details, see Antonio Viñao, "La historia material e inmaterial de la escuela: memoria, patrimonio y educación," *Educação* 35 (2012): 7–17.

"reality effect."[44] Objects do not speak for themselves. There are people of course for whom objects say nothing. But those who are receptive to them do not see or hear the same things. The uses and meanings of the material and immaterial remains and traces of the past differ, as do their meanings, depending on who is looking at them and on how, why and from where they are being looked at. Their mere cataloguing, description, and enumeration will not give us anything beyond a chronicle, a chronology or a record. Registering the existence of a series of objects is not the same as associating them, comparing them or putting them into a context. Just as events cannot be completely isolated from other events and from their contexts, neither can objects or their life story exist in a vacuum. Their relevance and interest do not derive from their condition as objects or stories, but from the meanings, connections and relationships that the historian establishes between them and the context of their production, reception, appropriation, and interpretation. For this type of study to mean something, they need to be integrated and contextualized by means of broader theoretical and conceptual approaches that are linked to notions such as school culture(s) or the grammar of schooling, continuities and changes in teaching, studies of the processes of school enrolment and teacher professionalization, among other possibilities. And they must be endowed with an interpretative narrative or discourse. That is the historian's job: to unite the empirical culture of the school with the life experiences, memory, patrimony and archeology of the school[45] and the social and cultural processes from inside and outside the school setting in which this culture is born, transmitted, and transformed.

Bibliography

Allen, Judith A. "The body and the senses." In *New Directions in Social and Cultural History*, edited by Sasha Handley, Rohan McWilliam, and Lucy Noakes, 65–83. London: Bloomsbury Academic, 2018.

Ball, Stephen. *Global Education Policy: Austerity and Profit*. La Laguna: Universidad de La Laguna, 2012.

Barthes, Roland. *El susurro del lenguaje. Más allá de la palabra y la escritura*. Barcelona: Paidós, 1987.

---

44 Roland Barthes, *El susurro del lenguaje. Más allá de la palabra y la escritura* (Barcelona: Paidós, 1987), 163–195. French edition: *Essais critiques IV. Le bruissement de la langue* (Paris: Editions du Seuil, 1984).

45 Agustín Escolano, *La cultura empírica della scuola. Esperienza, memoria, archeologia* (Ferrara: Volta la carta, 2016).

Boddice, Rob. "The history of emotions." In *New Directions in Social and Cultural History*, edited by Sasha Handley, Rohan McWilliam, and Lucy Noakes, 45–63. London: Bloomsbury Academic, 2018.

Braster, Sjaak, Ian Grosvenor, and María del Mar del Pozo Andres, eds. *The Black Box of Schooling. A Cultural History of the Classroom*. Brussels: Peter Lang, 2011.

Brigss, Asa, and Peter Burke. *A social History of the Media. From Gutenberg to the Internet*. Cambridge: Polity Press, 2002.

Broterton, Graham. "Key concept: Class." In *Education Studies. The Key Concepts*, edited by Dave Trotman, Helen E. Lees, and Roger Willoughby, 232–235. Abingdon, Oxdon: Routledge, 2018.

Burke, Peter. *A Social History of Knowledge*. Cambridge: Polity Press–Blackwell, 2000.

Chartier, Roger. "Intellectual history or sociocultural history? The French trajectories." In *Modern European Intellectual History. Reappraisals & New Perspectives*, edited by Dominick La Capra and Steven L. Kaplan, 13–46. Ithaca, New York: Cornell University Press, 1982.

Chervel, André. "Des disciplines scolaires à la culture scolaire." In *Education and Cultural Transmission*, edited by Johan Sturm, Jeroen Dekker, Richard Aldrich, and Frank Simon, 181–195. Gent: Paedagogica Historica. Supplementary Series (II), 1996.

Chervel, André. *La culture scolaire. Une approche historique*. Paris: Belin, 1998.

Chevallard, Yves. *La transposition didactique*. Paris: La Pensée Sauvage, 1985.

Darnton, Robert. *La gran matanza de gatos y otros episodios de la historia cultural francesa*. México D. F.: Fondo de Cultura Económica, 1987.

Depaepe, Marc, and Frank Simon. "Is there any place for the History of 'education' in the 'History of Education'? A plea for the history of every day educational reality in-and outside schools." *Paedagogica Historica* XXX (1995): 9–16.

Edgar, Andrew. "Culture". In *Key Concepts in Cultural Theory*, edited by Andrew Edgar and Peter Sedgwick, 101–103. London: Routledge, 1999.

Eggermont, Betty. "The choreography of schooling as site of struggle: Belgian primary schools, 1880–1940." *History of Education* 30 (2001): 129–140.

Escolano, Agustín. "Las culturas escolares del siglo. Encuentros y desencuentros." *Revista de Educación*, monographic issue on "La educación en España en el siglo XX" (2000): 201–218.

Escolano, Agustín, ed. *La cultura material de la escuela*. Berlanga de Duero, 2007.

Escolano, Agustín. *La cultura empírica della scuola. Esperienza, memoria, archeologia*. Ferrara: Volta la carta, 2016.

Geertz, Clifford. *The Interpretation of Cultures. Selected Essays*. New York: Basic Books, 1973.

Gómez García, Miguel Ángel. "La transposición didáctica: historia de un concepto." *Revista Latinoamericana de Estudios Educativos* 1 (2005): 83–111.

Hamilton, David. "Patents: a neglected source in the History of Education." *History of Education* 38 (2009): 303–310.

Hampel, Robert, William Johnson, David Plank, Diane Ravitch, David Tyack, and Larry Cuban. "History and Educational Reform." *History of Education Quarterly* 36 (1996): 473–502.

Handley, Sasha, Rohan McWilliam, and Lucy Noakes, eds. *New Directions in Social and Cultural History*. London: Bloomsbury Academic, 2018.

Handley, Sasha, Rohan McWilliam, and Lucy Noakes. "Introduction. Toward new social and cultural histories." In *New Directions in Social and Cultural History*, edited by Sasha

Handley, Rohan McWilliam, and Lucy Noakes, 1–18. London: Bloomsbury Academic, 2018.
Julia, Dominique. "La culture scolaire comme objet historique." In *Colonial Experience in Education. Historical Issues and Perspectives*, edited by António Nóvoa, Marc Depaepe, and Erwin V. Johanningmeier, 353–382. Gent: Paedagogica Historica. Supplementary Series (I), 1995.
Kliebard, Herbert M. *Changing Course. American Curriculum Reform in the 20th Century*. New York: Teacher College Press, 2002.
Lawn, Martin, ed. *Modelling the Future. Exhibitions and the Materiality of Education*. Oxford: Symposium Books, 2009.
Lawn, Martin, and Ian Grosvenor, eds. *Materialities of Schooling. Design – Technology – Objects – Routines*. Oxford: Symposium Books, 2005.
Loftus, Donna. "Markets and Culture." In *New Directions in Social and Cultural History*, edited by Sasha Handley, Rohan McWilliam, and Lucy Noakes, 109–128. London: Bloomsbury Academic, 2018.
Meda, Juri. *Mezzi di educazione di massa. Saggi di storia della cultura material della scuola tra XIX e XX secolo*. Milano: Franco Angeli, 2016.
Meda, Juri, and Antonio Viñao. "School memory: Historiographical balance and heuristic perspectives." In *School Memories. New Trends in the History of Education*, edited by Cristina Yanes-Cabrera, Juri Meda, and Antonio Viñao, 1–9. Cham: Springer, 2017.
Navickas, Katrina. "A return to materialism? Putting social history back into place." In *New Directions in Social and Cultural History*, edited by Sasha Handley, Rohan McWilliam, and Lucy Noakes, 87–108. London: Bloomsbury Academic, 2018.
Rockwell, Elsie. "Huellas del pasado en las culturas escolares." *Revista de Antropología Social* 16 (2007): 175–212.
Sarason, Seymour B. *The Culture of the School and the Problem of Change*. Boston: Allyn and Bacon, 1971.
Sarason, Seymour B. *Revisiting "The Culture of the School and the Problem of Change"*. New York: Teacher College Press, 1996.
Summerfield, Penny. "Subjectivity, the self and historical practice". In *New Directions in Social and Cultural History*, edited by Sasha Handley, Rohan McWilliam, and Lucy Noakes, 21–44. London: Bloomsbury Academic, 2018.
Terrón, Aida, and Ángel Mato. "Modifications des programmes et inertie institutionnelle: tradition et changement dans le modèle scolaire des classes homogènes." *Paedagogica Historica* XXXI (1995): 125–150.
Terrón Aida, and Violeta Álvarez. "Sobre la cultura escolar y los mitos en nuestra escuela." *Cultura y Educación* 14 (2002): 235–252.
Tyack, David, and Larry Cuban. *Tinkering toward Utopia. A Century of Public School Reform*. Cambridge Mss.: Harvard University Press, 1995.
Tyack, David, and William Tobin. "The 'grammar' of schooling. Why has it been so hard to change?" *American Educational Research Journal* XXXI (1994): 453–479.
Verret, Michel. *Le temps des études*. Paris: Librairie Honoré Champion, 1975.
Vincent, Guy, Bernard Lahire, and Daniel Thin. "Sur l'histoire et la théorie de la forme scolaire." In *L'éducation prisonnière de la forme scolaire? Scolarisation et socialisation dans les sociétés industrielles*, edited by Guy Vincent, 11–48. Lyon: Presses Universitaires de Lyon, 1994.

Viñao, Antonio. *Innovación pedagógica y racionalidad científica. La escuela graduada pública en España (1898–1936)*. Madrid: Akal, 1990.
Viñao, Antonio. "Culturas escolares, reformas e innovaciones: entre la tradición y el cambio." In *La construcción de una nueva cultura en los centros docentes*, 17–29. Murcia: Fórum Europeo de Administradores de la Educación, 1996.
Viñao, Antonio. "Por una historia de la cultura escolar: cuestiones, enfoques, fuentes." In *Culturas y civilizaciones. III Congreso de la Asociación de Historia Contemporánea*, 167–183. Valladolid: Universidad de Valladolid, 1998.
Viñao, Antonio. "Culturas escolares, reformas e innovaciones educativas." *Con-Ciencia Social* 5 (2001): 27–45.
Viñao, Antonio. "History of education and cultural history. Possibilities, problems and questions." In *Cultural History and Education. Critical Essays on Knowledge and Schooling*, edited by Thomas S. Popkewitz, Barry M. Franklin, and Miguel A. Pereyra, 125–150. New York: RoutledgeFalmer, 2001.
Viñao, Antonio. "Do education reforms fail? A historian's response." *Encounters on Education* 2 (2002): 27–47.
Viñao, Antonio. *Sistemas educativos, culturas escolares y reformas*. Madrid: Morata, 2002.
Viñao, Antonio. "La memoria escolar: restos y huellas, recuerdos y olvidos." *Annali di Storia dell'Educazione e delle Istituzione Scholastiche* 12 (2005): 19–33.
Viñao, Antonio. "El éxito o fracaso de las reformas educativas: condicionantes, limitaciones, posibilidades." In *La reforma necesaria: entre la política educativa y la práctica escolar*, edited by José Gimeno, 43–60. Madrid: Morata, 2006.
Viñao, Antonio. "La historial material e inmaterial de la escuela: memoria, patrimonio y educación." *Educação* 35 (2012): 7–17.
Williams, Raymond. *Keywords. A Vocabulary of Culture and Society*. Hammersmith: Fontana Press, 1988.

Index

À Kempis, Thomas   394
Adelung, Johann Christoph   299
Agazzi, Evandro   44
Albert I (King)   155
Aldrich, Richard   12f., 471
Alhadeff-Jones, Michael   87f.
Alonso Zapata, Manuel   411f.
Althusser, Louis   43
Amad, Paula   92f.
Andress, David   135f., 138
Ankersmit, Frank   26, 388, 390
Apple, Michael W.   198, 203
Arendt, Hannah   112
Ariès, Philippe   384, 400
Ash, John   302
Autenrieth, Ferdinand   323

Bachelard, Gaston   96
Bailey, Peter   436, 443
Bakanja Isidore   163
Baker, Bernadette   106, 329, 353
Bakker, Nelleke   23f., 27, 359, 364, 385, 445
Baldwin, James   143
Ball, Stephen   46, 473
Barad, Karen   2, 4f., 7f., 10, 108, 453
Bárczy, István   256
Barra, Valdenira Lopes de   452
Basedow, Johann Bernhard   298f., 301
Batthyány, Ervin   256
Baudouin (King)   159, 169
Becher, Tony   267f.
Becker, Carl Heinrich   220f., 224f., 228f., 233, 233f.
Becker, George Ferdinand   328, 329, 329f.
Beckstette, Sven   131, 134
Bedaux, Jan Baptist   389, 400
Béhar, Rachel   188
Bekhterev, Vladimir   338
Benchimol, Claire   189, 189f.
Benchimol, Hassiba   189, 189f.
Benjamin, Walter   83, 112, 117, 120, 136, 449–451, 461f.

Bentley W. Holman   158
Berger, Brigitte   106f.
Berger, Peter   106f.
Bergson, Henri   9f., 83f., 88–90, 92f., 95–97
Bérillon, Edgar   338f., 346f., 352
Bernheim, Hippolyte   346, 348
Beun, Gerarda (Sister)   433f., 443
Biesta, Gert   16f., 66, 268, 279
Binet, Alfred   338f.
Bismarck, Otto von   130
Bladergroen, Wilhelmina   363, 368, 371
Bloch, Marc   6, 40, 393
Blumenberg, Hans   119
Bognár, Cecil   258
Bogumil Jewsiewicki   155
Böhme, Günther   272
Bollen, Jean   162
Bontinck, François   158
Bosche, Anne   206
Bourdieu, Pierre   51, 282
Bovet, Pierre   410, 418
Bramwell, Milne   350
Braster, Sjaak   26–29, 46, 393, 405, 408f., 418f., 423–425, 483
Brémaud, Paul   345
Brezinka, Wolfgang   16, 250
Broterton, Graham   479
Burggraeve, Adolphe   342f.
Burke, Catherine   26f., 70, 70f.,112, 113, 113f., 410f., 419, 419f., 421, 421f.
Burke, Peter   480, 480f.
Buth, Peggy   131

Cabanel, Patrick   183, 187
Campe, Joachim Heinrich   294, 298f., 301
Camus, Jean-Pierre   299f.
Canales, Antonio   1, 6f., 39, 50, 436
Carr, Edward Halle   112f.
Caruso, Marcelo   19, 202, 289f., 294f., 304
Casement, Roger   163
Casid, Jill   118
Castelain, Leopold   339f., 349f.

Cats, Jacob 392–397, 399 f.
Cattier, Félicien 163
Chaltin, Louis 150
Chapron, Emmanuelle 206
Charcot, Jean-Martin 343, 345, 348
Charton, Albert 180
Cheri, Samba 152 f.
Christy, Agatha 170
Claparède, Edouard 23, 410, 418, 420
Clemens of Alexandria 297
Cody, Caroline 206
Coll y Cuchi, César 413
Comandon, Jean 92
Comenius, Jan Amos 17, 384, 400
Conklin, Alice 178
Conrad, Joseph Teodor (Konrad Korzeniowski) 20, 150
Cormier, Cléonisse 187
Corrigan, Philip 457
Cresswell, Tim 94
Cruickshank, William M. 367, 369 f., 372
Cuban, Larry 53, 331, 472, 474
Curtis, Sarah 185–187

Dagen, Philippe 147
Daston, Lorraine 454
Daughton, J.-P. 181
De Deken, Constant 152
De Gaulle (General) 169
De Jonghe, Edouard 157
de Vroede, Maurits 3
Deakin, Alfred 86
Debaise, Didier 95–98
Decroly, Ovide 11, 21–23, 28, 346, 409, 418
Dekker, Jeroen 24–26, 383–395, 397–399, 471
del Mar del Pozo Andrés, Maria 26–28, 46, 388, 393, 405, 408–411, 415, 417 f.
Delboeuf, Joseph 348–350
Deleuze, Gilles 1–4, 11, 88, 95, 109 f., 115, 453 f.
Denyn, Victor 157
Depaepe, Marc 1–4, 3 f., 5 f., 6 f., 7 f., 9 f., 11, 11 f., 15, 15 f., 17, 17 f., 19 f., 21–25, 28 f., 40, 40 f., 43–46, 48, 48 f., 49, 49 f., 52, 52 f., 53 f., 55, 55 f., 59, 59 f., 60, 60 f., 62 f., 65, 71, 71 f., 77, 77 f., 103–107, 109, 111, 113, 113 f., 121, 129, 129 f., 130, 130 f., 142 f., 175, 175 f., 176, 176 f., 184, 184 f., 190, 190 f., 218 f., 249 f., 255 f., 271 f., 273 f., 277, 278 f., 279 f., 282, 282 f., 284 f., 291 f., 294 f., 331 f., 337, 338 f., 339 f., 359, 359 f., 360, 360 f., 383, 384 f., 385 f., 388 f., 408 f., 449–453, 455, 455 f., 456 f., 470 f., 471 f., 484 f.
Depaepe, Maria Adonia 3, 3 f.
Deschamps, Pierre 180
Dewey, John 10 f., 22, 103 f., 109–111, 115, 313, 325–328, 330 f., 386
Dietrich, Theo 16, 242 f., 294 f.
Dikaka, Jean-Pierre 149
Dilthey, Wilhelm 48, 218–220, 229
Doane, Mary Ann 87 f.
Donato (Alfred Edouard D'Hont) 345, 348 f.
Donzwau, M.D. Nlemvo 158
Dörpfeld, Friedrich Wilhelm 330
Dufourcq, Elisabeth 186
Dulac, Germaine 9 f., 81, 83 f., 90–98
Dumas, Louis 301
Dussel, Inès 28 f., 108, 385, 409, 449, 456, 458 f.
Dyche, Thomas 300

Eddington, Arthur 87
Edgar, Andrew 476 f.
Edwards, Elizabeth 26, 415
Ekibondo 149
Elster, Jon 6, 39, 46 f., 50
Emin, Pacha 154
Ensor, Beatrice 418
Eötvös, József 249, 252, 257
Escolano, Agustín 452, 460, 472, 483, 485
Etambala, Zana 3, 13 f., 147, 151, 153, 159, 166
Evans, Walker 112, 406

Felbiger, Johann Ignaz von 301
Fendler, Lynn 6–9, 59, 72, 74, 119, 453
Ferrière, Adolphe 409 f., 413, 416, 418
Ferry, Jules 177, 180
Fielding, Michael 138
Fináczy, Ernő 254, 258

Fish, Gustave 162
Flitner, Wilhelm 16, 18, 232–235, 240, 245
Foucault, Michel 6, 40, 42, 54, 60–63, 67f., 107, 109, 119f., 360, 408, 449–451, 462f.
Franck, Louis 156
Francke, August Herrmann 298
Franco, Francisco 9, 44, 50, 90, 133, 290, 415, 452, 456, 483
François, Albert 40, 148, 162, 178f., 181, 186, 301, 348
Franits, Wayne 388f., 395
Fraser, James 303
Freire Méndez, Justa 411f.
Freud, Sigmund 340
Fuchs, Eckhardt 14, 176, 195, 201, 280, 282

Gallagher, Michael 434
García Férriz, Jesús 412
Gauss, Carl Friedrich 66
Geertz, Clifford 477f.
Gildea, Robert 141
Goodman, Joyce 5, 9f., 81–83, 87, 142, 453
Grewel, Frank 365f.
Grosvenor, Ian 1, 6, 13f., 25–29, 46, 70, 112f., 129, 132, 386, 410, 419, 421, 451f., 455, 483
Grosz, Elizabeth 81, 88, 93
Grunder, Hans-Ulrich 385
Gryseels, Guido 139
Guattari, Felix 1–4, 11, 110
Gudjons, Herbert 272

Hacking, Ian 44f., 45, 114
Halewood, Michael 90, 97f.
Hall, Granville Stanley 116, 117f.
Hall, James 395, 395f.
Halma, Nicholas 301
Hamilton, David 483
Hampel, Robert L. 474
Harding, Sandra 75f.
Hardy, Georges 178f.
Hart de Ruyter, Theo 364f., 371
Haskell, Francis 384, 389
Heidegger, Martin 2, 454

Heinrich, Gusztáv 62, 253, 323
Hellinckx, Bart 190
Hendy, David 436, 441
Herbart, Johann Friedrich 22, 253, 313–321, 323–325, 327
Herderschêe, Dirk 364
Herman, Frederik 1, 7, 14, 24, 28, 105, 323, 362, 451
Heydorn, Heinz-Joachim 16
Huizinga, Johan 388f.
Hulstaert, Gustaaf 157f.
Humboldt, Wilhelm von 140, 220, 289
Hutereau, Armand 157

Ingold, Tim 2f., 28, 453–455
Ismaa'il, Ibrahim 143

Jaklin, Ingeborg 206f.
Janet, Pierre 255, 348
Jaricot, Pauline 182
Johnson, Samuel 302f., 322, 474
Johnstone, Paul H. 406f.
Julia, Dominique 29, 73, 206f., 362, 469f.

Kalverboer, Alex 372–375
Kármán, Mór 252–254
Keiderling, Thomas 207
Kellner, Hans 106
Kenyeres, Elemér 258
Kerschensteiner, Georg 274
Ķestere, Iveta 269, 274, 277
Killingray, David 167
Kimbangu, Simon 165f.
Kipling, Rudyard 177
Kitcher, Philip 45
Kittel, Helmuth 234
Klebelsberg, Kunó 257
Klein, Astrid S. 131, 170, 241, 346
Kliebard, Herbert M.. 472
Kok, J.F.W. 371–374
Kornis, Gyula 250, 258
Koselleck, Rheinhart 112, 293, 295
Kruger, Paul 86
Kudláčova, Blanka 272
Kuhn, Thomas S. 44, 268

Labaree, David 6, 45

Lange, Dorothea 406
Lange, Joachim 298
Latour, Bruno, 28, 69, 74, 451, 453, 459
Laudan, Larry 44
Laurier, Wildrid 86
Le Bon, Gustave 340, 344f.
Le Brun, Charles 390f., 395, 398
Lefranc, Stanislas 163–165
Lehtinen, Laura E. 364, 370
Lejeune, Jules 343, 347
Lemaire Charles 156
Lempp, K. 371
Lennon, John 383
Leopold II (King) 13, 155
Leopold III (King) 150, 151f.,
Lesko, Nancy 108
Liébeault, Auguste Ambroise 346
Liégeois, Jules 349f.
Litt, Theodor 16, 18, 219, 223, 227f., 230, 233, 238, 240–242, 245, 273
Llorca y García, Ángel 410f., 413
Lods, Pierre 160
Lombroso, Cesare 348
López Velasco, Elisa 411f., 414–416
Lorand, Georges 165
Luambo 167
Lubrich, Ágost 253
Lusinga, Tumbwe 156f.

Mann, Horace 62
Marx, Karl 44, 454, 479
Masala 169
Masschelein, Jan 360, 449f.
Mato, Ángel. 470
Matthes, Eva 18, 203, 217–221, 225–227, 229, 232, 235f., 240
Mbunza 149
McCulloch, Gary 50, 55, 111f., 142
Mead, George Herbert 330f.
Meda, Juri 452, 456f., 483
Menzerath, Paul 340
Mercier (Cardinal) 163
Merkel, Angela (Chancellor) 139
Merton, Robert K. 52
Mesmer, Franz 341
Miani, Giovanni 149
Michaux, Oscar 151f., 156

Mobutu, Sese Seko 162, 165–167
Mollenhauer, Klaus 16
Montessori, Maria 23, 109, 273, 409
Morel, Edmond-Dene 163
Moreno, Antonio 412, 452
Morris, Richard 87f., 331
Muizniek, Nils 134f.
Mussolini, Benito 82, 85

Nagy, László 254f.
Navickas, Katrina 479–481
Németh, András 18, 249f., 252–256, 258, 262
Nietzsche, Friedrich 60f., 67
Nohl, Herman 16, 18, 229–232, 235f., 239f., 245
Nóvoa, António 6, 48, 90, 130, 142, 385, 470
Nwagbogu, Azu 131, 134

Oelkers, Jürgen 17, 21f., 207, 252, 313
Orwell, George 134
Ovid 392, 394
Ozola, Iveta 18, 267, 269, 275, 277f., 282

Paisant, Chantal 187
Panofsky, Erwin 389
Papastephanou, Maria 81, 86f., 89
Parijs, Philippe van 46
Parker, Gordon 385, 435
Pasold, Eric 143
Patrick, James 39, 45, 330
Pauer, Imre 254
Pauler, Ákos 255
Paulsen, Friedrich 220
Peeters, Louis 339, 346
Pekri-Pekár, Charles 338
Pénot, Sosthène 180
Pestalozzi, Johan Heinrich 62, 294
Petersen, Peter 242
Piaget, Jean 2 258, 273
Pineau, Pablo 451f.
Pöggeler, Franz 386
Popkewitz, Tom 10f., 22, 26, 42f., 70, 74, 89, 103–106, 108f., 115, 117–119, 284, 480
Popper, Karl 330

Prechtl, H.F.R. 366, 368, 370 f., 373
Presser, Jacques 386
Prohászka, Lajos 250, 258

Quetelet, Adolphe 66

Rajský, Andrej 258, 272
Rákosi, Mátyás, 249, 259, 262
Rancière, Jacques 107
Ranke, Leopold von 44, 393, 400
Reble, Albert 18, 240–245
Rée, Jonathan 442, 444
Reilly, Maura 136–138
Rein, Wilhelm 232, 253
Reyniers, Nele 27, 433
Rhodes, Cecil 86, 140
Rice, Tom 27, 434 f.
Rich, Adrianne 134, 280
Ringer, Fritz K. 48, 51
Ripa, Cesare 390
Robinson, Keith 88, 92 f., 95, 98, 218, 348
Rockwell, Elsie 474 f.
Rodrigue, Aron 184, 184 f.
Roemer, John 46
Rogers, Carl 273
Rogers, Rebecca 1, 14, 175, 176 f., 184 f., 185 f., 190 f.
Romein, Jan 386
Roth, Wolff-Michael 16, 251
Rousseau, Jean-Jacques 62, 294, 410
Rubene, Zanda 18, 267, 269, 272 f., 275, 278, 280, 282
Ruiz Berrio, Julio 207

Sarason, Seymour B. 472 f.
Schafer, Murray 434, 437, 439
Schleiermacher, Friedrich Daniel Ernst 240, 254, 322 f.
Schmidt, Dierk 131, 131 f.
Schmidt, Jenő 256
Schneller, István 254
Schollmayer, Friedrich 19, 289
Schröder, Carl August 205
Seddon, Richard 86
Serra, María Silvia 452
Serres, Michel 10, 81, 87, 94 f.
Shaviro, Steven 97 f.

Silva, Vera Gaspar da 108, 116 f., 199, 452, 456
Simon, Brian 50, 50 f., 250 f., 273, 279 f.
Simon, Frank 2, 11 f., 15 f., 21 f., 22, 23 f., 28 f., 40 f., 46, 46 f., 71 f., 77, 77 f., 184, 184 f., 190, 190 f., 359 f., 384 f., 450 f. – 452 f., 471 f., 484 f.
Slavin, Robert 273
Sluys, Alexis 410
Smeyers, Paul 9, 15, 17, 21, 24, 28, 53, 71, 104, 109, 282, 284, 360, 388, 452 f.
Southwell, Myriam 271, 282, 285
Spencer, Herbert 321 f., 330 f.
Spencer, William George 330 f.
Spener, Philipp Jacob 298
Spranger, Eduard 16, 18, 218–231, 233 f., 236, 238 f., 241, 243, 245, 258
Stanley, Henry-Morton 116 f., 150, 154 f., 164, 167
Steedman, Carolyn 455
Steen, Jan 398 f.
Storms, Emile 156 f.
Strauss, Alfred A. 364, 366 f., 370, 419
Stryker, Roy Emerson 406 f.
Szabó, Ervin 256 f.
Szabolcs, Éva 18, 249 f., 254 f., 258

Tamboukou, Maria 96, 98
Tarde, Gabriel 340
Terrón, Aida 470, 473
Thibaudeau, Antoine Claire 302
Thompson, Edward P. 42 f., 387
Thorndike, Edward Lee 22, 63–65, 323–326
Tibout, Nelly 364
Tisza, Kálmán 251
Tobin, William 331, 472
Tolia-Kelly, Divya P. 137 f.
Touwen, B.C.L. 370, 373 f.
Trott zu Solz, August von 218, 225
Tsing, Anna 81, 95
Tyack, David 53, 331, 472, 474

Valéry, Paul 96
Valk, J. 369 f.
Van Cauter 163
Van der Goes, Hugo 388

Van der Weijden, Rogier 388
Van Drenth, Annemieke 27, 437–440
Van Ecyk, Jan 388
Van Gorp, Angelo 1, 15, 20–23, 28, 147, 346, 359
Van Holsbeek, Henri 342f.
Van Kerckhoven, Willem 162, 162f.
Van Krevelen, D. Arnold 365, 365f.
Van Velsen, Prosper 350f.
Vandervelde, Emile 163, 164, 164f., 165
Vaudiau, M. 160f.
Vehkahlathi, Kaisa 27
Venne, Adriaan van de 392
Verdeil, Chantal 187
Vermeersch, Arthur 163, 164, 165
Vidal, Diana 456
Vigarello, Georges 457
Viñao, Antonio 29, 51–53, 206, 385, 457, 469f., 472, 480, 482–484
Vincent, Guy 472
Vinçotte, Thomas 154f.
Volper, Julien 156,

Waldapfel, János 254
Wandel, Paul 223, 295
Ward, Herbert 153f.
Ware, Caroline Farrar 406f.
Weber, Max 48, 479
Weniger, Erich 18, 218, 232f., 235–240
Weszely, Ödön 253–256
White, Owen 159, 177, 181, 183
Whitehead, Alfred North 10, 81, 84, 88, 90, 95–98
Williams, Raymond 83, 90f., 94, 476
Wils, Kaat 23, 337, 341, 344f., 348
Wissaert, Paul 153
Wolff, Christian 323
Wrench, Evelyn 9f., 81, 83–90, 94–98
Wright, Erik O. 46, 49
Wundt, Wilhelm 218, 255

Ziegler, Béatrice 198f., 203
Ziller, Tuiskon 253